The Empire Looks South

The Empire Looks South

Chinese perceptions of Cambodia before and during the Kingdom of Angkor

PETER HARRIS

Preface by

DAVID CHANDLER

Silkworm Books

ISBN 978-616-215-196-5 (Hardback)
ISBN 978-616-215-198-9 (Paperback)

First edition published in 2023 by
Silkworm Books
430/58 M. 7, T. Mae Hia, Chiang Mai 50100, Thailand
info@silkwormbooks.com
www.silkwormbooks.com

Typeset in Minion Pro 10 pt. by Silk Type

Cover images:
Top: The Tang emperor Taizong © The National Palace Museum, Taipei.
Bottom: Jayavarman VII, The National Museum Cambodia, Phnom Penh © Jean-Pierre Dalbéra, https://www.flickr.com/photos/dalbera/49956204771/

Printed and bound in Thailand by O. S. Printing House, Bangkok

5 4 3 2 1

Contents

Acknowledgments ix
A note on the presentation of the text x
Preface by David Chandler xi

Introduction 1
- Sources used in this work 3
- The standard histories 4
- Encyclopedias and compendiums 6
- The writings of envoys, officials, Daoists, Buddhists, and others 7
- Secondary sources 8
- On translation 12
- The transmission of texts 13
- The pronunciation of old names and words 14
- Placenames and nomenclature 14
- Locations and languages 17
- The layout of this book 18

Chapter 1: Early portraits: ambassadors going south, and others 21
- The earliest references to Funan 21
- Background to the journey south of Kang Tai and Zhu Ying 23
- Kang Tai and Zhu Ying's visits to the southern states 25
- The remnants of Kang Tai's account of Funan 28
- How Kang Tai portrays Funan, including its foundation story 32
- The poet Zuo Si and his prose–poem *The Three Capitals* 36
- The writer Wan Zhen's *Annals of Strange Things* 37
- One other early traveler, Zhu Zhi 40

Chapter 2: Buddhist voyagers, Daoist dreamers, early court annalists 42
- Buddhist and Daoist sources on Funan 43
- Buddhist voyagers 43
- Daoist dreamers 46
- Early annals: *The History of the Jin Dynasty* 50

New and old in the Jin history's account of Funan 52
After the Jin: *The History of the Liu Song Dynasty* 53
A monk-envoy glorifying Funan: *The History of the Southern Qi Dynasty* 54
What *The History of the Southern Qi Dynasty* tells us about Funan 61

Chapter 3: *The History of the Liang Dynasty* and its portrait of Funan **64**
Looking back on Funan from the vantage point of the Tang 64
The History of the Liang Dynasty on Funan's customs and kings 67
How *The History of the Liang Dynasty* adds to our knowledge of Funan 75
Two other early works of history on Funan 76

Chapter 4: The last of Funan during the seventh century CE **78**
A Sui dynasty embassy to Funan's offshoot Chitu (Red Earth) 79
The History of the Sui Dynasty on Funan's takeover by Zhenla 84
A Tang compendium on Funan's final tribute to China 85
An alternative record of Zhenla's annexation of Funan 87
Fragmentary accounts of the gold, iron and fragrances of Funan 88
Funan recollected in the two official Tang histories 89
Two more historical works on Funan 91
What we learn about Funan from later sources 92

Chapter 5: A history of Funan on the basis of Chinese sources **93**

Chapter 6: A contemporaneous Chinese portrait of early Zhenla **107**
The transition from Funan to Zhenla 107
The History of the Sui Dynasty's account of early Zhenla 110
Lineage linkages between Funan and Zhenla 116
How seventh-century Zhenla may have differed from Funan 117
The strengths and weaknesses of *The History of the Sui Dynasty* 118

Chapter 7: Distant images: Zhenla in Tang and Northern Song sources **119**
The account of Zhenla in *The Old History of the Tang Dynasty* 119
What *The Old History of the Tang Dynasty* tells us about Zhenla 123
A first official reference to the Khmers 124
The Old History of the Tang Dynasty on Land Zhenla and Water Zhenla 125
The whereabouts and nature of Water Zhenla 126
The whereabouts and nature of Land Zhenla, also called Wendan 126
Wendan's tribute to China 127
Purple pins and privacy: other sources on Zhenla during the Tang 128

The New History of the Tang Dynasty on an overland route to Wendan ... 132
The New History of the Tang Dynasty on other aspects of Zhenla ... 135
Zhenla during the Tang: what Chinese sources tell us and what is missing ... 136

Chapter 8: Perceptions of Angkor during the Southern Song ... 139
The three-century "freeze" in Zhenla's relations with China ... 140
Three Song gazetteers ... 142
Fan Chengda's *Cinnamon Sea* ... 142
Zhou Qufei's *Beyond the Five Mountains* ... 145
Zhao Rugua's *Various Foreigners* ... 149
Old and new in Zhao Rugua's account of Zhenla, also called Angkor ... 152
Zhao Rugua on Zhenla's deteriorating relations with Champa ... 153
Zhao Rugua on Zhenla's luxury goods ... 154
Glimpses of Zhenla in Song encyclopedias and histories ... 156
Song sources on Zhenla's resumption of tribute missions ... 160
Song sources on other issues, including Zhenla's other name Zhanla ... 162
Why official Song sources disregard Angkor's growing power and glory ... 165

Chapter 9: Angkor brought to life: the *Record* of Zhou Daguan ... 166
Zhou's *Record*: a newly arranged version ... 169
Zhou's *Record* compared to earlier sources ... 194

Chapter 10: After Zhou: selected accounts through the Ming ... 195
The merchant Wang Dayuan's depiction of Zhenla ... 195
Zhenla and the Ming voyages of Admiral Zheng He ... 197
The soldier Fei Xin's account of Zhenla ... 198
The scholar Huang Xingzeng's description of Zhenla ... 199
Four other Ming portrayals of Cambodia ... 200
Ming historical sources on Cambodia ... 206

Chapter 11: Conclusions ... 210
Some salient issues ... 211
The identity of Funan and its connection with Zhenla ... 211
The role of foreign trade ... 213
The extent of Funan's Indianization ... 214
The transition from Funan to Zhenla ... 215
The perception of Funan and Zhenla as states ... 215
The influence of imperial Chinese perspectives ... 216
Final remarks ... 218

Appendix 1: Official writings used as primary sources, listed chronologically 221
Appendix 2: Chinese dynasties and Cambodian rulers 222
Appendix 3: Tribute missions to China from Funan and Zhenla from the Han to the Song Dynasty 224
Appendix 4: A comparative table of the customs of Funan and Zhenla 226
Appendix 5: The elusive Linyi: Chinese sources revisited 228
Appendix 6: Glossary of names of people and places 260

Bibliography 285
Endnotes 306
Index 380

Acknowledgments

First I should like to thank Gloria Davies and David Chandler, who generously gave their time, insight, and expert advice through successive drafts of an earlier version of this work, submitted for a Ph D at Monash University (and subsequenrly amended and modified for this book). David Chandler's extraordinary knowledge of and contributions to Cambodian history and Gloria Davies' deep understanding of Chinese culture and history did much to prevent me from going astray. My thanks also go to Wang Gungwu and Penny Edwards for their thoughtful comments on an earlier version of this work.

I also want to thank Warren Sun for his careful critiques of my translations of difficult passages in the Chinese texts, and to Ian Mabbett for commenting on the whole work, especially with regard to the Indianization debate and the transliteration of Sanskrit terms. My thanks, too, go to Duncan Campbell and Catherine Churchman for their stimulating suggestions, and to Chen Jiarong, who found time in Hong Kong to discuss his many contributions to the study of China-Southeast Asian relations.

Thanks are also due to Margo Picken for first interesting me in Zhou Daguan, and to James Chin, Wendy Doniger, Keith Taylor, Li Tana, and Endymion Wilkinson for their expert comments, kindly and readily given, on textual and other issues. I am grateful to Nicholas Menzies and Li Tana for their advice on Chinese scholarship in the field of Southeast Asian studies. In addition I would like to convey my appreciation to the following: Reed Aeschliman, Nguyen Ngoc Anh, William Aspell, Alexander Bukh, Nguyễn Tuấn Cường, Kent Davis, Glenn Gibney, Srea Hak Kuoch, Minh Thu Nguyen, Daniel Reeve (for the two maps), Andrew Wilford, and Jason Young. I greatly appreciate the efforts of Trasvin Jittidecharak at Silkworm Books, and her editor Noel Perales-Estoesta, to see this work through to publication. Finally, a very special thank you to my wife Vicky Noble, who has been a fine editor as well as a constant source of encouragement and insight, as well as to Max, Ben, Alexis, Schyana, and Jane, ll of whom have, as always, been wonderfully supportive.

A note on the presentation of the text

Translations of Chinese texts are presented in a sans serif font.

People's names, placenames, and special terms and expressions that derive from Chinese are romanized using hanyu pinyin. The equivalent Chinese logograms, or characters, are provided in footnotes and in the glossary at the end. Transliterations of Khmer terms are those given in David Smyth and Tran Kien's Cambodian dictionary unless otherwise indicated.

Preface

by **David Chandler**

In *The Empire Looks South* Peter Harris has assembled, edited and deftly translated into English a trove of imperial Chinese documents that tell us almost all we know about that part of the world we call Cambodia in the first millennium CE.

This absorbing, clear-eyed book will be indispensable to scholars of Cambodian history and to readers interested in Chinese relations with the region long before it was 'discovered' by the West.

Readers will also be drawn into the book by Harris' crisp, accessible style, by the depth and range of his scholarship, and by his persuasive argumentation.

At another level, readers will enjoy meeting the ragtag cast of characters who visited or took an interest in the region for hundreds of years and recorded their impressions.

Intriguingly, the word Cambodia never appears in any of the early documents collected into this book. Instead, the Chinese sources refer to a pair of prosperous kingdoms that they call Funan and Zhenla.

Funan was a coastal, outward-looking civilization whose inhabitants for much of the period were Buddhist. Remnants of a Funanese city, probably not the capital, were excavated by the French in southern Vietnam in the 1940s.

Zhenla, on the other hand, was an inland, agricultural kingdom whose Khmer speaking inhabitants by the seventh century CE at least had adapted an Indian alphabet and worshipped Indian gods. Its early capital has been excavated in the Cambodian province of Takeo.

To express their inferiority and their admiration for the Chinese court, Funan and Zhenla periodically sent tributary gifts to China. At various times the gifts included elephants, rare birds and exotic musical instruments.

The Chinese documents that report these missions often provide the dates when the missions took place. These dates helped Peter Harris to frame the valuable sketch of Funan history which appears in this book as chapter five.

In the ninth century CE the powerful kingdom that we call Angkor gathered momentum in the Cambodian northwest. Angkor came to dominate much of mainland southeast Asia for the next five hundred years.

The documents in *The Empire Looks South* say less about Angkor. From the ninth century onward, with one indispensable exception, Chinese records of Cambodia become sparse. The exception is the detailed account written by a Chinese diplomat named Zhou Daguan, who spent nearly a year in Angkor in 1296–1297 and wrote a colorful, perceptive account of his experiences.

A well regarded French translation of the text appeared in the early twentieth century. Almost a hundred years later Harris translated the original memoir into English and published an annotated version, *A Record of Cambodia: The Land and its People.* The book was a critical and commercial success.

Peter Harris first visited Angkor in the 1960s, a few years after I had been posted to Cambodia as a fledgling American diplomat. He returned to Cambodia in the 1980s and again early this century as a development consultant in Phnom Penh. During this time he invited me to provide a preface to his new translation of Zhou Daguan, which I did.

The Empire Looks South originated as a PhD dissertation that Peter Harris submitted to Monash University in 2020. Its external readers, Professor Wang Gungwu and Professor Penny Edwards, praised the dissertation and urged Peter to publish it as a book. They made several suggestions that have been absorbed into the final version.

The rest, as they say, is history.

I am honored and delighted to introduce its readers to this pathbreaking, capacious historical study. *The Empire Looks South* alters the landscape of Cambodia's distant past. Beginning with sketchy accounts that describe local people as naked and black, the Chinese sources culminate in Zhou Daguan's recollections of a sophisticated, well managed city, less than a century before its multi-faceted, mysterious collapse.

David Chandler

Introduction

reality is in reality no more than the jumbled fragments of a shattered frieze behind which an altogether other order of things is serenely and immovably fixed, and of which on occasion the world, the metaworld, slyly grants a tantalising glimpse

—John Banville

Some time ago, when I was translating the Chinese envoy Zhou Daguan's account of thirteenth-century Angkor, I realised that there was much more to be discovered from early Chinese sources about life in the Kingdom of Angkor, and in Cambodia before Angkor. Zhou's *A Record of Cambodia: The Land and its People* is the most detailed description of the Kingdom of Angkor left to posterity. But it is not the only early Chinese portrait of Cambodia by any means. A number of other Chinese sources describe aspects of early Cambodia, going back a thousand years or more before the time of Zhou.

Some of these were translated into French over a century ago by the French savant Paul Pelliot. Since then scholars have translated various other individual texts into English and other languages. But there has still been the need for a full set of translations, an overview of all the Chinese texts relating to Angkorian and pre-Angkorian civilization. This set would disentangle the long historical record provided by Chinese sources, and convey in a coherent way the fascinating, sometimes vivid portraits of early Cambodia that the Chinese texts have left us. The purpose of this work is to meet that need.

The work has two aims. The first is to provide full, up-to-date, and readable translations into English of all the Chinese sources concerning Cambodia up to the time of Zhou Daguan, with a brief look at Chinese records in the centuries after Zhou.[1] These sources refer to Funan, the state that flourished from the first to seventh century CE around the lower reaches of the Mekong River, and to Zhenla, the name that Chinese chroniclers gave to the polity or polities that absorbed Funan, and that from the ninth to thirteenth century constituted what most modern historians call the Kingdom of Angkor.[2]

Taken together, the translations constitute a unique account of a near neighbor to China over the course of a millennium or so, as told from an imperial Chinese perspective. They add considerably to what we know about early Cambodia. Beyond that, they highlight the potential of imperial Chinese sources to provide new perspectives not only on Cambodia, but also on dozens of other polities beyond China's borders, from Japan to Java and Srivijaya to India.

The second aim of the book is to describe the contribution each of these Chinese sources makes to our understanding of early Cambodian history, and to assess the gaps and omissions in the Chinese record and the imperial Chinese attitudes that inform that record.

Early Chinese texts on Cambodia remain of enduring importance for both Cambodia and Southeast Asia today. For all their limitations, they are the sole written sources for the history of early Cambodia, and in certain respects they remain an integral part of contemporary Cambodia's constructed identity.[3] For instance, Cambodia's foundation story is often identified with the foundation story of Funan as described by the third-century Chinese envoy Kang Tai, who provided the first written record of that story.[4] Similarly, the account of Angkor that the envoy Zhou Daguan wrote after visiting from 1296 to 1297 remains critical to our understanding of daily life there.[5] The importance of this work is reflected in the fact that Zhou and his *Record* are now the subject of a new museum near Siem Reap, the city for tourists visiting Angkor.[6] His work gives a Chinese dimension to the centrality of Angkor in Cambodia's sense of modern nationhood at a time when China's relations with Cambodia, now increasingly close and overbearing, are again salient to Cambodia's identity.[7]

The texts retain their importance for other reasons too. Were it not for the accounts of it in Chinese texts, Funan would be a culture and society identifiable only through sparse archaeological findings.[8] The name Funan, perhaps derived from the Khmer *phnom* (hill), is the only name known for this culture and, *faute de mieux*, is a name still used in Western and Chinese histories and textbooks.[9] The name is sometimes used to refer to the whole region and era in which Funan flourished.[10]

The name and polity or polities of Zhenla, a proper noun whose meaning and origin have yet to be fully explained, also have enduring significance. With the exception of one long interval in the ninth and tenth centuries when references to Zhenla disappear from Chinese records, Zhenla culture and society are frequently referred to in Chinese writings from the seventh to the thirteenth century, and even after that.[11] Moreover, Zhenla is the principal Chinese name for Cambodia during the whole period from the demise of Funan to the establishment in 802 of the Kingdom of Angkor, and beyond that to the decline of Angkor in the fourteenth century.[12]

This being the case, accounts of Zhenla still feature largely in both Chinese and Western descriptions of early Cambodia. Some Western scholars apply the name Zhenla to Cambodia in the seventh and eighth centuries, the period between Funan and Angkor, rather than to the seven hundred years between Zhenla's first appearance and Angkor's decline, as Chinese historians do. Strictly speaking, the name Zhenla should refer to this entire seven-hundred-year span.[13] While Chinese accounts of Zhenla contribute less to our understanding of the pre-Angkor and Angkor periods than Chinese accounts of Funan do, they still add insights to information provided by other primary sources, such as inscriptions, buildings, and other archaeological findings—important from the seventh century on—as well as the recent findings of aerial surveys.

Sources used in this work

The bulk of the texts translated and commented on in this book date from the third century to the thirteenth century CE—that is, from the Later Han dynasty (25–220 CE) to the Yuan dynasty (1271–1368) up to the time of Zhou Daguan.[14] A final chapter also considers texts from the later Yuan dynasty and the Ming dynasty (1368–1644).

The book focuses largely on Chinese primary sources. Only a few Western scholars have drawn directly on these sources to complement other primary sources. The result has sometimes been a kind of "stir-fry" research, to use the memorable phrase of David Chandler, the leading historian of Cambodia—that is to say, research in which certain events and issues relating to early Cambodia, often attributed to Chinese sources, are recycled even when they are poorly substantiated or not substantiated at all.[15] One aim of this book is to help minimize "stir-fry" scholarship of this kind.

The primary sources used here consist of books written or compiled in China, both official and unofficial, during the period in question. Official writings—that is, writings approved and usually commissioned by Chinese emperors—include the so-called standard histories (*zhengshi*) of individual dynasties, as well as works sometimes known in English as universal histories (*tongshi*) because their contents transcend particular dynasties.[16] These official writings are listed in appendix one. Unofficial writings include those from Daoist and Buddhist traditions, and those by travelers and others describing conditions in countries beyond China's frontiers for the education and amusement of a wider Chinese audience rather than just the imperial court.

The standard histories

Among the official writings of China, the official histories of each dynasty, or "standard histories" as they are known in Chinese, are the most important resource for both the history of imperial China itself and accounts of its relations with other states. As the historian Kenneth Gardiner puts it, the standard histories "form a body of documentation . . . that is impressive both in quantity and quality, and one to which no other culture can offer a parallel."[17] They constitute the principal written source of information about Funan, and are complemented by scattered references to the same in other Chinese texts (such as encyclopedias), and by archaeological findings in Óc Eo in the Mekong Delta, in Angkor Borei in southeastern Cambodia, and other sites.

The standard histories also provide useful references to Zhenla. The information they provide about Zhenla is, however, more limited, and subordinate to other resources, notably Sanskrit and Khmer inscriptions from the seventh century onwards, as well as the abundant buildings, sculptures, and bas-reliefs that characterized the Kingdom of Angkor from the ninth to the fourteenth century.

While valuable, the standard histories are partial and incomplete. The principal objective of their authors was not to establish full and detached records of past events but to provide ruling emperors with a guide to past practices and a basis for present policy making. As the Sinologist Endymion Wilkinson explains, "It was an important part of the duties of a ruler [in imperial China] . . . to set the framework for right thinking about the past" by commissioning the histories of previous dynasties and seeing that they were edited according to the ruler's view of what was legitimate and correct.[18]

The standard histories were subject to what today would be described as heavy editing. Some of them—for example, *Jin shu* [*The History of the Jin Dynasty*]—were subject to several redactions before achieving their final, approved form.[19] Most of the histories went through a process of collecting and sifting, building up materials from three basic sources: previous dynastic histories, the "true records" or annals (*shilu*, often translated as "veritable records") of each reign in the dynasty concerned, and other historical materials.[20]

The nature of the authorship of the histories also changed over time. A number of early histories were written by individual scholar-officials, in seven cases by father-and-son teams, usually under official patronage of some kind. But it was not until early in the Tang dynasty (618–907) that emperors officially commissioned histories, usually from committees of scholars led by a scholar-official of particular merit.[21] It is not clear how this change in the way the histories were written affected their accounts of Southeast Asian states. In one early case, *Nan Qi shu* [*The History of the Southern Qi Dynasty*], the Buddhist faith of its author, Xiao Zixian, may have resulted in the Buddhist aspects of Funan being highlighted, reflecting the Buddhist beliefs not only of Xiao but also his master, Emperor Wu of the Liang dynasty (505–556).[22] But this seems to have been an isolated instance of such influence.

In some cases, there was a considerable gap between the Chinese dynasty concerned and the completed history of that dynasty. For example, *Liang shu* [*The History of the Liang Dynasty*]—which like *Nan Qi shu* is an important source on Funan—was finished in 636, eighty years after the Liang dynasty ended. This time difference means that even though the standard histories often read as if they are contemporaneous, their narratives, including their accounts of Funan and Zhenla, are written from the viewpoint of a later age. But there are exceptions, notably *Song shu* [*The History of the Liu Song Dynasty*], *Nan Qi shu* and *Sui shu* [*The History of the Sui Dynasty*], all of which were completed within a short time of the dynasty whose affairs they chronicle. *Nan Qi shu* was finished within twenty years of the end of the Southern Qi dynasty, while *Sui shu* with its detailed portrayal of early Zhenla was finished only eighteen years after the demise of the Sui dynasty in 618, and refers to a Zhenla king, Īśānavarman, who was probably still reigning when it was written. The *Nan Qi shu* and *Sui shu* accounts of Zhenla thus have an immediacy missing from some of the other histories.

The formats of the histories vary, but all of them employ the composite *ji zhuan* form.[23] The *ji* (annals) consist of chronological accounts of the main events of each reign in the dynasty, including tribute missions; the *zhuan* (biographies and other records, called *lie zhuan*, "ranked biographies," from *Song shu* onwards) include not only the lives of distinguished officials and other outstanding individuals, but also, importantly for us, accounts of foreign states.[24]

These accounts come towards the end of the *zhuan* sections and constitute the histories' main source of information about Funan and, to a decreasing extent, Zhenla as well. Perhaps because of changing trade patterns and diplomatic priorities (possible explanations are considered in chapter eight), accounts of Zhenla in the standard histories dwindle over time to the point that in *Yuan shi* [*The History of the Yuan Dynasty*], completed in 1370, decades after Zhou Daguan's visit to the Angkor capital, there is no longer any description of Zhenla at all.

Given the nature of the standard histories, it is clear that the purpose of these accounts, although never explicitly stated, was to portray those aspects of foreign states that were of interest to the Chinese emperor and his court: their location; their relations with the Chinese empire, including the tribute they submitted; the nature of their government and customs; and their local produce, including produce not available in China.

Encyclopedias and compendiums

Other officially commissioned books with material on Funan and Zhenla include the great compendiums and encyclopedias written during the Tang and Song dynasties, as well as *hui yao* (collected statutes).[25] Of the compendiums, which are collections of materials about Chinese government and government institutions, the most significant are the *San tong* [*Three Comprehensive Studies*]: the late eighth-century *Tong dian* [*A Comprehensive History of Institutions*], the twelfth-century *Tong zhi* [*A Comprehensive Treatise on Institutions*], and the fourteenth-century *Wenxian tongkao* [*A Comprehensive Study of Institutions on the Basis of Authoritative Documents*]. All three repeat material on Funan and Zhenla found in the standard histories and have little to add to our knowledge of them, although Western scholars have sometimes cited *Wenxian tongkao* as a source because its account of Zhenla, taken from the seventh-century *Sui shu*, was translated into French in the late nineteenth century, and so became accessible to scholars who did not know classical Chinese.[26]

Of the encyclopedias, two are important sources on Funan and Zhenla. These are the tenth-century *Taiping yulan* [*An Encyclopedia Compiled during the Era of Great Peace* {976–983} *and Read by the Emperor*] and the eleventh-century *Cefu yuangui* [*Outstanding Models from the Storehouse of Literature*]. Of these two, *Taiping yulan* is much the more significant. This voluminous work, consisting of a thousand *juan* (chapters), is named in acknowledgement of how the Song Emperor Taizong read through three chapters every day for a year, recalling to himself as he did the remark of the early poet Tao Yuanming that "it's always worthwhile, opening a book."[27] It is an important source for very early material on the state of Funan, including fragments from the firsthand account by the third-century Chinese envoy Kang Tai, which are scattered in different parts of the work and will be considered in detail in the following chapter. The other encyclopedia, *Cefu yuangui*, is mainly useful as a source for information about tribute missions, which it lists in some detail.

Of the *hui yao* (collected statutes), the most notable is the tenth-century *Tang hui yao* [*Essential Documents and Regulations of the Tang Dynasty*], which refers to an early date for the takeover of Funan by Zhenla.

These official sources have been subject to numerous redactions and published in various editions. For the standard histories, I have used here as my main source the punctuated and lightly annotated modern editions published in Beijing by the leading publishing house Zhonghua Book Company (Zhonghua shuju). I have also used the online texts of these works available through one of the various online databases now available, the Chinese Text Project.[28] The Chinese Text Project is not entirely free of flaws—in some instances, for example, phrases and passages are interpolated from elsewhere—but overall the project is an extraordinary achievement, and its search engines are most helpful. I have used various modern editions of other works, as listed in appendix one. My principal source of one work, *Taiping yulan*, is an early, unpunctuated Song dynasty edition, published as four large volumes in facsimile form by Zhonghua shuju in 1960, since this edition occasionally has readings that make better sense than those in later versions.

The task of identifying relevant texts has been made much easier by two important collections of early Chinese texts on Cambodia edited by contemporary Chinese scholars, both punctuated and lightly annotated.[29] These compilations have brought my attention to several texts that I would not otherwise have discovered, including textual material on Funan that Pelliot missed.

The writings of envoys, officials, Daoists, Buddhists, and others

References to Funan and Zhenla in unofficial writings are infrequent and scattered. Various books that may have included accounts of early Cambodia have been largely or wholly lost to posterity. Even the envoy Zhou Daguan's portrait of Angkor as we now have is evidently only part of what he originally wrote. One source suggests that perhaps two-thirds of the original has been lost.[30]

The earliest extant account of Funan comes from the writings of the third-century Chinese envoy Kang Tai. Being a firsthand observer, Kang Tai lends an attractive sense of reportage to his writings, although sadly only small parts of them remain. Kang Tai was an official envoy, and his writings must have derived from a report he submitted on his return to the imperial court. As such, they were unofficial only to the extent that they may also have been intended to appeal to an audience larger than just the emperor. While this is plausible, we do not know how widely these writings were distributed and read.

Other early works on Funan are now lost or exist only in tantalizing fragments. These include writings by Yang Fu, a second-century official in south China; a record by Kang Tai's traveling companion Zhu Ying; a work by Wan Zhen, a third-century chronicler of strange tales; and an account by the late fifth- or early sixth-century scholar Zhu Zhi of his foreign travels. Otherwise, there are some high-flown passages relating to Funan in Daoist writings attributed to the alchemist Ge Hong (283–343), and informative references to Funan in Buddhist writings, including records kept by traveling Buddhist monks, notably Buddhabhadra (fl. early sixth century) and Yijing (635–713).[31]

Surprisingly, perhaps, there is little about Funan or Zhenla in the stories about strange things and outlandish places that became popular in China from the Six Dynasties onwards. Extracts from various early works with *yi wu zhi* (annals of strange things) in their title appear in *Taiping yulan* and other encyclopedias and compendiums, attesting to a growing Chinese interest in the unusual and unfamiliar. But little on Funan and Zhenla remains to us in these works, now mostly lost, or in the short stories of strange events and legends (*chuan qi*) that came into their own during the Tang dynasty.[32]

During the latter part of the Song dynasty (960–1279), with its economic revolution in commerce and communications, unofficial accounts of Zhenla finally began to emerge.[33] By that time, Chinese scholar-officials were traveling more widely, and in some cases they wrote about their travel experiences.[34] In the twelfth and thirteenth centuries scholar-officials also wrote works of another related genre, unofficial treatises (*zhi*) or records of out-of-the-way peoples and places, mainly but not exclusively in China. The best known of these treatises—or gazetteers, as James Hargett helpfully calls them—all include material on Zhenla.[35] These are Fan Chengda (1126–1193)'s *Guihai yuheng zhi* [*The Treatise of the Supervisor and Guardian of the Cinnamon Sea*]; Zhou Qufei (1135–1189)'s *Lingwai daida* [*Representative Responses to Questions about Regions beyond Wuling* {the five mountains of southern China}]; and Zhao Rugua (1170–1231)'s *Zhu fan zhi* [*A Treatise on the Various Foreigners*].[36] Collectively, they constitute the main body of unofficial Chinese records relevant to Zhenla before the writings of Zhou Daguan.

Finally, the writings of Zhou Daguan himself, based on a visit he paid to Angkor from 1296 to 1297, remain a uniquely valuable source of information about the kings, religions, culture, and economy of Zhenla (the name Zhou uses), then ruled by Indravarman III and apparently in the final stages of its imperial power. Apart from a short final chapter on late Yuan and Ming dynasty sources, an updated translation of Zhou's record of his trip is the point at which this study concludes.[37]

Secondary sources

The western and Chinese secondary sources used in this work fall into two main categories. The first and most important consists of writings on the history, politics, foreign relations, society, economics, archaeology, and art of Funan and Zhenla, with special attention paid to what these writings have to say about Chinese primary sources. The second relates to the history of imperial China, particularly its historiography, tribute system, and trading practices, and its relations with foreign states, including Funan and Zhenla. A third, related group, less central to this work, concerns the history and development of Southeast Asia and of maritime trade and other activities involving Southeast Asian states, including Cambodia.

The first category of secondary sources encompasses a range of scholars with different views about the origins and early development of Funan. The pioneer in the study of Funan was the French sinologist Paul Pelliot. In two lengthy articles published in 1903 and 1925, Pelliot refuted an earlier view that Chinese sources had little to offer for the identification of Funan, translating all of the early Chinese texts on Funan that he could find.[38] He was a scrupulous scholar, but basing his assessment on these texts, he lent weight to the theory that from the outset of its recorded history Funan was under Hindu (or Indian, as the French term hindou is often misleadingly translated) influence. For example, he expressed the opinion that

Fig. 1 Paul Pelliot (1878–1945), circa 1920. The pioneer of Western studies of early Cambodia, Pelliot analysed and translated into French early Chinese texts on Funan. He also reassessed and retranslated the Yuan envoy Zhou Daguan's first-hand account of the kingdom of Angkor (Zhenla).

Source: Keystone-France/Gamma-Keystone via Getty Images, 2003–2020

Fig. 2 George Coedès (1886–1969), at an unknown date. In his time the doyen of Southeast Asian studies, Coedès shared and expanded on Pelliot's view that Funan was one of the early Southeast Asian states to have been 'Hinduized' under the influence of Indian culture.

the Funanese names that Kang Tai wrote about in the third century CE were Chinese versions of names that were "more or less Hinduized" (plus ou moins hindouisée).[39]

This theory was accepted by the archaeologists Étienne Aymonier and Louis Finot, and further developed by the historian George Coedès, then doyen of early Southeast Asian history. Coedès explained his views at length in his classic study *Les états hindouisés d'Indochine and d'Indonésie*, first published in 1948 and based on an earlier work published in 1944, then updated in 1964 and translated into English in 1968 as *The Indianized States of Southeast Asia*. In this work, Coedès portrayed Funan as one of a number of Southeast Asian states that formed as Indian civilization expanded to the east, first through merchants and later through "the first two castes," by which he meant *kṣatriya* (warrior-rulers) and brahmins, with Buddhism playing an enabling role. In Coedès' view, this peaceful expansion permitted early Southeast Asian states to preserve "the essentials of their individual cultures," but his emphasis was on their Indianization.[40]

In his comprehensive 1951 history *The Ancient Khmer Empire*, the historian Lawrence Palmer Briggs seemed to concur with Pelliot, Aymonier, and Finot, though he focused on the Funan's Indianization (as he called it) from the fifth century CE onwards, rather than earlier.[41] But other scholars took a more measured view. In 1955, Jacob van Leur published an influential paper in which he described Indian influence in the region as "a thin and flaking glaze" under which indigenous forms continued to exist.[42] In 1977, Ian Mabbett observed that "the conventional analysis of the problem of 'Indianization' . . . masks a complex and many-hued process;" compared Sanskrit lore to a great, unevenly-spreading stain; and cautioned against the view derived from "a few Chinese reports" of Funan being an empire or Indian-style state.[43]

In 1979, Claude Jacques warned against taking Chinese texts on early Cambodia too literally.[44] In his 2006 work *The Language of the Gods in the World of Men*, Sheldon Pollock traced the spread of Sanskrit through Southeast Asia but noted the absence of "anything remotely resembling colonization."[45] In more recent times, archaeologists such as Pierre-Yves Manguin and Miriam Stark, building on early work by Louis Malleret, have added depth to our understanding of the variegated nature of early Cambodia through their analysis of archaeological sites such as Óc Eo and Angkor Borei.

The Cambodia specialist Michael Vickery provided the basis for a quite different perspective on early Cambodia. In a carefully researched work on seventh- and eighth-century Cambodia, published in 1998, and in a long article published five years later, Vickery criticized Pelliot's "Indologist prejudice" and his tendency to give primacy to Chinese texts, as well as Coedès' and others' views on Hinduization.[46] He argued instead for a reappraisal of early Cambodian history emphasizing indigenous culture and pre-Angkorian epigraphy, especially Khmer language inscriptions that gave details of everyday life.[47] In contrast to the Chinese portrayal of Funan and early Zhenla as fully formed kingdoms, Vickery postulated the gradual emergence of numerous indigenous polities under chiefs with the Mon-Khmer title *poñ* (*fan* in Chinese) that slowly coalesced into the political and social foundations for Angkor.[48] This emphasis on local cultures and elites rather than external influences such as Indianization now characterizes much of the contemporary scholarship on early Cambodia as well as on other Southeast Asian polities.[49]

The historian David Chandler and the archaeologist Michael Coe have taken Vickery's and others' views into account in their overviews of Cambodia's early development, Chandler in his *History of Cambodia*, fourth ed. (2008), and Coe in his *Angkor and the Khmer Civilization*, second ed. (2018). For their part, modern Chinese historians—notably Chen Xiansi in his 1990 history of Cambodia, Chen Xujing in his 1992 history of Funan, and Chan Kai Wing (Chen Jiarong) in his 2003 work on historical sources for early communications across the South China Sea—have paid these views less attention. Instead, they have largely accepted the conceptions of Funan and Zhenla that appear in classical Chinese sources, and have devoted their research to a fuller account of what these sources reveal about them.

While early notions of wholesale Indianization have been discredited, debate over the historical import of Chinese sources has not entirely ended. A 2004 paper by the French archaeologist Éric Bourdonneau criticizes Vickery's distrust of Chinese sources and what Bourdonneau calls "the repeatedly distorted portrayal of Chinese sources [that] betrays the culturalist views lingering behind concepts in use in recent historiographical research"—in other words, the negative effects of anti-Chinese bias.[50]

The approach I have taken here is to present the textual evidence about early Cambodia chronologically and with reference to relevant contextual information. I accept clear signs of Indian influence—for example, when the names of Funanese kings are demonstrably based on Sanskrit—but avoid assumptions about Indian or Chinese agency or perceptions unless they can be substantiated.

Secondary sources on Cambodia from the eighth century onwards have less to offer this study, although Chen Xiansi and Tatsuo Hoshino provide valuable insights into the early Zhenla period.[51] They have less to offer partly because of the paradoxical fact, mentioned earlier, that as Angkor grew richer in architectural, archaeological, and epigraphic resources, Chinese sources on Zhenla diminished, and for nearly three centuries (the ninth to the late eleventh century) were virtually non-existent. Only with the emergence of Song dynasty gazetteers and the firsthand account of Angkor by Zhou Daguan do Chinese texts again become significant.

The other main group of secondary materials—those relating to imperial China's historiography, tribute, trade, and relations with foreign states—can be dealt with more briefly. The structures, prejudices, and purposes of China's standard histories and imperial encyclopedias and compendiums are the subject of studies, some of them generic and others of particular books, by many eminent scholars.[52] In the growing literature on imperial China's early foreign relations, Wang Gungwu's pioneering 1958 work "The Nanhai Trade," which makes extensive use of primary sources, remains an essential resource.[53]

The ideology of tribute—a system designed to combine acknowledgement of status and prestige with practical concerns of trade and security—and its relationship with commerce have yet to be fully explored. However, Robert Wicks on money and trade in early Southeast Asia, Tansen Sen on Buddhist-era diplomacy and trade, Jonathan Skaff on Sui-Tang China's external relations, Shiba Yoshinobu on Song dynasty commerce, and Derek Heng on Song dynasty tribute and trade (to mention but a few) have deepened our understanding of the Chinese tribute system and described how it was often though not always interconnected with trade. More generally, essays by John K. Fairbank, Lien-sheng Yang, and Wang Gungwu in *The Chinese World Order*, edited by Fairbank in 1968, are still valuable for their insights into imperial China's view of the *tianxia* (all-under-heaven) world order over which it presided. This view has subsequently been qualified by the studies of Morris Rossabi, David Heng, and others that show how during Song and Yuan times the Chinese government functioned as one state within a multi-state system.[54]

In outline, these are the primary and secondary sources I have used. Let me now discuss the approach I have taken in the work.

On translation

With the exception of the Ming era (chapter ten), I have worked on as many early Chinese texts concerning Cambodia as I can identify, engaging in minor collations but adhering largely to the texts as given in the Zhonghua shuju editions and other modern versions, as listed in the bibliography. Generally, I have translated relevant parts of these texts in full. With a few minor exceptions, translations appear chronologically, starting with texts relating to the Han dynasty and concluding with texts relating to the Yuan dynasty up to the time of Zhou Daguan, with a brief look at sources after Zhou.

My aim with regard to the relationship between source and target texts has been to translate the ancient language used in the source texts into clear, readable, and modern English without losing or obscuring the intended meaning or flavor of the originals. Classical Chinese is a terse medium, and too often translations of classical Chinese texts are made inaccessible by stilted language that strives to reflect particular words or turns of phrase in the original, or by bracketed additions or explanations that interfere with the flow of the text. I have tried to minimize such practices. Occasionally, expressions in Chinese sound awkward in English and have been modified accordingly. For example, the term *fan* (literally "foreign"), which is used to describe customs in non-Chinese states, has occasionally been translated as "local."[55]

Most of the texts translated here are written in a straightforward, detached tone. The standard histories in particular rarely diverge from a dispassionate narrative style, embellished here and there by more elaborate court language when imperial commands and records of meetings with emperors are recounted, as in the passage on Funan in *Nan Qi shu*. Conversations involving Cambodians are rarely recorded, and apart from kings and envoys, individual Cambodians are never mentioned or named. The content of the standard histories is sometimes formulaic, as when they describe Funan's customs, local produce, and royal courts, or when encyclopedists and gazetteers list local products one after another. With occasional exceptions, Zhou Daguan being one, even accounts by individual authors lack a clear authorial voice. Fortunately, the content of the texts is sufficiently informative, even engrossing, to make up for this absence.

The transmission of texts

Translating ancient texts from any language raises a number of issues, most of them very familiar to scholars in the field. In the case of classical Chinese texts, there are particular difficulties. One of these is the distorting effect of textual transmission. In China the transmission of primary sources over many centuries has led to scribal errors and sometimes unhelpful editorial interventions, particularly in texts dealing with proper names and other materials unfamiliar to Chinese scholars. One or two slips of the brush can easily transform one character into an entirely different one. In very early texts on Cambodia (for instance, the writings of Kang Tai, Zhu Ying, Wan Zhen, Ge Hong, and Zhu Zhi), the names of original works and their authors have also sometimes undergone changes, resulting in such issues as an author being cited under more than one title without it being clear how many works are involved, and whether the author indeed wrote the works attributed to him.[56]

Another concern is that in early encyclopedias and compendiums, fragments of a text are broken up to fit the categories established by their editors, who sometimes give incomplete references to the source and no indication of its original structure or of the order in which it was first written.

The pronunciation of old names and words

Another difficulty in translating early Chinese texts is pronunciation. Because the Chinese writing system is non-alphabetic and the spoken languages of China have evolved over time, the current pronunciation in standard Chinese (Putonghua) of old Chinese texts does not accurately convey the pronunciation used when they were written.[57] In this book such differences matter mainly with respect to proper nouns, whose Chinese pronunciation between the Han and Yuan dynasties was often quite different from what it is today. These pronunciations sometimes have to be reconstructed for these proper nouns to be properly understood. As a rough guide to pronouncing proper nouns from the Han to the Tang, I have used the Swedish linguist Bernhard Karlgren's reconstruction of what he calls Ancient Chinese, defined as the language of the capital Chang'an (now Xi'an) in 600 CE.[58]

Since he published it over sixty years ago, Karlgren's work has been updated and in some ways superseded by other efforts to reconstruct the sounds of Ancient Chinese (to stay with Karlgren's term) and ancient Chinese dialects, notably by Edwin Pulleyblank and more recently by William Baxter and Laurent Sagart. Pulleyblank has also provided a lexicon of reconstructed pronunciation for Chinese during the Yuan dynasty (1271–1368). Despite its shortcomings, Karlgren's work remains a valuable resource and is the main reference used to reconstruct pronunciations in this study. When citing Karlgren's reconstructed pronunciation, I have added the letter *K* after it. In those few cases when Karlgren does not provide a reconstructed pronunciation I have cited Pulleyblank's reconstructed pronunciation, adding the letter *P* after it.[59]

Placenames and nomenclature

Two other more far-reaching issues are to do with toponymy or placenames, and nomenclature.

The first of these has to do with, among other things, the origin and meaning of the names Funan and Zhenla.

There are at least two categories of names for foreign states in these records. The first consists of transliterations of local names bearing no other discernible meaning. The second consists of transliterations or other renditions of local names, but with characters that convey a meaning. There seems also to be a third category consisting of exonyms, but with occasional exceptions (for example, Da Qin or Great Qin for the Roman Empire, usually taken to mean the eastern Roman Empire), this is harder to provide evidence for.[60]

The name Funan (whose literal meaning in Chinese is "supporting the south") appears to belong to the second category. As mentioned earlier, Funan may be a transliteration of *bnam*, the Old Khmer word for "mountain," the modern word form of which is *phnom*. The pronunciation of the two characters for Funan in Ancient Chinese was Pi̯u nậm [K]; as Coedès points out, they bear a resemblance to *bnam*.[61] In writing about his sea voyage from India, the Buddhist monk Yijing (635–713), an accomplished linguist, adds weight to the identification of Funan with *bnam* by recording that his ship "reached the state of Ba'nan (Ba nam [P]), formerly called Funan."[62] The mountain in question was no doubt a sacred one, perhaps the mountain described by the monk Nāgasena during his visit to the Chinese court on behalf of the king of Funan in 484.[63]

As for the name Zhenla (Tśi̯ĕn lâp [K])—its meaning in Chinese being "true sacrifice" or, in a variant form of *la*, "true wax"—its etymology is uncertain.[64] The linguist Michel Atelme argues that "true wax" is indeed its meaning, given the importance the Chinese attached to Cambodian wax; but wax is not mentioned at all in the first, important Chinese description of Zhenla and its products provided by *Sui shu*, making this explanation unlikely.[65] Michel Ferlus proposes that the name derives from Vietnamese and means "people of the wax," but the same objection applies to his explanation as to Atelme's.[66]

In notes published after his death in 1945, Paul Pelliot put forward another, more adventurous idea, namely that Zhenla might translate to "China defeated." His argument was that *lâp* could represent the Khmer word *răp* (flatten), as in the name of the Cambodian city Siem Reap (pronounced Siem-răp in modern Khmer), which translates to "Siam flattened." Tśi̯ĕn, meanwhile, could be a local pronunciation of Qin, the third-century BCE dynasty from which the name China is thought to have derived.[67] Pelliot surmised that early Cambodian rulers might have found "a malicious pleasure" (un malin plaisir) in devising such a name following some conflict with the southern reaches of the Chinese empire. As it happens, there is at least one such conflict on record: an attack that Tang forces launched in or soon after 713 on a hostile southern alliance including forces from Zhenla. But this particular conflict cannot confirm Pelliot's theory, since by 713 the name Zhenla was firmly established in Chinese annals, and in any case the Chinese forces claimed victory. Nonetheless, it remains possible that there were other early, unrecorded conflicts between Chinese and Cambodians.[68] Pelliot's suggestion also has the merit of being consistent how in Song and Yuan times Zhenla took the alternative name Zhanla. According to *Ming shi* [*The History of the Ming Dynasty*], it did so to mark its defeat of the Cham (Zhan in Chinese). This shows that Zhang Tingyu, the lead author of *Ming shi*, accepted that the *la* of Zhanla did indeed mean "wiped out" or "defeated."[69]

Last but not least, the historian and translator Geoff Wade argues that Zhenla is a Hokkien rendition of the Khmer word *tonlé* (river), which in present-day Hokkien is pronounced *chinlah*, and so refers to Tonlé Sap, the freshwater lake and river in the center of the Cambodian plains.[70] This identification does not take into account that Zhang Tingyu took the *la* in Zhenla to mean "wiped out" or "destroyed." All the same, Wade's explanation of Zhenla's original meaning is perhaps the most plausible, even if Pelliot's suggestion is the most intriguing.

Nomenclature involves another far-reaching issue. A number of terms used in ancient Chinese texts reflect the worldview of imperial Chinese writers in ways that affect our understanding of their meaning. It is worth briefly considering two of them: *guo* (state or country) and *cheng* (city).[71]

Chinese usages of the term *guo* date back at least as far as the Zhou dynasty (1046–256 BCE), when it sometimes conveyed the sense of a city or enfeoffed territory and at others a more fully formed state.[72] In the Warring States period (675–221 BCE), *guo* referred to either to a capital city or state in a variety of sources, notably *Zuo zhuan* [*The Commentary of Zuo* or *The Tradition of Zuo*] and *Meng zi* [*Mencius*], both dating from the fourth century BCE. During that period China came to be divided among seven mutually antagonistic polities, all called *guo*.[73] These *guo* evolved into entities that more or less conformed to the notion of a state as defined by the sociologist Charles Tilly: a "coercion-wielding organization" with an army, an administration, and a capital city.[74] While they varied in size, each of these seven states controlled substantial territory and was ruled by a king (*wang*).[75] These circumstances match the definition of *guo* in the first extant Chinese dictionary, the first-century *Shuo wen jie zi*, where it is defined as *bang* (territory) and vice versa.[76]

Official Chinese descriptions of frontier and other non-Chinese *guo* in Tang and pre-Tang times indicate that these *guo* were also of different strengths and compositions. They ranged in size and authority, from polities as large as Persia to places that were little bigger than villages. *Jiu Tang shu* [*The Old History of the Tang Dynasty*], for instance, refers to "small cities (*xiao cheng*), all called *guo*" to the east of Shui Zhenla (Water Zhenla, the name *Jiu Tang shu* gives to the southern part of Zhenla in the eighth century).[77] Similarly, *Taiping yulan* quotes what may be a Six Dynasty source to describe a state called Xitu with ten or so dependencies, small states (*xiao guo*) numbering some two thousand foreign families in all.[78]

Descriptions such as these suggest that many early *guo* located on or beyond China's frontiers—including Funan and Zhenla before the Kingdom of Angkor—may have been no more than a cluster or clusters of small communities or chiefdoms, rather than more fully formed states as Chinese writers might have thought of them.[79]

Not all of them, moreover, were ruled by kings. Funan's founding queen Liuye, variously referred to as ruler (*zhu*) or monarch (*wang*), is repeatedly identified as a woman, while one Asian state, Nü guo (the Women's State), is said to have been ruled by queens (*nü wang*).[80] So while translating *guo* as "state" can be misleading, so too can the habit, adopted from Pelliot and others, of rendering the term *guo* as "kingdom."

The early meaning of the term *cheng* (city, or by extension city wall) is subject to similar considerations. Early usages of *cheng* seem to refer mainly to walled settlements, often housing the palaces of rulers, characteristic of state or regional capitals from the Warring States on.[81] But how much Chinese chroniclers identified these early models of *cheng* with those they mentioned in accounts of Southeast Asian states is uncertain. Some of the early Southeast Asian *cheng* referred to in official sources seem to amount to little more than large villages. In describing seventh-century Zhenla, for example, *Sui shu* records that the state had thirty large cities with several thousand families apiece, the adjective "large" suggesting that smaller cities would house much fewer people.[82]

It is not clear from Chinese accounts whether foreign *cheng* were always walled. Sometimes the walls of *cheng* are specifically mentioned. For example, the seventh-century *Liang shu* records that the state of Langyaxiu had city walls built of bricks. The sixth-century *Nan Qi shu* describes Funan's city walls as being made of fencing, a point also made by *Liang shu* about the city walls of the state of Panpan.[83] But whether these walls are mentioned because they were built with unusual materials or simply because they existed we cannot be sure. The most we can deduce is that beyond China, *cheng* referred to settlements varying considerably in size and structure. They ranged from what would today be regarded as large villages to sizeable walled settlements such as Īśānapura, described by *Sui shu* as a *cheng* with twenty thousand or more families under its outer walls.[84]

Locations and languages

Another cause for debate has been the locations of Funan and Zhenla. It is now widely accepted that Funan was centered on Óc Eo and Angkor Borei on and around the lower reaches of the Mekong River, while Zhenla developed into the Kingdom of Angkor. Chinese primary sources provide information, not always consistent, about the sizes and locations of both Funan and Zhenla. This issue is discussed at various points in the book and revisited in the conclusion. There is also some controversy as to whether the language and culture of Funan was Mon-Khmer or Austronesian, an issue touched on in the main text and revisited in the conclusion.

The layout of this book

This book consists of an introduction, ten chapters, a conclusion, and six appendices. Chapters one to ten are largely comprised of translated Chinese texts, accompanied by comments on the language and content of the texts, as well as discussions of what the texts tell us, what they omit, and what perspectives the texts bring to bear. The translated texts are connected by a historical narrative. Chapter five is an exception that draws on the first four chapters to provide a brief history of Funan on the basis of Chinese records.

More specifically, chapter one addresses the earliest sources on Funan, largely from the third century CE, including the fragmentary writings of the envoy Kang Tai. Chapter two considers early Daoist and Buddhist references to Funan, as well as the accounts of Funan in the first three of the standard histories of southern China (*Jin shu*, *Song shu*, and *Nan Qi shu*) during the period of disunity between the Han and the Sui dynasties.

Chapter three deals with the accounts of Funan in the remaining two standard histories of the southern dynasties (*Liang shu* and *Chen shu* [*The History of the Chen Dynasty*]), and the composite standard history of those dynasties (*Nan shi* [*The History of the Southern Dynasties*]). Chapter four consists of translations and analyses of Chinese texts from the remaining standard histories (*Sui shu*, *Jiu Tang shu*, and *Xin Tang shu* [*The New History of the Tang Dynasty*]) and other official works that mention or describe Funan. These works date from the early Tang to the later Yuan dynasty (seventh to fourteenth century).

Chapter five, as mentioned, reprises the content of records translated in the first four chapters to provide a brief history of Funan.

Chapter six focuses on the *Sui shu* rendition of Zhenla, the fullest and most contemporary account of Zhenla in the standard histories. Chapters seven and eight are concerned with shorter passages on Zhenla as it was during the Tang and Song dynasties. These are found mainly in the standard histories *Jiu Tang shu*, *Xin Tang shu*, and *Song shi* [*The History of the Song Dynasty*], as well as in the principal encyclopedias. Chapter eight includes translated passages on Zhenla in unofficial writings, including the three gazetteers mentioned earlier by Fan Chengda, Zhou Qufei, and Zhao Rugua.

Chapter nine assesses the writings of the Yuan envoy Zhou Daguan in light of the findings of earlier chapters. Chapter ten provides a brief overview of late Yuan and Ming sources on Cambodia, with selected extracts.

A conclusion summarizes the findings of chapters two through ten regarding the contributions they make to our understanding of early Cambodian history, their gaps and omissions, and the Chinese perspectives that inform them.

There are six appendices consisting of

1. a chronological list of official writings used as primary sources, in Chinese and English;
2. a list of Chinese dynasties and Cambodian rulers during Funan and Zhenla;
3. a table of tribute missions to China from Funan and Zhenla from the Han dynasty to the Song dynasty, with a note on the composition of the tribute;
4. a table comparing the subject matter of the four main early sources on Funan (Kang Tai, *Jin shu*, *Nan Qi shu*, *Liang shu*);
5. a note on Chinese sources on early Cambodia's neighbour Linyi;
6. a glossary of people and places referred to in the book.

The lists of books and rulers in appendices one and two may be useful for anyone bewildered by the many book titles and people encountered throughout this work. Likewise, the glossary in appendix six may be a helpful point of reference to search out an obscure historical player or location.

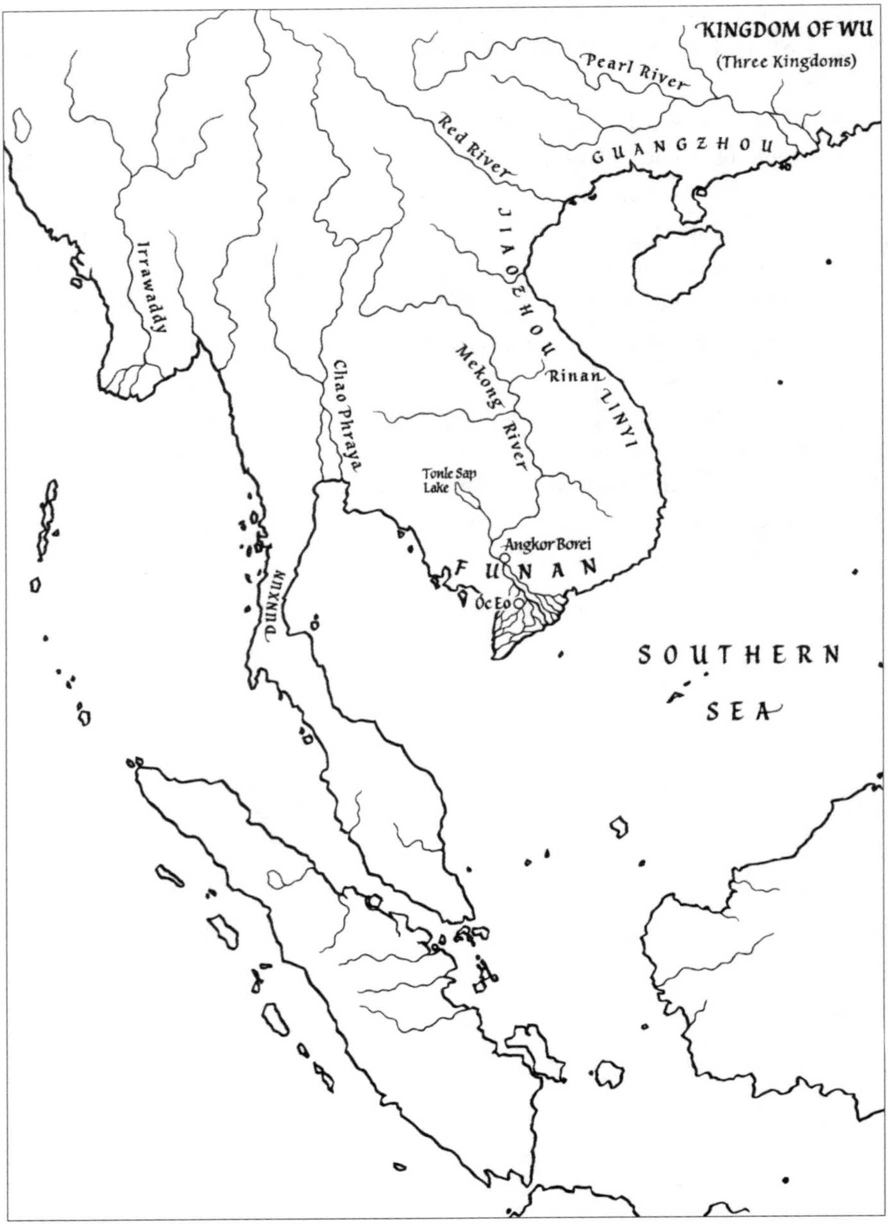

Map 1. Funan during the Three kingdoms (220–280 CE)

1

Early portraits: ambassadors going south, and others

In the early years of the third century CE, the Han dynasty (202–28 BCE, 27–220 CE) finally collapsed after a prolonged period of warfare. China was then divided for most of the third century into three states: Wei in the north, Shu in the southwest, and Wu in the southeast. This was the period of the so-called Three Kingdoms. The transitional era between the Han dynasty and the Three Kingdoms is still celebrated in China for its tales of swashbuckling heroes, subtle strategems, and mighty battles.[1] The capital city of the eastern state of Wu was Jianye, present-day Nanjing on the lower reaches of the Yangzi River. Jianye was close to the sea, and Wu came to develop maritime contacts with various southern states, including Funan. These southern states were known as the states of Nanhai, the Southern Sea—that is, the present-day South China Sea and waters beyond it.

Most of the Chinese texts translated and discussed in this chapter date from or refer to the Three Kingdoms period. They include the first mention of contact between China and Funan, as well as the writings about Funan by the Wu envoy Kang Tai and by another third-century Wu official, Wan Zhen. The available remnants of Kang Tai's and Wan Zhen's writings on Funan are gathered and translated into English here for the first time. The texts here also include a passage mentioning Funan by a renowned third-century poet, Zuo Si, and a short passage by a later traveler, Zhu Zhi.

The earliest references to Funan

Funan is mentioned twice in in *San guo zhi* [*The Annals of the Three States*, often called *The Annals of the Three Kingdoms*], the standard history of the Three Kingdoms period. This is the earlier reference to Funan in a reliable Chinese text.

San guo zhi was written in or around the 280s by the scholar-official Chen Shou (233–297).[2] There are other, even earlier references in Chinese texts to events or entities that might be identified with Funan or Cambodia, but these are either implausible or unsubstantiated. Legend tells us, for instance, of envoys from the ancient state of Yueshang, south of the Red River Delta, going to Funan after visiting the Chinese court in the early Zhou dynasty (1046–256 BCE). But there seems to be no reliable basis for the story.[3] Nor is there any good reason to suppose that envoys from a state called Jiubuzhi (Kjwi: pi̯əu: dz'i- [K]), who delivered tribute to the Han court in the first century CE, came from anywhere near Cambodia, despite the uncanny similarity between the names Jiubuzhi and Kambuja (born of Kambu), a term for Cambodia first used many centuries later.[4]

The view that *San guo zhi* was the first Chinese source to refer to Funan originated in Paul Pelliot's seminal 1903 study of Funan. Pelliot wrote that "before *San guo zhi* the official history [of China] does not provide us, I believe, with text in which the name Funan appears."[5] His view is corroborated by the two collections of old Chinese documents on Cambodia mentioned in the introduction, neither of which includes references to Funan earlier than those in *San guo zhi*.[6] For my part, I have undertaken a full search of the fourth century BCE *Zuo zhuan* and the first four standard histories—*Shi ji* [*The Record of the Historian*], *Han shu* [*The History of the Former Han Dynasty*], *Hou Han shu* [*The History of the Later Han Dynasty*], and *San guo zhi*—and have found no mention of Funan apart from the references in *San guo zhi*.

All the same, it is not yet possible to say for sure that references to Funan are absent from other early sources, given that archaeological discoveries in China continue to uncover extraordinary new texts and variants of previously discovered texts from the first millennium BCE.[7]

As things stand, the lack of any reference to Funan in Chinese records before those in *San guo zhi* is somewhat surprising, especially since one of the sites most associated with Funan, Angkor Borei, was probably settled by the fifth to fourth century BCE, while another, Óc Eo, started to develop in "a somewhat sudden manner," according to the archaeologist Pierre-Yves Manguin, in the first century CE.[8] The third-century envoy Kang Tai's descriptions further attest to the well-formed nature of the social and political culture of Funan by the time of his visit there.

It is quite possible, of course, that there were earlier accounts of Funan but that these no longer exist. The fragmentary condition of Kang Tai's and Wan Zhen's writings are reminders of the extent to which early Chinese records of other states, including those beyond the Southern Sea, have been lost.

There does exist one possible reference to Funan before *San guo zhi*: a very short passage—of no great significance in itself—about Funanese fans found in two tenth-century compilations, *Shi lei fu* [*A Prose Poem on Categories of Things*] and *Taiping yulan*.[9] The passage reads:

> Those in the state of Funan previously only knew how to make large fans, which they arranged for people to hold, not realizing that fans could be used by individuals for themselves. But now in the hot weather they each use their own.

It has been suggested that this passage dates from the first century CE and is the work of Yang Fu (fl. 76?–84? CE), an official in south China who may have served under Emperor Zhang (r. 76–88) of the Later Han dynasty.[10] But the evidence for Yang's authorship is uncertain. He is not officially recorded as serving the Later Han court until some six centuries later, when his name appears in the standard history *Sui shu* (636).[11] Neither this entry nor a subsequent entry about him in *Jiu Tang shu* (945) firmly establishes his authorship of the passage on fans. Nor is he mentioned as the author of the passage in either of the two compilations in which the passage appears.[12]

Background to the journey south by Kang Tai and Zhu Ying

Funan aside, we know from both Chinese textual evidence and archaeological findings that southern China was in touch with various foreign states, nearby and farther afield, from the Later Han dynasty on. A passage in *Han shu* describes five southern states (none of them Funan) as far away as Huangzhi in South India that could be reached by sea, noting that "from the days of Emperor Wu [r. 140–86 BCE] until now they have all come with tribute."[13] According to this same *Han shu* passage, Chinese merchants sailed to distant parts in search of goods, using foreign—probably Malay—rather than Chinese ships to do so.[14]

If Chinese merchants used foreign vessels, they did so despite the fact that by the time of Emperor Wu, Chinese boat-building skills were well developed, with Chinese naval operations taking place along the southern Chinese coast.[15] These operations included a naval attack by Emperor Wu in 112 CE on the kingdom of Nanyue, whose capital was at Panyu, the present-day city of Guangzhou.[16] Evidence for the Nanyue kingdom's wealth and access to foreign goods includes the sites of the royal palace and the tombs of the Nanyue kings, where gold and silver decorated with west Asian and Persian designs, glass beads, African ivory, and frankincense—among other exotic objects—have been excavated since 1983.[17]

Emperor Wu's attack on Nanyue led to the kingdom's absorption into the Han empire, and its division into nine commanderies or administrative divisions spanning the present-day Chinese provinces of Guangdong, Guangxi, and Hainan, and part of present-day Vietnam. Since several of these commanderies are mentioned in later texts on Cambodia, it is worth noting that their names were Daner, Zhuya, Nanhai, Cangwu, Yulin, Hepu, Jiaozhi, Jiuzhen, and Rinan.[18] The first two were discontinued in the first century CE. Of the remaining seven, Nanhai, Cangwu, Yulin, and Hepu were in the southernmost part of present-day China, while the other three—Jiaozhi, Jiuzhen, and Rinan—were located in the north of present-day Vietnam. The southernmost of these three, Rinan, was one of the points from which travelers later set off for Funan, as Kang Tai and *Nan Qi shu* confirm.

Responsibility for the nine commanderies, known collectively as Jiaozhou (the Jiao region, *zhou* being an administrative region), rested with a regional inspector, the first of whom was appointed in 106.[19] In the 220s, the Jiao region was divided into two regions, Jiaozhou and Guangzhou.[20] During the following three centuries, the commanderies in these regions grew in number, though the number of registered inhabitants in them remained quite small. For example, official Chinese data for the year 464 report 10,453 households for the whole of Jiaozhou, though this figure may have excluded local non-Chinese.[21]

Jiaozhou was a long way from the centers of Chinese power and authority. The sixth-century *Nan Qi shu* reflects what was no doubt the prevailing Chinese view when it describes Jiaozhou as being

> remote and far off, where the sea and the sky meet, in touch beyond with the southern foreigners, from whom come forth valuable goods, incomparably strange and precious things from distant places. Being far away, the people frequently like to rise up in revolt.[22]

By the 220s, the Three Kingdoms had succeeded the Later Han, and the "remote and far off" region of Jiaozhou was ruled, at least in name, by the kingdom of Wu with its capital at Jianye. The first ruler of Wu was Sun Quan (182–252). According to *San guo zhi*, Sun Quan appointed an official by the name of Lü Dai (161–256) as Jiaozhou's regional inspector in 220.[23] Lü Dai put down a local revolt, then turned his attention to the states south of Jiaozhou, evidently looking for ways to develop tribute and trade.[24]

In 226, a merchant from Da Qin—the Roman Empire, more specifically the eastern Roman Empire—visited Sun Quan in Jianye and told him about the glories of the Romans. Spurred on, perhaps, by this prospect of distant wealth, Lü Dai then dispatched an officer to the foreign states beyond China's southern frontiers. The title of the unnamed officer was Assistant Officer to Propagate the Civilization of the State—the state meaning China.[25] As *San guo zhi* notes, soon after this officer's trip south, the kings of three southern states—Funan, Linyi, and a place called Tangming—all sent tribute to Wu, probably to Lü Dai.[26] These tribute missions were probably sent before 231, the year Lü Dai ended his assignment in Jiaozhou. *San guo zhi*'s record of these missions constitutes the first clear mention of Funan in a Chinese source.

Funan appears elsewhere in *San guo zhi* when reference is made to a second tribute mission from the Funanese, sent by the king Fan Zhan in 243. According to *San guo zhi*, the tribute consisted of local produce and musicians.[27] Funanese music and musical performers, including dancers, are subsequently listed in various standard histories and encyclopedias, including *Song shu*, *Sui shu*, *Jiu Tang shu*, *Xin Tang shu*, *Tong dian*, and *Taiping yulan*, all of which have sections devoted to music and musical performers from foreign states.

Kang Tai and Zhu Ying's visits to the southern states

Sometime after that second mission from Funan, Sun Quan sent Kang Tai, a man from a Sogdian background—Sogdians being renowned traders—and a second man, Zhu Ying, as envoys to Funan and other southern states. This time Sun Quan's motive was quite clear: to find out about how to communicate through these southern states with India and the Roman Empire.[28]

The first official source to describe their trip, *Liang shu*, gives Kang Tai the title Gentleman of the Palace, and Zhu Ying the title Assistant Officer to Propagate Civilization. Zhu Ying's title suggests that in addition to investigating communications with countries to the west, Kang and Zhu—like the earlier, unnamed officer sent south by Wu—were charged with the task of spreading the word about Chinese civilization.

On their return to China, Kang Tai and Zhu Ying both reported of their journeys. Their reports are now mostly lost, but fragments survive in later collections.[29]

We do not know exactly where or when Kang Tai and Zhu Ying went on their journey, or how long they were away. *Liang shu* tells us they visited or heard second-hand about "some one hundred and twenty to thirty states."[30] This is a prodigious number of states—even if, as is likely, many of them were very small—and suggests the two men were a long time away. As for dates, their trip seems likely to have begun in the late 240s, the early 250s, or possibly the early 260s.[31]

We learn from *Liang shu* that while in Funan Kang Tai and Zhu Ying met an envoy from India called Chen Song. Chen Song was accompanying Su Wu, a kinsman of the previous Funanese king Fan Zhan. Su Wu had recently returned from a four-year trip to India. He had been sent there by Fan Zhan, whose interest in India had been aroused by the stories of a travelling merchant.[32] Chen Song had much to tell Kang and Zhu about India, including the fact that it was where

Buddhism originated—the first mention of Buddhism, chronologically speaking, in the context of Funan.

Liang shu describes Kang and Zhu's trip in three short, separate entries in a single chapter (*juan*).[33] The three entries are as follows, with the gaps between entries marked by ellipses.

> In the Yuanding period of the Han dynasty [116–110 BCE], Lu Bode, General for Pacifying the Waves, was sent to open up the Hundred Yue and established the commandery of Rinan.[34] From the time of Emperor Wu [141–87 BCE] onwards, the various states beyond the frontiers sent tribute to court. During the time of the Later Han Emperor Huan [147–167 CE], the Roman Empire and India both used this route to send envoys and tribute.[35] At the time of Sun Quan of Wu, Zhu Ying, Assistant Officer for Propagating Civilization, and Kang Tai, Inner Gentleman of the Palace, were sent to communicate with them. They experienced or heard about some one hundred and twenty or hundred and thirty states, on the basis of which they wrote accounts of them . . .
>
> During the time of Wu, Gentleman of the Palace Kang Tai and Assistant Officer Zhu Ying were sent as envoys to the state of [Fan] Xun. The people of the state were still naked, apart from the women wearing clothing that they put their heads through to wear. [Kang] Tai and [Zhu] Ying said to him, "Your state is truly fine, but it's strange that the people are indecent and go about naked." [Fan] Xun then ordered the men of the state to wrap themselves in strips of cloth. Now these strips of cloth are *ganman*, with everyone making them from embroidered material, and only the poor using plain cloth . . .[36]
>
> In the ninth year of the Yanxi reign period [166 CE] of Emperor Huan of the Later Han, King Andun [Marcus Aurelius Antoninus?] of the Roman Empire [Da Qin] sent envoys from beyond the frontiers of Rinan with tribute.[37] This was the only such communication during the time of the Han dynasty. Its people are merchants and frequently come to Funan, Rinan, and Jiaozhi, though people from the various states of the southern frontiers seldom go to the Roman Empire.
>
> In the fifth year of the Huangwu reign period [226 CE] of Sun Quan's rule, a merchant from the Roman Empire called Qin Lun came to Jiaozhi. The governor of Jiaozhi, Wu Miao, sent him to visit Sun Quan. Sun Quan asked him about the customs and habits of his country, and Qin Lun gave him a full reply. At the time, Zhuge Ke was carrying out a punitive attack on Danyang and had captured some dwarves from You and She. When Qin Lun saw them he said, "It's rare to see such people in the Roman Empire." Sun Quan dispatched his officer Liu Xian of Kuaiji with twenty dwarves, ten men, and

ten women to present to Qin Lun; but Liu Xian died on the road, and Qin Lun went straight back to his own country.[38]

During the time of the Han emperor He [r. 89–106 CE], India sent envoys with tribute several times; but after that the western frontier regions were in revolt and these missions ended. In the second and fourth years of the Yanxi reign period [159 and 161 CE] of Emperor Huan, there was frequent tribute from beyond the frontiers of Rinan, but during the Wei and Jin periods [the Three Kingdoms state of Wei (220–265 CE) and the Jin dynasty (265–420 CE)], it ended and there was no further communication.

Once during the time of the state of Wu, Fan Zhan, king of Funan, sent his kinsman Su Wu as an envoy to that state [India]. From Funan he set out from the mouth of Juli and followed the sea across a large bay, going directly northwest and entering in succession several states beside the bay. After perhaps a year or so, he came to the mouth of the great river of India and, going upstream, traveled seven thousand li before arriving.[39]

The king of India was astonished and said, "The shores of the sea are so very far away, and yet this man is here!" He gave orders for him to be given a full view of the country, then sent Chen Song and another person to go back with him with four horses from Yuezhi as recompense to [Fan] Zhan, together with other gifts.[40] After a total of four years, they reached home. At the time of their return, Wu had sent Gentleman of the Palace Kang Tai as an envoy to Funan. He met Chen Song and the other person with him and asked them all about the customs of India. [Chen Song gave Kang a glowing description of India, which he described as "the state where the Buddhist way arose."]

A rare early portrait of a Yuezhi horse. The Chinese greatly admired Yuezhi horses for their strength and size. The king of India is said to have sent four of them as a gift to Fan Zhan, king of Funan. The portrait here is on a silver coin the obverse of which shows Heraios, a king of the Yuezhi chiefdom of Kushan.

Source: https://www.wikiwand.com/en/Heraios

The remnants of Kang Tai's account of Funan

Kang Tai and Zhu Ying's records of their journey and the countries they heard about are two of the many "lost books of medieval China," to use the sinologist Glen Dudbridge's phrase—works that have been destroyed by fire, warfare, and the ravages of time.[41] What remains are mainly some passages by Kang Tai, including a few on Funan, scattered among later compilations, the so-called *lei shu* or "categorized works" compiled from Tang times onwards.[42] Most of the passages on Funan are in different parts of the 984 encyclopedia *Taiping yulan*, edited by the scholar Li Fang and others.

Reassembling Kang's writings on Funan involves surmounting a number of textual and editorial issues. The passages in *Taiping yulan* and other sources were arranged according to categories decided on by Li Fang and the other editors, not according to the order in which Kang originally wrote them. In addition, it is sometimes unclear whether a passage was sourced from a work by Kang or another author.[43] I have selected passages that can reasonably be attributed to Kang's own brush, and tried to present them in as coherent a narrative as possible.

The narrative starts with comments about Funan and nearby states, followed by a section on boat making potentially relevant to Funan's foreign relations. It goes on to tell the story of Funan's founding and anecdotes about several of its kings. It concludes with comments about the social customs of Funan, including its practices of trial by ordeal. Organized in this way, the material gives some coherence to the remnants of Kang's writings, though it is too fragmentary to give any sense of an authorial voice.

The narrative consists of twenty paragraphs, as follows.[44]

> From Linyi to the Rinan port of Lurong is perhaps two hundred li or so. To go south by sea to Funan and the other states, you usually set out from that port.[45]
>
> Dukun is in Funan. There is mint in its mountains.
>
> A sulphurous perfume comes from the state of Dukun, which is three thousand li or so to the south of Funan.[46]
>
> There is an island in the Great Sea east of Funan where there are multicolored parrots. White ones that look like hens have also been seen.
>
> There is a mountain in the sea west of Funan, a thousand li in circumference. In the middle of it there is a large rock called the Sea Drum, which is perhaps a hundred poles wide. If you are going by sea and want to know if the wind will blow fiercely, you first listen to the stirrings of this rock. When it rumbles like thunder, whales come up and the wind blows.[47]

To the northeast of Zhuzhuanbo [Java?] lies the island of Juji.[48] The people there have no fields to plant taro in, so they sail their boats in the sea and cut out whorled clamshell cups to take to Funan.

Southwest of Funan lies the state of Linyang, at a distance from Funan of seven thousand li.[49] The place pays homage to the Buddha, and there are several thousand monks.[50] They uphold Buddhist discipline and observe the six days of fasting, and do not allow fish or meat into the country. There are two markets each day—a morning market for all kinds of husked rice and other grains, sweet-tasting fruits, and cane sugar; and an evening market just for trading in aromatic substances and flowers.

The king of the state of Funan bequeathed some pure gold cups to the king of Piqian.[51]

In the state of Funan they cut down trees to make boats. These are twelve *xun* long and measure six feet in width. Their heads and tails are shaped like a fish and are decorated with hanging iron ornaments. Large ones carry a hundred people. Each of them uses a long and a short oar and a boat-pole. From head to tail there are fifty people on each side, or forty-two, depending on whether the boat is large or small. Standing they use the long oars, sitting they use the short ones; if the water is shallow, they use the boat-poles, all of them responding [to a helmsman] with one voice as they ply their poles.[52]

Originally the ruler of Funan was a woman called Liuye. A person from the state of Mofu by the name of Hun Shen [Hun Tian] liked to serve the gods, which he did with tireless devotion. They were moved by the depth of his feelings, and one night he dreamed someone gave him a sacred bow and told him to go to sea in a merchant ship. In the morning, Hun Shen went to the temple and found a bow beneath a sacred tree. He then set out to sea in a large ship. A whirling wind of the gods took him to Funan. Liuye wanted to stop him and seize him, but Hun Shen took up his sacred bow and shot at her, his arrow going right through her boat. Liuye was afraid and submitted to him. Thus it was that Hun Shen came to Funan.[53]

The state from which Hun Dian [Hun Tian] originally took a large merchant ship was the state of Wuwen.[54]

As a young man, King Pankuang of Funan was bold and brave. When he heard there were large elephants in the mountain forests, he captured them at once and had them trained for people to ride on. The various states heard about this and submitted to him.

Once during the time of Fan Zhan, a person called Jia Xiangli from the state of Tanyang went from that country to India, and then in the course of traveling as a merchant here and there came to Funan. He told [Fan] Zhan about the customs of India, its widespread dharma, its abundant riches, and its fertile mountains and rivers.[55] He said that it fulfilled one's every need, and that large countries nearby had respected it for generations. [Fan] Zhan asked, "Now if one goes there, when will one get there? And how many years will it take to get back?" [Jia] Xiangli replied, "India may be thirty thousand or so li from here; there and back will take some three years. Once you go, you won't come back in less than four years—it's regarded as the center of the world."

Fan Xun, king of Funan, uses iron to make fake spurs for his fighting cocks, and plays with them for bets with his generals.[56]

The Funan king Fan Xun rears tigers on a mountain. People who commit an offense are thrown to the tigers. If they are not eaten by the tigers, they are forgiven. So the mountain is called Great Creature or Great Spirit.[57] The king also keeps ten crocodiles, and people who commit an offense are thrown to the crocodiles. If the crocodiles do not eat them, they are pardoned. Innocent people never get eaten, so the crocodiles are kept in a pond.[58] Something else that is done is to have water heated and a golden finger ring thrown into the boiling water, where people then have to grope for it. Innocent people's hands do not get scalded, but when offenders put their hands in the hot water, they get burned.

In Funan it is the custom when managing disputes to do without prisons and flogging and beating, and just to decide on who is honest by having people search for something in hot water, or grasp a chopper, or be immersed in water. The persons concerned are first sent to bathe and fast, then they are made to put their hands in boiling water, or carry a hot chopper with both hands, or suffer being immersed in water.[59] Those who are innocent are not scalded or burned or drowned, while offenders are proved to be such.

With disputes in Funan, water is heated until it is boiling, then a gold finger ring is thrown into the water, after which the people concerned search for it with their hands. The hands of those who are honest are not scalded, but when offenders put their hands in the boiling water, they are burned.

With disputes in Funan, iron is heated until it is red hot, then taken up with tongs and given to those concerned to hold while they walk seven steps. The hands of those who have not offended are unscalded, while offenders' hands get burned.[60]

The people of Funan all wear decorated girdles made of hide.[61]

When killing people in their country, the kings of Funan use a knife to cut them up or stab them. Sometimes the knife does not penetrate, so they daub the blade of the knife with sweat, and then it cuts into them. The people of the country call this *chan*.[62]

Taiping yulan contains four other paragraphs on Funan that cite *Waiguo zhuan* [*A Record of Foreign States*], which may be Kang Tai's work or may derive from fifth century sources.[63]

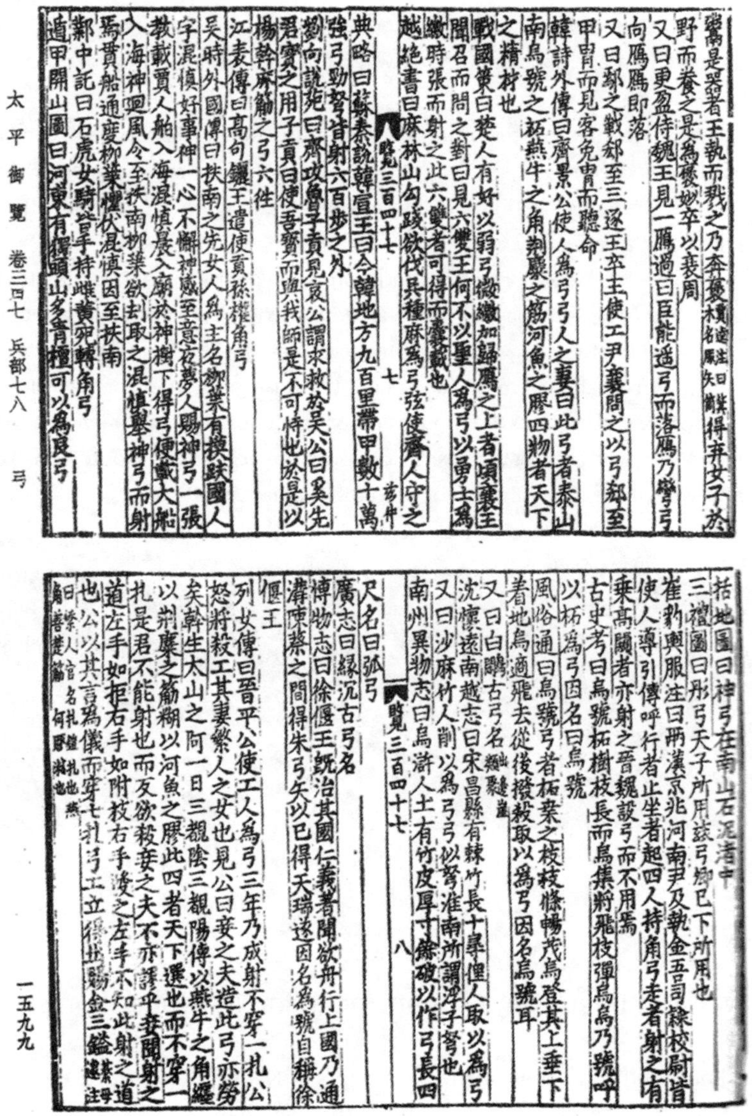
鷟爲是器者王執而戮之乃奔褒得弃女子於
野而養之是爲褒姒卒以喪周
又曰更羸侍魏王見一鴈過曰臣能虛弓而落鴈乃彎弓
向鴈鴈即落
又曰鄢之戰郤至三逐王卒王使工尹襄問之以弓郤至
甲胄而見客免胄而聽命
韓詩外傳曰齊景公使人爲弓弓人之妻曰此弓者泰山
南烏號之柘燕牛之角荊麋之筋河魚之膠四物者天下
之精材也
戰國策曰楚人有好以弱弓微繳加歸鴈之上者頃襄王
聞召而問之對曰見六雙王何不以聖人爲弓以勇士爲
繳時張而射之此六雙者可得而囊載也
越絶書曰麻林山句踐欲伐吳種麻爲弓弦使齊人守之
御覽三百四十七 七
典略曰蘇秦說韓宣王曰今韓地方九百里帶甲數十萬
強弓勁弩皆射六百步之外
劉向說苑曰齊攻魯子貢見哀公請求救於吳公曰吳先
君寶之用子貢曰使吾寶而與我師是不可恃也於是以
楊幹麻筋之弓六往
江表傳曰高句驪王遣使貢繖楛角弓
吳時外國傳曰扶南之先女人爲主名柳葉有摸趺國人
字混慎好事神一心不懈神感至意夜夢人賜神弓一張
教載賈人船入海混慎晨入廟於神樹下得弓便載大船
入海神迴風令至扶南柳葉欲去取之混慎舉神弓而射
焉貫船通度柳葉懼伏混慎因至扶南
鄴中記曰石虎女騎皆手持雌黃宛轉角弓
遁甲開山圖曰河東有猬頭山多青檀可以爲良弓
太平御覽 卷三百四十七 兵部七十八 弓

括地圖曰神弓在南山石泥渚中
三禮圖曰彤弓天子所用兹弓卿已下所用也
崔豹輿服注曰兩漢京兆河南尹及執金吾司隸校尉皆
使人導引傳呼行者止坐者起四人持角弓走者射之有
乘高闚者亦射之晉魏設弓而不用焉
古史考曰烏號柘桑枝長而烏集將飛枝彈烏烏乃號呼
以柘爲弓因名曰烏號
風俗通曰烏號弓者柘桑之枝枝條暢茂烏登其上垂下
着地烏適飛去從後撥殺取以爲弓因名烏號耳
又曰白鸊古弓名
沈懷遠南越志曰宋昌縣有棘竹長十尋俚人取以爲弓
又曰沙麻竹人削以爲弓弓似弩淮南所謂浮子弩也
南州異物志曰烏滸人土有竹皮厚寸餘破以作弓長四
尺名曰弧弓
御覽三百四十七 八
廣志曰綠沉古弓名
博物志曰徐偃王既治其國仁義著聞欲舟行上國乃通
溝陳蔡之間得朱弓矢以已得天瑞遂因名爲號自稱徐
偃王
列女傳曰晉平公使工人爲弓三年乃成射不穿一札公
怒將殺工其妻繁人之女也見公曰妾之夫造此弓亦勞
矣幹生太山之阿一日三覩陰三覩陽傳以燕牛之角纏
以荊麋之筋糊以河魚之膠此四者天下選也而不穿一
札是君不能射也而反欲殺妾之夫不亦謬乎妾聞射之
道左手如拒右手如附枝右手發之左手不知此射之道
也公以其言爲儀而穿七札弓工立得出賜金三鎰
一五九九

An entry in a facsimile of a Song edition of *Taiping yulan* that records Kang Tai's account of the Funan foundation story.The entry, on the top left, begins: '*Wu shi waiguo zhuan yue funan zhi xian nüren wei zhu* 吳時外國傳曰扶南之先女人為主 [*A Record of Foreign States during the Wu Period* says, Originally the ruler of Funan was a woman]'.

Source: Li Fang et al., eds., *Taiping yulan* (Beijing: Zhonghua shuju, 1960), vol.4

From Funan you go west to Jinchen, which you get to after two thousand li or so.[64]

In the Great Sea east of Funan, there is a large volcanic island. There are trees on the island whose bark is completely black when taken during spring rain and pure white when taken after being burned in the flames. They spin the bark to make handkerchiefs or wicks for lamps that are never known to burn out.

The largest residences of the people of the state of Funan have carved patterns and engravings.[65] They like giving alms. There are many birds and animals. The kings like hunting; they all ride elephants and spend more than a month at a time away.[66]

If a vessel or utensil goes missing from someone's house in Funan, they take a pint of rice and pay a visit to the temple where they entreat the god to expose the thief, putting the rice at the god's feet. The following day they take back the rice, call the women slaves of the house, and order them to chew it. Whoever bleeds from the mouth and ends up not crushing the rice is the thief; those who are not thieves can break up the rice in their mouth. It is like this everywhere from Rinan to beyond the frontiers.

Examples of excavation sites at Óc Eo, Mekong delta, showing typical structures of brick and stone

Sources: (above) www.semanticscholar.org, 2016; ThoughtCo, thoughtco.com/oc-eo-funan-culture-site-vietnam-172001, 11-02-2020

How Kang Tai portrays Funan, including its foundation story

Brief and partial though they are, the remnants of Kang Tai's writings give us some insights into what may have been Funan's formative phase.

Firstly, while the sentence describing Funan's location does not give its distance from China—more specifically, from Rinan—it does note that Funan lay to the south of Rinan and confirms that there was sea communication between Rinan and Funan by the middle of the third century CE.

Kang Tai also gives us a picture of Funan's maritime role in giving or exchanging local products. Notably, however, the only time he actually mentions trade as such is with reference to Jia Xiangli, the merchant who told King Fan Zhan about India. Kang refers to four states by name that were evidently of interest to or had contact with Funan for the purpose of trading local products: Dukun, a source of mint and perfume, located perhaps on the Malay Peninsula and possibly a constituent part of Funan in some sense; Zhuzhuanbo, which was probably Java, near an island that provided Funan with cups made of seashells; a more distant place called Linyang, possibly in present-day Myanmar, whose connection with Funan is unclear; and an unidentified state, Piqian, perhaps an island, that is described as a source of the gold used for royal gifts. Kang Tai also mentions two other islands to the east and west of Funan (three if the *Waiguo zhuan* passages are taken into account), one of them a source of brightly colored parrots, which were enduringly popular in China, and another the source of fireproof material for handkerchiefs.[67]

In addition to these places, there is a short but significant account of India, described to Fan Zhan by the merchant Jia Xiangli. Fan Zhan is portrayed as showing great interest in India but knowing little about it. As we have seen, *Liang shu* relates that Fan Zhan subsequently sent his kinsman Su Wu to India, where he met King Muruṇḍa (Maolun). Su Wu then returned to Funan with the Indian envoy Chen Song and with gifts that included four prized horses from Yuezhi.[68] The account by Kang Tai suggests that Funan's connection with India, at least at the royal or elite level, began comparatively late, in the third century CE.

Kang Tai's description of boat making in Funan gives a rare portrait of a well-developed skill in a society for which—judging by the canals excavated near Óc Eo—water transport played a considerable role. The passage's description of boats carrying rowing and punting crews of eighty-four or a hundred men suggests the vessels were used for unspecified military purposes. Perhaps they were the boats used by Fan Xun's predecessor, Fan Shiman, on his military campaigns abroad, as described in *Liang shu*.[69]

Kang Tai's writings on Funan also provide us with the earliest version of Cambodia's foundation story, in which the queen, Liuye, is cowed into submission by a foreigner, whom Kang calls Hun Shen or Hun Dian but later records suggest was named Hun Tian (see footnote 53). The foreigner arrives by boat with a god-sent mission and stays to rule. This foundation story has led to some controversy, not least about the degree to which Funan was subject to Indian influence at an early date. Kang Tai's account serves to remind us of what is clearly on record concerning the story, and what amounts to speculation or embellishment. The story is repeated more or less verbatim in subsequent Chinese histories, but Kang's account contains its essential features.

Before turning to this controversy, we should note that according to Kang Tai, Funan was originally ruled by a queen, not a king. It is possible that other queens ruled in the region, for the Chinese term *wang* is in fact gender-neutral, as is the Chinese term *zhu* (ruler), a term sometimes used instead of *wang* (for example, here in Kang Tai's account of Liuye, and in Zhou Daguan's thirteenth-century *Record* of Angkor).

That said, Chinese chroniclers tend to treat female sovereigns as uncommon enough to remark on—for example, by explicitly noting as Kang does that "the ruler was a woman."[70] For this reason, we can assume that most Southeast Asian *wang* and *zhu* were male, not female. Even so, it's notable that, as later standard histories show, women in Funan may have played a significant role in determining the line of royal inheritance, a point we shall return to later.

With regard to the controversy itself, Queen Liuye is sometimes portrayed as a serpent or naga queen called by the Sanskrit name Somā, while Hun Tian or Hun Shen is sometimes identified as a brahmin called by the Sanskrit name Kauṇḍinya. There are two issues to be considered here: the association between two individuals called Somā and Kauṇḍinya, and the identification of these two individuals with Liuye and Hun Tian.

The association between Somā and Kauṇḍinya goes back a long way, though its origin is hard to pinpoint. As Michael Vickery and Rüdiger Gaudes show, the names Somā and Kauṇḍinya occur together in various pre-Angkor and Angkor Sanskrit inscriptions. These include two that describe Somā and Kauṇḍinya as lineage ancestors of the seventh-century king Īśānavarman, and four that portray Somā and Kauṇḍinya as dynastic ancestors of the tenth-century Angkor king Rājendravarman and his son Jayavarman V.[71] This association between Somā and Kauṇḍinya has continued into contemporary times. A contemporary dance program in Phnom Penh, for example, writes of how "the traditional Khmer wedding . . . symbolizes and reflects the union of Preah Thong and Neang Neak, or Preah Bat Kaundyn [Kauṇḍinya] and Neang Soma."[72]

On the other hand, the identification of Liuye with Somā and Hun Tian with Kauṇḍinya does not seem to have been made until the twentieth century, more specifically until 1911. In that year the archaeologist Louis Finot published an article quoting a Sanskrit inscription from a stele at Mỹ Sơn in the center of present-day Vietnam that he dated to 658. The inscription tells of how, armed with a javelin, the greatest of brahmins Kauṇḍinya took as his wife Somā, daughter of the king of the nagas. Finot identifies Somā and Kauṇḍinya with Liuye and Hun Tian, and remarks that "thus the legend of Kauṇḍinya and Somā is originally from Funan."[73]

During the past century scholars have made this identification a number of times.[74] But whatever the merits of identifying the Liuye-Hun Tian story with the

Kauṇḍinya-Somā legend, there is little in Kang Tai's account to justify it. Nothing that Kang writes associates Liuye with a naga queen or with the name Somā. The name Liuye (Li̯əu: i̯äp [K]) bears no resemblance to Somā, and there is no mention of snakes or nagas.

Nor is there a compelling reason to take Hun Tian to be a brahmin. As a brahmin, he might have been expected to have come from India. But according to *Liang shu*—and possibly Kang Tai, if Pelliot's tentative identification of Mofu with Hengdie is correct—he came from the south. True, this does not preclude him from being a brahmin, since there may have been brahmins in states to the south of Funan from the early centuries CE onwards. *Taiping yulan* quotes sources from the fifth/sixth century and the seventh century remarking that two states, Panpan and Dunxun, were home by that time to many brahmins. In Dunxun, which like Panpan is thought to have been on the Malay Peninsula, there were said to be over a thousand of them, as well as five hundred families from India.[75] Nevertheless, the fact that Hun Tian came from the south raises a question about his brahminical identity.

There are other considerations as well. One is that Indian culture and religion may have been unknown to the Funan elite until the third century CE, long after Hun Tian, when Fan Zhan first learned about India from Jia Xiangli. Another is that Hun Tian is described as worshipping unnamed gods—gods that could have been part of the Hindu pantheon but could just as well have been local deities. As for Hun Tian's name, Pelliot suggests it may have been a transliteration of Kauṇḍinya, and Karlgren's reproduction of the Ancient Chinese pronunciation of Hun Tian as Yuən: D'ien can plausibly be construed as Kauṇḍinya, albeit with the final syllable missing.[76] But there are reasons to doubt whether this is the case. Firstly, the name Kauṇḍinya occurs later, in *Nan Qi shu* and *Liang shu*, with a different transliteration, one more suited to the Sanskrit original. Secondly, according to *Liang shu*, Hun Tian's successor Pankuang also bore the name Hun, with no suggestion from anyone that in Hun Pankuang's case the first part of his name could have been a transliteration of Kauṇ-.

Vickery offers an alternative explanation. He suggests that the word *hun* (yuən:) is not part of a transliterated Sanskrit name, but is rather a prehistoric Austronesian or Mon-Khmer title or clan name.[77] Vickery's argument is weakened by the possibility that the transliteration of Sanskrit names was a skill that Kang Tai did not have, and by the fact that Pankuang was given the name or title Hun in the seventh-century *Liang shu*, but not by Kang Tai or the sixth-century *Nan Qi shu*, both earlier sources that just call him Pankuang. Even so, Vickery offers a plausible alternative view of what the name Hun Tian might consist of.

It is worth adding here that Vickery brings a similar argument to bear when considering the character *fan* (b'i̯wɒm: [K]) in the Chinese transliterations of the names of subsequent Funanese kings, as well as in the names of the kings of Linyi from the third to the fifth centuries. He argues that *fan* may correspond to the local title *poñ*, which appears in inscriptions relating to the seventh and eighth centuries CE, and was perhaps used for local chiefs who combined political and ritual roles.[78]

Returning to Kang Tai's comments on Funan, Kang Tai introduces us to four of Funan's earliest kings: Hun Tian, Pankuang, Fan Zhan, and Fan Xun, though it will only be some three centuries later that *Liang shu*, discussed in chapter three, gives us a full list of Funan's early rulers and their offspring—Hun Tian, Pankuang (or Hun Pankuang), his son Panpan, the general Fan Shiman (who *Liang shu* calls Fan Man), Fan Shiman's nephew Fan Zhan (called Zhan in *Nan Qi shu*), and the general Fan Xun—and an account of when and how they ruled. It is possible, of course, that Kang originally gave a longer account of Funan's royal lineage but that it has not survived.

In his comments on Funan, Kang also describes scenes from everyday life that feature in subsequent Chinese accounts of both Funan and Zhenla. These include the training of elephants to carry people; people's fondness for cockfights; and trials by ordeal, descriptions of which may have appealed to Chinese readers, since they recur in later writings on Funan and Zhenla up to and including those of Zhou Daguan. The accounts of trial by ordeal given here are a bit repetitive, either because they come from different works by Kang Tai, or else because they all derive from one long passage that later sources have distorted.

The poet Zuo Si and his prose–poem *The Three Capitals*

We know nothing about what happened to Kang Tai and Zhu Ying after their return to China, or about how widely their works were distributed. However, we can speculate that Funan's name became current in learned circles, since it was mentioned in a third-century *fu*, or prose poem, written quite soon after the two men's return home.

The prose poem, *San du fu* [*A Prose Poem on the Three Capitals*], extolling the virtues of the capitals of the Three Kingdoms, was by Zuo Si (c. 253–c. 307 CE), a scholar and poet who came to enjoy a lasting reputation for his poetic skills. He probably wrote the long prose poem in the 270s and early 280s after moving to Luoyang, capital of the recently established Western Jin dynasty, where it became so popular that it was said to have driven up the price of paper.[79]

Zuo Si's composition consists of three prose poems, one for each of the Three Kingdoms' capitals. Funan is mentioned in the prose poem that describes Jianye, erstwhile capital of the Wu dynasty. The poem provides a sweeping panorama of a wealthy, vigorous city and court, and the reference to Funan comes in a description of the king of Wu out hunting:[80]

> The dew has gone, frost has come on,
> The days and months are leaving us.[81]
> The grasses wither, trees shed their leaves;
> The birds and beasts are fleshy and fat.
> With hawks and falcons carefully checked,
> Cautions issued to the troops,
> Armor put on, bound up with silk,
> Stately banners on display,[82]
> Junior officers are commanded to take up the bells,
> High-ranking officers to pursue the hunt in the Juqu marshlands.
> The chiefs of Wuhu, Langhuang,[83] and Funan,[84]
> Of Xitu, Daner, and Heichi,[85]
> The leaders of Jinlin and Xiang commandery,[86]
> Go whirling by, a mass of mighty horses,
> Hurtling on and dashing along,
> Striving to be the first on the road ahead.

Here Zuo Si portrays Funan—written in a variant form, with the character *fu* lacking the "hand" radical—not in the matter-of-fact prose of the standard histories, but in the elaborate, extravagant language of the *fu*, or prose poem, a genre then in its heyday.[87] In these lines, Funan serves as little more than one among a group of names intended to add a touch of the exotic to the poet's description of the hunt. This sense of the strange is enhanced by some of the other names, with their rhymed bisyllables (Wuhu, Langhuang) and slightly bizarre meanings: Daner means "pendant ears," Heichi "black teeth," and Xitu "western butchers."

We know that Zuo Si researched his poetry conscientiously, but nowhere in the *fu*, which has been well preserved thanks to its inclusion in the famous literary anthology *Wen xuan* [*Selections of Literature*], is there any indication that he knew anything more about Funan.[88]

The writer Wan Zhen's *Annals of Strange Things*

A contemporary or near-contemporary of Kang Tai and Zuo Si, the scholar-official Wan Zhen also wrote a book about exotic products and phenomena in the countries of the south, including Funan. Wan Zhen was a Governor of Danyang in southeast China, in the southern state of Wu, so he was a senior official as well as a scholar.[89] We know nothing else about him, so we have no way of assessing whether he wrote from firsthand experience or, as seems more likely, relied on hearsay or the experiences of others.[90]

Only fragments of Wan Zhen's book survive, but from them we can see that the book consists of a series of entries about exotic aspects of life beyond China's southern frontiers. These range from rhinoceroses with flaming horns to elephants as large as mountains, from skulls used as drinking cups to boys diving for sea pearls, and from boats with four sails catching the wind—an early reference, perhaps, to sailing with the monsoon wind—to ships carrying hundreds of people and large quantities of cargo.[91]

The book is usually known as *Nanzhou yi wu zhi* [*Annals of Strange Things in the Southern Regions*], though apparently it also went by other titles.[92] In *Taiping yulan*, as well as in other sources, there are a number of entries under the title *Nanzhou yi wu zhi*, but without mention of an author. Where these entries relate to Funan, I have made the tentative assumption that they are the work of Wan Zhen.[93]

Here are what seem to be the only remaining fragments of Wan Zhen's writings on Funan:[94]

> The state of Funan is three thousand or so li west of Linyi. It has put in place its own king; its various dependencies all have officers in charge.[95] Together with the senior officials serving the king these are all called Kunlun.[96]
>
> Linyang is seven thousand li or so west of Funan. The land is level and spread out, and the people comprise one hundred thousand or so families. The men and women conduct themselves according to the right and the good, and all of them serve the Buddha.[97]
>
> Dianxun is three thousand li or so from Funan. Originally it was a separate country, but the former king of Funan, Fan [Shi]man, was brave and strong and a man of strategy, and he attacked it and brought about its submission. Now it is a dependency of Funan.[98]
>
> In the Funan sea there are large seashells like bowls. Cut them open on the straight side to get a shape like a cup, or use them joined together. The shape of the shells is undulating and twisting. When wine is poured from them, it appears never to run dry. To have fun, people use the shells to pour wine and are penalized if they serve the wine wrongly.
>
> The king of Funan [Fan Xun?] is good at hunting with bows and arrows. There are often three hundred people with him riding elephants, with four or five thousand people following on.[99]

> By a corner of the Funan sea live people who are like animals. Their bodies are black like lacquer, their teeth as white as pure silk. They move round according to the seasons and do not live in one place all the time. They eat only fish and meat and do not know how to grow crops. In cold weather they wear no clothes, but cover themselves with sand. Sometimes they get together and mingle with pigs, dogs, and hens; sometimes they look human in a debased way but are no better than domestic animals.[100]

These fragments add a little to what we know from the writings of Kang Tai. The most significant comments are in the first passage. The description of Funan's location as "three thousand or so li west of Linyi" is the first account of the distance from Linyi to Funan. During this period, one li was the equivalent of perhaps half a kilometer, so three thousand li or so were equal to approximately one thousand five hundred kilometers.[101] Assuming Linyi was located somewhere in the center of present-day Vietnam, and the destination was Óc Eo, reached by sea and canal, this is a reasonable estimate of distance, though not of compass direction (Kang Tai's reference to Funan being south of Linyi is closer to the mark).

The comment in the same passage that the "officers in charge" of Funan's dependencies share the title Kunlun (Kuən li̯uĕn [K]) with the king's own senior officials is the first known mention of the word *kunlun* in the context of Funan. The comment is repeated later in the Daoist work *Tai qing jin ye shen dan jing* [*Scripture of the Divine Elixir of the Gold Liquor of Great Clarity*], which reproduces Wan Zhen's description in much the same words, except that it describes the dependencies as being under "rulers and high officials."[102]

It has long been recognized that the term *kunlun* has several different meanings. It was the name of a mythical Chinese mountain or mountain range, dating back to very early times. It was also used by Chinese writers from the seventh century onwards as a generic term for locations in the Southern Sea, as well as their languages and inhabitants, notably those described as having black skin and curly hair.[103] Wan Zhen seems to have used the term with a third meaning, as a name or title indicating royalty or social status, perhaps a kinship term.

This latter meaning of *kunlun* is also evident from references to the term in other texts from the third to seventh centuries. For instance *Taiping yulan* quotes the fifth-sixth century traveler Zhu Zhi as saying that the ruler of Dunxun is called Kunlun.[104] *Taiping yulan* also quotes *Liang shu* as giving local titles to the four most senior ranks of officials in the state of Panpan, the second, third, and fourth of which all have Kunlun as a constituent part of the title. This quotation from *Liang shu* goes on to remark that there is some confusion between the term Kunlun and another term, Gulong (Kuo: li̯wong [K]), noting that "when one says *kunlun* it is close in sound to *gulong*, so there are some who call it *gulong*."[105] In addition, *Taiping yulan* quotes *Sui shu* as suggesting that *kunlun* is a kinship term, one mistakenly used for the term *gulong*.[106] According to this quotation,

> the kings of the state of Funan have the family name Gulong, as is often the case with the family name [of kings] in the various states. When asked [whether that should be Kunlun], elders say there is no family name Kunlun, which is a mistake.

Lastly, the late eighth-century encyclopedia *Tong dian* and the twelfth-century encyclopedia *Tong zhi* both state that "in the time of the Sui dynasty the king of the state [of Funan] had the surname Gulong."[107]

So what are the meanings of *kunlun* and *gulong* as these terms are used here? A possible answer comes from considering contemporary equivalents in the Khmer language, as found in inscriptions from the seventh century onwards. One relatively close equivalent to *gulong* (though slightly less close if Karlgren's kuo: li̯wong is taken as *gulong*'s Ancient Chinese pronunciation) is the term *kuruṅ*, a term that Vickery describes as a title translated as "king" or "to rule."[108] Vickery himself notes that *gulong* is "easily understood" as the *kuruṅ* mentioned in *Sui shu*, adding that the term would have been "plausibly appropriate at that time for a chieftain, although it is not found at that time in any local inscriptions."[109]

Another term Vickery discusses is *kloñ* or *khloñ*, a term which seems to have meant 'chief' at differing hierarchical levels, sometimes in combination with other words. In Vickery's view, the term *ge kloñ*, for example, which occurs in seventh- and eighth-century inscriptions, may have been a title associated with elite women.[110] The linguistic equivalence between *kloñ* and either *kunlun* or *gulong* is less apparent than the equivalence between *kuruṅ* and *gulong*; even so, the contemporaneous use of the two titles might conceivably explain the confusion between *kunlun* and *gulong* on the part of Chinese chroniclers.

One other early traveler, Zhu Zhi

Before concluding this chapter, it is worth mentioning one other writer of records of Funan and southern places, since his writings, though they come later, seem comparable to those of Kang Tai and Wan Zhen. This is the scholar and traveler Zhu Zhi (fl. 450?–525?), whose work *Funan ji* [*Record of Funan*] includes accounts of both Funan and various other southern states, and can be dated to somewhere between 447 and 527.[111] Zhu's work is now lost, but it survives in fragments preserved in *Taiping yulan*, *Shui jing ji*, and other sources.[112]

Just as Kang Tai's surname suggests he came from a Sogdian background, so Zhu Zhi's surname suggests that he was Indian in origin, since the surname Zhu—as in the old Chinese name for India, Tianzhu—usually indicated that.[113] Otherwise we know nothing about him, other than that he must have traveled around the Southern Sea and written partly from firsthand knowledge. We can surmise this because a surviving passage from Zhu Zhi's book—about another place, not Funan—makes his firsthand experience clear. The passage reads.[114]

> The state of Linyang is two thousand li by pathway from the state of Jinchen. You go by horse and cart; there is no way there by water. The whole country serves the Buddha. There was a monk there who died and was cremated, burned with several thousand bundles of firewood. So he was seated within the fire, then he was moved and put in a stone building. Sixty years or so later, his body had not withered away in the slightest. I, Zhu Zhi, saw this with my own eyes.

Little is left of Zhu Zhi's writings, and almost nothing of his writings about Funan, which, judging from its title, was the main subject of his book. One significant thing he tells us is that "Funan is four thousand li from Linyi, and can be reached by water and by pathway."[115] This is the first time an early Chinese text mentions access by land to Funan from southern China (or, at any rate, from a point just south of southern China, as Linyi was).

Zhu also mentions two other states in relation to Funan: Dunxun and Piqian. Of Dunxun, the state apparently in the north of the Malay Peninsula first mentioned by Wan Zhen, Zhu writes that it was a dependency of Funan with a a ruler called Kunlun and "five hundred foreign families from India, two Buddhist temples, and more than a thousand Indian brahmins." Of Piqian, first mentioned by Kang Tai, Zhu tells us that it is "in the sea"—that is, on an island—eight thousand li from Funan, but without saying in which direction. Of the rest of Zhu Zhu's writings on Funan, nothing remains.[116]

2

Buddhist voyagers, Daoist dreamers, early court annalists

From the beginning of the third century on, China went through nearly four centuries of turmoil and disarray. The country was only reunited towards the end of the sixth century, when the Sui dynasty (581–618) paved the way for the glorious Tang dynasty (618–907).

For most of this period, China was divided between north and south, with each of the two regions ruled by a series of impermanent regimes. From the fourth century on, the north came to be controlled by the Mongolic Tuoba people, called Taghbač in their own language, meaning Lords of the Earth, while the south was ruled by five short-lived regimes or "dynasties" controlled by a succession of families.[1] The five southern dynasties were the Eastern Jin (317–420), Liu Song (420–479), Nan Qi or Southern Qi (479–502), Liang (502–556), and Chen dynasties (557–589).[2] With their capital city at Jianye, renamed Jiankang—present-day Nanjing on the Yangzi River—these southern dynasties oversaw a mixture of Chinese and local peoples or *ethnies*.[3] They tended to be outward-looking enough to develop relations with southern states beyond their frontiers, including Funan.

For the Chinese realm as a whole, the era was one of "astonishingly fertile" intellectual achievement, to quote the French historian Jacques Gernet, marked by both great cultural creativity and a burgeoning interest in Buddhism.[4] As far as Funan was concerned, it remained a local and perhaps regional power, at least until the sixth or seventh century, at which point it was absorbed by Zhenla. Funan's rulers came to assume Sanskrit names, evidently reflecting the influence of Indian political and religious ideas, and Buddhism became a strong feature of Funanese culture, one that enhanced Funan's relations with courts in Jiankang.[5]

In this chapter and chapter three, we shall be looking at Chinese sources that refer to or describe Funan during this era. The present chapter is devoted to a scattering of early texts related to early Daoist and Buddhist traditions, as well as material from the first three standard histories of the five southern dynasties. These histories are *Jin shu* [*The History of the Jin Dynasty*], *Song shu* [*The History of the Liu Song Dynasty*], and

Nan Qi shu [*The History of the Southern Qi Dynasty*].[6] The two remaining standard histories of the southern dynasties, *Liang shu* [*The History of the Liang Dynasty*] and *Chen shu* [*The History of the Chen Dynasty*], will be considered in chapter three.

At this point it is worth noting that *Jin shu*, *Liang shu*, *Chen shu*, *Bei shi* [*The History of the Northern Dynasties*], and *Nan shi* [*The History of the Southern Dynasties*] were all completed during the early years of the Tang dynasty.[7] This being the case, they were subject to a different method of history-writing, with scholarly committees under a lead scholar-official replacing the work of individual scholars. On the whole, this new method of writing histories does not seem to have affected the way foreign states were recorded. On the other hand, the example of one of the histories to be discussed in this chapter, *Nan Qi shu*, suggests that a single author could bring a history to life with his own views in a way a committee would not. In *Nan Qi shu*'s case its author Xiao Zixian was a convinced Buddhist, and his Buddhist beliefs—shared by his emperor, Wu of Liang—may have led him to highlight the Buddhist aspects of Funan. Had the history been written by committee, the outcome might have been different.[8]

Buddhist and Daoist sources on Funan

Entries on Funan in the official Chinese histories of this period describe its development as a polity that sent tribute missions to China, engaged in trade and military adventures, and experienced the growing influence of Buddhism—principally Buddhism of the Mahayana tradition—and of Sanskrit culture.[9] Entries in unofficial Chinese writings from this era also give a sense of Funan as an emerging, prosperous state. These unofficial writings include works with Buddhist content, as well as two important works of Daoism, *Bao pu zi* [*The Master who Embraces Simplicity*] and *Tai qing jin ye shen dan jing* [*The Scripture of the Divine Elixir of the Gold Liquor of Great Clarity*].[10]

These Buddhist and Daoist sources are worth looking at in more detail. They are limited in scope, but make an enjoyable contrast to official Chinese records, being focused on matters of spiritual concern rather than on issues of interest to the imperial Chinese court.

Buddhist voyagers

As is well known, Buddhism spread from India to China in the early centuries CE by two routes: overland through central Asia, and by sea via the South China Sea.[11]

As maritime trade between southern China and Southeast Asia increased from the third century onwards, so too did the number of seafaring Buddhist monks.[12] According to the Tang Buddhist monk Yijing, who recorded the biographies of sixty leading Buddhist monks in China, thirty-six of them had traveled by sea to India from China, and two more from Korea, by the time he wrote about them in the early eighth century.[13]

The first Chinese Buddhist monk to describe his sea journey was the celebrated Faxian (c. 337–c. 422), who went from China to India by land but returned by ship, leaving east India for Guangzhou in 411 and eventually being washed up after a storm way off his route in northeast China.[14] Faxian mentions his route taking him via a place called Yepoti, which was either Java or Sumatra, but unfortunately he makes no mention of Funan or other Southeast Asian polities.[15]

Funan does, however, feature in records of other fifth- and sixth-century monks traveling by sea, whether they were sailing from India to Funan, Funan to China, or China to Funan.[16] Some of these records are included in the two main collections of biographies of Buddhist monks from the Han to the early Tang, *Gao seng zhuan* [*Biographies of Eminent Monks*] by Huijiao (497–554) and *Xu gao seng zhuan* [*More Biographies of Eminent Monks*] by Daoxuan (597–667).[17] Among the earliest of these roaming monks was an Indian called Qiyu, whose biography is in *Gao seng zhuan*. In the early 300s, Qiyu is said to have traveled to Funan and thence to Luoyang, then capital of the Western Jin dynasty, subduing two wild tigers en route.[18] He apparently stayed in Luoyang until it fell into "the chaos of war," presumably when the Western Jin were overthrown by descendants of the nomadic Xiongnu, who occupied Luoyang in 311. At that point he returned to India.[19]

Of the monks mentioned in *Xu gao seng zhuan*, those from Funan included Saṃghapāla (Senggapoluo being his name in Chinese) and his colleague, Mandra (or Mantuoluo).[20] Both men traveled from Funan to the southern Chinese capital Jiankang in the early 500s and stayed there under the aegis of the Liang Emperor Wu (r. 502–549).[21] Mandra arrived in Jiankang in 503, probably as part of the first tribute mission from Funan to the Liang court as listed in *Liang shu*.[22] Between them, Saṃghapāla and Mandra translated a number of Buddhist texts, many of them brought by Mandra from Funan. They did this in various temples and other sites in Jiankang, one of them called the Funan Office.[23] With only one exception, the texts they translated were works of the Mahayana or Greater Vehicle tradition.[24]

Another monk, Paramārtha (Boluomotuo), who was originally from western India, went to Jiankang from Funan in 546 in response to a call from the Liang Emperor Wu for knowledgeable Buddhist scholars.[25] There he became what one Buddhist specialist calls one of the three greatest translators of Sanskrit Buddhist texts into Chinese who ever lived—the other two being Kumārajīva (344–413) and Xuanzang (c. 602–644).[26]

Regrettably, none of these monks seems to have left an account of Funan.[27] In the northern Chinese capital Luoyang, on the other hand, a sixth-century Buddhist monk called Buddhabadra (Putibatuo) described Funan briefly but glowingly after seeing it at first hand.[28] Buddhabadra is mentioned by the Chinese scholar Yang Xuanzhi (?–555) in his vivid portrait of Luoyang, *Luoyang galan ji* [*A Record of the Monasteries of Luoyang*], completed in five chapters in 530.[29] According to Yang, Buddhabadra came to Luoyang from a country in the far south called Geying, and his journey to Luoyang took him through Funan. Yang does not give us the date of the journey, but given that he completed his portrait of Luoyang in 530, Buddhabadra is likely to have traveled there sometime in the 520s.

Yang's account of Buddhabadra is in the fourth chapter of *Luoyang galan ji*, on the monasteries in Luoyang's western suburbs. It reads:[30]

> On the distant western frontiers you reach the Roman Empire [Da Qin], at the western edge of heaven and earth. There they farm the land and spin cloth. The common people live among the fields, their villages and houses in sight of one other; their clothes and horses and carts are similar to those of China. In the south lies the state of Geying, at a very great distance from the Chinese capital, a land and people that are completely cut off, and have not communicated with China for generations. Even during the two Han dynasties and the [Three Kingdoms] Wei dynasty they never came.[31]
>
> Now for the first time a Buddhist monk, Buddhabadra [Putibatuo] has come from there. As he himself puts it, "I traveled north for a month till I reached the state of Gouzhi. After going north for eleven more days, I arrived at the state of Diansun. From Diansun state I traveled north for thirty days, and reached the state of Funan, which is five thousand square li in size.[32] Among the states of the southern foreigners, it is the strongest and largest, its families wealthy and numerous. They produce rare and precious things, gems, gold, jade and crystals, and betel nuts in abundance. From the state of Funan, I went north for a month and reached the state of Linyi. Upon leaving Linyi, I entered the state of Xiaoyan [the personal name of the Liang Emperor Wu]."[33]

Buddhabadra's description from firsthand knowledge of Funan as the largest and strongest of the southern states is rare confirmation of Funan's regional importance in the sixth century.

Otherwise, early Buddhist writings refer now and then to Funan, though they do not tell us a great deal. Funan does feature in some fanciful Buddhist tales, for example stories found in the seventh-century Buddhist compilation *Fayuan zhulin* [*Forest of Gems in the Dharma Garden*], completed in 668 by the monk Daoshi (d. 683). One such tale—one of a number of stories about miraculous Buddhist statues and footprints—is said to date from the late fifth century, and tells of a timeless and extraordinarily heavy stone statue of the Buddha from Funan housed in a nunnery in Panyu, the present-day city of Guangzhou. A fire threatened to damage the statue, but when three or four people took hold of it, "it went floating up" and was easily moved to safety.[34] The one thing we learn from this story is that very large, heavy Buddhist statues from Funan were valued enough to be transported to southern China.[35]

The colossal fifth-century Buddha in Yungang, north China, an example of the monumentalism in Buddhist statuary found at that time. This monumentalism is reflected in a fifth-century Chinese story about an enormously heavy Buddhist statue from Funan in a southern Chinese nunnery.

Source: Andy Hill, "Admiring the Yungang Grottoes", gbtimes.com, 23-01-2015

Daoist dreamers

Turning to Daoist writings, Funan features in two early Daoist works, both of them attributed to the renowned alchemist Ge Hong (283–343). The two works address a range of Daoist beliefs and practices, including the search for an elixir of immortality, and for the cinnabar and other exotic substances thought to be necessary for its concoction.

The first of the two is Ge Hong's most famous book, *Bao pu zi* [*The Master who Embraces Simplicity*]. He completed this in 317, after living for many years in

Guangzhou and other parts of south China.[36] Subsequently he was given official appointments under the Eastern Jin, newly established in Jiankang after the Jin court had been driven out of north China; but he refrained from moving to Jiankang, despite the devotion to Daoism being cultivated by northern emigrés there.[37] Towards the end of his life, Ge Hong asked for an official appointment in Jiaozhi in the far south, apparently because he thought ingredients for the elixir of immortality might be found there. "I don't desire this post for the sake of honor," he explained to the emperor, "but merely because of the cinnabar." The emperor gave Ge Hong the appointment but he never took it up, and there is no record of him ever traveling to Jiaozhi or to states beyond China's frontiers, including Funan.[38]

The entry concerning *Bao pu zi* consists of a single fragment. Touching on early Cambodia's reputed wealth, it describes Funan's diamonds:[39]

> The state of Funan produces diamonds. These can be used to cut jade. They look like amethyst. They appear on large rocks a hundred poles deep in water, like stalactites. People go down into the water to take them, coming out at the end of a whole day. If you beat a diamond with iron you cannot damage it; rather, the iron itself will get spoiled; but if you knock it with the horn of a ram it will fall apart.[40]

The other work with passages about Funan, *Tai qing jin ye shen dan jing* [*The Scripture of the Divine Elixir of the Gold Liquor of Great Clarity*], is sometimes attributed to Ge Hong but seems to be a composite work.[41] The work is associated with the Great Clarity (*Tai qing*) corpus of Daoist scriptures on the search for immortality—scriptures written over many centuries from Han or even pre-Han times onwards—and neither its date nor its authorship has been clearly determined.[42] Fabrizio Pregadio, a specialist in the Great Clarity corpus, believes it includes writings by different authors at different dates, and was probably put together editorially at some point before the Tang dynasty.[43]

The parts of *Tai qing jin ye shen dan jing* that relate to Funan feature in four separate passages in the third and final chapter of the work. The passages all have a dream-like quality quite different from the matter-of-fact records of official histories. The first of the four reads:[44]

> Ge Hong said . . . "When I was small I wanted to study the Way and was determined to go roaming far and wide. Once when I had some time to spare I went traveling in the south. At first I thought about just seeing around Jiaozhou and Lingnan [southern China].[45] Then, as fate would have it I went to Funan.

> "The territory of Funan covers a thousand or so square li; its people are to be reckoned in the hundreds of thousands. Surrounding mountains are ranged beside the sea, and its lands stretch far into the distance. In my mind I see it as the farthest south of all the states there are . . . "

Ge Hong is then said to remark that "from India on"—meaning traveling eastwards from India—there were a dozen or so large states "like Funan," while from Da Qin (the Roman Empire) on there were innumerable small states in different places. Of these various states, Funan and four others—Dunxun, Linyi, Dubo, and Wulun—are credited with producing various ingredients suitable for medicines to promote long life. The five states are listed in the order just given, apparently without reference to geographical location. As we have seen, Dunxun was probably located in the northern part of the Malay Peninsula, and Linyi was in the central part of present-day Vietnam, while Dubo may have referred to Java. Wulun does not feature in *Tong dian*, *Taiping yulan*, or the Six Dynasties standard histories and cannot be identified.[46]

After a discussion of other issues, there is a passage about the sea voyage to Funan:

> Slowly, slowly you make your way along, sailing down the great expanse of river.[47] You set out from Xianglin [in southernmost China] with the Southern Sieve ahead of you and the Great Fire at your back.[48] You go with the winds and currents, rushing speedily on, not stopping day or night, the days mounting up until twenty days have gone by.
>
> Then you reach Funan. There are kings and rulers in that remote and distant state, with its ten thousand li of frontiers.[49] To the north it abuts on to Linyi, to the south it includes Dunxun. On the one hand it leads to Dubo, on the other it connects with Wulun. There are countless types of local produce, and markets everywhere . . .

In a later passage there is another version of the same journey, followed by a description of Funan:

> You set out from Shouling port in Rinan [in the far south of China] and go directly south by sea, so that the stars of the Great Fire are at your back and the stars of the Southern Sieve are ahead of you.[50] Without stopping day or night, you reach Funan in ten days or so.
>
> Funan is three thousand li or so southwest of Linyi. It has set up its own king; its various dependent states all have their rulers. The king is called

Paodao; the next-ranking king of the large state is called Potan; the rulers and high officers of the small states as well as the king's senior officials are all called Kunlun.[51]

The land of Funan has a great deal of cinnabar and many precious stones. Three thousand li north of Funan you get to Linyi, a rich and abundant land with a great deal of cinnabar and sulphur.[52] Dianxun is five thousand li to the south of Funan. It was originally a separate state, but a former king of Funan, Fan [Shi]man, who was brave and strong and a man of strategy, attacked it and brought about its submission. Now it is a dependency of Funan. Iron comes out of the ground there. Further south are the states of Dukun, Bisong, and Juzhi, all of which Fan [Shi]man crossed over to in his time to attack and bring to submission. This is why I say that [Funan's] name includes Dianxun.[53]

Dianxun is twenty thousand li from Rinan, and Funan cannot be more than three thousand seven hundred or three thousand eight hundred li from Linyi. How do I know that? When an oceangoing ship sets out from Shouling port, and with a northeasterly wind it does not call a halt day or night, in fifteen days it will get to Dianxun, sailing two thousand li each day and each night.

Ge Hong, or whoever the writer is, then describes Wulun and Linyang, both of which are said to lie two thousand li or so west of Funan.[54] Then, in a final passage mentioning Funan, the writer tells the story of a Chinese merchant who is swept away by the sea to Da Qin (the eastern Roman Empire).

Formerly a merchant from China went to Funan. From Funan he set sail in a ship, intending to go to the state of Gunu [?Kanadvīpa in India].[55] But the wind turned and he did not get to his destination, heading elsewhere instead. After sailing nonstop for sixty days and nights he reached a steep shore. He did not know where he was. Climbing up the shore he found someone to ask, and was told, "This is the Roman Empire".

This was not at all where the merchant had been heading, and he was quite terrified, afraid that he would come to grief. So he pretended to be an envoy from the king of Funan, and paid a visit to the king of the Roman empire [Da Qin].

When the king saw him he was astonished and said, "So there are people even on the very farthest shores. Tell me, sir, what country are you from? Why are you here as an envoy of Funan?" The merchant replied, "Your servant was dispatched by the king of Funan on the edge of the northern sea to come to your majesty's court to convey his deepest respects. Moreover we have heard that there are rare goods and treasures in your kingdom, and would beg of you some liquor made from Mysterious and Yellow [Clay] to add luster to our humble city."[56]

The king of the Romans [Da Qin] asked, "Tell me, sir, are you from the frontier people of the state of Zhou [the ancient Zhou dynasty]? You have braved the Great Sea to travel two hundred thousand li to my court—you must be tired out." [The king then gave the merchant some refined mercury as well as other substances, and four years later the merchant returned to Funan. The writer explains that the king of the Roman empire lived so far away that he did not realize that the Zhou dynasty had come to an end centuries earlier.]

In these narratives we encounter an exotic view of Funan that conforms to the principal purpose of the texts they are drawn from, namely the Daoist search for the elixir of immortality. The inconsistencies in the texts—the varying estimates of the time taken to sail from Rinan or Linyi to Funan (ten days, twenty days), the confusion between Xianglin and Linyi (the same location with different names in different parts of the texts), and the varying distances between Linyi and Funan—reinforce the supposition that the texts depended on secondhand knowledge drawn from various sources.

Still, they provide the occasional insight, as in their listing of official titles, though these may be garbled, and in their portrait of Funan as a large, beguilingly well-endowed country, with its diamonds, precious stones and other natural assets. The final passage also tells us, significantly, that a pre-Tang Chinese merchant was prepared to sail from China to Funan and from there to faraway India.

Early annals: *The History of the Jin Dynasty*

Turning now to the official or standard histories, the first to consider Funan—at least, in terms of the era it records—is *Jin shu* [*The History of the Jin Dynasty*], which comprises the history of the Eastern and Western Jin dynasties, dynasties that followed each other in succession immediately after the Three Kingdoms. In terms of its date of composition *Jin shu* is not, in fact, the first standard history, since it was only completed in its final form in 648, over a century after *Nan Qi shu*, which was finished in 520, and twelve years after *Liang shu*, completed in 636. The reason for its late completion is that Taizong (r. 627–649), the great second emperor of the Tang dynasty, regarded earlier fourth- and fifth-century versions of *Jin shu* as inadequate, and ordered a new version to be written instead. This task was undertaken by a committee under Taizong's direction and headed by the scholar-official Fang Xuanling (578–648). Taizong evidently allowed Fang and his colleagues to draw on material contained in earlier drafts, so we really do not know how far back much of *Jin shu* goes. Its record of Funan may, after all, be very old.[57]

In spite of this uncertainty, the extracts on Funan from the standard histories of this period are given below and in chapter three in chronological order of the dynasties concerned, with *Jin shu* coming first. *Jin shu*'s entries on Funan include a brief overview of the state, as well as records of envoys and gifts from Funan received during the Jin dynasty. *Jin shu*'s brief overview of Funan reads:[58]

> For Funan you go three thousand or so *li* west from Linyi. It is in a large bay of the sea. Its territory is three thousand li in extent.[59] There are cities, districts, palaces and houses.[60] The people are all ugly and black with curly hair. They go naked and walk barefoot. They are honest in character and do not rob or steal. They devote themselves to ploughing and planting, planting in one year and harvesting for three. They like carving patterns and making engravings. Their eating utensils are often made of silver, and they pay their levies and taxes with gold, silver, pearls, and aromatic substances. They also have written records for the content of their storehouses; the script is related to that of the Hu.[61] Their funerals and marriages are more or less the same as those of Linyi.
>
> Its monarch was originally a woman named Yeliu [Liuye]. At that time there was a foreigner, Hun Kui [Hun Tian], who had served the gods.[62] He dreamed that they gave him a bow and told him to go to sea in a ship. In the morning Hun Kui visited the gods' temple and obtained a bow. He then went to sea with a merchant and arrived at an outer district of Funan. Yeliu led her forces to resist him, but when Hui Kui raised his bow, Yeliu was fearful and submitted. Thereupon Hun Kui took her as his wife and occupied her state.
>
> His heirs were weak and his descendants did not inherit his position; instead the country's general Fan Xun restored the royal line of Funan.[63]

In addition to this brief overview, *Jin shu* records tribute from Funan received by the Western Jin (265–316 CE) in 268, four years after the Jin dynasty was founded, and in 285, 286, and 287, as well as by the Eastern Jin (317–420) in 357 and 389.[64] The envoy sent in 285 was part of a group dispatched from ten states, and the envoy in 286 was part of a group of envoys from twenty-one states. In both cases Funan is the only named state.

Jin shu's records of envoys include two very similar accounts of a single event: how in 357 Funan offered a live elephant—or perhaps elephants, the number not being specified—as tribute to the Eastern Jin emperor at his court in Jiankang. The emperor, Mu (r. 345–361), turned the gift down, ostensibly because of the harm the elephant might cause. This is explained in the second of the two accounts, which reads:

> At the beginning of the Taishi reign period [265–274 CE] of Emperor Wu [of the Western Jin], an envoy was sent with tribute. During the Taikang reign period [280–289], tribute came repeatedly. At the beginning of the Shengping reign period [357–361] of Emperor Mu, Zhu Zhantan, who was called king, again sent an envoy with tribute consisting of a trained elephant. The emperor commanded that it be returned, for fear of unusual animals from strange lands causing people harm.[65]

This was not the only time a Chinese emperor reacted against having trained elephants given as gifts to the court. According to *Jiu Tang shu*, the Tang emperor Dezong (r. 780–804) ordered the release of thirty-two tame elephants into the wilds soon after he acceded to the throne, an act the author of *Jiu Tang shu*, Liu Xu, records with apparent approval. We cannot be sure why Dezong and Mu acted as they did. One reason, conceivably, was that in the first millennium CE elephants were still roaming the forests of China, and the emperors and their courtiers did not regard them as being particularly useful or exotic.[66]

New and old in the Jin history's account of Funan

Like later descriptions of Funan in the standard histories, *Jin shu*'s short account clearly reflects the interest of the Chinese court in certain aspects of the Funan polity. These are its location and governance, its customs and beliefs, the quality of its tribute, and the extent of its loyalty to the Chinese imperial ecumene. The *Jin shu* record touches on topics addressed by the other two principal historical sources on Funan, *Nan Qi shu* and *Liang shu*, and to a lesser extent by Kang Tai, but it also mentions things that these other sources do not.[67]

For instance, *Jin shu*'s reference to the use of Hu script, probably of Indian origin, is the first such reference in the standard histories, and indeed the first such reference anywhere.[68] *Jin shu*'s description of Funanese farming practices—one year planting, three years harvesting, presumably of the rice mentioned by Kang Tai—is also new. It suggests fertile, well-watered land, and is unique to the standard histories' accounts of Funan. Similarly, the *Jin shu* reference to Funan's levies and taxes, *gong fu*, is rare.[69] The only other standard history to mention taxes in Funan is *Xin Tang shu* [*The New History of the Tang Dynasty*], written three centuries later.[70]

On the other hand, *Jin shu* echoes *Liang shu* when it describes the people of Funan as ugly and black.[71] and in its comment about carved patterns and engravings it repeats a comment made in *Waiguo zhuan*.[72]

One topic addressed by all four sources—Kang Tai, *Jin shu*, *Nan Qi shu*, and *Liang shu*—is the foundation story of Hun Tian and Liuye (whom *Jin shu* calls Hun Kui and Yeliu). The original source of the story is evidently Kang Tai, since the language used in every case is similar to his. All four sources also mention gold or silver cups or utensils, and the use of tamed elephants. In addition, *Jin shu* and the other two histories all deal with Funan's size and location. All three describe it as being three thousand li in extent. Their descriptions of its location vary but taken together indicate a location west or southwest of Rinan/Linyi, on or near a river flowing eastwards into the sea.

Jin shu treats Funan's royal lineage with a light touch, giving the names of only Hun Kui (that is, Hun Tian) and Fan Xun, but giving no account of the rulers that came between them. As with the remnants of Kang Tai's writings, we are left to wait for *Liang shu* (in the following chapter) to give us a full description of the rulers of Funan after Liuye.

After the Jin: *The History of the Liu Song Dynasty*

Apart from *Jin shu*, a special case because of its late completion, the first history of this period to mention Funan is *Song shu* [*The History of the Liu Song Dynasty*]. This was a brief fifth-century southern dynasty—it ruled from 420 to 479— that called itself Song but is usually referred to as the Liu Song dynasty after its ruling Liu family, thereby distinguishing it from the later, far more illustrious Song dynasty.

Song shu was completed in 488 by the scholar, poet, and prosodist Shen Yue (441–513), partly on the basis of work by others.[73] It is the longest of the histories of the southern dynasties, but contains only scattered references to Funan.[74] These include mention of the fact that in 431 the king of Funan refused an intriguing request for soldiers from the state of Linyi, which wanted to attack Jiaozhou, that is, southern China. This is a rare instance of an early Cambodian ruler running the risk of being embroiled in hostilities with the Chinese.

Song shu also gives a list of missions consisting of envoys and local produce sent by Funan to the Liu Song court.[75] These missions took place in 434, 435, and 438, and the king who sent them is named as Chilibamo.[76] Chilibamo's missions are also mentioned in *Liang shu*, where he is called Chilituobamo.[77] Wang Bangwei plausibly suggests that Chilituo was a transliteration of Dhṛta (Ď'i lji d'ie̯: [K]), making the king's Sanskrit name Dhṛtavarman, meaning Clad with Armor or a Shield.[78] (The locution *bamo* often occurs in Chinese texts as a transliteration of the Sanskrit *varman*, meaning "shield.")

A monk-envoy glorifying Funan: *The History of the Southern Qi Dynasty*

The Liu Song dynasty was succeeded by the Nan Qi or Southern Qi dynasty (479–502), whose standard history, *Nan Qi shu* [*The History of the Southern Qi*], was probably completed between 515 and 520.[79] It was written by the scholar Xiao Zixian (489–537), a scion of the Qi royal family who served the succeeding dynasty, the Liang. Xiao was a devoted Buddhist, as was his master, the Liang emperor Wu (r. 502–549).[80] Emperor Wu was an ardent follower of Mahayana Buddhism and an active preacher and performer of extraordinarily grand rituals.[81] One modern scholar has criticized Xiao for unduly promoting Buddhist thought and the existence of gods in *Nan Qi shu*. It could indeed be that the inclusion in the history of a long section on the Funan envoy Nāgasena, including Nāgasena's praise of the god Maheśvara—a god portrayed as having Buddhist attributes—is a reflection of Xiao's Buddhist beliefs as well as those of his emperor.[82]

The following is the account of Funan in *Nan Qi shu*.[83] It consists of a single long passage, much longer than the brief overview in *Jin shu*. It repeats aspects of the earlier account by Kang Tai, notably Funan's foundation story, but also provides us with a considerably enlarged portrait of the place.

> The state of Funan is on a western bay of the large sea south of Rinan. It is some three thousand li in extent. There is a large river whose waters flow from the west into the sea.[84]
>
> Originally Funan's monarch was a woman called Liuye. Then a person from the state of Jiao, Hun Tian, dreamed that the gods gave him a bow and told him to take to sea in a ship. In the morning Hun Tian got up and went to the gods' temple, where he found a bow under a tree. He then went by ship to Funan. Liuye saw the ship and led her forces out with the intention of resisting it. Hun Tian lifted up his bow and shot at them from a distance; his arrow went right through one side of her boat and struck someone full on. Liuye was afraid, and surrendered. Hun Tian took her as his wife. He abhorred the fact that she displayed her body naked, and folded up a cloth for her to wear by passing her head through it. He then ruled this state, and his descendants passed it down from one to another.

When King Pankuang died, the people of the state set up in his place his great general Fan Shiman. When Fan Shiman fell ill, his older sister's son Zhan usurped his position, killing Fan Shiman's son Jinsheng. After a decade or so, Fan Shiman's youngest son Chang carried out a surprise attack on Zhan and killed him. As he thrust his sword into Zhan's stomach he said, "You killed my older brother. Now I am taking revenge on you for my father and him." Zhan's great general Fan Xun then killed Chang, and the people of the state set him up as king.[85] This was during the time of the Wu and Jin dynasties. During the Jin and Liu Song dynasties, generations of rulers sent tribute to court.

Towards the end of the Liu Song dynasty, the king of Funan, whose family name was Kauṇḍinya [Qiaochenru] and whose name was Jayavarman [Sheyebamo], sent [people with] merchandise to Guangzhou. An Indian Buddhist monk [in Guangzhou], Nāgasena [Nagaxian], was going to travel back to Funan with them.[86] But the wind took them to Linyi, where their goods and effects were all stolen. Nāgasena then made it to Funan by an indirect route and told people there all about the sage ruler of China who had the mandate to rule.[87]

In the second year of the [Southern Qi] Yongming reign period [484 CE], [Kauṇḍinya] Jayavarman sent the Indian monk Nāgasena to the court [of Emperor Wu of the Southern Qi] with a memorial. It declared:

"The king of Funan, your subject Kauṇḍinya Jayavarman, bows deeply and says, 'Heaven's civilizing influence cherishes and nurtures us, moves the panoply of gods, and brings harmony to the four seasons in succession. I respectfully wish the wise ruler good health at all times for his august self, as well as every good fortune for the crown prince, pure blessings for the empress and her entourage, universal harmony amongst the various masters of the royal concubines and amongst ministers and officials in and outside the court, the allegiance of neighboring peoples and the myriad states, bountiful harvests from the five kinds of grain, the absence of disasters natural or manmade, and an unsullied, prosperous land and people, completely peaceful and secure. I, your subject, and my people owe our peace and prosperity entirely to the radiance of your majesty's civilizing influence, which encompasses the contented plenitude of our land, the harmony of our seasons, and the multitude of our devotees and lay people.'

"He also says, 'Previously, your subject dispatched envoys to present you with a variety of produce. They went [beforehand] to Guangzhou to engage in trade. A Buddhist monk from India, Nāgasena, was in Guangzhou and traveled back with them on my ship with the intention of coming to Funan.

But at sea the wind swept them into Linyi, where the king of that state stole my goods as well as Nāgasena's personal effects.

"[Nāgasena] told me everything that happened between China and here. He also respectfully described your majesty's sage virtue and humane governance, careful consideration of moral guidance, splendid display of Buddhist dharma, large populace of Buddhist monks, abundant daily observance of the dharma, stern regal authority, royal oversight of state procedures, and sympathy for the common people—how Heaven and earth, north, south, east, and west, and the four corners of the world all submit to you.

"To listen to what he said made being transformed through drawing near the heavenly devas pale by comparison.[88] When I heard it my heart leapt with pleasure, as if I had been afforded a brief moment at your feet to look up respectfully at your beneficence as it flows down to a small state—a moving effect that Heaven allows, enveloping the people throughout the land in your benign protection.

"For this reason your subject is now sending this Buddhist monk Nāgasena as an envoy to make this submission and pay our respects, offering some insignificant gifts to convey our sincerity and to inform you of our humble feelings. What I present here is, however, paltry and deeply shameful, and it is my respectful desire that Heaven's forbearance and encompassing kindness will discern my sincerity and refrain from dispensing blame.'

"In addition he says, 'Your subject has a slave called Jiuchouluo who ran away and went to live elsewhere.[89] He joined up with some rebels and destroyed Linyi, where he has set himself up as king. He has never shown any respect, turning his back on what is beneficent and right. Rebelling against one's master is a transgression Heaven does not tolerate. I respectfully recollect the time when Linyi was destroyed by [the Chinese General] Tan Hezhi and for a long time reverted to civilized ways.[90]

"The scope of Heaven's majesty is such that all within the four seas submit to it, yet Jiuchouluo now maintains his position as a slave rebel and very strongly asserts control over his own affairs. Moreover Linyi and Funan are neighbors whose lands are adjacent.[91] He is truly your subject's slave, yet still he rebels. Your court is far away, and no doubt that is why he shows it no respect. Our state is a dependency of your majesty's, and that is why I am humbly informing you about all this.

"With respect, I have heard that in recent years Linyi has reduced or ended its tribute and wants to cut itself off from the court for good. How can a rat be placed upon the throne of a lion? It is my humble desire that a general be sent to attack the rebels. With humble sincerity I also offer my own services to help the court punish them severely and ensure that the various states bordering on the sea submit to you altogether. If your majesty wishes to set up someone else in place of this king, I shall respectfully obey your command. If perhaps you are not pressingly disposed to raise troops to attack Linyi, it is my humble desire that you will do a special favor to us here and assist me at your convenience with a few soldiers so that availing myself of your heavenly majesty I can extirpate these wretches, striking at evil and following the good. On the day peace is restored, I shall submit to your majesty a gift of five *bhara* of gold.[92]

"If you now disparage this, your subject's sincere submission, as delivered by this envoy, my humble feelings have not been fully expressed, and I would respectfully supplement them with all that Nāgasena and those accompanying him can tell you by word of mouth.

"My respectful hope is that you will sympathize with what has been conveyed to you. I present as gifts a replica of a dragon king's throne carved in gold, an elephant made of white rosewood, two ivory pagodas, two pieces of cotton cloth, two glass vessels, and a tortoiseshell areca bowl."[93]

Nāgasena visited the capital [at Jiankang, bearing this memorial from Kauṇḍinya Jayavarman]. He told [Emperor Wu] how it was the custom in his state to serve the god Maheśvara [Moxishouluo], who frequently descended on to Mount Modan, where the weather was always warm, the grasses did not wither and the trees did not shed their leaves.[94]

Asram Maharosei on the slope of Phnom Da, a hill near Angkor Borei, probably the site of the capital of Funan. Asram Maharosei Is one of the few extant structures that may date in part from the Funan period.

Source: Tonbi Ko, Wikipedia Commons; commons.wikimedia.org/wiki/File:Wat_asram_moha_russei.jpg, 17-04-2016

[Nāgasena] offered up a written account, as follows:[95]

"Good fortune brings benefit to the world,
Moving and uplifting all living beings.
The reason this is so is that Heaven is moved
To bring light upon the font of transformation.
An immortal mountain by the name of Modan
Is finely spread about with auspicious trees.
Making use of this place, Maheśvara
lets his revered spirit descend,
Affording his assistance to the whole land,
The people all made peaceful and secure.
Given the protection of this benevolence,
Your subject submits with a loyal heart.
The Bodhisattva practices forbearance and mercy;
Originally from an ordinary place,
Once he put forth his Bodhi heart
He did not wait upon the Two Vehicles,
But through successive lives built up merit,
Practicing great compassion through the Six Pāramitās.[96]
Fearlessly spanning a number of kalpas,[97]
He gave up wealth and life, leaving nothing behind.
He had no dislike for either life or death,
Transforming his karma at the six levels of existence,
Attaining each of the ten stages of enlightenment.
His bequest is to let the living world cross over.[98]
Now that his merits are already determined,
His actions completed, his enlightenment achieved,
And countless acts of goodness and wisdom fulfilled,
A beneficent sun shines down on human life.
Sentient beings are moved by his responses to karma,
And timely provision of remedies of the dharma.
The Buddha's transformations reach in every direction;
There is none that does not enjoy his aid and succor.

"The emperor sanctifies the spacious Way,
Bringing vigor to the Three Treasures
And looking with concern upon countless matters,
His awesome benevolence stirs the farthest places.

Throughout the land, in cities and districts,
His humane ways turn things pure and bright,
Like Śakra, Lord of the Devas, supreme among gods.
Your Majesty surpasses the multitude of people,
And all within the four seas give you their loyalty.[99]
Your sage-like beneficence flows out without bounds
And gives deep-seated protection to your subject's small state."

In response the emperor declared, "When you describe how the spirit of Maheśvara descends and flows over your lands, though it is an alien custom and a strange manner of being, from a distance I deeply appreciate and approve of it.

"I understand that Jiuchouluo has rebelled in your land and has occupied Linyi by stealth, bringing together evildoers and pillaging without constraint, and it is entirely proper that I should punish him severely. Although yours is a distant place, it has long offered foreign tribute. From the time of the Liu Song dynasty there have been many difficulties, with obstacles in the way of getting maritime interpreters.[100] Now Heaven's civilizing influence has been renewed, but mistaken practices have yet to be done away with.[101] I am welcoming people from distant parts with refinement and virtue, and do not want to engage readily in warfare. Since the king has brought us sincere expressions of loyalty, asking from afar for military might, I shall now command Jiaozhou to respond at its convenience.[102]

"Chastising rebels and treating gently those that submit is truly the governing principle of the state, with every effort made to achieve outstanding merit and so assist in meeting expectations. Nāgasena, you have frequently dealt with interpreting for frontier peoples, and understand very well the strengths and weaknesses of our Central Land. All of this you are bidden to declare [to Kauṇḍinya Jayavarman]."

As recompense, the emperor gave [Kauṇḍinya Jayavarman] five pieces each of fine silk with dark red and purple bases decorated in yellow, blue and green.

The people of Funan are crafty, clever, and ingenious. They attack and capture people from neighboring districts who are not submissive and make them slaves. They trade with gold, silver, and colored silks. In the great families, the men cut up embroidered cloth to wrap around themselves; the women wear it by putting their heads through it. The poor use cloth to shade themselves with. They forge gold rings and bracelets and silver vessels for food. They cut down trees to build houses. The king of the state lives in a tiered, storeyed building. Their city walls are made of wooden fencing.

By the sea grow large, broad-leafed bamboos, their leaves eight to nine feet long. They bind these and thatch their houses with them. The people live in storeyed buildings as well. They make boats eight to nine poles long and cut six or seven feet wide, their heads and tails shaped like a fish.[103]

This sandstone statue of Śiva from southern Cambodia dates from the mid-seventh century, that is, during or soon after Funan's absorption by Zhenla. Śiva was the god eulogised by the Buddhist monk Nāgasena in the description of Funan he gave in an audience with Emperor Wu of the Southern Qi dynasty in 484.

Source: Metropolitan Museum of Art, New York; https://www.metmuseum.org/toah/works-of-art/1987.17/, 2020

When he goes out the king of the state rides an elephant, and his wives are capable of riding an elephant too. Entertainment consists of fighting cocks and fighting pigs.

There are no prisons. If there is a dispute, a gold ring or a hen's egg is thrown into boiling water and the disputants are told to take it out. Or again, a metal chain is heated until it is red hot, and they take it and hold it in both hands and walk seven paces with it. The offender's hands are badly burned, while the one who has not offended is not hurt. Or again, they are submerged in water, and the honest one does not sink down deep while the one who is dishonest does.

They have different kinds of sugar cane, pomegranates, mandarin oranges, and plenty of betel nuts.[104] Their birds and animals are like those of China. The people have a good nature, and are not inclined to go to war. They are often invaded by Linyi. They are not in communication with Jiaozhou, so their envoys come rarely.

What *The History of the Southern Qi Dynasty* tells us about Funan

The account of Funan in *Nan Qi shu* includes the first substantial account of the kings who came immediately after Hun Tian. Compared with the similar but longer account in *Liang shu* (see chapter three), the *Nan Qi shu* account is only missing Panpan, the middle son of Hun Tian's successor Pankuang.

Like Kang Tai and *Jin shu*, *Nan Qi shu* notes that Funan's first monarch, Liuye, was female. It also makes other references to the role and status of women in Funan. These include the implication that Zhan was entitled to the kingship because of his mother, Fan Shiman's older sister, and an observation that like the king, his wife or wives—or perhaps women of high status (the term *furen* here could mean any of these)—could ride on an elephant too.[105] It is worth noting in this context that according to *Nan Qi shu*, women in nearby Linyi were held in higher regard than men.[106] These fragmentary reports suggest leading social roles for women in both Linyi and Funan—roles that in the case of Funan, at least, had a political dimension as well. Citing Zhan as an early example, Vickery goes so far as to suggest that pre-Angkorian Cambodian society may have been characterized by matrilineal lineages of *poñ* (rulers, *fan* in Chinese), and that these were replaced by patriliny once the focus of society shifted inland.[107]

While longer than the account in *Jin shu*, *Nan Qi shu*'s account of Funan would still be quite brief were it not for its extended description of the monk-envoy Nāgasena's visit to Jiankang in 484. Still, several points in *Nan Qi shu*'s account of

Funan are worth noting. In terms of their dates of composition, this is the first time in official Chinese records that the name of the king of Funan is transliterated from Sanskrit—clear evidence of the spreading cultural influence of India, or at least of Indian norms of rulership.[108] In official Chinese records, the starting point for this influence was the Indian brahmin, also called Kauṇḍinya, who came to rule Funan with Indian law and custom many decades earlier, in the late fourth or early fifth century CE. He is mentioned in *Liang shu*, as we shall see in the following chapter, but not in *Nan Qi shu*.[109]

The reference to a royal envoy engaging in trade in Guangzhou is a rare allusion in official Chinese records to someone from Funan trading abroad.

King Kauṇḍinya Jayavarman's supplicatory language, including his description of Funan as a dependency of the Southern Qi dynasty, conveys a vivid sense of the protocol the Chinese court expected or at least hoped for from its tribute bearers. Even allowing for a predisposition on the part of Chinese historians to portray the Chinese emperor in a commanding role, Kauṇḍinya Jayavarman's way of expressing himself is remarkably submissive.

The naming of Modan, the still unidentified mountain on which the cult and culture of Nāgasena's Funan was concentrated, is the first time Chinese chroniclers provide the name of a place in Funan—and the only time they do so until *Xin Tang shu* calls the Funan capital Temu some five hundred years later.

The apparent melding of Hindu and Buddhist beliefs in Nāgasena's account of Maheśvara or Śiva, which moves smoothly from praising Maheśvara to eulogizing the (Mahayana Buddhist) Bodhisattva of compassion, is also noteworthy.[110] It seems to run counter to the view sometimes held on the basis of archaeological findings that in early Funan, cults devoted to Viṣṇu and others, including Śiva, ran in parallel with—but separate from—Buddhist cults.[111] It suggests an intermingling of Buddhist and Hindu precepts and practices, one that seems to mirror Buddhist-Hindu syncretism in other parts of Southeast Asia. That said, we should note that *Sui shu* and (much later) Zhou Daguan portray Buddhist and non-Buddhist—perhaps Hindu—devotees in Zhenla living and worshipping side by side, that is, in parallel rather than in a melded or syncretistic fashion.[112]

One final point to note is Emperor Wu's remark about the difficulties of communication and interpretation during the preceding Liu Song dynasty, suggesting that despite Funan sending tribute missions at that time (which it did in 434, 435, 438, and 442), the southern Chinese court had not paid it much attention.[113]

Most of the final part of *Nan Qi shu*'s account of Funan—its description of the people and their customs—is new to official Chinese records. This revealing information includes an important reference to the enslavement of people captured from districts neighboring Funan, confirming the existence of slavery in Funan, first mentioned in the *Wai guo zhuan* story about women slaves being accused of theft. *Nan Qi shu*'s comments on the country's clothing, gold rings and bracelets, silver vessels, wooden storeyed houses, wooden city walls, and bamboo leaves used for thatching are also new. Mention is made for the first time of gold, silver, and silks being used in trade, perhaps as forms of currency. These items may have been of foreign origin, but whether the trade concerned was mainly local or with foreigners is left unclear. On the other hand, references to other features of Funan life—its fighting cocks, its wooden boats, its trials by ordeal—reiterate points made over two centuries earlier by Kang Tai.

Given the propensity of early Chinese historians to look down on China's neighbours, *Nan Qi shu*'s author, Xiao Zixian, takes a relatively positive view of the Funanese, whom he calls crafty, clever, and ingenious. His tone is consistent with the approving remark made over a century later by the renowned Chinese scholar-commentator Li Shan, who describes the people of Funan as "especially talented and ingenious, unlike the other southern foreigners."[114]

The accounts of Funan in this chapter show that from the third to the sixth century, it gradually became a feature of both unofficial and official writings in China. It is clear from unofficial writings that it was regarded as a source of Buddhist learning in China, as well as being an impressionistic inspiration for Daoists in search of immortality. Official writings, particularly the standard histories of the Jin and Southern Qi dynasties, show that successive southern Chinese courts maintained a connection with Funan through its tribute missions, although the emperor's attention only seems to have really focused on Funan as a result of Nāgasena's tribute mission in 484. This focus was sustained and developed during the Liang dynasty (502–556), as we have seen from records of Buddhist monks in China, and as we shall consider further in the next chapter.

3

The History of the Liang Dynasty and its portrait of Funan

This chapter takes us on to the sixth century, which culminated in the 580s with the reunification of China under the Sui dynasty (581–618) and the glorious Tang dynasty (618–907).

Most of the chapter is devoted to the standard histories of the last of the short-lived southern Chinese dynasties during the Han-Sui interregnum, *Liang shu* [*The History of the Liang Dynasty*] and *Chen shu* [*The History of the Chen Dynasty*]. It also looks at the two composite standard histories for the whole period, *Bei shi* [*The History of the Northern Dynasties*] and *Nan shi* [*The History of the Southern Dynasties*]. Of all these works, much the most informative and engaging as a source of information on Funan is the history of the Liang dynasty, the brief Buddhist dynasty that ruled southern China during the first half of the sixth century.

As with the histories discussed in chapter two, the histories considered in this chapter were all completed in a later era—in these cases during the first decades of the Tang dynasty, under the supervision of the practically minded and ambitious second emperor of the Tang, Taizong (r. 627–649). Taizong was keen to leave his imprint on the past, and thus on the present.[1] He commissioned *Liang shu* and *Chen shu*, which were both completed in 636.[2] Much of the work on *Bei shi* and *Nan shi* was also undertaken under his aegis, though they were not completed until ten years after his death.[3]

Looking back on Funan from the vantage point of the Tang

The next histories are discussed in order of the dates of their composition. The first of them is *Liang shu*, which covers the period between 502 and 556, when the Liang court ruled from its capital Jiankang (Nanjing). The first forty-eight years of the dynasty were dominated by a single ruler, its founding emperor Wu (not to be confused with Emperor Wu of the Southern Qi, the ruler who met the monk-envoy

Nāgasena in 484). As we saw in the last chapter, Emperor Wu of the Liang was a fanatical devotee and practitioner of Mahayana Buddhism. Buddhist monks from India, Funan, and elsewhere came to his court, responding to his call for expertise and bringing classic Buddhist texts for translation.

Like *Nan Qi shu*, *Liang shu* includes several passages on the southern Chinese court's connections with states outside China, many of them far beyond China's southern frontiers. The passages referring to Funan include one quite long account and a number of shorter references, three of which—about the third-century visit to Funan by Kang Tai and Zhu Ying—were considered earlier, in chapter one.

The principal author of *Liang shu* was Yao Silian (557–637), a high-ranking official whose life straddled two dynasties. Yao served the Sui dynasty in its final years before going on to serve the Tang dynasty in its new capital at Chang'an (present-day Xi'an). Assisted by other scholars, Yao completed the work on *Liang shu* that had been started by his father Yao Cha.[4] In this respect he resembled the famous Han dynasty historian Sima Qian, who had taken over the work of his father on the first of the great Chinese histories, the first-century BCE *Shi ji* [*The Record of the Historian*]. While finishing *Liang shu*, Yao and his assistants also completed the work Yao's father had begun on the last of the Six Dynasty histories, *Chen shu*.[5]

Yao was already in his seventies when he undertook these momentous tasks, and died soon after completing them. Well-recognized as an outstanding historian while he was still alive, Yao was made a member of the prestigious College of Literary Studies, a body of eighteen pre-eminent officials and scholars who advised Taizong on matters of state. At Taizong's command the renowned court painter Yan Liben (c. 600–673) portrayed these eighteen men—and as always in such matters, they were all men—in a single famous scroll. Unlike other works by Yan, including a portrait of Taizong, the scroll of the eighteen scholars has not, sadly, survived in any form. So we are deprived of a rare chance to see a portrait of a leading early Chinese historian who wrote about Funan.[6]

Yao and others like him found themselves writing and editing at a busy and demanding time. Taizong was intent on consolidating Tang authority—meaning, in effect, his own—both at home and abroad.[7] One way of realizing this goal was by seeing that the standard histories of all the dynasties preceding the Tang were completed, which he did by establishing an official History Office.[8] In addition to Yao's histories of the Liang and Chen dynasties, Taizong commissioned historical accounts of the two most recent northern dynasties, the Northern Qi (550–577) and the Northern Zhou (557–581), as well as a history of the Tang dynasty's immediate predecessor, the Sui. He also arranged for the composition of a new history of the Jin dynasty, building on earlier, unsuccessful attempts to complete one. Over the course of seven years, from 629 to 636, Taizong thus presided over the unprecedented compilation of six histories of dynasties.[9]

The Tang emperor Taizong, in a copy of a portrait by an unknown Ming dynasty artist.

Source: The National Palace Museum, Taipei

Under Taizong, court historians also set to work on composite histories of the Northern and Southern Dynasties between the Jin and the Sui. A scholarly committee was set up to compile these two larger, more all-embracing histories, which became *Nan shi* and *Bei shi*. Their lead author was the scholar-official Li Yanshou (d. 680), who undertook work on both books in collaboration with other historians in the History Office. Like Yao Silian, Li based his work partly on earlier work done by his father. Comprehensive though they were, neither *Bei shi* and *Nan shi* pay much attention to remote Funan. *Bei shi* only mentions it four times, principally in a passage about the Funanese offshoot Chitu or Red Earth (which we shall return to in the next chapter), and in another passage about Funan's successor state, Zhenla. Both these references to Funan are taken verbatim from *Sui shu*.[10] *Nan shi* contains several passages devoted to Funan, but they are derived from *Liang shu* and contain very little that is new. We shall return briefly to *Nan shi* later.[11]

The History of the Liang Dynasty on Funan's customs and kings

Of all the histories of the Six Dynasties, *Liang shu* has some of the most revealing and engaging material on Funan. In addition to various short passages recording Funan's tribute missions, the history devotes quite a long passage to Funan's culture and history, notably its first queen Liuye and the various kings who came after her. All the same, it wouldn't do to overstate Funan's importance to *Liang shu*'s authors. Although relatively lengthy, their description of Funan still only amounts to a small part of the whole work, less than a chapter in a fifty-six-chapter book. So while Yao Silian and his colleagues evidently took some interest in Funan, it was only a distant one.[12]

As with *Jin shu* and *Song shu*, *Liang shu*'s first entries on Funan record the occasions on which the king of Funan sent envoys with tribute to the Liang court in Jiankang (today's Nanjing). A steady stream of envoys carrying gifts of local products were sent during the time of Emperor Wu of Liang, about nine times in total: in 503, 504, 511–512 (two dates that probably refer to the same mission), 514, 517, 519, 520, 535, and 539 (the last including tribute of one or more live rhinos). Although *Liang shu* does not say so, the mission in 503 probably included among its members the Buddhist monk Mandra, whose visit to Jiankang was mentioned in chapter two. During the course of this mission, the newly enthroned Emperor Wu bestowed on King Kauṇḍinya Jayavarman the title General Pacifying the South.[13] One other tribute mission, in 530, is not listed in these first entries but is mentioned in chapter fifty-four.[14] This steady flow of tribute missions is testamony to the good relations that must have existed between Funan and the Liang court, strengthened no doubt by a strong common faith in Buddhism.

Following the list of tribute missions, *Liang shu* makes no further mention of Funan until chapter fifty-four. This chapter begins with a passage describing the various states to the south of the sea—meaning the Southern Sea—as "generally being on large islands (*zhou*) to the south and southwest of Jiaozhou" at distances varying from three thousand to thirty thousand li.[15] The western ones among them are said to be "adjacent to the various states in China's western frontier regions." There follows the account of Kang Tai and Zhu Ying's southern travels, and a short passage on communications between southern China and the states of the Southern Sea during the preceding Jin, Liu Song, and Southern Qi dynasties.

This passage notes that during the Jin dynasty, communications between the states of the Southern Sea and China were rare, so no official records were kept of them. During the Liu Song and Southern Qi dynasties, the history continues, ten or so states sent representatives, and records began to be kept. Then during the Liang dynasty, with new arrangements for tribute in place, seafaring visitors began coming to China every year in greater numbers than before. According to *Liang shu*, "some rough writings about their customs have been put together in *Hainan zhuan* [*A Record of South of the Sea*, referring to the states south of the Southern Sea]."[16] It is not clear whether the *Hainan zhuan* referred to here is simply this section of the *Liang shu* or a separate work. The editors of the modern Zhonghua shuju edition of *Liang shu* seem to regard it as the latter.[17]

Either way, the comment is an interesting one. It suggests that the writings of Kang Tai and Zhu Ying were not the only sources for Chinese accounts of southern states in *Liang shu* and elsewhere during the Funan era. The existence of a collation of "rough writings" may also help explain why the entry on Funan in *Liang shu* is broader in scope than the entries in the earlier standard histories.

Liang shu then gives an account of the state of Linyi (a polity or polities discussed in greater detail in appendix five). It notes that Linyi "was originally Xianglin district of the Han dynasty commandery of Rinan, on the frontier of the old Yueshang," and suggests that Linyi and Funan have some things in common:[18]

> As for the customs of the state [of Linyi], the people live in storeyed buildings, which are called *ganlan*, and the entrances to them all face north.[19] They write on paper made from the leaves of trees. The men and women all wear horizontal strips of cotton, which they wrap around and below their waist and which are called *ganman* or *duman*.[20] They wear strings of small rings in their ears. The footwear of the people of high status is made of leather; those of low status go barefoot. This is how things are in the various states going south from Linyi and Funan.

Liang shu also suggests a strong Indian influence in Linyi, remarking that "its great family names are Brahmin."[21] After recording Linyi's tribute missions, *Liang shu* then turns its attention to Funan and other Southern Sea locations:[22]

> The state of Funan is south of Rinan commandery, in a large bay to the west of the sea. It is at a distance of about seven thousand li from Rinan, some three thousand li southwest of Linyi. The city is five hundred li from the sea.[23] There is a large river ten li in width that flows from the northwest and enters the sea in the east. The extent of the state is three thousand li or so. The territory is low lying, flat, and spread out, the weather, the land, and the people broadly comparable to those of Linyi. They produce gold, silver, copper, tin, lign-aloes, ivory, peacock, and kingfisher feathers, and multi-colored parrots.[24]
>
> Three thousand li or more from Funan's southern frontiers lies the state of Dunxun.[25] It is on a shore with winding cliffs, its territory a thousand li in extent, its city ten li from the sea.[26] It has five kings, all of them loosely dependent on Funan.[27] On its eastern frontier, Dunxun communicates with Jiaozhou, while its western frontier connects with the various states beyond the frontiers of India and Parthia [Anxi], which it trades with back and forth. The reason this is so is that in a thousand or so li, Dunxun curves back round to the sea.[28] The Great Sea has no limits, and boats and ships have not yet been able to go right across it. Dunxun's markets are meeting places for east and west, with more than ten thousand people in them every day, and every kind of fine things and precious goods available there.[29] They also have a liquor tree similar to the pomegranate. They leave the juice of the flowers in earthenware jars for a few days and it turns to liquor.
>
> Apart from Dunxun, there is the state of Piqian, lying at a distance of eight thousand li from Funan on a large island in the sea. It is said that the king is two poles tall, with a neck three feet long. He has stayed alive from olden times until now, and no one knows how old he is. The king is a godlike sage, and with respect to the people of the state he knows all about their ways good and bad, and what the future will bring, the consequence being that no one dares cheat him. In southern places they call him King Longneck.
>
> As for the customs of the country, they have houses and clothes and eat rice. The language of the people is similar to that of Funan. There is a mountain that produces gold; the gold is visible on the rock face, and there is an endless amount of it. Under the laws of the state, criminals are all punished by having their flesh eaten in the presence of the king. The country does not take in traveling traders, and if they go there they are killed and eaten too. So traveling merchants do not venture to go there. The king usually dwells

in a storeyed building. He eats no meat, and he does not serve the gods. His offspring live and die like other people; the king alone does not die.

The king of Funan frequently sends him envoys with letters, to each of which he responds. He often sends the king of Funan eating utensils for fifty people made of pure gold, shaped like round dishes or cups, which are called *duoluo*, each with a capacity of five pints, or like bowls, each with a capacity of a pint. The king can also write Indian [Tianzhu] script, and has written perhaps three thousand words explaining the origins of pre-destined fate in the manner of a Buddhist sutra, as well as discoursing on the good.[30]

It is also said that on the eastern frontiers of Funan is the Great Sea. In it there is a large island. On the island is the state of Zhubo [?Java], to the east of which lies Mawuzhou [?Maluku].[31] If you go farther east on the Great Sea for a thousand li or so, you reach the Great Island of Natural Fire. On it there are trees growing out of fire, and people nearby on the island scrape away their bark and spin it into cloth, and with several feet of it at most make handkerchiefs with it. It is the same as burned hemp but slightly green-black in color. If there is a small impurity they throw it back into the fire, and it comes out pure again. They also make wicks for lamps that are never known to burn out.[32]

The people of the state of Funan were originally accustomed to going naked, with tattooed bodies and their hair hanging loose.[33] They wore no clothing on the upper or lower parts of their body. They regarded a woman called Liuye as their monarch. She was young and strong, somewhat like a man. To their south was the state of Jiao, where a man named Hun Tian served the gods. He dreamed that the gods gave him a bow and that he took to sea in a merchant's ship. The next morning Hun Tian got up and visited the temple, where he found a bow under a sacred tree. Then he did as he had dreamed and took to sea in a ship, and in due course entered an outer district of Funan.

Liuye and her forces saw the ship arrive and wanted to seize it. Hun Tian drew his bow and shot an arrow at their ship; it went through the side of the ship and struck an attendant. Liuye was very fearful and had her forces surrender. Hun Tian then taught Liuye to wear a cloth by putting her head through it so that she was no longer uncovered. Then he governed her state, taking Liuye as his wife. The sons she bore were made the kings of seven districts.

The king who came after him, Hun Pankuang, deviously asserted his strength to divide the various districts and brought about doubt and confusion among them, at which point he raised an army, attacking and taking them over.[34] He then sent his sons and grandsons to divide up the rule of these various districts among themselves. They were known as second-ranking kings.[35]

Pankuang died when he was ninety or so. He set up his middle son, Panpan, to succeed him, delegating the affairs of state to his senior general, Fan [Shi]man.[36] Panpan died after being in place three years, and the people of the state together raised Fan Shiman up to be king. Fan Shiman was brave, strong, and a man of strategy, and again used military power to attack neighboring states, all of which submitted and became dependencies. He called himself the Great King of Funan. Then he prepared for and built large ships that sailed to the ends of the Great Sea, attacking ten or so states, including Qudukun, Jiuzhi, and Dianxun, opening up five to six thousand li of territory.[37] He was going on to attack the state of Jinlin, but he fell ill and sent the crown prince Jinsheng to carry on the attack in his place.

At that time, [Fan] Zhan, the son of Fan Shiman's elder sister, was a general in charge of two thousand men, and relying on this he usurped the throne and set himself up in Fan Shiman's stead, sending someone to dupe Jinsheng and kill him.

When Fan Shiman died, he left an infant son called Chang amongst the people. When this son reached the age of twenty, he joined up with some strong, valiant fellows and carried out a surprise attack on [Fan] Zhan, killing him.[38]

Zhan's senior general Fan Xun then killed Chang in turn and set himself up as ruler. He put right the governance of the country and constructed high buildings for his enjoyment, where in the morning and mid–afternoon he would receive guests three or four times a day.[39] The ordinary people gave him bananas, sugar cane, tortoises, and birds as gifts.[40]

In the law of the state, there are no prisons. People accused of an offense first fast for three days. An axe is then heated until it is red hot, whereupon those charged have to carry it in both hands for seven paces. Or a gold ring or a hen's egg is cast into boiling water, and they are told to fetch it out. If they are dishonest, their hands are scalded; if they have done right, they are not. Or the accused are fed without ado to crocodiles kept in the city moat, or to wild animals penned up outside the city gates. If the crocodiles and animals do not eat them, they are regarded as innocent, and after three days they are set free.

The crocodiles are two poles or more long and shaped like alligators.[41] They have four feet and a snout six or seven feet long, with teeth on either side as sharp as a knife or a sword. They usually eat fish, but if they happen upon river deer, deer, or people, they eat them too. They are found everywhere to the south of Cangwu and in foreign countries . . .[42]

During the Tai Kang reign period [280–289] of the emperor Wu of the [Western] Jin dynasty, [Fan] Xun began sending envoys with tribute. In the first year of the Shengping reign period [357] of Emperor Mu, the king Zhu Zhantan made a gift of a trained elephant together with a memorial he submitted. An imperial edict declared, "Presenting this animal has involved considerable effort; you are to refrain from doing this."[43]

The king who came after him, Kauṇḍinya [Jiaochenru], was originally an Indian brahmin.[44] The gods said to him, "You should be king of Funan."[45] He was very happy and went from the south to Panpan.[46] The people of Funan heard about him; the whole country was delighted and took him back to be greeted and set up as ruler.

He then changed the system of rules and customs and used Indian law instead.[47] When Kauṇḍinya died, the king after him was Dhṛtavarman [Chilituobamo].[48] During the time of Emperor Wen of the Liu Song dynasty [r. 424–453], he submitted memorials and offered up local produce as gifts.

During the Yongming reign period of the [Southern] Qi dynasty [483–493], the king, [Kauṇḍinya] Jayavarman [Shexiebamo], dispatched an envoy with tribute.[49] In the second year of the Tianlan reign period [of the Liang dynasty, 503], [Kauṇḍinya] [Jaya]varman [Bamo] again dispatched an envoy to present coral and Buddhist statuary, as well as gifts of local produce. An imperial command declared, "The king of Funan, Kauṇḍinya Jayavarman [Jiaochenru Shexiebamo], dwelling on the edges of the sea, has governed the south for a generation, his loyalty and probity known from afar. Speaking through more than one interpreter he presents us with treasures; it behoves us to provide recompense, and proclaim for him an illustrious title. May he be General Pacifying the South, King of Funan."[50]

Now the people of the state are all ugly and black with curly hair. They do not dig a well in the place they live in. Rather, twenty or thirty families share a pond and draw water from it. Their custom is to serve the gods, making bronze images of them, with two faces and four hands, or four faces and eight hands, each of the hands holding something, either a small boy, or a bird or animal, or the sun or moon.[51]

When the king goes in and out of his palace, he rides an elephant, as do the women of the palace and attendants.[52] When the king is seated, he squats aslant with his right knee cocked and his left leg hanging down to the ground. In front of him is spread a cotton cloth, with golden bowls and incense burners laid out on it.[53]

A copper alloy statue of the bodhisattva Avalokiteśvara (Guanyin), dating from the 8th-early 9th century and originally from Sumatra or the Malay peninsula. Perhaps this and other early statues, including ones of Viṣṇu with four or eight arms bearing objects, were the basis for the many-armed statues of Funan referred to in *Liang shu*.

Source: Metropolitan Museum of Art, New York; https://www.metmuseum.org/art/collection/search/38952

With regard to the customs of the country, when they are in mourning, they cut off their hair and beards. They have four ways of disposing of the dead: in water, by casting the body into the flowing waters of the Great River; by fire, by burning the body until it is reduced to ashes; in the ground, by burying the body; and by means of birds, in which case the body is thrown into the wilds.[54]

By nature the people are covetous and miserly, lacking in decorum and a sense of what is right. If a man or woman desires someone, they go after them.

In the tenth and thirteenth years [of the Tianlan reign period, 511, 514], [Kauṇḍinya] Jayavarman sent a succession of envoys with tribute. In the latter year he died. His concubine's son, Rudravarman [Liutuobamo], killed the younger brother of his principal wife and set himself up as king. In the sixteenth year [517] he sent an envoy, Zhu Dangbaolao, with a memorial and tribute.[55] In the eighteenth year (519), he again sent an envoy to present a statue of the Buddha made of Indian sandalwood, and leaves of the *poluo* tree, as well as gifts of glass pearls, turmeric, liquidambar, and other aromatic substances.[56] In the first year of the Putong reign period [520], the second year of the Zhongdatong reign period [530], and the first year of the Datong reign period [535], he sent a series of envoys with gifts of local produce.

In the fifth year [539], he again sent an envoy, this time with the gift of live rhinos, and said there was a hair of the Buddha in his country, twelve feet long. The emperor commanded the Buddhist monk Yunbao to go back with the envoy to receive it.[57]

Liang shu continues with brief accounts of other states, two of which it says share some characteristics with Funan. The first of these is the Buddhist state of Gantuoli, which Wang Gungwu tentatively locates on the island of Sumatra. *Liang shu* describes it as being "on an island in the Southern Sea, with customs that are similar to those of Linyi and Funan, and produce consisting of variegated cloth, cotton, and betel nuts of outstanding quality, the best of the various states" in the south.[58]

The other is the state of Langyaxiu, which *Liang shu* describes as being twenty-four thousand li from Guangzhou. It has been variously located astride the neck of the Malay Peninsula, or in the northeast of the Malay Peninsula, perhaps around Pattani. Assuming it was in the north of the Malay Peninsula, *Liang shu*'s estimate of Langyaxiu's distance from Guangzhou was highly inaccurate.[59] *Liang shu* describes the state as having a climate and produce that are "more or less the same as Funan's," and as having brick walls and a double entrance, and a king who rides out on an elephant "with soldiers and guards in full array."[60]

How *The History of the Liang Dynasty* adds to our knowledge of Funan

The *Liang shu* account of Funan adds considerably to what we know, while still leaving important aspects of Funanese state and society unexplained.

It provides the most comprehensive extant account of the royal lineage of Funan from Hun Tian onwards, enabling us to construct a fuller picture of when and how Funanese rulers succeeded one another.[61] That said, two issues regarding this lineage are left unresolved. Both result from ambiguities in the Chinese text.

The first issue arises from the phrase *sheng zi*, which can mean either "bore a son" or "bore sons," leaving unclear whether Liuye bore one son or seven. As noted earlier, the respected twelfth-century scholar Zheng Qiao read the phrase as "seven sons." If his interpretation was correct, it would suggest that at this juncture Funan was a group of small interconnected polities rather than just one.

The second issue stems from the phrase *qi hou wang*, which can mean either "a king who came after him," as in one of his successors, or "the king who came after him," as in his immediate successor. This small ambiguity means that we cannot be clear whether in three instances—Hun Pankuang, the first Kauṇḍinya, and Dhṛtavarman—the king named as *qi hou wang* was the immediate successor of the kings named before him or a more distant one.[62] This in turn has a significant effect on our ability to trace back Funan's royal chronology.

Another curious aspect of the *Liang shu* text is its account of the brahmin Kauṇḍinya, who came to Funan from the south after responding to a call from the gods to rule Funan, which he evidently did in the late fourth or early fifth century (since his immediate successor sent tribute to China from 434 on). This account seems to be a partial reprise of the story of Hun Tian, who was also called by the gods to rule Funan and who may also have come there from the south. It is impossible to explain the similarity between these two figures with any degree of certainty. Whether it represents a case of history repeating itself, a melding of the two stories, or some other construction or reconstruction of the events concerning them, we cannot say.

On a surer note, *Liang shu*'s account of King Kauṇḍinya Jayavarman (d. 514) being succeeded by his son Rudravarman establishes the first connection between early Chinese accounts of Funan and local archaeological evidence, since Jayavarman and Rudravarman are mentioned as father and son in K.40, a sixth-century inscription thirty kilometers south of present-day Phnom Penh.[63] As we shall see later, this is one of only two instances in which Chinese records are clearly substantiated by local evidence.

Turning from history to geography, *Liang shu* gives us a first brief picture of Funan's physical appearance. It describes the land as flat and low lying, which is consistent with Funan's location in or near the Mekong Delta. It also makes a first reference to water usage, mentioning that the people do not dig wells but rather share ponds. Taken with *Jin shu*'s reference to farming practices—one year planting, three years harvesting—this mention of ponds suggests a plentiful supply of water. However, it leaves unclear what relationship if any the ponds had to the network of canals that was a feature of Funan, as we know from archaeological findings and aerial surveillance.[64]

It is worth noting here that like earlier accounts of Funan, the *Liang shu* account makes no mention at all of Hun Tian drinking the country's water—a story that has erroneously found its way into some Western accounts of Funan and has been construed as a possible allusion to Funan's water management.[65]

The accounts in *Liang shu* of various trials by ordeal repeat those in the writings of Kang Tai. The mention of a city moat, echoing Kang Tai's reference to Fan Xun's water-filled ditch, is confirmed by archaeological evidence of an urban moat at Óc Eo, which, according to Manguin, had been dug by the early third century CE.[66]

Liang shu lists Funan's local produce and the items it sent as tribute to China. It has nothing to say about Funan's status as an entrepôt or trading center, although some of the local produce was clearly suitable for trade as well as tribute. We are left to infer Funan's involvement in foreign trade from *Liang shu*'s description of the "loosely dependent" state of Dunxun, with its busy, crowded markets and its important intermediate location, as it seems, astride the Kra Isthmus.

Liang shu contains the first reference in early Chinese records to religious statuary in Funan, though its description of many-handed bronze icons bearing small boys, birds, and animals seems improbable, and is not borne out by the Funan-era statues that have survived.[67]

Finally Yao Xilian, the author of *Liang shu* takes a stiffer, less accommodating view of the Funanese than his predecessor Xiao Zixian, author of *Nan Qi shu*. Xiao was quite complimentary of them, calling them clever and ingenious. In Yao's disapproving view, they were cowardly, miserly, improperly behaved, and carelessly drawn by sexual attraction.

Two other early works of history on Funan

The standard history following *Liang shu* was *Chen shu*, covering the last of the Southern Dynasties, the short-lived Chen dynasty (557–589). Its author, Yao Silian, completed the thirty-six chapters of this short history in 636, at the same time as he completed work on *Liang shu*.[68] *Chen shu* contains nothing on Funan apart from records of three tribute missions bearing local produce sent in 559, 572, and 588.[69]

The final standard history to be written about the Six Dynasties era, or at least most of it, was *Nan shi*. Work on this synoptic account of the four dynasties that ruled south China between 420 and 589 was begun by the scholar-official Li Dashi, who served the Sui dynasty until its collapse, and was then in exile before returning to the new Tang capital Chang'an to serve as a senior official there. It was completed by his son, Li Yanshou, who submitted it to the Tang emperor Gaozong in 659 together with *Bei shi*, a history of the northern dynasties that ruled during roughly the same period, which the two Li's also wrote.[70]

Nan shi includes an account of Funan but offers little beyond what the other standard histories provide.[71] It repeats nearly verbatim the account of Funan in *Liang shu*, with some minor amendments.[72] Otherwise it lists the tribute missions sent from Funan to China during the period in question, with one addition to the missions listed in the standard histories from Liu Song to Chen, a mission sent to the Liu Song court in 442.[73]

Taking the Six Dynasties era as a whole, Chinese records of Funan in the standard histories of the period are thus dominated by the accounts in Yao Silian's *Liang shu* and Xiao Zixian's *Nan Qi shu*. We do not know what materials Yao and Xiao relied on. It has sometimes been assumed that, like other early historians, they made extensive use of records left by Kang Tai and Zhu Ying.[74] They may indeed have done so. But as noted earlier, *Liang shu* seems to have drawn on more than one source for its information about southern states; *Nan Qi shu* certainly did for information about Funan, given its account of the Nāgasena mission in 484, more than two centuries after Kang Tai wrote about his trip south.

Whatever their sources were, both *Liang shu* and to a lesser extent *Nan Qi shu* tell us about Funan in sufficient detail to give us a valuable, if partial, portrait of its rulers, society, and history. To flesh out this portrait we must turn to subsequent Chinese sources on Funan, those dating from the Tang dynasty and later, some of them written after Funan ceased to exist or at least vanished from Chinese records. We'll look at these sources in chapter four.

4

The last of Funan during the seventh century CE

In this chapter we turn to the remaining official Chinese texts that contain records of Funan. By and large these texts, which were written from the Tang dynasty (618–907) onwards, reprise in short form earlier accounts of Funan. But they also contain some remarkable new material. This includes a vivid portrait of the state of Chitu or Red Earth, an offshoot or "different type" of Funan as it is called. They also include the first references to Funan being taken over by its hitherto unmentioned dependency Zhenla, later to become the Kingdom of Angkor, a polity or polities that will be the subject of chapters six to nine.

These remaining Chinese texts, discussed here in chronological order, consist of three standard histories and six other official works. The standard histories are *Sui shu* [*The History of the Sui Dynasty* (581–618)]—which was completed in 636, forty-seven years after the Sui dynasty ended—and two official histories of the Tang dynasty. These are *Jiu Tang shu* [*The Old History of the Tang Dynasty*], which was completed in 945 during the half-century interregnum between the Tang dynasty and the Song dynasty (960–1279), and a fully revised version of this history, *Xin Tang shu* [*The New History of the Tang Dynasty*], which was completed over a century later, in 1060, and differs substantially from its predecessor.

The other official works date from the Tang, Song, and Yuan dynasties. They consist of six massive works, namely: (1) the 801 historical compendium *Tong dian* [*A Comprehensive History of Institutions*]; (2) the 853 digest of Tang government institutions *Tang hui yao* [*Essential Documents and Regulations of the Tang Dynasty*]; (3) the 982 encyclopedia *Taiping yulan* [*An Encyclopedia Compiled during the Era of Great Peace* {976–983} *and Read by the Emperor*], which as we saw in chapter one is an important source for the very early history of Funan, including the writings of Kang Tai; (4) the geographical survey *Taiping huanyu ji* [*A Record of the World during the Era of Great Peace*], completed in the late tenth century; (5) the 1149 encyclopedic history of institutions *Tong zhi* [*A Comprehensive Treatise on Institutions*]; and (6) the historical survey of institutions *Wenxian tongkao*

[*A Comprehensive Study of Institutions on the Basis of Authoritative Documents*], presented to the emperor in 1319.

A Sui dynasty embassy to Funan's offshoot Chitu (Red Earth)

Sui shu, the history of the dynasty that reunited China and paved the way for the Tang, was written by three eminent early Tang scholars, Wei Zheng (580–643), Linghu Defen (583–666), and Zhangsun Wuji (d. 659).[1] Wei Zheng was a confidant of the Tang Emperor Taizong and lived in a ward of the cosmopolitan Tang capital Chang'an, quite close to the emperor's palace compound.[2] Wei and the others completed *Sui shu* and submitted it to Taizong in 636, the year their fellow historian Yao Silian finished work on *Liang shu* and *Chen shu*.[3]

Apart from a reference to performers of Funanese music, *Sui shu* contains four notable entries on Funan.[4] The first and most engaging of these is a lively portrait of the state of Chitu or Red Earth, which *Sui shu* describes as a *bie zhong* or "different type" of Funan, suggesting some kind of the kinship or racial affinity.[5] The location of Chitu is in dispute, but it is most likely to have been a polity in the northeast of the Malay Peninsula, although another intriguing possibility, suggested by Hoshino, is that it was located near the town of Kompong Cham in today's Cambodia.[6]

The *Sui shu* account of Chitu must have been based on a two-chapter report by a senior Chinese official, Chang Jun, on a visit he and a group of envoys paid to Chitu in 607, during the final years of the Sui dynasty. Chang Jun was the Sui officer in charge of state farms, an old Chinese system for managing agricultural production in distant places, sometimes under military control, and the other named officer accompanying him, Wang Junzheng, was in charge of forestry.

Chang Jun and his entourage were sent to Chitu by Emperor Yang of the Sui (r. 604–617), who is said to have wanted to restore Sui's relations with states cut off from China.[7] It is conceivable that one of the states Emperor Yang wanted to cultivate closer ties with was Funan. But by this time Funan's status was uncertain, its takeover by Zhenla either under way or imminent.[8] This uncertainty may explain why the emperor sent envoys to an offshoot of Funan, Chitu, rather than to Funan itself.

A further consideration may have been the condition of Funan's neighbor, the state of Linyi at the southern extremity of the Sui realm.[9] In the early 600s, Linyi was attacked by troops under the overall direction of Emperor Wen, Emperor Yang's father. Emperor Wen had engaged in huge, expensive public works projects, draining his court of resources, and according to *Sui shu* was lured into attacking Linyi by talk at court of its extraordinary wealth.[10]

In 605 the newly enthroned Emperor Yang followed up his father's assault by conquering Linyi and taking its capital city. (His troops later withdrew.)[11] Perhaps Chang Jun was sent on his mission farther south as a sequel to this conquest. *Sui shu* implies that his mission was a high-minded diplomatic démarche, but the fact that he and his colleague were in charge of state farms and forestry suggests that the mission had more mundane, perhaps exploitative intentions, even if for some reason these were not realized. In this instance, as in others, an account of the mission from those on the receiving end would be valuable to have, but as was usually the case no such local account exists.[12]

Here is *Sui shu*'s colorful account of Chitu and of Chang Jun's visit there:[13]

> The state of Chitu [Red Earth] is a different type of Funan. It is in the Southern Sea, and its capital takes a hundred days or so to reach by water. Much of its soil is red in color, hence its name. To its east is the state of Boluola, to the west the state of Poluosuo, and to the south the state of Heluodan. To the north it abuts on to the Great Sea.[14] Its territory is several thousand square li in size. The king's family name is Qutan, and his name is Lifuduosai.[15] He is not aware that there are [various other] states nearby and far away.
>
> The position of king passed to Lifuduosai after it had been announced that his father was abdicating to become a monk. He has reigned for sixteen years and has three wives, all of them daughters of kings of neighboring states. He lives in Sengzhi [Lion?] City.[16] It has gates three layers deep, each set of gates a hundred or so paces from the next. On every gate there are paintings of flying immortals, immortals, images of the Buddha, hanging gold flowers, and feathers with pendant bells.
>
> [Near the gates] there are several dozen women, some playing music, others holding up golden blossoms in both hands. Four women dressed like the guardian spirits by the sides of Buddhist pagodas stand on either side of the gates.[17] People outside the gates bear military weapons, while within them there are people carrying white whisks. The road is arrayed on either side with white nets and hanging blossoms.
>
> All the buildings in the king's palaces are multi-storeyed. The entrances are on the north side, and when sitting the king faces north, seated on a three-tier couch. He wears rose-colored cloth and is crowned in a gold-flowered crown with pendant jeweled tassels. Four young women stand and serve him, with a hundred or so guards to his left and right.
>
> Behind the king's couch is a wooden shrine, inlaid with gold, silver and various aromatic woods.[18] Behind the shrine hangs a golden flame. Set on either side of the king's couch are two gold mirrors, with gold jars laid out in

front of them. A gold incense burner stands in front of every jar. Up ahead is placed a gold reclining ox, before it a single jeweled canopy flanked by jeweled fans. Several hundred brahmins and others sit in lines on each side, facing each other across the middle.

The state's officials consist of one Satogaluo, two Tuonadayi, and three Galimiga, who are together in charge of affairs of state, and one Juluomodi, in charge of criminal law. Each city [in Chitu] has a Nayega and ten Bodi.[19]

Ordinary people all pierce their ears and cut their hair. They do not engage in ritual kneeling and bowing. They daub their bodies with perfumed oil. Their custom is to venerate the Buddha and to treat brahmins with even greater respect. Women wear their hair coiled at the back of the neck. Men and women alike dress in rose-colored, light grey, or multi-colored cloth.[20] The rich and powerful houses lead a luxurious life and use only gold locks [to secure their possessions?] and only those bestowed on them by the king.

Whenever a marriage takes place, an auspicious day is chosen. For five days in advance, the family of the bride provide music, food, and drink. The father gives the hand of his daughter to his son-to-be, and after seven days the match is made. Following the marriage, property is divided and [the elder son] live separately; only the father's younger sons still live with him. When someone's father, mother, elder brother, or younger brother dies, they cut their hair and put on plain white clothing, go to the riverside, and build a bamboo or wooden pavilion. In it they make a firewood pyre and place the body on it. To see the body on its way, they light incense and raise banners, blow conches and beat on drums. They set the pyre alight and lower it into the water. High and low are all treated in the same way, except for the king of the state. His ashes are gathered after his cremation and placed in a golden urn, which is stored in a temple building.

It is always hot, winter and summer, with frequent rain and few clear skies. The plants are not seasonal, and the place is especially suitable for rice, non-glutinous millet, white beans, and black hemp. Other products are mostly the same as those of Jiaozhi. They make wine from sugarcane mixed with the root of a purple gourd. The wine is yellowy-red in color and has a fine, aromatic taste. They also make wine from coconut juice.

When Emperor Yang came to the throne, he recruited people who could communicate with frontier regions cut off from China. In the third year of the Daye reign period [607], Chang Jun, Officer in Charge of State Farms, Wang Junzheng, Officer in Charge of Forestry and Crafts, and others asked if they could go as envoys to Chitu. The emperor was delighted. He gave each of them a hundred rolls of silk and a suit of clothes in the current style, and sent them on their way. He also sent five thousand items as gifts to the king of Chitu.

In the tenth month of that year [607], Chang Jun and the others took a ship from the Nanhai commandery, and after a journey of twenty days and nights, with the wind constantly behind them, they reached and passed by Jiaoshishan [Burnt Rock Mountain], then went southeast and anchored at Linggabobaduo [Liṅgaparvata] Island. Linyi was across from them to the west, a holy temple above it. On they went southwards, and came to Shizishi [Lion Rock], from which there ran a chain of islands. After two or three days' more travel they could see the mountains of the state of Langyaxu in the distance. From there they headed south as far as Jilong [Chicken Coop] Island, and thence to the frontier of Chitu.[21]

The king dispatched the brahmin Jiumoluo with thirty ships to greet them. Musicians blowing conches and beating drums welcomed the Sui envoys. Chang Jun was given a cable of gold locks to attach to his ship.

After a month or so [on their journey from Nanhai] they reached the capital. There the king sent his son Nayega to give Chang Jun and the others a ceremonial greeting.[22] Beforehand he had sent people with a gold tray holding fragrant flowers, a mirror and pincers, two gold boxes containing aromatic oil, eight gold vases holding scented water, and four strips of cotton, all for the envoys to bathe with. Early that afternoon, Nayega greeted the envoys with two elephants and peacock-feather parasols, and presented a gold tray with gold flowers to bear the emperor's edict.

With a hundred men and women blowing conches and beating drums, two brahmins led the way to the king's palace. Carrying the imperial edict, Chang Jun and the others went up into a storeyed building where the king and those ranking below him were all sitting. The edict having been proclaimed, Chang Jun and the others were taken to be seated, and Indian music was played. When the event was over, Chang Jun and the others returned to their hall. Brahmins were again sent there and gave them a meal served on platters made from leaves of grass, each one a square pole in size. As they did this they said to Chang Jun, "Now we are officers of the Great State, no longer the state of Chitu. Kindly partake of our meager food and drink with the Great State in mind."

A few days later, Chang Jun and the others were invited to a banquet. Guards with banners and other appurtenances went before and after them, as in the rituals of the previous encounter. Two divans were set out in front of the king, and on them were spread platters made of leaves of grass, each

> platter one and a half square poles in size. These carried pastries colored yellow, white, purple, and red, as well as a hundred or so varieties of beef, mutton, fish, tortoise meat, pork, and turtle meat. Chang Jun was invited to be seated on a divan, while those accompanying him sat on mats on the ground, each of them with a gold cup of wine. Female musicians performed in succesion for them, and they were given the finest gifts.
>
> Soon afterwards, Nayega was charged to go with Chang Jun, offering up local products as tribute [for Emperor Yang], as well as presenting a golden lotus crown, camphor, and a gold cast of a *duoluo* leaf with a memorial written on it in relief, enclosed in a gold box. Brahmins were sent to see the envoys off with fragrant blossoms, conches, and drums.[23]
>
> When they had put to the sea, they saw a shoal of green fish flying over the water. After being at sea for ten days or so, they sailed past southeastern Linyi with its mountains. There in the sea, a thousand or so paces wide, was a stretch of yellow, stinking fumes. These persisted for a whole day as the ship sailed on and were said to be the excrement of a huge fish. Skirting the sea's steep northern shores, they reached Jiaozhi.
>
> In the spring of the sixth year [of the Daye reign period, 610], Chang Jun went with Nayega to visit the emperor at Hongnong. The emperor was delighted and presented Chang Jun and the others with two hundred different items as gifts. They were all made Loyal Guards, and Nayega and other officials were each rewarded according to status.[24]

According to brief entries elsewhere in *Sui shu*, Chang Jun traveled on from Chitu to the state of Luosha. Luosha was said to be east of Poli, which Hsu tentatively locates on the island of Sumatra.[25] According to *Taiping yulan*, the inhabitants of Luosha were a degenerate people with red hair, dark bodies, animal teeth, and eagle claws. They engaged in trade, but only by night, covering their faces during the day. Given their unpreposessing nature, the items they traded in must have been well worth Chang Jun's trip, but *Taiping yulan* does not tell us what they were.[26]

Oddly, *Sui shu* does not describe Chang Jun's onward journey to Luosha after its account of his visit to Chitu, as we might expect it to. In another respect too, the last part of the *Sui shu* account of Chang Jun's visit to Chitu is unclear. It does not say explicitly whether Nayega traveled with Chang Jun back to China, or went later on his own. The fact that Nageya's gifts for Emperor Yang are mentioned while the two of them were still in Chitu suggests that Chang Jun left Nayega behind, only to meet him again over two years later in 610, when the two men went to see Emperor Yang in Hongnong near the Chinese capital. This would make sense if Chang Jun did not return to China directly but went to Luosha first.

Sui shu records that during Chang Jun's visit to Chitu in 608 and 609, Chitu sent envoys with local produce to the Sui court in Luoyang. *Sui shu* also records that Chitu sent an envoy in 610, presumably a reference to Nayega's visit in that year to Emperor Yang. *Xin Tang shu* records one further, much later mission from Chitu, sent in 669 by an otherwise unidentified king called Zhandabo. Thereafter there is no further mention of tribute missions or other activities relating to Chitu in Chinese records. There is one caveat: *Liang shu and Cefu yuangui* do list three other missions from a state called Shizi or Lion State, sent in 527, 670 and 711 (the latter being the last on record). In every case the missions are listed together with missions from Linyi. In a separate entry, *Liang shu* describes Shizi as "a state beside India." But given the name of Chitu's capital, it could conceivably have been Chitu.[27]

The History of the Sui Dynasty on Funan's takeover by Zhenla

Moving on from Chitu to *Sui shu*'s other three comments on Funan, one of them is a brief reference to a Funan book on or from Liang times—the text is unclear as to which—that was written in Hu script, evidently meaning a form of script from India.[28] As in the case of *Jin shu*, which also mentions writings in Funan derived from the Hu, this may be an early reference to writings in Khmer.

The third comment, mentioned earlier in this book, records that the kings of Funan have the surname Gulong, "as is often the case with family names in the various states."[29]

The last and most significant comment on Funan in *Sui shu* is a report that Funan was taken over (*jian*) by a king of the Funan dependency Zhenla whose name was Citrasena (Zhiduosina) and whose family name was Kṣatriyaḥ (Shali).[30] *Sui shu* does not give a date for the takeover, but it does record that Citrasena died and was succeeded by his son, so by this account the takeover would have taken place sometime before *Sui shu*'s completion in 636. In Vickery's carefully argued estimation, Citrasena "probably died in the first decade of the seventh century," having become king of a sizeable realm upon the death of his brother Bhavavarman I in or around 600. This would suggest that the takeover was completed by the early 600s.[31]

The *Sui shu* reference to Zhenla's takeover of Funan is the first known mention in official Chinese records of this crucial historical event. In the two modern compilations of Chinese documents on early Cambodia used in this study, both of which cite official sources in chronological order, the *Sui shu* account is the first official record of the takeover. Both compilations also include a number of unofficial writings, and while the editors do not list these in strict chronological order, it is clear from them that none of the writings that pre-date *Sui shu* makes any reference to the event.[32] For my part, I have searched the relevant standard histories and concluded that as far as these histories are concerned, *Sui shu*'s reference to Zhenla's takeover of Funan is the first.

A Tang compendium on Funan's final tribute to China

The next official work to include material on Funan was *Tong dian* [*A Comprehensive History of Institutions*]. Completed for the most part in 771 and submitted to the Tang emperor Dezong in 801, *Tong dian* was the first of what were eventually to be the *shitong*, "the ten comprehensive compendiums" on government institutions that were successively compiled from the eighth century right up to the 1930s.[33] Of these, the three most important were *Tong dian*, *Tong zhi*, completed in 1149 during the Song dynasty, and *Wenxian tongkao*, presented in 1319 to the Mongol emperor Renzong of the Yuan dynasty. In contrast to the standard histories, which by and large confined themselves to particular dynasties, these voluminous works covered historical developments from the remote past up to the time of their composition.[34]

The author of *Tong dian*, Du You (735–812), was a respected scholar-official from a renowned family—his grandson Du Mu was to be an acclaimed poet and commentator on *Sun Tzu's Art of War*—and he served as chief minister to three successive emperors.[35] His magnum opus, *Tong dian*, consists of two hundred chapters divided into nine major topics. The last of these topics, border defenses, deals with Funan.[36] The topic consists of sixteen chapters covering peoples and states located at all points of the compass, north, south, east, and west of China. Funan features in chapter 188, which describes southern foreigners in twenty-eight southern states. Of these only four—Linyi, Funan, Chitu, and Zhenla—are considered at any length.[37]

Apart from two brief mentions of Funan music elsewhere in the book, the entry in chapter 188 is the only information about Funan that *Tong dian* provides. It draws heavily on the account of Funan in *Liang shu*, though some parts of that account are omitted. Additional material is provided from *Nan Qi shu* and *Bao pu zi*.

Chapter 188 also contains two new passages on Funan. The second one in particular merits attention. The first passage reads:

> There are also eagles that go into the water for turtles. The turtles' shells can be cut up and made into halters for horses, called "ornamental bridles."[38]

And the second passage reads:

During the [Liu] Song, Southern Qi, and Liang dynasties, [Funan] submitted local produce as tribute. During the Sui dynasty, the king of the state had the family name Gulong, as was often the case with family names in the various states. When asked [whether that should be Kunlun], elders said there was no family name Kunlun, which was a mistake.[39]

A portrait of the Buddhist monk Xuanzang (602–664) with an Indian acolyte, done in Japan in the fourteenth century. In his account of his travels to India, Xuanzang mentions Zhenla, which he calls Īśānapura after its then capital. He also explains for his Chinese audience the meanings of the term brahmin and the four varna or classes in Indian society.

Source: Metropolitan Museum of Art, New York; www.metmuseum.org/art/collection/search/45372, 2020

> During the Sui dynasty, an envoy was sent with tribute.[40] After the [start of the] Wude reign period [618–626] of the great Tang, tribute came frequently. During the Zhenguan reign period [627–649], tribute was again presented in the form of two people from Baitou state sent to Luoyang.[41] That state is to the west of Funan, southwest of Canban.[42] The men and women are all born with white hair, and their bodies are pure white. They live in mountain caves with rocky cliffs on every side, and therefore inaccessible, adjacent to the state of Canban.

The final part of this second passage, recording the tribute from Funan of two people from Baitou, is significant not only because of the unprecedented nature of its tribute—Funan had never before sent human beings—but also, more importantly, because of its dates, 627–649. These dates make the mission the last datable event relating to Funan, other than a passing reference in the encyclopaedia *Cefu yuangui* to the effect that in 643 Funan still existed, since in that year Linyi asked Taizong for help against against an attack by Funan (which Taizong declined to give.)[43] Both the dates of the tribute mission and the *Cefu yuangui* report suggest that Funan was still active decades after the death of Citrasena, the Zhenla king said by *Sui shu* to have taken over Funan—suggesting in turn that for some time and in some form Funan and Zhenla coexisted.

An alternative record of Zhenla's annexation of Funan

Chronologically, the next official source to refer to Funan was *Tang hui yao* [*Essential Documents and Regulations of the Tang Dynasty*], the first in a series of official Chinese digests of regulations relating to imperial institutions, dynasty by dynasty, that were compiled from the tenth century onwards.[44] *Tang hui yao* was completed by the senior official Wang Pu (922–982), partly on the basis of earlier work done by others. Wang Pu's final text was presented to Taizu, the first emperor of the Song dynasty, in 961.[45]

Tang hui yao contains two notable remarks about Funan, made in the context of more extensive comments about Zhenla, which we will consider in chapter seven. The first and more significant of these is that

> Zhenla is to the southwest of Linyi and was originally a dependency of Funan . . . during the Datong reign period [535–545] of the Liang dynasty, it began to annex Funan and take possession of that state.[46]

This is by far the earliest date given in Chinese records for Funan's takeover by Zhenla, although by including the verb *shi*, "began," it suggests that the process was a gradual and possibly protracted one.[47] The date is compatible, although barely so, with the account in *Sui shu* of Funan being taken over by Citrasena of Zhenla in or by the early 600s. *Sui shu* does not say at which point in his life Citrasena began to take over Funan, or how long he lived. If he lived until his nineties, dying in the first decade of the seventh century as Vickery suggests, and began the process of taking over Funan when he was still very young, the date in *Tang hui yao* would just about be plausible.

The second notable remark in *Tang hui yao* occurs in its account of the five regions of India: north, south, east, west, and central. Eastern India is described as being on the edge of a "large sea connecting it with Funan, which was only separated from it by the Small Sea and nothing more."[48] The period this statement relates to is not specified; but while its wording is somewhat unclear, it suggests that at some point, perhaps in the sixth century, Funan's authority stretched as far west as the west coast of present-day Myanmar, with the large sea presumably being the present-day Bay of Bengal as a whole, and the Small Sea today's Gulf of Thailand.

Fragmentary accounts of the gold, iron and fragrances of Funan

In 982, some two decades after Emperor Taizu received the finalized version of *Tang hui yao*, work was completed on the monumental encyclopedia *Taiping yulan* [*An Encyclopedia Compiled during the Era of Great Peace and Read by the Emperor*]. The work had been undertaken by the senior scholar Li Fang (925–996), collaborating with a group of fourteen others.[49] A huge book of a thousand chapters divided into fifty-five large categories or topics, ranging far and wide from emperors to aromatic substances, Korea to India, *Taiping yulan* includes valuable fragments concerning early Funan, notably (as we saw in chapter one) fragments of the third-century records of the envoy Kang Tai and the writer Wan Zhen.

Apart from the writings of Kang Tai and Zhu Ying, various other references to Funan are scattered through the book.[50] These include extracts from Six Dynasties sources that allude to "Funan people who make a living by always using gold", including for the hire of ships over short or long distances, and that describe how foreign boats carry iron from a place called Danlanzhou to be sold in Funan.[51] There is also an anecdote from a Tang dynasty source about a finely made, priceless mirror brought to China by "a large Funan ship coming from western India"—another striking reflection of the distances Funan maritime traders were traveling.

In addition there are the following three passages from the Six Dynasties period, tentatively dateable to the third, third, and sixth centuries respectively:[52]

> In the state of Funan there are fine fresh-looking fish. They have black bodies five poles long, and they have heads like the heads of horses. When servants go into the water, the fish come and inflict injuries on them.
>
> Sandalwood comes from Funan and Linyi. Its color is purple-red.
>
> Taken together, the many aromatic substances of the state of Funan make a single tree. Its trunk is sandalwood, its branches are lign-aloes, its flowers are cloves, its leaves are mint, and its resin is frankincense.[53]

The third passage is revealing. Two of the elements of the fragrant tree said to constitute Funan (three if we include mint, from Dukun according to Kang Tai) come from distant places—cloves from Maluku and frankincense from India. So we are reading here of substances made available to China not only from Funan but also through it. This being so, the description seems to be an allusion, unusual in Chinese sources, to Funan's role as a regional trading center or entrepôt.[54]

At about the same time that Li Fang and his colleagues were working on *Taiping yulan*, another early Song scholar, Yue Shi (930–1007), was leading a group of scholars to compile the lengthy geographical gazetteer, *Taiping huanyu ji*, which they completed in the late tenth century. *Taiping huanyu ji* has an entry on Funan which with minor variations replicates the entry in *Tong dian*.[55]

One other Song encyclopedia containing material relevant to Cambodia was *Cefu yuangui*, completed in 1013 by a scholarly committee headed by Wang Qinruo (962–1025). *Cefu yuangui* has a number of entries on both Funan and Zhenla. By and large, the entries on Funan reproduce material available in other sources already cited here. We shall return to its entries on Zhenla in chapter seven.

Funan recollected in the two official Tang histories

In 1060, the standard history *Xin Tang shu* [*The New History of the Tang Dynasty*] was completed by the celebrated scholar-official Ouyang Xiu (1007–1072), working with Song Qi (998–1061) and others.[56] Consisting of 249 chapters, *Xin Tang shu* was intended to be an improvement on the first standard history of the Tang, the 214-chapter *Jiu Tang shu* [*The Old History of the Tang Dynasty*], completed by Liu Xu over a century earlier.[57] Both histories include short sections on Linyi, Zhenla and other southern states (chapter 197 in *Jiu Tang shu*, chapter 222 in *Xin Tang shu*). And in another rare reference to Funan's foreign trade and role as an entrepôt, both histories observe that Funan traded with India. As *Jiu Tang shu* notes,

> Central India . . . has relations with the eastern Roman empire [Da Qin], so its valuable goods can reach Funan and Jiaozhi, where they are traded.[58]

In their sections on foreign music, both histories mention Funanese dancers in the Chinese court dressed in rose-colored costumes, wearing red leather boots, and performing in pairs. *Jiu Tang shu* adds that there were also players on drums, flutes, and other Indian-style instruments.[59]

Of the two histories, only *Xin Tang shu* carries a full passage devoted to Funan.[60] This consists largely of material taken from *Liang shu* and *Jin shu*, with several modifications and omissions. The omissions include the absence of any reference to the city of Funan being five hundred li from the sea, or to a broad river flowing eastwards. The list of Funan's produce is also omitted, as is its royal history.

Xin Tang shu describes Funan's customs as being the same as those of Huanwang, the Austronesian polity or polities called Champa that emerged in parts of present-day Vietnam from the seventh century onwards. Huanwang—literally, King Huan, *huan* meaning ring and *wang* king—is the unexplained name that *Xin Tang shu* and other later Chinese chronicles give to Champa for several decades from 756–757 on, when they record that it superseded Linyi. (For more on Linyi becoming Huanwang, see appendix five.)[61]

With respect to Funan itself, *Xin Tang shu* describes its kings as having the family name Gulong, but without reference to any particular period. It refers briefly to the country's buildings and royal elephants, and repeats earlier descriptions of its people being "black and curly haired and going naked, and accustomed not to rob or steal." Mention is made, as in *Jin shu*, of their practice of planting in one year and harvesting for three. The passage about diamonds found in *Bao pu zi* is also repeated with minor variations.

Xin Tang shu then continues with a passage about the capital of Funan that is not recorded in earlier histories:

> The people get enjoyment from cockfights and pig fights, and treat gold, pearls, and perfumes as taxes.[62] The capital was Temu City, but in a very short time it was annexed by Zhenla, and it was to [Funan's] advantage to move south to Nafuna City.[63] During the Wude [618–626] and Zhenguan [627–649] reign periods [of the Tang], it repeatedly came to pay respects to the emperor and also presented tribute in the form of two Baitou people. [*Xin Tang shu* then repeats the *Tong dian* account of the Baitou or White Hair people.]

This is the first time Chinese sources give the name of the—or anyway a—capital of Funan, with the possible exception of Modan, the name of the holy mountain described by the fifth-century Funan envoy Nāgasena. *Xin Tang shu* gives no date for Temu's annexation and the move from Temu to Nafuna, so we cannot be sure when these developments took place.

The meaning of Temu (D'ək mi̯uk [K]) has not been satisfactorily explained. Coedès argues that d'ək mi̯uk is similar enough in sound to *dalmāk*, a Khmer word for "hunter," for it to refer to the ancient kingdom of Vyādhapura, City of the Hunter. But Vickery questions whether Coedès' argument is tenable. He acknowledges that Vyādhapura is given on some Cambodian inscriptions as the name of an ancient kingdom but makes the point that it is almost never found on inscriptions that predate the Angkor era—that is, before the ninth century.[64] This important point must cast doubt on attempts to identify Temu with Vyādhapura. Despite this, in tourist and reference materials Vyādhapura is still often described as the name of the capital of Funan.[65]

As mentioned in chapter three, a widely held view is that the capital of Funan—assuming there was a single capital, and regardless of its name or names—was located at present-day Angkor Borei.

Why does the name Temu feature for the first time in a standard Chinese history at such a late date, some four centuries after Funan's last recorded tribute to the Chinese court? There is no ready explanation. It can only be surmised that *Xin Tang shu*'s authors came across some new source, or else a source that had not earlier been used.

The meaning and location of Funan's new capital, Nafuna (Nâ pi̯uət nâ [K]) have not been identified. Pelliot suggests without explication that the name Nafuna City could be derived from the Sanskrit Navanagara, meaning New City. This is a plausible enough hypothesis, though if Nafuna is a Sanskrit name, it raises the question of why the name of its immediate predecessor, Temu, is apparently not.[66]

Two more historical works on Funan

Two other official works from the Song and Yuan dynasties contain passages on Funan. These are the historical compendium *Tong zhi* and the historical survey *Wenxian tongkao*. Neither text adds much to the information provided by earlier sources.

Tong zhi was completed in 1149 by the creative scholar Zheng Qiao (1104–1162) and consists of two hundred chapters, with only one small section of one chapter, chapter 198, on Funan.[67] The *Tong zhi* text follows the *Liang shu* account of Funan quite closely, with a few minor changes and rearrangements of the order of the text. The changes include stating more clearly that the great river of Funan flows from west to east, and explicitly mentioning that the sons of Hun Tian, whose name *Tong zhi* renders as Hun Kui, were seven in number.[68] Rhinos are listed among Funan's local produce, and the passages about underwater diamonds (as in *Bao pu zi*) and eagles searching for sea turtles (as in *Tong dian*) are both included.

Tong zhi also refers to the fact in Sui times the king of Funan had the surname Gulong and sent an envoy to Chang'an. This envoy would have visited Chang'an in 588, the date of the only mission from Funan to China during the Sui dynasty as recorded in *Chen shu*.[69] The passage concludes by reproducing the section of *Tong dian* about Funan sending two Baitou people to Luoyang during the period 627 to 649.

The author of the other work, *Wenxian tongkao*, was Ma Duanlin (1245–1322), a learned scholar who lived through the collapse of the Southern Song and its replacement by the Mongol Yuan dynasty. *Wenxian tongkao*, which Ma presented to the Song emperor Renzong in 1319, consists of 348 chapters in twenty-four sections, each dealing with a topic from early times onwards. The book's arrangement generally follow those of *Tong dian*.[70] There is a section on Funan in chapter 331, which reproduces almost word for word the entry on Funan in *Tong dian* and hence *Sui shu*—since *Sui shu* was *Tong dian*'s source for Funan—with only a couple of characters altered.

As mentioned earlier, *Wenxian tongkao* sometimes assumes undue importance in Western sources on early Cambodia. This is because it was translated into French in the late nineteenth century, and was therefore available to Western scholars who did not know Chinese and so had no direct access to *Sui shu* and other histories.[71]

What we learn about Funan from later sources

The later Chinese sources considered in this chapter add only a little to our knowledge of Funan. There is *Sui shu*'s revealing portrait of Funan's offshoot Chitu or Red Earth, and belated mention for the first time in *Xin Tang shu* of the name of the Funan capital, Temu. There are scattered references to hitherto unmentioned exotica—turtle-hunting eagles, huge black fish, dancers in rose-colored costumes and leather boots. There is a reference to Funanese kings having the surname Gulong, and the suggestion in *Tang hui yao* that Funan's influence may have stretched far to the west. Otherwise, much the most important role the sources play is to tell us about the timing and circumstances of Funan's takeover by Zhenla. We shall return to this topic in chapter six.

5

A history of Funan on the basis of Chinese sources

Before moving on to Funan's successor Zhenla, it may be helpful to review what early Chinese records tell us about the history of Funan. These records are the sole written source for this history, and taken as a whole they give us a portrait of Funan over six centuries or so that is surprisingly informative and coherent. Histories of Funan in leading secondary sources, notably the works of Coedès and Briggs, have combined Chinese records with other materials, interweaving discussions, sometimes speculative, about the influence of India.[1] The purpose of this chapter is to consider what we can learn about Funan from Chinese sources alone, with only limited reference to other points of view.[2]

Early Chinese records locate Funan variously to the south, southwest, and west of Linyi, and to the south of Rinan.[3] Linyi was the coastal state in the center of present-day Vietnam. Rinan was the southernmost part of China, in the center-north of present-day Vietnam.[4] The fullest account of Funan's location is in *Liang shu* [*The History of the Liang Dynasty*] (636).[5] It describes Funan as being a low-lying, flat country in a bay south of Rinan, about three thousand li—perhaps 1,500 kilometers—southwest of Linyi. According to *Liang shu*, Funan's main city was five hundred li inland, with a large river flowing eastwards into the sea.[6] A fifth-century Chinese traveler, Zhu Zhi, adds that Funan could be reached overland as well as by sea.[7]

The location of Funan given in these early sources corresponds broadly with archaeological sites at Óc Eo, Angkor Borei, and elsewhere in the Mekong Delta and the lower reaches of the Mekong River. Most modern scholars take the view that Funan was centered in this lower Mekong region.[8]

The name Funan occurs in all the standard histories of China from the third to eleventh century. In the early seventh century, the Buddhist monk Yijing, a noted linguist, remarked that in contemporary usage the name Funan was pronounced Ba'nan.[9] Yijing's observation reinforces the view that Funan was a transliteration of the Khmer word *phnom*, "hill"—perhaps a sacred hill of the kind described by the Funan envoy Nāgasena during his visit to China in 484 CE.[10]

The earliest portrait of Funan in Chinese sources is found in the writings of the Chinese envoy Kang Tai, who visited Funan with his fellow envoy Zhu Ying, probably in the late 240s or 250s CE. The purpose of their visit was to find out more about communicating with India (Tianzhu) and the Roman Empire (Da Qin), whose goods had reached China via Funan.[11] Both men left records of their visit. Fragments of Kang Tai's writings on Funan have survived.

According to Kang Tai, the first ruler of Funan was a woman called Liuye.[12] Liuye is Chinese for "willow leaf," and the name is an incongruous one, since willows do not grow in the lower reaches of the Mekong. It may be the transliteration of a local name, but if so the name has not been identified.

Kang relates that one day Liuye and her people saw a merchant ship approaching the shores of Funan. On board the ship was a man called Hun Tian.[13] Unlike Liuye, the name Hun Tian has no obvious meaning.[14] Like Liuye, it may be a transliteration of an unidentified local name. Vickery suggests that the first part of the name, Hun, may have been a clan name or title.[15]

Kang notes that Hun Tian came from a state called Wuwen. Other, later sources report that he came from a state called Jiao or Ji, located to the south of Funan.[16] Nothing more is known about either place. According to Kang, Hun Tian was devoted to unnamed gods, who came to him one night in a dream and urged him to go to sea.[17] The next day he found a bow and arrows lying near the gods' temple. Taking these he went to sea as bidden, traveling on a merchant ship that was carried by the sea to Funan.[18]

When the ship arrived off the shores of Funan, Liuye and her people went out from the shore by boat to prevent the ship from approaching. At that point Hun Tian shot an arrow right through Liuye's boat. Frightened, she gave in to him. Hun Tian married her and occupied Funan. They had, it seems, seven sons who became kings of seven districts of Funan.[19]

The story of Liuye and Hun Tian is Cambodia's earliest foundation story. A second, later foundation story is about Kambuja, meaning those born of Kambu, and dates from the ninth century CE.[20]

There is arguably as much myth as history in the Liuye-Hun Tian tale. It certainly foreshadows in a striking way a later, fifth-century account of a foreign brahmin who went to serve as king of Funan at the bidding of the gods, an account we shall return to. But if we take the Liuye-Hun Tian story at face value, and calculate back in time on the basis of what early Chinese histories tell us about their successors, Liuye and Hun Tian could have reigned sometime in the late first or early second century CE.

According to *Nan Qi shu* [*The History of the Southern Qi Dynasty*] (537) and *Liang shu*, Hun Tian was succeeded by a king called Pankuang or Hun Pankuang.[21]

It is not clear whether he was Hun Tian's immediate successor.[22] He is said to have died when he was some ninety years old,[23] so assuming he reigned directly after Hun Tian he would have ruled the kingdom for much of the second century CE.

Kang Tai describes Pankuang as a bold, brave man. He was enterprising enough to capture wild elephants and train them for people to ride on, causing various unnamed states to submit to him.[24] *Liang shu* describes him as causing disarray among "the various districts," presumably including the seven districts ruled by Liuye's and Hun Tian's sons, and then taking them over with an army raised for the purpose, doubtless one with soldiers mounted on elephants. Pankuang's sons and grandsons ruled these conquered districts as second-ranking kings.[25]

Liang shu relates that when Pankuang died he was succeeded by his middle son Panpan. Panpan must have been incapable or very young, since he did not manage the affairs of state himself. Instead, these were delegated to a senior general, Fan Shiman, who the people of Funan made their king when Panpan died three years later.[26] Calculating back on the basis of information in later records, Fan Shiman could have reigned sometime during the first half of the third century CE. Vickery proposes persuasively that the word "Fan" in Fan Shiman's name, as well as in the names of two subsequent rulers of Funan, corresponds to the Khmer title *poñ* used by chieftains.[27]

The third-century writer Wan Zhen describes Fan Shiman as brave, strong, and a good strategist.[28] According to *Liang shu*, Fan Shiman styled himself the Great King of Funan. He attacked nearby states, making them Funan's dependencies. He went on to build large ships and attack ten or so other states. These included the state of Diansun, also called Dunxun, which was ruled by five kings, all of whom became loose dependents of Funan.[29] Dunxun was probably located in the northern part of the Malay Peninsula, and judging from an account of it in *Liang shu* it served as a trading center and land bridge between the present-day Gulf of Thailand and the Andaman Sea.[30]

Among the other states Fan Shiman attacked were Dukun (also called Qudukun) and Jiuzhi (also called Juli), both of them also probably on the Malay Peninsula.[31] Kang Tai mentions Dukun as a source of mint and a sulphurous perfume.[32] Juli was where Su Wu, a kinsman of Fan Shiman's successor Fan Zhan, set out for India as an envoy from Funan.

While waging his maritime campaigns, Fan Shiman fell ill, and his eldest son Jinsheng was expected to take over from him. But Fan Shiman's nephew Fan Zhan, also a general, had Jinsheng murdered and became king instead. Fan Zhan was the son of Fan Shiman's older sister—an instance, perhaps, of matrilineal customs affecting Funan's royal succession.[33]

Nan Qi shu relates that Fan Zhan reigned for ten years or so.[34] Part of his reign, at least, was during the 240s, since he sent tribute to the southern Chinese kingdom of Wu in 243. The tribute consisted of local produce and musicians.[35] Reports of Funanese musicians and musical instruments occur in a succession of subsequent Chinese sources.[36]

Fan Zhan's reign ended suddenly when, as *Nan Qi shu* tells it, Jinsheng's youngest brother Chang stabbed him to death with his sword. "You killed my older brother," Chang told him. "Now I am taking revenge on you for my brother and my father."[37] Perhaps Chang daubed sweat on the blade of his sword to make it sharper, a curious practice of Funan royalty recorded by Kang Tai.[38]

Early Chinese sources make no mention of whether Dunxun and the other states that Fan Shiman conquered remained under Funan's control after his death. *Liang shu* devotes a separate passage to Dunxun, suggesting perhaps that it was still a dependency of Funan in Liang times, that is, in the first half of the sixth century.[39] But the *Liang shu* record of Dunxun contains no datable information and could relate to an earlier period, as accounts of southern states in standard Chinese histories sometimes do. So we cannot be sure that Dunxun remained a dependency of Funan, or that Fan Shiman's many conquests were upheld by his successors.

According to Kang Tai and *Liang shu*, King Fan Zhan took the initiative to engage with India. Fan Zhan's interest in India had been aroused by a traveling merchant called Jia Xiangli, who had been to India and who told Fan Zhan about its wealth, variety, and religious beliefs.[40] After meeting the merchant, Fan Zhan sent his kinsman Su Wu to India as an envoy.[41] Su Wu set off from Juli on the Malay coast, and made a boat journey up a long river, evidently the Ganges, until he reached northwest India. There he met the Indian king Muruṇḍa (Maolun), one of a line of kings called Muruṇḍa that ruled northern India at the time. Four years later, Su Wu returned to Funan with Chen Song, an envoy from King Muruṇḍa, and a gift of four prized horses from the Yuezhi (Tokharian) people of central Asia.[42]

By the time Su Wu arrived back in Funan, King Fan Zhan had died. Another general, Fan Xun, had killed Fan Zhan's assassin, and was reigning in Fan Zhan's place.[43] Fan Xun was the king that the Chinese envoys Kang Tai and Zhu Ying met when they visited Funan.[44] While in Funan, Kang Tai also met Chen Song, King Muruṇḍa's envoy from India, who told Kang about the glories of India, including the fact that it was the place where Buddhism had arisen.[45] Given that one of the purposes of his visit to Funan was to open communications with India, Kang must have listened to Chen Song's account of India with the greatest interest.[46]

In chronological terms, Chen Song's mention of Buddhism is the first reference to Buddhism in Chinese records of Funan. Another early reference relates the story of a Buddhist monk from India called Qiyu who traveled to Funan and then on to the Western Jin capital Luoyang in the early fourth century, subduing two tigers encountered en route.[47]

We do not know how long Fan Xun's rule lasted. From the 250s until the late 280s, either Fan Xun or whoever came after him sent a number of tribute missions to the Western Jin dynasty (265–316) in Luoyang. The first of these missions, in 265 or 268, was no doubt sent to congratulate the first Jin emperor on establishing a new dynasty.[48] A further three missions were reportedly sent in 270, 271, and 272.[49] Another three missions were sent in quick succession in 285, 286, and 287. After that Funan sent no further tribute missions to China until 357.[50]

Kang Tai and other early sources give us some idea of King Fan Xun's character. He showed his mettle by "putting right the governance of the country," as *Liang shu* puts it.[51] To amuse himself he enjoyed betting on cockfights with his fellow generals.[52] In response to a disparaging comment about the people of Funan going naked, he ordered his male subjects to wrap themselves in cloth.[53] (The comment, by Kang Tai and Zhu Ying, seems to be belied by Kang's observation elsewhere that the Funanese wore leather girdles, which suggests they wore other clothing as well.)[54]

Fan Xun built himself palatial buildings to relax and receive guests in.[55] Grand buildings like those in the palace were apparently decorated with carved patterns and engravings on wood and perhaps on metal.[56] Ordinary people brought Fan Xun gifts of bananas, sugar cane, tortoises, and birds. He reared tigers on a mountain and crocodiles in a pond or city moat, and had people who committed offenses thrown to these creatures. If the tigers or crocodiles failed to devour them, the offenders were forgiven.[57]

Other Funanese trials by ordeal in Fan Xun's time involved wrongdoers having to grope for a gold ring in boiling water, or being forced to hold a red-hot iron. Again, anyone who came away unharmed was judged to be innocent.[58] Such trials by ordeal must have intrigued Chinese readers, since there is a description of them a millennium later in the envoy Zhou Daguan's account of Angkor.[59]

Waiguo zhuan [*A Record of Foreign States*] recounts another, less extreme Funanese trial by ordeal. When householders suffered a theft and wanted to find out who was responsible, they made their female slaves chew rice that had been blessed in the temple. Whoever failed to crunch up the rice and was left with a bleeding mouth was deemed to be the thief.[60] This story not only tells us that households had female slaves, but also confirms that rice was part of the diet.

This story of thieving slaves is not the only account of slavery in Funan. Later, *Nan Qi shu* reports that the Funanese made slaves of recalcitrant people they captured. It also quotes the king of Funan as alluding to a slave in his possession.[61] Taken together, these references suggest that slavery was an integral part of Funanese society.

Kang Tai also describes the boats that the Funanese built. They were large boats, up to seventy (US) feet long and more than four feet wide, with prows and sterns shaped like the heads and tails of fish. Each boat was manned by eighty-four or a hundred oarsmen, depending on the boat's size. The oarsmen propelled the boat with long and short oars, or boat poles in shallow water.[62] Kang does not say so, but given that the boats carried so many men, it seems likely they were used in warfare—perhaps, for instance, to carry soldiers across the seas for Fan Shiman's maritime campaigns.

Wan Zhen describes another outdoor activity, royal hunts. He records that the king, presumably Fan Xun, was good at hunting with bows and arrows, which he did with large parties of hunters, often consisting of three hundred people mounted on elephants and four or five thousand others following along.[63] These huge hunting parties are said to have gone off on hunts for a month at a time.[64]

According to Wan Zhen, senior officials in Funan were all called *kunlun*.[65] *Kunlun* was a Chinese word later used for southern peoples and languages, but Wan seems to have regarded it as a name or title. There are also references in later Chinese sources to the kings and officials of southern states being called *kunlun*.[66] *Sui shu* [*The History of the Sui Dynasty*] (636) notes that Chinese chroniclers mistakenly used the term *kunlun* for Funanese and other royal surnames, rather than the correct term *gulong*.[67] *Gulong* is probably a transliteration of the Mon-Khmer title *kuruṅ*, used for chieftains. Its use, like the use of the term *poñ*, seems to reflect the endogenous nature of early Funan hierarchies.[68]

Kang Tai and Wan Zhen note various curiosities. During their visit to Funan, Kang Tai and Zhu Ying remark on the fact that the people of Funan were wearing no clothes.[69] Wang Zhen notes the existence of a backward people in an obscure part of Funan who led rough, itinerant lives, moving from place to place with the seasons. Perhaps these people were among the inhabitants of nearby places that the Funanese used to capture and enslave.[70] They were blackskinned and reportedly had white teeth, unlike the blackened teeth of people elsewhere, including presumably the Funanese themselves.[71] Why the people of Funan had black teeth is not clear. Perhaps like the nearby Heichi (Black Teeth) people, they cleaned their teeth with grass that stained them.[72] Another curiosity Wan Zhen remarks on, more lightheartedly, was undulating seashells that could hold wine and were used in wine-pouring games of challenge.[73]

Other Funan curiosities mentioned in pre-fifth-century Chinese sources include fans for individual use rather than large fans plied by someone, no doubt a slave, for a whole group; diamonds shaped like stalactites fetched up from deep under the water; dangerous black fish, huge with heads like the heads of horses; and sandalwood.[74]

Were the fans, diamonds, and sandalwood all items of foreign trade and tribute? Kang Tai and other early Chinese records leave this question unaddressed. But when writing about Funan, Kang refers to other states having mint, parrots, and cups made of clamshells and gold—all items with potential for tribute or trade.[75]

After Fan Xun, there is a gap in the records. The next recorded king was Zhu Zhantan, who sent tribute to the Eastern Jin dynasty (317–420) in 357.[76] The Eastern Jin ruled from Jiankang, present-day Nanjing on the lower reaches of the Yangzi River. Zhu Zhantan's tribute, an elephant, was presented as a gift to the emperor Mu (r. 345–361). We do not know how it reached Jiankang, but like later live tribute, it probably traveled the long journey by boat across the Southern Sea, along the coastal waters of southeast China and up the Yangzi.

The emperor rejected the gift and had the elephant sent back, ostensibly because it involved too much effort and might harm people, but also perhaps because China still had plenty of elephants of its own.[77] King Zhu Zhantan's surname Zhu indicates that he was from India; his standing as king may have been in doubt, since the account of his mission in *Jin shu* [*The History of the Jin Dynasty*] (648) notes that "he was called king," an unusual turn of phrase.[78] Perhaps his dubious status was another reason why his tribute was not welcome. Nothing more is known about him.

According to *Liang shu*, the king who succeeded Zhu Zhantan, either directly or after an intervening period, was an Indian brahmin called Jiaochenru, Kauṇḍinya in Sanskrit. In a partial reprise of the Hun Tian story, *Liang shu* recounts that the gods told Kauṇḍinya to go to Funan and serve as its king. He willingly did as he was told, traveling northwards from his home to Panpan, a state on the Malay Peninsula.[79] From there he went to Funan, where he was made king by popular acclaim. To quote *Liang shu*, he "then changed the system of rules and customs and used Indian law instead," the law presumably being the dharma.[80] The new customs evidently included the use of Sanskrit names by Funan's kings, since from his time on the names of Funanese kings in Chinese sources were Chinese transliterations of names in Sanskrit.

Kauṇḍinya seems to have ruled in the early fifth century, during and perhaps after the final years of the Eastern Jin dynasty (317–420). This dating is based on the fact that according to *Song shu* [*The History of the Liu Song Dynasty*] (488) and *Liang shu*, his immediate successor sent tribute to China from 434 on.

Before moving on to his successor, one other source of information about third- and fourth-century Funan should be mentioned. That is *Jin shu*, the standard history of the Western and Eastern Jin dynasties (265–420). Completed in 648 on the basis of earlier drafts, *Jin shu*'s portrait of Funan is brief, and while it is ostensibly about Funan during the late third and fourth centuries, it gives no real indication as to which period of time its account refers to. *Jin shu* describes Funan as being three thousand li in extent, and its people as being naked, curly-haired, ugly, and black—a formulaic description also found in *Liang shu*. It adds that the people liked carving and engraving, and ate off silver. They ploughed one year and harvested for three, no doubt a reflection of the fertile, well-watered soil of the lower Mekong region. What they harvested is not specified, but as the story of thieving slaves implies, one crop was clearly rice. They paid levies and taxes with gold, silver, pearls, and aromatic substances, a rare mention of taxes being levied in Funan. They maintained storehouses and kept records using a Hu or Indian script, the first reference to a Funanese writing system.[81]

When Kauṇḍinya died he was succeeded by Chilituobamo, probably Dhṛtavarman in Sanskrit.[82] Dhṛtavarman repeatedly sent memorials and tribute to the Liu Song dynasty, which succeeded the Eastern Jin dynasty and ruled from Jiankang between 420 and 479. He sent missions in 434, 435, and 438, all of them during the reign of the Liu Song's third ruler, Emperor Wen (r. 424–453).[83]

In 479 the Liu Song dynasty was replaced by the Nan Qi or Southern Qi dynasty, which governed southern China between 479 and 502. Its second and longest-serving ruler was Emperor Wu (r. 483–493). In 484 a king of Funan by the name of Qiaochenru Sheyebamo, Kauṇḍinya Jayavarman in Sanskrit, sent an envoy to the Southern Qi capital in Jiankang.[84] The envoy was an Indian Buddhist monk called Nāgasena (Nagaxian).

Nāgasena presented Emperor Wu with gifts made of gold, rosewood, ivory, cotton, and some form of glass, and had a lengthy audience with him. In the course of this meeting the emperor complimented his guest on his language skills and remarked on the fact that a lack of interpreters had previously hampered communications between China and states to its south.

On behalf of Kauṇḍinya Jayavarman, Nāgasena asked the emperor for military help in bringing to heel a Funanese slave who had seized Funan's neighbor Linyi. The emperor demurred, referring the matter to his officers in the southern Chinese region of Jiaozhou, who appear to have taken no further action.[85]

Nāgasena also told the emperor about Funan's spiritual beliefs. He described how Funan served a god called Maheśvara, whose spirit dwelt on a mountain called Modan. Maheśvara was a common name at the time for the Hindu god Śiva, but by Nāgasena's account Maheśvara seems to have been a Bodhisattva with a Bodhi heart, so the deity he described embodied both Buddhist and Hindu attributes. The emperor was impressed. "When you describe how the spirit of Maheśvara descends and flows over your lands," he told Nāgasena, "though it is an alien custom and a strange manner of being, from a distance I deeply appreciate and approve of it."[86]

In addition to describing Nāgasena's visit, *Nan Qi shu* provides us with a short account of the Funanese people. It describes them as good natured and peaceable, but also crafty and ingenious, enslaving neighboring peoples when they did not submit to them. They traded in gold, silver, and colored silks, though whether the trade was local or foreign is not made clear. The king rode an elephant, and women, presumably high-ranking women, did the same. The men and women of the country's great families were dressed in embroidered cloth. People wore gold rings and bracelets and used silver vessels for food. They lived in storeyed houses built of wood, the roofs thatched with outsized bamboo leaves, and built their city walls out of wood rather than stone, the material later used for the walls of Angkor.[87]

Other remarks in *Nan Qi shu*, including an account of Funan's trials by ordeal, are taken from Kang Tai, though he is not mentioned by name. The fact that *Nan Qi shu* includes comments from Kang, a third century source, indicates that while it is primarily a history of the fifth-century Southern Qi dynasty, its descriptions of Funan, like those of *Jin shu* and *Liang shu*, are at best very loosely related to the dynastic period it was supposed to record.

Kauṇḍinya Jayavarman, who may possibly have been Indian in origin, reigned for three decades or more.[88] He seems to have maintained good relations with China, dispatching at least four tribute missions to the Liang dynasty, which succeeded the Southern Qi and ruled from Jiankang from 502 to 556. These missions were sent to the first Liang ruler, Emperor Wu (not to be confused with Emperor Wu of the preceding Nan Qi dynasty), a devout Buddhist whose long reign lasted from 502 to 549. The missions took place in 503, 504, 511–512, and 514, the year of Kauṇḍinya Jayavarman's death.[89]

According to *Liang shu*, the younger brother of Kauṇḍinya Jayavarman's principal wife was meant to succeed him, but a concubine's son murdered the wife's brother and became king instead. The new king called himself Liutuobamo, Rudravarman in Sanskrit.[90] Rudravarman was the last king of Funan to be named in Chinese sources.

Rudravarman maintained Kauṇḍinya Jayavarman's good relations with the Liang court, sending six more tribute missions to Emperor Wu between 517 and 539. He plied the emperor with glass pearls, aromatic substances, live rhinos, and a sandalwood Buddha, and even offered him a ten-foot-long strand of the Buddha's hair.[91] The last two items would have been particularly welcome, given Emperor Wu's Buddhist leanings. He was a great patron of Mahayana Buddhism, an ardent believer and a preacher who organized large, elaborate Buddhist rituals.[92]

Funan evidently made considerable contributions to Emperor Wu's Buddhist devotions. In the early 500s two Buddhist monks from Funan, Saṃghapāla (Senggapoluo) and Mandra (Mantuoluo), went to Jiankang and translated into Chinese a number of Mahayana Buddhist texts, many of them brought from Funan.[93] Among the places in Jiankang where they worked was a centre set up specially for Funanese scholars, The Funan Office.[94] In 546, towards the end of his life, Emperor Wu put out a call for knowledgeable Buddhist scholars, and in response another monk from Funan, Paramārtha (Boluomotuo), originally from India, went to Jiankang and became a leading translator of Sanskrit Buddhist texts into Chinese.[95]

With one exception—two if we include the envoy Nāgasena—none of the Buddhist monks who traveled from Funan to China described Funan. The exception was a monk named Buddhabadra (Putibatuo), who came from an unidentified place far to the south of China and in or around the 520s traveled to Luoyang, then capital of the Northern Wei dynasty. On his way to Luoyang, Buddhabadra passed through Funan. He described the kingdom to a Luoyang listener in glowing terms, calling it "the strongest and largest" of the southern states, five thousand square li in size, with many wealthy families and gems, gold, jade, crystals, and betel nuts in abundance.[96]

The Northern Wei dynasty was famous for its Buddhist grottos at Longmen and Yungang, with their colossal stone statues. These massive images found an echo in a contemporary story relating to Funan. The story was set in a nunnery in Panyu, the present-day city of Guangzhou. Standing in the nunnery was a huge statue of the Buddha that had come from Funan long before. The statue was too heavy to move, but when a fire swept through the nunnery it became weightless and could be carried to safety with ease.[97] Among the things we learn from this story is that very large Buddhist statues carved in Funan were greatly valued in south China.

Although Rudravarman was the last named king of Funan and sent his last mission in 539, Chinese sources continue to record tribute missions from Funan for a century or more after that. *Chen shu* [*The History of the Chen Dynasty*] (636) records two missions from Funan to the Chen dynasty, which ruled briefly between 557 and 581, and one to its successor, the Sui dynasty. The missions were sent in 559, 572, and 588.[98] *Tong dian* [*A Comprehensive History of Institutions*] (801) and subsequent sources record a number of missions from Funan during the first decades of the Tang dynasty (618–907). According to *Tong dian*, there were frequent missions from Funan between 618 and 626, and a final mission during the Zhenguan reign period (627–649). This final mission presented the Tang court with a gift of two white-haired people—albinos, perhaps?—rarities from a remote, mountainous region west of Funan. This tribute of human beings may be a reflection of the slavery that was part of Funan and subsequently Zhenla life.[99]

In other respects, the information about Funan in the sixth and seventh centuries that we gain from Chinese sources is very patchy. We finally learn the name of Funan's capital. According to *Xin Tang shu* [*The New History of the Tang Dynasty*] (1060) it was called Temu. If this a transliteration of a local name, the name has not been identified.[100] *Xin Tang shu* tells us nothing about Temu's location or duration, or why its name was mentioned only at this late stage. *Xin Tang shu* also records that at an unspecified date, perhaps in the early seventh century, Funan moved its capital from Temu to another city called Nafuna *cheng*—Navanagara or New City in Sanskrit, perhaps—because Temu was suddenly taken over by the Funan dependency Zhenla.[101]

We have no way of assessing how far Funan's control or influence stretched during these later centuries. Without specifying dates, *Tang hui yao* [*Essential Documents and Regulations of the Tang Dynasty*] (961) mentions that Funan was only separated from eastern India by the present-day Gulf of Thailand, implying that its authority extended a long way from east to west.[102] The *Tang hui yao* comment could be taken to mean that in these later centuries, as during Fan Shiman's time, Funan's geographical reach was considerable. But this single piece of textual evidence is too flimsy to draw firm conclusions from.

Similar considerations apply to Funan's status as a trading center during these later centuries—and earlier as well. Chinese sources on Funan include scattered allusions to its foreign trade, but not enough to build up a full picture. An early reference dates from the third century CE, when Kang Tai and Zhu Ying went to Funan to find out how goods from India and the Roman Empire were reaching southern China via Funan.[103] These goods would clearly have been not only for tribute but also for trade. At that point, then, Funan already played some kind of role as a regional entrepôt. This early reference is complemented by scattered references to Funan's foreign trade in later centuries. A sixth-century Chinese source compares Funan to a single tree with a sandalwood trunk, branches made of lign-aloes, flowers that were cloves, and frankincense as its resin. Since cloves were native to Maluku and frankincense came from India, the metaphor suggests that at that time, too, Funan was an entrepôt or center for foreign trade.[104]

Other sources dating from Funan's later centuries refer to the Funanese using gold, including for the hire of long-distance ships, and to iron being taken by ship to Funan for sale there. One account describes how a large Funanese ship brought a valuable mirror to China all the way from western India.[105] In addition to these scattered references, the lists of Funanese products provided by Buddhabadra, *Nan Qi shu*, and *Liang shu*—its pomegranates, mandarin oranges, betel nuts, and lign-aloes, its gems, gold, jade, silver, copper, and peacock feathers, the latter much prized in China—all seem to suggest that Funan was seen as a fruitful source of items for tribute and no doubt trade too. But early Chinese sources do not give a full or clear account of Funan's role as a regional trading center.[106]

Of the standard histories, *Liang shu* has the most to tell us about conditions in Funan in these later centuries, although as in the cases of *Jin shu* and *Nan Qi shu*, its description of Funan is only loosely related to the Liang period, and some of its material is clearly drawn from earlier sources.

The author of *Liang shu*, Yao Silian, observes that for their water supplies the Funanese shared ponds, twenty or thirty families to a pond, rather than digging wells. Like other early histories, *Liang shu* makes no mention of irrigation. It also reports on Funan's spiritual beliefs, portraying its inhabitants as worshipping bronze images of gods with two faces and four hands or four faces and eight hands, each hand holding an object—a vague allusion, perhaps, to the early Cambodian statues in bronze and stone of Viṣṇu, Śiva, the two-faced Harihara and other deities, many of which have survived to the present day.[107]

Liang shu describes Funan's king and court, and its funeral rites. Outside his palace the king rode an elephant, as did his attendants and the women of the palace (a point also made by *Nan Qi shu*).[108] When in audience, he sat with golden bowls and incense burners arrayed in front of him, his right knee cocked and his left leg hanging down to the ground. This posture was similar to the often-portrayed pose of the bodhisattva Avalokiteśvara (Guanyin) when seated at ease.[109] When in mourning, the people of Funan cut off their beards, moustaches, and hair. They disposed of the dead in earth, air, fire, or water, by burying the bodies, exposing them to birds in the wild, cremating them, or consigning them to river waters.[110]

Liang shu's author Yao Yilian takes a censorious view of the Funanese. He calls them covetous, miserly, and lacking in decorum and morality, ready to follow their sexual desires without restraint.[111]

Sui shu adds to *Liang shu*'s portrait of Funan by providing a glimpse of another aspect of late Funanese culture, an offshoot or "different type" of Funan called Chitu or Red Earth, reportedly called that after the color of its soil.[112] Chitu may conceivably have been described as a different branch because it was under a ruler related to Funan royalty. Its location is in dispute, but may have been the northeast of the Malay Peninsula.[113] In 607 the Sui Emperor Yang (r. 605–616) sent a mission to Chitu, led by a senior official called Chang Jun. It is unclear why the emperor, keen to improve his overseas connections, selected Chitu as the place to send a mission. Perhaps it filled a gap caused by Funan's pending annexation by Zhenla, or perhaps the mission was a sequel to the Sui's recent assault on Linyi in search of wealth.[114]

Chang Jun and his colleagues wrote an account of their visit to Chitu, parts of which are apparently reproduced in *Sui shu*.[115] They relate that Chitu's capital city, a month's journey by boat from the Chinese frontier, was called Sengzhi *cheng*, meaning Lion City or possibly Eternal City.[116] The inhabitants of Chitu were devout Buddhists, but revered even more the hundreds of brahmins living in their midst. The king's name was Qutan Lifuduosai, the transliteration of an unidentified Sanskrit or local name, or name and title. He had a son called Nayega, Sanskrit for Nayaka, "guide."

Chang Jun gives us a lively portrait of the welcome his delegation received in Chitu, and the lavish reception laid on by the king. The king lived in a multi-storeyed palace, and during audiences he seated himself on a three-tiered couch near a gold reclining ox, perhaps Śiva's mount Nandi.[117] Chitu's produce included rice, millet, beans, hemp, and wines made from sugarcane and coconut juice. Marriage involved a seven-day ceremony, after which the bridegroom took a share of his parents' property and went with the bride to live elsewhere. The dead were cremated and consigned to river waters, except for the king, whose ashes were stored in a temple.

Following Chang Jun's mission to Chitu, Nayega and Chang Jun went to Hongnong near the Chinese capital Luoyang, where Emperor Yang met them in 610.[118] There is no account in official Chinese records of Chitu's subsequent history. Nor do *Sui shu* or other histories mention any connection between Chitu and Dunxun or other early states on the Malay Peninsula.

Sometime between 535 and the 650s, Funan was taken over by Zhenla, a previously unmentioned dependency of Funan. In the ninth century, Zhenla was to become what western historians call the Kingdom of Angkor. Its takeover of Funan may have been peaceful, at least in part, since the language that Chinese sources use to describe it does not include words associated with conflict or war.

Tang hui yao claims that the takeover began in 535–545. *Sui shu* indicates that it occurred later and was carried out by the Zhenla king Citrasena, who by Vickery's estimate reigned during the first decade of the seventh century.[119] *Sui shu* was a near-contemporary record, being completed in 636, within a few decades of Citrasena's death, a fact that adds credibility to its account. The *Sui shu* and *Tang hui yao* accounts are just about compatible, but only if we assume that Citrasena lived to a very old age, and began taking over Funan long before he became king. An alternative account of the takeover is given in *Xin Tang shu*, which records that it began between 627 and 649, during the rule of Citrasena's son and successor Īśānasena (r. ?616–late 630s). The *Xin Tang shu* text is flawed, and may be less dependable. On the other hand, its dates conform with a *Cefu yuangui* report indicating that in 643 Funan was still in existence, since in that year Linyi sent an envoy to China with a request for Taizong's help against an attack by Funan (the outcome of which is not known).[120]

Chinese sources make no further reference to tribute missions or other activities involving Funan after 649. Later Chinese records go on referring to Funan, but only by recording earlier events or by repeating earlier accounts of its activities. In this manner, Funan disappears from the historical record.

This brief history shows that we can draw on early Chinese records to construct a simple chronological narrative of Funan over the course of six centuries, one that is built on scattered references to Funan's rulers and to its customs and ways of life. The records portray a society whose norms and practices clearly included endogenous elements, but whose political culture came under Indian influence, at least from the time of King Kauṇḍinya in the early fifth century onwards. They also convey some sense of Funan's role as a center of Buddhist belief and probably trade, and as a subordinate, tribute-bearing state keen to maintain relations with successive imperial courts in south China.

There is much that is missing from this history. The records provide little clear information about Funan's economy, the geographical extent of its authority, its belief systems, and the precepts and practices of its kings, elites, and ordinary people, including its slaves. Above all they give us little if any sense of Funan's evolution over time. Early Chinese records thus leave us with a portrait of Funan that offers valuable insights but is far from complete, and will remain so pending further documentary, archaeological, or epigraphic discoveries.

6

A contemporaneous Chinese portrait of early Zhenla

In the remaining chapters of this book we move on to Zhenla, the Cambodian polity or polities that absorbed Funan in the sixth or seventh century. In Chinese sources the name Zhenla encompasses both the pre-Angkorian period of the seventh and eighth centuries and the Kingdom of Angkor from the beginning of the ninth century onwards. Some Western scholars use the name Zhenla to refer only to the pre-Angkorian era, a usage that can be confusing. In fact Chinese sources go on using the name Zhenla even in Ming times (1368–1644), though from the Yuan dynasty (1279–1368) on they also use the name Cambodia (Jianpuzhai, Ganbozhi, and other, similar names in Chinese).[1]

This and the following two chapters will look at the Chinese texts on Zhenla that date from the Sui (581–618), Tang (618–907) and Song (960–1279) dynasties. The focus of this chapter is the engaging and detailed description of Zhenla in *Sui shu* [*The History of the Sui Dynasty*]. This is the first account of Zhenla in official Chinese sources, is close to being contemporaneous (as we noted earlier), and remains the fullest portrait of Zhenla until the envoy Zhou Daguan's description of it over six centuries later.

The transition from Funan to Zhenla

Before turning to *Sui shu*, we should give further consideration to the relationship between Funan and Zhenla, and how the first was replaced by the second. Modern historians have devoted a good deal of attention to this issue.[2] In contrast, imperial Chinese sources give only very brief consideration to it, and to the connections between Funan and Zhenla. This applies not only to their political relations—that is, the diplomatic dealings and ties among the kings and elites of Funan and Zhenla—but also to their geographical, religious, and other interconnections.

With regard to political relations between the two, and in particular how Zhenla took over Funan, official Chinese sources leave us with little to work on. We have only a few brief and inconsistent accounts of the takeover. These were reviewed at the end of chapter four. To go over them again: *Tang hui yao* dates the start of the takeover of Funan to 535–545. *Sui shu* records that Funan was taken over by the Zhenla king Citrasena, who (as we know from other sources) reigned over a sizeable realm from about 600 until his death in the first decade of the seventh century, having earlier been a local ruler of some authority. *Xin Tang shu* relates that it was Īśānasena (r. ?616–late 630s) rather than his father Citrasena who annexed Funan, starting the process during the period 627–649, when the Tang emperor Taizong was on the throne. The account in *Xin Tang shu* may be garbled—it somewhat misrepresents the name Īśānasena—and this casts some doubt on its reliability. On the other hand, its dates conform with a *Cefu yuangui* report suggesting that in 643 Funan still existed, since in that year Linyi sent envoys to Emperor Taizong asking for military help against an attack by Funan (which the emperor declined to give).[3]

Xin Tang shu also describes Zhenla's annexation of the capital of Funan, which it calls Temu, as having occurred "in a very short time," after which the Funanese moved to a city called Nafuna. It does not, however, give a precise date for the annexation or record any subsequent events, other than noting that the last tribute mission from Funan took place during Taizong's reign.[4]

We should add to these official accounts one other remark about Funan that may be relevant. This is a comment by the Chinese Buddhist monk Yijing, who spent the years 671 to 695 visiting some thirty countries to collect Buddhist scriptures. In this remark, in which he refers to Funan as Ba'nan, Yijing relates that Buddhism in Ba'nan has "now" been eradicated by "an evil king."[5] This dramatic development might conceivably be connected to the takeover of Funan by Zhenla.

Yijing's comment is in his work *Nanhai jigui neifa zhuan* [*A Record of Buddhist Precepts Sent Home from the Southern Sea*]. We do not know precisely when this work was written, but it evidently refers to the period during which Yijing was traveling—that is, sometime before 695. Here is Yijing's remark in full:[6]

> Going on foot directly south from Huanzhou you get to Bijing after perhaps fifteen days or so.[7] If you go by ship it takes five or six days. Then you go south to Champa—that is, Linyi. In this state the majority are of the [Buddhist] School of Correct Measures [Zhengliang], while the minority are of the School of the Reality of all Phenomena [Youbu].[8] Going for a month to the southwest you then reach Ba'nan, formerly called Funan. Originally the people of this state went naked and devotedly served heaven, then later the Buddhist

> dharma flourished there. An evil king has now eradicated this. There are no Buddhist monks whatsoever, and those of other beliefs dwell together there. This place is in the southern corner of Jambudvipa [the southern continent in Buddhist geography], not an island in the sea.[9]

The unidentified evil king who eradicated Buddhism in Funan foreshadows the king, also unidentified, who presided over an anti-Buddhist iconoclasm in Cambodia in the thirteenth century.[10] Both stand in contrast to the apparent blending or coexistence of different faiths that according to *Nan Qi shu* and Zhou Daguan seems to have characterized Funan and Zhenla at other times.[11] The fact that Yijing wrote his account sometime before 695 suggests that the evil king was either Jayavarman I (r. ?657–?681) or an unknown predecessor or near-contemporary. On the basis of local inscriptions Vickery portrays Jayavarman I as a strong ruler and centralizer, but neither Vickery nor Jacques, who writes that Jayavarman I was "remembered as a great king", suggests that he was hostile to Buddhists.[12] Whoever was responsible, it is tempting to see the eradication of Buddhism reported by Yijing as the kind of dramatic step that might characterize the transition from one state to another, in this instance from Funan to Zhenla.

Chinese texts tell us little about other aspects of the relationship between Funan and Zhenla. We learn nothing, for example, about what Zhenla's takeover of Funan actually consisted of—whether it was violent or peaceful, for example. The fact that the Funanese had to move their capital suddenly from Temu to Nafuna suggests that some conflict may have been involved. On the other hand, neither of the two Chinese terms used to describe Funan's takeover by Zhenla—*bing* in *Tang hui yao* and *Xin Tang shu*, meaning "annex," "take over," "unite with" or "come together with," and *jian* in *Sui shu* and other later texts, meaning "take over" or "combine with"—has obvious military overtones, while verbs descriptive of military aggression such as *gong* ("attack"), *xi* ("carry out a surprise attack"), or *ji* ("strike") are notable for their absence.[13]

All we can deduce from these disparate data is that Funan was taken over by Zhenla some time between 535 and 650 or even later, either over a short period of time or in a more gradual process, perhaps peaceful or partially peaceful. One possibility, alluded to earlier, is that Citrasena began taking over Funan while he was still very young, so that the takeover was nearly complete by the time he died. Another is that it spanned the years in which he and his son Īśānasena lived. A third—given the *Xin Tang shu* account, the tribute sent between 627 and 649, and Yijing's comment about the suppression of Buddhism sometime in the second half of the seventh century—is that the process did not end until the time of Īśānasena's successor Bhavavarman II (r. late 630s–mid-650s) or even later.[14]

Official Chinese sources tell us that Zhenla first communicated with China during the Sui dynasty, and that it sent its first tribute to China in 616, during the final years of the Sui dynasty.[15] In addition, we learn that during the Sui, the Chinese imperial court lost touch with some of the southern states that had been sending tribute, one of them possibly being Funan, although Funan or some part of it briefly resumed sending gifts to the Tang court during the reign of Taizong.[16]

We know little about the extent to which the realms of Zhenla and Funan overlapped geographically. It is reasonable to assume there was some geographical continuity between the two, particularly between Funan and the southern part of Zhenla later known to the Chinese as Water Zhenla.[17]

Similarly, Chinese sources convey little sense of which political, religious, social, and other practices Zhenla may have inherited from Funan. With the exception of one indirect allusion to a royal lineage connecting Funan and Zhenla, which we shall consider shortly, there is a complete absence of comment on such matters. This is particularly notable since in its account of Zhenla, *Sui shu* explicitly compares certain Zhenla practices and products with those of Linyi, Chitu (admittedly, an offshoot of Funan), and the southern Chinese regions of Jiuzhen and Rinan.

In the case of Chitu, the authors of *Sui shu* may have found comparisons easier to make because of Chang Jun's report on his 607 mission to Chitu, which they presumably had access to. Chang Jun did not visit Zhenla, but perhaps his report on Chitu contained hearsay accounts of Zhenla that the authors of *Sui shu* drew on.

The History of the Sui Dynasty's account of early Zhenla

Sui shu contains two entries on Zhenla. *Sui shu*'s record of Zhenla is close to being contemporaneous, since it records that Zhenla's king was Īśānasena [Yishe'naxian], generally identified with Īśānavarman I, who was probably still reigning when *Sui shu* was completed in 636.[18] The first of *Sui shu*'s two entries records the fact that in 616, the twelfth year of the Sui emperor Yang, Zhenla sent an envoy to the Sui court with a tribute of local produce.[19] The second, much longer entry—the most important Chinese source on the early years of Zhenla—is one of the passages on "southern foreigners" found in the eighty-second of *Sui shu*'s eighty-six chapters.[20]

As an introduction to their account of Zhenla, Wei Zheng and the other authors of *Sui shu* begin chapter eighty-two with some comments about southern foreigners in general. They note the existence of "southern foreigners of various different kinds, living intermingled with Chinese"—an early reference, it seems, to Chinese living or trading overseas—and "somewhat dependent on China."[21] They go on to write that *Sui shu* will not be providing detailed accounts of all of these "far-off southern states," adding that while ten or so came to the Sui court with tribute during the reign of emperor Yang (605–617), in many cases all traces of them later disappeared, with no further news of them.[22]

The emperor Yang of the Sui dynasty (r. 604–618), from a portrait attributed to the seventh-century Tang court painter Yan Liben. The portrait is part of a scroll by Yan Liben that contains portraits of thirteen Chinese emperors and their staff. In 607 the emperor Yang sent the envoy Chang Jun and others to the state of Chitu, and it is conceivable that the passages on Zhenla in *Sui shu* drew on material they gathered.

Source: Attributed to Yan Liben, Museum of Fine Arts, Boston; collections.mfa.org/objects/29071, 2020

As noted earlier, it is conceivable that Funan was one of these disappearing states, having sent only one mission to the Sui court, in 588. True, it again sent missions to China between 618 and 649, during the reign of the Tang emperor Taizong, overlapping with the first missions from Zhenla. But Wei Zheng and the other authors of *Sui shu* make no mention of these final missions from Funan—either because they did not know about them, or else because they saw them as beyond their remit, which was write the history of the Sui.

After their introductory remarks about southern foreigners, Wei Zheng and his colleagues go on to say that they are recording the affairs of just four southern states, Linyi, Chitu, Poli, and Zhenla. Linyi was the precursor to Champa, and is discussed in appendix five, while Chitu was the state, probably located in the north of the Malay Peninsula, that was visited by the Sui envoy Chang Jun. As for Poli, whose customs *Sui shu* describes as being similar to those of Zhenla, it may have been a polity located in north-central Sumatra.[23]

Prasat Yeay Peau, one of the ruined temples in the Sambor Prei Kuk temple complex.The seventh-century Zhenla capital Īśānapura, mentioned in *Sui shu*, was probably located near Sambor Prei Kuk

Source: Ian Pitwood, overland-underwater.com; www.overland-underwater.com/media/20060506/Images/Sambor_Prei_Kuk03.jpg, 18-06-2006

When it comes to Zhenla, *Sui shu* gives us the following partial but engaging portrait:[24]

> The state of Zhenla lies to the southwest of Linyi. It was originally a dependency of Funan. Going from Rinan commandery it takes sixty days by boat to get there.[25] To the south it is adjacent to the state of Chequ; to the west is the state of Zhujiang.[26] The family name of the [first] king was

Kṣatriyaḥ [Shali], and his name was Citrasena [Zhiduosina].[27] His ancestors grew gradually stronger and more prosperous, so that when it came to Citrasena's time he annexed Funan and took possession of it. After his death his son Īśānasena [Yishe'naxian] took his place.[28]

He resides in Īśānapura [Yishe'na *cheng*].There are twenty thousand or more families beneath the city's outer walls. Within the city there is a large hall where the king gives audiences on matters of government. There are altogether thirty large cities with several thousand families apiece, each under a regional leader. The titles of officials are the same as in Linyi.[29]

The king holds audiences once every three days. He sits on a couch made of various aromatic woods and precious stones, with a bejeweled screen spread above him.[30] The screen is on poles of carved wood, with walls of ivory and inlaid gold shaped like a small building, and dangling gold that flickers with light, much the same as in Chitu. In front of him there is a gold incense burner, with an attendant on either side. The king wears rose-colored cotton with jeweled tassels around his waist that fall to below his knees. His head is adorned with an ornamental crown set with gold and precious stones, and he is draped in pearls and jewelery. His footwear is made of leather, and gold pendants hang from his ears. Ordinarily he is clad in fine white cotton and ivory footwear, and when his hair is uncovered he does not wear jeweled tassels. Generally speaking the clothing that his officials have to wear is of the same type.[31]

There are five senior officials: the first is called Guluozhi [Kurāk], the second Gaoxiangping, the third Poheduoling, the fourth Shemoling, and the fifth Randuolou.[32] When the various minor officials have an audience with the king, they hastily touch their heads to the ground three times before the steps to the throne. The king then summons them up the steps. They kneel, clasping their arms with both hands, and sit in a semicircle around the king. When their discussion of the affairs of government is over, they kneel again, bow deeply, and leave. At the gates to the courtyard in front of the steps there are over a thousand guards wearing armor and bearing staffs.

The state has close and friendly relations with Canban and Zhujiang,[33] and is frequently in conflict with Linyi and Tuohuan.[34]

In their daily life, the people all carry armor and staffs, ready for use if they need to go into battle. It is the custom that only a son of the king's principal wife can be his heir. On the day the king is instated, all his older and younger brothers are punished with mutilation by having one of their fingers removed or their nose cut off. They are sent elsewhere and are provided for, but they cannot take up office.

The people are small and black in appearance, though some of the women are white.[35] They all have curly hair and pendant ears.[36] By temperament they are alert and strong. The places where they live and their vessels and utensils are quite similar to those of Chitu. They treat their right hand as clean and their left hand as unclean. They bathe every day, cleaning their teeth with twigs from the willow, and recite prayers. They also wash before eating, and when they have finished eating they again use willow twigs to clean their teeth, and again recite prayers.[37] For food and drink they have a lot of milk products, granular sugar, rice, millet, and rice cakes.[38] When they are going to have a meal, they mix the cakes in a sauce of mixed meats then eat them, all by hand.

When taking a wife they just send a piece of clothing, choose a day, and dispatch a matchmaker to greet the bride. Then for eight days the man's and the woman's family both refrain from going out, and keep lamps lit all the time, day and night. When the marriage ceremony is over, the man and his parents divide their property, and the man goes elsewhere to live.[39] If parents die and leave behind young sons who are not yet married, what is left of the property goes to them. If their sons are already married, the property goes to the authorities.

At the time of funerals, the sons and daughters of the deceased all fast for seven days, cut off their hair and weep.[40] Monks, nuns, holy men, relatives, and old friends gather together for the occasion, and see off the deceased with music.[41] The corpse is burned with wood of various perfumes; the ashes are taken and kept in a gold or silver vase and sent off on the great waters.[42] The poor sometimes use earthenware which they paint a variety of colors. There are those that do not cremate corpses but rather take them into the mountains, where they are left for the wild animals to eat.

The north of the state is very mountainous. In the south there are rivers, lakes, and marshes, and the climate is really hot. There is no frost or snow, but pestilences and poisonous creatures abound. The soil is good for growing large-grained millet and rice, and there are small amounts of broomcorn millet and foxtail millet.[43]

The fruits and vegetables are similar to those of Rinan and Jiuzhen.[44] Unusual products include jackfruit, which have no flowers, leaves like a persimmon's, and fruit like wax gourds; and mango trees, which have blossoms and leaves like a date palm's and fruit like plums.[45]

There are *piye* trees, which have blossoms like quinces, leaves like apricots, and fruit like paper mulberry fruit, and *potianluo* trees, whose blossom, leaves, and fruit are all very much like those of the date. There are also wood apples, which blossom like crab apples and have leaves like those of the elm, only thick and large. Their fruit are like plums, but as large as pint measures. Of the rest, many are the same as those of Jiuzhen.[46]

In the sea there is a fish called *jiantong*, which has four feet, no scales, and a trunk like an elephant's. It sucks in water and squirts it out to a height of fifty to sixty feet. There is also a fish called *fuhu*, which has a body like an eel and a beak like a parrot, and has eight feet.[47] There are a number of large fish whose bodies come half out of the water, and that are like mountains to look at.

During the fifth and sixth month each year, when noxious vapors become widespread, white pigs, white oxen, and white goats are sacrificed outside the west gate of the city. If this is not done, the various grains do not grow, a lot of domestic animals die, and a large number of people fall sick from pestilential disease.[48]

Near the capital [*du*] [Īśānapura] is Mount Liṅgaparvata [Linggabopo], on which there is a sacred temple, normally protected by a five thousand-strong army. To the east of the city is a deity called Bhadreśvara [Poduoli][Śiva], to which sacrifices are made using human flesh. [49] Every year the king kills someone in a nighttime sacrifice and prayer ritual, again with a thousand-strong guard.[50] This is how they revere the spirits and gods. They greatly respect the Buddhist dharma and place even more faith in their holy men.[51] The Buddhists and holy men both set up statues in halls of worship.

In the twelfth year of the Daye reign period (616), an envoy was sent with tribute, which the emperor received with the greatest courtesy. Thereafter it came to an end.

The temple at Wat Phu in present-day Laos. In a line of argument rejected by Vickery, Coedès believed that this was the temple to Bhadreśvara mentioned in *Sui shu*, and that the founders of the state of Zhenla originated there before moving south and establishing the capital at Īśānapura near present-day Sambur Prei Kuk.

Source: Lonely Tours, Luang Prabang; www.luangprabang-laos.com/Wat-Phou-festival#&gid=1&pid=3, 2020

Sui shu's description of Zhenla, with its reference to the still-living king, Īśānasena, that is Īśānavarman I, gives it an appeal offered by few other Chinese accounts of early Cambodia, with the exception of the fragments left by Kang Tai and Wan Zhen, parts of Zhao Rugua's *Zhu fan zhi*, and the thirteenth-century record of Zhou Daguan.[52] Other accounts, written decades or even centuries after the periods they refer to, lack the immediacy of *Sui shu* and other records that were based on first-hand knowledge or—as in the case of *Sui shu*—written soon after the conditions they described.

Lineage linkages between Funan and Zhenla

The *Sui shu* reference to Īśānasena or Īśānavarman and his father Citrasena is significant for another reason as well. Apart from the allusions in *Tang hui yao*, *Sui shu*, and *Xin Tang shu* to Funan being taken over by Zhenla, it is the only reference in official Chinese sources that allows us to make a relatively reliable connection between Funan and Zhenla, and more specifically between their rulers. The connection is between the last named king of Funan, Rudravarman (r. 514–?539), as mentioned in *Liang shu*, and the first named kings of Zhenla, Citrasena and his son Īśānavarman, as mentioned in *Sui shu*.[53]

This connection is made explicit in an important epigraphic source, a 667 Sanskrit inscription numbered K. 53 found near Ba Phnom.[54] This inscription names five kings served by four generations of a prominent family, the kings being Rudravarman (r. 514–?539), Bhavavarman (I) (r. late sixth century), Mahendravarman (another name for Citrasena) (r. ?600 for some years), Īśānavarman (I) (r. ?616–late 630s), and Jayavarman (I) (r. ?657–?681?—the latter not to be confused with the Kauṇḍinya Jayavarman referred to in *Nan Qi shu*, Rudravarman's father.

In a detailed analysis of the relationships among these five kings, drawing on local inscriptions, Vickery argues that they were all likely to have belonged to or married into a single lineage, one that was dominant in an area of southern Cambodia that Funan must have included.[55] In other words, the evidence of inscriptions suggests that the last-named king of Funan, Rudravarman, was closely related to Citrasena-Mahendravarman, the Zhenla king who allegedly took over Funan.

Sui's account of Īśānavarman being Citrasena's son and heir appears to be supported by other palaeographic evidence as well. As Vickery relates, in addition to their two names featuring on K. 53, Citrasena-Mahendravarman's name occurs in a number of Sanskrit inscriptions dating back to the sixth century. These are found in Stung Treng and Kratié, both in present-day Cambodia; Korat, Khon Kaen, Phimai, Surin, Ta Phraya, and Ubon, all in present-day Thailand; and Basak in present-day Laos. In these inscriptions Citrasena is referred to either as a prince or as Mahendravarman, the latter evidently being the royal title he took when he succeeded his brother Bhavavarman in about 600, after which he probably ruled from a location near Sambor Prei Kuk.[56] Local inscriptions do not make an explicit connection between Citrasena-Mahendravarman and Īśānavarman, but according to Vickery Īśānavarman is mentioned as a living king in two inscriptions dated 627 and 637.[57] Taking all this into account, the royal succession described by K. 53 seems to be consistent with *Sui shu*'s description of Īśānavarman as Citrasena's son.

Such linkages are rare. In fact the linkages discussed here mark only the second time information about Cambodian rulers in Chinese sources seems to correspond with local epigraphic records. The first time, as noted earlier, was the match between a sixth-century inscription found near Phnom Penh and the names of the early sixth-century Funanese king Jayavarman (that is, Kauṇḍinya Jayavarman) and his son Rudravarman.[58]

It is worth noting in passing that when considering the *Sui shu* passage on Citrasena and Īśānavarman, Vickery, Coedès, and other non-China specialists cite as their Chinese source the *Sui shu* account as given in Ma Duanlin's fourteenth-century *Wenxian tongkao*.[59] They do so because the *Wenxian tongkao* account was available to them in translation—the somewhat slipshod French version done in 1883 by Marie-Jean-Léon Lecoq, the Marquis d'Hervey de Saint-Denys—whereas the *Sui shu* account had not then been made available in a European language.[60]

How seventh-century Zhenla may have differed from Funan

In other respects *Sui shu*'s account of Zhenla, while comparable in certain respects to previous historians' accounts of Funan, is fuller than them and also differs from them in a number of ways. These differences are as follows.

Unlike earlier accounts of Funan, *Sui shu* gives a detailed description of Zhenla's king and mentions by name his capital, Īśānapura, with its nearby temple to Poduoli, which Coedès plausibly identifies with the Bhadre- of the name Bhadreśvara, a name for the god Śiva. It gives an account of the the human sacrifices made there, and makes reference to monks, nuns, and holy men. By recording that "only a son of the king's principal wife can be his heir" it indicates that patrilineal succession was the practice in Zhenla, in contrast to succession practices in Funan that may have been subject to matrilineal influences.[61] It describes the king's banishment of his brothers once he has taken office, the rituals of the king's audiences, and the titles of the five senior officials or types of official. It mentions the existence of thirty other cities, each with a regional leader. And it relates that the people go armed and that armed soldiers protect the sacred temple. In all these respects, its account of Zhenla differs from earlier accounts of Funan.

The social customs of early Zhenla that *Sui shu* describes also differ from those of Funan. It mentions two ways of disposing of the dead: cremation and exposure to animals in the wild. This contrasts with *Liang shu*'s account of four methods used in Funan—consignment to river waters, cremation, burial, and exposure to birds. *Sui shu* describes what people eat, said to include both rice and millet and, improbably, milk products, and also their washing habits, which seem similar to those of people in India. Finally it mentions three kinds of livestock—pigs, oxen, and goats, all used in sacrifices—and lists local fruits and vegetables, including jackfruit and mangos. The names of several of these evidently derive from Sanskrit, suggesting that some elements of this language, at least, were in day-to-day use, and not just restricted to religious matters.[62] In all these respects, too, *Sui shu*'s account of Zhenla differs from earlier accounts of Funan.

The strengths and weaknesses of *The History of the Sui Dynasty*

Sui shu still leaves us with a very incomplete picture. There is no mention of people's livelihoods, including fishing, agriculture, and trade, though from the references to rice and millet it is clear that farming, at least, was an everyday part of life. There is no account of the slaves that are referred to in Chinese accounts of Funan, and that Zhou Daguan later portrays as an essential part of Zhenla society.[63] There is no record of buildings, carvings, or statuary, as there was in Chinese records of Funan.[64]

Passing references to soldiers and to people being armed suggest that armed conflict may have been part of daily life, but if so there is little explanation as to why, apart from a brief mention of perennial enmity with Linyi and Tuohuan (which may have been Dawei in the south of present-day Myanmar). Finally, as noted earlier, *Sui shu* does not discuss how Zhenla differs from or resembles Funan, despite its apparent absorption of Funan.[65]

For all its limitations, *Sui shu*'s portrait of early Zhenla helps give substance to its life and customs. It is also of considerable historical value. One of the most contemporary Chinese accounts of early Cambodia, it provides the most substantial Chinese portrait of pre-Angkorian Cambodia until the late thirteenth-century *Record* of Zhou Daguan.[66] In addition, it is the first Chinese source to confirm that Funan's dependency Zhenla took over Funan. Finally, it enables us to establish a royal connection between Funan and Zhenla, and between the Zhenla of Chinese chronicles and local epigraphic records.

7

Distant images: Zhenla in Tang and Northern Song sources

During the centuries following the *Sui shu* account of Zhenla, Chinese descriptions of Cambodia contain much to entertain and inform, but they tend to be patchy and selective, and are often quite short.

They do include records of one much-debated development, Zhenla's reported division in the early eighth century into two parts, Water Zhenla and Land Zhenla, the latter sometimes called Wendan—a division that Chinese sources suggest lasted over a hundred years. Beyond that, none of them describes Zhenla in much detail, and surprisingly none of them provides any record at all of Zhenla from the early ninth to the late eleventh centuries (a point we shall return to later.) Only in the twelfth and thirteenth centuries does Zhenla start to come alive again in Chinese writings, culminating in the record by the envoy Zhou Daguan of his visit to Angkor in 1296–1297.

This chapter considers Chinese accounts of Zhenla that date from the Tang dynasty (618–907), the period of disorder between the Tang and Song dynasties (907–960), and the early or Northern Song dynasty (960–1127), when the Song had its capital in the inland city of Bianliang, present-day Kaifeng. They consist of records in the two standard histories of the Tang (945 and 1060), as well as the digest of Tang government institutions *Tang hui yao* [*Essential Documents and Regulations of the Tang Dynasty*] (961). They also include records of Zhenla in five monumental encyclopedias.[1] The few scattered references to Zhenla in unofficial sources for this period are considered in the context of these official sources.

The account of Zhenla in *The Old History of the Tang Dynasty*

Aftert *Sui shu* the next official Chinese source to provide a new perspective on Zhenla is *Jiu Tang Shu* [*The Old History of the Tang Dynasty*]. This was completed in

945, more than three centuries after *Sui shu*, during the half-century interregnum between the Tang and the Song dynasties.

Before turning to *Jiu Tang shu*, we should mention in passing the first of the five great encyclopaedias, *Tong dian* [*A Comprehensive History of Institutions*]. This was completed by the eminent scholar Du You in the late eighth century. Chronologically speaking, it thus came roughly half-way between *Sui shu* and *Jiu Tang shu*.

There is a section on Zhenla in *Tong dian*. Disappointingly, however, it has nothing to add to the account of Zhenla in *Sui shu*. Indeed, it reproduces the *Sui shu* entry on Zhenla almost verbatim, with only a brief additional comment to the effect that Zhenla began communicating with China during the Sui. *Tong dian*'s author Du You makes no attempt to update the information on Zhenla, for example by recording the kings who succeeded Īśānavarman I. Such information would have been available from the tribute missions from Zhenla that visited the Tang court at frequent intervals between 616 and 801 (see appendix three for details). But for reasons unknown to us, Du You did not have it to hand, or at any rate did not choose to use it, when he compiled his great encyclopaedia.[2]

The next official record of Zhenla is contained in *Jiu Tang shu* [*The Old History of the Tang Dynasty*], completed nearly a century and a half after *Tong dian* in 945. *Jiu Tang shu* was the first of the two standard histories of the Tang dynasty, the other being the 1060 *Xin Tang shu* [*The New History of the Tang Dynasty*]. The long break in official records between *Sui shu* and *Jiu Tang shu* is explained by the simple fact that the Tang dynasty enjoyed over three centuries in power, so that court historians no longer had to record the affairs of short-lived dynasties, as they had done when compiling the histories of the Six Dynasties.[3]

Written by the scholar-official Liu Xu and others, *Jiu Tang shu* is a work in two hundred chapters. It includes several short references to Zhenla as well as a longer entry describing Zhenla's location and customs. This longer entry is quite succinct, and contains no record at all of activities relating to Zhenla during the last ninety years or so of Tang rule. This reflects the lapse in communications between Zhenla and the Chinese empire that began in the early 800s and lasted until the late eleventh century, a lapse whose causes will be considered later.[4]

Jiu Tang shu's short references to Zhenla include an intriguing report on Zhenla's participation with Linyi in a plan to join a rebellion against the Tang authorities, who had established a protectorate in Annan (An Nam or Annam in Vietnamese) in the far south of China, with its headquarters in Jiaozhi. The rebellion, which broke out in 713, was led by a person called Mei Shuluan (Mai Thúc Loan in Vietnamese) (?–722), who styled himself the Black Emperor. The Black Emperor and his rebels seized Annan with a force of four hundred thousand men before being put down by the Tang general Yang Sixu.[5] This is a rare allusion in early Chinese sources to the prospect of a military conflict between Chinese forces and forces from Zhenla.

There is also a short report of Zhenla sending tribute to the Tang court in 814. This mission came shortly after—or may have been the same as—a mission from Water Zhenla in 813. The mission in 813, led by an envoy called Li Mona, is recorded in the longer *Jiu Tang shu* entry on Zhenla, which also mentions missions from Zhenla in 623 and 628, and an unspecified number of missions from Water Zhenla and Land Zhenla in the period 650 to 755.[6]

A third brief reference to Zhenla is a listing in *Jiu Tang shu*'s bibliography of an unattributed book on Zhenla, *Zhenla guo shi* [*Matters relating to the State of Zhenla*].[7] This book is now lost, but its listing suggests that substantial information on Zhenla was available to the Tang court and its historians.

Jiu Tang shu's longer entry on Zhenla comes towards the end of the history, in chapter 197, which deals with fifteen southern states and peoples.[8] The entry on Zhenla reads:

> The state of Zhenla is northwest of Linyi. Originally a dependent state of Funan, it is a variety of [the southern states whose people are known as] *kunlun*, and lies twenty thousand seven hundred li south of the capital [of the Tang, Chang'an].[9] To get from there [Zhenla] to Aizhou [the name at this time for Jiuzhen in the far south of China] is a sixty-day journey north.
>
> The family name of its king is Kṣatriyaḥ [Shali]. There are thirty or so large cities, and the royal capital [*du*] is Īśānapura [Yishe'na *cheng*]. The customs and clothing are the same as Linyi's. The land is fertile, and the humid air gives rise to noxious diseases. In the sea there are large fish that sometimes half emerge from the water, which are like mountains to look at. During the fifth and sixth month of each year, when noxious vapors become widespread, oxen and pigs are sacrificed. If this is not done the various grains fail to grow.
>
> It is the custom there to have doors opening to the east, and to give priority to the east. They have five thousand fighting elephants, and feed rice and meat to the superior ones among them. If they do battle with a neighboring state the elephants are arrayed at the front. On their backs they carry tiered wooden structures, each with four people on them, all carrying bows and arrows.[10] The state reveres the way of the Buddha and the heavenly deities, with the latter being of greater importance and the way of the Buddha ranking next.[11]
>
> In the sixth year of the Wude reign period [623], it sent an envoy to court with local produce as tribute. In the second year of the Zhenguan reign period [628], it again came to pay its respects to the emperor with tribute,

> this time together with the state of Linyi. The emperor Taizong commended the envoys on their long and exhausting journey, and conferred very generous gifts on them.[12]
>
> People in southern places refer to the state of Zhenla as the Jimie [Khmer] state.[13] From the Shenlong reign period [705–706] onwards, Zhenla was divided into two. The southern half near the sea with its many lakes and marshes was called Water Zhenla, and the northern half with its many mountains was called Land Zhenla, also called the state of Wendan.[14] During the reigns of Emperor Gaozong [r. 650–683], [Empress Wu] Zetian [r. 684–704], and Emperor Xuanzong [r. 713–755], they both sent envoys with tribute for the emperor.[15]
>
> The northern, southern, eastern and western boundaries of the state of Water Zhenla were each about eight hundred li long.[16] In the east it reached the region of Bentuolang, in the west the state of Dvaravati [Duoluobodi].[17] In the south it extended to the Small Sea, and in the north to Land Zhenla. The name of the city its king lived in was Poluotiba [?Purandarapura]. On the eastern frontier of the state there were some small cities, all called states. The state had a large number of elephants. In the eighth year of the Yuanhe reign period [813] it sent Li Mona and others to pay its respects to the emperor.[18]

Local epigraphic evidence suggests several possible Sanskrit and Khmer equivalents for the name Poluotiba (Ba la dɛj bəɨt [P]). One is Varadagrāma or Varada village or town, *grāma* meaning village or town and Varada meaning Bestower of Wishes, often with reference to Śiva. According to Vickery, Varadagrāma was the home of Īśānasena I near Ba Phnom, southeast of present-day Phnom Penh. As an alternative, Coedès suggests the name Bālādityapura or Bālāditya City, named after a southern chieftain "of undetermined date" (as he acknowledges) called Bālāditya. But Dupont casts doubt on this idea, pointing out that no such place is mentioned in local inscriptions.

A third and more likely equivalent, one that local inscriptions do mention, is Purandarapura, Purandara (Poluotiba) referring to Indra and *pura* being the Sanskrit for city. In Jacques' view Purandarapura may have been the capital of Jayavarman I (r. 657?–681?), a suggestion that Vickery regards as plausible. As for Purandarapura's location, Jacques notes that it was long thought to be in the south of Cambodia, but prefers a location near Angkor, whereas Vickery tentatively suggests a location further south than Angkor, possibly at the site of Banteay Prey Nokor near present-day Kompong Cham. This latter location—which incidentally is the site Hoshino proposes for the capital of Chitu or Red Earth—would be more suitable geographically as a capital for Water Zhenla.[19]

If the name Poluotiba is indeed a rendition of Purandara as in Purandarapura or Purandara City, it is one of only two cases of a Chinese name for an early Cambodian city corresponding with local palaeographic evidence, the other being Īśānasena's capital Īśānapura (Yishe'na *cheng*).

Elsewhere in chapter 197, *Jiu Tang shu* gives a little more information about Zhenla vis-à-vis its neighbors.[20] It records that "the state of Duoheluo is adjacent to Zhenla to its east," while the state of Heling, "which is located on an island in the Southern Sea . . . is adjacent to Zhenla, which is to its north." As noted earlier, Duoheluo was probably an alternative form of Duoluobodi, Dvaravati in present-day Thailand, while Heling was the name of a state on Java. *Jiu Tang shu* also records that "the state of Zhenla is the eastern neighbor" of the state of Piao. If Piao was the equivalent of the Old Burmese name Pyū, it was the polity or polities that flourished in the middle reaches of the Ayeyarwady (Irrawaddy) River during the first millennium CE.[21]

What *The Old History of the Tang Dynasty* tells us about Zhenla

Jiu Tang shu's comments on Zhenla partly repeat what is contained in *Sui shu*, but they also provide new information, some of it perhaps from the lost book *Zhenla guo shi*. This new information consists of a few remarks about Zhenla's social customs, as well as a new account of Zhenla's identity and location, including its significant report of the division of Zhenla into two parts, Water Zhenla and Land Zhenla, in the early eighth century.

With respect to Zhenla's social customs, *Jiu Tang shu* adds to earlier Chinese accounts by telling us about the east-facing locations of Zhenla's doors; its elephants and their howdahs bearing armed people—men and perhaps women too, though it is not specific; and the relative weight given to the worship of both Buddhist and other deities, presumably both Indian and local, the other deities outweighing the Buddhist ones in importance.

The new information about Zhenla's regional location is more substantial than the information given in *Sui shu*, though it still raises questions. Liu Xu and the other authors of *Jiu Tang shu* describe Zhenla—by which they mean, perhaps, early Zhenla, before Zhenla's division into Land Zhenla and Water Zhenla—as being a very long way south of the Chinese capital Chang'an. They may have had in mind a route involving journeys by land, since they refer to Zhenla being sixty days' travel south of Aizhou in the center-north of present-day Vietnam—or to be more precise, to Aizhou being sixty days' journey north of Zhenla, a curious formulation suggesting that Zhenla is the starting-point. This leaves open the possibility that this leg of the journey, at least, was seen as being traversible overland, rather than by river and sea. (As we shall see shortly, *Xin Tang shu* clearly documents the existence by mid-Tang times of an overland route linking Zhenla and the coast of present-day Vietnam.[22])

Liu Xu and his colleagues are unconvincingly specific about the distance from Zhenla to Chang'an, which they record as being twenty thousand seven hundred li. This is far too much for the distance concerned, which is no more than a quarter of that as the bird flies—or say a third of that, if the journey is a circuitous one by water and land. Moreover the number two thousand seven hundred is unnaturally precise, with two round thousands plus some hundreds. We can assume it is the result of a clerical error or misunderstanding of some kind.

Jiu Tang shu's description of early Zhenla's location vis-à-vis Linyi is also awkward. It is the only official Chinese record to place Zhenla northwest of Linyi, rather than southwest of it.[23] Locating it northwest of Linyi makes no sense if, as seems likely, Īśānapura was located at Sambor Prei Kuk, and perhaps, again, "northwest" is an error.

The fact that *Jiu Tang shu* locates Zhenla's capital in only one place, Īśānapura (or two, if Poluotiba/Purandarapura, the capital of Water Zhenla, is included) highlights another curious fact. This is the absence from *Jiu Tang shu* of any record of events relating to the founding of subsequent Zhenla capitals, culminating in the accession to the throne of Jayavarman II (r. 802–835) at his royal capital Mahendraparvata, a glorious event customarily taken to mark the beginning of the Kingdom of Angkor.[24]

A first official reference to the Khmers

Jiu Tang shu notes that Zhenla is referred to regionally as the Jimie (Kiḙ̂t miet [K]) or Khmer state.[25] This is the first known reference to the ethnonym Khmer in official Chinese records, although the name occurs earlier in unofficial writings. It is found, for example, in a slightly different form—Gemie (Kập miet [K]) rather than Jimie—in two passages in *Yiqie jing yinyi* [*The Pronunciations and Meanings of All the Sutras*], a Buddhist dictionary by two monks, Huiying and Huilin, that was completed by 820 at the latest.[26] The first passage relates that the *kunlun* language, also commonly called *gulun*, is that of

> the foreigners of the islands in the Southern Sea. They are very dark, go naked, and can tame wild animals, rhinos, elephants, and so on. There are various kinds of them, Sengzhi [the people of Red Earth], Tumi, Gutang, Gemie [Khmer], and so on, all of them lowly peoples.[27]

The second passage reads:

> Gemie is a *kunlun* language. The old name [of the place] was the state of Yixin [?Īśānapura]. Of all the *kunlun* states, this state is the largest, and devoutly believes in the Three Treasures.[28]

The Old History of the Tang Dynasty on Land Zhenla and Water Zhenla

The most important new information in *Jiu Tang shu* is its much debated claim that early in the eighth century Zhenla divided into two parts, Lu Zhenla or Land Zhenla, also known as Wendan (Mi̯uən tân [K]), and Shui Zhenla or Water Zhenla.[29] Assuming they existed in some form or other, it is not clear how long these two entities may have lasted. The information given in Chinese records suggests that they endured for a hundred years or more, perhaps a few decades longer than that. *Jiu Tang shu* dates the division from 705–706, but records that the two entities both sent missions earlier than that, and reports that the last tribute from Water Zhenla was sent to China in 813. *Xin Tang shu* provides no further information. *Cefu yuangui* makes one last mention of Water Zhenla in a brief report for the year 838, when it records that in that year a prince of Water Zhenla led an army to protect Huanzhou from being taken over by Annan, at that time a Chinese protectorate.[30]

From these dates we can assume that within decades of the establishment of the Kingdom of Angkor by Jayavarman II in 802, Chinese chroniclers ceased to regard the two entities as functioning polities—a significant juncture in the history of Zhenla in Chinese sources.

The locations and identities of Land Zhenla and Water Zhenla have been the cause of some controversy. In the first half of the twentieth century, leading European scholars concurred with the account given in *Jiu Tang shu*. They accepted the assumption implicit there and in other official Chinese sources that the two entities existed as two distinct states, an assumption still accepted by the Chinese historian Chen Xiansi as recently as 1990.[31]

In 1943 Dupont questioned this consensus by asking whether Land Zhenla and Water Zhenla could in fact be seen as comprising two distinct states. In an influential paper, he suggested instead that by the eighth century there were two blocs of disaggregated power, one southern and the other northern, ruled by a total of six dynasties.[32] Since then, others including Jacques and Vickery have expressed similar doubts about Land Zhenla and Water Zhenla being two discrete states. Jacques suggests that in fact they constituted a multiplicity of realms. Vickery argues that political power in eighth-century Zhenla, an entity he locates in the north-central part of present-day Cambodia, was far from being divided into two. Rather, he proposes, Zhenla continued to undergo a process of consolidation from an earlier state of fragmentation, a process begun under Īśānavarman I and Jayavarman I and later intensified under Jayavarman II.[33]

The whereabouts and nature of Water Zhenla

By contrast, Chinese sources give a relatively clear description of the location of Water Zhenla and, to a considerable extent, of Land Zhenla too. With respect to Water Zhenla, *Jiu Tang shu* records it as having the sea to its south, Land Zhenla to its north, the southern reaches of the Cham people, perhaps, to its east, and the emergent polity Dvaravati in present-day Thailand to its west. The description is concrete enough to give us a sense of a coherent polity. Importantly, however, *Jiu Tang shu* describes Water Zhenla's eastern frontier as consisting of small city states—echoing, perhaps, *Sui shu*'s report that in the seventh century Zhenla had thirty large cities under regional leaders—thus reflecting an awareness that at its periphery, anyway, Water Zhenla was fragmented.

One further point worth noting is *Jiu Tang shu*'s estimation of the size of Water Zhenla, eight hundred li square, which sounds realistic enough to suggest a relatively well-defined area under the control of at least one of the Water Zhenla polities. While perhaps smaller in size than the Funan described by early Chinese chroniclers, it also suggests the possibility of an overlap between Water Zhenla and Funan.

One other early Chinese reference to the location of Water Zhenla can be found in a passage in *Man shu* [*Book of the Southern Foreigners*], a description of Nanzhao in present-day Yunnan written by the late Tang scholar Fan Chuo (fl. 860–870).[34] Without being explicit, *Man shu* implies that Land Zhenla lay immediately to the south of Nanzhao, and that beyond it lay Water Zhenla, and through it an overland route south to the sea. The *Man shu* passage reads:

> Water Zhenla and Land Zhenla are adjacent to the southern foreigners' [city of] Zhennan [in Yunnan]. The southern foreign rebels led an army on horseback to the shores of the sea, but when they saw the great breakers of dark blue waves they were cast down. Withdrawing their forces, they turned back.[35]

The whereabouts and nature of Land Zhenla, also called Wendan

With respect to Land Zhenla, which *Jiu Tang shu* and *Xin Tang shu* both describe as having the alternative name Wendan (Mi̯uən tân [K]), Chinese sources seem to suggest a location in the northeast of present-day Thailand, across the Mekong River from today's Laos. This corresponds quite well with various locations on or near the mid to upper reaches of Mekong that have been suggested by Western historians.

Writing in 1904, Pelliot suggested that Wendan could have been in the region of Sambor. In the 1940s Briggs suggested that it may have had its capital near Thakhek. In 1947 Stein, following Maspero, located it around Pak Hin Boun, a short distance north of Thakhek.[36] More recently Chandler, following Jacques, has suggested that it was "apparently somewhere on the upper reaches of the Mekong," perhaps near Wat Phu in southern Laos.[37] Some scholars have identified Wendan with Vientiane (Wanxiang in Chinese), reading *dan* with its alternative Chinese pronunciation *chan* and arguing that the name of Wenchan approximates that of Wanxiang.[38] Perhaps most persuasively, Hoshino has argued on the basis of his firsthand knowledge of the area that Wendan was a Dai polity, its name derived from the Daic *man sem* (Siamese villages) and that it was located in Kantharawichai and Fa Daet in the north-east of present-day Thailand.[39]

Chinese sources, specifically *Xin Tang shu* and *Taiping huanyu ji*, seem to indicate that of these locations, the one proposed by Hoshino is the most likely. *Xin Tang shu* and *Taiping huanyu ji* both report that Wendan was fifteen or sixteen days' overland travel southwest from Huanzhou, which was probably situated near the present-day Vietnamese city of Vinh. *Taiping huanyu ji* adds that the distance from Huanzhou to Wendan was three hundred and fifty li. These reports seem to locate Wendan either on or across the Mekong. In its detailed account of the overland journey, *Xin Tang shu* also seems to suggest—though its wording is imprecise—that overland travelers heading southwest to Wendan had to go not just as far as the Mekong, but beyond it.[40] This is a tentative assessment of the *Xin Tang shu* account, but if it is tenable the northeast of present-day Thailand, which is the site of a number of Angkor-era buildings, seems the most likely location for Wendan—always assuming, of course, that it was a single polity.

Wendan's tribute to China

Jiu Tang shu makes several other references to Wendan. These relate mainly to a tribute mission sent from Wendan in 771, led by a king of Wendan called Pomi (B'uâ mjię: [K]). *Xin Tang Shu* also mentions this mission, describing Pomi as a deputy king. In an unusual reference—women are rarely mentioned in accounts of envoys—*Xin Tang shu* adds that Pomi traveled to Chang'an with a wife, who is not named. This rare reference to a woman may conceivably indicate (as Hoshino suggests) that the wife accompanying Pomi was the real source of authority in Wendan.[41]

This is not the first record of a tribute mission to China from Wendan. *Cefu yuangui* records missions from Wendan in 710, 717, and 753. The unnamed leader of the mission from Wendan in 753 went on to support the Tang in "carrying out a punitive attack [on the recalcitrant state of Nanzhao] in Yunnan." But the visit by Pomi and his wife in 771 seems to have been a particularly notable occasion, perhaps because Pomi's host, the Tang emperor Daizong (r. 763–780), wanted to thank him for Wendan's support in the conflict with Nanzhao.[42]

As recounted in both *Jiu Tang shu* and *Cefu yuangui*, the emperor welcomed Pomi warmly, treated his delegation to a banquet, and accepted his gift of eleven dancing elephants.[43] (Later, Wendan continued to ply Daizong with elephants. By the time of Daizong's death there were said to be thirty-two Wendan elephants in the possession of the Chinese court—by one count, forty-two of them.[44]) Daizong also awarded Pomi with two imperial titles, one of them high-ranking. The titles were Commander Unequaled in Honor and Provisional Director of Palace Administration.[45] The first title conferred very high status, since Commanders ranked second in the thirty tiers of the Chinese administrative hierarchy—more senior, for example, than provincial governors.[46] After the death of Daizong, *Jiu Tang shu* relates, his successor Dezong (r. 780–804) "ordered that the thirty-two dancing elephants given by Wendan be released on to the southern slopes of the Jing mountains," reflecting, perhaps, the aversion to elephants being brought as tribute that apparently became a hallmark of imperial policy during the Song dynasty (960–1279).[47]

Purple pins and privacy: other sources on Zhenla during the Tang

Five official Chinese records that followed soon after *Jiu Tang shu* carry comments on Zhenla, although they are of a limited nature. In chronological order these records are: (1) *Tang hui yao*, the digest of Tang official regulations presented to the newly-established Song court in 961; (2) *Taiping guangji*, the second of the five great encyclopedias mentioned at the beginning of this chapter, this one consisting of a huge collection strange tales put together by a committee under the scholar Li Fang and completed in 978; (3) the third of the great encyclopedias, *Taiping yulan*, an important source of information about early Funan, also compiled by a committee under Li Fang and completed four years later, in 982; (4) the fourth encyclopaedic collection, the geographical compendium *Taiping huanyu ji*, completed by the scholar Yue Shi in the late tenth century; and (5) the fifth encyclopedia *Cefu yuangui*, completed by a committee led by Wang Qinruo in 1013.[48] Despite the limited information they provide, it is worth reviewing each of their comments on Zhenla. The comments do not always refer to any particular period, but it seems reasonable to suppose that most of them relate to Zhenla during the Tang.

Tang hui yao [*Essential Documents and Regulations of the Tang Dynasty*] repeats in an abbreviated form the entry on Zhenla in *Sui shu*, with a few additions taken from *Jiu Tang shu*. It also records at least six tribute missions sent to the Chinese court. It reports that envoys from Zhenla "repeatedly brought tribute" during the reign of the Tang emperor Taizong (627–649); that an envoy from Zhenla brought a trained elephant or elephants as tribute in 651; and that envoys brought rhinos and other tribute in 698, 717, and 750. The listings all refer to Zhenla, and it is not clear whether the later missions were from Water Zhenla or Land Zhenla/Wendan.[49]

With regard to the treatment of these missions, *Tang hui yao* notes that in 695 and 700 Empress Wu—imperial China's one and only empress, who ruled from 684 to 704—issued orders calling for the envoys of foreign states within a defined perimeter beyond China's borders, including Zhenla, to be given provisions according to requisite regulations. In the case of Zhenla these were to be five months of provisions, a reflection, perhaps, of its perceived importance.[50]

Turning to the encyclopedias, *Taiping guangji* [*Extensive Records Compiled during the Era of Great Peace* {976–983}] has three entries on Zhenla. Each of them relates a curious story. The first tells of a huge bird, the size of a camel and the shape of an owl, that once lived in a cave halfway up an enormously high mountain. The king of Zhenla killed it by feeding it beef that concealed a small sharp spear. The other two entries are about a tree that produces "purple pins," perhaps a type of fungus, and about how Zhenla people treated their guests and how they engaged in sexual relations. The latter is a rare reference in early Chinese sources to the sexual behaviour of early Khmers.[51]

As the sources for the two latter entries, *Taiping guangji* cites two Tang dynasty works, the first a ninth-century miscellany, the second a collection of anecdotes dating perhaps from the early eighth century.[52] The two entries are as follows:

> One product of the state of Zhenla is the *zifei* or purple pin tree. In Zhenla they call it *lequ*.[53] It is also a product of the state of Persia [Bosi]. The tree is a pole in height, and its boughs are covered in luxurious growth. The leaves are like those of the mandarin orange and do not wither in winter. It blossoms

> in the third month of the year; its flowers are white and do not seed. When the sky is filled with mist and rain that moisten its twigs and branches, it puts out purple-colored pins . . . The monk Tuosha'nibatuo, Garrison Militia Commandant and envoy from Zhenla, says that the ants move earth to the tree to make their nest there, and when the soil of the ants gets moist from the rain and mist it congeals and forms purple pins.[54] The best of these are found in the *kunlun* states; the next best are from the state of Persia . . .
>
> The state of Zhenla is five hundred li south of Huanzhou.[55] When they have guests it is customary for them to serve small pieces of betel nuts, camphor fruit, clams, and so on for them to enjoy.[56] They regard drinking wine as being a depraved thing to do, except with their wives in the privacy of their homes, away from their elders. Again, when men and women have sexual intercourse they do not want to let people see—the same custom as in China.[57]

The entries on Zhenla in the encyclopedia *Taiping yulan* [{*An Encyclopaedia*} *Compiled during the Era of Great Peace and Read by the Emperor*] (984), are all taken from *Sui shu* and *Jiu Tang shu*, which *Taiping yulan* refers to as *Tang shu*. Unhappily, given what a rich source *Taiping yulan* is for Funan, they contain nothing new.

The geographical compendium *Taiping huanyu ji* [*A Record of the World during the Era of Great Peace*] provides in a shorter form the *Sui shu* entry on Zhenla, with supplementary material from *Jiu Tang shu* and other minor changes and additions.[58] These additions include one point of interest. This is the comment that Water Zhenla "has very many elephants, but otherwise products and a language that are the same as those of Land Zhenla"—the first mention in official Chinese records of Zhenla's language (*yuyan*), and one that suggests that Water Zhenla and Land Zhenla had a language in common. This was almost certainly Khmer, and if true makes it less likely that the people, or at least the elite, of Land Zhenla spoke some other language—Tai, for instance, as Hoshino suggests they might have.[59]

Otherwise, in what might have been a clerical error, *Taiping huanyu ji* omits the word "city" in in its account of the location of the Bhadreśvara site, so that the text reads less precisely as "To the east is a deity called Bhadreśvara [Boduoli]." It also gives a list of six missions, in 623, 628, 651, 698, 717, and 750, noting that in 698, 717, and 750 the envoys offered rhinos as tribute.[60]

The fifth and last of the great encyclopaedias mentioned at the beginning of this chapter, *Cefu yuangui* [*Outstanding Models from the Storehouse of Literature*] contains three passages on Zhenla that reproduce almost verbatim the passages on Zhenla in *Sui shu* and *Jiu Tang shu*.[61] The only new comment is that in Zhenla "the writing commonly used is the same as that of brahmins," a clearer formulation than the *Jin shu* reference to the people of Funan writing with Hu script (Hu probably being India)—the only other mention of writing systems in early Cambodia.[62]

Apart from that, *Cefu yuangui*'s main contribution is to add to the list of Zhenla-related missions given variously in *Sui shu*, *Jiu Tang shu*, *Tang hui yao*, and *Taiping huanyu ji*.[63] Missions noted in *Cefu yuangui* took place in 616, 623, 625*, 628, 635*, 651, 682*, 698, 707*, 710*, 717, 750, 753*, 771, 798*, 813 and 814* (those hitherto unrecorded being marked with an asterisk). The mission in 798 was the last in the name of Wendan; the Tang emperor Dezong (r. 780–804) gave the envoy in charge of the mission, Li Touji, the relatively senior title of Commandant.[64] The mission in 814 was the last tribute mission from Zhenla to China for three centuries—a gap whose causes we shall consider later.

The record in *Cefu yuangui* of one particular mission—the mission sent in 717—is worth considering further. It reads:[65]

> In the fifth month, Zhenla, Wendan, Xinluo, Mohe, and central India all sent envoys to pay their respects to the emperor and present local products as tribute . . .[66]
>
> On the *bingzi* day of the sixth month, the envoys from the states of Wendan and Zhenla who had brought tribute to court returned to their foreign homes.[67] They were each given a letter from the emperor and five hundred pieces of silk to present to the king of their state. Zhenla and Wendan were each small southern states. They pledged their loyalty to each new emperor and submitted tribute regularly; that pleased the emperor, hence this beneficence.[68]

Two points here are worth highlighting. The first is that Zhenla and Wendan are recorded together, as they were earlier in missions recorded in *Cefu yuangui* for the year 710. This is most plausibly explained by treating Wendan as Land Zhenla and Zhenla as Water Zhenla. The second, more important point is the reference to the size of (Water) Zhenla and Wendan, which are both described as small states. This statement is not related to any particular point in time, but perhaps refers to their size in 717, the year of the mission. If this is the case, it suggests that the growth in size and influence of a more united Zhenla, evident from the ninth-century establishment of the Kingdom of Angkor onwards, was not yet appreciably under way.

Like *Jiu Tang shu* and *Tang hui yao*, *Cefu yuangui* records a mission from Zhenla (according to *Jiu Tang shu*, Water Zhenla) in 813, led by Li Mona. It also confirms *Jiu Tang shu*'s record of a mission from Zhenla—the same mission, perhaps?—the following year, 814.[69] This 814 mission was probably sent by the great Jayavarman

II (802–835), first ruler of the Kingdom of Angkor. As just mentioned, it was the last recorded tribute mission from Zhenla before the demise of the Tang dynasty in 907, and indeed for over three centuries. The next mission, recorded in *Song shi* [*The History of the Song Dynasty*] and *Song hui yao jigao* [*A Draft Edition of the Essential Documents and Regulations of the Song Dynasty*], did not take place until 1117, some three centuries later.[70]

The New History of the Tang Dynasty on an overland route to Wendan

As mentioned earlier, the fact that the authors of *Jiu Tang shu* calculate Zhenla's distance from Chang'an by reference to Aizhou in today's Vietnam suggests that they may have in mind a route involving travel by land. The next standard history to consider Zhenla—*Xin Tang shu* [*The New History of the Tang Dynasty*], completed in 1060 as a quite new history of the Tang—gives firmer evidence of an overland route connecting Zhenla with China, more specifically with the southernmost part of China in what is now north-central Vietnam.

This route is a section of one of seven or so routes connecting China with other parts of Asia that were famously mapped out by the Tang court geographer Jia Dan.[71] Jia Dan's routes originally comprised a book that he researched and wrote during the Zhenyuan reign period (785–804) of the Tang dynasty. The purpose of the book was to provide the emperor Dezong (r. 780–804) with a detailed guide to China's main means of communications with the foreigners of its frontier regions.

Judging from the account of his work in *Xin Tang shu*, Jia Dan was a diligent geographer. He undertook thorough research, carrying out careful investigations and interviewing foreign envoys with the help of interpreters. He also included local placenames and the names of places never before recorded. His book is now lost, but the seven major routes it maps out are not, being described in the last part (*xia*) of chapter forty-three of *Xin Tang shu*.[72]

According to this entry in *Xin Tang shu*, Jia Dan's seven routes were: (1) an overland route to the northeast; (2) a maritime route to Korea and the Bohai Sea; (3) a route northwards to Datong and Yunzhong, both in present-day Shanxi province; (4) a route to the western frontier regions; (5) a route to the Uyghurs in the north; (6) a route from Annan to India (Tianzhu), Annan or Annam being the protectorate governing the north of present-day Vietnam; and (7) a maritime route from Guangzhou in south China to "the foreigners of the [Southern] Sea".[73]

Zhenla, or to be more precise Wendan, features in the sixth of these routes, the overland one from Annan to India. Given that *Jiu Tang shu* describes Water Zhenla as a seaboard state, Jia Dan might have been expected to mention Zhenla or Water Zhenla in the seventh route, the maritime one running south from Guangzhou; but in fact Zhenla does not feature in that route.[74] A likely explanation for this is the diminished roles that Funan's successor states were playing in Chinese maritime communications.

The references Jia Dan makes to Wendan are to be found in one of two subsidiary land routes included in the Annan-India route. One of these subsidiary routes leads to Champa, the other to Wendan. While the Annan-India route begins from Jiaozhi, the headquarters of the Annan protectorate, both subsidiary routes actually start farther south, from Huanzhou. At this time Huanzhou was at the southern tip of the Tang empire, probably at or near Vinh on the north-central coast of today's Vietnam.[75]

Here is Jia Dan's account of the two subsidiary routes:[76]

> By one route, if you go east for two days from Huanzhou, you get to Anyuan district of Tanglin prefecture. Then going southwards you pass by the Guluo river; after two days' travel you reach the Tandong river in the state of Huanwang [Champa]. After another four days you get to Zhuya, then go past Danbu garrison and after two days get to the city of Huanwang state. This is where the old Han dynasty commandery of Rinan was.
>
> [By the other route,] if you travel southwest for three days from Huanzhou and cross the Wuwen Mountains, after another two days' journey you get to Riluo district in Tangzhou. Then you pass by the Luolun river and get to the Shimi mountains with their Gulang caves. After a further three days' journey you reach Wenyang district in Tangzhou. Then you pass through the Chichi gorge, and after four days' travel you reach Suantai district in the state of Wendan. A further three days' journey gets you to the outer city of Wendan, and with one more day's travel you reach its inner city.[77] It is also known as Land Zhenla, with Water Zhenla to its south.
>
> If you carry on south you reach the Small Sea [the Gulf of Thailand]. South of that is the state of Luoyue; going farther south still you reach the Great Sea [the Southern Sea].[78]

Jia Dan's itinerary tells us that Wendan lay fifteen to sixteen days' journey overland to the southwest of Huanzhou. As mentioned earlier, Jia Dan also seems to indicate—though his language is a little vague—that Wendan lay across the Mekong in the northeast of present-day Thailand.

Was Jia Dan's overland route from Huanzhou to Wendan much used? The route would not have been an easy one to follow, passing as it did through the Annamite Mountain Rrange separating present-day Vietnam from Laos. But by including it in his list of routes Jia Dan is clearly indicating that it was an important artery of communication. This is underlined by the fact that even before *Xin Tang shu*, the late-tenth century *Taiping huanyu ji* locates Wendan with reference to Huanzhou, while (as we saw earlier in this chapter) *Taiping guangji* cites a reference to Huanzhou in relation to Zhenla that dates back over two centuries before that.[79]

Maspero suggests that the Huanzhou–Wendan route was in use as early as 722, during an expedition Zhenla carried out against the Black Emperor Mai Thúc Luan (having earlier sided with him).[80] Hoshino surmises that the route was used to deliver the elephants Wendan sent as tribute to China, since they would have been difficult to transport by boat.[81] Most interestingly, Li Tana argues that in Song times the route was Cambodia's primary point of access to the South China Sea for trade and other purposes.[82]

To support her case, Li points out that during the Song dynasty Zhenla sent tribute far more often to the newly independent Đại Việt (present-day Vietnam) than it did to China.[83] In the eleventh and twelfth centuries, tribute missions from Zhenla to Đại Việt were certainly a frequent occurrence. The fourteenth-century history of Vietnam, *Việt Sử Lược* [*A Brief History of Vietnam*] lists seventeen such missions between 1012 and 1195.[84] *Việt Sử Lược* also mentions an official Vietnamese order in 1025 calling for a crossing point for foreigners to be set up on the southern edge of Huanzhou, suggesting that some of these missions, at any rate, took an overland route rather than traveling by river and sea.[85]

Zhenla's tribute missions to Đại Việt could well have been motivated by more than just trade. Security would surely have been a concern. When the Vietnamese leader Đinh Tiên Hoàng (924–979) declared himself emperor in the 960s and created the independent state of Đại Cồ Việt, later Đại Việt, the kings of Angkor (Zhenla) would no doubt have thought it prudent to acknowledge Vietnamese authority, given how uncertain Zhenla's own security was.[86] Threats to Zhenla's security are well attested to in Chinese records. *Xin Tang shu*, repeating *Sui shu*, states that Zhenla was frequently in dispute with Champa and Tuohuan/Gantuohuan. The Song gazetteer *Lingwai daida* notes that Champa and Zhenla were in a state of constant enmity, and that in 1173 Champa defeated Zhenla in war, while another Song gazetteer, *Zhu fan zhi*, in an account repeated by *Wenxian tongkao*, reports that Champa carried out a destructive naval attack on Angkor in 1177.[87] In view of these various conflicts, good relations with the Vietnamese would clearly have been in Zhenla's interest.

The New History of the Tang Dynasty on other aspects of Zhenla

Apart from its description of Jia Dan's route to Wendan, *Xin Tang shu* carries other short entries on Zhenla, as well as a longer passage on Zhenla's location, customs, and history.

The short entries include a reference to Zhenla's location north of two polities, Heling (on Java) and Touhe, an unknown state, and east of three other polities—Duoheluo (Dvaravati), Piao (Pyū), and the unidentified state of Xiuluofen.[88] Another short entry describes how Zhenla consolidated its rule after a period in which various small states in the Zhenla region sent tribute missions to China. According to this entry, in 638 four hitherto unmentioned states—Senggao, Wuling, Jiazha, and Jiumo—sent envoys with tribute to the Chinese court, with more tribute being sent later by the kings of Jiumo and another state called Funa (whose name in Chinese is different from Funan). Then sometime after 655, "Zhenla took over Senggao and [the?] other states".[89]

While this lapidary description is too brief to read much into, it suggests that Zhenla's absorption of Funan was accompanied by a period of political uncertainty, followed by an effort by the ruler of Zhenla—presumably Bhavavarman II's successor, Jayavarman I (r. ?657–?681), a strong centralizer—to consolidate his control.[90] If this was the case, Jayavarman I seems to have been confident enough to do so without needing to explain anything to the Chinese, since during his reign he did not send a single tribute mission to the Tang court in Chang'an.[91]

The longer passage on Zhenla in *Xin Tang shu* reads:[92]

> Zhenla, also called Jimie [Khmer], was originally a dependency of Funan. It is twenty thousand seven hundred li from the capital [Chang'an].[93] To the east it reaches Chequ, to the west it touches on Piao [Pyū], to the south it is next to the sea, in the north it is adjacent to Daoming, and to the northeast it abuts on to Huanzhou.[94] During the Zhenguan reign period [627–649] its king Kṣatriyaḥ Īśānasena [Shali Yijinna] started to annex Funan and take possession of it.[95]
>
> Its houses all face east, and seating someone to face east affords them the greatest respect. When guests come, they give them small pieces of betel nuts, camphor fruit, and clams. They do not drink wine, seeing it as depraved, except in their homes with their wives, away from their elders. There are five thousand war elephants, the high quality ones being fed on meat. For generations they have had cordial relations with Canban and Piao [Pyū], but they have several times fought with Huanwang [Champa] and Gantuohuan [?Dawei].[96]

From the Wude reign period [618–626] to the Shengli reign period [698–699], they came four times to pay their respects to the emperor. After the Shenlong reign period [705–706] the country divided into two; the northern half with its many mountains was called Land Zhenla, and the southern half bordering the sea, with its abundance of lakes and marshes, was called Water Zhenla. The Water Zhenla half had eight hundred li of territory, and its king lived in the city of Poluotiba [?Purandarapura].[97] Land Zhenla was also called Wendan or Polou, and had a territory of seven hundred li. Its king was called Daqu.[98]

During the Kaiyuan and Tianbao reign periods [713–741, 742–755], the prince [of Land Zhenla] led a retinue of twenty-six people to pay his respects to the emperor, and had the title of Courageous Commandant conferred on him. During the Dali [766–779] reign period, the deputy king Pomi and his wife came to pay his respects to the emperor [Daizong] and presented him with eleven trained elephants as tribute. Pomi was promoted to Provisional Director of Palace Administration and had the name Distinguished Guest conferred on him. [As recounted in *Jiu Tang shu*, Daizong's successor Dezong had the elephants set free in the Jing mountains.] . . . During the Yuanhe reign period [806–820], Water Zhenla again sent an envoy with tribute.[99]

To the northwest of Wendan there was a dependent state called Canban. In the eighth year of the Wude reign period [625] its envoys came to court. Daoming was another dependency. Its people went without clothing, and when they saw people wearing clothes they all laughed at them. They had no salt or iron, and provided for themselves by shooting birds and animals with crossbows made of bamboo.

Zhenla during the Tang: what Chinese sources tell us and what is missing

This *Xin Tang shu* account of Zhenla reiterates parts of *Sui shu* and *Jiu Tang shu* while adding a few new insights.

Its report about Īśānasena and his initial absorption of Funan, while potentially useful, includes dates that are later than the dates indicated in *Sui shu*, *Tang hui yao*, and the section on Funan in *Xin Tang shu*. *Xin Tang shu*'s apparent misrepresentation of Īśānasena's name raises a question about its reliability on this matter.

New names are given for states on either side of Zhenla, reflecting, perhaps, changed circumstances by the mid-eleventh century when *Xin Tang shu* was written. In its description of Water Zhenla's location, *Jiu Tang shu* refers to Bentuolang—

perhaps part of Champa?—being to the east of it, and Dvaravati being to the west. In *Xin Tang shu*'s description of the location of Zhenla (without the Water element of its name), Bentuolang is replaced by the unknown polity Chequ—possibly another name for part of Champa?—and Dvaravati is supplemented by Piao, probably Pyū, the polity or polities in the middle reaches of the Irrawaddy River.

Xin Tang shu gives the dimensions of both Water Zhenla and Land Zhenla. It records that Water Zhenla was eight hundred li in extent (a less clear figure than the one given in *Jiu Tang shu*, which records that Water Zhenla was eight hundred li square). Land Zhenla is recorded as being seven hundred li or perhaps three hundred and fifty kilometers in extent (if that is the correct way to construe the measurement given in the text)—the first time Land Zhenla's size is to be found in a Chinese source. Its size is consistent with *Cefu yuangui*'s description of it as a small state. *Jiu Tang shu* also mentions two dependencies of Land Zhenla—Canban and Daoming—neither of which appears in later official records. Another new piece of information is the reference to Daqu, the undeciphered name or title of the king of Wendan.

What is missing from *Xin Tang shu*, as from *Jiu Tang shu* and indeed all the Chinese sources considered in this chapter, is any substantial account of the habits and customs of Zhenla of the kind provided in *Sui shu*. Nor is there any record of events relating to Zhenla's history after the reign of Īśānasena (d.?late 630s), apart from the brief report of Zhenla taking over several states after 655, and the account of Zhenla dividing for a century or more into two parts from 705–706 onwards. There are, of course, the records of the twenty or so tribute missions that Zhenla, including Land and Water Zhenla, sent to the Tang court between 623 and 814, but these add little to what we know of Zhenla itself. So from the eighth century until the end of the Tang dynasty in 907, Chinese sources provide little information about Zhenla's political, social or cultural evolution.

This is particularly disappointing given the extraordinary changes Zhenla was starting to undergo. The ninth century was a transformative period in the development of Zhenla, which was ruled by a line of notable kings including Jayavarman II (r. 802–835), whose reign is usually taken to mark the beginning of the Kingdom of Angkor; Indravarman I (r. 877–c. 889); and Yaśovarman I (r. 889–c. 900).[100] What accounts for the silence of official Chinese sources? The lapse in Chinese records continues after the fall of the Tang and lasts until the late eleventh century. It is a lapse matched by a three-century gap in tribute missions from Zhenla to China from 814 to 1117. In the next chapter we will consider likely explanations for this remarkable hiatus.

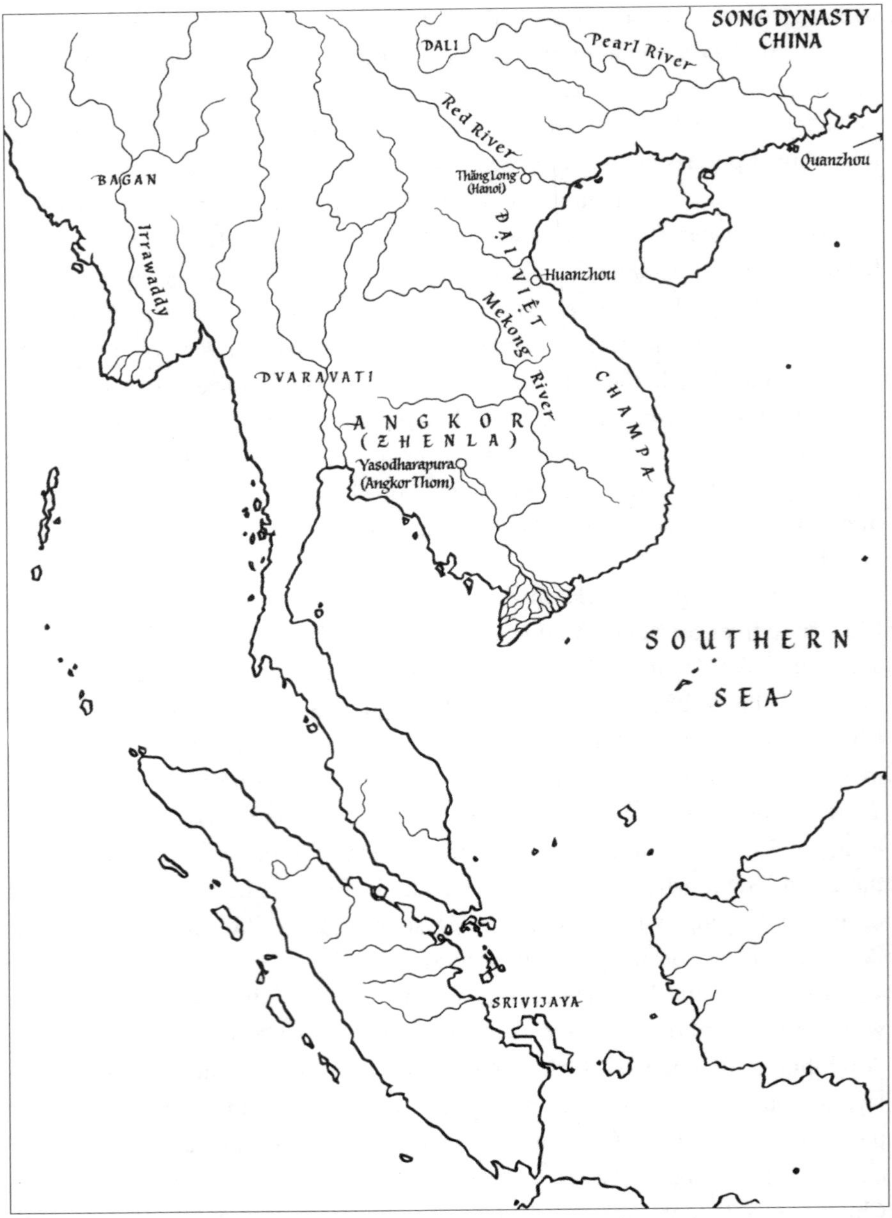

Map 2. Angkor/Zhenla during the Song dynasty (960–1279)

8

Perceptions of Angkor during the Southern Song

In 1127 the Jurchens of northeast Asia, the precursors of the Manchus who ruled China in late imperial times, ended a period of uneasy coexistence with the Song court, and occupied the Song capital Kaifeng.[1] Thus ended the period of Song rule known as the Northern Song. The Song court fled south and eventually settled in the city of Hangzhou, then called Lin'an, on the coast of southeastern China. In this impressive city they established the capital of the Southern Song (1127–1279).[2]

During the Southern Song, Hangzhou was not only home to the Song court, but also a vibrant center of domestic and foreign trade, one of several bustling port cities in southeast and south China. The city remained a trading center even after it was captured in 1276 by troops loyal to the Mongol emperor Kublai Khan. It was greatly admired by foreign visitors such as Marco Polo, who visited it in Kublai Khan's time and described it in glowing terms in his *Travels*.[3]

During the Southern Song, unofficial Chinese sources resumed reporting on Zhenla. Subsequently, during the Mongol Yuan dynasty (1271–1368), official Chinese historians and encyclopedists provided further information about Zhenla as it was perceived to be during the Southern Song.

The principal unofficial sources on Zhenla as it was during the Southern Song were twelfth- and thirteenth-century gazetteers by scholar-officials who spent time in or near the city ports of southeast China. Official sources consisted of the standard history *Song shi* [*The History of the Song Dynasty*] (1345) and the huge compilation of Song court documents, *Song hui yao jigao* [*A Draft Edition of the Essential Documents and Regulations of the Song Dynasty*] (finally published in 1936), as well as two more encyclopedias, *Tong zhi* [*A Comprehensive Treatise on Institutions*] (1161) and *Wenxian tongkao* [*A Comprehensive Study of Institutions on the Basis of Authoritative Documents*] (1319).

The three-century "freeze" in Zhenla's relations with China

Before considering these sources in detail, we should return to the questions raised in the last chapter. Why did Chinese accounts of Zhenla dwindle after the seventh century, to the point where there were scarcely any Chinese references to Zhenla at all from the ninth to the late eleventh century? And why was there apparently no tribute from Zhenla to China from the early ninth to the early twelfth century?

There are several possible answers to these questions. A leading Chinese historian of Cambodia, Chen Xiansi, devotes a whole section of his history to analyzing what he calls this "frozen" period in relations between China and Zhenla. He believes there were two principal reasons for the "freeze."[4] The first was the unsettled state of China during the period concerned. This lasted, Chen argues, from the late Tang dynasty, which never fully regained its authority after the devastating An Lushan rebellion in 755, through the unstable Five Dynasties and Ten Kingdoms period that came after the Tang, to the end of the Northern Song, during which time the Song court was preoccupied with retaining power in the face of Jurchen pressure.[5] Chen's argument has particular merit for the pre-Song period, since Chinese official records show a steep decline in tribute missions from southern states, followed by their almost complete cessation during the period 760 to 960.[6] It is reasonable to believe that a major reason for this was the political unrest affecting China during that time.

The second cause of the "freeze" in China's relations with Zhenla, in Chen's view, was the need for the rulers of Angkor to consolidate their power and put a priority on establishing good working relations with their immediate neighbors. Only when these neighbors seriously threatened them, Chen argues, did the kings of Angkor seek to improve relations with the Chinese.[7]

Chen also argues that as an inland state Zhenla no longer played the pivotal maritime role taken earlier by Funan, a role diminished by the rise of the Sumatra-based polity Srivijaya.[8] Others agree that in the sixth and seventh centuries Funan's maritime role grew less important, although not so much because of the rise of Srivijaya—notable as that was—but for other reasons, among them improved seagoing skills, including the use of monsoon winds, that enabled sailors to bypass it.[9]

With its growing importance, Srivijaya became the most significant of the Song's southern trading partners, and the only one among them to maintain continuous contact with the Song court. This it did through a series of tribute missions sent between 960, when the Song dynasty was established, and 1178, when Srivijaya's importance for China's maritime economy began to wane.[10] By the early eleventh century the Song dynasty's leading trading partners to the south and southwest were Srivijaya, Java, Dashi (the Arabs), and Chola (southern India). The Song court afforded the status of first-class trading state to all of these.[11] Zhenla was not among them.

There can be little doubt that as a polity or polities based inland, Funan's successor Zhenla was less engaged in maritime trade than Funan itself had been. Several historians have emphasized this point. Vickery suggests that the centers that developed in Cambodia between the seventh and thirteenth century were "prototypical inland agrarian state[s]" in which foreign trade seems to have played only a limited role. He also notes that in the Angkor region after the 870s "the dispersal of inscriptions indicates almost total disinterest in southern Cambodia and its coast, and concentration on exploitation of land and labour."[12]

Robert Wicks writes that while Angkor between the ninth and twelfth centuries engaged in some regional trade, its economy was largely agricultural and—unusually for the region—based on barter rather than monetary transactions, with taxes paid in kind.[13] Victor Lieberman notes that "there is no indication that maritime commerce was central to patronage structures [in Angkor] or to the general economy, certainly not in the critical period 950–1150."[14] Even Kenneth Hall, while arguing that Suryavarman I (r. 1002–1049) sought to promote Angkor's commercial expansion, acknowledges that "Khmer rulers were primarily committed to developing their agrarian base around Angkor."[15]

Another, less tangible factor may have been the growing pride of pre-Angkorian and Angkorian kings, whose sense of their own importance and the cosmic significance of their realm may have deterred them from paying homage to another imperial power. An early example of these increasingly proud kings may have been Jayavarman I (r. ?657–681), who as we saw in the last chapter apparently declined to send a single tribute mission to China during his twenty-odd-year reign.[16]

Of the factors mentioned here, two especially—the turmoil and uncertainty of China in transition, and the low priority given to foreign trade in Zhenla's inland agrarian economy, at least until the twelfth century—offer the most persuasive explanation for the apparent lack of Chinese interest in Zhenla from the seventh to the eleventh century, and for the lapse in formal relations between Zhenla and China from the early ninth to the late eleventh century.[17]

This lack of interest is evident in the fact that in their records of this "frozen" period none of the official Chinese sources even mentions Zhenla. The two historical works *Song shi* and *Song hui yao jigao* do refer to Zhenla, but only with respect to events from 1062 onwards, while *Tong zhi* and *Wenxian tongkao* add little to what these two historical sources provide, and record nothing new relating to Zhenla before the 1060s.

Three Song gazetteers

When discussing Chinese sources on Zhenla in later Song times, it is best to start with the unofficial sources, since these come before the official sources chronologically, and in one instance (Zhao Rugua's *Zhu fan zhi*) relate a sequence of events in Zhenla-Champa relations, the destruction of Champa by Zhenla at the end of the twelfth century, to which *Song shi*, the official history of the Song, also alludes.

The principal unofficial sources are three gazetteers written during the twelfth and early thirteenth centuries by the scholar-officials Fan Chengda, Zhou Qufei, and Zhao Rugua. These three works were written against the backdrop of major changes in China, particularly in the economic sphere.[18] One aspect of these changes was an increase in both domestic and foreign trade. From the late eleventh century on, the Song court relaxed official controls on foreign trade, a move that encouraged the growth of southern port cities, including not only Hangzhou, but also Mingzhou (present-day Ningbo), Wenzhou, Quanzhou, and the city of Guangzhou. Here and elsewhere, maritime trade, until this point the domain of foreign shippers, was increasingly undertaken by seagoing Chinese merchants, deploying large trading ships and steering with magnetic compasses.[19]

These developments were accompanied by new trends in Chinese society and culture. In the literary domain these included the emergence of two new forms of writing: travel diaries and gazetteers (*zhi*, "treatises").[20] While both forms of writing are principally concerned with describing locations within China, three gazetteers by Fan Chengda, Zhou Qufei, and Zhao Rugua also include material on foreign places, including Zhenla. The works in question are Fan's *Guihai yuheng zhi*, Zhou's *Lingwai daida*, and Zhao's *Zhu fan zhi*.[21]

Fan Chengda's *Cinnamon Sea*

The author of the first of these works, Fan Chengda, is principally remembered today as one of the great masters of Southern Song poetry. But he also wrote three travel diaries and the gazetteer *Guihai yuheng zhi* [*A Treatise of the Supervisor and Guardian of the Cinnamon Sea*].[22] The *Guihai* in the title of his gazetteer, meaning "Cinnamon Sea," is a name for the Southern Sea, since fragrant forests of cinnamon or cassia (*gui* can mean either) had a long association with the far southwest of China and the sea beyond it. Much earlier, in the sixth-century literary anthology *Wen xuan*, the respected commentator Li Shan noted that "there are cinnamon trees by the Southern Sea, so it is called Guihai."

Fan Chengda was brought up in Suzhou near the southeastern coast of China. He served as an official in various central and local posts, and also as an envoy to the Song's foes the Jurchen.[23] He wrote *Guihai yuheng zhi* after a distant posting in 1173 to present-day Guangxi in southern China, and probably completed it by 1175. Fan was "deeply attached" to the Guangxi region, at that time a remote spot inhabited mainly by tribal peoples, and it is the main subject of his gazetteer. But the gazetteer also briefly considers places farther afield, including Zhenla.[24]

In his gazetteer Fan makes three references to Zhenla. The first is in a passage on lign-aloes, the aromatic wood encountered much earlier in the *Liang shu* description of Funan. It is not surprising that Fan devotes some attention to this product. By Song times, it featured largely among the aromatic substances that had become the most valuable and sought-after commodities imported into China.[25]

Fan starts by describing the varieties of lign-aloes available from southern states, then goes on:[26]

> Personages in China bring this aromatic substance only from Champa, Zhenla, and so on, using ships from Guangzhou.[27] In recent years they have also treated with respect [the type of] this aromatic substance that comes from Dingliumei. I have tried it, but it is not as good as even the medium- or poor-quality products from Hainan. When it is brought by ship it is often musty smelling and strong, and when it is not so very musty its smell is short lived, with a woodiness to it, and the last of it to be burned is inevitably charred.

Dingliumei, also called Dengloumei and Dengliumei, seems to have been in the upper Malay Peninsula.[28] Fan's second reference is a comment found only in *Wenxian tongkao*.[29] The comment suggests that at one point Zhenla may have controled the Champa coastal city called Vijaya. It reads:

> Xinzhou [Vijaya?] was once Zhenla territory but was taken in an aggressive attack.

The later gazetteers *Zhu fan zhi* describes Xinzhou, which means New City, as the capital of Champa, and *Zhu fan zhi*'s modern editor Yang Bowen identifies New City with Foshi, citing a *Song shi* record of a "new" king of Champa taking power in Foshi in 990. Following Coedès, Foshi is usually taken to refer to Vijaya, the coastal Champa city or entity mentioned in local twelfth- and thirteenth-century inscriptions, and customarily located in Bình Định province of present-day Vietnam.[30]

If Zhenla controlled Vijaya at some time before Fan wrote this in the 1170s it would add a significant piece to the mosaic of the growing Zhenla realm. It is unclear from Fan's short comment when and how Zhenla's authority stretched as far as east as Vijaya, if that was indeed the identity of New City, and when it lost control of it. Its writ in Vijaya clearly preceded the conflicts between Champa and Zhenla in the late twelfth century, which we shall come to shortly. Fan wrote his comment in the course of an account of Annan, by this time the independent Vietnamese state of Đại Việt, and this would suggest that the Vietnamese carried out the attack. But Taylor and Coedès both write of a king of Champa occupying Vijaya at the end of the tenth century, so if the takeover of New City/Vijaya occurred soon after 990, when its new king assumed power, the aggressors may have been from Champa.[31]

Finally, a third passage in Fan's gazetteer gives us a vague sense of Zhenla's location. Again, the passage is not included in the received text, but is found quoted in the diary of a later Chinese scholar.[32] It reads:

> After crossing a river from Jiaozhi you get to Champa state, which was Linyi during the Han dynasty. On the south bank of the river are the mountains with Ma Yuan's bronze pillars on them. To the east and west is the Great Sea. Champa is separated from Zhenla by a river. Beyond another river is a place called Dengloumei. The Great Sea [also] lies to the west of these few states, where it goes by the name of Ceylon [Xilan] and forms the western frontier of Jiaozhi, Dali, and Tufan [Turfan]. To the south it is next to a great ocean, at the entrance to which is the state of Ceylon. To its west are the five Indias [north, south, east, west, and central India].[33]

Later in this passage, by the way, Fan notes that

> Sanfoqi [Srivijaya] is regarded as the largest of the states in the great southern ocean, the trading center for the various foreigners' valuable goods.[34]

This comment, which Zhou Qufei also makes, tends to confirm Srivijaya's primacy at that time among the maritime trading states of the region.[35]

Fan's impressionistic geography betrays his lack of firsthand knowledge of the places he mentions. The Great Sea or South China Sea would have been to the east—not the west—of Champa. The river dividing Champa from Zhenla was presumably the Mekong, but the river dividing Zhenla from Dengloumei/Dingliumei could have been one of several, and the ocean called Ceylon—no doubt the Bay of Bengal—could not have been a frontier for Jiaozhi, Dali, and Turfan in any realistic sense.

Zhou Qufei's *Beyond the Five Mountains*

The second of the three gazetteers, Zhou Qufei's *Lingwai daida* [*Representative Responses to Questions about Regions Beyond Wuling* {*the Five Mountains of South China*}], is also partly about Guangxi, but includes references to distant places as well. Zhou Qufei seems to have come originally from Yongjia county near Wenzhou, one of the port cities of southeast China.[36] Yongjia was the home county of Zhou Daguan, the Yuan chronicler of Angkor,[37] and while there is no record of the two men coming from the same family, the fact that they shared the same surname suggests they could have done.

Zhou Qufei spent about six years of his adult life as a junior official in Guangxi, some of the time under Fan Chengda, and drew on his experiences there to write *Lingwai daida*, which he completed in 1178.[38] The book was subsequently lost, but later retrieved from the massive Ming dynasty collection *Yongle dadian* [*Great Compendium of the Yongle Era* {1403–1424}], completed in 1407. Since then it has survived intact.[39]

In its present form *Lingwai daida* consists of 294 entries in ten chapters on places, countries, peoples, local customs, products, plants, animals, insects, and strange phenomena. There is a short entry specifically on Zhenla, one of twenty-four entries on foreign states and peoples. The entry reads:[40]

> The state of Zhenla is far from Champa and near all the various foreigners. Next to it are the states of Wali, Xipeng, Sanbo, Malan, Dengliumei, and Dilata, for which Zhenla serves as the trading center, abutting on Champa to the north.[41] Of the well-known aromatic substances it produces the most, though the aromatic substances that Dengliumei produces are of the rarest quality that none of the other foreign states match.
>
> The incantations of sacred texts by the country's Buddhist monks and holy men are highly spiritual. Monks in yellow robes live with their wives; monks wearing red dwell in monasteries, where they follow strict monastic rules. The holy men use the leaves of trees as clothing.
>
> When you are in the country and look up at one corner of the sky, there are often a few scar-like marks there. People there say that in time gone by this was a place that Nüwa [the mythical Chinese figure who repaired the collapsing sky] never reached.
>
> In the second year of the Xuanhe reign period of Emperor Huizong [1120] envoys were sent with tribute.

None of the states listed as being next to Zhenla can be identified with any degree of certainty. As we have seen, Dengliumei (mentioned in Fan Chengda's *Treatise*) was probably in the north of the Malay Peninsula. Wali could have been in the Karen region of present-day Myanmar, or else on the northwest coast of the Kra isthmus.[42]

With regard to Xiping, Sanbo, Dilata, and Malan,[43] *Lingwai daida*'s modern editor Yang Wuquan cites various sources to suggest that Xipeng may have been located at Suphan in the center of present-day Thailand; Sanbo (also pronounced Sanpo) may have been the state called Canban, perhaps Sambor in Kratié province of present-day Cambodia; Dilata may have been at Trat in the southeast of present-day Thailand; and Malan may have been at Pailin in the west of present-day Cambodia. Malan is probably the place Zhou Daguan refers to as Moliang, known in inscriptions as Malyan. Vickery locates it in present-day Battambang rather than Pailin.[44] Wali and Xipeng are mentioned later in *Zhu fan zhi*, which appears to mention Sanbo and Malan too, though by slightly different names.[45]

"The incantations of sacred texts" translates the more literal "incantations of the [scriptures of the] dharma (*zhou fa*)."[46] For *daoshi* (masters of the Way) I have again used the term "holy men." By the Song dynasty Chinese readers might have taken *daoshi* to refer to Daoists; but there is no evidence of Chinese Daoism ever reaching Cambodia, and (as earlier in *Sui shu* and later in Zhou Daguan) the reference to masters of the Way may be to Hindu holy men. "Highly spiritual" (*ling shen*) suggests the incantations had magical powers.[47] The mention of married monks is rare. Zhou Daguan mentions monks dressed in yellow, but neither he nor anyone else in Chinese sources describes yellow-clad monks as being married.[48]

Nüwa was a familiar figure in Chinese creation myths. According to old beliefs, she restored order by repairing the sky after it collapsed and brought chaos to the world. By Southern Song times she was apparently regarded as a historical rather than a mythical figure. Her story is unlikely to have reached Zhenla unless by means of Chinese merchants or settlers there; this being the case, Zhou Qufei's allusion to "people there" talking about her may be the first, albeit indirect, reference to Chinese in the Kingdom of Angkor.[49]

Zhou Qufei's other references to Zhenla include the telling comment that Champa and Zhenla were "the trading centers for Wali and the various states", located "near the south of the Jiaozhi sea, not even half as far away as the state of Srivijaya [Sanfoqi] and Java [Shepo]."[50] This is the first reference in a Song source to Zhenla being a trading center, and is complemented by later descriptions of Zhenla's trade by Zhao Rugua and Zhou Daguan. By Zhou Qufei's time, then, Zhenla was evidently developing an interest in trade, including foreign trade. The reasons for this are not entirely clear. A significant factor must have been Angkor's markedly increased influence and geographical extent, which according to Zhao Rugua, writing in the 1220s, had grown to encompass southern Champa and coastal locations on the Kra isthmus, as well as Lopburi in present-day Thailand and Pagan in Myanmar.[51]

Zhou Qufei also describes Zhenla as being the best source of lign-aloes and as having palanquins (*jianyu*). On palanquins he writes:[52]

> From Annan to Champa and Zhenla, they all have palanquins. They make the palanquin with cloth, putting it together like a cloth sack and lifting it with a long pole. A long awning is spread above it, decorated with leaves and the scales of fish. It is like the top of a sedan chair in China. Two people lift up the long pole and two more walk along holding it up.[53]

Palanquins shown on a frieze on the Bayon temple, the temple at the centre of Angkor Thom mostly built by Jayavarman VII (r. 111–c.1218). Zhou Qufei and Zhou Daguan both mention the use of palanquins in Zhenla.

Source: Peter Harris, 17-03-2005

In addition Zhou Qufei relates that in 1173—five years before he completed *Lingwai daida*—a Chinese official introduced cavalry to Champa, enabling it to achieve victory in a conflict with Zhenla. Here is the passage, from the section of Zhou's work on Champa:[54]

> Champa . . . abuts on Zhenla to its south. It is a vassal of Jiaozhi [by this time under Vietnamese rule] and a constant enemy of Zhenla. In the Guiyi year of the Qiandao reign period [1173], a Min [Fujian] man was selected to be a senior military official and gained the position of Military Director-in-Chief of the Jiyang Army [on Hainan Island].[55] While traveling by sea, the official was carried by a high wind to Champa. There he saw Champa and Zhenla fighting each other on elephants, with neither side securing a clear victory.

He then explained to the king [of Champa] the advantage of fighting with cavalry, and taught him how to shoot a crossbow while riding on horseback. The Champa king was delighted and arranged for a ship to escort the officer back to Jiyang, taking plenty of resources with him. With these several dozen horses were purchased and used in battle to defeat the enemy [Zhenla].

The following year [a delegation from Champa] came again with a very large number of men, but the Jiyang Army turned them away, not having any more horses, so they went round to Qiongguan [on another part of Hainan Island]. But Qiongguan would not receive them, so they went home angry and did not return.[56]

Zhou Qufei's account of elephants being used by Zhenla in a battle with Champa was one among many Chinese reports of elephants in Funan and Zhenla. These elephants served as tribute to China, as mounts for the king and his hunters, and to carry soldiers in battle. Their ivory was also prized. Shown here is a lightly caparisoned stone elephant at East Mebon, the Angkor temple built by Rājendravarman II (r. 944–968).

Source: Peter Harris, 17-03-2005

Finally, Zhou Qufei writes that "according to tradition the Buddha appeared in the world in the city of Zhanlipo in the state of Zhenla."[57] He relates that the Buddha was a woman with miraculous powers who gave birth to a son and cast him into the sea as a gift to the king of the dragons. Earlier the king had rescued her from a storm at sea, one that he had stirred up himself, securing a promise from her to give him a son before conveying her ship to land at Zhanlipo.[58]

Zhanlipo seems to be Zhenlifu, which is mentioned in a passage in *Wenxian tongkao* (reproduced in *Song shi*) as a dependency of Zhenla in the southwestern corner of Zhenla. Rockhill and Hirth locate Zhenlifu/Zhanlipo in Chanthaburi, southwest of Battambang in present-day Thailand.[59] The Buddha referred to here may have been the Bodhisattva of compassion Avalokiteśvara, given that this Bodhisattva assumes a female form, Guanyin, in China.[60] But why did she appear in a dependency of Zhenla? Could this story of a tryst between a dragon king and a woman with magic powers conceivably be a distorted echo of the Cambodian foundation story of a tryst between a brahmin and a naga king's daughter?[61]

Zhao Rugua's *Various Foreigners*

The third of the three main gazetteers, and the most informative about Zhenla, is Zhao Rugua's *Zhu fan zhi* [*A Treatise on the Various Foreigners*]. Zhao Rugua—or Zhao Rukuo, according to an alternative pronunciation of his name—was a scholar-official descended from the second Song emperor, Taizong (r. 976–997, not to be confused with the second emperor of the Tang, also called Taizong).[62] He held a series of official posts, serving for some time from 1225 on as Supervisor of Maritime Trade in the bustling, cosmopolitan port city of Quanzhou in southeastern China. This important role would have given him rare access to knowledge and information about southern states. It seems that he completed his gazetteer sometime between his posting in Quanzhou and his death in 1231 near Taizhou, a small port not far north of Quanzhou.[63]

Like *Guihai yuheng zhi*, Zhao Rugua's *Zhu fan zhi* was included in the 1407 Ming compendium *Yongle dadian*, after which it became a leading source of information about foreigners for Chinese readers.[64] As noted by Rockhill and Hirth, who published a well-annotated English translation of the work in 1911, Zhao's book consists partly of material taken from maritime traders, and partly of texts copied from other sources. These include the standard histories and *Guihai yuheng zhi*, which Zhao repeats more or less verbatim in several places.[65]

Zhao Rugua devotes a relatively long passage to Zhenla. He also includes a number of short passages on local products from Zhenla and other southern states. Zhao's long passage on Zhenla is the last substantial account of Angkor before Zhou Daguan's, and includes some revealing details of life in twelfth-century Zhenla. So it is worth citing here in full, even though some of it reproduces material in earlier sources:[66]

> Zhenla is adjacent to southern Champa. To the east it extends to the sea, to the west it reaches Pugan [Pagan], and to the south it stretches to Jialuoxi [on the Kra Isthmus?]. Traveling by ship from Quanzhou you can get there with a favorable wind in a little more than a month. Its territory is roughly

seven thousand or so li in area, and its capital is called Luwu [Angkor?].[67] The weather is never cold.

For the most part the king's attire is the same as that of Champa, but when he goes to and from his palace his ceremonial entourage is greater. He rides in a carriage drawn by a pair of horses or by oxen.

Its districts and towns are also the same as Champa's.[68] The houses of officials and ordinary people are all made of woven bamboo with thatched roofs. Only the king of the state has a residence made out of hewn stone, with a magnificent granite lotus pool crossed by a golden bridge some thirty poles or so long, and imposing palace buildings of the greatest beauty.[69]

The king sits on a couch made of aromatic woods and precious stones, with a bejeweled screen spread out on poles of carved wood and supporting walls of ivory. When officials come to pay their respects to the king, they first touch their heads to the ground three times before the steps to the throne, then mount the steps and kneel, clasping their arms with both hands, and sit in a semi-circle around him. When their discussion of the affairs of government is over, they kneel again, bow deeply and leave.

On a bronze terrace in the southwest corner [of the city] are arrayed twenty-four bronze towers guarded by eight bronze elephants, each of them weighing four thousand catties.

There are about two hundred thousand elephants for use in battle, and many horses, though they are small in size. They are strict in their devotion to the Buddha, and every day some three hundred local women dance and present food to the Buddha. They are called *a'nan*, that is, dancing girls.[70]

If people engage in lewd and depraved behavior it is not the custom to question it. Those committing theft are punished by having a hand or foot cut off or their chest branded.[71]

The incantations of sacred texts by the country's Buddhist monks and holy men are highly spiritual. Monks in yellow robes have wives; monks wearing red dwell in monasteries, where they follow strict monastic rules. The holy men use the leaves of trees as clothing. They have a god called Bhadreśvara [Poduoli], which they worship with sacrifices most reverently. They regard their right hand as clean and their left hand as unclean. They combine rice with a broth of mixed meats, then take it and eat it with their right hand.

The soil there is fertile. The fields are not divided up—people plough and sow as much as their strength allows. The price of rice and grain is low and fair; with an ounce of lead you can buy two pecks of rice.[72] The local products are ivory, three kinds of lign-aloes—fine lign-aloes of the types called *zan* and *su*, and coarse ripe lign-aloes—beeswax, kingfisher feathers, which Zhenla has the most of, dammar, gourd dammar [that is, gourds filled with dammar resin], local oil, ginger peel, benzoin, sappan wood, raw silk, cotton cloth, and so on.[73] The local merchants trade in exchange for things like gold and silver, porcelain ware, fine embroidery, parasols, leather drums, wine, sugar, and pickled meat or fish.

Dengliumei, Bosilan, Luohu, Sanluo, Zhenlifu, Maluowen, Lüyang, Tunlifu, Pugan [Pagan], Wali, Xipeng, Duhuai, and Xunfan are all dependent states of Zhenla.

Formerly this state had good neighborly relations with Champa, sending tribute of gold every year. Then on the fifteenth day of the fifth month of the fourth year of the Chunxi reign period [1177], the ruler of Champa carried out a surprise attack with a naval force on the state capital. He refused their petition for peace and put them to death. As a result [Zhenla] felt a great sense of grievance, and swore that it had to be avenged. In the *yimou* year of the Qingyuan reign period [1199], it carried out a great attack on Champa, imprisoned its ruler, killed his ministers and retainers, and came close to completely exterminating its people. Someone from Zhenla was put in place as the ruler, and now Champa is also a dependent state of Zhenla.

During the Wude reign period [618–626] of the Tang dynasty, Zhenla began having relations with China.[74] In the second year of the Xuanhe period [1120] of this dynasty, it sent an envoy with tribute. To the south the state is adjacent to Jialuoxi, a dependent state of Srivijaya [Sanfoqi].

The use of the name Luwu (Ləwk ŋut [P]) for the capital of Zhenla is potentially important but puzzling, since epigraphic evidence suggests that at the time Zhao wrote this in the late 1220s the capital of the Kingdom of Angkor was known to the Khmers as Yaśodharapura, after king Yaśovarman I (r. 889–c. 900). It has been argued that Luwu refers to Lovek, the place near Udong that later became the capital of Cambodia, but Pelliot rightly rejects this, pointing out that Lovek did not become the capital until the fifteenth century, and noting that when Zhao wrote *Zhu fan zhi* the capital was located at the place now known as Angkor (meaning Angkor Thom and the region around it). Instead Pelliot argues that Luwu derives from a dialect pronunciation of *nagara*, the Sanskrit word for "city" on which the name of Angkor is thought to be based. His line of reasoning, which he spells out in some detail, is fairly plausible, and I have followed it as the most likely explanation of the derivation of an otherwise obscure name. If accepted, it means that by the thirteenth century the name Angkor was already taking hold, at least among traders.[75]

The locations of some but not all the thirteen dependent states that Zhao Rugua mentions can be identified with varying degrees of certainty. One of them, Pugan, is clearly Pagan. This was firmly established as an independent polity by the time Zhao wrote *Zhu fan zhi*, so its status as a dependency on Zhenla must be in serious doubt.[76] Five others were mentioned earlier in *Lingwai daida*—Dengliumei, Wali, Xipeng, Sanluo, and Maluowen (assuming Zhao's names Sanluo and Maluowen are variants for Sanpo and Malan)—so we need not dwell on them here. The remaining seven are Bosilan, Luohu, Zhenlifu, Lüyang, Tunlifu, Duhuai and Xunfan.[77]

Considering each of these in turn: Bosilan, perhaps the same place as the Basili mentioned by Zhou Daguan, was somewhere to the south of Zhenla, though where is not clear. It is described in a passage in *Wenxian tongkao* (repeated in *Song shi*) as being adjacent to Zhenlifu to its southeast. In the same passage, Zhenlifu is described as being in the southwest corner of Zhenla.[78] Luohu was a Mon-Khmer polity with its capital at Lopburi on the lower Chao Raya River; it was destroyed by the northern state of Xian in 1349, resulting in the state of Xianluo, which remained the Chinese name for Siam, now Thailand, until the twentieth century.[79] Lüyang and Tunlifu have not been identified, though Lüyang's name (which means Green Ocean) suggests a location near the sea. Duhuai and Xunfan may have been on the Kra Isthmus. The two names could be taken to constitute a single name, but the translation here follows Yang Bowen, who takes the them to represent two separate names.[80] If this is the case, Duhuai may be a variant of Tuohuan, perhaps Dawei in present-day Myanmar, while Xunfan may conceivably have been located in today's Chumphon, on the Kra Isthmus not far from Dawei.[81]

Old and new in Zhao Rugua's account of Zhenla, also called Angkor

In his account of Zhenla Zhao Rugua mixes up old and new materials. The second paragraph about the king and his courtiers is taken from *Sui shu*, with minor changes. In the fifth paragraph, the description of the country's Buddhist monks and holy men comes from *Lingwai daida*, and the rest of that paragraph, with its accounts of Bhadreśvara, clean right hands and rice eaten with a meat broth, is taken largely unchanged from both *Sui shu* and *Lingwai daida*.

Most of the rest of the text appears to be new, in the sense that it does not appear to be based on earlier extant written sources. The name Angkor (if Pelliot is correct, and that is what Luwu alludes to), the account of the king's residence and palace buildings, the list of local products, the use of barter for trade, probably including foreign trade, and some of the polities listed as dependent states are all recorded for the first time. So is the account of a bronze terrace in the southwest corner of the city with twenty-four bronze towers guarded by eight bronze elephants.

Strikingly, this is the first reference in Chinese texts to the magnificent buildings that graced Angkor.[82] It is hard to know whether Zhao had a particular building in mind. One candidate is the sandstone structure now called Phnom Bakheng constructed by Yaśovarman I (r. 889–c. 900) as the state temple for his new city, Yaśodharapura, and located to the southwest of the walled city built by Jayavarman VII in the twelfth century.[83] Today Phnom Bakheng gives no evidence of terraces, towers, or elephants made with bronze. Nor were there any when an early European traveler, the Frenchman Henri Mouhot, described Phnom Bakheng after visiting it in 1860.[84] But the pyramid below the quincunx towers at the peak of Phnom Bakheng consists of five levels, each marked out with twelve small towers, and if the towers on, say, the top two levels were originally adorned with bronze, Phnom Bakheng might have been what inspired Zhao's description.

An aerial view from the west of the ninth-century Phnom Bakheng, showing the five levels with twelve towers (apart from those now lost) on each level. Could this have been the bronze terrace Zhao Rugua refers to?

Source: Claude Jacques with René Dumont, Angkor (Cologne: Könemann, 1999), 61

Zhao Rugua on Zhenla's deteriorating relations with Champa

In the final part of his account of Zhenla, Zhao records—in the only such account in a Chinese source—that before Zhenla and Champa became enemies in the last part of the twelfth century, Zhenla used to send Champa an annual tribute of gold. He then adds to *Lingwai daida*'s account of Zhenla's 1173 defeat by Cham cavalry a record of two more events in the conflict between these two states: a surprise attack carried out by Champa on Zhenla in 1177, and Zhenla's virtual eradication of Champa in 1199.[85]

Zhao's record of these significant events only partly resembles the accounts given by Western historians, including Maspero, Vickery, and Anne-Valérie Schweyer.[86] Maspero accepts the Chinese narrative with regard to 1171 and 1177, but goes on to recount that in 1190 the Angkor king Jayavarman VII (r. 1181–c. 1218) responded to Cham aggression by sending troops to take the Champa capital Vijaya.[87] By Maspero's account Champa was subsequently divided into two, then reunited under a king whom Jayavarman VII deposed in 1199, turning Champa into a Khmer province. Thirty years after that, Maspero concludes, the Khmers left Champa for good, preoccupied by "a new enemy, Siam."[88]

According to Vickery's account, the future Jayavarman VII was based in Vijaya in the 1160s and 1170s, and led Cham allies in raids on Angkor, which he conquered sometime in the decade before 1181.[89] The 1177 Champa attack on Angkor, Vickery argues, is not recorded in local inscriptions and has to be seen as "a bit of academic folklore."[90] After Jayavarman's conquest of Angkor, Vickery continues, the central and southern parts or polities of Champa were under his control, with one rebellion there apparently put down in 1190.[91]

Schweyer's account effectively picks up where Vickery leaves off. According to Schweyer, citing Cham inscriptions, after Jayavarman VII suppressed a rebellion in Vijaya in 1190 Champa consisted of several polities and was partly under Angkor's control. But an enemy of Jayavarman took Vijaya and remained there until 1203, despite repeated attacks on him by Jayavarman's army. War between part of Champa and Angkor then apparently persisted until around 1220, when Jayavarman VII's son Indravarman II became king of Angkor and the Khmer army withdrew from Champa territory.[92]

Zhao Rugua on Zhenla's luxury goods

The only other references to Zhenla are in the second part of *Zhu fan zhi*. They are concerned with local products. In addition to products already mentioned—ivory, different varieties of lign-aloes, beeswax, kingfisher feathers, benzoin, dammar, and sappan wood—Zhao Rugua describes Zhenla as a source of cardamom, used in China for medicinal purposes, and a substance called musk wood (*shexiangmu*), which is hard to identify.[93]

For his entries on lign-aloes and its varieties as well as on dammar, Zhao appears to have relied on an earlier work on aromatic fragrances. The work, *Xiang lu* [*A Record of Aromatic Substances*], was by the scholar Ye Tinggui (fl. 1120–1150). In it Ye mentions at least two other aromatic products from Zhenla that Zhao does not include. These were a yellow "gourd fragrance" made from the sap of a tree that locals smeared their bodies with, and a paste for the skin and hands made from Borneo camphor, musk, and other scents that Ye tell us was popular in Guangzhou. Ye's work highlights how much Southern Song consumers enjoyed these fragrant substances from Zhenla.[94]

This famous stone sculpture is often described as a portrait of the Angkor king Jayavarman VII (r. 1181–c.1218), though there is some disagreement about whether this identification is correct. According to *Zhu fan zhi*, Jayavarman VII was responsible for a savage attack on Champa in 1199, undertaken in reprisal for an earlier Champa attack on Angkor.

Source: Musée Guimet, Paris; www.guimet.fr/collections/asie-du-sud-est/jayavarman-vii, 2020

Apart from the three gazetteers by Fan, Zhou, and Zhao, there are occasional references to Zhenla in other Song sources. Of these, one is worth noting. This is an essay by the scholar-official Lou Yue (1137–1213) that includes mention of "ships of big merchants from Zhenla," showing that by his time, anyway, merchants from Zhenla were engaging in substantial maritime trade.[95] One other late Song or early Yuan source worth mentioning is the eclectic compilation *Yu hai* [*Sea of Jade*] by the scholar Wang Yinglin (1223–1296), who died the same year Zhou Daguan took up residence in Angkor. *Yu hai* gives an unsourced list of tribute missions from Funan and Zhenla which includes three from Funan in 270, 271, and 272 not recorded elsewhere.[96]

Glimpses of Zhenla in Song encyclopedias and histories

We turn now to official sources of information about Zhenla as it was in Song times. These are the encyclopedias *Tong zhi* (1161) and *Wenxian tongkao* (1319), and the historical works *Song shi* (1345) and *Song hui yao jigao* (1936). Apart from *Tong zhi*, these works were all composed after the end of the Song, but refer back to the Song period.

Neither of the two encyclopedias adds much to earlier accounts of Zhenla. Both reproduce almost unchanged the account of Zhenla in *Sui shu. Wenxian tongkao* adds passages about Water Zhenla and Land Zhenla (or Wendan) from the two Tang histories, *Jiu Tang shu* and *Xin Tang shu*, as well as remarks in *Zhu fan zhi* about Zhenla's size and location, terraces and towers, and conflict with Champa. It also records the tribute missions sent by Zhenla in 1117 and 1120, and a court award bestowed on the king of Zhenla in 1129.[97] These events are also recorded in *Song shi* and *Song hui yao jigao*, and will be considered shortly In addition *Wenxian tongkao* has an entry about the Zhenla dependency Zhenlifu, the entity—a very small one, according to *Wenxian tongkao*, consisting of only sixty or so villages—mentioned by Zhao Rugua. The entry is repeated with variations in *Song shi* and *Song hui yao jigao*.[98] The *Wenxian tongkao* entry on Zhenlifu is as follows:

> Zhenfuli is a dependent state of Zhenla. The state is in the southwest corner [of Zhenla], adjacent to Bosilan to its southeast and a neighbor of Dengliumei to the southwest. It controls sixty or so villages. In the sixth year of the Qingyuan reign period [1200], the Qingyuan prefecture said that as its king had been in place for twenty years, he was sending an envoy with a memorial to the throne, and tribute of two auspicious elephants and local products. The emperor commanded that the envoy be favorably treated and that as

> usual the state concerned be exempted from submitting further tribute, the journey by sea being such a long one.[99]

I have opted for the translation "auspicious elephants" for the term *rui xiang*, but it is an odd phrase and may be a copying error for the homophone "statues of the Buddha," used by *Liang shu* in its account of Funan.[100] The emperor Ningzong (r. 1195–1224)'s polite but dissuasive response to the gifts from Zhenfuli may reflect the Southern Song's nascent policy of trying to distinguish between trade and diplomacy.[101]

Although *Wenxian tongkao* was completed by 1319, more than two decades after the Yuan dynasty envoy Zhou Daguan visited Cambodia in 1296–1297, there is no sign that its author Ma Duanlin was aware of Zhou's trip or had any knowledge of Zhou's *Record* of his journey. Perhaps this shows that Zhou's book was not written, or more likely not made widely available, until sometime after his return to China.

The two main official accounts of Song history, *Song shi* [*The History of the Song Dynasty*] and *Song hui yao jigao* [*A Draft Edition of the Essential Documents and Regulations of the Song Dynasty*], give only limited consideration to Zhenla. But they contain revealing material.

Song shi, completed in 1345 by a group of Yuan dynasty scholars led by the Mongol senior minister Tuotuo or Toqto'a (1314–1356), is the longest of the standard histories, being forty percent larger than the next largest, *Ming shi* [*The History of the Ming Dynasty*].[102] *Song hui yao jigao* is even longer, being over a quarter of the length of the twenty-four standard histories combined. It is a collection of court documents compiled during successive reigns of Song emperors and was only finally published in 1936, having been partly lost during the Ming dynasty, then reconstructed by the scholar Xu Song (1781–1848) and others during the nineteenth century. A facsimile copy of their text was eventually published by the Beiping (Beijing) Library in 1936.[103]

In spite of their great length, the references to Zhenla in these two historical works are few and far between, and include nothing comparable to the accounts of Zhenla in *Sui shu* or even the Tang histories. This means, in effect, that the official Chinese chroniclers of Song affairs neglected to portray the Kingdom of Angkor during the time of its greatest power and glory. Why this may have been so we shall return to later.

Considered chronologically, the first reference to Zhenla in the two historical works is a short account in *Song hui yao jigao* of how in 1008 emperor Zhenzong (r. 998–1022) responded to what seems to have been a rare event involving Zhenla, one that highlighted its exotic remoteness.[104]

> In the Dazhongxiangfu reign period . . . in the ninth month of the first year [1008], Gaozhou [a county on the south coast of China] informed the emperor that two merchants from Zhenla had been driven away by Jiaozhou [the Vietnamese] and then lost their way at sea and arrived at the frontiers of the prefecture. It wanted to send them to do slave labor in the prefecture, but the emperor's response was, "With respect to people from distant places who submit themselves to us in their extremity, the prefecture in question should be ordered to give them clothes of the kind currently worn and strings of cash, and assign someone to escort them to the frontier, there to let them return to their own country."

Song shi's first reference to Zhenla relates to the year 1062. In that year, *Song shi* records, the Military Commissioner for the Guangxi region reported that Champa was preparing for war with Jiaozhi (the Vietnamese). The Commissioner mentioned Zhenla, which he called Zhanla, noting that it was peaceable but implying that it might have an interest in Champa winning the war.[105]

> Zhanla does not customarily engage in warfare, and often suffers aggression from Jiaozhi, which is its neighbor.

According to Taylor, Champa and Đại Việt did indeed go to war soon after, when in 1069 the Vietnamese king Lý Thánh Tông sent troops to capture the king of Champa, Rudravarman III, and razed his city Vijaya.[106] Zhenla/Zhanla's role in the war, if there was one, is not on record.

Both *Song shi* and *Song hui yao jigao* report that seven years later in 1076, the Chinese emperor, at that time Shenzong (r. 1067–1085), proclaimed that Champa and Zhenla (which *Song shi* again calls Zhanla) should carry out a joint attack on the Vietnamese. Shenzong no doubt envisaged the joint attack as part of the full-scale war that he was about to wage on Đại Việt, which took place in 1077–1079.[107] There is no Chinese record of Champa and Zhenla taking the action that Shenzong urged on them. But both his proclamation and a subsequent mention of gifts for the ruler of Zhenla, at that time King Harṣavarman III (r. c. 1066–1080), suggests that by the 1070s there was some form of communication between Angkor and the Song court.

Song hui yao jigao's account of the imperial proclamation is as follows:[108]

> In the Xining reign period [1068–1077] . . . on the second day of the second month of the ninth year [1076] the emperor issued the following command: "The two states of Champa and Zhenla, having long been encroached upon

> by Jiaozhi [the Vietnamese], should take advantage of the opportunity provided by the punitive attack on it that our royal army is now launching, and join forces to dispose of it completely. When peace is restored they will be endowed with high rank and large rewards. As we have often heard, their people are frequently taken prisoner by Jiaozhi, and we have ordered the Chief Attendant of the Bandit Suppression Commission to search these people out once he is in the country and have them sent home. With regard to the former territories of Champa, circumstances are such that it will be hard to return them there, so we should order them instead to come to court to enjoy our great benevolence . . ."

The emperor then commands that the two states be given medicines, matériel, and cash. *Song hui yao jigao* continues:[109]

> On the fourteenth day of the fourth month [of the same year, 1076], an imperial command was issued that gifts be variously conferred on the kings of Zhenla and Champa, and on the generals of Zhenla and their deputies. As the emperor was intent on punishing Jiaozhi, warships were sent to patrol the country to help suppress the rebels and make them submit.

The Bandit Suppression Commission was an ad hoc military force under the Song sent to suppress disorder in a particular area. Mention of warships here is unusual; it is not clear whether they were from Zhenla, Champa, or China.[110] The passage continues with a brief account of an envoy from Champa leading a twenty-one person tribute mission in that same year, and remarking that "the journey from Champa to [the capital of] Zhenla is estimated to take a month by water, that being the way to go, the journey to the [Zhenla] port being eighteen days."[111]

In another noteworthy passage, *Song hui yao jigao* goes on to record that two years later, in 1078, Zhenla and the Chinese court of emperor Shenzong were again in communication.[112]

> On the fifth day of the seventh month of the first year [1078] of the Yuanfeng reign period of the emperor Shenzong [r. 1067–1085], an imperial proclamation noted that in view of the rebellion by the southern foreigners in Jiao [the Vietnamese] and the recent order of the court to Liu Fu, officer in Guangzhou responsible for military recruitment, to take and present to Zhenla state an imperial command [ordering it to supply troops], it was acceptable to decide on recompense [for Zhenla], since the sea journey to and fro was understood to be arduous.

> Later, a memorial was submitted that the imperial command should not be taken [after all]. Initially the Visitors' Bureau reported that Liu Fu had presented the command to the ruler of Zhenla and overseen the submission of items of tribute from Zhenla to the capital [Kaifeng], in light of which the Bureau dared not send it away again. The Secretariat proposed that the Visitors' Bureau send it back the way it had come; it did not propose giving recompense, so ordered that the imperial command be disregarded.

During the Song dynasty the Secretariat was one of two predominant agencies in the central Chinese government, the other being the Bureau of Military Affairs. The Visitors' Bureau was a unit under the Secretariat charged with welcoming foreign envoys and arranging for them to have audiences with the emperor.[113] This convoluted entry in *Song hui yao jigao* is significant in two respects.

First, it refers to what seems to have been an abortive tribute mission sent from Zhenla to China in or around 1078, during the reign at Angkor of Harṣavarman III. This was nearly forty years before the tribute mission from Zhenla to China in 1117, a mission usually taken to mark the restoration of diplomatic relations between the two states after a break of over three centuries.[114] Second, it confirms an existing relationship between China and Zhenla, one in which the Chinese court adopted a familiar, even patronizing manner towards Zhenla, ordering it to raise troops against the Vietnamese, then turning away its tribute when it was no longer needed.

Taken together, the events of 1076–1078 recorded in *Song hui yao jigao*—the imperial Chinese proclamation in 1076, the imperial edict delivered to Zhenla in 1078, and Zhenla's unaccepted offer of tribute to the Chinese court in that year—suggest that by the final decades of the eleventh century the royal courts of Zhenla and China were in touch with one another again.

Song sources on Zhenla's resumption of tribute missions

Both *Song shi* and *Song hui yao jigao* go on to record three tribute missions from Zhenla, sent in 1117, 1120, and 1155. The mission sent in 1117 appears to have been the first successfully completed tribute mission from Zhenla in over three centuries. According to *Song shi* the mission consisted of fourteen people, and presented Emperor Huizong (r. 1101–1125) with various unnamed books, staying in the Chinese capital, still Kaifeng at this point, for three to four months (five months according to *Song hui yao jigao*).

The mission was led by someone named Xinzhumosengge, also called Jiumosengge, who is recorded as having the (Chinese) title Civilization-Promoting

Commandant, together with his deputy Mojunmingjisi, entitled Civilization-Pacifying Commandant.[115] *Song hui yao jigao* notes that when the mission first arrived it was dealt with by lower-ranking officials, since it was concerned only with trade. Presumably it was upgraded when its diplomatic intentions were established.[116]

A second mission in 1120 was led by an envoy whose name *Song shi* records as Molamotu, also entitled Commandant. During that mission Huizong "invested his king with a title," which is unnamed, doing the same for Champa and others. Commandant was a title bestowed on tribal chiefs, and together with the other title was evidently intended as a courtesy conveying the court's respect for the king of Zhenla's envoys and the king himself.[117]

Both *Song shi* and *Song hui yao jigao* note that in 1129 the emperor, by this time Gaozong (1127–1162) of the Southern Song, added to the king of Zhenla's privileges and named him distinguished Honorary Senior Minister, a very senior title.[118] Thereafter *Song shi* and *Song hui yao jigao* record only one other mission from Zhenla, in 1155, with no further record of Zhenla missions during the final century or so of Southern Song power. The 1155 mission is recorded as presenting the emperor Gaozong with tame elephants.[119]

Though they are not named, the Angkor kings responsible for the missions in 1117, 1120, and 1155 were Sūryavarman II (r. 1113–c. 1149), "one of the greatest Khmer rulers" (to quote Coe), renowned for commissioning Angkor Wat, and his successor Tribhuvanādityavarman (r. 1149–c. 1177).[120] These two rulers seem to have presided over a period of renewed warmth in relations between Angkor and the Song court, perhaps because of a shared hostility towards the Vietnamese. (According to Taylor, during his reign Sūryavarman II directed allied Khmer and Cham forces to attack the Vietnamese four times, though each time without success.)[121]

Elephants are cumbersome animals, hard to transport. As with all the elephant tribute from early Cambodia, we have no idea how the elephants sent by Tribhuvanādityavarman in 1155 were transmitted to the Chinese court, or how they were presented there. The final stage of their journey, at least, was doubtless undertaken by sea, since by 1155 Gaozong was ruling from the port city of Hangzhou. Whether the rest of their journey was undertaken by river or overland we do not know. Likewise, we can only guess at the elephants' appearance when they were finally presented to the emperor at court.

Fortunately, in his gazetteer *Guihai yuheng zhi* Fan Chengda has left us a vivid description of five elephants that the Vietnamese sent as a gift to Gaozong's successor Xiaozong (1163–1189) some years later, in 1173.[122] Fan's description is probably an eye-witness account, since during his 1173 posting to Guangxi he was responsible for the Song court's day-to-day dealings with the Vietnamese.[123]

Here is Fan's portrait of the elephants from the Vietnamese, conveying some idea, perhaps, of how the Cambodian elephants from Tribhuvanādityavarman looked when presented to the Chinese court in Hangzhou in 1155.[124]

> Caparisoned as ceremonial gifts, their elephants had a gold imperial *luowo* for those riding on them, the *luowo* being shaped like the frame of a saddle. Their tusks were encased in gold, and their foreheads adorned with colored thread interwoven with gold. Elephant hooks encased in gold and silver were attached to knotted sashes. Their foreheads were adorned with silver inlaid with gold, and they wore vermilion-bound rattan strips decked in gold and silver. On their feet were small bells enclosed in gold-plated bronze, and [their bodies] were clad in elephant bells attached to iron chains. The emperor's riding seat consisted of an embroidered mat of fine bamboo.
>
> The elephants as well as domestic yaks were garlanded with flowers. There was a vermilion ladder for getting to the imperial *luowo*, with sashes knotted in the shape of dragons' heads, and so on.[125]

Song sources on other issues, including Zhenla's other name Zhanla

In addition to its record of tribute missions, *Song shi* devotes several brief passages to Zhenla. One of them repeats the story about Cham cavalry being used to defeat Zhenla in *Lingwai daida*, dating the event to 1171 rather than 1173, and adds the account of Zhenla's revenge attack on Champa in 1199 given in *Zhu fan zhi*. This differs slightly from the account in *Zhu fan zhi* and reads as follows:[126]

> From the Qingyuan reign period [1195–1200] onwards, Zhenla carried out a great attack on Champa by way of revenge. It killed almost everyone, and imprisoned its ruler and took him back [to Zhenla]. Champa then perished, and all its territory became Zhenla's.

Two brief passages give accounts of Zhenla's location and customs. One passage reads:[127]

> In the ninth year [of the Xining reign period {1076}], [Champa] again sent an envoy. He said that it was a month's journey by sea from his country to Zhenla, and forty days, all by mountainous roads, to reach Jiaozhou to the northwest.

The other passage repeats in briefer form the information given in *Zhu fan zhi*, including its passing reference to a bronze terrace and towers.[128] Apart from this reference, *Song shi*'s authors show no sign of being aware of Angkor's many extraordinary architectural and engineering achievements, notably the construction of Angkor Thom with its Bayon temple, mostly built during the reign of Jayavarman VII (r. 1181–c. 1218). Nor do the *Song shu* authors betray any knowledge of Zhou Daguan's firsthand account of his visit to Zhenla in 1296–1297, despite the fact that this account may have preceded the completion of *Song shi* by decades.

One point of interest in the second passage, which is taken from *Zhu fan zhi* is an additional comment—not included in *Zhu fan zhi*—about Zhenla's name. This notes that "the state of Zhenla is also called Zhanla."[129] (As mentioned earlier, the name Zhanla was first used in *Song shi* in its record of a passing comment about Zhenla/ Zhanla by a southern Chinese official in 1062.) The Chinese word *zhan* means "occupy," but can also refer to Champa. *Song shi* does not discuss the etymology of Zhanla, and it is left to *Ming shi* [*The History of the Ming Dynasty*], completed centuries later in 1739, to offer an ex post facto explanation. As *Ming shi* puts it,[130]

> During the Qingyuan reign period of the Song dynasty [1195–1200] Zhenla wiped out Champa and took over its territory. Because of this it changed its name to Zhanla; during the Yuan dynasty it was still called Zhenla.

There must be some doubt about this explanation, given that it is provided some five centuries after the event in question, not to mention the fact that *Song shi* first refers to the name Zhanla in 1062. That said, as we noted in the introduction, the syllable *la* (lâp [K]) in Zhenla and Zhanla resembles *reap* (răp [K]), meaning "flattened" or "defeated" in Khmer. Since Zhan in Chinese can refer to Champa, it is thus plausible to construe Zhanla as meaning "Champa defeated", as *Ming shi* does.[131] Perhaps the name came into use in Zhenla after an earlier conflict with Champa, rather than the conflict in 1195–1200, or perhaps the etymology is simply mistaken.

The name Zhanla occurs again in Zhou Daguan's account of Angkor, as well as in *Yuan shi* [*The History of the Yuan Dynasty*] (1370), although both sources also use Zhenla. *Ming shi* reverts to the term Zhenla. In a first reference to the name Cambodia, Zhou Daguan notes that the country is also called Ganbozhi or Ganpuzhi.[132] *Ming shi* goes a step further, and refers to Jianpuzhai, the term for Cambodia still used by the Chinese today. To quote *Ming shi* again,[133]

> The state's name for itself was Ganbozhi [Kambuja], or later in error Ganpozhe. After the Wanli reign period [1573–1619] it changed again to Jianpuzhai [Cambodia].

This is the first reference in official Chinese sources to the name Jianpuzhai, although it appears earlier in Ming sources such as Zhang Xie's *Dongxi yangkao* (1617), as discussed in chapter ten. In the Hokkien dialect spoken in Quanzhou and elsewhere in southeastern China, the pronunciation of the *jian* in Jianpuzhai is *kan*, and the changes noted by *Ming shi* were probably changes in the Chinese written form of the name, rather than a change to the underlying name in Khmer.

A final passage in *Song hui yao jigao* describes the dependency Zhenlifu, whose people, it says, "love the Buddhist dharma." The passage is notable for its account of the sea journey, still, it seems, hazardous, from Zhenla to southern China. Here is the relevant part of the passage:[134]

> It is not known when Zhenlifu was first established as a state. It is in the southwest corner [of Zhenla], adjacent to Bosilan in the southeast, and a neighbor of Dengliumei in the southwest. It controls some sixty or so villages. Its products are ivory, rhino horn, native wax, lakawood, local oil, coarse incense, cardamom, black ebony, and so on.[135]
>
> Its ruler lives in a place like a Buddhist temple, with gold utensils everywhere in use, and curtains made of fine red Tang dynasty silk. The ruler wears white, which is honored, and is screened by fine white silk inlaid with gold. When his officials come to him in court, they bow their heads and bring their hands together to convey the utmost respect . . . A written script is in general use, with writing done with white chalk on writing material made of black bark. There are officials in charge of every village . . .
>
> Someone wanting to travel to China from this state goes by sea to Bosilan, which they reach after five days. Then they sail the Kunlun Sea past the state of Zhenla, and after several days arrive at the state of Bindalang [Phan Rang]. In a few more days they reach the frontier of Champa. Then for ten days they cross the ocean, with rocky outcrops called Wanli on their southeastern side, where the ocean is sometimes deep and sometimes shallow, with rapid water and numerous reefs. Seven or eight out of ten boats capsize and sink there, and there are absolutely no hilly shores [for shipwrecked sailors to make for]. Only then do they get to the frontier of Jiaozhi. A further five days brings them to Qin[zhou] and Lianzhou [on the south coast of China]. These estimates are all based there being favorable winds.[136]

Song hui yao jigao also records tribute missions sent by Zhenlifu in 1200, 1202, and 1205. The 1200 tribute, also described in *Wenxian tongkao* and *Song shi*, was sent to mark the twentieth anniversary of the rule of the king of Zhenlifu.[137]

Why official Song sources disregard Angkor's growing power and glory

The cursory records of Zhenla provided by *Song shi* and *Song hui yao jigao* reinforce the impression that except during wartime the Song court, more specifically the Southern Song court, had limited interest in Angkor and less knowledge. Judging from *Song shi*'s brief coverage of all the Southeast Asian states, this was also the case with respect to the rest of Southeast Asia. As Wang Gungwu puts it, "It is remarkable that the *Sung shih* [*Song shi*] has almost nothing to say about official relations between the Southern Sung and the Southeast Asian countries."[138]

Given the commercial ties between China and Southeast Asia during the Southern Song, this neglect is not easy to explain. Perhaps one factor was an elite culture that treated trade, including foreign trade, as an inferior activity, not worthy of serious scholar-officials' attention.[139] To the extent that this was so, it was clearly an elite worldview at odds with the popular culture of China's port cities and the outlook of authors such as Zhao Rugua.[140] Another consideration may have been changing attitudes towards foreign trade at the Song court, which resulted in a more laissez-faire approach to maritime trade beyond China's borders, and therefore more limited official interest in it.[141]

A further, more speculative explanation is that the temples and other buildings that helped make Angkor so noteworthy had limited appeal to an elite culture ill-attuned to such splendors. According to this line of argument, put forward among others by the Belgian Sinologist Simon Leys, buildings were not of primary concern in the imperial Chinese view of the world, immersed as it was in other, less tangible aspects of civilization.[142] As Leys puts it, in China "what strikes the educated visitor is the monumental absence of the past", since in the Chinese view of the world "eternity should not inhabit the building, it should inhabit the builder". Chinese culture and history, and their textual representations, were quintessential; buildings were ephemeral.

Whatever the explanation, this lack of appreciation of Angkor was partly remedied during the Yuan dynasty (1271–1368), when the envoy Zhou Daguan visited the Kingdom of Angkor and described what he saw there, including some of its buildings. Zhou's *Record* of his visit is unique, being the only substantial firsthand account of the daily life and customs of Angkor. Zhou and his *Record*—presented here in a revised format—are considered next.

9

Angkor brought to life: the *Record* of Zhou Daguan

This chapter reviews what is known about Zhou Daguan, as well as the textual history and main features of his *Zhenla fengtu ji* [*A Record of Zhenla: The Land and its People*].[1] It also includes an updated version of the annotated translation of Zhou's work that I published in 2007 under the title *A Record of Cambodia: The Land and its People*.[2] The text of the version given here is slightly rearranged to make its sequencing more coherent.

Most of what little we know about Zhou Daguan is gleaned from references to him in other works. He was from Yongjia county in the administrative region of Wenzhou, a major port in southeast China.[3] Yongjia was evidently the county that Zhou Qufei, author of the gazetteer *Lingwai daida*, came from, and given their common surname it is conceivable the two men were from the same family.

By his own account, Zhou accompanied an unnamed envoy sent on a mission to Champa and Zhenla in 1296 by the Chinese emperor, who at that time was Chengzong (Temür Khan, r. 1295–1307), the second emperor of the Mongol Yuan dynasty. Chengzong's decision to send the mission should be seen in the light of the repeated attacks on Champa and the Vietnamese carried out by his father Kublai Khan. Chengzong, a more cautious man than his father, seems to have been averse to further military action, and may have been trying to shore up diplomatic relations with Champa and Zhenla instead.[4]

The king of Angkor during Zhou's visit was Indravarman III (r. 1296?–1308).[5] Zhou spent just under a year in Cambodia, then returned to China, where he wrote *Zhenla fengtu ji* at some point between 1297 and 1312. The year 1312 can be established as an end date because, as Pelliot points out, a contemporary of Zhou's—a Hangzhou scholar named Wu Qiuyan who died in 1312—included three poems to Zhou in an anthology he compiled. He describes Zhou as an envoy to Zhenla and the author of a book about its customs.[6]

We do not know whether Zhou originally wrote his work as a report submitted to the emperor, but it is clear from later references to it that in due course it gained a wider circulation.[7] At the time of his visit to Angkor, Zhou was almost certainly still young, since nearly fifty years later in 1346 he wrote a preface to a miscellany by a fellow southerner called *Cheng Zhai zaji* [*Cheng Zhai's Miscellany*].[8]

According to Pelliot and Zhou's modern editor Xia Nai, the original text is lost.[9] The text we now have was transmitted in at least fifteen later works.[10] Of these four are relatively well known, and one is of critical importance. In chronological order these four works are:

1. The fourteenth-century scholar Tao Zongyi's anthology *Shuo fu* [*Environs of Stories*], a sizeable compilation completed in 1361, presumably soon after Zhou's death. Much of the original version of Tao's one hundred–chapter *Shuo fu* was later lost, but a seventeenth-century version included Zhou's text, apparently copied from (2).[11]
2. An anthology comparable to *Shuo fu*, *Gujin shuo hai* [*A Sea of Stories Old and New*], compiled by the scholar Lu Ji in 1544.[12] In *Gujin shuo hai*, Zhou's text is divided into forty sections with titles. This text is critically important because it is the earliest complete text that we have.[13]
3. A late sixteenth-century compilation called *Gujin yishi* [*Other Histories Old and New*] by a scholar called Wu Guan, in which Zhou's text appears largely the same as as it did in *Gujin shuo hai*.[14]
4. The lengthy Qing dynasty encyclopedia *Qin ding gujin tushu jicheng*, or *Tushu jicheng* for short [*A Collection of Illustrations and Books Old and New, Imperially Authorized*], compiled by Chen Menglei and others in 1726–1728. Pelliot believes the text of *Zhenla fengtu ji* in this work was copied from the seventeenth-century edition of *Shuo fu*.[15]

The extant text seems far from complete. The seventeenth-century bibliophile Qian Zeng (1629–c. 1699) made an entry about Zhou's text, referring to Zhou as Zhou Jianguan, in a catalogue he drew up of books in his library. He wrote:[16]

> Zhou Jianguan's *Record of Zhenla: The Land and its People*: one *juan*. From 1295 to 1297 [Zhou] Jianguan went as an envoy to Zhenla, after which he set out for home. He wrote a very detailed account of the land and its people and of the state's affairs. The work was copied from a properly collated Yuan text. The *Shuo fu* version has contradictions, errors, and omissions, with six- or seven-tenths missing, and does not really constitute a book.

It is not clear from this whether Qian Zeng knew the Yuan-era text firsthand, but his confident remarks about the *Shuo fu* version suggest that he did.

The first to translate Zhou Daguan into a European language was the French Sinologist Jean-Pierre Abel-Rémusat (1788–1832), who used the *Tushu jicheng* version.[17] In 1902 Paul Pelliot published an improved French version, largely on the basis of the *Gujin shuo hai* text. This was republished posthumously in 1951 with minor updates and detailed annotations on the first three chapters, which appear to be all Pelliot had completed before his death in 1945.[18] Pelliot's translation was twice translated into English before I published my own English translation from Chinese, based on Xia Nai's annotated Chinese edition, in 2007. Xia Nai's edition drew mainly on the text in *Gujin yishi*.[19] Another English translation from Chinese by Beling Uk and Solang Uk, published in 2016, was also based on the *Gujin yishi* text.

Given what Qian Zeng writes, the text of *Zhenla fengtu ji* as we now have it may be as disorganized as, say, Kang Tai's extant writings are. Some of the forty sections of the text certainly seem to be out of sequence, or unnecessarily divided up.

The following is a slightly updated version of my earlier translation of *Zhenla fengtu ji*, with the text rearranged and the number of its sections halved so that it reads sequentially. Rearranged in this way, Zhou's text describes Angkor's capital city and governance; its ruler, palace, officials, and annual events; its social outcasts, including its slaves; its practices relating to birth, coming of age, and death; its religious doctrines; its writing and language; its means of resolving disputes; its agriculture, local products, and trade; its transport; and a few curious facts. Following this sequence, the rearranged text is divided into twenty rather than forty sections. The headings of these twenty sections are drawn from the headings of the old, forty-section text (headings that I have retained, even though they may have been added by a later editor) with minor modifications.[20]

The twenty sections of the rearranged text, with the numbers of the forty old sections in brackets, are as follows:

1. General preface (General preface, 1, 18)
2. The city, prefectures, and villages (2, 33, 34)
3. The king and his palace (3, 40)
4. The women of the palace and others (6)
5. Officials and official dress (4, 3, 39)
6. The New Year and other special events (13)
7. Slaves and savages (9, 11)
8. Young girls (8)
9. Childbirth (7)
10. Illness and death (15, 16)
11. The three doctrines (5)
12. Writing and language (10, 12)
13. Settling disputes (14)

14. Cultivating the land (17)
15. Products (19, 29)
16. Trade (20, 21)
17. Flora and fauna (22, 23, 24, 25, 26, 27, 28)
18. Utensils (30)
19. Boats, palanquins, and carts (31, 32)
20. Taking gall, and other curious facts (35, 36, 37, 38)

Zhou's *Record*: a newly arranged version

Here, then, is the text of Zhou's *Record*, as rearranged along the lines described above.

1. General preface

The state of Zhenla, also called Zhanla, calls itself by the name of Ganbozhi [Cambodia]. The present sacred dynasty follows the scriptures of the Western foreigners and calls it Ganpuzhi, which sounds almost the same as Ganbozhi.[21]

If you set sail from Wenzhou and go south-southwest by the compass past Min, Guang and the various overseas ports, then cross the Seven Islands Sea and the Jiaozhi Sea, you come to Champa; and with the wind behind you, you will then get from Champa to Zhenpu [Vung Tao?] on the border [of Zhenla] in about fifteen days. Then from Zhenpu you go west southwest by the compass, cross the Kunlun Sea, and enter a river estuary.[22]

There are dozens of estuaries, but you can only enter the fourth one, as the rest are all so silted up that large boats cannot get through. As it is, there are tall bamboos, old trees, yellow sand, and white reeds as far as the eye can see. As you move swiftly along, it is not easy to make out where you are, and the sailors reckon it is a hard thing to do to find the right estuary.

From Zhenpu onwards, you skirt many tree-covered plains and forests.[23] To traverse the huge estuary of the long river, you go several hundred li from one end to the other.[24] Birds and animals make a riot of sound in the dark, shadowy forests with their old trees and tall bamboos. Halfway across the estuary you start to see spacious fields completely bare of trees. As far as the eye can see there is nothing but a thick, matted carpet of millet. Herds of wild oxen, countless thousands strong, gather there.[25] There are also slopes of bamboo stretching hundreds of *li* from end to end. Thorns grow in the joints of the bamboo, and the bamboo shoots have a most bitter taste. On all four sides there are high mountains.

From the mouth of the estuary you sail north. With a favorable current you reach a place called Zha'nan, a prefecture of the state, in about fifteen days. For the trip from Zha'nan you change on to a small boat. With a favorable current it takes about ten days or so to go through Halfway Village and Buddha Village, cross the Freshwater Sea [Tonlé Sap Lake], and reach a place called Ganpang, fifty li from the [capital] city.[26]

According to *Zhu fan zhi*, [Zhenla] is seven thousand li in breadth.[27] Going north, it is fifteen days by road to Champa, and to the southwest it is fifteen days' journey to Xianluo [Siam]. In the south it is ten days' journey to Panyu, and to the east there is the ocean.[28] It has long been a trading state.

The great mandate of heaven that the sacred dynasty has received includes everywhere within the four seas. Marshal Suodu set up a province in Champa and sent out a general and a senior commander who went to this state together. In the end they were seized and did not return. In the sixth month of the year *youwei* [1295] in the Yuanzhen reign period [1295–1296], the sacred Son of Heaven dispatched an envoy with an imperial edict and ordered me to accompany him.[29]

In the second month of the following year, the year *bingshen* [1296] in the Yuanzhen reign period, we left Mingzhou, and on the twentieth day of that month we set sail from the harbor at Wenzhou. On the fifteenth day of the third month, we reached Champa, having been set back by adverse winds mid-journey. We arrived [at our destination] at the beginning of the seventh month, in the autumn, and duly secured the submission of local officials. In the sixth month of the year *dingyou* [1297] in the Dade reign period [1297–1307], we turned our boat around, and by the twelfth day of the eighth month we were back at Siming [Mingzhou], anchored off the coast.[30]

Although I could not get to know the land, customs, and affairs of state in every particular, I could see enough to get a general sense of them.

2. The city, prefectures, and villages

The walls of the city are about twenty li in circumference.[31] There are five gateways, each of them with two gates, one in front of the other. There are two gateways facing east, and one gateway facing in each of the other directions. Around the outside of the walls there is a very large moat. This is spanned by big bridges carrying large roads into the city. On either side of every bridge there are fifty-four stone deities. They look like stone generals, huge and fierce-looking.

The five gateways are all alike. The parapets of the bridges are all made of stone and carved into the shape of snakes, each snake with nine heads.[32] The fifty-four deities are all pulling at the snake with their hands, and look as if they are preventing it from escaping. Above the gateways in the city wall there are five stone Buddha heads. Four of them face towards the four cardinal points, and one of them is placed in the middle. It is decorated with gold.[33] On either side of the gates the stones are carved into the shape of elephants.

The walls are all made of piled-up stones, and are about twenty-two feet high. The stones are very tightly packed and firm, so there are no weeds growing. There are no battlements either. Here and there sugar palms have been planted on and in the walls, and there are empty chambers at frequent intervals.

The inside of the walls is built as a slope, and is probably well over a hundred feet in width. The slopes all have big gates on them that shut at night and open early in the day. There are guards, too, though only dogs are not allowed in—and also criminals who have had their toes amputated.

The city walls form an exact square, with a stone tower on each of its four sides.[34]

In the center of the state is a gold tower [Bayon], flanked by twenty or so stone towers and a hundred or so stone chambers. To the east of it is a golden bridge flanked by two gold lions, one on the left and one on the right. Eight gold Buddhas are laid out in a row at the lowest level of stone chambers.[35]

About a li north of the gold tower there is a bronze tower [Baphuon].[36] It is even taller than the gold tower, and an exquisite sight. At the foot there are, again, several dozen stone chambers. About one li further north again there is the residence of the king. There is another gold tower [Phimeanakas] in his sleeping quarters.[37]

I suppose all this explains why from the start there have been merchant seamen who speak glowingly about "rich, noble Zhenla".

Half a li or so beyond the south gate is Stone Tower Mountain [Phnom Bakheng]. According to legend Lu Ban built it in a single night. Lu Ban's tomb [Angkor Wat] is about one li beyond the south gate. It is about ten li in circumference, and has several hundred stone chambers.[38]

Ten li east of the city wall lies the East Lake [East Mebon]. It is about a hundred li in circumference. In the center of it there is a stone tower with stone chambers. In the middle of the tower is a bronze reclining Buddha with water constantly flowing from its navel.[39]

Five li to the north of the city wall lies the North Lake [Jayatataka]. In the middle of it is a gold tower, square in shape, with several dozen stone chambers [Neak Pean]. A gold lion, a gold Buddha, a bronze elephant, a bronze cow, and a bronze horse—these are all there.[40]

The country has ninety or so prefectures. There are Zhenpu, Zha'nan, Bajian, Moliang, Baxue, Pumai, Zhigun, Mujinbo, Laigankeng, and Basili. I cannot record all the others. They all have their officials, and they all have walls consisting of wooden stockades.[41]

In every village there is a Buddhist temple or a pagoda. Where the population is quite dense there is normally an official called *maijie* who is responsible for the security of the village.[42] Resting places called *senmu*, like our posting houses, are normally found along the main roads. As a result of repeated military conflicts with the people of Xian [precursor of Siam], the land has been completely laid to waste.[43]

3. The king and his palace

I have heard that during the time of the previous king, he was so concerned to guard against unanticipated events that there were no chariot tracks out of his residence.

The new king [Indravarman III] is the old king's son-in-law.[44] Originally he was in charge of the soldiers. When his father-in-law died, the daughter secretly stole the gold sword and gave it to her husband.[45] The old king's own son was thus deprived of the succession. The son then planned a military uprising, but the new king found out about it, cut off his toes, and put him away in a dark room. The new king had a sacred piece of iron embedded in his body, so that if anything like a knife or an arrow touched him he could not be injured. With this to rely on he ventured out of his residence.

I stayed a year or so, and saw him come out four or five times. Each time he came out all his soldiers were gathered in front of him, with people bearing banners, musicians and drummers following behind him. One contingent was made up of three to five hundred women of the palace. They wore clothes with a floral design and flowers in their coiled-up hair, and carried huge candles, alight even though it was daylight. There were also women of the palace carrying gold and silver utensils from the palace and finely decorated instruments made in exotic and unusual styles, for what purpose I do not know. Palace women carrying lances and shields made up another contingent as the palace guard. Then there were carts drawn by goats, deer and horses, all of them decorated with gold.

All the ministers, officials, and royal relatives were in front, riding elephants. Their red parasols, too many to number, were visible in the distance.[46] Next came the king's wives and concubines and their servants, some in palanquins and carts, others on horses or elephants, with well over a hundred gold filigree parasols. Last came the king, standing on an elephant, the gold sword in his hand and the tusks of his elephant encased in gold. He had more than twenty white parasols decorated with gold filigree, their handles all made of gold. Surrounding him on all four sides were elephants in very large numbers, with soldiers to protect him as well.

If he was going to a place nearby, he just rode on a gold palanquin carried by palace women. He only used a gold cart, I heard, if the place he was visiting was quite a distance away.[47] Generally when leaving or returning to the palace he had to visit a small gold stupa, with a gold Buddha in front of it. Onlookers all had to kneel down and touch their head on the ground in a gesture called *sanba*.[48] If they did not, they were arrested by officers of protocol, who did not lightly let them off.

Twice a day the king sat in his outer palace and dealt with matters of government, and did so without anything fixed in writing.[49] All the ministers and ordinary people that wanted to see him had to sit in a row on the ground and wait for him. After a while you heard the muffled sound of music from the inner palace, while outside a conch shell blew to welcome him. In a moment you saw the delicate hands of two palace women rolling up a curtain to reveal the king, sword in hand, standing framed in a golden window. Ministers, officials, and people of lower rank all put their hands together in greeting and bowed to the ground. They were only allowed to lift their head when the sound of the conch stopped. The king then proceeded to sit down. I heard that where he sat there was a lion skin, a national treasure he had inherited.

When he had finished speaking about official matters, the king at once turned away. Two palace women lowered the curtain again, and everyone rose.

We can see from this that although this is a country of uncouth foreigners, they all know at first hand that they have a supreme ruler.[50]

The royal palace, officials' residences, and great houses all face east. The palace lies to the north of the gold tower [Bayon] with the gold bridge near the northern gateway. It is about five or six li in circumference. The tiles of the main building are made of lead; all the other tiles are made of yellow clay. The beams and pillars are huge, and are all carved and painted with images of the Buddha. The rooms are really quite grand-looking, and the long corridors and complicated walkways, the soaring structures that rise and fall, all give a considerable sense of size.

In the place for doing official business there is a gold window, with rectangular pillars to the left and right of the crosspieces. At the top of the window about forty or fifty mirrors are arranged on either side; the lower part is made of images of elephants. I have heard that there are many wonderful places in the inner palace, but it is very strictly out of bounds and I could not get to see them.

In the inner palace there is a gold tower [Phimeanakas], at the summit of which the king sleeps at night. The local people all say that in the tower lives a nine-headed snake spirit which is lord of the earth for the entire country. Every night it appears in the form of a woman, and the king first shares his bed with her and has sex with her. Even his wives do not dare go in. At the end of the second watch he comes out, and only then can he sleep with his wives and concubines. If for a single night this spirit does not appear, the time has come for the foreign king to die. If for a single night the foreign king stays away, he is bound to suffer a disaster.[51]

Next come the dwellings of the royal relatives, senior officials, and so on. These are large and spacious in style, very different from ordinary people's homes. The roofs are made entirely of thatch, except for the family shrine and the main bedroom, both of which can be tiled. In every house the rooms are also made to a regulation size, according to the rank of the official living there.

At the lowest level come the homes of the common people. They only use thatch for their roofs, and dare not put up a single tile. Although the sizes of their homes vary according to how wealthy they are, in the end they do not dare emulate the styles of the great houses.

4. The women of the palace, and others

The one thing people know about southern foreigners is that they are coarse, ugly, and very black.[52] I know nothing at all about those living on islands in the sea or in remote villages, but this is certainly true of those in the ordinary localities [in Zhenla]. When it comes to the women of the palace and women from the *nanpeng*—that is, the great houses—there are many who are as white as jade, but that is because they do not see the light of the sun.[53]

Generally, men and women wrap a cloth around their waist, but apart from that they leave their smooth chests and breasts uncovered.[54] They wear their hair in a topknot and go barefoot. This is the case even with the wives of the king.

The king has five wives, one principal wife, and one for each of the four cardinal points. Below them, I have heard, there are several thousand concubines and other women of the palace.[55] They also divide themselves up by rank. They only go out of the palace on rare occasions.

Every time I went inside the palace to see the foreign king, he always came out with his principal wife, and sat at a gold window in the main room. The palace women all lined up by rank in two galleries below the window. They moved to and fro to steal looks at us, and I got a very full view of them. Any family with a female beauty is bound to have her summoned to the palace.

At the lower level there are also the so-called *chenjialan*, servant women who come and go providing services inside the palace, and number at least a thousand or two. In their case they all have husbands and live mixed in among ordinary people. They shave their hair at the front of the top of their head, which gives them the look of northerners with their "open canal" style. They paint the area with vermilion, which they also paint on to either side of their temples. In this way they mark themselves out as being *chenjialan*.[56] They are the only women who can go into the palace; no one else below them can go in. There is a continuous stream of them on the roads in front of and behind the inner palace.

Apart from wearing their hair in a topknot, ordinary women do not have ornaments in their hair like pins or combs. They just wear gold bracelets on their arms and gold rings on their fingers. The *chenjialan* and the women in the palace all wear them too. Men and women usually perfume themselves with scents made up of sandalwood, musk, and other fragrances.

Every family practices Buddhism.

The country has a lot of epicene individuals who go round the markets every day in groups of a dozen or so.[57] They frequently solicit the attentions of Chinese in return for generous gifts. It is shameful and wicked.

5. Officials and official dress

As in China, the state has officials with the rank of chief minister, commander-in-chief of the army, astronomer, and so on. Below them are various kinds of junior officials, but they are not called by the same titles as ours. In general those who take on these positions are royal relatives. If they are not, they give him a daughter as a concubine as well.

In going out and about, the insignia and retinues of these officials vary by rank. The most senior are those with a palanquin with gold poles and four parasols with gold handles. Next in rank are those that have a palanquin with gold poles and two gold-handled parasols. Next down are those with a palanquin with gold poles and one gold-handled parasol; and next again, those with just one gold-handled parasol. At the lowest level are those who just have a parasol with a silver handle and nothing else. There are also those who have a palanquin with silver poles.

The senior officials with gold-handled parasols are all called *bading* or *anding*. Those with silver-handled parasols are called *siladi*.[58] The parasols are all made of a strong, thin red Chinese silk, with fringes that hang down and trail on the ground—except for oiled parasols, which are made of the same silk, but green, and have short fringes.[59]

From the king down, the men and women all wear their hair wound up in a knot, and go naked to the waist, wrapped only in a cloth.[60] When they are out and about they wind a larger piece of cloth over the small one.

There are very many different grades of cloth. The materials the king wears include some that are extremely elegant and beautiful, and worth three or four ounces of gold a piece. Although cloth is woven domestically, it also comes from Xianluo [Siam] and Champa. Cloth from the Western Seas is often regarded as the best because it is so well-made and refined.[61]

Only the king can wear material with a full pattern of flowers on it. On his head he wears a gold crown, like the crown worn by the Holder of the Diamond.[62] Sometimes he goes without a crown and simply wears a chain of fragrant flowers such as types of jasmin wound round the braids of his hair. Around his neck he wears a large pearl weighing about three catties. On his wrists and ankles and all his fingers and toes he wears gold bracelets and gold rings, all of them inlaid with cat's-eye gemstones. He goes barefoot, and the soles of his feet and the palms of his hands are dyed crimson with a red preparation. When he goes out he has a gold sword in his hand.

Among ordinary people only the women can dye the soles of their feet and the palms of their hands. The men do not dare to.

Senior officials and relatives of the king can wear cloth with a scattered floral design, while junior officials and no others can wear cloth with a two-flower design. Among the ordinary people, only women can wear cloth with this design. However, if newly arrived Chinese wear it, people do not make so bold as to take offense, on the grounds that they are *anding basha*, meaning that they do not understand what is right and proper.[63]

The soldiers also go naked and barefoot. In their right hand they carry a lance, and in their left hand a shield. They have nothing that could be called bows and arrows, trebuchets, body armor, helmets, or the like.[64] I have heard reports that when the Luo people [the Siamese] attacked, all the ordinary people were ordered out to do battle, often with no good strategy or preparation.

6. The New Year and other special events

The first month of the year is always the tenth month of the Chinese calendar. The month is called Jiade.[65] A large stage is set up in front of the state palace. There is room on it for a thousand or more people. It is hung everywhere with globe lanterns and flowers. Facing it on a bank more than twenty or thirty poles away are some tall structures that are made of wood joined and bound together, like the scaffolding used to make a pagoda.[66] These are perhaps some twenty poles high. Every night they put up three or four of these, or five or six of them, and set out fireworks and firecrackers on top of them.[67] The various provincial officials and great houses take care of all the costs.

When night comes, the king is invited to come out and watch. He lights the fireworks and firecrackers—the fireworks can all be seen a hundred li away. The firecrackers are as big as the rocks thrown by trebuchets and make enough noise to shake the whole city. Officials and noble families all give their share of huge candles and betel nuts, and spend a very great deal. The king also invites foreign envoys as spectators. Things go on in this way for fifteen days before coming to an end.

Every month there is always an event. For example, in the fourth month there are ball games. In the ninth month there is *ya lie*.[68] *Ya lie* involves everyone in the state gathering together in the city and being reviewed in front of the state palace. In the fifth month there is "water to welcome the Buddha," when Buddhas throughout the country, far and near, are all brought together and taken into the water, where they are bathed in the company of the king. There is also "dry land boating," which the king goes up a tower to watch.

The seventh month is the time for "rice burning," when new rice that is ready for harvesting is received outside the south gate and burnt as an offering to all the Buddhas. Countless women in chariots and on elephants come and watch, though the king does not appear. In the eighth month there is *ailan*, a dance that selected female dancers perform daily in the palace.[69] There are boar fights and elephant fights as well, and again the king invites foreign envoys as spectators. Things go on like this for ten days.

The events of the other months I cannot record in detail.

In the state there are also people who are expert astronomers. They can predict all the partial eclipses of the sun and the moon. But their long and short months are quite different from China's. Like China they have years with intercalary months, but they only intercalate a ninth month, which I cannot understand at all. They divide the night into only four watches; and every seven days is a cycle, similar in kind to China's so-called "open, shut . . . set up, take away" cycle of twelve days.[70]

Since none of the locals has a surname or given name, they do not keep a record of their birthdays. Many of them call themselves by the name of the day they were born on. Two days in their cycle are the luckiest; three days are ordinary; and four are the most unlucky. Which day you can travel east on, which day you can go west on—even the women all know how to work these out.

Their twelve calendar animals are also the same as China's, only they call them by different names. For example, horse is *busai*, rooster is *man*, pig is *zhilu* and ox is *gu*.[71]

7. Slaves and savages

Family slaves are all savages purchased to work as servants. Most families have a hundred or more of them; a few have ten or twenty; only the very poorest have none at all. The savages are people from the mountains. They have their own race, but are commonly called "thieving Zhuang."[72] When they come to the city, none of them dares go in and out of people's homes. The Zhuang are so despised that if there is a quarrel between two city dwellers, it only takes one of them to be called a Zhuang for hatred to enter into the marrow of his bones.

A strong young slave is worth perhaps a hundred pieces of cloth; a weak old one can only fetch thirty or forty.[73] They are only allowed to sit and sleep under the house. If they are carrying out their tasks then they can come up into the house, but they must kneel, join their hands in greeting, and bow down to the floor before they can venture forward. They address their master as *batuo* and their mistress as *mi*. *Batuo* is "father" and *mi* is "mother."[74] If they do something wrong they are beaten, and take their caning with heads bowed, not venturing to move even a little.

The males and females mate, but the master would never have reason to have intercourse with them. Sometimes a Chinese arrives and having been single a long time acts carelessly, but as soon as he has had relations with one of them the master will hear of it, and the following day he will refuse to sit with the Chinese, on the grounds that he has come into contact with a savage.

Sometimes one of them will have intercourse with an outsider, to the point of becoming pregnant and having a baby. But the master will not try and find out where it is from, since the mother has no status and he will profit from the child, who can eventually become his slave.

Slaves sometimes run away. Those that are caught and taken back must carry a dark blue tattoo on their face, and sometimes an iron shackle around their neck, or between their arms and legs.

There are two kinds of savage. The first know how to deal with people and talk to them, and are sold into the towns as slaves. The second are uneducated and cannot talk.

This second kind have no homes to live in, but move from place to place in the mountains, taking their family with them and carrying a clay pot on their head as they walk. When they come across a wild animal they shoot it with a bow and arrow, then take it, make a fire by striking stones, roast it, and eat it together before setting off again. By nature they are very ferocious; their herbal concoctions are highly poisonous; and within their own groups they frequently kill one another.

On land that is closer by there are also some who grow cardamom and kapok and weave cloth for a living, but the cloth is very coarse and thick, and the floral designs on it are very odd-looking.

8. Young girls

When a family is bringing up a daughter, her father and mother are sure to wish her well by saying, "May you have what really matters—in future may you marry thousands and thousands of husbands!"

When they are seven to nine years old—if they are girls from wealthy homes—or only when they are eleven—if they come from the poorest families—girls have to get a Buddhist monk or a holy man to take away their virginity, in what is called *zhentan*.[75]

So every year, in the fourth month of the Chinese calendar, the authorities select a day and announce it countrywide. The families whose daughters should be ready for *zhentan* let the authorities know in advance. The authorities first give them a huge candle. They make a mark on it and arrange for it to be lit at dusk on the day in question. When it reaches the mark, the time for *zhentan* has come.

A month, fifteen days, or ten days beforehand, the parents have to choose a Buddhist monk or a holy man. This depends on where the Buddhists' and holy men's temples are. The temples often also have their own clients. Officials' families and wealthy homes all get the good, saintly Buddhist monks in advance, while the poor do not have the leisure to choose.

Wealthy and noble families give the monks wine, rice, silk, and other cloth, betel nuts, silverware, and the like, goods weighing up to a hundred piculs and worth two or three hundred ounces of Chinese silver. The smallest amount a family gives weighs between thirty or forty piculs or ten to twenty piculs, depending on how thrifty the family is.[76]

The reason poor families only start dealing with the matter when their girls reach eleven is simply that it is hard for them to manage these things. Some wealthy families do also give money for poor girls' *zhentan*, which they call doing good work. Moreover in any one year a monk can only take charge of one girl, and once he has agreed to and accepted the benefits, he cannot make another commitment.

On the night in question a big banquet with drums and music is laid on for relatives and neighbors. A tall canopy is put up outside the entrance to the house, and various clay figurines of people and animals are laid out on top of it. There can be ten or more of these, or just three or four—or none at all in the case of poor families. They all have to do with events long ago, and they usually stay up for seven days before people start taking them down.

At dusk the monk is met with palanquin, parasol, drums, and music, and brought back to the house. Two pavilions are put up, made of colorful silk. The girl sits in the middle of one, and the monk sits in the middle of the other. You cannot understand what he is saying because the drums and music are making so much noise—on that night the night curfew is lifted. I have heard that when the time comes the monk goes into a room with the girl and takes away her virginity with his hand, which he then puts into some wine. Some say the parents and neighbors mark their foreheads with it, others say they all taste it. Some say the monk and the girl have sex together, others say they do not. They do not let Chinese see this, though, so I do not really know.

Towards dawn the monk is seen off again with palanquin, parasol, drums, and music. Afterwards, silk, cloth, and the like have to be given to the monk to redeem the body of the girl. If this is not done the girl will be the property of the monk for her whole life, and will not be able to marry anyone else.

The instance of this that I saw took place early on the sixth night of the fourth month of the year *dingyou* [1297] in the Dade reign period.[77]

Before this happens, the parents always sleep together with their daughter; afterwards she is excluded from the room and goes wherever she wants without restraint or precaution. When it comes to marriage, there is a ceremony with the giving of gifts, but it is just a simple, easy-going affair. There are many men who get married only after leading a dissolute life, something local custom regards as neither shameful nor odd.

On a *zhentan* night, up to ten or more families from a single alley may be involved. On the city streets people are out meeting Buddhists monks and holy men, going this way and that, and the sounds of drums and music are everywhere.

9. Childbirth

As soon as they give birth the local women prepare some hot rice, mix it with salt, and put it into the entrance of the vagina. They usually take it out after a day and a night. Because of that women do not fall sick when they are giving birth, and usually contract so as to be like young girls again.

When I first heard this I was surprised by it, and seriously doubted whether it was true. Then a girl in the family I was staying with gave birth to a child, and I got a full picture of what happened to her. The day after the birth, she took up the baby right away and went to bathe in the river with it. It was a truly amazing thing to see.

Then again, I have often heard people say that the local women are very lascivious, so that a day or two after giving birth they are immediately coupling with their husbands. If a husband does not meet his wife's wishes he will be at once be abandoned, as [the Han dynasty official] Zhu Maichen was.[78] If the husband happens to have work to do far away, if it is only for a few nights that is all right, but if it is for more than ten nights or so the wife will say, "I'm not a ghost—why am I sleeping alone?" This is how strong their sexual feelings are. That said, I have heard that there are some who have the will to restrain themselves.

The women age very quickly indeed, the reason being that they marry and have children young. A twenty or thirty-year-old woman is like a Chinese woman of forty or fifty.

10. Illness and death

The people of this country are frequently ill, and can often cure themselves by immersing themselves in water and repeatedly washing their head. At the same time, there are a lot of lepers—they are everywhere on the roads—and local people think nothing of sleeping and eating in their company.[79] They sometimes say the disease occurs because of particular local conditions. It is also said that a king once contracted the disease, so people are not troubled by it.

In my humble opinion people contract the disease because they so often go into the water and bathe after making love. I have heard that local people always go and bathe as soon as their love-making is over.

Out of every ten people that contract dysentery, eight or nine die.

They also have people who sell medicines in the markets, as with us, but the medicines are not the same kinds as in China, and I do not know what they are made of.

There are also witchdoctors of some kind that give people their help. It is really most amusing.

When people die there are no coffins. The body is just kept on a kind of bamboo mat and covered with a cloth. When it is taken out for the funeral it is preceded by banners, drums, and music, as with us. Two dishes are filled with fried rice, and this is scattered along the route. The body is carried out of town to a remote, uninhabited spot, where it is thrown down and left. After that vultures, crows, dogs, and other village animals come and eat it. If it is quickly consumed, that means the father and mother of the dead person are blessed, and so gained this reward. If it is not eaten, or only partly eaten, on the other hand, it means the father and mother have come to that because of their wrongdoings.

Nowadays they also have more and more cremations, mainly of the descendants of Chinese.

When a father or mother dies, there are no special clothes for mourning. Sons show their respect for their parent by shaving off all their hair, daughters by shaving a space the size of a coin in the hair on the top of their head.

The kings are still buried in towers, though I do not know if their corpses are buried or just their bones.

11. The three doctrines

Those who are learned men are called *banjie*. Those who are Buddhist monks are called *zhugu*. Holy men are called *basiwei*.[80]

With regard to *banjie*, I do not know what the source of their doctrine is. They have nowhere that can be called an academy or place of learning, and it is hard to find out what books they study. All I have seen is that they dress like other people, except that they hang a white thread around their neck. This is all that distinguishes them as learned men. Those among the *banjie* who take up official positions become men of high status. They keep the thread round their neck till the end of their life.

Zhugu shave their heads and dress in yellow. They leave their right shoulder uncovered, and otherwise wrap themselves in a robe made of yellow cloth and go barefoot. For their temples they too can use tiles for roofing. In the middle of the temple there is just one icon, an exact likeness of the Sakyamuni Buddha, which they call Bolai.[81] It is clothed in red, sculpted from clay, and painted in many colors. Apart from that there are no other icons. In the pagodas, the Buddhas are all different in appearance, and all cast in bronze. There are no bells, drums, clappers, or cymbals, and no hanging curtains, fine canopies, and the like.

The monks all eat fish and meat—they just do not drink wine. They also make offerings of fish and meat to the Buddha. They take one meal a day, which they get from the home of an almsgiver, as there are no kitchens in the temples. They chant a very large number of scriptures, which are all written on piles of palmyra leaves put together in a very orderly way.[82] They write on them with a black script, using not brush and ink to write with but something else, though I do not know what. The monks also have palanquins with gold and silver poles, and parasols. If the king is dealing with important matters of government, he also seeks their advice. There are no nuns, though.

The *basiwei* dress just like ordinary people, except that they wear a red or white cloth on their head. It looks like the tall headdress of Tartar women, except it is somewhat shorter.[83] They have temples, too, though these are rather smaller than the Buddhist temples. In general the holy men are less prosperous than the Buddhists. They do not make offerings to an icon, only to a block of stone, like the altar stones for the gods of the earth in China. Again, I do not know what the source of their beliefs is. There are also holy women, though. Their temples can be roofed with tiles too. *Basiwei* do not eat other people's food and do not let other people see them eat. Again, they do not drink wine. I have never seen them chanting scriptures or engaging in devotional studies.

When young boys from lay families go to school, they all start by being trained by Buddhist monks. Only when they have grown up do they return to lay life. I could not look into this in detail.

12. Writing and language

The country's language consists of sounds that are its own, and despite being nearby neither the Chams nor the Siamese speak in a way that is understood. Thus the word for one is *mei*, two is *bie*, three is *bei*, four *ban*, five *bolan*, six *bolanmei*, seven *bolanbie*, eight *bolanbei*, nine *bolanban*, and ten *da*. Fathers are called *batuo*, and even paternal uncles are, too. A mother is called *mi*, and so are paternal and maternal aunts and the wives of fathers' younger brothers, and even older women in the neighborhood. Elder brothers are called *bang*, and so are elder sisters. Younger brothers are called *buwen*, and maternal uncles are called *chilai*, as are the husbands of paternal and maternal aunts.[84]

In general many of the words that come afterwards, they put in front. For example, we may say that that man is Zhang San's younger brother; they say he is "*buwen* Zhang San". We say that this man is Li Si's maternal uncle; they say he is *chilai* Li Si.[85]

To give another example, China is called Beishi, an official is called *bading*, and a scholar is called *banjie*.[86] But a Chinese official is not called Beishi *bading*; rather, he is called *bading* Beishi. And a Chinese scholar is not called Beishi *banjie*; rather, he is called *banjie* Beishi. On the whole, it is all like that.

This is just a brief general outline. When it comes to specifics, officialdom has its official debates and deliberations, scholars have their scholarly literary conversations, and the Buddhists and holy men have their own language of Buddhism and the holy Way. The towns and villages all have particular ways of speaking—but then again, that is no different from China.

Everyday writing and official documents are all done on the skin of muntjaks, deer, and so on that is dyed black. Depending on whether it is big or small, broad or narrow, the skin is cut in whatever way is desired. People use a kind of powder like Chinese chalk, which is rolled into a little stick called *suo* and held between forefinger and thumb, to draw shapes on the parchment and make words.[87] These stay fast forever. When they have finished with the chalk they stick it behind their ear. From the form of the words people can also make out whose handwriting it is. It can only be erased by being wiped with something wet.

For the most part the shape of the words is just like the shape of words written in Uyghur.[88] The writing is always from left to right, not from top to bottom. I have heard Esen Khaya say that the letters of the alphabet are pronounced in exactly the same way as in Mongolian, with two or three exceptions.[89]

Official seals are non-existent. For families petitioning the authorities there are no shops with writers for hire, either.[90]

13. Settling disputes

If there is a dispute among the ordinary people, it must be referred up to the king, even if it is a small matter. There are never any floggings by way of punishment, only fines as I have heard. Nor do they hang or behead anyone guilty of a serious crime. Instead they just dig a ditch in the ground outside the west gate of the city, put the criminal in it, fill it up solid with earth and stones, and leave it at that. Otherwise people have their fingers or toes amputated, or their nose cut off.

There is, however, no prohibition against adultery or gambling. If a husband finds out that his wife has committed adultery, he has her lover's feet squeezed between two pieces of wood. When he is unable to bear the pain the lover gives the husband everything he owns, and only then can he get his release. Given this practice, some people set things up so as to defraud people.

If a person finds a dead body by his doorway, he himself drags it with a rope to wasteland outside the city. There is never anything that could be called an inquest or official inspection.

When a family catch a thief, they can also impose their own punishment, whether it is detention, torture, or beating. There is however one standard process for the use of, say, a family that have lost something, and suspect it has been stolen by someone who will not own up. They heat some oil in a cauldron until it is extremely hot, and make the person concerned put their hand in it. If they are the thief, their hand turns putrid; if they are not, their skin and flesh stay the same as before. Such are the strange laws of foreigners.

Then again, if two families have a dispute to resolve and cannot agree on right and wrong, there are twelve small stone towers [Prasat Suor Prat] on a bank opposite the palace, and the two people concerned are sent to sit in two of them.[91] Outside, members of each family keep guard against the other. They may sit in the towers for a day or two, or for three or four days. Then for sure the one who is in the wrong becomes visibly ill, and leaves. He may have sores, or a cough or fever or something of the kind. The one who is in the right is absolutely fine. Thus right and wrong are assessed and decided on, in what is known as the judgment of heaven. Such is the spiritual power of the local gods.

14. Cultivating the land

In general, crops can be harvested three or four times a year, the reason being that all four seasons are like our fifth and sixth months, with days that know no frost or snow. For six months the land has rain, for six months no rain at all. From the fourth to the ninth month it rains every day, with the rain falling only in the afternoon. The high water mark around the Freshwater Sea [Tonlé Sap Lake] can be seven or eight poles, completely submerging even very tall trees except for the tips.[92] Families living by the shore all move to the far side of the hills.

From the tenth to the third month there is not a drop of rain. Only small boats can cross the Sea, whose lower depths are only three to five feet down. The families move back down again, and the farmers work out when the paddy will be ripe and when the waters will have spread where, and sow their seed accordingly.

For ploughing they do not use cows. Their ploughs, sickles, and hoes are quite similar to ours, but of course they are not made in exactly the same way.

There is also a kind of uncultivated field, where rice usually grows even though it is not planted. If the water in the field gets to be ten feet high, the rice grows at that height too. I assume this is a different variety of rice.

They do not use night soil for manuring the fields or growing vegetables, thinking it is unclean. Chinese who come to this place never talk to people about matters relating to manure and fertilizer, for fear of being looked down on.[93]

To make a latrine, groups of two or three families get together and dig a hole, which they cover with grass. When it is used up they fill it in and dig another one. Whenever they go to the lavatory they always go and wash themselves in a pond afterwards. They only use their left hand, keeping their right hand for taking food. When they see a Chinese going to the lavatory and wiping themselves with paper they all laugh at them, to the point where they do not want them in their home. Among the women there are some who also urinate standing up—and that really is laughable.

15. Products

In the mountains there are exotic trees in plenty. Where there are no trees, rhinos and elephants come together and bring up their young. There are precious birds and wonderful animals too numerous to count. Fine things include kingfisher feathers, elephant tusks, rhinoceros horns, and beeswax. Less refined things include lakawood, cardamom, gamboge, lac, and chaulmoogra oil.[94]

Kingfishers are really quite hard to catch. Where there is a lake in a forest and there are fish in the lake, the kingfisher flies out of the trees in search of them. The locals cover their bodies with leaves and sit by the edge of a lake, where they catch a female kingfisher in a cage as a lure for the males. They wait for the males to come, then trap them with a small hand-held net. Sometimes they take four or five birds in a day; sometimes they get absolutely nothing all day.

Elephant tusks come from families living in remote mountain areas. When any elephant dies it still has its two tusks; there is no truth in the old saying that elephants change their tusks once a year. The best ivory comes from an elephant killed with a lance; the next best from an elephant whose tusks people have collected soon after it has died a natural death; the least good from elephants lying dead in the mountains for many years.

The locals get beeswax from a kind of bee with a narrow waist like an ant's that lives inside rotten trees in the villages. Every junk can carry two or three thousand honeycombs of beeswax, and each comb weighs thirty to forty catties for a large one, and eighteen or nineteen catties for a small one.[95]

Better-quality rhino horns are white with veining; the less good ones are dark.

Lakawood grows in the forest. The locals expend a great deal of effort chopping up the trees, as the wood comes from the heart of the trees. They are white on the outside and about eight or nine inches thick. Even the small ones are no less than four or five inches thick.[96] Cardamom is cultivated entirely by the savages in the mountains. Gamboge is resin from a kind of tree. The locals cut the tree with a knife a year in advance, letting the resin drip out, then start collecting it a year later. Lac grows on the branches of a kind of tree, looks just like mulberry mistletoe, and is also quite hard to obtain. Chaulmoogra oil comes from the seeds of a large tree. The fruit is round and shaped like a coconut; inside there are several dozen seeds. In some places there are also peppers. They grow on a twisting vine that forms clusters like wild hops. When they are fresh the dark green ones are hotter than the others.[97]

None of the locals produces silk. Nor do the women know how to stitch and darn with a needle and thread. The only thing they can do is weave cotton from kapok. Even then they cannot spin the yarn, but just use their hands to gather the cloth into strands. They do not use a loom for weaving. Instead they just wind one end of the cloth around their waist, hang the other end over a window, and use a bamboo tube as a shuttle.

In recent years Luo people [Siamese] have come to live there, and unlike the locals they engage in silk production. The mulberry trees they grow and the silkworms they raise all come from Luo. (They have no ramie, either, only hemp.)[98] They themselves weave the silk into clothes made of a black, patterned satiny silk. Siamese women do know how to stitch and darn, so when local people have torn or damaged clothes they ask them to do the mending.

16. Trade

The local people who know how to trade are all women. So when a Chinese goes to this country, the first thing he must do is take in a woman, partly with a view to profiting from her trading abilities.

There is a market every day from around six in the morning until midday. There are no stalls, only a kind of tumbleweed mat laid out on the ground, each mat in its usual place. I gather there is also a rental fee to be paid to officials.

Small market transactions are paid for with rice or other grain and Chinese goods. Next up in size are paid for with cloth. Large transactions are done with gold and silver.

In years gone by local people were completely naïve, and when they saw a Chinese they treated him with great respect and awe, addressing him as a Buddha and falling prostrate and kowtowing when they saw him. Lately, though, as more Chinese have gone there, there have been people who have cheated and slighted them.

They do not produce gold or silver, I believe, and so they hold Chinese gold and silver in the highest regard.

Next they value items [from China] made of fine, double-threaded silk in the five main colors.[99] Next after that they value such things as pewter ware from Zhenzhou, lacquer dishes from Wenzhou, and celadon ware from Quanzhou and Chuzhou, as well as mercury, cinnabar, writing paper, sulphur, saltpetre, sandalwood, lovage, angelica, musk, hemp, yellow grass cloth, umbrellas, iron pots, copper dishes, glass balls, tung tree oil, fine-toothed combs, wooden combs, and needles—and of the ordinary, heavier items, mats from Mingzhou.[100] Beans and wheat are particularly sought after, but they cannot be taken there.[101]

17. Flora and fauna

All they have in common with China are pomegranates, sugar cane, lotus flowers, lotus roots, starfruit, and bananas.[102] Their lychees and oranges are the same shape as ours, but have a sour taste. The rest are all things we in China have never seen. And their trees really are very different from ours, while their grasses and flowers are fragrant and beautiful and more plentiful than ours. There are also more varieties of aquatic flowers, though I do not know any of their names.

As for peaches, plums, apricots, flowering apricots, pines, cypresses, firs, junipers, jujubes, poplars, willows, cassias, orchids, and angelica—these they have none of. They do have lotus flowers in the first month of the year, though.[103]

Of their birds, peacocks, kingfishers and parrots do not exist in China. Otherwise they have birds like vultures, crows, egrets, sparrows, great cormorants, storks, cranes, wild ducks, siskins, and so on.[104] They do not have magpies, wild geese, orioles, cuckoos, swallows, or pigeons.

Of their animals, rhinos, elephants, wild oxen, and mountain horses do not exist in China. Otherwise they have very many kinds of animals, including tigers, leopards, different kinds of bear, wild boar, elk, deer, water deer, muntjaks, apes, foxes, and gibbons.[105] The only animals that aren't seen are lions, orang-utangs, and camels. And of course there are chickens, ducks, cows, horses, pigs, and goats.

The horses are very short and small. There are a great many cows. People do not venture to ride on them when they are alive, eat them when they are dead, or flay their hides for leather, and—I hear—their carcasses are left to rot away, all because they exert their best efforts for people. They are used to haul carts and nothing else.[106]

Previously, they had no geese, but in recent times sailors from China brought them into the country, so now they are being raised.

They have rats as large as cats; there is also a kind of rat whose head looks exactly like a new-born puppy's.

For vegetables they have onions, mustard, chives, eggplants, watermelons, winter gourds, snake gourds, and amaranth.[107] They do not have radishes, lettuce, chicory, or spinach. Watermelons, gourds, and eggplants are also available in some places as early as the second month of the year. Some eggplants can be left for several years without being uprooted.

There are kapok trees higher than a room that are not replaced for more than ten years at a time.

There are very many vegetables whose names I do not know. There are also many kinds of vegetable that grow in water.

Of their fish and turtles, black carp are the commonest. Other fish that are plentiful include common carp, goldfish, and grass carp. There are gudgeons—the large ones weigh two catties or more.[108] Otherwise there are very many fish whose names I do not know, all of them coming from the Freshwater Sea.

As for saltwater fish, they have every different kind.

The local people do not eat swamp eels, the freshwater eels from the lakes, or the frogs, which go this way and that across the roads at night.

There are giant softshell turtles and alligators as big as large pillars.[109] The turtles are eaten up, offal and all. Prawns from Zha'nan weigh a catty or more. The goose-necked barnacles from Zhenpu may be eight or nine inches long.[110]

There are crocodiles as big as ships. They have four feet and look exactly like dragons except that they have no horns.

The razor clams look very fine and are very crisp-tasting.[111] They get frogs, freshwater clams, and pond snails by just scooping them out of the Freshwater Sea. The only things I did not see were crabs. They do have crabs, I believe, but people do not eat them.

They have four kinds of wine. The first is what the Chinese call "honey-sweet wine", made by mixing a fermenting agent into honey and water. The next, which the local people call *pengyasi*, is made from the leaves of a kind of tree, the leaves being known by that name. The third is made from husked rice, or rice left over after a meal. It is called *baolengjiao*, which means husked rice. The last is "sugar-shine wine", which is made from sugar.[112] Down by the banks of the estuary they also have a palm starch wine, which they make from the starch of the leaves of a type of palm that grows in on the river bank.

There is no prohibition on salt works in the country, and from Zhenpu to Bajian and other locations along the coast, most places heat seawater to make salt.[113] In the mountains there is also a kind of rock that tastes even better than salt and that can be carved into objects.

The local people cannot make vinegar. If they want to give a sauce a sour taste they add some leaves from the tamarind tree—or berries from the tree if it has produced berries, or seeds from the trees if it has produced seeds.[114]

They do not know how to make soy sauce either. This is because they have no soy beans or wheat, and have never made a fermenting agent. So they make wine from honey, water, and the leaves of a tree, and use a wine yeast that looks like the spirit yeast used in our villages.[115]

18. Utensils

Ordinary people have houses but nothing else by way of tables, chairs, jars, or buckets. They use an earthenware pot to cook rice in, and make sauce with an earthenware saucepan. For a stove they sink three stones into the ground, and for spoons they use coconut husks.

When serving rice they use earthenware or copper dishes from China; sauce comes in a small bowl made from the leaves of a tree, which does not leak even when it is full of liquid. They also make small spoons from the leaves of the nipa palm, which they spoon liquid into their mouth with and throw away after using. Even when they are making offerings to the gods and to the Buddha they do things the same way.

They also have a tin or earthenware bowl on one side which they fill with water and dip their hands in. They do this because they eat rice with just their hands, and it sticks to their hands and will not come off without water.

When they drink wine they do so from a pewter vessel called *qia*[116] that holds about three or four small cupfuls. When serving wine they do so with a pewter pot, though poor people use a clay jug. In the great houses and wealthy homes, silver or even gold is used for everything. In the palace they often use receptacles of gold, different from others in style and shape.

On the ground they lay out grass mats from Mingzhou, or rattan matting, or the pelts of tigers, leopards, muntjaks, deer, and so on. Lately people have started using low tables, about a foot high. When they sleep they just lie on the ground on bamboo mats. Lately, again, they have taken to using low beds, usually made by Chinese.

At night there are a lot of mosquitoes, so they use cloth nets. In the king's quarters the nets are made of fine silk with gold filigree work, all of them the gifts of seafaring merchants.

For husking rice they do not use millstones, just pestle and mortar.

19. Boats, palanquins, and carts

Very large boats are made from hard wood broken into planks. The carpenters have no saws, and just chisel the wood with axes so as to make the planks. This is very cumbersome, a waste of wood and a waste of effort. For anything needing wood cut into lengths, including house building, the wood is chiselled and cut into pieces in the same way. To make ships they also use iron nails. The awning consists of palm leaves, held down with strips of areca wood. The ships, which they call *xinna*, use oars. The grease they spread on the boats is fish oil, and they use lime for mortar.

Small boats, on the other hand, are made from a single very large piece of wood, hollowed out by chiseling. They treat the wood with smoke from a fire, which makes it soft, then use timber to stretch it out. The boats, which they call *pilan*, are large in the middle and pointed at either end. They do not have a sail, can hold several people, and have to be rowed with oars.[117]

Their palanquins are made of pieces of wood that bend in the middle and point upwards at either end.[118] They are carved with floral designs and girdled with gold or silver, which is what I meant by gold and silver palanquin poles. One foot down from each end of the palanquin pole is a hook nailed into the wood. A large strip of thick cloth folded in two is tied to the hooks with a rope. A person sits in the cloth and is carried by two people, one at either end. In addition palanquins come with a thing like the sail of a boat, except broader, which is decorated with fine silk done in many colors. It is carried by four men, who follow along with it.

For long distances they also ride on elephants and horses or use carts. The carts are made in the same way as in other places, but the horses have no saddles. The elephants, on the other hand, carry benches to sit on.

20. Taking gall, and other curious facts

Previously, gall bladders were taken from people in the eighth month in response to an annual demand from the king of Champa for an urn filled with human gall bladders—perhaps a thousand or more of them.[119] At night men were sent out in many directions to well-frequented places in towns and villages. When they met people out at night they snared their head with a rope and took out their gall bladder by sticking a small knife into their lower righthand side. When there were enough of these they were given to the Champa king.

The only gall bladders they did not take were those of Chinese, since one year they took one from a Chinese and put it in with the others, only to find that the gall bladders in the urn all turned rotten and could not be used.

Recently the practice of taking gall bladders was done away with. The officials who took the gall bladders have been reassigned, and reside inside the north gate of the city.

The place is unbearably hot, and no one can go on without bathing several times a day. Even at night you have to bathe once or twice. They may never have had bathrooms, buckets, or the like, but every family is sure to have a pool or at least a pool to share among two or three families.

Everyone, male and female, goes naked into the pool. The only exceptions are when there are parents or elderly people in the pool, in which case children and youngsters do not venture in, or when there are young people in the pool, in which case elderly people have to stay away too. For people from the same generation there are no constraints, though women do cover their vagina with their left hand when they go into the water.

Every three or four days, or every four or five days, women in the capital get together in groups of three to five and go out of the city for a river bathe. When they get to the river bank they take off the cloth they are wrapped in and go into the water. Those gathering together in the river often number in thousands. Even the women from the great houses join in, and without the slightest embarrassment. You get to see everything, from head to toe.

In the big river outside the city not a day passes without this happening. On their leisure days Chinese regard it as quite a pleasant thing to do to go along and watch; and I have heard that there are those who go into the water for a surreptitious encounter.

A side view of Angkor Wat, the great temple and also perhaps mausoleum built during the time of Sūryavarman II (r. 1113–c. 1149). No Chinese record mentions Angkor Wat until it is alluded to by Zhou Daguan.

Source: Peter Harris, 18-03-20

The river is always warm like heated water. Only in the fifth watch does it get a little cooler. But as soon as the sun appears it warms up again.

Inside the east gate there was a southern foreigner who had sex with his younger sister. Their skin and flesh stuck together and would not come apart. After three days without eating they both died. My fellow countryman Mr Xue has lived in this place for thirty-five years, and says he has seen this same thing happen twice.[120] Such, then, is the spiritual power of the holy Buddha in this country.

Chinese sailors do well from the fact that in this country you can go without clothes, food is easy to come by, women are easy to get, housing is easy to deal with, it is easy to make do with a few utensils, and it is easy to do trade. They often run away here.

Zhou's *Record* compared to earlier sources

Zhou Daguan's description of Angkor covers many of the same topics as earlier Chinese accounts of Zhenla, but does so far more richly and extensively.[121] There are omissions—there is no local history, for example, and no mention of Zhenla's foreign affairs beyond passing references to foreign envoys and wars with the Siamese. But otherwise his account is much more detailed than earlier Chinese records. It also addresses several hitherto unexplored subjects. These include slaves, the role of women, language and writing—Zhou clearly gained some proficiency in Khmer, local Chinese, and trade, as well as the great buildings of Angkor.

Taken overall, Zhou's *Record* gives the cumulative impression of a slave-based society with a fine royal capital, whose mainstay was agriculture complemented by trade, whose women played a major role in trade and also in the palace, and whose frequent armed conflicts with Xian (Siam) had laid to waste its villages.[122]

Zhou's portrait of Zhenla is thus far more informative than any other Chinese account, even *Sui shu*,[123] the most detailed of any Chinese description of Zhenla before Zhou's. Now and then Zhou's *Record* is also slightly more personal in tone than other Chinese records. He mentions witnessing particular events (a family's experience of childbirth, the coming of age ritual for young girls), laughs at an odd local practice (women urinating while standing up), and casually refers to an otherwise unidentified person, Esen Khaya, who may perhaps have led his mission.[124]

Finally, we should mention again Zhou's descriptions of Angkor's architecture. He refers to six of Angkor Thom's most dramatically beautiful buildings.[125] To identify them by the terms he uses, while giving their present-day names in brackets, these are the royal palace and its gold tower (Phimeanakas); a stone tower mountain (Phnom Bakheng), which may also have been mentioned in *Zhu fan zhi*; a tomb ten li in circumference with hundreds of stone chambers (Angkor Wat), which Zhou misguidedly claims was the burial place of the Chinese carpenter Lu Ban; a gold tower with stone chambers set in a northern lake (Neak Pean); and a gold tower with a gold bridge (Bayon).[126] Here, at last, is some recognition by a Chinese chronicler of the Kingdom of Angkor's architectural glories.

10

After Zhou: selected accounts through the Ming

The main aim of this work has been to consider Chinese texts on Cambodia up to the time of Zhou Daguan. But while Zhou's *Zhenla fengtu ji* represents a high point in the Chinese empire's understanding of the Khmers, it by no means marks the end of China's dealings with them. During the later Yuan dynasty and the following Ming dynasty (1368–1644), Chinese scholars and officials continued to write about Zhenla, while in early Ming times Khmer rulers frequently sent tribute to the Chinese court and received Chinese envoys in Cambodia, exchanges recorded in *Ming shi* [*The History of the Ming Dynasty*], the standard history of the Ming, and *Ming shi lu* [*Ming Veritable Records*], official records of the Ming emperors' reigns.

To conclude the main part of this work, this chapter will review a selection of the Chinese writings on Zhenla that relate to the late Yuan and Ming periods.

The merchant Wang Dayuan's depiction of Zhenla

The first Chinese writer to describe Cambodia after Zhou Daguan was a merchant called Wang Dayuan (c. 1311–?), who gave an account of Zhenla a few decades later. Wang was active in the last chaotic decades of the Mongol Yuan dynasty, before its final collapse in 1368. He lived in the great southeastern port of Quanzhou, and traveled widely abroad, spending two long periods amounting to a total of seven or eight years outside China.[1]

Wang's main work was a record of foreign countries entitled *Dao yi zhi lüe* [*A Brief Record of the Foreigners of the Islands*]. He completed it in 1350. In it he describes a hundred foreign states, territories, and peoples, apparently drawing on both personal experience and hearsay.[2] One of these states is Cambodia, which he still calls Zhenla.

Here is Wang's account of Zhenla:[3]

The gate to the south of the city [that is, the capital of Zhenla] is actually the main marketplace.[4] There is a city wall seventy li or so in circumference, with a stone river surrounding it that is twenty poles wide. They have some four hundred thousand elephants for use in warfare, and thirty or so very grand and imposing temple buildings.[5] These are adorned with walls of gold and tiles made of flattened silver.

There is a chair made of precious stones for the ruler, and the nobles and their relatives all sit on gold stools. Every year there is a gathering in which jade monkeys, golden peacocks, white elephants with six tusks, and three-horned oxen with silver hooves are arrayed before them. Ten gold lions are displayed on a bronze terrace, and an array of twelve silver towers is guarded by bronze elephants. Everyone has to eat and drink from gold teacups, ornate bamboo and wooden baskets, and golden bowls.

It is known elsewhere as the city of a hundred towers, for they have built a hundred golden Buddhist pagodas. One of these was attacked by dogs, so its finial has not been completed. There is another called the Masi Green Lake, where five pagodas have been built, their spires done in gold. Another is called the Sangxiang Buddha Hall. They have made a stone bridge encased in gold forty or so poles long. There is a saying, "Rich, noble Zhenla".[6]

The weather is always warm, and it is customary to live a life of luxurious plenty. The yield of the land is bountiful. The people get salt from the sea, and ferment millet to make liquor. Men and women wear their hair bound in a knot.

When a young girl is nine years old, a Buddhist monk is asked to apply Buddhist doctrine and pierce her body with his finger.[7] He then makes a mark in red on the foreheads of the girl and her mother. They call this "good fortune", saying that in this way when she marries someone later it will bring good fortune to the family. A girl marries at the end of her tenth year.

If a wife has depraved relations with a guest, her husband is very happy, boasting to others that "my wife is clever, she gets others to love her".

They wrap themselves in silk brocade and put pearls on their eyebrows and foreheads. When their chief goes out and about, he travels in a golden cart with feather banners, his body wrapped in jeweled tassels, a sword in his left hand and a deer's tail in his right.[8]

Punishments under the law consist of cutting off the nose or foot, or banishment after being branded on the face. If people in the state engage in a robbery, their arm or leg is cut off and they are branded on their chest or back or with a black mark branded on their forehead. Anyone killing a

> Chinese is put to death. If a Chinese kills a local he pays a heavy fine in gold. If he has no gold he sells himself to redeem the debt.
>
> Locally produced beeswax, rhino horns, peacocks, lign-aloes, sappan wood, chaulmoogra, and kingfisher feathers are better than those of other foreign parts. Trading is done with gold and silver; yellow and red beads; dragon-patterned satins; silk brocade from Jianning; silk, cloth, and the like.

Wang's description of Zhenla is similar in outline to the accounts of Zhao Rugua and Zhou Daguan, and contains some of the same material—the royal review, fro instance, young girls' coming-of-age ritual, and the saying about rich, noble Zhenla. These are all topics taken from Zhao and Zhou. But it differs from Zhao and Zhou in many details. These include the number of fighting elephants—surely exaggerated—the number of towers guarded by statues of elephants, the local name of "good fortune" for the coming-of-age ritual, the (indecipherable) names of structures in the capital, the practice of wives having sex with visitors, and the penalties for crimes involving Chinese.

Wang Dayuan's early translator William Rockhill remarks that Wang "must have had [Zhou Daguan's *Record*] before him when he wrote about Kamboja, for much of the information he gives seems to be derived from or inspired by that work."[9] Given the numerous discrepancies between Wang's account and the accounts of both Zhou Daguan and Zhao Rugua, it seems more likely that Wang drew on their work from an imperfect memory, and depended at least in part on the recollections of other informants as well.

Zhenla and the Ming voyages of Admiral Zheng He

Like the imperial records before them, Chinese records of Zhenla during the Ming dynasty fall into two main categories, official and unofficial.

Notable among the official records are the historical works *Ming shi* and *Ming shilu*, completed long after the Ming dynasty ended.[10] We shall return to these works shortly.

Unofficial sources include various Chinese accounts of states beyond China's southern borders, including those with ties of trade and tribute with the Chinese imperium. Trade relations between southern China and states to the south and southwest continued during the Ming, albeit it in restricted form as a result of periodic efforts by the Ming court to curtail them. As for tributary relations with southern states, these were well maintained during the early decades of the Ming, when its capital was in Nanjing, but dwindled after the Ming relocated its capital to Beijing in 1420.[11]

One celebrated feature of the early Ming was the sea journeys to foreign lands by the Ming admiral Zheng He, who led huge, imposing fleets of ships on six overseas expeditions between 1405 and 1431.[12] Most of the expeditions were commissioned by the Yongle Emperor (r. 1402–1424), a son of the founding emperor of the Ming and an assertive man determined to put his stamp on his rule.[13] Admiral Zheng's expeditions took him to a number of far-flung locations, including Java, Ceylon, India, Arabia, and East Africa—and according to *Ming shi*, Zhenla.[14] The purposes of the expeditions are still not entirely clear, but a major aim was clearly to enhance the prestige of the Ming and its rulers, especially the Yongle Emperor himself. This they were to do by making an impressive and if need be coercive display of China's wealth and power.[15]

Zheng's journeys resulted in several well-known books that describe places along his routes. The author of the best-known of these, Ma Huan (c. 1380–1460), was a linguist from the Hangzhou region who served as Zheng's interpreter during his fourth, sixth, and seventh voyages. Ma's book, *Yingyai shenglan*, [*An Overall Survey of the Ocean's Shores*], published two decades after Zheng's final voyage, describes twenty-one countries, from Champa and Java in southeast Asia to Hormuz and Mecca in the Arab world.[16] Unfortunately Zhenla is not one of the countries in the book.

The soldier Fei Xin's account of Zhenla

Zhenla does, however, feature in a book by another member of Zheng He's entourage. This is an account of foreign lands written by a soldier from Suzhou called Fei Xin (1388?–?), who served on three of Zheng's expeditions.[17] Fei's work, *Xingcha shenglan* [*An Overall Survey of the Star Raft*], completed in 1436, gives descriptions of forty-five foreign states and other locations. Nineteen of these are among the locations described by Ma Huan, while the remaining twenty-six are places Fei either visited himself or learned about from other sources. One of these twenty-six places is Zhenla. Unhappily, it is clear from what Fei Xin writes that he did not experience Zhenla firsthand.

Fei's description of Zhenla (the name he uses), the first to feature in a major Ming work, is in effect a shorter version of the description given in Wang Dayuan's *Dao yi zhi lü*, parts of which Fei reproduces, though without acknowledgement. Fei only makes three small additions to what Wang recorded.[18] He notes that Zhenla is "reachable from Champa in three days and nights, given a favorable wind." He remarks that the people of Zhenla "wear short upper garments and wrap themselves in elegant cloth."[19] And he concludes—as he does after every country he describes—with a short poem. In the case of Zhenla the poem is a. short eulogy to

> Zhenla, distant among the lowly hills,
> Its rustic city by the shores of the sea
> With its many glorious animals and birds
> And people living in luxury
> Amid an array of wondrous towers . . .

The scholar Huang Xingzeng's description of Zhenla

One other Ming work, completed decades later in 1520, explicitly builds on Zheng He's expeditions and Ma Huan's record of foreign lands. Written by the scholar Huang Xingzeng (1490–1540), who does not seem have traveled abroad himself, the work is called *Xiyang chaogong dianlu* [*Records of Tribute from the Western Ocean*], and is a survey of states to the south and west of China.[20]

Over half the twenty-three states Huang describes featured earlier in Ma Huan's *Yingyai shenglan*. Of the remainder, one is Zhenla (so called in Huang's work).[21] Huang begins his account of Zhenla by noting that Zhenla "has Champa to its south and the sea to its east, and is the market place for Hainan"—that is, the states to the south of the Southern Sea. He goes on to give a brief portrait of Zhenla that is, once again, a shorter version of Wang Dayuan's *Dao yi zhi lüe*, which is again left unacknowledged.

Huang makes a few minor changes and additions. He describes "the city where the king lives" as being "some seventy li square" as opposed to Wang's "some seventy li in circumference." He also mentions (as Fei Xin does) that the people wear "short upper garments." And he writes that Zhenla is suitable for "the five kinds of grain," but without specifying which ones.

The only part of Huang's account of Zhenla that diverges from Wang Dayuan's comes towards the end, when he describes its local products and tribute, and goes on to allude to its history. He concludes his description with a "discussion" of what he regards as Zhenla's main features. Here is what he writes:

> Beeswax, peacocks, and kingfisher feathers abound, and there is plenty of *su* and *zan* lign-aloes. There are three types of lign-aloes, *lüyang*, the best, *sanle*, the next best, and *boluo*, the next after that.[22] There are trees called dammar that look like pines. When they are old they exude resin that has a clean, pure

> aroma. The locals collect it in gourds. Another tree, wood apple, has flowers like the Chinese crabapple, the leaves of an elm, and fruit like plums. There is *piye* [possibly bael fruit], which has the leaves of an apricot tree and fruit like paper mulberry. There is a tree that looks like a mango tree, with elm leaves, long branches, yellow flowers, and dark seeds. Its produce, sappan wood, can be used for dyeing.
>
> They have a fish called *jiantong* that has a trunk like an elephant's, can blow water into the air, and has four feet and no scales. Another fish called *fuhu* looks like an eel, has a beak like a parrot's, and has eight feet.[23]
>
> Its tribute missions are infrequent. In the sixth year [1373] of the Hongwu reign period [1368–1398], its king Huerna sent his officer Naiyiji and others to present local products as tribute.[24] Since then their tribute has been infrequent. It consists of elephants, ivory, sappan wood, pepper, beeswax, rhino horns, ebony, yellowflower wood, local lakawood, gemstones, and peacock feathers.
>
> Discussion: it is clear that Zhenla began with a person with the family name Shali [Kṣatriyaḥ, referring to Kṣatriyaḥ Īśānasena]. During the Qingyuan reign period [1195–1200] it undertook a great attack on Champa, reduced it to ruins, and changed its king to one of the ruling family of Zhenla. At this time it had about two hundred thousand elephants for use in warfare. Its territory is seven thousand or so square li; in the Southern Sea it is a prosperous, strong state. From the Hongwu period on it has paid tribute to the court, working through more than one interpreter.[25]

Like Fei Xin's description of Zhenla, Huang Xingzeng's portrait of Zhenla is significant not for what it says, but for what it leaves unsaid. Apart from the final section, Huang takes all his material from Song and Yuan sources. This suggests that, like Fei Xin, he had little or no access to contemporary information about Cambodia.

Four other Ming portrayals of Cambodia

A number of other Ming works include records of or allusions to Cambodia. Four of these are relatively well-known. They are *Shuyu zhouzi lu* [*A Record of Various Views on Distant Regions*], *Xian bin lu* [*A Record of All Foreign Guests*], *Dongxi yang kao* [*On the Eastern and Western Oceans*], and *Huangming xiangxu lu* [*The Record of an Interpreter of the August Ming Dynasty*]. All four consist of portraits of various foreign states, listed one by one in broadly the same format used by Wang Dayuan,

Fei Xin and Huang Xingzeng. Like the works by these writers, these four books add little to what earlier sources tell us, although they do contain a few pieces of new and interesting information.

The first of the four, *Shuyu zhouzi lu*, was completed in 1583 by Yan Congjian, a learned scholar from the city of Jiaxing to the northeast of Hangzhou, on the Grand Canal. We know nothing about Yan other than that he passed the highest grade of the imperial examination in 1559.[26] *Shuyu zhouzi lu* is made up of twenty-four chapters containing accounts of thirty-nine places. Zhenla—named as such—is sixth among them.[27]

Yan's description of Zhenla is quite long, but apart from a section on Ming-era tribute adds little to earlier records. He begins with a brief history of Funan, which he treats unquestioningly as the precursor to Zhenla. In a passing remark he identifies Funan with Xiangpu (a Ming name for the region of Champa), but without explaining why.[28] He then gives a short account of Funan from its founding queen Liuye to the takeover of Funan by the Zhenla ruler Kṣatriyaḥ Īśānasena, whom he calls simply Yijinna, the name used in *Xin Tang shu*. He goes on to mention the division of Zhenla into Water Zhenla and Land Zhenla, Zhenla's "ninety or so dependencies," ten of them named (with the names taken from Zhou Daguan), and Zhenla's "large-scale revenge attack" and takeover of Champa in the late twelfth century.

Turning to tribute during Ming times, Yan relates that when the first emperor of the Ming came to the throne in 1368 he sent an envoy to Zhenla. Soon after, the ruler of Zhenla, Huerna (the king mentioned earlier by Huang Xingzeng), sent his officer Naiyiji to the Ming court. In 1373 the emperor presented Huerna with gifts that included an imperial almanac, a work entitled *Tongyi li* [*The Almanac of Great Unity*], and multicolored silks.[29]

In 1387, Yan continues, the first emperor of the Ming dispatched another envoy, Tang Jing, to Zhenla.[30] In response, an unnamed ruler of Zhenla (still King Huerna?) presented the Ming court with fifty-nine elephants—a very large consignment, one that would surely have posed considerable transport problems—and sixty thousand catties of aromatic substances, an enormous amount weighing in excess of thirty-eight tons.

According to Yan, when the Yongle Emperor came to the throne in 1403 he sent yet another envoy to Zhenla as part of his effort to notify foreign states of his enthronement—his self-aggrandizing effort, for as we have seen Yongle was intent on having his authority stamped on all those who encountered it, near and far. The envoy, an official called Yin Shou who bore the title Imperial Historian, traveled by ship from Guangzhou to Champa.[31] From there he crossed, perhaps by land, to an unidentified city (*zhou*) called Putisa on Tonlé Sap Lake, and went on from there to

Zhenla via the Lu Ban Temple.[32] This temple seems to have been Angkor Wat, since as we saw earlier, Zhou Daguan believed that Angkor Wat was the tomb of Lu Ban, the semi-mythical Chinese carpenter. After Yin Shou had delivered the emperor's edict, which the Cambodian king "received with awed respect," he returned home by sea. On arriving in Nanjing he delighted Yongle by presenting him with a map of the various islands, mountains, rivers, lands, and capital cities he had seen en route. So far as we know, the map no longer exists.

Yan also notes that in the following year the king of Cambodia sent nine people with tribute to the Ming court. Yan calls the king Canlie Popiya. Canlie may be the Khmer honorific Samdach, but the Khmer equivalent of Popiye is unclear. When Popiya died in 1405 the Yongle Emperor enfeoffed his eldest son Canlie Zhaopingya as king. Coedès suggests that the Khmer title and name of this king was Samdach Chao Ponhea Yat. In 1421 Zhaopingya sent further tribute to the Ming, with Cambodia's last tribute to the Ming being sent in 1452.[33]

Yan goes on to describe the people and customs of Zhenla, drawing extensively on Zhou Daguan and mentioning both Zhou and his book by name. Yan quotes at length from the book, while adding a few lively asides of his own. In one of these he expresses incredulity at the idea that an ancient Chinese carpenter, Lu Ban, was entombed at Angkor.[34] In another, he questions a description—in a different source, not Zhou—of Pagan as a dependency of Zhenla, arguing that Pagan was ranked too high in Song protocol to have had that status. On this issue Yan was surely right; by Song times Pagan was a strong, independent state, too strong to be under Zhenla's aegis, even if it later faded away.[35]

Yan concludes by describing Zhenla's local products and tribute. The products he describes, several of them in some detail, are all mentioned in earlier sources, namely the work of Zhou Daguan and Zhao Rugua as well as *Sui shu* and *Liang shu*, though at this point Yan does not acknowledge his sources by name. The products are copper, benzoin, dammar, lign-aloes, musk wood, cardamom, elephants, sappan wood, kingfisher feathers, chaulmoogra, *piye* trees (possibly bael fruit), *potianluo* trees (perhaps date palms), mangoes, and the types of fish called *jiantong* and *fuhu*. The tribute from Zhenla that Yan lists is exactly the same as the tribute from Zhenla listed earlier by Huang Xingzeng.

In closing, Yan gives a somewhat vague account of Zhenla's location, which he describes as having the sea to its east, Pagan to its west, Jialuoxi to its south—Jialuoxi being a dependency of Srivijaya, possibly on the Kra Isthmus—and Champa to its north.

To sum up, Yan Congjian depends almost entirely on earlier sources, particularly Zhou Daguan, for his description of Zhenla. The only original material in his work are his occasional asides, and his accounts of the official missions to and from Cambodia from 1368 to 1452. These accounts are interesting for two reasons. First, the tribute the king of Cambodia sent to China in 1387 was enormous, even allowing for exaggeration, and shows how seriously he treated his relations with China at that time—largely, no doubt, because of threats posed by the Siamese, but also perhaps because by the fourteenth century the Cambodians had acquired a considerable respect for the power of Chinese itself.[36] Second, the route taken by the Yongle Emperor's second ambassador to Zhenla in 1403 suggests that until the early 1400s the king of Cambodia still lived in the region of Angkor Wat.

The second of the four works, *Xian bin lu* [*A Record of All Foreign Guests*] was completed around 1591 by Luo Yuejiong, an otherwise unknown scholar from Nanchang in Jiangxi province in central-south China.[37] An account of foreign peoples as well as countries, *Xin bin lu* consists of descriptions of a hundred and eight different states and peoples, one of which is Zhenla. We have no reason to believe Luo ever went abroad or visited the country.[38]

Luo begins with a short overview of the history of Zhenla, and before it Funan, from Queen Liuye to King Huerna. His only additions to earlier sources are two brief stories, one from the Han, the other from the Tang. The first tells how Funan sent Emperor Cheng of the Han dynasty (r. 33–7 BCE) a gift of ancient clams—presumably clamshells—and translucent pearls, which the emperor gave to his consort and favorite concubine. This putative event is not found in any Chinese source before *Xian bin lu*, and is probably a late fabrication. The other story is about a priceless mirror from Funan, sent by the gods. An earlier version of the story featured in a Tang dynasty work, now lost (see chapter four).[39]

Luo quotes extensively from Zhou Daguan. Like Yan Congjian, he acknowledges Zhou and his work by name, and with enthusiasm. He remarks that of all the histories and other works he has read, "nothing is as extraordinary" as Zhou's record, and nothing in the record "as extraordinary as the king lying each night in a gold tower with a nine-headed snake spirit in female form."

Luo provides a partial list of Zhenla products that includes several fanciful or obscure items. The products are *jiantong* and *fuhu* fish, another large fish that spouts water, an animal called *fengmu* (described in *Taiping yulan* as a hairless, red-eyed, ape-like creature), another creature called *quechenshou* ("the dust-dispelling animal"), as well as *piye* (possibly bael fruit), *potianluo* (perhaps date), wood apple, crocodiles, and "beauties' wine," an otherwise unknown name for a Cambodian wine.[40]

Luo concludes by remarking that Zhenla stands out among the countries of the southwest for the way it dispenses justice, a fact explained, in his view, by its proximity to India and its strict devotion to Buddhism.

The third of the four works, *Dongxi yang kao* [*On the Eastern and Western Oceans*], conveys slightly more up-to-date knowledge of Cambodia than its two predecessors. Completed in 1617, in the last decades of the Ming, it is a full account of the maritime routes known to late Ming traders.[41] Its author Zhang Xie (1574–1640) was a writer and poet from a well-regarded local family in Zhangzhou, a city near the coast to the southeast of the port of Quanzhou. Perhaps because of the tumultuous period Zhang was living through—the Ming government was sinking into terminal decline—he did not pursue an official career. But he was persuaded to write *Dongxi yang kao* by two officials in his locality, one of them a magistrate responsible for taxation.[42] This was a time when foreign trade was burgeoning despite periodic Ming efforts to curb it, and the officials clearly saw a growing need for information of the kind Zhang could provide.

Zhang's work falls into two parts. The first part describes some twenty-one places and peoples, from Jiaozhi (the Vietnamese) and Champa to Japan and "the Red-Haired Foreigners"—the latter being the Dutch, first reference to Westerners in Ming accounts of maritime trade. The second part discusses aspects of foreign trade and specific conditions in certain locations in more detail.

Cambodia is one of the twenty-one places in the first part of Zhang's book.[43] In a break from precedent, he calls it Cambodia (Jianpuzhai), recording that

> This is the old Zhenla. The state's name for itself is Ganbozhi, which was later mistakenly rendered as Ganpozhe. Now the term Jianpuzhai is again an error for Ganpozhe.[44]

After reviewing Cambodia's history from the time "it was a dependency of Funan," Zhang writes that "for merchant ships arriving there nowadays, the main capital is on the territory of [the former] Water Zhenla"—in other words, somewhere much closer to the coast than Angkor. Later he scatters through his text several other remarks about conditions for merchants in Cambodia.[45] At one point he notes that

> nowadays merchant ships do not go to the royal city, but just to a dependent state at a corner of the sea, so they do not see the city's glories.

Which royal city Zhang is referring to he does not say, but his reference to its glories suggests he means Angkor. Zhang also refers to a *zhou* (city) called Limu or Bamboo Fence Wood, and explains that it is a city made of wood where Chinese guests are housed, and where merchants go to conduct trade through a chieftain (*qiuzhang*).[46] Although he does not say so, it seems that Limu was part of the dependent state by the sea. Towards the end of his description of Cambodia, he comments again on local trading conditions, remarking that

> the foreigners [Cambodians] are quite honest by nature. They use official coinage they have minted to trade with us, and after taking their money we use it some other time to buy their local goods.

In addition to these scattered remarks about trade, Zhang describes some of the diplomatic and tribute missions involving Cambodia and China in Song and Yuan times, repeating information available in earlier sources, including Yan Congjian.[47]

Zhang also gives a full account of the lives and customs of Cambodians, quoting at length from Zhou Daguan. He repeatedly mentions Zhou's *Zhenla fengtu ji* as his source, while also drawing extensively from it.

In conclusion, Zhang provides a list of local products. Most of these are from *Sui shu* and *Zhenla fengtu ji*, which Zhang duly notes as his sources. The other products that Zhang lists include "crane crest" plums, copper, benzoin, dammar, lign-aloes, cloth, otter skin, local jars, coconut, swallows' nests, musk wood, and sappan.[48]

The last of the four works, *Huangming xiangxu lu* [*The Record of an Interpreter of the August Ming Dynasty*], also a late Ming work, was completed in 1629 by Mao Ruizheng (fl. 601–631), a member of a leading family in Guian county in Zhejiang province. Mao was an accomplished scholar-official, having passed the highest level of the imperial examination in 1601, and served for some twenty-seven years in different branches of government, including the Ministry of War. The "Interpreter" in the name of his book was the title given to senior Ming officials responsible for taking care of foreign envoys.

Mao wrote fourteen books, nearly all of them on geographical topics, and many on foreign countries and peoples.[49] *Huangming xiangxu lu* contains accounts of ninety-seven countries and regions, including Cambodia, which Mao again calls Zhenla. The entry on Zhenla does not, however, add anything to records already available in earlier sources. Aside from giving a brief account of Zhenla's history as far back as Citrasena, and repeating reports of Zhenla's tribute missions to China in Song, Yuan, and Ming times, Mao repeats many of the main points made in Zhou Daguan's *Zhenla fengtu ji*, whose author and title he again acknowledges by name.

To sum up, the sources discussed here, while not the only unofficial works that describe or refer to Zhenla, can be taken as representative of what educated Chinese knew about Cambodia during the late Yuan and Ming. This knowledge was surprisingly limited, given the opportunities to learn more about Cambodia from maritime traders visiting China's ports, and from the numerous missions traveling to and from Cambodia and China in the period concerned. The fact that so few knew so little was probably a reflection of Angkor's decline, and the diminishing significance of Cambodia in regional affairs.

Ming historical sources on Cambodia

Two official Ming historical sources, *Ming shi* [*The History of the Ming dynasty*], completed in 1739, nearly a century after the establishment of the Qing dynasty, and *Ming shilu* [*The Veritable Records of the Ming Dynasty*], not fully published until modern times, have some modest value with respect to records of Cambodia, still called Zhenla. They are mainly useful for their records of the tribute missions and other exchanges between Zhenla and China during the early years of the Ming dynasty, before the Ming capital moved from Nanjing to Beijing in 1421. Otherwise, neither source has anything new to say about Cambodia's customs and conditions. *Ming shi* does contain a short section with a general description of Zhenla, but it consists entirely of extracts from Zhou Daguan's *Zhenla fengtu ji* and other earlier materials.[50]

The tribute missions and other exchanges recorded by *Ming shi* and *Ming shilu* are concentrated into the half-century between 1370 and 1420—that is, from the founding of the Ming in 1368 to its move to Beijing, when exchanges petered out. Zhenla was not the only southern state to send a large number of tribute missions during this period.[51] But it was certainly one of the most active. Between 1371 and 1436 it dispatched nineteen tribute missions to the Ming court.[52] For its part, the Ming court sent six missions to Zhenla between 1370 and 1406.[53]

Despite their sparseness, the records of these exchanges—a small component of the large and complex tribute principles and practices that characterized the Ming[54]—are informative in various ways. Firstly, they raise a question, albeit obliquely, about Zhenla's location and identity. In 1371 Zhenla sent a tribute mission to the Hongwu Emperor (r. 1368–1398), evidently in response to envoys that the emperor sent out to Zhenla and elsewhere the year before to mark his accession. The 1371 mission was recorded as being from "King Huerna of Bashan in the state of Zhenla." This is an unusually specific formulation. Bashan (Ba Mountain) may mean Ba Phnom, referring perhaps to the venerable hill southeast of present-day Phnom Penh (*phnom* being "hill" or "mountain" in Khmer).[55] Assuming it does, the records could be interpreted to suggest that the Ming court recognized Huerna as king in one particular location, Ba Phnom, while allowing for the possibility of other Cambodian rulers elsewhere.[56]

The records also convey a sense of the importance Zhenla attached to its tribute relationship with China. In 1372–1374 the Hongwu Emperor renounced military aggression, affirmed that China would refrain from invading Zhenla and other named states, and instructed Zhenla and other distant states to submit tribute only occasionally and without extravagance. Despite this, the Zhenla king Canda Ganwuzhe Chidazhi (a transliteration perhaps of Samdach Kambuja-dhirāja) sent envoys with tribute to the Ming court in 1377–1378, and again in 1380, setting the trend for continual tribute missions from Zhenla to China that lasted for decades.[57] The kings of Zhenla clearly regarded their tribute missions to China as being too important to curtail.

The records show how inordinately large the tribute could be. In 1383, the Hongwu Emperor sent envoys to Zhenla and other states to collate official tallies so as to ensure against fraud. (As we saw in references to tallies in Zhou Daguan's *Record*, split tallies were used in China for military and civil officials, one part held by the person in command, one part by the subordinate.) What the background to this initiative was is unclear—perhaps tallies carried by envoys had been misused. To thank them for their help, as it seems, in that same year Hongwu sent each of the kings of Zhenla, Champa, and Siam thirty-two pieces of gold-embroidered and decorated silk and nineteen thousand pieces of porcelain—the latter a very substantial gift indeed.[58]

The records also describe continuing friction between Zhenla and Champa. In 1386 the Hongwu Emperor sent Tang Jing and others as envoys to Zhenla and elsewhere. They returned from Zhenla the following year with fifty-nine elephants and sixty thousand catties of aromatic substances—another huge gift, mentioned earlier by Yan Congjian. Champa is said to have set up "bandits" to steal up to thirteen of the elephants, along with fifteen slaves. This angered the emperor, who sent an envoy to reprimand the Champa king; before the envoy arrived, the king of Champa returned the stolen tribute and apologized.[59] Later, in 1414, an envoy sent to China by the then king of Zhenla, Canlie Zhaopingya (a transliteration perhaps of Samdach Chao Ponhea Yat), complained that Champa was repeatedly subjecting Zhenla to encroachment and plunder. The envoy was eventually escorted home from Nanjing by Zhu Yuan, a senior Ming official. En route there or back, Zhu Yuan stopped off in Champa to reprimand the king of Champa again and to tell him, in effect, that he had to be a more responsible neighbor.[60]

The records mention slaves as being part of Zhenla's tribute. In 1388 King Baopiye Ganpuzhe sent a mission to China that consisted of envoys with twenty-eight elephants, thirty-four slaves to care for them, and thirty-five other "foreign" slaves, presumably people from Cambodia.[61] The provision of slaves is reminiscent of the tribute of two people from Baitou sent by Funan in the early seventh century, and shows that slavery was still part of Cambodian life.

On a lighter note, the records suggest that exchanges were sometimes characterized by mishaps. In 1403 the Yongle Emperor marked his accession to the throne by sending envoys to nine states including Zhenla. Three soldiers in the group sent to Zhenla went missing, lured away, perhaps, by the idyllic life that (according to Zhou Daguan) Chinese could enjoy there. The king, Canlie Popiya, resolved this awkward issue by substituting three of his own people for the three who had gone missing. His action was not appreciated. "What use are these three to me," the emperor expostulated, "with no language to communicate with them, and their unfamiliar customs?" The three were sent back, and in 1404 Canlie Popiya sent gifts to the emperor, no doubt to appease him.[62]

Finally, the records reflect the readiness of both sides to observe that proper protocol, one that affirmed good working relations, but also Cambodia's subservience to China. In 1405 an envoy was sent from Zhenla to the Ming court to convey the news that Canlie Popiya had died. The Yongle Emperor not only sent an envoy to Zhenla to offer sacrifices for the late king, but also dispatched two other envoys to enfeoff Canlie Popiya's eldest son Canlie Zhaopingya. The two envoys arrived back in China a year later, accompanied by another envoy from Zhenla who submitted tribute in thanks, and was given gifts in return.[63]

It is not entirely clear why missions from Zhenla petered out in the fifteenth century. The main reason seems to have been the Ming court's move to its new capital in Beijing. Following this move, tribute missions from southern states quickly diminished in number, though Siam was an exception, since it continued to send tribute missions now and then until the last years of the Ming.[64]

One point about these various records of exchanges between Zhenla and China stands out. Whereas Champa is portrayed as a source of instability, there is no mention of aggression towards Zhenla on the part of Xianlo, that is, Siam. This is remarkable, given that Zhou Daguan made it clear in *Zhenla fengtu ji* that by the end of the thirteenth century Siamese depredations were taking their toll on the life of Angkor, while according to Coedès, Siamese annals suggest that in the fourteenth century Angkor repeatedly came under attack by Siamese forces.[65] By contrast, *Ming shi* does not mention any Siamese attack on Zhenla until two centuries later, during the Wanli reign period (1572–1620).[66] At that time, it records,

> Siam . . . moved its army and attacked Zhenla, deposing its king. From then on, it deployed its troops every year, and became the greatest power among the various states.

Despite this lacuna, an important reason for Zhenla's vigorous involvement in tribute missions during the early Ming would undoubtedly have been concern about the threat to its security posed by the Siamese.[67] Not that theirs was the only threat the Khmers of Angkor faced during the Yuan and Ming era. Champa was troublesome, as the records show. China itself was also a cause for concern, although not one that was likely to feature in Chinese records. The Hongwu Emperor may have had pacific intentions, but other events—Kublai Khan's campaigns in Southeast Asia, the Yongle Emperor's occupation of Vietnam between 1407 and 1427, Admiral Zheng He's awe-inspiring and overbearing naval fleets—all served to remind the rulers of Zhenla that China's intentions were not always benign.

Nonetheless, the threat from Siam would have been foremost in Khmer rulers' minds. Perhaps the silence of Ming annals on this score can be explained, at least in part, by Siam's assiduous cultivation of the Ming court through the submission of tribute.[68]

11

Conclusions

This work has endeavored to provide full, up-to-date translations into English of all the significant early Chinese texts on Çambodia up to the time of the thirteenth-century envoy Zhou Daguan, with a brief review of relevant texts from then until the end of the Ming dynasty. It has also analyzed these texts to assess the contributions they make to our understanding of early Cambodian history, their gaps and omissions, as well as the imperial Chinese perspectives that inform them.

The process of translating these texts has highlighted the fact that, apart from a period between the eighth and the late eleventh century, Funan and subsequently Zhenla featured almost continually in Chinese sources. Some of these sources are humdrum, but many are informative and original, in the sense that they provide new points of view and new materials.[1] Taken as a whole the texts amount to a cumulative historical narrative stretching over most of a millennium, one that entails different Chinese voices speaking from differing perspectives, official and unofficial.

One particular conclusion to be drawn is that the texts rely on a variety of sources. In the case of Funan, a passing comment in *Liang shu* as well as the differing accounts of Funan in *Jin shu*, *Nan Qi shu*, and *Liang shu* suggest that the reports of the third-century envoys Kang Tai and Zhu Ying, while important, were not the only source of information about Funan in later texts.[2] Similarly, in the case of Zhenla, whichever source—perhaps the report of the Sui dynasty envoy Chang Jun to Red Earth—informed the first account of Zhenla in *Sui shu*, it was clearly not the only source of information for several later passages about Zhenla written well before the visit there of Zhou Daguan.

Some salient issues

Otherwise, it may be useful to sum up the comments and analyses provided in the course of this work. There are a number of salient issues, several of them particularly notable. These are: the identity of Funan and its connection with Zhenla; the role of foreign trade; the extent of Funan's Indianization; the nature of the transition from Funan to Zhenla; the perception of Funan and Zhenla as states; and the influence of imperial Chinese perspectives.

The identity of Funan and its connection with Zhenla

While Zhenla in its later stages is clearly the polity known to modern historians as Angkor, an enduring question relating to Funan is whether, and if so why it should be regarded as part of Cambodian history. Chinese texts on Funan show that this question can be considered from four perspectives: geographical, linguistic, cultural, and historical.

Geographically, the locations for Funan given in early Chinese sources are consistent with the archaeological sites—at Óc Eo, Angkor Borei, and elsewhere—that modern historians and archaeologists have identified with Funan. Early Chinese sources locate Funan south of Rinan (as in Kang Tai, *Nan Qi shu*, and *Liang shu*) or west or southwest of Linyi (as in *Tai qing jin ye shen dan jing*, *Jin shu*, and *Liang shu*). The extent or size of Funan is hard to judge from Chinese sources. This is partly because of the difficulty in defining relevant Chinese terms—notably *guangmao*, whose meaning as we have seen is debatable—and partly because it is not clear what the *shu* (dependencies) of Funan mentioned by Wan Zhen and Zhu Zhi and in *Tai qing jin ye shen dan jing*, *Liang shu*, and *Tang hui yao* consisted of or how long they lasted.

The *Liang shu* account of Fan Shiman's conquests of neighboring states suggests that during his reign (in the early third century?) Funan's authority was geographically widespread, but there is little in Chinese records to confirm that his conquests were enduring other than a passing reference in *Tang hui yao* to Funan's authority reaching as far west as present-day Myanmar. As for the geographical relationship between Funan and Zhenla, Chinese accounts of the takeover of Funan by Zhenla make no mention of the two overlapping territorially, though it is reasonable to suppose a sizeable overlap between Funan and the eighth-century Water Zhenla.

Linguistically, doubts remain as to whether Funan's people were speakers of a Mon-Khmer or Austroasiatic language, or speakers of an Austronesian language related to Cham, or indeed both.[3] Vickery notes that seventh-century inscriptions show that Khmer had been the language of central and southern Cambodia for centuries.[4] If the fragmentary evidence in Chinese sources suggests anything, it is that the people associated with Funan spoke a form of Mon-Khmer. The name of the Funan dependency of Dunxun may have been derived from Mon.[5] More importantly, the royal title or surname Gulong, mentioned in *Liang shu* and subsequent Chinese texts, may have been the equivalent of the Mon-Khmer title *kuruṅ*. Similarly, if Vickery's argument is accepted, the royal title or surname Fan mentioned in *Liang shu* and later Chinese texts may have been the equivalent of the Mon-Khmer title *poñ*. Otherwise, the linguistic origins of other proper names in Chinese texts, other than those derived from Sanskrit, have yet to be identified. Moreover the Chinese term Jimie, probably meaning Khmer, does not occur until after the disappearance of Funan from Chinese texts, being first mentioned in the Buddhist text *Yiqie jing yinyi* (820?), and so has no bearing on the case.

Culturally, *Sui shu* describes Zhenla as having originally been a dependency of Funan, and in terms of broad categories official Chinese accounts of Funan and Zhenla are quite similar. For example, if we compare the accounts of Funan in *Liang shu* and Zhenla in *Sui shu*—both quite full accounts in Chinese histories dating from the same year, 636—we find that they have at least eight broad topics in common.[6] In detail, however, their accounts differ. Several aspects of the two states—the conduct of their kings, their people's daily habits, their funeral rituals—are portrayed differently.[7] The accounts in *Liang shu* and *Sui shu* are too brief and selective for us to attach too much importance to such differences. All the same, it is notable that with one possibly important exception—*Sui shu*'s comparison between the living arrangements of the people of Zhenla and those of Chitu—imperial Chinese historians never make an explicit comparison between Funan and Zhenla, as they do with respect to other states. This could suggest that they regarded Funan and Zhenla as quite distinct from one other.

Historically, there are two reports in Chinese sources, probably related, that connect Funan and Zhenla. The first is the description in *Sui shu*, repeated in later texts, of Zhenla originally being a dependency of Funan. The second is the lineage that, according to local epigraphic evidence, seems to have been shared by the last named king of Funan Rudravarman, mentioned in *Liang shu*, and Citrasena, described in *Sui shu* as the king of Zhenla who took over Funan.

In themselves these two reports give only limited ground for claiming a broader continuity between the polities of Funan and Zhenla. The Chinese term *shu* or dependency is too vague for us to know what the dependent relationship between Zhenla and Funan might have consisted of, while a lineage shared by two generations of local kings is not in itself enough to justify an assumption that the peoples and territories they preside over have a shared history or culture.[8]

To sum up, the evidence from Chinese texts suggests that Funan may have been a Khmer-speaking polity with royal lineage connections to Zhenla, while its social and economic conditions were in some broad senses portrayed as similar to those of Funan but may have differed from them in detail.

The role of foreign trade

An unexpected aspect of Chinese texts on Funan and Zhenla prior to the twelfth century is how infrequently they refer to foreign trade. This is not the case from the late Song on, when there are references to foreign trade involving Zhenla, most extensively in Zhou Daguan's *Zhenla fengtu ji*.

In the case of early Zhenla, this omission can be tentatively explained by the fact that from the eighth to the tenth century Zhenla's economy was primarily based on agriculture and had little to do with foreign trade, and by the arguably related fact that Chinese records during that period barely mention Zhenla at all.[9]

But with respect to Funan the paucity of Chinese references to foreign trade is more surprising, given that Funan's strength is often portrayed as deriving largely from its role as a center of regional commerce.[10] Putting aside remarks about trade and traders elsewhere—the merchant whose ship Hun Tian sailed on, the merchant Jia Xiangli who told Fan Zhan about India, the thriving markets in the Funan dependency of Dunxun—there are only a limited number of allusions in official Chinese texts to Funan engaging in trade beyond its frontiers.

These consist of: (1) references to goods from Da Qin (the eastern Roman empire) being sent via Central India to be traded through the southern states including Funan, initially given as an explanation of Kang Tai and Zhu Ying's trip south in the third century CE, and much later included in accounts of Funan in both the Tang standard histories; (2) the reference in *Liang shu* to the merchants from Da Qin who "frequently" went to Funan in the second century CE; (3) the *Nan Qi shu* account of how in 484 Kauṇḍinya Jayavarman sent people to Guangzhou to engage in trade there; (4) the reference in *Nan Qi shu* to trade in Funan, perhaps foreign trade, being done with gold, silver, and silks; (5) Six Dynasty fragments in *Taiping yulan* referring to people making a living with gold and hiring ships with it, presumably for trading purposes, and to iron being taken by ship from an unidentified place called Danlanzhou to Funan for sale there; and (6) the description of Funan cited in *Taiping yulan* as being like a tree made up of aromatic substances, at least two of them—cloves and frankincense—foreign to Funan and presumably available to it only through foreign trade.

Kang Tai and *Nan Qi shu* also both refer to various products that might have served Funan as objects of either tribute or foreign trade. In addition, of course, the standard histories and other official sources list tribute missions, and it is arguable that such tribute was frequently associated with trade.[11]

The relatively few references to trade by Funan could perhaps be explained by the attitude of official Chinese chroniclers, the principal sources of information on Funan, who may have regarded trade as an unsuitable subject for official records.[12] But in their accounts of other locations—Dunxun is a notable example—chroniclers are willing to report trade activities when they occur. Another consideration could be that modern scholars have emphasized Funan's status as a regional trade center at the expense of other explanations, such as Funan's role of Funan as a regional center of Buddhist learning, as can be evinced from several official and other Chinese sources.

The extent of Funan's Indianization

In his 2003 essay "Funan Reviewed," Vickery famously challenged the view held by Coedès that Funan's founding story, first related by Kang Tai, is the retelling of an Indian legend about a brahmin coming together with a local ruler, and as such represented Funan's first Indianization (or Hinduization, Coedès' original French term, and a more suitable one).[13] There is certainly good reason to question whether, as Pelliot tentatively suggested, the name of the story's male protagonist, Hun Tian, derived from the Sanskrit Kauṇḍinya. Moreover, Kang Tai recorded that people in Funan first learned about India not through Hun Tian but during the reign of one of Hun Tian's successors, Fan Zhan (fl. 243 CE), who learned about the riches of India from the visiting merchant Jia Xiangli.

Admittedly, this record of Fan Zhan's encounter with Jia Xiangli cannot readily be reconciled with growing evidence of cultural contacts and networks of exchanges between India and Southeast Asia dating back many centuries before the time of Fan Zhan. But it is consistent with the fact that the first record in Chinese sources of an overt Indian influence in Funan is found much later, in *Liang shu*'s account of the late fourth- or early fifth century brahmin Kauṇḍinya, who came to Funan, became king there, and "changed the system of rules and customs and used Indian law [?dharma] instead."[14]

Kauṇḍinya's story bears a resemblance to Hun Tian's, with both men apparently coming to Funan from a location to the south of it, after being bidden to do so by a god or gods. So perhaps parts of the Hun Tian story adumbrate the story of Kauṇḍinya, even if Hun Tian's name and other elements of his story owe their origins to local rather than Indian influences. In any case, from the time of Kauṇḍinya on, Indian influences in Funan—and subsequently Zhenla—become more evident. Thenceforth the names of Funan kings are derived from Sanskrit. There are also other references to Sanskrit names, titles and Indian beliefs, such as the title Maheśvara and the deity it refers to, Śiva, and to local products whose names seem to derive from Sanskrit. As for the extent of Indian influence before the fifth century, the limitations of Chinese sources on Funan make it difficult to determine with any degree of certainty.

The transition from Funan to Zhenla

Judging from the brief and disparate reports in *Tang hui yao*, *Sui shu*, *Xin Tang shu*, and the Buddhist monk Yijing's *Nanhai jigui neifa zhuan*, it seems clear that Funan was taken over by Zhenla sometime between 535 and 650 or even later, probably in a gradual process. The language of the Chinese texts, the sole sources of information about this transition, suggests that the takeover could have been effected relatively peacefully; but again, Chinese textual sources are too cryptic for us to be able to say for sure.[15]

The perception of Funan and Zhenla as states

Jacques, Vickery, and others have questioned whether Funan and Zhenla constituted single states rather than scattered polities, at least until the rise of the Kingdom of Angkor (Zhenla from the ninth century onwards), and have argued that in this respect Chinese sources are misleading.[16] It is true that Chinese descriptions of Funan and Zhenla as states reflect a Chinese imperial view of the world beyond China as being largely made up of states (*guo*). But Chinese chroniclers knowingly applied this term to a wide range of polities, from entities no larger than large villages to states that amounted to unified "coercion-wielding organizations" (to use Tilly's term) of the kind familiar to modern political scientists. The question is: what type of *guo* did they perceive Funan and Zhenla to be?

Chinese accounts of these two polities allow for the fact that at least until the time of the Kingdom of Angkor, they were both often either loosely connected or disunited. With respect to Funan, *Liang shu* relates that from early days it consisted of seven districts with seven rulers, albeit all under one overarching king, and that the

Funan king Pankuang (?second century CE) seems to have divided these districts up among his sons and grandsons. Subsequently Fan Shiman attacked neighboring states and made them Funan's "dependencies (*shu*)", but what this arrangement consisted of and how long it lasted is unclear. *Liang shu* describes one such dependency, the trading polity of Dunxun, as being ruled by five kings "loose dependent" on Funan, implying a cluster of small entities with a high degree of autonomy. Later, *Sui shu* refers to the state of Chitu, located perhaps in the north of the Malay Peninsula, or possibly near present-day Kampong Cham, as being an offshoot of Funan. In one passage the Daoist text *Tai qing jin ye shen dan jing* seems to refer to "the kings and rulers" of Funan.[17] These comments all suggest that other than during the time of Fan Shiman, Chinese chroniclers and other writers accepted that Funan was a loosely connected polity or set of polities rather than a homogeneous state.

Similarly, Chinese sources not only describe the division of Zhenla into Land Zhenla and Water Zhenla during the eighth century, but also portray early Zhenla as a polity or polities of many parts. *Sui shu* notes that seventh century Zhenla comprised thirty large cities, each under its own regional leader. *Xin Tang shu* relates that in 638 and thereafter five states sent tribute to China before some or all of them were taken over by Zhenla, suggesting a degree of political disunity during that period. *Jiu Tang shu* records that on the eastern frontier of Water Zhenla there were "small cities, all called states." *Xin Tang shu* mentions that Wendan or Land Zhenla had two dependencies, Daoming and Canban. While fragmentary, these references suggest that Chinese perceptions of Zhenla before the ninth century allowed for a degree of fragmentation.

It is arguable, therefore, that Chinese chroniclers' understanding of what the polities of Funan and Zhenla consisted of in some ways resembled that of modern historians.

The influence of imperial Chinese perspectives

In the words of Michael Loewe, the standard histories of dynastic China were "irretrievably [S]ino-centred", designed to display the splendor of the Chinese imperium and lacking in other sources that might provide different points of view.[18] The same applies to other official records. This single-minded Sinocentrism had a profound effect on the Chinese worldview. As the contemporary Chinese philosopher Ge Zhaoguang puts it, "the Chinese of ancient times always believed that . . . Han civilization was the pinnacle of world civilization, and that the races surrounding them were barbarous and uncivilized," the sole challenge to this sense of civilizational superiority having come from Buddhism.[19]

These Sinocentric attitudes influenced Chinese accounts of early Cambodia, especially those in official records, in two ways. They seem to have affected the substance and content of what was recorded. They also influenced its tone.

In official accounts, the substance and content of what was recorded clearly reflected the desiderata of successive imperial Chinese courts. Until the Song dynasty, when such accounts came to an end, accounts in official records were concerned with up to six aspects of the state, whether Funan or Zhenla. These were: (1) its geographical location vis-à-vis China; (2) its system of governance, specifically its rulers and their officials; (3) its relations with other states; (4) its local produce, especially exotic goods unobtainable in China; (5) its customs, including matters of ritual and worship; and (6) the nature and frequency of its tribute missions. Most unofficial sources—notably Wan Zhen, Zhao Rugua, and Zhou Daguan—also tended to deal with these topics, though in certain cases, particular the Daoist writings attributed to Ge Hong, one topic was considered at the expense of others: in the case of the Daoist writings, the perennial search for the elixir of immortality.

As a result, there are notable omissions in even the fullest Chinese sources—*Nan Qi shu*, *Liang shu*, *Sui shu*, and the works of Zhao Rugua and Zhou Daguan. We have already noted the omission of any substantial account of trade before Zhou Daguan. Again, with the exception of Zhou's *Record*, Chinese sources give little account of farming techniques and make only two references to taxation, evidently for state revenue.[20] With respect to Zhenla, there is no account of Angkor's great water management schemes, apart from a passing mention by Zhou of two lakes in the Angkor capital (evidently Yaśovarman I's East Baray or reservoir, and Jayavarman VII's Jayatataka Baray).[21]

Gender bias is also a persistent feature of these Chinese sources, which were written by men for men, including successive emperors. With the exception of an allusion to possible matriliny in Funan, these sources generally portray the societies of Funan and Zhenla as solidly patriarchal and male centered.[22] This is misleading, as we know from the many portraits of women in social roles provided in Khmer inscriptions, and by Zhou Daguan's account of the women of Angkor, whom he describes as confident, knowledgeable about trade, and active in large numbers in the king's palace.[23]

There are occasional hints of other perspectives. Kang Tai and later sources acknowledge that the original ruler of Funan was a woman. *Nan Qi shu* and *Liang shu* allude to the authority enjoyed by Funan women or palace women, who could ride elephants along with the king. The Tang histories relate the unusual fact that the (unnamed) wife of a ruler of Wendan, or Land Zhenla, accompanied him when he paid a visit to the Chinese court. Zhou Daguan mentions holy women as well as holy men at Angkor, and Zhao Rugua seems to allude to temple *devadāsīs*. *Waiguo zhuan* and Zhou Daguan also refer to female slaves. But these are straws in the wind. The problem of gender bias is compounded by the paucity of gender-specific nouns and pronouns in classical Chinese, which inhibits our understanding of the possible roles of women in other settings, for example as guards and soldiers.

A final comment should be added about the tone of the Chinese texts. The tone of official sources, in particular, is marked by an attitude of *de haut en bas*. This is reflected in the Chinese terms used for southern peoples, notably the term *nan man*. Part of the lexicon of Chinese words for "foreigner", *man* is written with a disparaging "insect" radical.[24] It is reflected, too, in the benevolent condescension of the emperor Wu of the Southern Qi towards his Funan visitor Nāgasena, and also, perhaps, in the view expressed by Emperor Shenzong of the Song that Zhenla could and would do his bidding for a suitable reward. It is also evident in the repeated description of early Cambodians as "ugly and black", and in Zhou Daguan's patronizing amusement at a local practice he found odd. More generally it informs the assumptions of the tribute system, with its preconceptions of respect paid and patronage given, and in the *mission civilisatrice* implicit in the work of Chinese envoys such as Kang Tai and Zhu Ying, with their appointed task of *xuanhua* ("propagating civilization").[25] As the Chinese empire looked south, the presumption of its scholar-officials and other writers was that states such as Funan and Zhenla were not-yet-civilized entities being portrayed for the interest and information of the civilized Chinese imperium.

Final remarks

By translating and assessing the corpus of Chinese writings on Cambodia up to (and to a more limited extent beyond) the time of Zhou Daguan, this work has, I hope, added in several ways to our understanding of what we know, and do not yet know, about Cambodia's early history.

First, the study makes clear that most of the Chinese texts on Funan and Zhenla draw on new sources to add to records provided in earlier Chinese texts. Their portrayals of Funan and to a lesser extent Zhenla should be viewed as cumulative rather than merely repetitive.

Second, this work has identified and translated into English for the first time all the known fragments of the third-century envoy Kang Tai's record of Funan. These provide an important benchmark, or originary standard, against which to consider later reports of Funan.

Third, the study reaffirms the fact, earlier observed by Mabbett, that no certain conclusion can be drawn from Chinese texts as to whether Funan was in any sense an empire, in spite of the expansionist conquests of Fan Shiman.[26] Indeed, depending on how ambiguous Chinese terms such as *guangmao* are interpreted, Funan's geographical extent or influence may have been quite small, even if one early sixth-century source (Buddhabadra) describes it as the largest of the southern states. At some points of time it held sway over dependencies, but we know little about what this relationship of dependency consisted of.

Fourth, consideration of Chinese sources raises a new question about the role of foreign trade. While Chinese texts on Funan and Zhenla before the twelfth century include descriptions of the local products of Funan and Zhenla, including those presented to the Chinese court as tribute, there are relatively few explicit references to foreign trade. In the case of Zhenla, especially early Zhenla, this is understandable, given its inland agrarian economy. In the case of Funan it suggests that it was not just Funan's function as a regional trading center that drew Chinese chroniclers' attention, but also, perhaps, other facets of its existence, notably its role as a center of Buddhist learning.

Fifth, with respect to the political culture of Funan, the study confirms that apart from the uncertainty of Hun Tian's origins, no extant Chinese sources convey a sense of a significant Indian or Sanskritic influence on Funan before the early fifth century CE.[27] It is notable, however, that these sources do give some sense of Funan, and also pre-Angkorian Zhenla, being a loosely structured polity or polities.

Sixth, Chinese sources suggest that the linguistic identity of Funan seems more likely to have been more Mon-Khmer than Austronesian, although in this respect the evidence is flimsy.

Seventh, the language of Chinese records suggests that while the nature of the transition from Funan to Zhenla in the seventh century is unknown, there are grounds for arguing that it may have been a relatively peaceful and gradual process. Chinese sources also suggest that political connections between Funan and Zhenla may have amounted to little more than a single royal lineage, and that culturally the polities of Funan and Zhenla had considerable differences as well as similarities.

Eighth, the study confirms the disappointing absence from Chinese sources of accounts of Zhenla or Angkor as it developed from the eighth to the twelfth centuries, an absence matched by the long gap in tribute missions from Zhenla from 814 to 1117. This state of affairs can be explained, at least in part, by the turbulent conditions in China in late Tang, Five Dynasties, and Northern Song times, and by the fact that Zhenla's inland agrarian economy allowed only a limited role for trade, at least until the twelfth century.

Finally, an understanding of the body of Chinese records relating to early Cambodia gives us a clearer perception of not only the value of these records but also their shortcomings. Written by members of a small educated male elite to meet the needs for historical and cultural documentation of the Chinese empire's foreign relations, the records have left us with a precious portrait of Funan and Zhenla. But they are irrefutably partial, incomplete, and influenced by a condescendingly Sinocentric worldview.

An important aim of this work has been to identify and contextualize early Chinese records of Funan and Zhenla, highlighting not only what they omit and distort, but also how they add to our knowledge of early Cambodian civilization. More broadly, the work serves as an illustration of how Chinese historical sources can enhance our understanding of Chinese perspectives on regional history, and of the role China has played in it. An increasingly confident, powerful China is now casting a growing shadow over Cambodia, not to mention other parts of Southeast Asia. This trend will, I think, sharpen the salience of this work.

Appendix 1:
Official writings used as primary sources, listed chronologically

Author or Compiler	Work	Date of completion (or presentation to the emperor)
Sima Qian 司馬遷	*Shi ji* 史記 [*The Record of the Historian*]	87 BCE
Ban Gu 班固	*Han shu* 漢書 [*The History of the Former Han Dynasty*]	96 BCE
Chen Shou 陳壽	*San guo zhi* 三國志 [*Annals of the Three States or Three Kingdoms*]	297 CE
Fan Ye 范曄 et al.	*Hou Han shu* 後漢書 [*The History of the Later Han Dynasty*]	445
Shen Yue 沈約	*Song shu* 宋書 [*The History of the Liu Song Dynasty*]	488
Xiao Zixian 蕭子顯	*Nan Qi shu* 南齊書 [*The History of the Southern Qi Dynasty*]	537
Yao Silian 姚思廉	*Liang shu* 梁書 [*The History of the Liang Dynasty*]	636
Yao Silian 姚思廉	*Chen shu* 陳書 [*The History of the Chen Dynasty*]	636
Wei Zheng 魏徵 et al.	*Sui shu* 隋書 [*The History of the Sui Dynasty*]	636
Fang Xuanling 房玄齡 et al.	*Jin shu* 晉書 [*The History of the Jin Dynasty*]	648
Li Yanshou 李延壽 et al.	*Nan shi* 南史 [*The History of the Southern Dynasties*]	659
Du You 杜佑	*Tong dian* 通典 [*A Comprehensive History of Institutions*]	801
Liu Xu 劉昫 et al.	*Jiu Tang shu* 舊唐書 [*The Old History of the Tang Dynasty*]	945
Wang Pu 王溥, ed.	*Tang hui yao* 唐會要 [*Essential Documents and Regulations of the Tang Dynasty*]	961
Li Fang 李昉 et al.	*Taiping guangji* 太平廣記 [*Extensive Records Compiled during the Era of Great Peace* {976–983}]	978
Li Fang 李昉 et al.	*Taiping yulan* 太平御覽 [{*An Encyclopedia*} *Compiled during the Era of Great Peace and Read by the Emperor*]	984
Yue Shi 樂史 et al., ed.	*Taiping huanyu ji* 太平寰宇記 [*A Record of the World during the Era of Great Peace*]	Late tenth century
Wang Qinruo 王欽若 et al., ed.	*Cefu yuangui* 冊府元龜 [*Outstanding Models from the Storehouse of Literature*]	1013
Ouyang Xiu 歐陽修 et al.	*Xin Tang shu* 新唐書 [*The New History of the Tang Dynasty*]	1060
Zheng Qiao 鄭樵	*Tong zhi* 通志 [*A Comprehensive Treatise on Institutions*]	1161
Ma Duanlin 馬端臨	*Wenxian tongkao* 文獻通考 [*A Comprehensive Study of Institutions on the Basis of Authoritative Documents*]	1319
Tuotuo 脫脫 (Toqto'a) et al.	*Song shi* 宋史 [*The History of the Song Dynasty*]	1345
Zhang Tingyu 張廷玉 et al.	*Ming shi* 明史 [*The History of the Ming Dynasty*]	1739
Liu Lin 劉琳 et al., ed.	*Song hui yao jigao* 宋會要輯稿 [*A Draft Edition of the Essential Documents and Regulations of the Song Dynasty*]	1936
Li Jinhua 李晉華 et al., ed.	*Ming shilu* 明實錄 [*The Veritable Records of the Ming Dynasty*]	1962–1968

Sources: Wilkinson, *Chinese History*, 694, 718, 724, 826, 1081; Johannes Kurz, "*Taiping yulan* 太平御覽" in Chennault et al., *Early Medieval Chinese Texts*, 342–343; Wang, *Tang hui yao*, i.

Appendix 2:
Chinese dynasties and Cambodian rulers

Chinese Dynasties	Dates
Zhou 周 Warring States 戰國	1046–256 BCE 475–256 BCE
Qin 秦	221–206 BCE
Han 漢 Former (Western) Han 前(西)漢 Later (Eastern) Han 後(東)漢	202 BCE–220 CE 202–8 BCE 27–220 CE
Three Kingdoms (Wei, Shu, Wu) 三國 (魏, 蜀, 吳) Wei 魏 Shu (or Shu Han) 蜀 (蜀漢) Wu 吳	220–280 220–265 221–263 222–280
Jin 晉 Western Jin 西晉 Eastern Jin 東晉	265–420 265–316 317–420
Northern and Southern Dynasties 南北朝 Six Dynasties 六朝	420–589 222–589
Southern Dynasties 南朝 Song (or Liu Song) 宋 (劉宋) Qi (or Nan Qi, that is, Southern Qi) 齊 (南齊) Liang 梁 Chen 陳	420–579 420–479 479–502 502–556 557–589
Sui 隋	581–618
Tang 唐	618–907
Five Dynasties and Ten Kingdoms 五代十國	907–960
Liao 遼	916–1125
Song 宋 Northern Song 北宋 Southern Song 南宋	960–1279 960–1127 1127–1279
Jin 金	1115–1234
Xia 夏	1038–1227
Yuan (Mongol) 元 (蒙古)	1271–1368
Ming 明	1368–1644
Qing (Manchu) 清 (滿洲)	1636–1912

Some dates in both categories are uncertain or disputed.

Source for Chinese dynasties: Wilkinson, *Chinese History*, 5, 767, 815.

Sources for (a) Funan: Li et al., *Taiping yulan*, 1599; Chen, *San guo zhi*, 920; Fang et al., *Jin shu*, 202; Xiao, *Nan Qi shu*, 1014–1015; Yao, *Liang shu*, 788–790; Vickery, *Society, Economics, and Politics*, 50. (b) pre-Angkor and Angkor: Coe and Evans, *Angkor and the Khmer Civilization*, 281; Vickery, *Society, Economics, and Politics*, 22, 124.

Cambodian rulers (kings except for Queen Liuye)	Dates
Funan	
Liuye	?Late first to early second century CE
Hun Tian	Late first to early second century CE
(Hun) Pankuang	Mid to late second century
Panpan	?End of the second century
Fan (Shi)man	?Early third century
Fan Zhan	fl. 243
Fan Xun	r. ?c.250–?c.290
Zhu Zhantan	fl. 357
Kauṇḍinya (Jiaochenru)	r. ?late fourth to early fifth century
Dhṛtavarman (Chili[tuo]bamo)	fl. 424–453
Kauṇḍinya Jayavarman (Qiaochenru Sheye[/xie]bamo)	r. late 470s–514
Rudravarman (Liutuobamo)	r. ?514–?539
Zhenla (1) pre-Kingdom of Angkor	
Bhavavarman I	late sixth century
Citrasena-Mahendravarman (Zhiduosina)	r. ?600–?610
Īśānavarman I (Yishe'naxian)	r. ?616–late 630s
Bhavavarman II	r. late 630s–mid 650s
Jayavarman I	r. ?657–?681
Jayadevi	fl 713
Zhenla (2) Kingdom of Angkor	
Jayavarman II	r. 802–835
Jayavarman III	r. c.835–?877
Indravarman I	r. 877–c. 889
Yaśovarman I	r. 889–c. 900
Harṣavarman I	r. c.900–c.923
Īśānavarman II	r. c.923–c.928
Jayavarman IV	r. c.928–941
Harṣavarman II	r. 941–944
Rājendravarman II	r. 944–968
Jayavarman V	r. 968–c.1000
Udayādityavarman I	r. 1001–1002
Sūryavarman I	r. 1002–1049
Udayādityavarman II	r. 1050–1066
Harṣavarman III	r. c.1066–1080
Jayavarman VI	r. 1080–1107
Dharanindravarman	r. 1107–1113
Sūryavarman II	r. 1113–c. 1149
Tribhuvanādityavarman	r. 1149–?c.1177
Yaśovarman II	r. c.1149–?c.1165
Jayavarman VII	r. 1181–c.1218
Indravarman II	r. c.1218–1243
Jayavarman VIII	r. 1243–1295
Indravarman III	r. c.1296–1308
Indrajayavarman (Indravarman IV)	r. 1308–1327
Jayavarmādiparameśvara	r. 1327–?

Appendix 3:
Tribute missions to China from Funan and Zhenla from the Han to the Song Dynasty

Sender	Date	Source
Funan	Pre-231	*San guo zhi*
Funan	243	*San guo zhi*
Funan	268 (?265)	*Jin shu*
Funan	?270	*Yu hai*
Funan	?271	*Yu hai*
Funan	?272	*Yu hai*
Funan	285	*Jin shu*
Funan	286	*Jin shu*
Funan	287	*Jin shu*
Funan	357	*Jin shu, Liang shu*
Funan	389	*Jin shu*
Funan	434	*Song shu*
Funan	435	*Song shu*
Funan	438	*Song shu*
Funan	442	*Nan shi*
Funan	484	*Nan Qi shu*
Funan	503	*Liang shu*
Funan	504	*Liang shu*
Funan	511/512	*Liang shu*
Funan	514	*Liang shu*
Funan	517	*Liang shu*
Funan	519	*Liang shu*
Funan	520	*Liang shu*
Funan	530	*Liang shu*
Funan	535	*Liang shu*
Funan	539	*Liang shu*
Funan	559	*Chen shu*
Funan	572	*Chen shu*
Funan	588	*Chen shu, Tong dian* (581–618)
Funan	618–649	*Tong dian, Taiping huanyu ji, Xin Tang shu*
Zhenla	616	*Sui shu, Cefu yuangui, Wenxian tongkao*
Zhenla	623	*Jiu Tang shu, Tang hui yao, Taiping huanyu ji, Cefu yuangui*
Zhenla	625	*Cefu yuangui*
Zhenla	628	*Jiu Tang shu, Tang hui yao, Taiping huanyu ji, Cefu yuangui*

Sender	Date	Source
Zhenla	635	*Cefu yuangui*
Zhenla	627–649	*Tang hui yao* ("repeatedly")
Zhenla	651	*Tang hui yao, Taiping huanyu ji, Cefu yuangui*
Zhenla	682	*Cefu yuangui*
Zhenla	698	*Tang hui yao, Taiping huanyu ji, Cefu yuangui*
Zhenla	707	*Cefu yuangui*
Wendan, Zhenla	710	*Cefu yuangui*
Wendan, Zhenla	717	*Tang hui yao, Taiping huanyu ji, Cefu yuangui* (both states listed)
Land Zhenla/?Wendan	741–?742	*Xin Tang shu*
Land Zhenla/?Wendan	750	*Tang hui yao, Taiping huanyu ji, Cefu yuangui*
Wendan	753	*Cefu yuangui*
Wendan	771	*Jiu Tang shu, Cefu yuangui, Xin Tang shu*
Wendan	798	*Cefu yuangui*
Water Zhenla/Zhenla	813	*Jiu Tang shu* (Water Zhenla), *Tang hui yao, Cefu yuangui*
Zhenla	814	*Jiu Tang shu, Cefu yuangui*
Zhenla	1117	*Song shi, Wenxian tongkao, Song hui yao jigao*
Zhenla	1120	*Lingwai daida, Song shi, Wenxian tongkao*
Zhenla	1155	*Song shi, Song hui yao jigao*

As noted in the main text, tribute consisted of various local products and specialities, including live elephants. Chinese sources sometimes specify these local products and specialities, sometimes not.

Itemized tribute from Funan included (a) a gold throne, a white rosewood elephant, two ivory pagodas, two pieces of cotton, and two glass vessels sent in 484; (b) a statue of the Buddha made of Indian sandalwood, leaves of the *poluo* tree, glass pearls, turmeric, liquidambar, and other aromatic substances sent in 519; (c) a live rhinoceros sent in 539; and (d) two white-haired people sent at some point between 627 and 649.

Itemized tribute from Zhenla included (a) eleven dancing elephants sent in 771; (b) books, presumably Buddhist texts, sent in 1117; (c) trained elephants sent in 1155; (d) tribute from Zhenla's dependency Zhenlifu or Zhenfuli sent in 1200, 1202, and 1205 that consisted in all of five elephants, two drapes to cover them, twenty-two elephant tusks, sixty rhino horns, fifty pieces of local cloth, and ten lengths of Indian cotton.

According to Bielenstein, tribute from Southeast Asian states from the seventh to the thirteenth centuries included human beings, mostly musicians; elephants (the largest item of tribute); rhinoceroses; elephant tusks and rhino horns; unusual animals and birds; kingfisher feathers; tortoiseshell; aromatic substances, including frankincense, rosewater, sandalwood, lign-aloes and camphor; spices, including cardamom and cloves; betel nuts; minerals, ores, and naphtha; gold and silver vessels and other manufactured objects; pearls, glass, hides, cotton, and silk; garments; and Buddhist texts. Items provided by Chinese courts in recompense included gold, silver, copper cash, silk, brocade, garments, caps, ornamental belts, vessels made of copper, porcelain and lacquerware, tea, banners, armor, military equipment, and Buddhist and Daoist texts. Bielenstein, *Diplomacy and Trade*, 82–94, 97–98.

What Bielenstein's analysis of tribute to China does not tell us is what tribute-bearing envoys received in return. As we have seen in official accounts, notably during the Ming dynasty, tribute was not a one-way street, and those bearing tribute often benefited from the emperor's largesse. Chinese sources often fail to describe the emperor's gifts to tribute-bearers in detail, leaving us with a probably unwarranted impression of exchanges of gifts being weighted heavily in China's favour.

Appendix 4:
A comparative table of the customs of Funan and Zhenla

Funan				
Topic	***Kang Tai*** **(*****Wai guo zhuan*****)**	***Jin shu***	***Nan Qi shu***	***Liang shu***
Distance from Linyi		✓		✓
River			✓	✓
History	✓	✓	✓	✓
Monarchs	✓	✓	✓	✓
Buildings	✓*	✓	✓	
Elephants, including for hunts		✓	✓	✓
Lie of land, weather				✓
People, character, appearance		✓	✓	✓
Marriages, funerals				✓
Women			✓	✓
Farming practices		✓		
Wells and ponds				✓
Carving, engraving	✓			
Almsgiving, temples	✓*			
Gods, holy statuary				✓
Utensils, cups of silver, gold	✓	✓	✓	✓
Taxes		✓		
Script		✓		
Slaves	✓*		✓	
Storehouses		✓		
Merchandise, produce			✓	✓
Clothing, cloth			✓	
Walls of wood, bamboo thatch			✓	
Boats	✓		✓	
Fighting cocks	✓		✓	
Trials by ordeal, crocodiles	✓		✓	✓

Zhenla					
Topic	***Sui shu***	***Jiu Tang shu***	***Xin Tang shu***	***Zhu fan zhi***	***Zhou Daguan***
Distance from Linyi, location	✓	✓	✓	✓	✓
River, lakes		✓			✓
History	✓				
King or kings	✓	✓	✓	✓	✓
Palace				✓	✓
Officials	✓			✓	✓
Cities, dependencies	✓	✓		✓	✓
Foreign relations	✓		✓	✓	✓
Soldiers, battle	✓	✓	✓	✓	✓
Elephants		✓	✓	✓	✓
People, habits, appearance	✓	✓	✓	✓	✓
Local Chinese					✓
Language, writing					✓
Other buildings				✓	✓
Weather	✓	✓		✓	✓
Women	✓		✓	✓	✓
Slaves					✓
Marriage	✓				✓
Illness, death	✓				✓
Farming, farming practices	✓		✓	✓	✓
Temples, monks, priests, Buddhist worship	✓	✓		✓	✓
Clothing, utensils	✓			✓	✓
Produce, including food and drink	✓		✓	✓	✓
Trade				✓	✓
Boats					✓
Carts, palanquins					✓
Trials by ordeal, punishments	✓			✓	✓

Appendix 5:
The elusive Linyi: Chinese sources revisited

Linyi is sometimes treated as the first stage of the history of Champa; but it is questionable whether this is a suitable way to consider it.[1] Chinese sources treat it as a distinct state up to the eighth century. Assuming there is some justification for this, we are bound to ask: in what sense was it distinct? Did its governance and society have particular qualities, and if so what were they? Did its ruling elite or elites consist of a single ethno-linguistic group? If so, was its identity mainly Mon-Khmer, as Vickery is inclined to argue?[2] Or was it primarily Cham, Chinese, proto-Vietnamese or something else, or a mixture of all these, at least during the third, fourth and fifth centuries CE? Moreover, did Linyi consist of a single entity, or at least a single dominant entity, as Chinese sources indicate, or of several entities or more?

A vital source of information about Linyi, whose name—like that of Funan—derives solely from Chinese sources, is the corpus of Chinese historical records. This is true not only of the first three centuries or so of Linyi's existence, when Chinese records are the principal historical source, but also from the fifth to the mid-eighth century, during which time Sanskrit and Cham inscriptions come to play a significant role, though without ever mentioning Linyi as such.[3]

While Chinese sources on Linyi have been extensively drawn upon, notably by Maspero, Coedès, Stein, Taylor, Southworth and Schweyer, they have yet to be considered in full, and free of any preconceptions (such as those entertained by Maspero and Coedès) about Linyi being an early stage of Champa. Moreover, significant parts of the early Chinese record have yet to be translated into English. The purpose of this note is to take a first step towards filling this gap. In it I have translated and commented on the principal records on Linyi in the standard Chinese histories up to and including *Xin Tang shu*, and have also considered briefly one other important source, Li Daoyuan's early sixth-century *Shui jing zhu*.

This note is by no means comprehensive. The *Shui jing zhu* entries on Linyi need more research, and other later Chinese sources on Linyi, including *Tang hui yao*, *Taiping youlan* and *Cefu yuangui*, have yet to be examined. But it will, I hope, be a first step towards a fuller appraisal of what Chinese sources offer.

The first account of Linyi in a standard history is the record given in *Jin shu*, the history of the Western and Eastern Jin dynasties (266–420 CE). *Jin shu* was completed in 648 by a group of scholars led by Fang Xuanling. As noted in chapter two, this was much later than the completion dates of the histories of the two dynasties that followed, *Song shu*, completed in 488, and *Nan Qi shu*, completed in 537. It was also later than the histories of the three subsequent dynasties, *Liang shu*, *Chen shu* and *Sui shu*, all of which were completed in 636. That said, *Jin shu* was to an unknown extent written on the basis of materials compiled earlier. So parts or indeed all of its entry on Linyi may predate these other histories.[4]

In any event, if we consider the standard histories in dynastic order, *Jin shu* comes first. Linyi is, it is true, mentioned in a reference in the earlier history *San guo zhi*. This records that the king of Linyi together with the kings of Funan and the unknown state of Tangming sent envoys with tribute to the Three Kingdoms state of Wu, evidently at some point during the late 220s. The *San guo zhi* record reflects the fact that by that time Linyi had broken away from China to become an independent or at least highly autonomous tributary state.[5] But *Jin shu* is the first history to provide us with a substantial account of Linyi as a state.

The *Jin shu* account of Linyi

The *Jin shu* record reads as follows.[6]

> The state of Linyi was originally Xianglin district during the Han dynasty, where the pillars Ma Yuan cast are located. It is three thousand li from Nanhai.[7] At the end of the Later Han Dynasty [which ended in 220 CE], the administrator of the district's Labour Section whose family name was Ou had a son called Lian. He killed the District Magistrate and set himself up as king.[8] His sons and grandsons succeeded him, and when a king coming after them had no successor, a daughter's son, Fan Xiong, became king instead. When Xiong died his son Yi took his place.[9]
>
> With regard to their customs, the doors [of the palace?] all open to the north, facing the sun. As to their dwelling places, they sometimes open to east or west, with nothing fixed. The people are cruel and fierce by nature, so get embroiled in fighting, and are used to living among mountains and rivers, rather than taking life easy on flat land. It is warm all the year round, without frost or snow, and the people all go naked and walk barefoot. In their view it is beautiful to be black in appearance.
>
> They treat women as having high status and men as having low status.[10] Marriage is between those with the same family name. As a first step women get female slaves to find them a husband.[11] When a woman marries she is clothed in cotton, with strips of cloth sewn around her like the railings of a well, and wears precious flowers on her head.[12] When mourning the loss of parents, people shave the sides of their head, this being said to show filial respect. Bodies are burned in the wilds; this is what is called disposing of the dead. The king wears a crown with tassels at the back. When he attends to affairs of state, none of his sons and younger brothers or his officials can come near him.
>
> From the time of Sun Quan [founder of the kingdom of Wu, r. 229–252], they did not come to court.[13] During the Taikang reign period [280–289 CE] of Emperor Wu [of the Eastern Jin dynasty], they began to submit tribute.[14] In the second year of the Xiankang

reign period [336, the reign period being 335–342] Fan Yi died, and the slave Wen usurped his position. Wen had been a slave to Fan Chui, the foreign military commander of the Xijuan district of Rinan.[15] Once, when tending cattle by a mountain stream, Wen caught two carp and changed them into iron, which he used to make knives. After doing this he faced a great stone ridge and uttered an incantation, saying, "The carp were transformed, and I smelted them into two knives. He who splits this ridge asunder possesses a spirit." He then went up and cut into the rocks, which fell to pieces.

Wen understood his spirit, and cherished it. He went with merchants here and there, and saw the laws and customs of the [Chinese] court.[16] Going to Linyi, he taught Fan Yi how to build a palace and a city and make weapons. Fan Yi placed his devoted trust in him, and made him a general.

Wan slandered Fan Yi's various sons, who either moved away or fled. When Fan Yi died, he had no successor, and Wen set himself up as king.[17] Wen put Fan Yi's wife and concubines in a high building.[18] Those who followed him he took as his; those who did not he deprived of food. Leading a forty- to fifty-thousand-strong army, he then attacked and took over various states including Greater and Lesser Qijie, Shipu, Xulang, Qudu, Qianlu and Fudan.[19] He sent an envoy with a memorial and tribute to the emperor [perhaps emperor Cheng of the Eastern Jin, r. 326–342], his writing all being in Hu script.[20] In the third year of the Yonghe reign period [347, the reign period being 345–356, and the emperor being Mu of the Eastern Jin, r. 345–361] Wen led his forces to attack and defeat Rinan, killing its Governor Xia Houlan and five or six thousand others. The remainder fled to Jiuzhen.[21] Having offered Xia Houlan's body as a sacrifice to Heaven, he razed the city of [his old home] Xijuan district and occupied Rinan. He told Zhu Fan, Regional Inspector of Jiaozhou, that he wanted the frontier to be the Heng Mountains on the northern border of Rinan.[22]

Previously, the various states beyond the frontiers brought precious goods by sea to trade with. The regional inspectors of Jiaozhou and governors of Rinan were very keen to profit from this, and behaved in a grossly interfering and insulting way, taking for themselves two or three parts out of ten. During the time of Regional Inspector Jiang Zhuang and his appointee Han Ji, Governor of Rinan, Han Ji set the official price for goods at more than half their value, and set upon merchant ships with beating drums and the sounds of war.[23] This enraged the various states. Besides this, Linyi lacked cultivated land and coveted the land of Rinan. Upon his death Han Ji was succeeded by Xie Zhuo, who was as grossly interfering as his predecessor.[24] At this point Xia Houlan came to the commandery. He was befuddled by drink, and his government pronouncements became increasingly chaotic. This is why Wen did away with him.

Having done so, Wen went back to Linyi. In that same year [347], Zhu Fan sent Protector-General Liu Xiong to guard Rinan.[25] Wen again carried out an attack and defeated him. In the fourth year [of the Yonghe reign period, 348], Wen went on to attack Jiuzhen, killing eighteen or nineteen people, some of them officials. The following year the Protector-General of the West, Teng Jun, led an army from the regions of Jiaozhou and Guangzhou and attacked Wen at [the port of] Lurong.[26] Wen defeated him, whereupon he withdrew to encamp in Jiuzhen.[27]

That year [349] Wen died,[28] and was succeeded by his son Fo. At the end of the Shengping reign period [357–361], the Regional Inspector of Guangzhou, Teng Han, led out a force to attack Fo, who was fearful and sought to surrender.[29] Teng Han reached an agreement with him, then returned home. In the Ningkang reign period of the emperor Xiaowu [373–375], Fo sent envoys with tribute.[30] Subsequently, during the Yiji reign period [405–418, of the emperor An], he again invaded Rinan, Jiuzhen, Jiude and other commanderies every year, killing and injuring large numbers of people.[31] Jiaozhou became enfeebled, while Linyi was worn out, too.

When Fo died, his son Huda took his place.[32] He submitted tribute of gold plates and bowls, gold gongs and other goods.

Notable features of the *Jin shu* account

Limited though it is, the *Jin shu* record is notable on several counts. First, its description of the rise to power of the slave Wen—whose status confirms the existence of slaves at the time—can be seen as a typical foundation myth of a hero achieving a superhuman feat to become leader of his people. Other such stories include the Greek myth of Odysseus stringing his massive bow, a feat beyond his rivals, and the English fable of Arthur pulling a sword from a rock.[33] Beckwith lists several comparable feats of strength and daring in national origin myths, as he calls them, from the cultures of central Asia.[34] There are also, of course, the foundation stories of the mythical emperors of China. Wen's case is complicated by a report in *Shui jing zhu* that he came from a Chinese city, the port of Yangzhou on the lower Yangzi River, moving from there to become a slave in Jiaozhou before escaping to join maritime traders.[35] Nonetheless, his charmed life suggests a form of foundation story, with a prequel consisting of the stories of Ou Lian, Fan Xiong and Yi. Unfortunately, if it is a foundation story it is too sketchy to reflect any particular ethno-linguistic or cultural roots.

Another remarkable feature of the *Jin shu* account is the fact, often commented on, that the names of several leaders include the name or title Fan.[36] These are Fan Xiong, the son of a daughter (notably) of one of Ou Lian's royal line; his son Fan Yi; and Fan Chui, a "foreign", that is, non-Chinese, military commander. The name or title Fan is not given to Wen, although later, for example in the early sixth-century *Shui jing zhu* [*A Commentary on the Classic of the Waterways*], he is called Fan. Fan was sometimes a Chinese surname; but as we saw earlier, Vickery suggests plausibly in the context of Funan that the name Fan could have been the Mon-Khmer honorific or title *poñ*.[37] The text also notes that marriage "is between those of the same family name". If Fan was a family name, the Fan clan could have been large enough to accommodate this form of endogamy. If Fan was a title, the comment about marriage could reflect a garbled understanding of a practice among those within the ruling group bearing the same title.

A third feature of the passage is the status of women, who are explicitly described as being seen as superior to men. This description is consistent with other references to the importance of women. In preparing for marriage the women, not the men, sought out prospective partners among members of the opposite sex (a practice that *Liang shu* explicitly explains as deriving from the superior status of women).[38] Fan Xiong secured the kingship of Linyi on the basis of being a son of a daughter of Ou Lian—or one of his successors, the text being unclear on this point—not of a son. Whilst the rulers were all male—Fan Yi and Wen had a wife or wives and concubines—these passing references suggest that matriarchical influences were a factor in Linyi society, just as there were signs of matrilineal influences in Funan.[39]

The *Jin shu* account locates the northern border of Rinan along the Hoành Sơn range (Heng shan in Chinese), thus placing Linyi some way to the south of them.

One other aspect of the *Jin shu* account worth noting is the unusually frank description of the corruption and decadence of Chinese officials in the far south. Three successive governors of Rinan commandery are described as venal and incompetent, and Governor Xia Houlan is portrayed as such an incapable drunkard that Wen's action in killing him is recorded without censure. These descriptions clearly reflect official Chinese discomfort at the behaviour of the Chinese court's distant representatives, though exactly whose discomfort—the Jin court's? the *Jin shu* lead author Fang Xuanling's?—it is hard to say.

Before moving on from *Jin shu*, we should note one other intriguing reference to Lin yi. The reference, which is often quoted, was first noted by Pelliot. It is in an earlier part of *Jin shu*, in the biography of the southern official Tao Huang.[40] Tao was Regional Inspector of Jiaozhou during the final years of the kingdom of Wu, and was reappointed to this position by the Western Jin founder, Emperor Wu, after his army had conquered Wu in 280. According to *Jin shu*, Tao sought Emperor Wu's permission to retain his military forces rather than having them disbanded, pointing out the difficulty of upholding peace in the far south. He petitioned the emperor as follows:[41]

> Linyi is just seven hundred li away, and during this time its foreign general Fan Xiong has sneaked about engaging in banditry. He calls himself king, and frequently attacks the ordinary people. Moreover he connects up with Funan. The clans are numerous, and their bands depend on each other and rely on the perilous terrain not to submit.

It is not clear whether the clans are Fan Xiong's, or relate to both Linyi and Funan. Assuming they are the latter, Tao seems to be suggesting a tribal affinity between Funan and Linyi. If so, and if, as seems plausible, the Funanese elite was primarily Mon-Khmer, then this would suggest that Linyi's elite (or elites) was, too. Taken on its own, however, the passage is too short to warrant any firm conclusion.

Jin shu and subsequent standard histories enable us to list some of the rulers of Linyi, with possible dates, as given in the table below.[42]

Ruler	Dates of rule
Ou (or Qu) Lian (or Da or Kui)	?220–?
[unknown successor(s)]	
Fan Xiong	fl. 280s
Fan Yi	?–336
Fan Wen	?336–349
Fan Fo	349–?early 400s
Fan Huda (?or Xuda)	?early 400s–?413
Dizhen	?–?
Wendi	?–420/21?
Fan Yangmai I	?420/21–?
Fan Yangmai II, born Duo	?–?446
[unknown successor(s)]	
Fan Shencheng	450s–?
Fan Danggenchun	?early 480s–early 490s
Fan Zhunong	492–498
(?Fan) Wenkuan/?Wenzan	?498–?500's

Ruler	Dates of rule
Tiankai (? = Devavarman)	fl. early 510's
Bicuibamo (? = Vijayavarman)	?late 510's–?mid-520's
Gaoshi Shengkai (? = Kū Śri Jayavarman)	fl. late 520's
Gaoshi Lutuoluobamo (= Kū Śri Rudravarman I)	fl. late 540s–early 550s
Fan Fanzhi	fl. 605–?late 620's
Fan Touli	?630–late 630's
Fan Zhenlong	?639–645
[Fan Touli's son-in-law, a brahmin]	?645–?
[Fan Touli's daughter]	?late 640's–?
Zhugedi/Jagaddharma	653–?
Bogashebomo/ Prakāśadharma	fl. 650s–660s
[unknown successor(s)]	
Jianduodamo	fl. 710s–740s
Lutuoluo/Rudravarman II	fl. 749

Song shu on the tribulations of Fan Yangmai

The next official account of Linyi is in *Song shu*, the history of the short Liu Song dynasty (420–478) completed in 488. *Song shu*'s author Shen Yue notes Linyi's frequent tribute missions, which he records as taking place in 430, 433, 434, 438, 439, 441, 446, 458 and 472,[43] but does not provide us with any information about Linyi's customs and culture. Instead he confines himself largely to narrating the tumultuous events relating to the Linyi king Fan Yangmai, portrayed as a successor to Huda—*Shui jing zhu* calls him Huda's son[44]—and his relations with the Liu Song regime. Given that *Song shu* was nearly contemporary with the events described, we can take the narrative as relatively reliable, compared, say, with later records of this period such as the account in *Liang shu*.[45]

The narrative begins by noting that in the first year of the Liu Song dynasty (420), Du Huidu, Regional Inspector of Jiaozhou, having defeated Linyi in battle five years earlier, attacked Linyi with ten thousand soldiers and officials, killing more than half of those he dealt with and securing from Linyi human captives, elephants, gold, silver, cotton and other goods. The following year, 421, Fan Yangmai sent envoys with tribute to court.[46] This is the first reference to Fan Yangmai, and presumably refers to Fan Yangmai the elder, rather than his son Duo, also called Fan Yangmai, who is mentioned in *Nan Qi shu* and elsewhere. The son was apparently Fan Yangmai's successor, but we do not know when he took over or what the dates for his reign are.[47]

Three years later, in 424, Fan Yangmai—either father or son—"violently attacked" various commanderies including Rinan and Jiude.[48] *Song shu* does not discuss the motives for his about-face. Was he simply seeking to extend his writ, or was he, perhaps, responding to provocations of the kind that had vexed his predecessor Wen? In 430, Fan Yangmai sought the Liu Song emperor's forgiveness for his hostility to Jiaozhou. But in the following year he "again sent a hundred or more storied ships to plunder Jiude", storied ships (*lou chuan*) being large ships built on more than one level. The Regional Inspector of Jiaozhou, by this time an official called Yuan Mizhi, sent a force of three thousand men in retaliation. In 431 they attacked Ousu, but were unable to overcome it, and turned back.[49] *Song shu* relates that

> Linyi wanted to attack Jiaozhou, and to borrow soldiers from the king of Funan, but Funan did not concur.[50]

This unusual proposal suggests, again, a special connection between Linyi and Funan.

In 433 Fan Yangmai sent envoys with local gifts and a memorial to the Liu Song court, and asked if he could take charge of the Jiaozhou region, a request the emperor rejected. In 435, 438, 439 and 441 "he repeatedly sent tribute, but his pillaging continued, and the gifts he sent were of poor quality".[51] In 446 Emperor Wen became angry at Fan Yangmai's disobedience, as *Song shu* puts it, and instructed Tan Hezhi, by then Regional Inspector of Jiaozhou, to attack him.[52]

Tan's forces were led by the renowned general Zong Que, with Xiao Jingxian commanding their vanguard.[53] Learning of the impending assault, Fan Yangmai sent the emperor precious goods and asked if he could return households in Rinan that he had earlier seized. The emperor agreed and told Tan to accept his submission. A delegation of twenty-eight men led by the Governor of Rinan, Qiang Zhongji, went to meet Fan Yangmai at a fortress called Zhuwu, and told him of the emperor's decision.[54] Fan Yangmai detained the delegates while sending one of them back to confirm receipt of the emperor's order.

As *Song shu* puts it, Fan Yangmai was seen to need further constraint. Forces led by Xiao Jingxian were despatched to Ousu, for the defence of which Fan Yangmai sent a senior general, Fan Fulongda (called Fan Fulong in *Shui jing zhu* and *Liang shu*), as well as infantry and a naval force.[55] Xiao Jingxian's men took Ousu, beheaded Fan Fulongda, and seized "incalculable amounts of gold, silver and other goods". Fan Yangmai and an unnamed son escaped and fled.

Elsewhere in *Song shu* there is another account of this or perhaps a related battle, dated as taking place a year earlier.[56] According to this, forces under Zong Que were unable to cope with a mass of armored elephants fighting on Fan Yangmai's side. Undeterred, Zong declared, "I hear lions frighten every living creature into submission," and had images of lions made for his forces to use. Faced with these, Fan Yangmai's elephants fled in fright and his soldiers scattered. (The story is typical of the clever military strategems beloved of Chinese commentators on Sun zi's *Art of War*.)[57]

Song shu concludes its report on Linyi by noting that following this it sent envoys with trubute again in 455, 458 and 472. A king, Fan Shencheng, is mentioned as sending the 458 mission. The fact that he is not mentioned in the context of the 455 tribute mission, which was headed by an aide called Fan Longba, suggests that he took office sometime between 455 and 458. *Liang shu* lists him as sending several envoys between 454 and 472, but as we shall see later, *Liang shu*'s record is not always reliable.[58]

The principal conclusion to be drawn from *Song shu* is that at least three of Linyi's kings, Fan Huda, Fan Yangmai and his son Fan Yangmai, were embroiled in frequent and bloody clashes with the Liu Song authorities, culimating in a war in or about 446 that resulted in Fan Yangmai's flight and (according to *Shui jing zhu*) his subsequent death.[59] The causes of these conflicts are, again, largely left unexplained. Mention is made of Linyi engaging in plunder, but while this may have been a motive, it is hard to believe that a small polity struggling to maintain itself in the shadow of an overbearing northern neighbour would have been so foolhardy as to provoke it. The *Jin shu* account of King Wen's experiences with predatory southern Chinese officials suggests an alternative explanation. A further consideration is that successive southern Chinese emperors and their Jiaozhou representatives, notably the powerful Du family, may have been reluctant to acquiesce in Linyi's recently acquired status as an independent or quasi-independent state.

With respect to the name of the city or fortress attacked in 446, called here Ousu (though commonly transliterated Qusu), Li Tana argues persuasively that Qusu is a misnomer, and that the name should in fact be Ouli, 區 being pronounced *ou* rather than *qu*, and *su* 粟 being an error for *li* 栗. Li points out that *li* is the second character of the name as given in *Nan Qi shu*, which is a relatively early and perhaps therefore a relatively reliable source. She identifies Ouli with a place called Wuli 烏里, later associated with aromatics. Since most of the Chinese sources discussed here write *su* 粟 rather than *li* 栗, I shall continue to refer to the place as Ousu, while accepting that Li may well be correct.[60]

As far as Ousu's location is concerned, Southworth and Taylor follow Stein in placing it in the basin of the Gianh River, which flows into the Southern Sea on the north-central coast of present-day Vietnam to the north of Hué.[61] The *Song shu* account seems to portray Ousu with its store of treasure as Linyi's principal city, but it appears from comments in *Shui jing zhu*, *Nan Qi shu* and *Liang shu* that at that time Ousu may have been distinct from Linyi's capital. *Shui jing zhu* seems to make this distinction several times, though in none of its references is its wording entirely clear. In one of two descriptions it gives of Linyi's city, it notes that the city being remote and inaccessible, Linyi's weapons were kept at Ousu, implying, it seems, that Ousu was a separate place. And in an account of Tan Hezhi's 446 attack on Linyi, *Shui jing shu* notes that the attack involved an assault on Ousu, followed by a battle near a river called Dianchong, to the west of which lay the Linyi capital.[62] Later, in a comment on the river Huai, described as being upstream from Dianchong, *Shui jing zhu* remarks:[63]

> The river flows from the northeastern corner of the city [of Linyi]. Going over to the north bank of the Huai on a high bridge hanging over the river, you come to the crossroads leading to Penglong and Ousu. That is where in Tan Hezhi's great Battle of the East Bridge, Yangmai was injured and fell from his elephant.

Taken together, the standard histories *Nan Qi shu* and *Liang shu* also seem to distinguish between Ousu and the capital city. *Nan Qi shu* describes Ousu as being on Linyi's northern frontier, that is, on its frontier with Rinan, while *Liang shu* places the city (*cheng*) of Linyi four hundred li from the Rinan frontier.

There have been various opinions about the location or locations of this second, capital city, assuming there was one. In his careful review of these opinions, Southworth argues that in 446 it was probably situated south of the Hương river in the region of Hué, while by 605 it was "almost certainly" located further south, at present-day Trà Kiệu in the Thu Bồn river valley.[64]

Descriptions of Linyi in *Shui jing zhu*

At this point we should turn from the standard histories to consider in more detail the work just referred to, *Shui jing zhu* [*A Commentary on the Classic of Waterways*]. This is a very useful source on Linyi. The work as a whole is a rare, even unique, survey of the geography, history and culture of early China, which its author Li Daoyuan considers in commentaries appended to brief accounts of waterways provided in the now-lost work *Shui jing* [*The Classic of Waterways*]. Li's commentaries are interspersed with valuable extracts from various Six Dynasties sources, all of them also now lost. Li died in 527, and he probably composed his work in the early 500s, after *Song shu* and before *Nan Qi shu*.[65]

The section on Linyi in chapter 36 of *Shui jing zhu* consists of a narrative interpersed with citations from various other works including the lost book *Linyi ji* [*A Record of Linyi*].[66] The citations from other works are scattered through the narrative, and sometimes overlap or more or less repeat themselves.

The narrative reviews various events in Linyi's history, covering much the same ground as the standard histories, though sometimes in more detail. These include the story of Fan Wen and his magic feat of strength; Fan Wen's death in battle and succession by his son Fo; Fo's defeat by his Chinese adversaries; and Du Huidu's battle with Fan Huda. The narrative also includes two accounts of Tan Hezhi's conflict in 446 with Fan Yangmai, including Tan's seige of Ousu, his defeat of Fang Yangmai, and his devastation of the Linyi capital, resulting in Fan Yangmai's grief–stricken death. On the latter, *Shui jing zhu* relates that:

> When Yangmai returned to the state [having fled to the mountains], he found families and the state devastated and laid to waste. The people of the time were no longer there. Irresolute and broken, his pent-up fury was barely endurable, and in the twenty-

> third year of the Yongjia reign period [446, the reign period being 424–453 of the Liu Song emperor Wen] he died.[67]

Shui jing zhu also includes two descriptions of the layout of "the city", that is, the main city of Linyi. The first, an extract from *Linyi ji*, reads:[68]

> Its city is situated between two rivers, with mountains close by on three sides. From the north and south sides you look down on their waters, while to the east and west there are mountain tributaries flowing down below the city. The western city wall is bent into eight corners [following a river in zigzag fashion?]. The city is six li and one hundred and seventy paces in circumference, spanning six hundred and fifty paces from east to west.[69] Its city walls, brick–built, are two poles in height, and on top of them are built brick walls measuring a further pole in height, with square holes opened up in them. There are boards resting on the bricks, and on the boards five-storey buildings. On these buildings there are houses with towers contructed on them, the tallest of them being seven or eight poles high, the smallest, five to six poles high.
>
> The city walls have thirteen gates. The whole palace faces south, and there are two thousand one hundred or so houses. There are markets and people living on all four sides. It is precipitous and a perilous place, and Linyi's armaments and weaponry are all kept at Ousu.
>
> There are a number of fortifications that date back to the time of King Fan Huda of Linyi. Following the Qin dynasty people migrated there and were transformed by local influences, the old ways of Rinan being changed and completely lost. Living so remotely, perched among the trees, in a poor place by the mountains, vast and impenetrable, the surging forests touching the clouds among distant and mysterious mists—this is not a place for people to pass their lives in.

This account portrays the city as a relatively large, long walled settlement tucked into mountains and between two rivers, a settlement that was well protected—the holes in the walls and the towers were no doubt for military use—but that was, it seems, distinct from Ousu. The size of its palace is unclear. The two thousand one hundred or so houses (*wuyu*) may have been part of the palace, or the city as a whole.[70]

The remark about the palace facing south is anomalous. Other early references to Linyi suggest that buildings faced north. To be more specific, in its second account of the capital, given below, *Shui jing zhu* notes that southern walls are closed off, and that "the south, it seems, has its back to the sun"— suggesting that the north had the primary position facing the sun. Elsewhere in chapter 36 *Shui jing zhu* notes that in Ousu doors open north, a comment consistent with the *Jin shu* remark about Linyi's doors usually opening to the north.[71]

Finally, the remark about post-Qin migrants to the region being assimilated by local cultural influences is notable for its ambiguity. It meets the requirement of connecting Linyi culturally with southern China, but at the same time it allows that Linyi's way of life was quite foreign.

The second, more detailed account of Linyi's city, which Li Daoyuan does not attribute to any particular source, repeats some of the first account, but differs from it in certain respects, and adds a good deal of new material.[72]

It starts by recording that Linyi is two thousand five hundred li west of Guangzhou, and that in the southwest corner of its city there was a long, high mountain range, from which the Huai river wound its way, joining another, smaller river also called Huai before flowing into Dian Chong.[73] It continues:

> On its south and west, the city is close to the mountains, while it looks down on the waters [of the Huai]. Double channels flow into the [Dian Chong] estuary, going round below the city walls. Apart from the channels to the south and east, they run close to the city wall, so the city is long from east to west and narrow from north to south. At the western end of its northern side [the city wall] twists and turns in and out.
>
> The circumference of the city is eight li and one hundred paces long. Its walls of brick are two poles high, and on top of them are built brick walls measuring a further pole in height, with square holes opened up in them. There are boards resting on the bricks, and on the boards there are storeyed buildings. On these buildings are structures with towers constructed on them, the tallest of these being seven or eight poles high, the lowest five to six poles high. Flying turrets and owls' tails greet the wind and brush the clouds.[74] They follow the line of the mountains and look down on the river, soaring aloft. Their construction is solid and crude, in keeping with old local customs.[75]
>
> Four gates open into the city walls, the east gate being the front one. It faces the banks of the two Huai,[76] and down a winding road there is an old stele carved in foreign script that extols the virtue of the former king Huda. The west gate faces two double channels; to its north, up in the distant mountains, the Huai flows down from the mountainous west. By the south gate, across two double channels, is a rampart of Duke Wen, the Jiaozhou Regional Inspector Wen Fangzhi, who in the second year of the Shengping reign period [358] . . . attacked Linyi and engaged in a series of land and sea battles with [Fan] Fo.[77] Fo defended himself and his city, then repeatedly sought to submit, and this was agreed to. Now five li south of Linyi's eastern city wall there is a second rampart that was Duke Wen's. The north gate is on the bank of the Huai, and there the road is cut, with no way through.
>
> Within the city there is a smaller city, three hundred and twenty paces in circumference. In this whole court with its tiled-roof halls, the southern walls have no

> openings. There are two long buildings whose roof ridges run from north to south. The south, it seems, has its back to the sun. In the western sector of the [smaller?] city[78] a stone hill aligned with the Huai faces the sunny side of the river. There is an east-facing hall with flying eaves and owls' tails, deep green ring-patterned windows, red stairs, projecting rafters and square rafters, many of them drawing on old methods of doing things. The palace has pillars that are higher than the city wall by at least a pole and a half, and are plastered with cow dung. It has brilliantly glistening, deep green walls, intricately made side rooms, finely decorated purple windows, and quarters for the king's wife and concubines, there being no distinctions among the palace women.[79] The ancestral temple, the principal hall, and the long walkway from the women's quarters are all in the upper part of the palace, so sitting by the eastern balcony [the king] can talk straight down to his sons, younger brothers, officials and attendants, none of whom is allowed to go up.[80]
>
> There are houses in some fifty quarters, their purlins connecting, ridgepoles touching, and eaves supporting one another. There are eight temples and pagodas, large and small, thickly wooded with high towers, similar in form to Buddhist monasteries. In the outer city there are no markets or neighbourhoods, and few people live in the district, the sea cliffs being cold and lonely, not a place where people live.[81] Yet for perpetual peace its chiefs have nurtured the state for ten generations—not, after all, such a long time.

This second account of the city of Linyi includes such realistic details—the king talking down from a balcony to his relatives, houses so close together that their eaves support each other, a stele outside a city gate commemorating Fan Fo's virtue—that it seems to be an eye-witness account, at least in large part. That said, many questions are left unanswered. Were the high towers on the city wall purely defensive, or did they also have religious significance? What was the system of beliefs that informed the placing of windows and the alignments of buildings? Given the significance that the north seems to have had in Linyi, why was the north gate to the city blocked (presumably to prevent enemy access from the river)? Does the fact that there were no distinctions among the palace women imply an enhanced status for elite women, whatever their role? If much of the building work followed old methods, what methods were they? Some of what is described, for example the layout of the palace, recalls Chinese precepts, but some could equally well reflect local architectural customs, or Chinese practices adapted for local use—by Fan Yi, say, under the tutelage of Wen.[82]

In some respects, the two accounts of the city are similar or identical, for example in their descriptions of a city with water flowing around it and high towers built above its walls. In certain other respects they differ, as in the number of city gates recorded, thirteen in one account, four in the other. One possible explanation for these discrepancies is that the accounts relate to different periods of the city's history. If that is the case, it is hard to know which of the two came first. Both accounts refer retrospectively to Fan Huda, who may have died in the early 400s, while the second account mentions the state of Linyi enduring for ten generations. Assuming each generation spanned twenty to twenty-five years, the tenth generation after Ou Lian would have been some time in the fifth century. So given that Li Daoyuan died in 527, both accounts probably date from the fifth or early sixth century— perhaps from some time before 446, the year the city of Linyi was laid to waste by Tan Hezhi.

An alternative explanation of the differences between the two accounts is that they refer to roughly the same era, but derive from different sources—*Linyi ji* for the first, and some other unacknowledged work or works that Li Daoyuan drew on for the second. What seems less likely, given their common features and only limited divergences, is that the two accounts portray two or more quite different cities.[83]

Towards the end of its account of Linyi, *Shui jing zhu* adds a few words about the state of Xitu. Citing a lost source, *Shui jing zhu* records that Xitu originally consisted of ten or so military families left behind by the Han general Ma Yuan. They were all surnamed Ma (after Ma Yuan) and "through intermarriage are now two hundred families." They lived on the southern banks of the Shouling river, across from Ma's bronze pillars on the north bank. These remainers were known in Jiaozhou as "Ma stay-behinds". Their language, food and drink were the same as those of the Hua (Chinese). Since the lie of the land changed over time and Ma Yuan's bronze pillars ended up in the sea, the Xitu people were relied on to know where the bronzes had once been. *Shui jing zhu* also cites *Linyi ji* as recording that "the southern border of Xianglin on which Ma Yuan set up two bronze pillars divided [Xianglin from] the state of Xitu, and constituted the southern frontier of the Han dynasty. Local inhabitants call those who have stayed on [in Xitu] 'Ma stay-behinds.' They are generally said to be of Han descent."[84]

The Nan Qi shu record of Linyi

The next standard history, *Nan Qi shu*, completed by Xiao Zixian in 537, has a single entry on Linyi.[85] By and large, its contents are similar to the records of Linyi in *Jin shu*, *Song shu* and *Shui jing zhu*, but include some new information, especially in the first section, which reads as follows:

> The southern foreigners' state of Linyi lies to the south of Jiaozhou, and is reached by a sea journey of three thousand li. To the north it connects with Jiude. In Qin times it was the old district of Linyi. At the end of the Han dynasty [its ruler came to be] called king. In the fifth year of the Taikang reign period of the Jin dynasty [284 CE] it began submitting tribute.
>
> In the first year of the Yongchu reign period of the Liu Song dynasty [420], Fan Yangmai, king of Linyi . . . [?submitted tribute, as *Song shu* records him doing in 421]. At

> his birth his mother dreamt that someone offered him on a gold mat, bright-looking and strangely beautiful, made of what in China is called pure gold, and the foreigners [that is, people in Linyi] call *yangmai*. For this reason he was called Yangmai.[86] When he died his son Duo took his place, changing his name to Yangmai out of respect for his father.[87]
>
> There are gold mountains in Linyi, with liquid gold that flows down and out to sea.
>
> They are followers of the way of Nirgrantha, and smelt gold and silver to make enormous statues.[88]

The fact that *yangmai* was the term used locally for pure gold shows that Fan Yangmai's given name was a transliteration of a local word. The term *yang* is not identifiable; as for *mai*, the modern term for gold in Khmer is *mee-ah* and in Cham is *mo'ḥ*, so *mai* could have been a transliteration of either.[89]

Nan Qi shu continues with a brief account of Fan Yangmai's conflict with Tan Hezhi. It describes Tan's destruction of "Quan (Dog) fortress [and?] the city of Ouli [sic]," described as being on Linyi's northern frontier, as well as his seizure from Linyi of "incalculable amounts of gold and treasure."[90] Much of the gold, *Nan Qi shu* relates, came from statues Tan destroyed. It goes on to record that when Tan grew sick and died he "saw a foreign spirit, which he paid reverence to"—making up, no doubt, for his earlier iconoclasm, though *Nan Qi shu* does not say so.[91]

Nan Qi shu records that the sons and grandsons of Fan Yangmai succeeded him in succession, while noting that it had no titles or names for them. It then describes the seizure of Linyi by a foreigner (*yi*) called Fan Danggenchun.[92] In 491, *Nan Qi shu* records, Danggenchun sent a tribute mission with gifts to the Chinese court, which acknowledged him as king. One of Fan Yangmai's offspring, Fan Zhunong, led members of his clan in an attack on Danggenchun, and "regained the state as it had been originally", securing recognition of his own status as king in 492 and imperial titles in 492 and 495. Three years after that, *Nan Qi shu* continues, Fan Zhunong drowned when his ship hit high winds on its journey to court, and was succeeded by his son Wenkuan.[93]

Nan Qi shu concludes by returning in time to the history of the slave Wen, whose emergence it dates to the final years (313–316) of the Western Jin, and by giving a description of Linyi's customs that more or less repeats what is recorded in *Jin shu*. It makes a few changes and additions. The king's precious crown is said to be "like the crown of the Buddha," and—more significantly—the country's "lordly teachers are called brahmins".[94] During weddings, a brahmin is said to draw the bride and bridegroom together and wish them "good fortune".[95] A couple of strange creatures are mentioned, sea creatures that blow spouts (whales?) and magic vultures that know when people are dying, eat their flesh and drop their ashes into the sea. Finally, *Nan Qi shu* records an eight-foot gauge set up in "Ouli city" that shows "the shadow of the sun crossing eight inches to the south", evidently a form of gnomon.[96]

With respect to Linyi's customs and culture, the four most notable features of the *Nan Qi shu* account are (1) the fact that Yangmai's name derives from a local term for pure gold, *mai* evidently derived from a Khmer or Cham word for gold; (2) Linyi's belief in Nirgrantha, a heterodox form of Buddhism rarely referred to in any context in early official sources; (3) the presence in Linyi of brahmins, and (4) the name Ouli for the city elsewhere called Ousu (and usually called Qusu by historians). The reference to Nirgrantha may reflect some specialist knowledge on the part of *Nan Qi shu*'s author Xiao Zixian, a devout Buddhist.[97]

Liang shu's account of Linyi

The next two standard histories, *Liang shu* and *Chen shu* were both completed by Yao Silian in 636, in the early years of the Tang dynasty. Both histories include records of envoys and tribute sent by Linyi. *Liang shu* lists these as being in 502, the first year of the long-reigning founder of the Liang dynasty, Emperor Wu; 510, when the Linyi envoys presented a white monkey; and the years 512, 513, 526, 527, 530, 534 and 540.[98] *Chen shu* records tribute missions in 568 and 572, from a king or kings unnamed, and nothing more. (Maspero claims that these last two missions were sent by Rudravarman, but does not substantiate his claim.)[99]

Liang shu also contains a section on the history and customs of Linyi. It contains much of the same information as recounted by *Jin shu* and *Nan Qi shu*, but there are some changes and additions, including a questionable account of Linyi's royal lineage.

Liang shu describes Linyi as being "originally Xianglin district of the Han commandery of Rinan, on the frontier of the old Yueshang"—an ancient state mentioned in *Hou Han shu*—the district having been established by General Ma Yuan "when he opened up the southern frontier of the Han."[100] It continues:

> The depth and breadth of its territory is perhaps six hundred li, with its city one hundred and twenty li from the sea, and four hundred or so li from the frontier with Rinan. To the north it is adjacent to the commandery of Jiude. By sea or on foot it is two hundred or so li [from the city] to the southern frontier, where there are the foreigners of the state of Xi[tu], also with a ruler called king. That is where Ma Yuan set up two bronze pillars to mark the frontier of the Han dynasty.[101]
>
> In the state there are gold mountains. Their rocks are all red in appearance and gold comes out of them. At night it comes flying out, looking like fireflies. The state also produces tortoiseshell, cowrie shells, cotton and lign-aloes.

Liang shu explains the last two items in more detail before going on to review the early history of Linyi. Its account of this history is very similar to that of *Jin shu*, except that Ou Lian is called Ou Da, the year of Yi's death is given as 337 rather than 336, and the story of the slave Wen's story is told with a few variations.[102] For example, Wen is said to have declared that if his knives cut through the mountain rock he would become king of the state, rather than be shown to possess a spirit. And when Yi died without a successor, Wen took action against the king's sons. "In neighboring states he spuriously invited the kings' sons for a drink and killed them by lacing it with poison, then coerced the people of Linyi to set him up as king."[103]

Liang shu then relates the history of Linyi after Wen's death, repeating some of the history given in *Song shu*, with embellishments. It describes how after Wen died in 349 his son Fo seized Rinan, then put up a sturdy defence of his (unnamed) city against soldiers sent from Jiaozhou and Guangzhou, before his being thwarted by a surprise attack from the rear. Driven back to Linyi, he surrendered there. In 357,[104] *Liang shu* continues, Fo again took to violent plundering, and was attacked and defeated by the Regional Inspector of Jiaozhou. In 399 his grandson Xuda (perhaps Huda) again plundered Rinan and Jiude, taking the governors of both places, and was again attacked and defeated by forces under the governor of Jiaozhi commandery, Du Yuan, subsequently the Regional Inspector of Jiaozhou. Later, we are told, Xuda/?Huda was in conflict with Jiaozhou after carrying raids on Rinan in 407 and Jiuzhen in 413, and following Du Yuan's death in 410 he plundered and killed in Rinan, Jiude and other southern commanderies on an annual basis.

When Xuda/?Huda died, *Liang shu* continues, he was replaced by his son Dizhen. Dizhen's younger brother Dikai took their mother and fled, and full of remorse at allowing this to happen, Dizhen abdicated and went to India, passing on his position (again, notably) to his sister's son.[105] Because of this trip to India, Maspero and Southworth identify Dizhen with Gaṅgārāja, the founder of a dynasty mentioned in a Mỹ Sơn inscription who is described as going on a pilgrimage to the Ganges.[106] Dizhen's sister's son is then said to have killed a senior official who had urged Dizhen not to abdicate, and was killed in turn by a son of the senior official. The latter set up Wendi, Dikai's younger half-brother, as king.[107] *Liang shu* claims that Wendi was then killed by Fan Danggenchun, who is described as "a son of the king of Funan," with the subsequent turmoil being suppressed by a senior official called Fan Zhunong, who then became king. According to *Liang shu* his son Yangmai succeeded him, submitting tribute in 421, and—in phrasing that replicates the phrasing in *Nan Qi shu*—was succeeded in turn by his son Duo, who took his father's name Yangmai out of respect.

This passage in *Liang shu* is puzzling, since it contradicts the earlier and so perhaps more reliable records in *Song shu* and *Nan Qi shu*. To recap, *Song shu* begins its history of Linyi during the Liu Song dynasty with an account of Fan Yangmai's life from his first tribute to the Chinese court in 421 to his defeat by General Tan Hezhi in 446, and his eventual replacement by Fan Shencheng, who sent tribute in 458. For its part, *Nan Qi shu* reports that at some point after the reigns of Fan Yangmai and his son Duo, also called Fan Yangmai, Danggenchun took power in Linyi, sending tribute to the Chinese court in 491. Some time after that Danggenchun was overthrown by Fan Zhunong, one of Fan Yangmai's offspring, who drowned on a visit to China in 498.

Compared with these earlier accounts, *Liang shu's* assertion that when Fan Zhunong died his son Yangmai replaced him makes little sense. As *Nan Qi shu* has it, Fan Zhunong was an offspring of Fan Yangmai, not the other way round. As for Dizhen and his half-brother Wendi, it is not clear where they would fit into the scheme of things, since the *Liang shu* narrative—that Dizhen was the son of Xuda/?Huda, and that Dizhen's half-brother Wendi was killed by Danggenchun—leaves no time for the intervening reign of Fan Yangmai and his son Duo. If Dizhen and Wendi were indeed historical figures, and Huda was Dizhen's father, their (brief) reigns would have had to precede that of Fan Yangmai. In that case *Liang shu*'s claim that Wendi was killed by Danggenchun is improbable.[108]

To explain these incongruities, Southworth suggests plausibly that *Liang shu* may have conflated two separate historical narratives relating to two local lineages. According to this suggestion, Dizhen (Gaṅgārāja, in Southworth's estimation) and Fan Yangmai were probably contemporaries, the former ruling from the Thu Bồn River valley, the latter from "the traditional territory of Linyi north of the Hải Vân pass". *Liang shu* claims that Fan Yangmai came some time after Dizhen; but confusingly it also records Yangmai as sending a tribute mission in 421, and if that was the case he and Dizhen could indeed have been contemporaries. Southworth's underlying idea—that the confusion in *Liang shu* could reflect an attempt on Yao Silian's part to deal with reports of two separate lines of rulers in the Linyi region—is certainly worth considering.[109]

After a break to describe Linyi's customs, which we shall return to, *Liang shu* goes on to repeat, more or less, the accounts in *Song shu*, *Shui jing zhu* and *Nan qi shi* of Tan Hezhi's defeat of Fan Yangmai. It then records a series of tribute missions to the courts of the Liu Song, Southern Qi and Liang dynasties. The missions are significant in that *Liang shu* names the kings who sent them.

The missions are recorded as follows. Between 454 and 464 Fan Shencheng repeatedly sent envoys with tribute to the Liu Song court, and did so again in 472. At some point between 483 and 493 someone called Fan Wenzan (perhaps Fan Zhunong's son Wenkuan) sent envoys with tribute to the Southern Qi court.[110] Thereafter the following kings sent envoys and tribute to the Liang court: (1) Fan Wenzan's son Tiankai (?Devavarman), who sent a white monkey in 510—for which the emperor awarded him the title of General Overawing the South—and further tribute in 511 and 514; (2) Tiankai's son Bicuibamo (?Vijayavarman), who succeeded Tiankai after the latter's sudden death through illness, and submitted a memorial and tribute; (3) Gaoshi Shengkai (?Kū Śri Jayavarman), who sent envoys with tribute in 526—when the emperor bestowed on him the title General Soothing the South—and 527; and (4) Gaoshi Lutuoluobamo (Kū Śri Rudravarman, that is, Rudravarman I) who sent envoys with tribute in 530 and again in 534, and was awarded the same title.[111]

As Vickery notes, the name Lutuobamo/Rudravarman is the first case in which a name in the Chinese records of Linyi seem to agree with the name of a ruler given in a local inscription.[112]

A notable feature of this record of tribute is the change from names beginning Fan to names that are evidently translations or transliterations of Sanskrit names. (As noted earlier the name Dikai could also conceivably have been a translation of a Sanskrit name.)[113] No doubt the change reflected a growing Indian influence in the Linyi court, exemplified by the presence of brahmins. But it is not clear whether the change represented a serious disruption of elite culture of the kind reported to have been brought about by Kauṇḍinya, the first king with a Sanskrit name in Funan. Indeed, the allusion in *Jiu Tang shu* to the Fan family or clan ruling continually over Linyi until over a century later, in 645, suggests continuity in the elite culture of this period, rather than disruption to it.[114]

All the same, one unexplained oddity in the Chinese use of Sanskrit names in Linyi is why Rudravarman's successors Fan Fanzhi, Fan Touli and Fan Zhenlong do not have Sanskritized names. By contrast, Sanskritized names for royalty in Funan continued uninterrupted once they had been introduced. Could this oddity reflect some further—or continued—ambiguity or division of the type Southworth envisages for the Dizhen–Wendi era, with two lineages laying claim to the name Linyi, one with Sanskrit names and the other bearing the name or title Fan, confusing the Chinese court and its record-keepers in the process?

Liang shu concludes its history of Linyi by noting in another section of the work that in 543 Linyi attacked the rebel Li Bi (Vietnamese Lý Bi) in Jiude, but Linyi's unnamed king, perhaps Rudravarman, was defeated and withdrew.[115]

Liang shu then turns to Linyi's customs. It gives a description of its location, housing and clothing, already translated in Chapter three, then goes on:[116]

> Its king wears Buddhist attire adorned with jewelled tassels, like those on Buddhist statuary.[117] When he goes out and about he rides an elephant, with conch shells blowing and drums beating, sheltered under cotton umbrellas with banners made of cotton.[118] The state has no regulations or laws; those who commit crimes are trampled to death by elephants. The great families have the family name Brahmin.
>
> They have to marry in the eighth month, when women seek out men, a practice stemming from the fact that women enjoy high status and men low status. Those with the same family name still get married. They get a brahmin to take a husband to meet his wife and hold hands together, chanting "Good fortune, good fortune".[119] That constitutes the marriage ceremony.
>
> The bodies of the dead are burned in the wilds, a practice called disposing of the dead with fire. Their widows live alone, and wear their hair hanging loose into old age. The king of the state follows the way of Nirgrantha, and has huge statues forged from gold and silver.

In *Liang shu* Yao Silian gives us some fresh details—the king clad in Buddhist clothes like a Buddhist statue, and riding out on an elephant under cotton umbrellas and banners; elephants trampling criminals to death; widows living alone with loosened hair, rather than (presumably) hair done up in the prevailing style. These details apart, his account resembles the accounts in *Jin shu* and *Nan Qi shu*, and suggests that Yao Silian did not have much new material to draw on.

Sui shu's portrait of Linyi

The next history, *Sui shu*, was completed by Wei Zheng and others in 636, in the same year as *Liang shu*. It is a more contemporary record than *Liang shu*, being the official history of the Sui dynasty, which reunited China in the 580s and was replaced by the Tang in 618. *Sui shu* is relatively informative about Linyi, just as (as described in chapters four and six) it was quite rich in detail when portraying Zhenla and the Funan offshoot Chitu.

One new source of information for *Sui shu*'s authors could conceivably have been material gained as a result of the Sui invasion of Linyi in 605, which we shall consider shortly. Another source, perhaps related to that invasion, may have been *Linyi ji*, the lost work cited in *Shui jing zhu*. In *Sui shu*'s bibliography there is a listing of an otherwise unknown work, *Linyi guo ji* (*A Record of the State of Linyi*), and this may have been *Linyi ji* by another name. Either way, this work may have been available to *Sui shu*'s authors.

Sui shu starts by reviewing Linyi's history from its first ruler Ou Lian to its defeat by General Tan Hezhi. It notes that originally Ou Lian set himself up as king during the rebellion led by the Trưng sisters. It describes this rebellion as occurring at the end of the Han dynasty, although in fact it took place during the first century CE.[120]

Sui shu then provides a portrait of Linyi and its people:[121]

> The state is several thousand li in area.[122] Its land has plenty of fragrant wood, gold and other precious things. Its products are basically the same as those of Jiaozhi. Its brick-built city walls are plastered with the ash of burnt clamshells. The doors face east. There are two [types of?] senior officials, called Sinapodi and Sapodige.[123] There are three grades of officials below them, the first called Lunduoxing, the next Gelunzhidi, and the next after that Yitagalan.[124] Local officials are divided into two hundred or so sections. The official in charge is called Foluo, with the next down called Kelun. The difference in rank between them is comparable to that of our heads of regions and districts.[125]
>
> The king has a gold flowered crown shaped like a scholar's cap, and wears rose-colored cloth and pearly tassels.[126] He has leather footwear and sometimes wears an embroidered robe. The sons of well-to-do families each have two hundred or so guards, bearing knives clad with gold. There are bows and arrows, knives, lances, and bamboo crossbows whose arrows are dipped in poison. For music they have lutes, flutes, pipas and five-stringed pipas, much as in China.[127] In general they use drums to alert their forces, and blow conch shells as they go into battle.
>
> Its people have deepset eyes, large noses and curly hair, and are black in appearance.[128] It is their custom to go barefoot, and wrap their body in a piece of cloth. In winter they wear a robe. The women wear their hair bound up in a knot.[129]

They use coconut leaves as mats. Whenever they get married, they get a go-between to present the woman's family with gold and silver bracelets, two jugs of wine and several fish, whereupon a suitable day is selected and the bridegroom's family meet relatives and guests, singing and dancing together. The bride's family invite a brahmin to take her to the bridegroom's home. After washing his hands, the bridegroom takes the bride as his wife.

When he dies the king is cremated after seven days. In the case of officials this period is three days, and in the case of ordinary people a single day. In every instance the body is placed in a casket, and carried forth with drums and dancing and taken to the [unnamed] river's edge, where it is burned on a pyre. The left-over bones are gathered together, and in the case of the king are placed in a gold jar that is immersed in the sea. In the case of officials they are placed in a bronze jar that is immersed at the mouth of the river; in the case of ordinary people they are put in a plain jar that is sent off down the river. Men and women all cut off their hair and go with the funeral procession to the water's edge. Their mourning over, they return home and weep no more. Every seventh day they light incense and scatter blossoms and again weep until the day's mourning ends. They do this up to the seventy-seventh day, when they desist. On the hundredth day and in the third year they do the same.

They are all Buddhists, and their script is the same as India's.

Sui shu relates that when Emperor Wen (r. 581–604), founding emperor of the Sui, had completed his conquest of the preceding Chen dynasty, Linyi sent envoys with local products, but stopped doing so thereafter. (Earlier, in a separate entry, *Sui shu* records without detail that Linyi sent tribute in 595.)[130] Towards the end of Emperor Wen's reign, *Sui shu* goes on, his officials described Linyi to him as a place of rare wealth and plenty. He must have listened with great interest, having spent out the Sui's economic resources.[131] He put his officer Liu Fang in charge of the frontier district of Huanzhou, then had him and other senior officials attack Linyi with a large army, consisting of ten thousand or so infantrymen and cavalrymen and several thousand criminals.[132]

As the army's southward journey got under way Emperor Wen died, and was succeeded in 605 by his son, Emperor Yang. Under the new emperor, Liu Fang's southern campaign continued. The king of Linyi at the time, named in this context for the first time as Fanzhi, countered Liu Fang's forces with an army mounted on large elephants.[133] Liu Fang prevailed over Fanzhi by constructing a number of small grass-covered pits into which Fanzhi's men were lured by a feint, causing fear and turmoil among them. In an alternative account of the Liu Fang campaign,[134] *Sui shu* records that his army crossed a river called Duli, driving the enemy from its stockades on the south bank, then battled on past Ousu and Ma Yuan's bronze pillars as far as the state capital (*guo du*), which was "eight days' journey south of Ma Yuan's bronze pillars."[135] Fanzhi abandoned the city and fled to sea. Liu Fang's forces destroyed the city, and

> seized eighteen ancestral tablets from their ancestral temple, all cast from gold, there being eighteen generations of the state.[136]

Liu Fang carved an account of his victory on stone, then turned his forces back, dying en route home. After that, *Sui shu* concludes,

> Fanzhi came back to his old territory, and sent envoys to ask forgiveness for his wrongdoings, thereafter submitting tribute continually.[137]

From its much later perspective, being written several centuries afterwards, *Xin Tang shu* describes what happened to Fan Fanzhi a little differently. According to *Xin Tang shu*,

> Its king Fan Fanzhi retreated, and its territory was divided into three commanderies, each with a governor. But the roads there were hazardous, preventing communication, and Fanzhi gathered together his remaining forces and set up another city of the state.[138]

Several points in the *Sui shu* account are noteworthy. The capital is described as being eight days' journey south of Ousu, a relatively long distance that is consistent with Southworth's view that it was no longer near Hué but in the Thu Bồn river valley. (Given the single brief reference to it, it is not possible to locate the new city that Fan Fanzhi set up after his defeat in 605.) Doors in Linyi were said to open to the east, as in early Zhenla, in contrast to earlier accounts of Linyi suggesting or stating outright (as in the case of *Liang shu*) that entrances faced north.[139] Some officials, at least, had titles derived from Sanskrit, but more importantly a number of local officials were called *kelun*, which is similar to the title *kloñ/khloñ*, perhaps a Mon-Khmer term. Judging from the account in *Sui shu*, the term seems to have referred to village-level officials. If it did, its use suggests a strong element of Mon-Khmer culture at the local level.

Sui shu's allusions to women suggest that their social standing was less elevated than it had been in the Linyi described in *Jin shu* and *Liang shu*. Specifically, its account of marriage practices describes go-betweens approaching women, presumably on behalf of prospective husbands, rather than women seeking out men. This fragmentary report may reflect a shift in social norms away from the high status that Linyi women enjoyed earlier.

Finally, it is curious that in *Sui shu*, Fanzhi, the king who fought Liu Fang, has neither a Sanskritized name— though the first part of his name, Fan 梵, has Indian overtones—nor the title or name Fan 范 characteristic of most earlier Linyi kings. Writing some three centuries later the author of *Jiu Tang shu*, followed later still by *Xin Tang shu*, restore this name or title, calling him Fan Fanzhi.

There are two other seventh-century Chinese histories that contains material on Linyi, and those are the composite histories *Bei shi and Nan shi*, both completed in 659. Neither work contains anything new. *Bei shi* repeats the history of Liu Fang's attack on Linyi given by *Sui shu*. *Nan shi* reproduces the entry on Linyi in *Liang shu*, including its confusing royal chronology.

Late historical records: *Jiu Tang shu*, *Xin Tang shu* and others

The last two standard histories containing substantial references to Linyi are the two histories of the Tang dynasty, *Jiu Tang shu* and *Xin Tang shu*, completed in 945 and 1060 respectively.

Jiu Tang shu begins its account of Linyi by placing it ten thousand or so li from Jiaozhou, a highly inaccurate estimate.[140] Like *Sui shu*, it records its area (*yanmao*) as being "several thousand li", abutting to the north on Huanzhou.[141] It notes that "the city where the king lives has a wooden palisade"—the defences of the city Fan Fanzhi built after 605, perhaps?—as opposed to the high brick walls described in *Shui jing zhu*, and the ash-covered brick walls described in *Sui shu*. The description of the king and queen is similar to that of *Sui shu*, but differs in detail. The king is said to wear white felt and cotton, while it is his wife who wears rose-colored cotton in the form of a short skirt. *Jiu Tang shu* goes on,[142]

> The king has five thousand soldiers as bodyguards. They can use crossbows and small spears, wear armour made of cane, and have bamboo bows. They go to battle riding on elephants. When the king goes out and about, a thousand elephants and four hundred horses are arrayed before and after him. Its people have curly hair and are black in appearance, and it is their custom to go barefoot. They plaster their bodies with musk, repeatedly applying it and washing during the course of a day. When visiting a superior they put their hands together and bow down to the ground. For marrying they find someone with the same surname. They have a writing system, and they are Buddhist, many of them becoming monks.
>
> When their father or mother dies, the children cut off their hair and weep. They put the body in a coffin and burn it on a pyre, gathering up the ashes and storing them in a gold jar, which they send off on the [unnamed] river. It is the custom to treat the second month as the start of the year, and they have two crops of rice a year. From here on south, there is an abundance of vegetation, with everyone eating fresh vegetables the year round, and liquor made from betel nut juice. There are mynah birds that can understand what people say . . . from Linyi southwards, they all have curly hair and black bodies, and are generally known as *kunlun*.

Jiu Tang shu recounts that in 623 and 625 Fan Fanzhi—as it calls the Linyi king—sent tribute and received in return a gift of fine silks from Gao zu (r. 618–626), founding emperor of the

Tang. Tribute consisting of a tame rhinoceros was sent in 627 on the accession of Gao zu's successor Taizong (r. 627–649), and once again in 630, when king Fan Touli, presumably Fan Fanzhi's successor, sent a magnificent glittering white crystalline pearl the size of a hen's egg. The following year he sent a multi-colored parrot, which Taizong was greatly taken by, and then another parrot, white in color, which was so clever that Taizong felt sorry for it and released it into the wilds.[143] Thereafter Fan Touli sent tribute continually, no doubt partly in recognition of the Sui and Tang's renewed assertiveness in the region. Fan Touli's attentions clearly touched Taizong, for when the latter died he had the king's image carved in stone and placed outside his resting place in his tomb.[144]

When Fan Touli died he was succeeded by his son Fan Zhenlong.[145] In 645, *Jiu Tang shu* records, Fan Zhenlong was killed by a high official, Mohemanduogadu, who "massacred his ancestral clan, so that the Fan family was brought to an end". In *Xin Tang shu*'s account, Mohemanduogadu "destroyed the ancestral temple, and the Fan family name came to an end".[146] The language here suggests that the death of Fan Fanzhi and his two successors was a significant juncture in Linyi's royal history, marking the end of long rule by one family or clan—one that up to Fanzhi's time had, according to *Sui shu*, lasted eighteen generations. If Fan 范 was a title rather than a family or clan name, an alternative interpretation of Fan Zhenlong's death could be that it marks the end of a line of rulers bearing the title Fan.[147]

Given that the demise of the Fan clan or title occurred not long before Linyi changed its name to Huanwang, it is possible that the two events were related. This possibility may be reflected in a cryptic comment in *Jiu Tang shu* that "now the rulers of the state of Huanwang are those coming after Fanzhi."[148] While loosely expressed, there being no reference to Fanzhi's successors, this comment seems to imply a shift in the nature of Linyi's, or at any rate local, rulership at some point quite soon after Fanzhi's death.

Jiu Tang shu ends its account of the royal affairs of Linyi[149] by recording that after Fan Zhenlong's assassination, the people of Linyi gave the kingship to a brahmin, the husband of a daughter of Fan Touli.[150] "Later," *Jiu Tang shu* goes on, "the great officers and people of the state were moved by the thought of their old ruler." Dispensing with the brahmin, they made as their queen a daughter of Fan Touli by his principal wife. As Fan Touli's daughter she might have been thought to represent a resumption of rule by the Fans, but evidently she did not, for reasons unknown to us—conceivably because she was a woman.

Xin Tang shu adds an account of what happened after that, albeit from an even later vantage point. It records: [151]

> Zhugedi [Jagaddharma] was the son of Fan Touli's father's sister.[152] After his father committed an offence, he fled to Zhenla. When the queen [of Linyi] was unable to settle the state, its great officers all invited Zhugedi to become king, which he did, marrying the queen.

> From the Yonghui reign period [650–655] to Tianbao reign periods [742–755] its envoys came to court with tribute three times. [In 713 it also participated with Zhenla and other states in a rebellion against the Tang led by the self-styled Black Emperor, Mei Shuluan.][153] After the Zhide reign period [756–757], it changed its name to Huanwang. [In 793 it sent tribute, but] at the beginning of the Yuanhe reign period [806, the reign period being 806–820] it did not send tribute [despite the accession of a new emperor, Xianzong].[154] [It then took over Huanzhou and Aizhou. In response] the Protector-General of Annan, Zhang Zhou, seized the illicit commanders of Huanzhou and Aizhou prefectures, beheaded thirty thousand men, took fifty-nine princes prisoner, and captured war elephants, small ships and armour.[155]

According to *Cefu yuangui*, Zhugedi sent tribute to China in 653 when he became king.[156] Otherwise we learn nothing more about him from *Cefu yuangui*, *Xin Tang shu* or any other source. Nor does *Xin Tang shu* explain why the name Linyi fell out of use. It does, however, make explicit the connection between Linyi, Huanwang and Champa, in the following passage.[157]

> Huanwang was originally Linyi. It is also called Zhanbulao and Zhanpo [two names for Champa]. It is a three thousand li journey by sea from Jiaozhou, going directly south. Its territory is three hundred li or more from east to west, a thousand li from north to south. To the west you get to the Wuwen Mountains of Zhenla; to the south you reach Benlangtuo *zhou* [Phan Rang]. In the south is a great river estuary where there are five bronze pillars.[158] The mountains there are shaped like leaning canopies, rising to majestic heights in the west, and forming cliffs to the sea in the east. The pillars were set up by Ma Yuan of the Han dynasty.
>
> Then there are the foreign Xitu people. When Ma Yuan went back they stayed behind. There were just ten households, but by the end of the Sui dynasty these had multiplied to three hundred. They all have the family name Ma, and living there as they do they are commonly called 'the Ma stay-behinds'. They and Linyi divide the southern Tang frontier between them.[159]

As noted earlier, Huanwang means King Huan or King Ring, *huan* being ring and *wang* king. The provenance of this name, found only in Chinese sources, is a mystery. Perhaps it refers to a forgotten king who ruled in the Linyi region in the first part of the eighth century. One fragment of *Linyi ji* preserved in the fourteenth-century anthology *Shuo fu* hints at a possible explanation. This records that "Mingda [Huda?], king of Linyi, made a tribute gift of gold finger rings". Mingda is probably a clerical error for Huda, the characters for *ming* and *hu* being similar, rather than the name of some forgotten king from a later era. But conceivably an eighth century king drew on Linyi's gold ore to present gold rings to the Chinese court, and so gained a temporary name for his kingdom.[160]

Xin Tang shu follows this with an account of the customs of Linyi, now Huanwang or Champa, that is similar in content to those of *Liang shu*, *Sui shu* and *Jiu Tang shu*. One addition is the titles given to the king and others. The king is called *yangpubu*, his principal wife *tuoyang'axiong*, the crown prince *achangpu* and the most senior official *pomandi*. The king's main residence, *Xin Tang shu* adds, is called Zhancheng (Cham city, usually rendered Champa in English), and his other residences Qiguo and Pengpilao. After descriptions of royal dress and soldiers that are similar to earlier accounts, *Xin Tang shu* ends by recording that those who have offended are either trampled to death by elephants, left in the Champa Mountains, or made to commit suicide.[161]

The *pubu* of *yangpubu* may be *pu poṅ*, a Cham term for court. Otherwise the terms for queen, crown prince, and senior official have not been identified. Nor have the names for the king's alternative residences—or cities?—of Qiguo and Pengpilao. Could they suggest that the former Linyi, now Huanwang or Champa, was a fractured polity?[162]

In contrast to these skimpy records in *Xin Tang shu*, two other sources, *Tang hui yao* (961) and *Cefu yuangui* (1013), both conclude early Chinese accounts of Linyi by recording frequent tribute missions from Linyi to the Tang court between 650 and 749.[163] (*Cefu yuangui* also records that in 643 Linyi sent envoys to Emperor Taizong to ask for military in countering an attack by Funan, which he declined to give.)[164] The tribute sent from Linyi, some of it very substantial, attests to a lively period of tribute and no doubt tribute-related trade between China and Linyi—soon to be officially designated Huanwang/Champa—in the late seventh and early eighth century.[165]

Tang hui yao gives the names of three of the kings of Linyi who sent tribute, with dates for the missions they sent. Their names are the last three names of Linyi kings on record, and are all evidently transliterations of Sanskrit. They are: Bogashebomo, who repeatedly sent tribute of trained elephants in 650–655 and 668–669 (*Cefu yuangui* records the second of these missions as being in 669); Jianduodamo, who sent tribute of trained elephants, lign-aloes, glass and other goods between 712 and 741 (*Cefu yuangui* records the first of these missions as being in 713); and Lutuoluo (*Cefu yuangui* calls him Lutuo, and describes him unusually as "ruler of the city of the state of Linyi"), who sent a large gift of tribute in 749 that included a hundred pearls and twenty trained elephants. Maspero makes a plausible case for Bogashebomo being a transliteration of Prakāśadharma, a king mentioned on an inscription whose royal name was Vikrāntavarman.[166] The equivalent of Jianduodamo is unclear, although Maspero identifies him with Vikrāntavarman's successor, also called Vikrāntavarman. Lutuoluo is clearly a transliteration of the name Rudra[varman], a ruler about whom nothing else is known.[167]

What can be deduced about Linyi from the Chinese record?

The review of Chinese sources undertaken here has, I hope, clarified certain aspects of Linyi's history and culture as conveyed by Chinese records. With respect to the questions raised at the outset, the sources do not, however, offer much clarification. Still, several points are worth making.

The obvious one, often neglected, is that Chinese historians with access to court records and other materials did not hesitate to treat Linyi as a separate entity. This applies throughout Linyi's recorded history, from the third to the eighth century CE. It suggests that Chinese court annalists perceived it as such, even in later centuries, when inscriptions bear out the fact that the Cham presence in the region was becoming more established. It is difficult to accept the view that Chinese historians continued to do so even after Champa had emerged as a separate entity, turning a blind eye to this devclopment and using "the old name 'Linyi' for what was really the new 'Chan-po'", as Vickery puts it.[168] Court officials are unlikely, for instance, to have registered the three tribute missions that came to the Chinese court between 650 and 750 as bearing the name Linyi if the missions did not actually do so.

A more plausible explanation is that an entity or entities called Linyi became more influenced over time by Cham culture, especially once its capital had moved south to Trà Kiệu. If this was the case, the persistence of the Fan name or title through more than eighteen generations until 605 and beyond—perhaps up to 645, when Fan Zhenlong was murdered, and even as fas as the reign of Zhugedi/Jagaddharma—suggests that the ruling lineage of Linyi was somehow sustained until at least the seventh century despite growing Cham influence. Chinese accounts do seem to reflect changing conditions in Linyi. This is notably the case in Chinese records of the events of 645, when they treat the demise of the Fan clan (or title) as a significant, perhaps terminal point in Linyi's existence. Changing conditions may also be reflected in *Liang shu*'s apparent confusion over fifth-century Linyi history, and the fact that in Chinese records Linyi kings took Sanskrit names in the sixth century, only to revert to Fan names in the seventh.

The relationship between Linyi and Funan was evidently close, though sometimes fractious. The two states are quite frequently recorded as submitting tribute to the Chinese court in the same year, even jointly. At the same time, *Nan Qi shu* reports that the people of Funan were peaceable, but often subject to Linyi's aggression.[169] In contrast to this, several events recorded by Chinese annalists suggest relations that were both close and relatively positive, at least from the third to the fifth century.

The first of these events was Tao Huang's request to the imperial court in the third century to let him to retain his military forces, on the grounds (as it seems from Tao's request) that the clans of Funan and Linyi connected up and relied on one another to harass Chinese authorities. Ths second event occurred in 431, when the king of Linyi, evidently Fan Yangmai, asked to borrow soldiers from Funan to help in a conflict with the Chinese. His request was not successful, but the fact that he made it at all suggests a special relationship between Linyi and Funan. The third event took place in 484, when the monk Nāgasena went from Funan to the Chinese court to ask for help in ousting the king of Funan's son (or slave—accounts differ), who had seized the throne of Linyi. The fact that a son or slave of the king of Funan had taken power in Linyi, and that the king of Funan conveyed such a strong sense of betrayal, could suggest, again, a special connection between Funan and Linyi.

There are several possible reasons for this special connection, assuming there was one. One could have been a common Khmer-based culture and language. The evidence for this in Chinese sources is, however, limited and fragmentary. There is the fact that at least until Fan Zhunong at the end of the fifth century, and from Fan Fanzhi to Fan Zhenlong in the first half of the seventh century, the kings of Linyi and certain others connected to Linyi bore the name or title Fan. This may just have been a clan or family name—Chinese annalists clearly took it to be such—or it may have been the Khmer honorific or title *poñ*. Then there is the name Fan Yangmai, which includes the local term *mai* for gold (in its modern Chinese pronunciation), a term that could have been Khmer, although it could also have been Cham. Finally, there are the titles of local officials in use in later Linyi, as recounted by *Sui shu*. These included *kelun*, which seems to be derived from *kloñ/khloñ*, a title used in early Cambodia. In this context it is notable that *Sui shu* describes the titles of officials in early Zhenla as being the same as those in Linyi.[170]

As described in the earliest relevant histories, *Jin shu*, *Nan Qi shu* and *Liang shu*, early Linyi culture had various other distinctive features. Two, possibly three of these may perhaps have been comparable in some sense or other to aspects of the culture of Funan. The first was a foundation story concerning a feat of god-given strength undertaken with a fighting instrument. In Funan's case it was the story of Hun Tian defeating Liuye with the help of a sacred bow. In Linyi's case it was the story of Wen splitting mountain rock using knives mysteriously obtained.

The second was the relatively high status of women. In some respects the standing of women in early Linyi was evidently higher than the standing of men. Even in the seventh century, when their social standing may have diminished, elite women were still in a position to influence royal succession, as shown by the leading roles played by one of King Fan Touli's aunts and two of his daughters. This suggests that matriarchical influences may have been a factor in Linyi society. Similarly, there were signs of matrilineal influences in Funan.

The third was the orientation of entrance doors. In early Linyi doors usually seem to have opened towards the north (even if the *Shui jing ji* records are ambivalent on this score).[171] Doors in the Funan branch state of Chitu (Red Earth) also opened to the north, although the report on this in *Sui shu* refers to a somewhat later date; we know nothing about the direction doors faced in Funan itself.

Otherwise, Chinese records suggest that Linyi culture had various specific features, although so far as we know these were not ones shared with Funan. They include the fact that in the early centuries the people of Linyi followed the way of Nirgrantha, a heterodox form of Buddhism known later in India as Jainism. This was a rare, perhaps unique, instance of a state being recorded in Chinese sources as adhering to this form of Buddhism. The brick walls city of Linyi destroyed by Chinese assault in 446 had unusually high towers, constructed (according to *Shui jing zhu*) in a solid, rough way according to local custom. There were also distinctive aspects of Linyi's royal courts and its disposal of the dead.

As an aside, Chinese records make the nature of the neighbouring state of Xitu and its dependent states or statelets a little clearer—or at least offer one possible explanation of their identity. They were said to be polities created by early settlers from Ma Yuan's army, though as in the case of Linyi itself, what the true ethno-linguistic identities of their inhabitants were, Chinese records reveal little.

Partial and Sinocentric though they are, the fragmentary records of Linyi thus serve to qualify the view that Linyi had little substantive identity of its own, even if they do not go far in elucidating the nature of that identity, or in documenting similarities between Linyi and Funan.

Epilogue: the story of Linyi retold

To conclude, here is a brief account of the history of Linyi according to Chinese sources, comparable in the way it is put together to the account of Funan given in chapter five.

During the final years of the Han dynasty in the early 200s CE, the son of a local official in the district of Xianglin in the south of Rinan, the southernmost commandery of the Han, killed the head of the district and set himself up as king. The name of the official's son was Ou Lian, sometimes known as Qu Lian, and his kingdom was called Linyi, meaning Forest City in Chinese.[172]

Chinese sources suggest that Linyi divided a frontier between itself and a small state called Xitu. Xitu, it is said, consisted of a handful of families left behind by the army of Ma Yuan, the Han general who erected bronze pillars to mark the southern frontier of the Han. These families are reported to have settled near the bronze pillars after Ma left the area. The state of Xitu initially consisted of just ten households, but over the centuries it grew in size and acquired small dependencies. Ma's bronzes were washed out to sea, and anyone wanting to know where they had once been had to ask the people of Xitu.[173]

Ou Lian was succeeded by his offspring. When there was no immediate successor, the son of a daughter of his (or possibly of a kinsman) became king instead. This man, Yi or Fan Yi, acquired a local slave, Wen, who had been brought up in southern China and travelled widely, including with overseas merchants. Wen was endowed with a supernatural spirit, which he demonstrated by splitting open a mountainside with two knives that he had forged from iron obtained from two carp. How the two fish were the source of this iron is not explained.

Wen taught Fan Yi how to build a palace and a city and make weapons of war. When Yi died, Wen murdered Yi's sons and replaced Yi as king. He led a large army to attack and take over six or so nearby states, or perhaps statelets. Provoked by southern Chinese officials' predatory greed, Wen also killed the governor of Rinan. Wen was keen to acquire cultivable land, rather than depend on a habitat of mountains and rivers, so he occupied Rinan, and drove his men on as far as the adjacent commandery, Jiuzhen.[174]

In 349 Wen died from injuries sustained while fighting, and was succeeded by his son Fo.[175] Fo continued to attack Rinan, Jiuzhen and other southern Chinese commanderies. In 361 a force under the Regional Inspector of Guangzhou launched a punitive attack on Fo, who gave way. Fo was eventually replaced by his son Huda, who built fortifications, and whose virtues were extolled on a stele outside the east gate of the capital of Linyi.[176]

After Huda the succession of Linyi rulers is sketchy. Huda is said to have been succeeded by his son Dizhen, who abdicated and went to India. Dizhen has been identified with Gaṅgārāja, the founder of a lineage mentioned in a local inscription. Dizhen gave his position to his nephew, who was murdered and replaced by Dizhen's sibling Wendi. But there are uncertainties about Dizhen and his two successors. They are first mentioned in *Liang shu*, whose account of Linyi's royal lineage is somewhat confused. Perhaps their appearance reflects the coexistence of two (or more) lineages in the Linyi region, lineages that Yao Silian, the author of *Liang shu*, tried to make sense of by integrating.[177]

In its early centuries, Linyi's rulers and senior figures all had the surname Fan, which may have been a family or clan name, or may have been the Khmer title *poñ*. Marriage was between people of the same family name, that is, within the same clan or elite group. According to one local Chinese official, reporting to the Chinese emperor, "The clans [of Funan and Linyi] are numerous, and their bands depend on each other and rely on the perilous terrain not to submit" to Chinese rule.[178]

In some ways women were of higher status than men, reflected in the fact that they took the initiative in sending out slaves—who were evidently part of Linyi life—to find suitable husbands. The people wore no clothes, though when they were married the women wore cotton. Entrances usually faced north. The king was treated with deference, no official or close male relative being allowed close to him. In the early centuries the country adhered to the heterodox Nirgrantha sect of Buddhism, later to become Jainism in India, though by the sixth century, it seems, Linyi's great families were brahmins.[179]

In the early 400s Linyi and southern China remained at loggerheads. In 420 the Regional Inspector of Jiaozhou, Du Huidu, scion of a powerful local family, attacked Linyi, securing its defeat and obtaining human captives, gold, and other goods. Four years later the Linyi king, Fan Yangmai—whose name meant Pure Gold in a local language—struck back. He (or perhaps his son, also called Yangmai) attacked Rinan and the nearby commandery of Jiude. In 431 he undertook a further attack on Jiude with a hundred or so large ships, provoking a Chinese counterattack on the Linyi fortress of Ousu. At that point, it seems, he wanted to borrow soldiers from Funan for an attack on the Chinese regional headquarters in Jiaozhou. But the king of Funan, evidently Dhṛtavarman, demurred.[180]

Further tensions ensued. In 446 Emperor Wen of the Liu Song dynasty decided to bring Linyi to heel. He ordered the then Regional Inspector of Jiaozhou, Tan Hezhi, to attack and defeat it. Forces under Tan's overall direction took the Linyi fortress of Ousu, beheading its commander and seizing "incalculable amounts of gold and treasure".[181] These items were presumably acquired by Linyi through local production, tribute exchanges, trade, and plunder—though Chinese sources rarely mention trade. Linyi's greatest local asset was gold, including molten gold, found in one or more of its mountains.[182] When Tan Hezhi's soldiers seized "incalculable" amounts of gold in 446, they did so by melting down Linyi's huge gold Buddhist statues.[183] For tribute and (presumably) trade, Linyi was also reported to be a source of tortoiseshell, cowrie shells, cotton, and the much-favored fragrant wood lign-aloes.[184]

According to the account of Tan Hezhi's campaign in *Shui jing zhu*, Tan's forces went on from Ousu to the Linyi capital, which they devastated. Fan Yangmai fled with his people to the mountains. Later he returned to his city, where in that same year, 446, he died of rage and anguish at the desolation he found there.[185]

Judging from *Shui jing zhu*'s two accounts of the city of Linyi—written, perhaps, before its destruction in 446—it was a well designed fastness.[186] Nestled into the mountains, its five-meter-high city walls, built of brick, were surrounded by river waters. The city walls were surmounted by a further layer of brick walls, on which were built tall towers, probably for military use. A high palace with pillars plastered with cowdung housed the king and the women of the palace, among whom "there were no distinctions". To preside over his court the king kept his distance and his dignity by sitting on an elevated balcony, from where he looked down on relatives and ministers.

The city had some fifty quarters in which houses were crammed together, their eaves overlapping. It had eight temples and pagodas, similar to Buddhist monasteries. These were no doubt used to celebrate Nirgrantha beliefs. Judging by one of the two accounts in *Shui jing zhu*, there were markets in the city, though the other account casts doubt on that. Beyond the city walls, in addition to a stele commemorating Fan Huda, lay two ramparts constructed by a senior Jiaozhou official who defeated Fan Fo in battle in about 358.[187]

Some years after the death of Fan Yangmai, Linyi resumed sending tribute to China. In the 450s the tribute was sent by a new king, Fan Shencheng, evidently Fan Yangmai's son. Fan Shencheng was followed by others of the same lineage.[188] In the 480s a foreigner called Fan Danggenchun (also, it seems, known by the name Jiuchouluo) seized Linyi and set himself up as its king. He was apparently a son or a slave of Kauṇḍinya Jayavarman, king of Funan, who was enraged at his lese-majesty, and pleaded with the Chinese emperor to send a military force to oust him. This the emperor declined to do.[189]

In due course another of Fan Yangmai's offspring, Fan Zhunong, ousted Danggenchun, regained Linyi and became its king. In the 490s Fan Zhunong was drowned while taking tribute by ship to China, and was succeeded by his son Wenkuan, also called Wenzan.[190]

By this time, it seems, brahmins had come to play a leading role in Linyi life.[191] So, too, had the practice of taking Sanskrit names for the kings. Wenkuan's son Tiankai, who succeeded him, may have had the Sanskrit name Devavarman. Tiankai was succeeded by others with

Sanskrit names—his son Vijayavarman, followed by a king called Jayavarman (unless, as is possible, Vijayavarman and Jayavarman were the same person), followed by a king called Rudravarman, who sent tribute to China in 530 and 534.[192] This Rudravarman I was the first king of Linyi whose name accords with the name of a king given in a local inscription.

The practice of taking Sanskrit names demonstrates the growing Sanskrit influence on Linyi's elite culture, exemplified by its brahmins. At the same time it is notable that in the first half of the seventh century—following a half-century gap in Chinese accounts of Linyi—three Linyi kings, Fan Fanzhi, Fan Touli and Fan Zhenlong, reverted to having non-Sanskrit names. Thereafter Chinese annalists again called the kings of Linyi by Sanskrit names. The annalists give no explanation for the temporary change of name styles. Maspero and Coedés assume that the three Fans had Sanskrit names which the Chinese did not record. But perhaps there are other explanations—for example, that the change again reflected fractured or diverse lineages during a period of transition.

In 605 the Chinese general Liu Fang invaded Linyi at the behest of the emperors Wen and Yang of the Sui dynasty (r. 589–604 and 605–616), who had expended their wealth and wanted to seize Lingyi's reputed riches to refill their coffers. The king of Linyi at the time was Fan Fanzhi.[193] By this time, to judge from *Sui shu*, conditions in Linyi had altered somewhat. Its city's walls, still built of brick, were plastered with clamshell ash. (*Jiu Tang shu* records that the city was surrounded by a wooden palisade, not a wall, but if its report is accurate it may perhaps refer to Fan Fanzhi's, new, post-605 city.) Doors faced east, not north. The people were Buddhist still, but without Nirgrantha being mentioned. Women no longer took the lead in arranging their marriage, instead being sought out by go-betweens sent by the family of the prospective husband. Sons of well-to-do families had their own corps of armed guards. Local officials seem to have been called *kloñ/khloñ*, perhaps a Mon-Khmer title. (*Sui shu* also gives terms for senior officials, two of them identifiably Sanskrit in origin. These differ from terms for Linyi officials of high rank given in the later *Xin Tang shu*, one of which, the term *yangpupu* for king, partly resembles the Cham term *pu poṅ* for court.)[194]

In his 605 campaign, General Liu Fang battled on past the Linyi fortress at Ousu and reached as far as the capital of Linyi, eight days' journey south of Ma Yuan's bronze pillars. This long journey south suggests that the city lay further south than the city of Linyi razed by Chinese troops in 446. Fan Fanzhi retreated. General Liu's men destroyed his capital and purloined eighteen gold tablets from its ancestral temple, one for each of eighteen generations.[195] These eighteen tablets evidently attested to a single Fan lineage tracing itself back some four centuries, perhaps to the time of Ou Lian.

According to the two Tang histories, Fan Fanzhi gathered his remaining forces and set up another city.[196] He submitted tribute to the newly-established Tang dynasty in the 620s, a practice maintained by Fan Touli, who succeeded him. Fan Touli nurtured good relations with the Tang; he sent the great Tang emperor Taizong (r. 627–649) a huge white pearl and two fine parrots, making such an impression that Taizong had a carved image of Fan Touli placed in his imperial tomb.[197]

In 645 Fan Touli's son and successor Fan Zhenlong was killed for unexplained reasons by a high Linyi official. The official massacred Fan Zhenlong's relatives and destroyed his ancestral temple.[198] These acts brought the Fan clan or title to an end. Judging from a cryptic comment in *Jiu Tang shu*, the effective end of Linyi had come earlier, with the demise of Fan Fanzhi. After him, *Jiu Tang shu* remarks, came Huanwang—meaning Champa.[199]

The history of Linyi was not yet quite over. A brahmin and son-in-law of Fan Touli assumed power, to be replaced by a daughter of Fan Touli. This unnamed queen evidently failed to qualify as a member of the Fan lineage, conceivably because she was a woman in what was now a more male-oriented culture. Unable to "settle the state," she was replaced by Jagaddharma, Zhugedi in Chinese, who was the son of Fan Touli's aunt.[200] Jagaddharma is the second king of Linyi whose name accords with a name on a local inscription.

From then on, Linyi gradually fades from Chinese records, although tribute records show that during its final century its tribute relations with China were particularly active. According to *Cefu yuangui*, Linyi sent 25 or 26 tribute missions to China between 650 and 750, much more than any other southern state.[201] Why Linyi sent so many tribute missions at this juncture is not clear. Three Linyi kings are mentioned by name as having sent tribute—Bogashebomo/Prakāśadharma (fl. 650s to 660s), Jianduodamo (fl. 710s to 740s), and Lutuoluo/Rudravarman (that is, Rudravarman II, fl. 749). Bogashebomo/Prakāśadharma is the third and last king of Linyi whose name accords with a name on a local inscription.

After 757 Linyi's name in Chinese records changed to Huanwang, which as *Xin Tang shu* notes, "was also called . . . Champa."[202] Nothing more about Linyi is recorded, or explained.

Appendix 6:
Glossary of names of people and places
Relating to Funan and Zhenla (not including contemporary names)

Aizhou 愛州 During the early Tang dynasty, the name for the southern commandery Jiuzhen in the north-center of present-day Vietnam. See Nanhai.

An Lushan 安祿山 The general who led a devastating rebellion in China from 755 to 763 that ended the long reign of the Tang emperor Xuanzong 玄宗. See also Xuanzong.

Andun 安敦 The king of Da Qin 大秦 (the Roman Empire) who according to *Liang shu* sent tribute to the emperor Huan 桓帝 of the Later Han Dynasty in 166 CE. Andun is thought to refer to the Roman emperor Marcus Aurelius (r. 161–180 CE).

Angkor The name of the Khmer civilization centered on the temple complex to the north of the present-day city of Siem Reap, including the twelfth-century temple Angkor Wat. The name Angkor seems to derive from the Sanskrit *nagara* (city). Many historians date the Kingdom of Angkor from the ninth to fourteenth century. Chinese records refer to the state of Zhenla, which they date from the seventh century and continue to refer to until the Ming dynasty. See Kingdom of Angkor, Zhenla.

Angkor Borei A site in southeast Cambodia associated with Funan. See also Óc Eo.

Angkor Thom Meaning Great Angkor. The name given to the last great capital city of the Kingdom of Angkor, founded by King Jayavarman VII (r. 1181–c. 1218) and located at the heart of the Angkor temple complex near present-day Siem Reap. See Jayavarman VII, Bayon.

Angkor Wat The temple and perhaps mausoleum of King Sūryavarman II (r. 1113–c. 1149), located to the south of the city walls of Angkor Thom. See also Sūryavarman II.

Annam, An Nam See Annan.

Annamite Mountains The mountains separating present-day Vietnam from Laos.

Annan 安南 A Tang dynasty protectorate in the far south of China, also referred to as Annam or An Nam (the Vietnamese pronunciation), with its headquarters at Jiaozhi 交阯, in the north of present-day Vietnam. See Jiaozhi.

Anxi 安息 A Chinese name for Parthia, the historical region centered on the northeast of present-day Iran.

Anyuan 安遠 The first stop on the eighth-century Chinese geographer Jia Dan 賈耽's overland route map from Huanzhou 驩州 to Huanwang (Champa). The other stops were Tanglin 唐林, Guluo 古羅, Tandong 檀洞, Zhuya 硃崖, and Danbu 單補.

Austronesian A large language family and the people who speak its languages. They include languages spoken on the Malay Peninsula, and in Taiwan, Madagascar, maritime Southeast Asia, and the islands of the Pacific.

Baitou 白頭 A state to the west of Funan, first mentioned in the late eighth-century *Tong dian*, whose name means "white head" or "white hair."

Bajian 巴澗 One of ten Zhenla prefectures (*jun* 郡) named by Zhou Daguan 周達觀. Located on the southeastern coast of present-day Vietnam, south of Zhenpu. See Zhenpu, Zhou Daguan.

Ban Gu 班固 (32–92 CE) The author of *Han shu*.

Ba'nan 跋南 See Funan.

Basili 八斯里 See Bosilan.

Baxue 八薛 One of ten Zhenla prefectures (*jun* 郡) named by Zhou Daguan 周達觀. Perhaps Pakse in the south of present-day Laos. See Zhou Daguan.

Bayon Jayavarman VII's state temple at the center of Angkor Thom. See Angkor Thom, Jayavarman VII.

Bentuolang 奔陀浪 Also called Bindalang 賓達榔, Benlangtuo 奔浪陀. Identified with Panduranga or Phan Rang, the southernmost part of Champa.

Bhadreśvara A title given to the god Śiva. In Coedès' generally accepted view, it was the Sanskrit equivalent of Poduoli 婆多利, the Zhenla deity mentioned in *Sui shu*. See Śiva.

Bhavavarman (I) (r. late sixth century) A king of Zhenla prior to the Kingdom of Angkor.

Bhavavarman II (r. late 630s?–mid-650s) The Zhenla king who succeeded Īśānasena I prior to the Kingdom of Angkor. See Īśānasena.

Bijing 匕景 A port south of Huanzhou 驩州, in the area of present-day Danang. See Huanzhou.

Bindalang 賓達榔 See Bentuolang.

Bisong 比嵩 An unidentified southern state in the Funan era.

Black Emperor 黑帝 See Mai Thúc Loan.

Boluola 波羅剌 An unidentified state to the east of Chitu. See also Chitu.

Boluomotuo 波羅末陀 See Paramārtha.

Bosi 波斯 A Chinese name for Persia from the fifth century CE onwards.

Bosilan 波斯蘭 One of the dependencies of Zhenla listed by Zhao Rugua 趙如适. According to *Wenxian tongkao*, Bosilan lay south of Zhenla. Perhaps it was the Basili 八斯里 mentioned by Zhou Daguan 周達觀. See Zhao Rugua, Zhou Daguan.

Brahmā A Hindu god, one of the supreme trinity Brahmā, Viṣṇu, and Śiva.

Buddhabadra (fl. early sixth century) A Buddhist monk, called Putibatuo 菩提拔陀 in Chinese, who went from his home in Geying 歌營, probably located on the Malay Peninsula, to the Chinese city of Luoyang 洛陽, traveling via Funan.

Cambodia A name derived from Kambuja, which means "born of Kambu," used as a term for the Khmer people. It is found in epigraphy from the ninth century CE onwards. See also Kambuja, Ganbozhi, Jianpuzhai.

Canban 參半 A dependency of Wendan 文單, located perhaps somewhere to the west of Zhenla. See Wendan, Land Zhenla.

Cangwu 蒼梧 An early commandery in the far south of China. See Nanhai.

Canlie Popiya 參烈婆毗牙 An early fifteenth-century king of Cambodia.

Canlie Zhaopingya 參烈昭平牙 A king of Cambodia, eldest son of Canlie Popiya.

Champa Zhancheng 占城 (Cham City) in Chinese. Champa is also referred to in Chinese as Zhanbulao 占不勞 and Zhanpo 占婆. The name for the state or states that held sway in central and southern parts of present-day Vietnam from the seventh-eighth century to the fifteenth century. See also Linyi.

Chang 長 (r. 250?) The youngest son of King Fan Shiman, and briefly, perhaps, a king of Funan. According to *Liang shu*, Chang killed Fan Shiman's successor, Fan Zhan, and was killed in turn by Fan Xun. See Fan Zhan, Fan Xun.

Chang Jun 常駿 (fl. early seventh century) A Sui dynasty envoy sent with another envoy, Wang Junzheng 王君政, to the state of Chitu 赤土. See Chitu.

Chang'an 長安 The capital of northern China during part of the Six Dynasties era, and capital of China during the Sui and Tang dynasties. Present-day Xi'an 西安.

Chen Shou 陳壽 (233–297) The author of *San guo zhi*, a history of the Three Kingdoms period. See Three Kingdoms.

Chen Song 陳宋 An Indian envoy who visited Funan in the mid-200s CE.

Chengzong 成宗 (r. 1295–1307) Temür Khan, second emperor of the Yuan dynasty (1271–1368).

Chequ 車渠 Also pronounced Juqu. A place mentioned in *Sui shu* as being south of Zhenla, and in *Xin Tang shu* as being east of Zhenla, and so possibly part of Champa.

Chikuang 絷誆 See Wuwen (2).

China In Chinese, Zhongguo 中國 translates to Central State or, in earlier usages, Central States. In early texts China is also referred to as Zhongtu 中土, Central Land(s), and Zhongzhou 中州, Central Region(s).

Chitu 赤土 Literally, Red Earth. A seventh-century state located perhaps in the north of the Malay Peninsula, perhaps with a kinship tie to Funan. *Sui shu* calls it a *bie zong* 別種, "a different type" of Funan. The Sui emperor Yang 煬帝 sent two envoys—Chang Jun 常駿 and Wang Junzheng 王君政—to Chitu in 607. Their report, much of it apparently preserved in *Sui shu*, may possibly have contained material on Zhenla that *Sui shu* drew on.

Chola The Tamil dynasty of south India that ruled during the first millennium CE.

Citrasena (r. ?600–?610) In Chinese, Zhiduosina 質多斯那; family name Kṣatriyaḥ (Shali 剎利). According to *Sui shu*, Citrasena was the king of Zhenla who took over Funan. Also called Mahendravarman, Citrasena-Mahendravarman.

College of Literary Studies See Wen xue guan.

Cui Xuan 崔鉉 See Wang Pu.

Da Qin 大秦 Literally, Great Qin (as in Qin dynasty), usually taken to refer to the Roman Empire, especially the eastern Roman Empire.

Dai Part of the Kra-Dai language group, whose languages include Tai and Thai.

Daizong 代宗 (r. 763–780) The emperor Daizong of the Tang dynasty.

Dali 大理 See Nanzhao.

Danbu 單補 See Anyuan.

Daner 儋耳 An early commandery in the far south of China. See Nanhai.

Danggenchun 當根純 Also called Fan Danggenchun 范當根純, a prince of Funan said to have usurped the throne of Linyi 林邑, probably in the 480s. Usually identified with the usurper Jiuchouluo 鳩酧羅. See Jiuchoulou, Linyi, appendix five.

Danliumei 丹流眉 See Dengloumei.

Danmeiliu 丹眉流 See Dengloumei.

Danqu See Daqu.

Daoming 道明 A dependency of Wendan 文單. See Wendan, Land Zhenla.

Daoshi 道世 (d. 683) A Buddhist monk and author of *Fayuan zhulin* 法苑珠林 [*A Forest of Gems in the Dharma Garden*]. Not to be confused with the term *daoshi* 道士 (follower of the Way, holy man or woman).

Daoxuan 道宣 (597–667) A Buddhist monk and author of *Xu gao seng zhuan* 續高僧傳 [*More Biographies of Eminent Monks*].

Daqu 笡屈 Also pronounced Danqu. A name or title of the king of Wendan 文單, according to *Xin Tang shu*. See Wendan.

Dashi 大食 An old Chinese term for the Arabs.

Dengliumei 登流眉 See Dengloumei.

Dengloumei 登樓眉 Also called Dengliumei 登流眉, Dingliumei 丁流眉, Danliumei 丹流眉, Danmeiliu 丹眉流. A dependency of Zhenla to its southwest, apparently on the northeast coast of the Malay Peninsula, mentioned by Zhao Rugua 趙汝适 and others. See also Zhao Rugua.

Dezong 德宗 (r. 780–804) The emperor Dezong of the Tang dynasty, successor to the emperor Daizong 代宗.

Dhṛtavarman (fl. 424–453) A king of Funan, called Chilituobamo 持梨陁跋摩 or Chilibamo 持梨跋摩 in Chinese.

Diansun 典孫 See Dunxun.

Dianxun 典遜 See Dunxun.

Dilata 第辣撻 A place adjacent to Zhenla mentioned by Zhou Qufei 周去非. Possibly Trat in the southeast of present-day Thailand. See Zhou Qufei.

Dingliumei 丁流眉 See Dengloumei.

Đinh Tiên Hoàng (924–979) The Vietnamese ruler who in the 960s founded the state of Đại Cồ Việt, later called Đại Việt (Da yue 大越 in Chinese).

Du You 杜佑 (735–812) The author of *Tong dian*.

Dubo 杜薄 See Zhuzhuanbo.

Duhebodi 杜和鉢底 See Dvaravati.

Duhuai 杜懷 Perhaps a variant of Tuohuan 陀桓, 陀洹. A place listed as a dependency of Zhenla by Zhao Rugua 趙汝适. See Tuohuan.

Dukun 都昆 Called Qudukun 屈都昆 in *Liang shu*, a state to the south of Funan, probably on the Malay Peninsula.

Dunxun 頓遜 Also Dianxun 典遜, Diansun 典孫. A dependency of Funan, apparently located in the northern part of the Malay Peninsula.

Duoheluo 墮和羅 See Dvaravati.

Duoluobodi 墮羅鉢底 See Dvaravati.

Durgā A Hindu goddess.

Dvaravati Duoluobodi 墮羅鉢底, Duoheluo 墮和羅, or Duhebodi 杜和鉢底 in Chinese. The Mon state or states located in present-day Thailand, especially in the Chao Praya Basin, that was or were active during the second half of the first millennium CE.

East Baray A lake or reservoir built by the Angkor king Yaśovarman I (r. 889–c. 900) and alluded to by Zhou Daguan 周大觀. See Yaśovarman I and Zhou Daguan.

East Mebon An Angkor temple built by the Angkor king Rājendravarman II (r. 944–968).

Fa Daet See Kantharawichai.

Fan Chengda 范成大 (1126–1193) The author of the gazetteer *Guihai yuheng zhi* 桂海虞衡志 [*The Treatise of the Supervisor and Guardian of the Cinnamon Sea*].

Fan Shiman 范師蔓 (?early third century) The self-styled Great King of Funan who attacked and conquered neighboring states. *Nan Qi shu* calls him Fan Shiman 范師蔓; *Liang shu* calls him Fan man 范蔓.

Fan Xun 范尋 (c. 250?–c. 289?) The king of Funan who hosted the Chinese envoys Kang Tai 康泰 and Zhu Ying 朱應.

Fan Ye 范曄 (398–c. 445 CE) The principal author of *Hou Han shu*.

Fan Zhan 范旃 (fl. 243) A king of Funan, a nephew of King Fan Shiman 范師蔓. Called Zhan 旃 in *Nan Qi shu*.

Fang Xuanling 房玄齡 (578–648) The principal author of *Jin shu*.

Faxian 法顯 (337–c. 422) A Buddhist monk who went from China to India overland, returning to China by sea, and left a record of his travels.

Foshi 佛逝 A Chinese name for (1) the trading state Srivijaya on Sumatra, (2) the coastal city of Champa called Vijaya. See Srivijaya, Vijaya.

Funa 富那 See Senggao.

Funan 扶南 The Chinese name for the state located in the Mekong Delta and the southeast of present-day Cambodia that flourished between the first or second century and the seventh century CE. The name means "supporting the south." The name Funan (or Ba'nan 跋南,

according to the seventh-century Buddhist monk Yijing 義) may derive from the Khmer word *phnom* (hill).

Funan Office Funan guan 扶南館 in Chinese, a place in the southern Chinese capital Jiankang 健康 where Buddhist monks from Funan worked in the early sixth century.

Fusang 扶桑 A Funan-era state located far to the east of China.

Gan Bao 干寶 (fl. 315) Author of *Sou shen ji* 搜神記 [*A Record of the Search for Spirits*].

Ganbozhi 甘孛智 A Chinese name for Cambodia in the Yuan and Ming dynasties, according to the Yuan envoy Zhou Daguan and *Ming shi*. Alternative forms of the name were Ganpozhe 甘破蔗 and Ganpuzhi 澉浦只. See also Cambodia, Jianpuzhai, Kambuja.

Gaṇeśa A Hindu god with an elephant's head.

Ganpozhe 甘破蔗 See Ganbozhi.

Ganpuzhi 澉浦只 See Ganbozhi.

Gantuohuan 乾陀洹 Also pronounced Qiantuohuan. See Tuohuan.

Gantuoli 干陁利 A state mentioned in *Liang shu*, probably on the island of Sumatra.

Gaozhou 高州 A Song dynasty county on the south coast of China.

Gaozong 高宗 (r. 650–683) The emperor Gaozong of the Tang dynasty.

Gaozong 高宗 (r. 1127–1162) The emperor Gaozong of the Song dynasty.

Ge Hong 葛洪 (283–343) A Daoist thinker and alchemist. The author of *Bao pu zi* 抱朴子 [*The Master who Embraces Simplicity*] and putative author of *Tai qing jin ye shen dan jing* 太清金液神丹經 [*The Scripture of the Divine Elixir of the Gold Liquor of Great Clarity*].

Gelang 葛浪 A mountain in Zhenla that was home to a huge bird, according to a story that may have originated during the Tang dynasty.

Gemie 閤蔑 See Jimie.

Geying 歌營 See Buddhabadra.

Gouzhi 勾稚 See Juli.

Great Island of Natural Fire In Chinese, Ziran dazhou 自然大洲. An island mentioned in *Liang shu*, apparently to the east of present-day Indonesia.

Guangzhou 廣州 An administrative region in south China from the third century CE on; also a port city called Guangzhou, especially from Song times on. The present-day capital of Guangdong province.

Guangxi 廣西 A region in south China, west of present-day Guangdong. The name Guangxi came into use during the Song dynasty.

Gulang 古朗 See Wuwen (2).

Gulong 古龍 See Kunlun.

Guluo 古羅 See Anyuan.

Gunu 古奴 Short for Gunusitiao 古奴斯調, tentatively identified with Jia'natiao 伽那調 / 迦那調, perhaps Kanadvīpa in India.

Gunusitiao 古奴斯調 See Gunu.

Gutang 骨堂 Mentioned with Gemie 閣蔑 (Khmer) as an example of a Kunlun language in an eighth to ninth century Chinese Buddhist dictionary. See Jimie.

Hainan 海南 "South of the sea," in English. A term used to refer to regions near the Southern Sea; (also) an island south of Guangxi 廣西.

Hangzhou 杭州 Capital of the Southern Song Dynasty (1127–1279), also known as the Temporary Capital (Xingzai suo 行在所). One of the prosperous port cities of south and southeast China during the Southern Song dynasty. Other ports included Mingzhou 明州 (later Ningbo 寧波), Quanzhou 泉州, Wenzhou 溫州, and Guangzhou 廣州.

Harihara The Hindu gods Viṣṇu and Śiva in a combined representation.

Hariharalaya See Jayavarman II.

Harṣavarman III (r. c. 1066–1080) A king of Angkor.

He di 和帝 (r. 89–106 CE) The emperor He of the Later Han dynasty.

He Lüguang 何履光 One of the Tang dynasty officers leading a Chinese assault on the state of Nanzhao 南詔 to the southwest of China in the late eighth century. See Nanzhao.

Heichi 黑齒 Meaning "black teeth." A small state in the far south of China, mentioned by the third-century poet Zuo Si 左思. Perhaps the same as Xitu 西屠. See Zuo Si, Xitu.

Heling 訶陵 A ninth-century state on the island of Java.

Heluodan 訶羅旦 An unidentified state to the south of Chitu. Also written 訶羅單, 呵羅單. See also Chitu.

Hengdie 橫跌 See Mofu.

Hepu 合浦 An early commandery in the far south of China. See Nanhai.

History Office See Shi guan.

Hoàng Sa See Xi sha.

Hu 胡 An old Chinese term for the peoples to the north and west of China. During the Six Dynasties the term evidently included the peoples of India.

Huan di 桓帝 (r. 147–167 CE) The emperor Huan of the Later Han dynasty.

Huangzhi 黃支 A state in south India, one of the maritime states that according to *Han shu* sent tribute to China from the days of the Han emperor Wu 武帝 (r. 140–86 BCE) on.

Huanwang 環王 The name given to Champa by *Xin Tang shu* and other works for the period from 756–757 to the early ninth century. See Champa.

Huanzhou 驩州 The eastern terminus of an overland route to Wendan 文單 or Land Zhenla, as described by the eighth-century Tang court geographer Jia Dan 賈耽. Located in the area of Vinh on the northern coast of present-day Vietnam.

Huerna 忽兒那 (fl. 1370s) A king of Cambodia.

Huijiao 慧皎 (497–554) A Buddhist monk and author of *Gao seng zhuan* 高僧傳 [*Biographies of Eminent Monks*].

Huilin 慧琳 (737–820) A Buddhist monk. See Huiying.

Huiying 慧英 (fl. mid-seventh century) A Buddhist monk who with a fellow monk, Huilin 慧琳 (737–820), compiled the Buddhist dictionary *Yiqie jing yinyi* 一切經音義 [*The Pronunciations and Meanings of All the Sutras*].

Huizong 徽宗 (1101–1125) The emperor Huizong of the Song dynasty.

Hun Dian 混滇 See Hun Tian.

Hun Kui 混潰 See Hun Tian.

Hun Pankuang 混盤況 See Pankuang.

Hun Shen 混慎 See Hun Tian.

Hun Tian 混填 (?first century CE) Also called Hun Shen 混慎, Hun Dian 混滇, Hun Kui 混潰. A seaborne foreigner who invaded Funan, married its queen Liuye 柳葉, and became Funan's first king. His story and name are given in various forms in the writings of Kang Tai 康泰, *Nan Qi shu* (where his name in the form Hun Tian 混填 first occurs), *Liang shu*, and other sources. See Liuye.

Indra A Hindu god.

Indravarman I (r. 877–c. 889) A king of Angkor.

Indravarman II (r. c.1218–1243) A king of Angkor, son of Jayavarman VII. See Jayavarman VII.

Indravarman III (r. ?1296–1308) The king of Angkor during Zhou Daguan 周達觀's visit there. See Zhou Daguan.

Īśānapura Yishe'na *cheng* 伊奢那城 in Chinese. Īśānavarman I's capital city. In his record of his journey from China to India, the Buddhist monk Xuanzang 玄奘 refers to the city, which he calls Yishangnabuluo 伊賞那補羅. It is thought to have been located near Sambor Prei Kuk, near Kampong Thom in present-day Cambodia. See Īśānasena, Xuanzang.

Īśānasena (?616–late 630s) Another name for Īśānavarman I, Īśānasena is mentioned in Chinese sources as an early king of Zhenla. In Chinese he is called Yishe'naxian 伊奢那先, and his family name is given as Kṣatriyaḥ (Shali 刹利). According to *Xin Tang shu*, it was Īśānasena, rather than his father Citrasena (as *Sui shu* relates), who took over Funan. See Citrasena.

Īśānavarman I See Īśānasena.

Jambudvipa Zhanbu[*zhou*] 瞻部[洲] in Chinese. The southern continent in the early Buddhist geography of the world.

Jayatataka Baray A lake or reservoir built by Jayavarman VII (r. 1181–c. 1218), and mentioned by Zhou Daguan 周大觀. See Jayavarman VII, Zhou Daguan.

Jayavarman See Kauṇḍinya, Kauṇḍinya Jayavarman.

Jayavarman (I) (r. 657?–681?) A king of Zhenla prior to the Kingdom of Angkor.

Jayavarman II (802–835) The king who is regarded as founding the Kingdom of Angkor. He was consecrated as king in Mahendraparvata, on the Kulen Plateau north of Siem

Reap. Later he made his capital at Hariharalaya, near Siem Reap, where he died. See Kingdom of Angkor.

Jayavarman VII (r. 1181–c. 1218) The king of Angkor said to have attacked and defeated Champa in the late twelfth century. He was principally responsible for building Angkor Thom. See Angkor Thom.

Ji 激, 徼 See Jiao.

Jia Dan 賈耽 (730–805) A Tang court geographer who wrote a detailed description of six overland routes and one maritime route in and out of China, including an overland route to Wendan, for the Tang emperor Dezong 德宗. See Wendan.

Jia Xiangli 家翔梨 The name of a seafaring merchant, perhaps just called Xiangli 翔梨, who came from the unknown state of Tanxiang 嘾楊 and told Fan Zhan, third-century king of Funan, about the glories of India. See Fan Zhan.

Jialuoxi 加羅 (囉) 希 A thirteenth-century dependency of Srivijaya to the south of Zhenla. Its location has not been clearly identified, though it may possibly have been on the east coast of the Kra Isthmus.

Jia'natiao 伽 (迦) 那調 See Gunu.

Jiankang 健康 The capital of successive southern dynasties between the Han and the Sui dynasties; present-day Nanjing 南京. See also Jianye.

Jianpuzhai 柬埔寨 The Chinese name for Cambodia from the late sixteenth or early seventeenth century until the present day. See Cambodia.

Jianye 建鄴 The capital of the Three Kingdoms state of Wu, later to become Jiankang 健康 and later still Nanjing 南京. See Jiankang.

Jiao 激, 徼 Also pronounced Ji. The state where Hun Tian 混填 set out from to sail to Funan, according to *Nan Qi shu* and *Liang shu*. *Liang shu* locates it to the south of Funan. See Hun Tian, Mofu.

Jiaobu 交部 See Jiaozhou.

Jiaochenru 憍陳如 See Kauṇḍinya.

Jiaoling 交嶺 A name meaning either (1) Jiaozhou 交州 and Wuling 五嶺 or (2) Jiaozhou 交州 and Lingnan 嶺南. See Jiaozhou, Wuling, Lingnan.

Jiaozhi 交阯 An early commandery in the far south of China, located in the Red River Delta. See Nanhai.

Jiazha 迦乍 See Senggao.

Jiaozhou 交州 During and after the Han dynasty, an administrative region of south China; from the 220s on, one of two administrative regions in south China, the other being Guangzhou 廣州.

Jimie 吉蔑 Also Gemie 閣蔑. A Chinese term for Khmer, first mentioned as one of several Kunlun languages in the eighth-ninth century Buddhist dictionary *Yiqie jing yinyi*. See Kunlun.

Jinchen 金陳 See Jinlin.

Jing Mountains 荊山 Jingshan 荊山, mountains in the west of present-day Hubei province in central China. Where the Tang emperor Dezong released thirty-two elephants given in tribute by Wendan.

Jinlin 金林, 金鄰 Also called Jinchen 金陳. A state located perhaps on the mainland west of Funan.

Jinsheng 金生 The son of Fan Shiman, king of Funan, killed by Fan Shiman's nephew Fan Zhan. See Fan Shiman, Fan Zhan.

Jinshuaibinshen 金衰賓深 The undeciphered Chinese name or title for the king of Zhenla in 1129, when the Song emperor Gaozong 高宗 conferred honors on him. The king of Angkor at the time was Sūryavarman II, whose name bears no relation to this Chinese name or title.

Jiubuzhi 究不事 A state mentioned in *Hou Han shu* that sent tribute to China in the first century CE, and is sometimes erroneously identified with Cambodia.

Jiuchouluo 鳩酎羅 A slave of King Kauṇḍinya Jayavarman (r. late fifth to early sixth century?), said to have usurped the throne of Linyi 林邑 in the late fifth century. Identified with the usurper Danggenchun 當根純. See also Danggenchun, Linyi, appendix five.

Jiumo 鳩摩 See Senggao.

Jiumosengge 鳩摩僧哥 See Xinzhumosengke.

Jiuzhen 九真 An early commandery in the far south of China. See Nanhai.

Jiuzhi 九稚 Also called Juzhi 句稚, Juli 拘利, Gouzhi 勾稚. The place, probably on the Malay Peninsula, from which King Fan Zhan of Funan's kinsman Su Wu 蘇物 set out to go to India in the third century CE. See Fan Zhan.

Jiyang 吉陽 A place on the south side of Hainan Island. A twelfth-century Chinese military commander based there taught the king of Champa how to defeat Zhenla in battle using crossbowmen on elephants.

Juji 巨迹 Also called Juyan 巨延. An island northeast of Zhuzhuanbo (Java?) that in the Funan era was a source of cups made from clam shells.

Juli 拘利 See Jiuzhi.

Juqu 車渠 See Chequ.

Jurchen In Chinese, Nüzhen 女真. Tungusic-speaking peoples living in the northeast of present-day China; predecessors of the Manchus.

Juyan 巨延 See Juji.

Juzhi 句稚 See Jiuzhi.

Kaifeng 開封 Capital of the Northern Song dynasty (960–1127).

Kainan 開南 See Zhennan.

Kambuja Meaning "born of Kambu." A term that was first used for Cambodia in the ninth century CE and that is the basis of the modern name Cambodia. Jianpuzhai 柬埔寨 in Chinese.

Kambuja-dhirāja An early thirteenth-century Cambodian king, called Ganwuzhe Chidazhi 甘武者持達志 in Chinese.

Kanadvīpa See Gunu.

Kang Tai 康泰 (fl. 240s–250s CE) A Chinese envoy sent with another envoy, Zhu Ying 朱應, to Funan and other southern states by the Three Kingdoms state of Wu. Kang and Zhu left records of their trip, fragments of which are still extant.

Kantharawichai A place in northeastern Thailand. In Tatsuo Hoshino's view, Kantharawichai and Fa Daet constituted a possible location for Wendan 文單. See Wendan.

Kauṇḍinya Jiaochenru 憍陳如 or Qiaochenru 僑陳如 in Chinese. The Sanskrit name of (1) a late fourth- or early fifth-century king of Funan, said by *Liang shu* to have been an Indian brahmin; (2) a late fifth- to early sixth-century king of Funan, Kauṇḍinya Jayavarman (Shexie[ya]bamo 闍邪[耶]跋摩), who sent the Buddhist monk Nāgasena on a mission to the southern Chinese capital Jiankang. Pelliot suggests questionably that the name of Funan's founding king, Hun Tian 混塡, was also a transcription of the name Kauṇḍinya. See Hun Tian.

Khmer A language that is part of the Austroasiatic family of languages; also the people who speak it. The official language of present-day Cambodia. See also Jimie.

Kingdom of Angkor A term used by some historians to refer to the period of Cambodian history from the ninth to the fourteenth century. See Angkor, Zhenla.

Kṛṣṇa The Hindu god Krishna.

Kumārajīva (344–413) A leading translator of Sanskrit Buddhist texts into Chinese, from Kucha in central Asia.

Kunlun 崑崙, 昆侖 In the context of the Southern Sea, a kinship or status term used by Wan Zhen 萬震 and other Chinese writers during the Funan era. Sometimes apparently confused with the kinship term *gulong* 古龍. Later used by Chinese writers as a generic term for places in the Southern Sea region, their languages, and their inhabitants, notably those described as having black skins and curly hair. See also Wan Zhen.

Laigankeng 賴敢坑 One of ten Zhenla prefectures (*jun* 郡) named by Zhou Daguan 周達觀. Its location is not known. See Zhou Daguan.

Land Zhenla Lu Zhenla 陸真臘 in Chinese. One of the two parts into which Zhenla is said to have been divided during the eighth century, according to *Jiu Tang shu* and later sources. Alternative names for Land Zhenla are Wendan 文單 and (according to *Xin Tang shu*) Polou 婆鏤. The other part of divided Zhenla was called Water Zhenla or Shui Zhenla 水真臘. See Water Zhenla, Wendan.

Langkasuka See Langyaxiu.

Langyaxiu 狼牙脩 (須) A state referred to in *Liang shu* and *Sui shu*. It was probably situated in the north of the Malay Peninsula, though Hoshino locates it in the Chao Phraya

Valley. Identified with Langkasuka, an old Arab, Javanese, Indian, and Malay placename (variously written).

Li Daoyuan 酈道元 (c. 470–527) The author of *Shui jing zhu* 水經注 [*A Commentary on The Classic of Waterways*].

Li Dashi 李大師 (570–628) See Li Yanshou.

Li Fang 李昉 (925–996) The principal editor of the encyclopaedias *Taiping yulan* and *Taiping guangji*. *Taiping yulan* is the main source for Kang Tai 康泰's writings. See Kang Tai.

Li Mona 李摩那 (fl. 813) An envoy sent by Water Zhenla to the Tang court in 813.

Li Touji 李頭及 An envoy sent by Wendan 文單 to the Tang court in 798.

Li Yanshou 李延壽 (d. 680) The principal author of *Nan shi* and *Bei shi*, completing work on both histories started by his father Li Dashi 李大師 (570–628).

Lianzhou 廉州 A place on the coast of Guangxi 廣西 in southern China.

Lin Kun 林坤 (fl. 1340s) Author of a 1346 miscellany which Zhou Daguan 周達觀 wrote a preface for.

Liṅgaparvata Linggabopo 陵伽缽婆 or Linggabobaduo 陵伽缽拔多 in Chinese. A linga or Śaivaite mountain; also, the Linga Mountain near Īśānapura. See Īśānapura.

Linghu Defen 令狐德芬 See Wei Zheng.

Lingnan 嶺南 A name for southern China and for the states to the south of it, meaning "south of the mountains."

Linyang 林陽 A state in the Funan era, possibly in the center or south of present-day Myanmar.

Linyi 林邑 An independent state, said to have evolved from the southernmost Han dynasty district of Xianglin 象林. It was located in the central coastal area of present-day Vietnam, and flourished from the third to the eighth century CE. Often known today by its Vietnamese name, Lâm Ấp, it is sometimes described as the precursor to, or the early stage of, Champa. See appendix five.

Liu Fu 劉富 (fl. late eleventh century) A Chinese officer in Guangzhou 廣州 in charge of military recruitment in the late eleventh century.

Liu Lin 劉琳 (fl. 1930s) The principal editor of *Song hui yao jigao*.

Liu Xu 劉昫 (887–946) The principal author of *Jiu Tang shu*.

Liuye 柳葉 (first century CE?) A queen of Funan, its first monarch. Her name, meaning "willow leaf", is given as such in Kang Tai 康泰, *Nan Qi shu*, *Liang shu*, and other sources; *Jin shu* inverts the name to Yeliu 葉柳 (leafy willow).

Lokeśvara The Bodhisattva of compassion, also known as Avalokiteśvara and Guanyin 觀音.

Lou Yue 樓鑰 (1137–1213) A Song dynasty essayist who refers to Zhenla.

Lu Ban 魯班 A semi-mythical Chinese carpenter who made his tomb at Angkor Wat according to a fanciful story of Zhou Daguan 周大觀's. See Zhou Daguan, Angkor Wat.

Lu Bode 路博德 The second-century BCE general who opened up the far south for the Han dynasty and established the Rinan 日南 commandery there. See Rinan.

Lü Dai 呂岱 (161–256 CE) A Regional Inspector in Jiaozhou 交州 in south China who was engaged in the first exchanges between China and Funan.

Lu Ji 陸楫 The editor of the sixteenth-century anthology *Gujin shuo hai* 古今說海 [*A Sea of Stories Old and New*].

Lu Zhenla 陸真臘 See Land Zhenla.

Luohu 羅斛 A Mon-Khmer state with its capital at Lopburi on the lower Chao Raya river of present-day Thailand. Destroyed by the northern state of Xian 暹 in 1349, it became part of the state of Xianluo 暹羅, which remained the Chinese name for Siam (now Thailand) until the twentieth century. Luohu is listed as a dependency of Zhenla by Zhao Rugua 趙汝适. See Zhao Rugua.

Luolun 羅倫 See Wuwen (2).

Luoyang 洛陽 At times the capital of northern China during the Six Dynasties era; during the Tang dynasty the eastern capital of China, the principal capital being Chang'an 長安. See Chang'an.

Luoyue 羅越 A place mentioned by the Tang geographer Jia Dan, and likely to have been on the Malay side of the present-day Malacca Strait.

Lurong 盧容 The port in Rinan 日南 from which the third-century Chinese envoys Kang Tai and Zhu Ying set sail for Funan. See also Shouling.

Luwu 祿兀 The capital of Zhenla, according to Zhao Rugua 趙汝适. Pelliot argues it could be a form of the name Angkor. See Zhao Rugua.

Lüyang 綠洋 Meaning "green ocean." A place listed as a dependency of Zhenla by Zhao Rugua 趙汝适. Its location has not been clearly identified. See Zhao Rugua.

Lý Thánh Tông (r. 1054–1072) A Vietnamese king who in 1069 sent troops to capture the then king of Champa, Rudravarman III, and raze his city Vijaya.

Ma Duanlin 馬端臨 (1245–1322) The author of *Wenxian tongkao*.

Ma Huan 馬歡 (c. 1380–1460) The chronicler who accompanied the Ming dynasty admiral Zheng He 鄭和 on three of his overseas voyages. The author of *Ying ya sheng lan*.

Ma Yuan 馬援 (14 BCE–49 CE) A Chinese general who crushed a southern rebellion by the Trưng sisters (Zheng 徵 in Chinese)—now regarded as national heroes in Vietnam—then erected bronze or copper pillars to mark the southern extremity of the Han dynasty. See Trưng sisters, Xitu, appendix five.

Mahendraparvata Meaning The Mountain of Great Indra. The city where Jayavarman II was consecrated as king in 802. See Jayavarman II.

Mahendravarman See Citrasena.

Maheśvara Meaning Great Lord, a title given to the god Śiva. Moxishouluo 摩醯首羅 in Chinese.

Mai Thúc Loan (?–722) Mei Shuluan 梅叔鸞 in Chinese. The Vietnamese leader of a rebellion against the Tang dynasty, who called himself the Black Emperor 黑帝.

Malan 麻蘭 Alternatively, Maluowen 麻羅問 and Moliang 莫良. A place mentioned by Zhou Qufei 周去非, Zhao Rugua 趙汝适 (as Maluowen 麻羅問), and Zhou Daguan 周達觀. Perhaps Malyan, a name on inscriptions that may refer to a place in Battambang in the west of present-day Cambodia. See Zhou Qufei, Zhao Rugua, Zhou Daguan.

Maluowen 麻羅問 See Malan.

Malyan See Malan.

Mandra A Buddhist monk, called Mantuoluo 曼陀羅 in Chinese, who went from Funan to the southern Chinese capital Jiankang in the early sixth century.

Maolun 茂論 The Indian king Muruṇḍa who met the third-century Funanese envoy Su Wu.

Mawuzhou 馬五洲 Literally Ma Five Islands, probably a name for Maluku.

Mei Shuluan 梅叔鸞 See Mai Thúc Loan.

Mingzhou 明州 See Hangzhou.

Modan 摩躭 The mountain in Funan on to which Śiva (Maheśvara) descended, as described by the monk Nāgasena during his mission from Funan to the southern Chinese capital Jiankang in 484.

Mofu 模趺 The unidentified state that according to Kang Tai 康泰 was the home state of Hun Shen 混慎 (Hun Tian 混塡). Paul Pelliot suggests it may possibly have been Hengdie 横趺, a state on the east coast of the Malay Peninsula. See also Jiao, Wuwen.

Mohe 靺鞨 Thought to be an early name for the far eastern Jurchen people.

Mojunmingjisi 摩君明稽毘 See Xinzhumosengke.

Molamotu 摩臘摩禿 The name (possibly garbled) of the leader of the tribute mission sent from Zhenla to the Song court in 1120.

Moliang 莫良 See Malan.

Mon A language that is part of the Austroasiatic family of languages and a recognized language in present-day Thailand and Myanmar; also, the people who speak it.

Mu di 穆帝 (r. 345–361) The emperor Mu of the Jin dynasty.

Mujinbo 木津波 One of ten Zhenla prefectures (*jun* 郡) named by Zhou Daguan 周達觀. Its location is not known. See Zhou Daguan.

Muruṇḍa See Maolun.

Nafuna 那弗那 The city that Funan moved to when its capital Temu 特牧 was annexed by Zhenla, according to *Xin Tang shu*. Pelliot suggests that Nafuna is a transcription of the Sanskrit word *navana* (new), so that Nafuna *cheng* means Navanagara, New City.

Nāgasena The Indian Buddhist monk, called Nagaxian 那伽仙 in Chinese, who was sent in 484 on a tribute mission to the Southern Qi court in Jiankang by Kauṇḍinya Jayavarman, king of Funan.

Nanhai 南海 (1) Southern Sea, the present-day South China Sea and beyond. (2) One of the nine commanderies (*jun* 郡, administrative divisions) that the Han dynasty established in the far south of China in the second century BCE. The other eight were Yulin 鬱林, Cangwu 蒼梧, Jiaozhi 交趾, Hepu 合浦, Jiuzhen 九真, Rinan 日南, Daner 儋耳, and Zhuya 珠崖.

Nanyue 南越 An independent kingdom in south China with its capital at Panyu 番禺, later the city of Guangzhou 廣州. The kingdom lasted from 204 BCE until its defeat by the Han dynasty in 112 BCE.

Nanzhao 南詔 An independent state in present-day Yunnan in southwest China, in power from the eighth to the tenth century. It was succeeded by the kingdom of Dali 大理, which was reabsorbed into China under the Mongols in the thirteenth century.

Navanagara See Nafuna.

Neak Pean A Buddhist temple set on a small island to the northeast of Angkor Thom, described by Zhou Daguan 周大觀 as a square gold tower with stone chambers. See Zhou Daguan.

Ningbo 寧波 See Mingzhou.

Ningzong 寧宗 (r. 1195–1224) The emperor Ningzong of the Song dynasty.

Norodom Sihanouk (1922–2012) The ruler of Cambodia at various times between 1941 and 2004; king of Cambodia from 1941 to 1955 and again from 1993 to 2004.

Noutuohuan 耨陀洹 See Tuohuan.

Nüwa 女媧 A Chinese goddess who repaired the sky when it collapsed in primeval times.

Óc Eo A major archaeological site in the Mekong Delta associated with Funan. See also Angkor Borei.

Ouyang Xiu 歐陽修 (1007–1072) The principal author of *Xin Tang shu.*

Ouyang Xun 歐陽詢 (557–641) The author of *Yi wen lei ju.*

Pankuang 盤況 Called Hun Pankuang 混盤況 by *Liang shu.* A king of Funan who was a successor to the founding king Hun Tian, perhaps in the second century CE.

Panpan (1) **盤盤** (Hun) Pankuang's son, who ruled Funan for three years, perhaps in the late second century CE.

Panpan (2) **槃槃, 盤盤** A state on the Malay Peninsula in the Funan era, perhaps present-day Pranburi or Surat Thani in southern Thailand.

Panyu 番禺 See Nanyue.

Paramārtha An Indian monk, called Boluomotuo 波羅末陀 in Chinese, who went to the southern Chinese capital Jiankang in 546 to become a leading translator of Buddhist texts into Chinese.

Phimeanakas The tenth-century temple in the royal palace in Angkor Thom, mentioned as a gold tower by Zhou Daguan 周大觀. See Jayavarman VII, Zhou Daguan.

Phnom Bakheng A state temple to the southwest of Angkor Thom built by the Angkor king Yaśovarman I (r. 889–c. 900). Perhaps alluded to by Zhao Rugua 趙汝适. See Angkor Thom, Zhao Rugua.

Piao 驃, 剽 The state or states in the middle reaches of the Irrawaddy River in present-day Myanmar, active during the first millennium CE. Piao is often identified with the Old Burmese name Pyū.

Piqian 毗騫 An unidentified state, perhaps an island state, with a preternaturally tall king who sent gifts made of gold to the king of Funan.

Poli 婆利 A state described in *Sui shu*, located perhaps in north-central Sumatra.

Polou 婆鏤 An alternative name for Land Zhenla. See Land Zhenla.

Poluosuo 婆羅娑 An unidentified state to the west of Chitu. See also Chitu.

Poluotiba 婆羅提拔 See Purandara.

Pomi 婆彌 A king or deputy king of Wendan 文單 who led a tribute mission to China in 771, accompanied by his (unnamed) wife.

Popiya 婆毘牙 (d. 1405) A Cambodian king, perhaps Chao Ponhea. Also called Baopiye Ganpuzhe 寶毘耶甘菩著.

Prasat Yeay Peau A temple in the temple complex at Sambor Prei Kuk, likely location of Īśānapura. See Īśānapura.

Pugan 蒲甘 The eleventh-to-thirteenth-century state of Pagan or Bagan, in the center-west of present-day Myanmar on the Ayeyarwady (Irrawaddy) River.

Pumai 蒲買 One of ten Zhenla prefectures (*jun* 郡) named by Zhou Daguan 周達觀. Likely to be Phimai, the walled temple complex south of Nakhon Ratchasima in present-day Thailand. See Zhou Daguan.

Purandara Possibly the Sanskrit equivalent of Poluotiba 婆羅提拔, mentioned by *Jiu Tang shu* as the capital city of Water Zhenla. Jacques suggests that Purandarapura (the city of Purandara), a name found in local inscriptions, was the capital of King Jayavarman I (?657–?681).

Putibatuo 菩提拔陀 See Buddhabadra.

Qian Zeng 錢曾 (1629–c. 1699) A bibliophile who saw an early, much fuller version of Zhou Daguan 周達觀's *Zhenla fengtu ji*.

Qiaochenru 僑陳如 See Kauṇḍinya.

Qin Lun 秦論 A traveling merchant who visited Sun Quan 孫權, ruler of the kingdom of Wu, in 226 CE and told him about Da Qin (the eastern Roman Empire).

Qingyuan 慶元 A county in the Chinese port city of Mingzhou 明州. See Mingzhou.

Qinzhou 欽州 A place on the coast of Guangxi 廣西 in southern China.

Qiongguan 瓊管 Also called Qiongzhou 瓊州. A place on the north side of Hainan Island.

Qiongzhou 瓊州 See Qiongguan.

Qiyu 耆域 (fl. early fourth century) A Buddhist monk who traveled from India to Luoyang via Funan.

Quanzhou 泉州 See Hangzhou.

Rājendravarman II (r. 944–968) The Angkor king who built East Mebon.

Rama A Hindu god.

Renzong 仁宗 (r. 1312–1320) The emperor Renzong of the Yuan dynasty.

Riluo 日落 See Wuwen (2).

Rinan 日南 An early commandery in the far south of China, a place from which travelers set off for Funan and farther afield. See Nanhai.

Rudravarman (?514–?539) The last-named king of Funan, as mentioned in *Liang shu*. Called Liutuobamo 留陀跋摩 in Chinese.

Rudravarman III (fl. 1068–1070) A Champa king. See Lý Thánh Tông.

Śaivaite Of, pertaining to, or worshipping the god Śiva. See Śiva.

Śakra Lord of the Devas. Shitihuan 釋提洹 or Shittihuanyin 釋提桓因 in Chinese. A title of Indra, lord protector of Devas (Hindu or Buddhist deities).

Saṃghapāla A Buddhist monk from Funan, called Senggapoluo 僧伽婆羅 in Chinese, who went from Funan to the southern Chinese capital Jiankang in the early sixth century.

San bao 三寶 Meaning The Three Treasures, Triratna in Sanskrit. The Three Treasures in Buddhist belief are the Buddha, the dharma (Buddhist law or teachings), and the sangha (the Buddhist monastic community).

San guo 三國 See Three Kingdoms.

Sanbo 三泊 Also pronounced Sanpo; alternative form Sanluo 三濼. A place next to Zhenla mentioned by Zhou Qufei 周去非 and Zhao Rugua 趙汝适, who describes it (calling it Sanluo 三濼) as a dependency of Zhenla. Possibly another name for the Wendan 文單 dependency Canban 參半. See Canban, Zhou Qufei, Zhao Rugua.

Sanfoqi 三佛齊 See Srivijaya.

Sanluo 三濼 See Sanbo.

Sea Drum Hai gu 海鼓 in Chinese. A rock on an island mountain west of Funan whose rumblings were said to warn sailors of storms.

Senggao 僧高 A state northwest of Zhenla that sent tribute to the Tang court in 638 and thereafter, along with four other states. Some or all of these states were subsequently taken over by Zhenla. The other four states, all otherwise unknown, were Wuling 武令, Jiazha 迦乍, Jiumo 鳩摩, and Funa 富那.

Senggapoluo 僧伽婆羅 See Saṃghapāla.

Sengzhi 僧祇 The capital of Chitu (Red Earth), probably meaning Lion City. Mentioned as an example of a Kunlun language in the eighth-ninth century Buddhist dictionary *Yiqie jing yinyi*—a reference perhaps to the language of Chitu. See Jimie, Chitu.

Shen Yue 沈約 (441–513) The author of *Song shu*.

Shenzong 神宗 (r. 1068–1085) The emperor Shenzong of the Song dynasty.

Shepo 闍婆 See Zhuzhuanbo.

Shi guan 史館 A Chinese term meaning History Office. Set up for court historians in 629 by the Tang emperor Taizong 太宗.

Shimi 石蜜 See Wuwen (2).

Shouling 壽泠 A river and port in Rinan 日南, perhaps the same as a place called Lurong 盧容. See also Lurong.

Shui Zhenla See Water Zhenla.

Siam An old name for Thailand. See Xianluo.

Siem Reap The present-day Cambodian city near Angkor. The popular etymology of the name is "Siam flattened."

Sima Qian 司馬遷 (c. 145–c. 86 BCE) The author with his father Sima Tan 司馬談 of *Shi ji*, a history of China from earliest times to the Han dynasty.

Sima Tan 司馬談 (c. 165–110 BCE) See Sima Qian.

Śiva A Hindu god, one of the supreme trinity consisting of Brahmā, Viṣṇu, and Śiva. Played a prominent role in Funan and Zhenla belief systems. See Maheśvara, Bhadreśvara.

Six Dynasties The period in China between the Han dynasty and the Sui dynasty, 222–589 CE.

Skanda A Hindu god.

Somā A naga or serpent queen sometimes identified with Liuye 柳葉. See Liuye.

Southern Sea See Nanhai.

Srivijaya The Sumatra-based trading state that rose to prominence from the seventh century on; apparently the state or city called Foshi 佛逝 and Sanfoqi 三佛齊 in Chinese.

Su Bian 蘇弁 See Wang Pu.

Su Mian 蘇冕 See Wang Pu.

Su Wu 蘇物 A kinsman of King Fan Zhan of Funan, who sent him to India in the third century CE. See Fan Zhan.

Suantai 算臺 See Wuwen (2).

Sun Quan 孫權 (182–252 CE) The founder of the Three Kingdoms state of Wu 吳 on whose behalf the envoys Kang Tai 康泰 and Zhu Ying 朱應 went to Funan. See Three Kingdoms.

Sūryavarman II The king of Angkor who the Song emperor Gaozong 高宗 apparently conferred honors on. See Jinshuaibinshen.

Suzhou 蘇州 A city near Hangzhou 杭州 in southeastern China.

Taizhou 台州 A small port city north of Quanzhou. See Quanzhou.

Taizong 太宗 (1) (r. 627–649) The emperor Taizong, second emperor of the Tang dynasty.

Taizong 太宗 (2) (r. 976–997) The emperor Taizong, second emperor of the Song dynasty.

Taizu 太祖 (r. 960–975) The emperor Taizu, first emperor of the Song dynasty.

Tan Hezhi 檀和之 (fl. 440s) A Chinese general and governor of Jiaozhou who carried out a punitive attack on Linyi 林邑 in 446. See Jiaozhou, Linyi.

Tandong 檀洞 See Anyuan.

Tanglin 唐林 See Anyuan.

Tangming 堂明 An unidentified southern state that sent tribute to the Three Kingdoms state of Wu 吳 in the third century CE.

Tang ren 唐人 Meaning "people of the Tang." A term used for Chinese living abroad by Zhou Daguan 周達觀, and still in use today among overseas Chinese communities.

Tangzhou 棠州 See Wuwen (2).

Tanxiang 嘾楊 See Jia Xiangli.

Tao Zongyi 陶宗儀 The editor of the fourteenth-century anthology *Shuo fu* 說郛 [*Environs of Stories*].

Temu 特牧 The name of the capital of Funan as given in *Xin Tang shu*.

Thakhek A possible location for Wendan 文單, on the Mekong River in the center of present-day Laos. See Wendan.

Three Kingdoms San guo 三國 (Three States) in Chinese. The three states were Wei 魏, Shu 蜀, and Wu 吳. Three Kingdoms is also the name given to the period (220–280 CE) when China was divided among the three states.

Three Treasures See San bao.

Tianzhu 天竺 A widely used old Chinese name for India.

Tonlé Sap Lake, Tonlé Sap Tonlé Sap Lake is the large, seasonally inundated freshwater lake in Cambodia south of Siem Reap. The river Tonlé Sap connects it to the Mekong River.

Touhe 投和 An unidentified place to the south of Zhenla, mentioned in *Xin Tang shu*.

Tribhuvanādityavarman (r. 1149–c. 1177) A king of Angkor. He evidently sent a tribute mission to the Song court in 1175 and may have died in a Champa military attack on Angkor in 1177.

Trưng sisters (c. 12–43 CE) Two sisters, Trưng Trắc and Trưng Nhị (徵側 Zheng Ce and 徵貳 Zheng Ni in Chinese), who led a revolt against the Han dynasty's occupation of the northern part of present-day Vietnam in the first century CE. They are now national heroes in Vietnam. See Ma Yuan.

Tufan 吐番 See Turfan.

Tumi 突彌 Mentioned with Gemie 閣蔑 (Khmer) as an example of a Kunlun language in an eighth-to-ninth century Chinese Buddhist dictionary. See Jimie.

Tunlifu 呑里富 A place listed as a dependency of Zhenla by Zhao Rugua 趙汝适. Its location has not been clearly identified. See Zhao Rugua.

Tuoba 拓拔 The Chinese name for the Mongol people who ruled north China in the in the fifth and sixth centuries, called Taghbač in their own language, meaning Lords of the Earth.

Tuohuan 陀桓, 陀洹 Also called Noutuohuan 耨陀洹, Gantuohuan (or Qiantuohuan) 乾陀洹, and Duhuai 杜懷. A place west of Zhenla mentioned in *Sui shu*, *Xin Tang shu*, and *Zhu fan zhi*, which calls it Duhuai and describes it as a dependency of Zhenla. Perhaps Dawei (Tuwa 土瓦 in Chinese) in the south of present-day Myanmar.

Tuoshanibatuo 陁沙尼拔陁 The Chinese version of the unidentified Sanskrit name of a Buddhist monk and envoy from Zhenla to the Chinese court, mentioned in a ninth-century story about a tree in Zhenla that sprouts purple pins.

Tuotuo 脫脫 (1314–1356) The Chinese version of the Mongol name Toqto'a. The author of *Song shi*.

Turfan 吐番 Tufan in Chinese. A Turkic name used in Song times to refer to the Himalayan plateau; today, a town on the northern rim of the Taklamakan desert in Xinjiang 新疆.

Uyghurs The Turkic-speaking people called Huigu 回鶻 in Chinese in Tang times, known today in Chinese as Weiwuer 維吾爾. The Uyghur people now live mainly in Xinjiang 新疆 in the far west of China.

Varuṇa A Hindu god.

Vientiane Wanxiang 萬象 in Chinese. The present-day capital of Laos. A possible location for Wendan 文單. See Wendan.

Vijaya A coastal city of Champa. Identified with Foshi 佛逝; also perhaps Xinzhou 新州, New City, mentioned by the Song dynasty writer Fan Chengda 范成大.

Viṣṇu A Hindu god, one of the supreme trinity Brahmā, Viṣṇu, and Śiva.

Vyādhapura The name for an ancient city of Funan. Despite the fact that it is sometimes located at Ba Phnom in the southeast of present-day Cambodia, Vickery argues that its location and identity are uncertain.

Wali 窊裏 A state next to Zhenla mentioned by Zhou Qufei 周去非 and Zhao Rugua 趙汝适, who lists it as a dependency of Zhenla. See Zhou Qufei, Zhao Rugua.

Wan Zhen 萬震 The third-century CE author of *Nanzhou yi wu zhi* 南州異物志 [*Annals of Strange Things in the Southern Regions*].

Wang Junzheng 王君政 A Chinese envoy sent to the state of Chitu in the early seventh century. See Chitu.

Wang Pu 王溥 (922–982) The principal editor of *Tang hui yao*, who drew on earlier work by Su Mian 蘇冕 (d. 805), Su Bian 蘇弁 (fl. 760–805), and Cui Xuan 崔鉉 (fl. 840s–860s).

Wang Qinruo 王欽若 (962–1025) The principal editor of *Cefu yuangui*.

Wang Yinglin 王應麟 (1223–1296) A Song dynasty scholar who compiled a list of missions to China from Funan and Zhenla.

Wanli 萬里 A place with dangerous rocks in the sea between Champa and Jiaozhi 交阯, described in *Song hui yao jigao*. See Jiaozhi.

Wanxiang 萬象 See Vientiane.

Wat Phu A temple in present-day Laos, once a shrine to Śiva. In a view Vickery casts doubt on, Coedès argues that it was the Zhenla temple to Bhadreśvara or Śiva mentioned in *Sui shu*.

Water Zhenla Shui Zhenla 水真臘 in Chinese. One of the two parts that Zhenla divided into during the eighth century, according to *Jiu Tang shu* and later sources, the other being Land Zhenla or Lu Zhenla 陸真臘. See also Land Zhenla.

Wei Zheng 魏徵 (580–643) The principal author of *Sui shu*, working with the scholars Linghu Defen 令狐德芬 (583–666) and Zhangsun Wuji 長孫無忌 (d. 659).

Wen xue guan 文學舘 A Chinese term meaning College of Literary Studies, a center for leading officials and scholars in the early Tang dynasty.

Wendan 文單 Also pronounced Wenchan. An alternative name for Land Zhenla. According to *Xin Tang shu*, Wendan had two dependencies, Canban 參半 and Daoming 道明. See Land Zhenla, Canban, Daoming.

Wenyang 文陽 See Wuwen (2).

Wenzhou 溫州 The port city Zhou Daguan 周大觀 set out from to go to Zhenla. See Zhou Daguan, Hangzhou.

Wu di 武帝 (1) The emperor Wu of the Former Han Dynasty (r. 140–86 BCE).

Wu di 武帝 (2) The emperor Wu of the Western Jin dynasty (r. 265–289).

Wu di 武帝 (3) The emperor Wu of the Southern Qi dynasty (r. 483–493).

Wu di 武帝 (4) The emperor Wu of the Liang dynasty (r. 502–549).

Wu Guan 吳琯 The editor of the sixteenth-century compilation *Gujin yishi* 古今逸史 [*Other Histories Old and New*].

Wu Qiuyan 吾邱衍 (d. 1312) Author of an anthology that mentions Zhou Daguan 周達觀's account of his visit to Cambodia. See Zhou Daguan.

Wu Shu 吳淑 (947–1002) The author of *Shilei fu* 詩類賦 [*A Prose Poem on Categories of Things*], an early work containing a passage on fans in Funan.

Wu Zetian 武則天 (r. 684–704) The empress Wu Zetian, during whose reign the name of the Tang dynasty was temporarily changed to Zhou.

Wuhu 烏滸 A wild region in the far south of China, mentioned by the third-century poet Zuo Si 左思. See Zuo Si.

Wuling (1) **五嶺** Translating to "five mountains," Wuling refers to the mountain range formed by the five mountain peaks of south China.

Wuling (2) **武令** See Senggao.

Wulun 無倫 An unidentified southern state in the Funan era.

Wuwen (1) **烏文** According to Kang Tai 康泰, the unidentified state that Hun Shen 混慎 (Hun Tian 混填) set out from when he sailed to Funan. See Hun Tian; see also Mofu.

Wuwen (2) **霧溫** The first stop on the eighth-century Chinese geographer Jia Dan 賈耽's overland route from Huanzhou 驩州 to Wendan 文單. The other stops were Riluo 日落,

Tangzhou 棠州, Luolun 羅倫, Shimi 石蜜, Gulang 古朗, Wenyang 文陽, Chikuang 絺誆, and Suantai 算臺. See Huanzhou, Wendan.

Xianglin 象林 See Linyi.

Xianluo 暹羅 See Luohu.

Xiao Tong 蕭統 (d. 531) The editor of *Wen xuan*, which included Zuo Si 左思's *San du fu* [*A Prose Poem on the Three Capitals*]. See Zuo Si.

Xiao Zixian 蕭子顯 (489–537) The author of *Nan Qi shu*.

Xiaozong 孝宗 (1163–1189) The emperor Xiaozong of the Song dynasty, the emperor Gaozong 高宗's successor.

Xilan 细蘭 Probably the island of Ceylon, present-day Sri Lanka, as referred to by Fan Chengda 范成大. See Fan Chengda.

Xinluo 新羅 Silla, the kingdom that ruled Korea from 668 to 935.

Xinzhou 新州 See Vijaya.

Xinzhumosengke 新祝摩僧可 Also called Jiumosengge 鳩摩僧哥 (Monk-Elder Brother Jiumo). The name of the leader of the tribute mission sent from Zhenla to the Song court in 1117. His deputy was Mojunmingjisi 摩君明稽毘. Both names seem to be transliterations of unidentified local names.

Xiongnu 匈奴 A nomadic people north of China, adversaries of the Former Han dynasty.

Xipeng 西棚 A state next to Zhenla mentioned by Zhou Qufei 周去非 and Zhao Rugua 趙汝刮, who lists it as a dependency of Zhenla. Perhaps located at Suphan in the center of present-day Thailand. See Zhou Qufei and Zhao Rugua.

Xitu 西屠 Also written 西圖. A small state with ten small dependencies said to have been founded by households of soldiers who stayed behind on the southern frontier of China when General Ma Yuan returned home. See also Heichi, Ma Yuan.

Xiuluofen 修羅分 An unidentified place west of Zhenla, mentioned in *Xin Tang shu*.

Xuanzang 玄奘 (c. 602–644) A Chinese Buddhist monk who went overland to India and back, leaving a record of his journey; a leading translator of Buddhist texts into Chinese.

Xuanzong 玄宗 (r. 713–755) The emperor Xuanzong of the Tang dynasty. His long reign was brought to an end by the devastating An Lushan 安祿山 rebellion. See An Lushan.

Xunfan 潯番 A place listed as a dependency of Zhenla by Zhao Rugua 趙汝适. Its location is not known. See Zhao Rugua.

Yan Liben 閻立本 (c. 600–673) A renowned court painter during the early Tang dynasty.

Yang di 煬帝 (r. 605–616) The emperor Yang, second emperor of the Sui dynasty. See Chitu.

Yang Fu 楊孚 (fl. 76?–84 CE) A Han dynasty official in south China who some argue was the first person whose comments on Funan, in a short passage on fans, have survived.

Yang Xuanzhi 楊衒之 (?–555) The author of *Luoyang galan ji* 洛陽伽藍記 [*A Record of the Monasteries of Luoyang*].

Yao Cha **姚察** (533–606) See Yao Silian.

Yao Silian **姚思廉** (557–637) The author of *Liang shu* and *Chen shu*, who completed work begun on both histories by his father Yao Cha 姚察.

Yaśodharapura The name that Angkor Thom was known by from the ninth century on, based on the name of its founder Yaśovarman. See Yaśovarman I.

Yaśovarman I (r. 889–c. 900) A king of Angkor, founder of the ninth-century city called Yaśodharapura, named after himself. The city was centered on the temple Phnom Bakheng near Angkor Thom. See Phnom Bakheng.

Ye Tinggui **葉廷珪** (fl. 1120–1150) The author of a book on aromatic substances found among southern foreigners.

Yeliu **葉柳** See Liuye.

Yepoti **耶婆提** A place the Buddhist monk Faxian passed en route from India to China, evidently Sumatra or Java. See Faxian.

Yijing **義淨** (635–713) A Buddhist monk who traveled by sea from China to India and back, and left a record of his travels.

Yishangnabuluo **伊賞那補羅** See Īśānapura.

Yongjia **永嘉** A county near the city of Wenzhou 溫州, the home county of both Zhou Qufei 周去非 and Zhou Daguan 周達觀. See Zhou Qufei and Zhou Daguan.

Yu Shinan **虞世南** (558–638) The author of *Bei Tang shu chao* 北堂書鈔 [*Excerpts from Books in the Northern Hall*].

Yue Shi **樂史** (930–1007) The principal editor of *Taiping huanyu ji*.

Yueshang **越裳** An ancient state in the Red River Delta, mentioned in *Hou Han shu*.

Yuezhi **月支** A Tokharian-speaking people from the Tarim Basin in present-day Xinjiang 新疆. In the third century CE a king of India sent four of the Yuezhi's much-prized horses to King Fan Zhan in Funan. See Fan Zhan.

Yulin **鬱林** An early commandery in the far south of China. See Nanhai.

Zha'nan **查南** One of ten Zhenla prefectures (*jun* 郡) named by Zhou Daguan 周達觀. A Mekong River town, perhaps the present-day town of Kampong Chhnang. See Zhou Daguan.

Zhanbulao **占不勞** See Champa.

Zhancheng **占城** See Champa.

Zhang di **章帝** (r. 76–88 CE) The emperor Zhang of the Later Han Dynasty.

Zhang Tingyu **張廷玉** (1672–1755) The author of *Ming shi*.

Zhanghai **漲海** Meaning Great Sea. Evidently another name for Nanhai 南海 or the southern part of Nanhai and beyond. Also called Dahai 大海. See Nanhai.

Zhangsun Wuji **長孫無忌** See Wei Zheng.

Zhanla **占臘** Another name for Zhenla, first used in *Song shi* in 1062. In a comment inconsistent with this date, *Ming shi* records that the name refers to Zhenla wiping out

Champa in 1195–1200. If that is the case, the meaning of Zhanla could be "Champa Defeated". See Zhenla.

Zhanlibo 占里波 See Zhenlifu.

Zhanlipo 占里婆 See Zhenlifu.

Zhanpo 占婆 See Champa.

Zhao Rugua 趙汝适 (1170–1231) Also pronounced Zhao Rukuo. The author of the gazetteer *Zhu fan zhi*. Zhao listed thirteen Zhenla dependencies of Zhenla: Dengliumei 登流眉, Bosilan 波斯蘭, Luohu 羅斛, Sanluo 三濼, Zhenlifu 真里富, Maluowen 麻羅問, Lüyang 綠洋, Tunlifu 吞里富, Pugan [Bagan] 蒲甘, Wali 窊裹, Xipeng 西棚, Duhuai 杜懷, and Xunfan 潯番. See each name for details.

Zhao Rukuo 趙汝适 An alternative pronunciation of Zhao Rugua. See Zhao Rugua.

Zhaowa 瓜哇 The Chinese name for Java, used from the fifteenth century to the present day. See also Zhuzhuanbo.

Zhenfuli 真富里 See Zhenlifu.

Zheng He 鄭和 A renowned Ming admiral. See Ma Huan.

Zheng Qiao 鄭樵 (1104–1162) The author of *Tong zhi*.

Zhenla 真臘, 真蠟 The Chinese name for a state that took over Funan in the seventh century, and from the ninth to the fourteenth century constituted what is often called the Kingdom of Angkor. The etymology of the name is uncertain. Wade argues that it derives from the word Tonlé in Tonlé Sap. Pelliot suggests that it could mean "China defeated". See Angkor, Kingdom of Angkor, Tonlé Sap, Zhanla.

Zhenlifu 真里富 Also called Zhanlipo 占里婆, Zhenfuli 真富里. A dependency of Zhenla mentioned by Zhao Rugua 趙汝适 and others, located in the southwest corner of Zhenla, perhaps at Chanthaburi in present-day Thailand. See Zhou Qufei, Zhao Rugua.

Zhennan 鎮南 A Chinese name meaning "guarding the south." Alternatively, Kainan 開南 (opening the south). According to *Man shu*, one of seven cities in the state of Nanzhao 南詔 in present-day Yunnan. See Nanzhao.

Zhenpu 真蒲 One of ten Zhenla prefectures (*jun* 郡) named by Zhou Daguan 周達觀. A frontier town on the southeastern coast of present-day Vietnam. See Zhou Daguan.

Zhenxi 鎮西 A Chinese name meaning "guarding the west." One of seven cities in the state of Nanzhao 南詔. See Zhennan.

Zhenzong 真宗 (r. 998–1022) The emperor Zhenzong of the Song dynasty.

Zhigun 雉棍 One of ten Zhenla prefectures (*jun* 郡) named by Zhou Daguan 周達觀. Possibly Saigon, now Ho Chi Minh City in the south of present-day Vietnam. See Zhou Daguan.

Zhongguo 中國 See China.

Zhongtu 中土 See China.

Zhongzhou 中州 See China

Zhou Daguan 周達觀 (fl. 1290s–1340s) Also called Zhou Dake 周達可, Zhou Jianguan 周建觀. The envoy who visited Angkor/Zhenla in 1296–1297 as part of a mission sent by the Yuan dynasty (Mongol) emperor Temür Khan. After returning to China, Zhou wrote *Zhenla fengtu ji*. Zhou mentioned by name ten prefectures (*jun* 郡) in Zhenla: Zhenpu 真蒲, Zha'nan 查南, Bajian 巴澗, Moliang 莫良, Baxue 八薛, Pumai 蒲買, Zhigun 雉棍, Mujinbo 木津波, Laigankeng 賴敢坑, and Basili 八斯里. See these names for details.

Zhou Qufei 周去非 (1135–1189) The author of the gazetteer *Lingwai daida*.

Zhu Dangbaolao 竺當抱老 An envoy sent to the southern Chinese court by Rudravarman, king of Funan, in 517.

Zhujiang 朱江, 硃江 Vermilion River in English. A river west of Zhenla mentioned in *Sui shu*. Its identity is unclear.

Zhu Ying 朱應 (fl. 240s–250s) A Chinese envoy sent with another envoy, Kang Tai 康泰, to Funan and other southern states by the Three Kingdoms state of Wu 吳. See Kang Tai.

Zhu Zhantan 竺旃檀 (fl. 357) A king of Funan, apparently of Indian origin.

Zhu Zhi 竺芝, 竺枝 Also perhaps called Zhu Jian'an 竺建安. Author of the late fifth-century (?) *Funan ji* 扶南記 [*A Record of Funan*], now mostly lost.

Zhubo 諸薄 See Zhuzhuanbo.

Zhuya 珠崖 An early commandery in the far south of China. See Nanhai, Anyuan.

Zhuzhuanbo 諸轉薄 Also called Zhubo 諸薄, Dubo 杜薄. An island across the Southern Sea from Funan, perhaps Java. Also perhaps called Shepo 闍婆, another way of writing Zhubo.

Ziran dazhou 自然大洲 See Great Island of Natural Fire.

Zuo Si 左思 (c. 252–c. 307 CE) The author of *San du fu*.

Bibliography

Primary sources

Note: When a modern Chinese edition of an old text includes in its title terms such as *jiao zhu* 校注 (*Collated and Annotated*) I have omitted these terms from the title, while describing the person responsible for doing the collating etc. as the editor. For instance, the 1986 edition of Fan Chengda's *Guihai yuheng zhi* is published under the title *Guihai yuheng zhi jiaozhu* 桂海虞衡志校注, followed by the names of the author Fan Chengda and the "collator and annotator" Yan Pei. Since Yan Pei is in effect the editor, I have described him as such.

Ban Gu 班固. *Han shu* 漢書 [*The History of the Former Han Dynasty*]. Beijing: Zhonghua shuju, 1962.

Chao Yuanfang, *Zhubing yuan hou lun* 諸病源候論 [*On Investigating the Origins of the Various Illnesses*]. ctext.org/wiki.pl?if=gb& res=836980

Chen Shou 陳壽. *San guo zhi* 三国志 [*The Annals of the Three Kingdoms*]. Beijing: Zhonghua shuju, 1977.

Daoshi 道世. *Fayuan zhulin* 法苑珠林 [*A Forest of Gems in the Dharma Garden*]. Edited by Zhou Shujia 周叔迦 and Su Jinren 蘇晋仁. Beijing: Zhonghua shuju, 2003.

Daoxuan 道宣. *Xu gao seng zhuan* 續高僧傳 [*More Biographies of Eminent Monks*]. Beijing: Zhonghua shuju, 2014.

Du You, 杜佑. *Tong dian* 通典 [*A Comprehensive History of Institutions*]. Beijing: Zhonghua shuju, 1988.

Fan Chengda 范成大. *Guihai yuheng zhi* 桂海虞衡志 [*The Treatise of the Supervisor and Guardian of the Cinnamon Sea*]. Edited by Yan Pei 嚴沛. Nanning: Guangxi renmin chubanshe, 1986.

Fan Chuo 樊綽. *Man shu* 蠻書 [*The Book of the Southern Foreigners*]. Edited by Xiang Da 向達. Beijing: Zhonghua shuju, 1962.

Fan Ye 范曄 et al. *Hou Han shu* 後漢書 [*The History of the Later Han Dynasty*]. Beijing: Zhonghua shuju, 1965.

Fang Xuanling 房玄齡 et al. *Jin shu* 晉書 [*The History of the Jin Dynasty*]. Beijing: Zhonghua shuju, 1974.

Faxian 法顯. *Fo guo ji* 佛國志 [*A Record of Buddhist States*]. Taipei: San min shuju, 2004.

Fei Xin 費信. *Xingcha shenglan* 星槎勝覽 [*An Overall Survey of the Star Raft*]. Edited by Feng Chengjun 馮承鈞. Beijing: Zhonghua shuju, 1954.

[Gan Bao 干寶 and Liu Yiqing 劉義慶.] *Sou Shenji* 搜神記 [*A Record of the Search for Spirits*], *Shi shuo xin yu* 世說新語 [*Well-known Tales Newly Told*]. Edited by Qian Zhenmin 錢振民. Changsha: Yuelu shushe, 2006.

Ge Hong 葛洪. *Bao pu zi nei wai pian* 抱朴子内外篇 [*The Master who Embraces Simplicity, the Inner and Outer Chapters*]. Taibei: Taiwan shangwu yinshuguan, 1965.

———. [attr.] *Tai qing jin ye shen dan jing* 太清金液神丹經 [*The Scripture of the Divine Elixir of the Gold Liquor of Great Clarity*]. In *Zhonghua Daozang* 中華道藏 [*Chinese Daoist Canon*], vol. 18, 1–18. Edited by Zhang Jiyu 張繼禹. Beijing: Huaxia chubanshe, 2003.

Huang Xingzeng 黄省曾. *Xiyang chaogong dianlu* 西洋朝貢典錄 [*Records of Tribute from the Western Ocean*]. Edited by Xie Fang 謝方. Beijing: Zhonghua shuju, 2000.

Hui Jiao 慧皎. *Gao seng zhuan* 高僧傳 [*Biographies of Eminent Monks*]. Beijing: Zhonghua shuju, 1992.

Kang Tai 康泰. *Wu shi waiguo zhuan* 吳時外國傳 [*A Record of Foreign States during the Wu Period*]. Edited by Xu Yunqiao 許雲樵. Singapore: ISEAS, 1971.

Kang Tai 康泰, Zhu Ying 朱應. *Waiguo zhuan* 外國傳 [*A Record of Foreign States*]. Edited by Chen Jiarong 陳佳榮 and Tan Guanglian 譚廣濂. Hong Kong: Xianggang haiwai jiaotong shi xuehui, 2006.

Legge, James, ed. and trans. *The Chinese Classics II: The Works of Mencius.* Taipei: SMC Publishing, 1991 [1871].

Legge, James, ed. and trans. *The Chinese Classics III: The Shoo King*. Taipei: SMC Publishing, 1991 [1865].
————. *The Chinese Classics IV: The She King*. Taipei: SMC Publishing, 1991 [1871].
————. *The Chinese Classics V: The Ch'un Ts'ew with the Tso Chuen*. Taipei: SMC Publishing, 1991 [1872].
Li Daoyuan 酈道元. *Shui jing zhu* 水經注 [*A Commentary on the Classic of Waterways*], edited by Chen Qiaoyi 陳橋驛. Beijing: Zhonghua shuju, 2017.
Li Fang 李昉 et al., eds. *Taiping guangji* 太平廣記 [*Extensive Records Compiled during the Era of Great Peace*]. Beijing: Zhonghua shuju, 2013.
————. *Taiping yulan* 太平御覽 [*{An Encyclopaedia} Compiled during the Era of Great Peace and Read by the Emperor*]. Beijing: Zhonghua shuju, 1960.
Li Yanshou 李延壽 et al. *Bei shi* 北史 [*The History of the Northern Dynasties*]. Beijing: Zhonghua shuju, 1974.
————. *Nan shi* 南史 [*The History of the Southern Dynasties*]. Beijing: Zhonghua shuju, 1965.
Liu An 劉安 et al. *Huainan zi* 淮南子 [*Master Huainan*]. Jilin: Jilin wenshi chubanshe, 1990.
Liu Lin 劉琳, Diao Zhongmin 刁忠民, Shu Dagang 舒大剛, Yin Bo 尹波 et al., eds. *Song hui yao jigao* 宋會要輯稿 [*A Draft Edition of the Essential Documents and Regulations of the Song Dynasty*]. Shanghai: Shanghai guji chubanshe, 2004.
Liu Xu 劉昫 et al. *Jiu Tang shu* 舊唐書 [*The Old History of the Tang Dynasty*]. Beijing: Zhonghua shuju, 1977.
Lu Ji 陸楫. *Gujin shuo hai* 古今說海 [*A Sea of Stories Old and New*]. Shanghai: Shanghai wenyi chubanshe, 1989 [1909 facsimile].
Luo Yuejiong 羅曰褧. *Xian bin lu* 咸賓錄 [*A Record of All Foreign Guests*]. Edited by Yu Sili 余思黎. Beijing: Zhonghua shuju, 2000.
Ma Duanlin 馬端臨. *Wenxian tongkao* 文獻通考 [*A Comprehensive Study of Institutions on the Basis of Authoritative Documents*]. Beijing: Zhonghua shuju, 2006.
Ma Huan 馬歡. *Ying ya sheng lan* 瀛涯勝覽 [*An Overall Survey of the Ocean's Shores*]. Edited by Wan Ming 萬明. Beijing: Haiyang chubanshe, 2005.
Mao Ruizheng 茅瑞徵. *Huangming xiangxu lu* 皇明象胥录 [*The Record of an Interpreter of the August Ming Dynasty*]. Chengdu: Sichuan minzu chunbanshe, 2002.
Ouyang Xiu 歐陽修 et al. *Xin Tang shu* 新唐書 [*The New History of the Tang Dynasty*]. Beijing: Zhonghua shuju, 1975.
Ouyang Xun 歐陽詢. *Yi wen lei ju* 藝文類聚 [*Literature Assembled by Topic*]. Shanghai: Shanghai guji chubanshe, 1965.
Shen Yue 沈約. *Song shu* 宋書 [*The History of the Liu Song Dynasty*]. Beijing: Zhonghua shuju, 1974.
Siku quanshu zhenben erji 四庫全書珍本二集 [*Rare Works from The Complete Library of the Four Branches, vol. 2*]. Edited by Wang Yunwu 王雲五. ?Shanghai: Shangwu yinshuguan, n.d..
Sima Qian 司馬遷. *Shi ji* 史記 [*The Record of the Historian*]. Beijing: Zhonghua shuju, 1965.
Song Lian 宋濂 et al. *Yuan shi* 元史 [*The History of the Yuan Dynasty*]. Beijing: Zhonghua shu ju, 1976.
Tuotuo 脫脫 [Toqto'a] et al. *Song shi* 宋史 [*The History of the Song Dynasty*]. Beijing: Zhonghua shuju, 1985.
Wan Zhen 萬震. *Nanzhou yi wu zhi* 南州異物志 [*Annals of Strange Things in the Southern Regions*]. Edited by Chen Zhifu 陳直夫. Hong Kong: Chen Zhifu jiaoshou jiuzhi rongqing menren zhuhe weiyuanhui, 1987.
Wang Dayuan, 汪大渊, *Dao yi zhi lüe* 島夷志略 [*A Brief Record of the Foreigners of the Islands*]. Edited by Su Jiqing 蘇继廎. [Beijing: Zhonghua shuju, 1981].
Wang Pu 王溥. *Tang hui yao* 唐會要 [*Important Documents of the Tang Dynasty*]. Shanghai: Shanghai guji chubanshe, 2006.
Wang Qinruo 王欽若 et al. *Cefu yuangui* 冊府元龜 [*Outstanding Models from the Storehouse of Literature*]. Hong Kong: Zhonghua shuju, 1960.
Wei Zheng 魏徵 et al. *Sui shu* 隋書 [*The History of the Sui Dynasty*]. Beijing, Zhonghua shuju, 1973.
Wu Shu 吳淑. *Shi lei fu* 事類賦 [*A Prose-poem on Categories of Things*]. Edited by Ji Qin 冀勤, Wang Xiumei 王秀梅, and Ma Rong 馬蓉. Beijing: Zhonghua shuju, 1989.
Xiao Tong 蕭統, ed. *Wen xuan* 文選 [*Selections from Literature*]. Hong Kong: Shangwu yinshu guan, 1936.
Xiao Zixian 蕭子顯. *Nan Qi shu* 南齊書 [*The History of the Southern Qi Dynasty*]. Beijing: Zhonghua shuju, 1996.

[Xu Shen 许慎.] *Shuo wen jie zi* 說文解字 [*An Explanation of Writing and Characters*]. Edited by Duan Yucai 段玉裁. Beijing: Zhonghua shuju, 1963.

[Xuanzang 玄奘 and Bianji 辯機.] *Da Tang xi yu ji* 大唐西域記 [*A Great Tang Dynasty Record of the Western Regions*]. Edited by Dong Zhiqiao 董志翹. Beijing: Zhonghua shuju, 2012.

Yang Fu 楊孚. *Yi wu zhi* 異物志 [*Annals of Strange Things*]. Edited by Wu Yongzhang 吳永章. Guangzhou: Guangdong renmin chubanshe, 1991.

Yan Congjian 嚴從簡. *Shuyu zhouzi lu* 殊域周咨錄 [*A Record of Various Views of Different Frontier Regions*]. Edited by Yu Sili 余思黎. Bejing: Zhonghua shuju, 1993.

Yang Xuanzhi 楊衒之. *Luoyang galan ji* 洛陽伽藍記 / *A Record of Buddhist Monasteries of Luoyang* [bilingual text]. English translation by Wang Yitong 王伊同. Beijing: Zhonghua shuju, 2007.

Yao Silian 姚思廉. *Chen shu* 陳書 [*The History of the Chen Dynasty*]. Beijing: Zhonghua shuju, 1972.

————. *Liang shu* 梁書 [*The History of the Liang Dynasty*]. Beijing: Zhonghua shuju, 1973.

Yijing 義淨. *Nanhai jigui neifa zhuan* 南海寄歸内法傳 [*A Record of Buddhist Precepts Sent Home from the Southern Sea*]. Edited by Wang Bangwei 王邦維. Beijing: Zhonghua shuju, 1995.

————. *Da Tang xiyu qiu fa gao seng zhuan* 大唐西域求法高僧傳 [*Great Tang Dynasty Biographies of Eminent Monks who went to the Western Regions in Search of the Dharma*]. Edited by Wang Bangwei 王邦維. Beijing: Zhonghua shuju, 1988.

Yu Shinan 虞世南. *Bei Tang shu chao* 北堂書鈔 [*Excerpts from Books in the Northern Hall*]. Beijing: Xueyuan chubanshe, 1998.

Yue Shi 樂史. *Taiping huanyu ji* 太平寰宇記 [*A Record of the World Compiled in the Era of Great Peace*]. Edited by Wang Wenchu 王文楚. Beijing: Zhonghua shuju, 2008.

Zhang Tingyu 張廷玉 et al. *Ming shi* 明史 [*The History of the Ming Dynasty*]. Beijing: Zhonghua shuju, 1974.

Zhang Xie 張燮. *Dongxi yang kao* 東西洋考 [*On the Eastern and Western Oceans*]. Edited by Xie Fang 謝方. Beijing: Zhonghua shuju, 2000.

Zhao Rugua 趙汝适. *Zhu fan zhi* 諸蕃志 [*A Treatise on the Various Foreigners*]. Edited by Yang Bowen 楊博文. Beijing: Zhonghua shuju, 2000.

Zheng Qiao 鄭樵. *Tong zhi* 通志 [*A Comprehensive Treatise on Institutions*]. Beijing: Zhonghua shuju, 1987.

Zhou Daguan 周達觀. *Zhenla fengtu ji* 真臘風土記 [*Zhenla: The Land and its People*]. Edited by Xia Nai 夏鼐. Beijing: Zhonghua shuju, 2000.

Zhou Qufei 周去非. *Lingwai daida* 嶺外代答 [*Representative Responses to Questions about Regions Beyond Wuling*]. Edited by Yang Wuquan 楊武泉. Beijing; Zhonghua shuju, 1999.

Zuo Si 左思. "San du fu 三都賦 [A Prose-poem on the Three Capitals]." In *Wen xuan* 文選 [*Selections from Literature*]. Edited by Xiao Tong 蕭統. Hong Kong: Shangwu yinshu guan, 1936.

Secondary sources

Abel-Rémusat, Jean-Pierre. *Description du royaume de Cambodge par un voyageur chinois qui a visité cette contrée à la fin du XIII siècle . . .* [*Description of the Kingdom of Cambodia by a Chinese traveller who visited this country at the end of the 13th century . . .*]. Paris: imprimerie de J. Smith, 1819.

Acri, Andrea, Roger Blench, and Alexandra Landmann, "Introduction: Re-connecting Histories across the Indo-Pacific." In *Spirits and Ships: Cultural Transfers in Early Monsoon Asia*, edited by Andrea Acri, Roger Blench, and Alexandra Landmann, 1–37. Singapore: ISEAS Yusof Ishak Institute, 2017.

Allsen, Thomas. "The Rise of the Mongolian Empire and Mongolian Rule in North China." In *The Cambridge History of China, Volume. 6: Alien Regimes and Border States, 907–1368*, edited by Herbert Franke and Denis Twitchett, 321–413. Cambridge: Cambridge University Press, 1994.

Antelme, Michel. "Quelques nouvelles pistes de recherche sur l'étymologie du nom Tchen-la" ["Some new avenues of research on the etymology of the name Zhenla"]. *Péninsule: Etudes Interdisciplinaires sur l'Asie du Sud-Est Péninsulaire*, 61, 18–19 (2010): 11–43.

Aspell, William. *Southeast Asia in the* Suishu*: A Translation of Memoir 47 with Notes and Commentary*. Singapore: NUS Asia Research Institute Working Paper no. 208, 2013.

Aung-Thwyn, Michael and Maitrii Aung-Thwyn. *A History of Myanmar since Ancient Times: Traditions and Transformations*. London, Reaktion Books, 2012.

Aymonier, Étienne. *Le Cambodge* [*Cambodia*] (3 volumes). Paris: Ernest Leroux, 1901–1904.

Backus, Charles. *The Nan-chao Kingdom and T'ang China's Southwestern Frontier*. Cambridge: Cambridge University Press, 1981.

Bacus, Elizabeth, Ian Glover, and Peter Sharrock, eds. *Interpreting Southeast Asia's Past: Monument, Image and Text*. Singapore: National University of Singapore, 2008.

Baldanza, Kathlene. *Ming China and Vietnam: Negotiating Borders in Early Modern Asia*. Cambridge: Cambridge University Press, 2016.

[Ban Gu 班固.] *The History of the Former Han Dynasty*. Translated and edited by Homer H. Dubs. Baltimore: Waverley Press, 1938.

Barrett, Timothy. "Diana Y. Paul: Philosophy of Mind in sixth-century China: Paramārtha's 'Evolution of Consciousness'" (book review). *Bulletin of the School of Oriental and African Studies*, vol. 50, no. 1 (1987): 175.

Baxter, William and Laurent Sagart. *Old Chinese: A New Reconstruction*. Oxford: Oxford University Press, 2014.

Becker, Elizabeth. *You Don't Belong Here: How Three Women Rewrote the Story of War*. New York: Public Affairs, 2021.

Beckwith, Christopher. *Empires of the Silk Road: A History of Central Eurasia from the Bronze Age to the Present*. Princeton: Princeton University Press, 2009.

Bellina, Bérénice, et al. *50 Years of Archaeology in Southeast Asia: Essays in Honour of Ian Glover*. Bangkok: River Books, 2010.

Bellina, Bérénice. "Southeast Asia and the Early Maritime Silk Road." In *Lost Kingdoms: Hindu-Buddhist Sculpture of Early Southeast Asia*, edited by John Guy, 22–24. New York: Metropolitan Museum of Art, 2014.

Bellwood, Peter. *First Migrants: Ancient Migration in Global Perspective*. Oxford: Wiley-Blackwell, 2013.

Benjamin, Walter. "The Task of the Translator." In Walter Benjamin, *Illuminations*, 69–82. New York: Harcourt Brace Jovanovich, 1968.

Berkowitz, Alan. *Patterns of Disengagement*. Stanford: Stanford University Press, 2000.

Bielenstein, Hans. *Diplomacy and Trade in the Chinese World 589–1276*. Leiden: Brill, 2005.

Bizot, François, ed. *Recherches nouvelles sur le Cambodge* [*New Research on Cambodia*]. Paris: École française d'Extrême Orient, 1994.

Boisselier, Jean. *La statuaire khmère et son évolution* [*Khmer Statuary and Its Evolution*]. Saigon: École française d'Extrême-Orient, 1955.

Bols, Peter. "*This Culture of Ours*": *Intellectual Transitions in T'ang and Sung China*. Stanford, Stanford University Press, 1992.

Boltz, Judith. "*Daozang* and Subsidiary Compilations." In *The Encyclopedia of Taoism*, vol. 1., edited by Fabrizio Pregadio, 28–33. Abingdon, UK: 2008.

Boltz, William. "*Shuowen jiezi* 說文解字." In *Early Chinese Texts, A Bibliographical Guide*, edited by Michael Loewe, 429–442. Berkeley: University of California, 1993.

Borell, Brigitte, Bérénice Bellina, and Boonyarit Chaisuwan, "Contacts between the Upper Thai-Malay Peninsula and the Mediterranean World." In *Before Siam: Essays in Art and Archaeology*, edited by Nicolas Revire and Stephen Murphy, 98–117. Bangkok: River Books and The Siam Society, 2014.

————. "Isthmus von Kra: Im Schnittpunkt maritimer Routen [The Kra Isthmus: at the Intersection of Maritime Routes]." In *Im Schatten von Angkor: Archäologie und Geschichte Südostasiens* [*In the Shadow of Angkor: Southeast Asian Archaeology and History*], edited by Mai Lin Tjoa-Bonatz and Andreas Reinecke, 45–54. Darmstadt: Philipp von Zabern, 2015.

Bourdonneau, Éric. "Culturalisme et historiographie du Cambodge ancient: à propos de la hiérarchisation des sources de l'histoire khmère/Ranking Historical Sources and the Culturalist Approach in the Historiography of Ancient Cambodia." *Mousson—Recherche en sciences humaines sur l'Asie du Sud-Est*, 7 (2004): 1–26.

————. "Réhabiliter le Funan. Óc Eo ou la première Angkor [Rehabilitating Funan. Óc Eo or the First Angkor]." *Bulletin de l'École française d'Extrême Orient*, vol. 94 (2007): 111–158.

Braddell, Roland. "An Introduction to the Study of Ancient Times in the Malay Peninsula and the Straits of Malacca (continued)." *Journal of the Malayan Branch of the Royal Asiatic Society*, vol. 19 no. 1. (138) (February 1941): 21–74.

Bray, Francesca. *Science and Civilization in China, Volume VI, Biology and Biological Technology, Part II, Agriculture*. Edited by Joseph Needham. Cambridge: Cambridge University Press, 1984.

Briggs, Lawrence Palmer. *The Ancient Khmer Empire*. Bangkok: White Lotus Press, 1999 [1951].
Brindley, Erica Fox. *Ancient China and the Yue: Perceptions and Identities on the Southern Frontier, c.400 BCE–50 CE*. Cambridge and New York: Cambridge University Press, 2015.
Brook, Timothy, et al. "Interpolity relations and the tribute system of Ming China". In *Sacred Mandates: Asian International Relations since Chinggis Khan*, edited by Timothy Brook et al., 58–89. Chicago: University of Chicago Press, 2018.
Brook, Timothy. *Great State: China and the World*. London: Profile Books, 2019.
———. *The Troubled Empire: China in the Yuan and Ming Dynasties*. Cambridge and London: Harvard University Press, 2010.
Bunker, Emma and Douglas Latchford. *Khmer Bronzes: New Interpretations of the Past.* Chicago: Art Media Resources, 2011.
Buswell, Robert and Donald Lopez. *The Princeton Dictionary of Buddhism*. Princeton: Princeton University Press, 2014.
Campany, Robert. *To Live as Long as Heaven and Earth: A Translation and Study of Ge Hong's Traditions of Divine Transcendents*. Berkeley: University of California Press, 2002.
Carter, Alison, Piphal Heng, Miriam Stark, Rachna Chhay and Damian Evans. "Urbanism and Residential Patterning in Angkor." *Journal of Field Archaeology*, 43/6 (2018): 492–506.
Chaffee, John and Denis Twitchett, eds. *The Cambridge History of China Volume 5: Sung China, 960–1279 AD, Part 2*. Cambridge: Cambridge University Press, 2015.
Chaffee, John. "Song China and the multi-state and commercial world of East Asia." *Crossroads*, vol. 1–2 (September 2010): 34–54.
Chan, Elisabeth. *Tropical Plants of Indonesia*. Singapore: Periplus, 1998.
Chandler, David. "Michael Vickery, 1931–2017." *Journal of the Siam Society*, 106 (2018): 371–374.
———. "Royally Sponsored Human Sacrifices in Nineteenth Century Cambodia—the Cult of *nak tā* Me Sa (Mahisāsuramardini) at Ba Phnom." In *Brajum Rioeh Breh* [*Collected Old Stories*], vol. 8, comp. Institute Bouddhique. Phnom Penh: Institute Bouddhique, 1971: 208–222.
———. "The Legend of the Leper King (1978)." In David Chandler, *Facing the Cambodian Past: Selected Essays, 1971–1994*. Silkworm Books: Chiang Mai, 1996: 3–14.
———. *A History of Cambodia*, 4th edition. Boulder and Oxford: Westview Press, 2007.
———. *The Tragedy of Cambodian History: Politics, War and Revolution since 1945*. New Haven: Yale University Press, 1993.
Chang, Kang-I Sun and Stephen Owen, eds. *The Cambridge History of Chinese Literature*, vol. 1. Cambridge and New York: Cambridge University Press, 2010.
Chassende, Damien. "*Chen shu* 陳書." In *Early Medieval Chinese Texts*, edited by Cynthia Chennault et al., 44–47. Berkeley: University of California, 2015.
Chassende, Damien. "*Liang shu* 梁書." In *Early Medieval Chinese Texts*, edited by Cynthia Chennault et al., 167–170. Berkeley: University of California, 2015.
Chen Jiarong 陳佳榮, ed. *Nan ming wang* 南溟網 [*Southern Seas Network*]. www.world10k.com.
Chen Jiarong 陳佳榮, et al. "Song yu Zhenlifu, Dengliumei, Pugan deng guo zhi guanxi 宋與真里富、登流眉、蒲甘等國之關係 [Relations between the Song and the states of Zhenlifu, Dengliumei, Pugan, etc.]". In *Nan ming wang* 南溟網 [*Southern Seas Network*], ed. Chen Jiarong 陳佳榮. www.world10k.com.
———. "Gudai Nanhai diming huishi 古代南海地名匯釋 [Gazeteer of Southern Sea Placenames in Ancient Times]." In *Nan ming wang* 南溟網 [*Southern Seas Network*], edited by Chen Jiarong 陳佳榮. www.world10k.com.
Chen Jiarong 陳佳榮. "Kang Tai, Zhu Ying shoushi Funan zhi tanjiu 康泰, 朱應首使扶南之探究 [Research into Kang Tai's and Zhu Ying's embassy to Funan]." In Kang Tai 康泰 and Zhu Ying 朱應, *Waiguo zhuan* 外國傳 [*A Record of Foreign States*], edited by Chen Jiarong 陳佳榮 and Tan Guanglian 譚廣濂, 309–332. Hong Kong: Xianggang haiwai jiaotong shi xuehui, 2006.
———. *Suiqian Nanhai jiaotong shiliao yanjiu* 隋前南海交通史料研究 [*Research on Historical Materials on Communications in the Southern Sea before the Sui Dynasty*]. Hong Kong: University of Hong Kong, 2003.
Chen Jiarong 陳佳榮 and Tan Guanglian 譚廣濂, ed. "Funan ji 扶南記 [Record of Funan]." In Kang Tai 康泰 and Zhu Ying 朱應, *Waiguo zhuan* 外國傳 [*A Record of Foreign States*]], edited by Chen Jiarong 陳佳榮 and Tan Guanglian 譚廣濂, 3–18. Hong Kong: Xianggang haiwai jiaotong shi xuehui, 2006.

Chen Xiansi 陳顯泗, Xu Zhaolin 許肇琳, Zhao Heman 趙和曼, Zhan Fangyao 詹方瑤 and Zhang Wansheng 張萬生, eds. *Zhongguo gujizhongde Jianpuzhai shiliao* 中國古籍中的柬埔寨史料 [*Historical Materials on Cambodia in Old Chinese Books*]. Zhengzhou: Henan renmin chubanshe, 1985.

Chen Xiansi 陳顯泗. *Jianpuzhai erqiannian shi* 柬埔寨二千年史 [*A Two Thousand Year History of Cambodia*]. Nanjing: Zhongzhou guji chubanshe, 1990.

Chen Xujing 陳序經. "Funan shi chu tan 扶南史初探 [Initial Enquiry into the History of Funan]." In Chen Xujing 陳序經, *Dongnan ya gushi huiji* 東南亞古史會集 [*Collected Writings on the Ancient History of Southeast Asia*], 509–730. Shenzhen: Haitian chubanshe, 1992.

———. *Dongnan ya gushi huiji* 東南亞古史會集 [*Collected Writings on the Ancient History of Southeast Asia*]. Shenzhen: Haitian chubanshe, 1992.

Chen Zhengxiang 陳正祥. *Zhenla fengtu ji yanjiu* 真臘風土記研究 [*Research on* {*Zhou Daguan's*} Record of Zhenla: The Land and its People]. Hong Kong: Chinese University Press, 1975.

Chen, Jinhua. "*Pañcavārṣika* Assemblies in Liang Wudi's Buddhist Palace Chapel." *Harvard Journal of Asiatic Studies*, vol. 66 no. 1 (June 2006): 43–103.

Chennault, Cynthia, Keith Knapp, Alan Berkowitz and Albert Dien, eds. *Early Medieval Chinese Texts.* Berkeley: University of California, 2015.

Chevance, Jean-Baptiste, Damian Evans, Nina Hofer, Sakada Sakhoeun, and Ratha Chhean. "Mahendraparvata: an early Angkor-period capital defined through airborne laser scanning at Phnom Kulen." *Antiquity*, vol. 93 issue 371 (October 2019): 1303–1321.

Chin, James. "Ports, Merchants, Chieftains and Eunuchs: Reading Maritime Commerce of Early Guangdong." In *Guangdong: Archaeology and Early Texts* (*Zhou-Tang*), edited by Shing Müller et al., 217–240. Wiesbaden: Harrassowitz Verlag, 2004.

Chittick, Andrew. "*Song shu* 宋書." In *Early Medieval Chinese Texts*, edited by Cynthia Chennault et al., 320–323. Berkeley: University of California, 2015.

———. *Vernacular Languages in the Medieval Jiankang Empire.* Sino-Platonic Papers no. 250. Philadelphia: Department of East Asian Languages and Civilizations, University of Philadelphia, 2014.

Churchman, Catherine. "Where to Draw the Line? The Chinese Southern Frontier in the Fifth and Sixth Centuries." In *China's Encounters on the South and Southwest*, edited by James Anderson and John Whitmore, 59–77. Brill: Leiden, 2014.

———. *The People Between the Rivers: The Rise and Fall of a Bronze Drum Culture, 200–750* CE. New York and London: Rowman & Littlefield, 2016.

Churchman, Michael. "Before the Chinese and Vietnamese in the Red River Plain: The Han-Tang Period." *Chinese Southern Diaspora Studies*, vol. 4 (2010): 25–37.

Ci hai 辭海 [*Sea of Words*]. Shanghai: Shanghai cishu chubanshe, 1989.

Clark, Joyce, ed. *Bayon: New Perspectives.* Bangkok: River Books, 2006.

Coe, Michael, and Damian Evans. *Angkor and the Khmer Civilization.* London: Thames and Hudson, 2018.

Coedès, George. "La Fondation de Phnoṃ Péñ au XVe siecle d'après la chronique cambodgienne [The Foundation of Phnom Penh in the 15th century according to the Cambodian chronicle]." *Bulletin de l'École française d'Extrême-Orient*, 1913, 6, 6–11.

———. "La Tradition généalogique des premiers rois d'Angkor d'après les inscriptions de Yaçovarman et de Rājendravarman [The genealogical tradition of the first kings of Angkor according to the Inscriptions of Yaśovarman and Rājendravarman]." *Bulletin de l'École française d'Extrême-Orient*, vol. 28 no. 1 (1928): 124–144.

———. "Le Royaume de Çrīvijaya [The Kingdom of Srivijaya]." *Bulletin de l'École française d'Extrême-Orient*, vol. 18 (1918), 6: 1–36.

———. "Le Site Primitif du Tchen-la [The Original Site of Zhenla]." *Bulletin de l'École française d'Extrême-Orient*, vol. 18 (1918), 9: 1–3.

———. "Notes sur Tcheou Ta-Kuan [Notes on Zhou Daguan]." *Bulletin de l'École française d'Extrême-Orient*, vol. 18 (1918), 9: 4–9.

———. "Nouvelles Notes sur Tcheou Ta-kouan [New Notes on Zhou Daguan]." *T'oung Pao*, 2/30 (1933): 224–226.

———. "The Ancient Khmer Empire by Lawrence Palmer Briggs (review article)." *Diogenes*, vol. 1 issue 1 (January 1953): 115–118.

———. *Angkor: An Introduction.* Oxford: Oxford University Press, 1963.

Coedès, George. *Inscriptions du Cambodge* [*Inscriptions of Cambodia*] (8 volumes). Hanoi: Imprimerie d'Extrême-Orient, 1937–1966.

———. *The Indianized States of Southeast Asia*. Translated by S. Cowing. Honolulu: University of Hawai'i Press, 1968.

Cooke, Nola, Li Tana and James Anderson, eds. *The Tongking Gulf Through History*. Philadelphia: University of Pennsylvania Press, 2011.

Coomaraswamy, Ananda, *History of Indian and Indonesian Art*. New Delhi: Munshiram Manoharlal, 1972 [1927].

Cort, Louise Allison and Paul Jett, eds. *Gods of Angkor: Bronzes from the National Museum of Cambodia*. Washington DC and Seattle: Smithsonian Institution and University of Washington Press, 2010.

Crespigny, Rafe de. "Universal Histories." In *Essays on the Sources for Chinese History*, edited by Donald Leslie et al., 64–70. Canberra: Australian National University Press, 1973.

———. *A Biographical Dictionary of Later Han to the Three Kingdoms (23–220 AD)*. Leiden: Brill, 2007.

———. *The Men who Governed Han China*. Leiden: Brill, 2004.

Crowell, William. "*Nan Qi shu* 南齊書." In *Early Medieval Chinese Texts*, edited by Cynthia Chennault et al., 202–208. Berkeley: University of California, 2015.

Cunin, Olivier. "The Bayon: an archaeological and architectural study". In *Bayon: New perspectives*, edited by Joyce Clark, 136–229. Bangkok: River Books, 2007.

Cutter, Robert. "*San guo zhi* 三國志." In *Early Medieval Chinese Texts*, edited by Cynthia Chennault et al., 250–257. Berkeley: University of California, 2015.

Dagens, Bruno et al. *Archéologues à Angkor: Archives photographiques de l'École française d'Extrême-Orient* [*Archaeologists at Angkor: Photographic Archives of the École française d'Extrême-Orient*]. Paris: Paris musées, 2010.

Denecke, Wiebke, Wai-Yee Li and Xiaofei Tian, eds. *The Oxford Handbook of Classical Chinese Literature (1000 BCE–900 CE)*. Oxford and New York: Oxford University Press, 2017.

Dennis, Joseph R. *Writing, Publishing and Reading Local Gazetteers in Imperial China, 1100–1700*. Cambridge and London: Harvard University Asia Center, 2015.

Dien, Albert. *Six Dynasties Civilization*. New Haven and London: Yale University Press, 2007.

Dikötter, Frank. *The Discourse of Race in Modern China*. London: Hurst & Co, 1992.

Drège, Jean-Pierre. "À propos des sources chinoises concernant l'histoire du Cambodge [Regarding Chinese Sources on the History of Cambodia]." *Siksacakr Journal of Cambodia Research*, Centre for Khmer Studies, Siem Reap, number 11, 2009: 12–21.

Dreyer, Edward. *Zheng He: China and the Oceans in the Early Ming Dynasty, 1405–1433*. New York and London: Pearson Longman, 2007.

Dubs, Homer H, tr. *The History of the Former Han Dynasty by Pan Ku*. Baltimore: Waverley Press, 1938.

Dudbridge, Glen, "Reworking the World System Paradigm." *Past and Present*, 2018, Supplement 13: 297–316.

Dudbridge, Glen. "Libraries, Book Catalogues, Lost Writings." In *The Oxford Handbook of Classical Chinese Literature* (1000 BCE–900 CE), edited by Wiebke Denecke, Wai-Yee Li and Xiaofei Tian, 147–159. Oxford and New York: Oxford University Press, 2017.

Dudbridge, Glen. *Lost Books of Medieval China*. London: British Library, 1999.

Dung, Lâm Thị Mỹ. "Champa Settlements of the First Millennium: New Archaeological Research." In *Champa: Territories and Networks of a Southeast Asian Kingdom*, edited by Arlo Griffiths, Andrew Hardy and Geoff Wade, 23–46. Paris: École française d'Extrême Orient, 2019.

Dupont, Pierre. "La dislocation de Tchen-la et la formation du Cambodge angkorien (VIIe–IXe siècle [The Disruption of Zhenla and the Formation of Angkorian Cambodia (7th to 9th Centuries)]." *Bulletin de l'École française d'Extrême-Orient*, vol. 43 (1943): 17–55.

Durrant, Stephen. "Histories (史)." In *The Oxford Handbook of Classical Chinese Literature* (1000 BCE–900 CE), edited by Wiebke Denecke, Wai-Yee Li and Xiaofei Tian, 184–200. Oxford and New York: Oxford University Press, 2017.

Durrant, Stephen, Wai-yee Li and David Schaberg, tr. *Zuo Tradition—Zuozhuan 左傳: Commentary on the "Spring and Autumn Annals"* (3 volumes). Seattle and London: University of Washington Press, 2016.

Edwards, E.D. and C.O. Blagden. "A Chinese Vocabulary of Cham Words and Phrases." *Bulletin of the School of Oriental and African Studies*, vol. 10 no. 1 (1939): 53–91.

Elvin, Mark. *The Pattern of the Chinese Past*. London: Eyre Methuen, 1973.

————. *The Retreat of the Elephants: An Environmental History of China*. New Haven: Yale University Press, 2004.

Empson, William. *The Face of the Buddha*. Edited by Rupert Arrowsmith. Oxford: Oxford University Press, 2016

Evans, Damian, et al. "Uncovering archaeological landscapes at Angkor using lidar." *PNAS* (*Proceedings of the National Academy of Sciences of the USA*), 110 (31) (July 30, 2013): 12,595–12,600.

[Fan Chengda 范成大.] *Treatises of the Supervisor and the Guardian of the Cinnamon Sea*. Translated and edited by James Hargett. Seattle and London: University of Washington Press, 2010.

[Fan Chuo 樊綽.] *The Man shu* [*Book of the Southern Foreigners*]. Translated by G. H. Luce. Ithaca: Cornell University Southeast Asia Data Paper no. 44, 1961.

[Faxian 法顯.] *A Record of Buddhistic Kingdoms, Being an Account by the Chinese Monk Fa-Hien of His travels in India and Ceylon* (*A.D. 399–414*) *in Search of the Buddhist Books of Discipline*. Translated by James Legge. New York: Dover Publications, 1965 [1886].

Fairbank, John K., ed. *The Chinese World Order: Traditional China's Foreign Relations*. Cambridge: Harvard University Press, 1968.

Ferlus, Michel. "Origine des noms anciens du Cambodge: Fou-nan et Tchen-la. L'interprétation des transcriptions chinoises [Origin of the old Cambodian names Funan and Zhenla. Interpreting the Chinese transcriptions]." *Péninsule: Études Interdisciplinaires sur l'Asie du Sud-Est Péninsulaire*, 2012, 65 (2): 47–64.

Finot, Louis. "Notes d'Épigraphie, III: Stèle du Çaṃbhuvarman a Mỹ Sơn [Epigraphical Note III: Stele of Śaṃbhuvarman at Mỹ Sơn]". *Bulletin de l'École française d'Extrême Orient*, 1903 (3): 206–21.

————. "Notes d'Épigraphie, XI: Les inscriptions de Mỹ Sơn. [Epigraphical Note XI: the Inscriptions of Mỹ Sơn." *Bulletin de l'École française d'Extrême Orient*, 1904 (4), 897–977.

————. "Sur quelques traditions Indochinoises [On some Indochinese Traditions]." *Bulletin de la commission archéologique de l'Indochine*, 1911: 20–37.

————. "The Temple of Angkor Wat" [1929] in Zhou Daguan, *The Customs of Cambodia*, ed. and tr. Michael Smithies, 125–147. Bangkok: The Siam Society, 2001.

Fitzgerald, C. P. *The Southern Expansion of the Chinese People*. Bangkok: White Lotus, 1993 [1972].

Franke, Herbert and Denis Twitchett, "Introduction". In *The Cambridge History of China, vol. 6: Alien regimes and border states, 907–1368*, edited by Herbert Franke and Denis Twitchett, 1–42. Cambridge: Cambridge University Press, 1994.

Franke, Herbert and Denis Twitchett, eds. *The Cambridge History of China: Volume 6, Alien Regimes and Border States, 907–1368*. Cambridge: Cambridge University Press, 1994.

Franke, Herbert. "A Sung Embassy Diary of 1211–1212: the 'Shih-chin lu' of Ch'eng Cho." *Bulletin de l'École française d'Extrême-Orient*, vol. 69 (1981): 171–207.

Freeman, Michael and Claude Jacques. *Ancient Angkor*. Bangkok: River Books, 2003.

Freeman, Michael. *A Guide to Khmer Temples in Thailand and Laos*. New York and Tokyo: Weatherhill, 1998.

Gardiner, K.H.J. "Standard Histories, Han to Sui." In *Essays on the Sources for Chinese History*, edited by Donald Leslie et al., 42–52. Canberra: Australian National University Press, 1973.

Garnier, Francois. *Voyage d'Exploration en Indo-chine effectué par une Commission Française présidée par le capitaine de frégate Doudart de Lagrée* [*Voyage of Exploration in Indochina carried out by a French Commission led by the Frigate Captain Doudart de Lagrée*]. Paris: Hachette and Co., 1885.

Gaudes, Rüdiger. "Kauṇḍinya, Prey Thaong, and the 'Nagi Somā': Some Aspects of a Cambodian Legend." *Asian Folklore Studies*, Vol. 52 No. 2 (1993): 333–358.

Ge Zhaoguang, *Here in 'China' I Dwell: Recontructing Historical Discourses of China for our Time*. Translated by Jesse Field and Qin Fang. Leiden: Brill, 2017.

Ge Zhaoguang 葛兆光, *Zhai zi Zhongguo: Chongjian youguan "Zhongguo" de lishilunshu* 宅兹中國：重建有関"中國"的歷史論述 [*This China We Reside In: Reconstructing Historical Discourses Relating to "China"*]. Beijing: Zhonghua shuju, 2011.

Gernet, Jacques. *A History of Chinese Civilization*. Cambridge: Cambridge University Press, 1996.

Gibb, H. A. R., ed. and tr. *Ibn Battuta: Travels in Asia and Africa, 1325–1354*. Delhi: LPP, 1999.

Glaize, Maurice. *Les Monuments du Groupe d'Angkor* [*The Monuments of the Angkor Group*]. Paris: J. Maisonneuve, 2003.

Glahn, Richard von. *The Economic History of China from Antiquity to the Nineteenth Century*. Cambridge: Cambridge University Press, 2016.

Glover, Ian and Peter Bellwood, eds. *Southeast Asia: From Prehistory to History*. Oxford and New York: Routledge Curzon 2004.

Glover, Ian. "Contacts between India and Southeast Asia". In *Tradition and Archaeology: Early Maritime Contacts in the Indian Ocean*, edited by Himanshu Prabha Ray and Jean-François Salles, 129–158. Delhi: Manohar, 2012 [1996].

Goble, Geoffrey. *Maritime Southeast Asia: The View from Tang-Song China*. Nalanda-Sriwijaya Centre Working Paper no. 16. Singapore: ISEAS, 2014.

Goodman, Howard. "Jin shu 晉書." In *Early Medieval Chinese Texts: A Bibliographical Guide*, edited by Cynthia Chennault et al., 136–145. Berkeley: Institute of East Asian Studies, University of California, 1995.

Goscha, Christopher. *Vietnam: A New History*. New York: Basic Books, 2016.

Graff, David. "*Bei shi* 北史." In *Early Medieval Chinese Texts*, edited by Cynthia Chennault, et al., 18–23. Berkeley: University of California, 2015.

Green, Gillian. "Angkor Vogue: Sculpted Evidence of Imported Luxury Textiles in the Courts of Kings and Temples." *Journal of the Economic and Social History of the Orient*, vol. 50, no. 4 (2007): 424–451.

————. "Indic Impetus? Innovations in Textile Usage in Angkorian Period Cambodia." *Journal of the Economic and Social History of the Orient*, vol. 43, no. 3 (2000): 277–313.

Griffiths, Arlo, Andrew Hardy and Geoff Wade, ed. *Champa: Territories and Networks of a Southeast Asian Kingdom*. Paris: École française d'Extrême Orient, 2019.

Groslier, Bernard and Jacques Arthaud. *Angkor, Art and Civilization*. London: Thames and Hudson, 1957.

Groslier, Bernard. "Pour une Géographie historique du Cambodge [For a Historical Geography of Cambodia]." *Les Cahiers d'Outre-Mer*, Presses Universitaires de Bordeaux, no. 104, Oct–Dec 1973: 337–379.

————. *Indochina*. London: Barrie and Jenkins, 1970.

————. *The Art of Indochina: including Thailand, Vietnam, Laos and Cambodia*. New York: Crown Publishers, 1962.

Guy, John, ed. *Lost Kingdoms: Hindu-Buddhist Sculpture of Early Southeast Asia*. New York: Metropolitan Museum of Art, 2014.

Haendel, Alexandra, ed. *Old Myths and New Approaches: Interpreting Ancient Religious Sites in Southeast Asia*. Melbourne: Monash University Publishing, 2012.

Hall, Kenneth. "An Introductory Essay on Southeast Asian Statecraft in the Classical Period." In *Explorations in Early Southeast Asian History: The Origins of Southeast Asian Statecraft*, edited by Kenneth Hall and John Whitmore, 1–24. Ann Arbor: Michigan Papers on South and Southeast Asia, 1976.

————. "Champa Ports and Trade Networking on the Coastline c.300–1599 CE." In *Vibrancy in Stone: Masterpieces of the Đà Nẵng Museum of Cham Sculture*, edited by Trần Kỳ Phương, Võ Văn Thắng and Peter D. Sharrock, 19–30. Bangkok: River Books, 2018.

————. "Economic History of Early Southeast Asia." In *The Cambridge History of Southeast Asia, Volume One: From early times to c.1500*, edited by Nicholas Tarling, 183–275. Cambridge: Cambridge University Press, 1999.

————. *A History of Early Southeast Asia: Maritime Trade and Societal Development, 100–1500*. Lanham Maryland: Rowman and Littlefield, 2011.

————. *Maritime Trade and State Development in Early Southeast Asia*. Honolulu: University of Hawai'i Press, 1985.

Hardy, Andrew, Mauro Cucarzi and Patrizia Zolese, eds. *Champa and the Archaeology of Mỹ Sơn (Vietnam)*. Singapore: NUS Press, 2009.

Hardy, Andrew and Nguyễn Tiến Đông, "The Peoples of Champa: Evidence for a New Hypothesis from the Landscape History of Quảng Ngãi". In *Champa: Territories and Networks of a Southeast Asian Kingdom*, edited by Arlo Griffiths, Andrew Hardy and Geoff Wade, 121–143. Paris: École française d'Extrême Orient, 2019.

Harris, Peter, ed. and trans. *Sun Tzu, The Art of War*. London and New York, Everyman's Library, 2018.

Haw, Stephen. "The Maritime Routes Between China and the Indian Ocean During the Second to Ninth Centuries C.E." *Journal of the Royal Asiatic Society*, vol. 27 no. 1: 53–81.

Heng, Derek. "Pre-Modern Island Southeast-Asian History in the Digital Age: Opportunities and Challenges through Chinese Textual Database Research." *Bijdragen Tot den de Taal-, Land-en Volkenkunde*, 172 (2019): 29–57.

————. "Shipping, Customs Procedures and the Foreign Community: the 'Pingzhou ketan' on Aspects of Guangzhou's Maritime Economy in the Late Eleventh Century." *Journal of Song-Yuan Studies*, 38 (2008): 1–38.

————. "State formation and the evolution of naval strategies in the Melaka Straits, c. 500–1500 CE." *Journal of Southeast Asian Studies*, vol. 44 no. 3 (October 2013): 380–399.

————. "Trans-Regionalism and Economic Co-Dependency in the South China Sea: the Case of China and the Malay Region (tenth to fourteenth century AD)." *The International History Review*, vol. 35 no. 3 (2013): 486–510.

————. *Sino-Malay Trade and Diplomacy from the Tenth through the Fourteenth Century*. Athens: Ohio University Press, 2009.

Heng, Piphal. "Transition to the Pre-Angkorian Period (300–500 CE): Thala Borivat and a regional perspective." *Journal of Southeast Asian Studies*, 47(3) (October 2016): 484–505.

Higham, Charles. "The Long and Winding Road that Leads to Angkor." *Cambridge Archaeological Journal*, 22: 2 (2012): 265–289.

————. *The Civilization of Angkor*. Berkeley and Los Angeles: University of California Press, 2001.

————. *The Origins of the Civilization of Angkor*. London and New York: Bloomsbury, 2013.

Hirth, Friedrich. *China and the Roman Orient: Researches into their Ancient and Medieval Relations as Represented in Old Chinese Records*. Leipzig and Munich: Georg Hirth, 1885.

Hodos, Tamar, ed. *The Routledge Handbook of Archaeology and Globalization*. London and New York: Routledge, 2017.

Holm, David. *'Crossing the Seas': Indic Ritual Templates and the Shamanic Substratum in Eastern Asia*. Sino-Platonic Papers no. 281. Philadelphia: Department of East Asian Languages and Civilizations, University of Pennsylvania, 2018.

Holmgren, Jennifer. *Chinese Colonisation of Northern Vietnam: Administrative Geography and Political Development in the Tongking Delta, First to Sixth Centuries A.D.* Canberra: Australian National University Faculty of Asian Studies, 1980.

Homer. *The Odyssey.* Translated by Robert Fitzgerald. London and New York: Everyman's Library, 1991.

Hong Quan. "Archaeological Discoveries Relating to the Maritime Trade of the Kingdom of Nanyue." In *The Search for Immortality: Tomb Treasures in Han China*, edited by James C.S. Lin, 37–42. Cambridge, New Haven and London: Yale University Press, 2012.

Hoshino, Tatsuo. "The Kingdom of Red Earth (Chitu Guo) in Cambodia and Vietnam from the Sixth to the Eighth Centuries." *Journal of the Siam Society*, vol. 84 part 2, 1996: 55–74.

————. "Wen Dan and its Neighbours: the Central Mekong Valley in the Seventh and Eighth Centuries." In *Breaking New Ground in Lao History: Essays on the Seventh to Twentieth Centuries*, edited by M. Ngaosrivathana and K. Breazeale, 25–72. Chiang Mai: Silkworm Press, 2002.

Hou Liqiang and Li Yingqing, "Yunnan Firm Eyes Cambodian Park" in *China Daily*, 11 March 2017.

Hsu Yun-ts'iao [Hsu Yun-ch'iao, Xu Yunqiao]. "A Study on Ch'ih-t'u or the Red Land." *Nanyang xuebao*, vol. II, no. 3, 1946: 1–14.

————. "Notes on Tan-tan." In *Southeast Asia-China Interactions*, edited by Geoff Wade, 38–50. Singapore: NUS Press, 2007.

Hucker, Charles. *A Dictionary of Official Titles in Imperial China*. Stanford: Stanford University Press, 1985.

Hudson, G.F. *Europe and China*. London: Edward Arnold, 1931.

Hui, Victoria Tin-bor. *War and State Formation in Ancient China and early Modern Europe*. New York: Cambridge University Press, 2005.

Huesemann, J. Henning. "*Shui jing zhu* 水經注". In *Early Medieval Chinese Texts*, edited by Cynthia Chennault et al., 311–317. Berkeley: University of California, 2015. Chennault, *Early Chinese Medieval Texts*, 311–314

Hung, Hsiao-chun. "Cultural Interactions in Mainland and Island Southeast Asia and Beyond, 2000 BC–AD 200." In *Handbook of East and Southeast Asian Archaeology*, edited by Junko Habu et al., 633–665. Berlin: Springer, 2017.

I-Tsing [Yijing, 義淨]. *A Record of the Buddhist Religion as Practised in India and the Malay Archipelago A.D. 671–695*. Translated and edited by J. Takakusu. Oxford: Clarendon Press, 1896.

Idema, Wilt and Lloyd Haft. *A Guide to Chinese Literature*. Ann Arbor: University of Michigan, 1997.

Indrawooth, Phasook. "The Archaeology of the Early Buddhist Kingdoms of Thailand." In *Southeast Asia: from Prehistory to History*, edited by Ian Glover and Peter Bellwood, 120–136. London and New York: Routledge Curzon, 2004.

Ishizawa, Yoshiaki. "Chinese Chronicles of the 1st–5th Century A.D. Funan, Southern Cambodia." In *South East Asia and China: Art, Interaction and Commerce*, edited by Rosemary Scott and John Guy, 11–31. London: School of Oriental and African Studies, 1995.

Jacob, Judith. "The Ecology of Angkor: Evidence from the Khmer Inscriptions." In *Cambodian Linguistics, Literature and History*, edited by D.A. Smyth, 280–298. London: School of Oriental and African Studies, 1993.

Jacobsen, Trudy. *Lost Goddesses: The Denial of Female Power in Cambodian History*. Copenhagen: NIAS Press, 2008.

Jacq-Hergoualc'h, Michel. *The Malay Peninsula: Crossroads of the Maritime Silk-Road (100 BC–1300 AD)*. Leiden: Brill, 2002.

Jacques, Claude and Michael Freeman. *Angkor Cities and Temples*. Bangkok: River Books, 2006.

Jacques, Claude and Philippe Lafond. *The Khmer Empire: Cities and Sanctuaries from the 5th to the 13th Century*. Bangkok: River Books, 2007.

Jacques, Claude, with René Dumont. *Angkor*. Cologne: Könemann, 1999.

Jacques, Claude. "'Funan', 'Zhenla': The Reality Concealed by these Chinese Views of Indochina." In *Early South East Asia: Essays in Archaeology, History, and Historical Geography*, edited by R.B. Smith and W. Watson, 371–379. New York: Oxford University Press, 1979.

————. "China and Ancient Khmer History." In *South East Asia & China: Art, Interaction and Commerce*, edited by Rosemary Scott and John Guy, 32–40. London: School of Oriental and African Studies, 1995.

————. "Le pays Khmer avant Angkor [The Country of the Khmers before Angkor]." *Journal des savants* (1986): 59–95.

Jenner, W.F.J., tr. *Memories of Loyang: Yang Hsüan-chih and the lost capital (493–534)*. Oxford: Clarendon Press, 1981.

Jessup, Helen Ibbitson. *Masterpieces of the National Museum of Cambodia: An Introduction to the Collection*. Norfolk, USA: Friends of Khmer Culture Inc., 2006.

————. *Art and Architecture of Cambodia*. London: Thames and Hudson, 2004.

Johnson, Ian. "A Revolutionary Discovery in China." *The New York Review of Books*, Vol. LXIII No. 7 (April 21–May 11, 2016): 53–56.

Kalia, Ravi. *Bhubaneswar: From a Temple Town to a Capital City*. Carbondale and Edwardsville: Southern Illinois University Press, 1994.

Kang, David. *East Asia Before the West: Five Centuries of Trade and Tribute*. New York: Columbia University Press, 2010.

Karlgren, Bernard. *Grammata Serica Recensa [A New Study of Chinese Characters]*. Stockholm: Museum of Far Eastern Antiquities, 1964.

Kathirithamby-Wells, J. and John Villiers, eds. *The Southeast Asian Port and Polity*. Singapore: Singapore University Press, 1990.

Khai, Vo Si. "The Kingdom of Fu Nan and the Culture of Oc Eo." In *Art and Archaeology of Fu Nan, Pre-Khmer Kingdom of the Lower Mekong Valley*, edited by James C.M. Khoo, 35–86. Bangkok: Orchid Press, 2003.

Khoo, James C.M., ed. *Art and Archaeology of Fu Nan, Pre-Khmer Kingdom of the Lower Mekong Valley.* Bangkok: Orchid Press, 2003.

Knechtges, David. "From the Eastern Han through the Western Jin (AD 25–317)." In *The Cambridge History of Chinese Literature*, Vol. 1: to 1375, edited by Kang-I Sun Chang and Stephen Owen, 116–198. Cambridge: Cambridge University Press, 2010.

Krishnan, Gauri Parimoo, ed. *Nalanda, Srivijaya and Beyond: Re-exploring Buddhist Art in Asia.* Singapore: Asian Civilizations Museum, 2016.

Kuhn, Dieter. *The Age of Confucian Rule: The Song Transformation of China.* Cambridge and London: Harvard University Press, 2009.

Kurtz, Johannes. "*Taiping yulan* 太平御覽." In *Early Medieval Chinese Texts*, edited by Cynthia Chennault et al., 342–346. Berkeley: University of California, 2015.

Lavy, Paul. "As in Heaven, so on Earth: The Politics of Viṣṇu, Śiva and Harihara Images in Preangkorian Khmer Civilization." *Journal of Southeast Asian Studies*, vol. 34 no. 1 (Feb 2003): 21–39.

[Lê Tắc.] *Ngann-nann-tche-luo* [*An Nam chí lược*] 安南志略: *Mémoires sur l'Annam* [*Memoirs of Annam*]. Translated by Camille Sainson. Beijing: Imprimerie des Lazaristes au Pé-t'ang, 1896.

Lee, Thomas, ed. *The New and the Multiple: Sung Senses of the Past.* Hong Kong: Chinese University Press: 2004.

Leslie, Donald, Colin Mackerras and Wang Gungwu, eds. *Essays on the Sources for Chinese History.* Canberra: Australian National University Press, 1973.

Leur, J.C. van. "On Early Asian Trade". In J.C. van Leur, *Indonesian Trade and Society: Essays in Asian social and economic history*. The Hague: W. van Heuve, 1967.

Lewis, Mark Edward. "Warring States: Political History." In *The Cambridge History of Ancient China*, edited by Michael Loewe and Edward Shaughnessy: 587–650. Cambridge: Cambridge University Press, 1999.

————. *China Between Empires: The Northern and Southern Dynasties.* Cambridge and London: Harvard University Press, 2009.

————. *China's Cosmopolitan Empire: The Tang Dynasty.* Cambridge and London: Harvard University Press, 2009.

————. *The Early Chinese Empires: Qin and Han.* Cambridge and London: Harvard University Press, 2007.

Leys, Simon. "The Chinese Attitude towards the Past". In Simon Leys, *The Hall of Uselessness: Collected Essays.* New York: New York Review Books, 2013 [1986].

Li Feng. *Early China: A Social and Cultural History.* Cambridge: Cambridge University Press, 2013.

Li Tana. "A View from the Sea: Perspectives on the Northern and Central Vietnamese Coast." *Journal of Southeast Asian Studies*, vol. 37 no. 1 (Feb. 2006): 83–102.

————. "Jiaozhi (Giao Chi) in the Han Period Tongking Gulf". In *The Tongking Gulf Through History*, edited by Nola Cooke, Li Tana and James Anderson, 39–52. Philadelphia: University of Pennsylvania Press, 2011.

————. "The Tongking Gulf Through History: A Geopolitical Overview". In *The Tongking Gulf Through History*, edited by Nola Cooke, Li Tana and James Anderson: 1–21. Philadelphia: University of Pennsylvania Press, 2011.

————. *The Changing Landscape of the Former Linyi in the Provinces of Quảng Trị and Thừa Thiên-Huế.* Nalanda-Sriwijaya Centre Working Paper no. 30. Singapore: ISEAS, 2019.

Lieberman, Victor. *Strange Parallels—Southeast Asia in Global Context, c.800–1830, volume 1: Integration on the Mainland.* Cambridge: Cambridge University Press, 2003.

Lin, James C.S., ed. *The Search for Immortality: Tomb Treasures in Han China.* Cambridge, New Haven and London: Yale University Press, 2012.

Liu, Shufen. "Jiankang and the Commercial Empire of the Southern Dynasties: Change and Continuity in Medieval Chinese Economic History". In *Culture and Power in the Reconstitution of the Chinese Realm, 200–600*, edited by Scott Pearce, Audrey Spiro and Patricia Ebrey, 35–52. Cambridge: Harvard University Asia Centre, 2001.

Liu, Xinru. *Ancient India and Ancient China: Trade and Religious Exchanges AD 1–600.* Oxford and Delhi: Oxford University Press, 1988.

Lo Jung-pang. *China as a Sea Power 1127–1368*. Edited by Bruce Elleman. Singapore: National University of Singapore Press, 2012 [1957].

Loewe, Michael, ed. *Early Chinese Texts, A Bibliographical Guide*. Berkeley: University of California, 1993.

Loewe, Michael. "Guangzhou: the Evidence of the Standard Histories from the *Shi ji* to the *Chen shu*, a Preliminary Survey". In *Guangdong: Archaeology and Early Texts (Zhou-Tang)*, edited by Shing Müller et al., 51–80. Wiesbaden: Harrassowitz Verlag, 2004.

————. "Knowledge of Other Cultures in China's Early Empires." In *Perceptions of the World: Geography and Ethnography in Pre-Modern Societies*, edited by Kurt Raaflaub and Richard Talbert, 74–88. New Jersey: Wiley-Blackwell, 2010.

Lu Junling 陸峻嶺 and Zhou Shaoquan 周紹泉, eds. *Zhongguo gujizhong youguan Jianpuzhai ziliao huibian* 中國古籍中有関柬埔寨資料匯編 [*Collection of Materials on Cambodia in Old Chinese Books*]. Beijing: Zhonghua shuju, 1986.

Luo Zhufeng 羅竹風 et al., eds. *Hanyu da cidian* 漢語大詞典 [*A Large Dictionary of Chinese*], CD ROM edition. Hong Kong: Commercial Press, 2002.

Ma Duanlin 馬端臨. *Ethnographie des peuples étrangers à la Chine* [*Ethnography of Foreign Peoples as seen in China*]. Translated by Marie-Jean-Léon Lecoq, le Marquis d'Hervey de Saint-Denys. London and Geneva: H. Georg and Trübner & Co, 1883.

Ma Huan 馬歡. *Ying-yai Sheng-lan, 'The Overall Survey of the Ocean's Shores' [1433]*. Translated by J.V.G. Mills. Bangkok: White Lotus, [1970] 1997.

Mabbett, I. W. "The 'Indianization' of Southeast Asia: Reflections on the Historical Sources." *Journal of Southeast Asian Studies*, vol. 8, no. 2 (Sept. 1977): 143–161.

Malleret, Louis. *L'archéologie du delta du Mékong: 3. La culture du Founan* [*The Archaeology of the Mekong Delta: 3. The Culture of Funan*] (2 vols). Paris: École française d'Extrême-Orient, 1962.

Malory, Thomas. *Le Morte Darthur* [*The Death of Arthur*], edited by R.M. Lumiansky. London: London MacMillan, 1982.

Manguin, Pierre-Yves, A. Mani and Geoff Wade, eds. *Early Interactions between South and Southeast Asia: Reflections on Cross-Cultural Exchange*. Singapore: ISEAS, 2011.

————. "Pan-Regional Responses to Southeast Asian Inputs in Early Southeast Asia." In *50 Years of Archaeology in Southeast Asia: Essays in Honour of Ian Glover*, edited by Bérénice Bellina et al., 171–181. Bangkok: River Books, 2010.

————. "The Archaeology of Fu Nan in the Mekong River Delta: The Oc Eo Culture of Vietnam." In *Arts of Ancient Viet Nam: From River Plain to Open Sea*, edited by Nancy Tingley, 101–108. New Haven and London: Yale University Press, 2010.

————. "The amorphous nature of coastal polities in Insular Southeast Asia: Restricted centres, extended peripheries." *Moussons*, 5 (2002): 73–99.

Marglin, Frédérique, *Wives of the God-King: The Rituals of the Devadasis of Puri*. Delhi and Oxford: Oxford University Press, 1985.

Marr, David and Anthony Milner, eds. *Southeast Asia in the 9th to 14th Centuries*. Canberra: Australian National University and Singapore: ISEAS, 1986.

Maspero, Georges. *The Champa Kingdom: The History of an Extinct Vietnamese Culture*. Bangkok: White Lotus, 2002 [1928].

————. "Le Royaume de Champa: Chapitre III. Le Linyi (Suite) [The Kingdom of Champa: Chapter III. Linyi (Continued)]", *T'oung Pao*, 2nd series, vol. 11 no. 4: 489–526.

————. "Le Royaume de Champa: Chapitre VII (Suite) [The Kingdom of Champa: Chapter VII (Continued)]". *T'oung Pao*, 2nd series, vol. 12 no. 3 (1911): 291–315.

Maspero, Henri. "Études d'Histoire d'Annam [Studies in the History of Annam]." *Bulletin de l'École française d'Extrême-Orient* (1918), 3: 1–36.

————. "La Frontière de l'Annam et du Cambodge du VIIe au XIVe Siècle [The Frontier between Annam and Cambodia from the Seventh to the Fourteenth Century]." *Bulletin de l'École française d'Extrême-Orient*, vol. 18 no. 3 (1918): 29–36.

McGregor, R. S. *The Oxford Hindi-English Dictionary*. Delhi: Oxford University Press, 1993.

Mehta, V.R. *Foundations of Indian Political Thought—an Interpretation (From Manu to the Present Day)*. New Delhi: Manohar, 1992.

Miksic, John. "Review of Michael Aung-Thwyn and Maitrii Aung-Thwyn, 'A History of Myanmar Since Ancient Times.'" *Asian Perspectives*, vol. 53 no. 2 (2015): 226–228.

————. *The Buddhist-Hindu Divide in Premodern Southeast Asia*. Nalanda-Sriwijaya Centre Working Paper no. 1. Singapore: ISEAS, 2010.

Monier-Williams, Monier. *English-Sanskrit Dictionary*. Delhi: Munshiram Manoharlal, 1995 [1851].

Moore, Elizabeth. "Place and Space in Early Burma: A New Look at 'Pyu' Culture." *Journal of the Siam Society*, vol. 97 (2008): 1–27.

Mote, F.W. *Imperial China, 900–1800*. Cambridge: Harvard University Press, 1999.

Mouhot, Henri. *Travels in Siam, Cambodia, Laos, and Annam*. Bangkok: White Lotus, 2000 [1862].

Müller, Shing, et al., eds. *Guangdong: Archaeology and Early Texts (Zhou-Tang)*. Wiesbaden: Harrassowitz Verlag, 2004.

Murphy, Stephen and H. Leedom Lefferts. "Globalizing Indian religions and Southeast Asian localisms: Incentives for the adoption of Buddhism and Brahmanism in first millennium CE Southeast Asia." In *The Routledge Handbook of Archaeology and Globalization*, edited by Tamar Hodos, 768–788. London and New York: Routledge, 2017.

Murphy, Stephen. "Ports of call in ninth-century Southeast Asia: The route of the Tang Shipwreck." In *The Tang Shipwreck: Art and exchange in the 9th century*, edited by Alan Chong and Stephen Murphy, 238–249. Singapore: Asian Civilizations Museum, 2017.

————. "The case for proto-Dvaravati: a review of the art historical and archaeological evidence." *Journal of Southeast Asian Studies*, vol. 47, no. 3 (Oct. 2016): 366–392.

Mus, Paul "Les Balistes du Bàyon [The Ballistae of Bayon]." *Bulletin de l'École française d'Extrême-Orient*, vol. 29 (129): 331–341.

Needham, Joseph and Wang Ling. *Science and Civilization in China, Vol. IV Physics and Physical Technology, Part I: Physics*. Cambridge: Cambridge University Press, 1962.

Needham, Joseph. *Science and Civilization in China, Volume III: Mathematics and the Sciences of the Heavens and the Earth*. Cambridge: Cambridge University Press, 1959.

————. *Science and Civilization in China, Vol. IV: Physics and Physical Technology, Part III: Civil Engineering and Nautics*. Cambridge: Cambridge University Press, 1971.

————. *Science and Civilisation in China, Vol. V: Chemistry and Chemical Technology, Part IV, Spagyrical Discovery and Invention—Physiological Alchemy*. Cambridge: Cambridge University Press, 1983.

Ng, On-cho and Q. Edward Wang. *Mirroring the Past: the Writing and Use of History in Imperial China*. Honolulu: University of Hawai'I Press, 2005.

Nienhauser, William, Jr, ed. *The Indiana Companion to Traditional Chinese Literature, Vol. 1*. Bloomington and Indianapolis: Indiana University Press 1986.

Ninh, Lương. "Óc Eo—Cảng thị quốc tế của Vương quốc Phù Nam [Óc Eo—International port city of the state of Funan]." *Khảo cổ học/Vietnam Archaeology*, 3-2011: 39–44.

O'Reilly, Dougald, *Early Civilizations of Southeast Asia*. Plymouth: AltaMyra Press, 2007.

Olivelle, Patrick. *King, Governance and Law in Ancient India: Kauṭilya's* Arthaśāstra. Oxford: Oxford University Press, 2013.

Owen, Stephen. "The Cultural Tang (650–1020)." In *The Cambridge History of Chinese Literature, Volume I: To 1375*, edited by Kang-I Sun Chang and Stephen Owen, 286–372. Cambridge and New York: Cambridge University Press, 2010.

Paine, Lincoln. *The Sea and Civilization: A Maritime History of the World*. London: Atlantic Books, 2013.

Papelitzky, Elke. "Gui-an as a Centre for Writing about the World during the Late Ming Dynasty". *Monumenta Serica*, vol. 68, no. 1, 2020: 107–135.

Pelliot, Paul. "Deux itinéraires de Chine en Inde à la fin du VIIIe siècle [Two Itineraries from China to India at the end of the 8th Century]." Bulletin de *l'École française d'Extrême-Orient*, vol. 4, 1904: 131–413.

————. "Friedrich Hirth et W.W. Rockhill, 'Chau Ju-kua: His Work on the Chinese and Arab Trade in the Twelfth and Thirteenth Centuries, Entitled Chu-fan-chi', traduit et annoté [translated and annotated]" (book review). *T'oung Pao*, Second Series, vol. 13, no. 3 (1912): 446–481.

————. "Le Fou-nan [Funan]." *Bulletin de l'École française d'Extrême Orient*, vol. 3, 1903: 248–303.

————. "Mémoire sur les coutumes du Cambodge [Memoir on the Customs of Cambodia]." *Bulletin de l'École française d'Extrême-Orient*, vol. 2, 1902: 123–177.

Pelliot, Paul. "Quelques Textes Chinois concernant L'Indochine Hindouisée [Some Chinese Texts Concerning Hinduized Indochina]". In *Etudes asiatiques, publiées à l'occasion du 25e anniversaire de l'École française d'Extrême-Orient* [*Asian Studies, published on the Occasion of the 25th Anniversary of l'École française d'Extrême-Orient*]. Hanoi and Haiphong: Imprimerie d'Extreme Orient [1925].

————. *Mémoires sur les Coutumes du Cambodge de Tcheou Ta-kouan* [*Zhou Daguan's Memoirs on the Customs of Cambodia*]. Paris: Adrien Maisonneuve, 1997.

————. *Notes on Marco Polo* (3 volumes). Paris: Librairie Adrien-Maisonneuve, 1959.

Phương, Trần Kỳ and Bruce Lockhart, eds. *The Cham of Vietnam: History, Society and Art*. Singapore: NUS Press, 2011.

Phương, Trần Kỳ, Võ Văn Thắng and Peter D. Sharrock, eds. *Vibrancy in Stone: Masterpieces of the Đà Nẵng Museum of Cham Sculture*. Bangkok: River Books, 2018.

Pollock, Sheldon. *The Language of the Gods in the World of Man: Sanskrit, Culture and Power In Pre-Modern India*. Berkeley: University of California Press, 2006.

Polo, Marco. *The Travels of Marco Polo*. Edited by Peter Harris. London and New York: Everyman's Library, 2008.

————. *The Travels of Marco Polo: the Complete Yule-Cordier Edition*. Edited by Henry Yule. New York: Dover Publications, 1993 [1920].

Porée-Maspero, Éveline. "Nouvelle Étude sur la Nāgī Somā [A New Study of the Nāgī Somā]." *Journal Asiatique* 238 (1950): 237–267.

————. *Étude sur les rites agraires des cambodgiens* [*Study of the Agrarian Rites of the Cambodians*] (3 volumes). Paris: Mouton, 1962–69.

Pregadio, Fabrizio, ed. *The Encyclopedia of Taoism*. London: Routledge, 2008.

Pregadio, Fabrizio. *Great Clarity: Daoism and Alchemy in Early Medieval China*. Stanford: Stanford University Press, 2005.

Ptak, Roderich. *Die Maritime Seidenstrasse. Küstenräume, Seefahrt und Handel in vorkolonialer Zeit* [*The Maritime Silk Road. Its Coastal Areas, Seafaring and Trade in Pre-Colonial Times*]. Munich: C. H. Beck, 2007.

Pulleyblank, Edwin. *Lexicon of Reconstructed Pronunciation in Early Middle Chinese, Late Middle Chinese, and Early Mandarin*. Vancouver: UBC Press, 1991.

Rachewiltz, Igor de and May Wang, *Repertory of Proper Names in Yüan Literary Sources*. Taipei: Southern Materials Center, 1988.

Rawson, Philip. *The Art of Southeast Asia*. London: Thames and Hudson, 1967.

Ray, Himanshu Prabha and Jean-François Salles, eds. *Tradition and Archaeology: Early Maritime Contacts in the Indian Ocean*. New Delhi: Manohar, 1996.

Ray, Himanshu Prabha. *The Archaeology of Seafaring in Ancient South Asia*. New York: Cambridge University Press, 2003.

Reid, Anthony and David Marr, eds. *Perceptions of the Past in Southeast Asia*. Sidney: Heinemann, 1979.

Reid, Anthony, ed. *Sojourners and Settlers: Histories of Southeast Asia and the Chinese*. Honolulu: University of Hawai'i Press, 1996.

Reid, Anthony. "Approaching 'Asia' from the Southeast: Does the Crisis Make a Difference?" (inaugural lecture). Wellington: Asian Studies Institute, Victoria University, 1997.

————. *A History of Southeast Asia: Critical Crossroads*. Oxford: Wiley Blackwell, 2015.

————. *Charting the Shape of Early Modern Southeast Asia*. Chiang Mai: Silkworm Books, 1999.

Reinecke, Andreas, Vin Laychour and Seng Sonetra. *The First Golden Age of Cambodia: Excavation at Prohear*. Bonn: Thomas Müntzer, 2009.

Ren Jiyu, 任繼愈, ed. *Fojiao da cidian 佛教大詞典* [*A Large Buddhist Dictionary*]. Nanjing: Jiangsu chubanshe, 2002.

Revire, Nicolas and Stephen Murphy, ed. *Before Siam: Essays in Art and Archaeology*. Bangkok: River Books and The Siam Society, 2014.

Reynolds, Frank. "Three Ramayana, Rama Jataka, and Ramakien: A Comparative Study of Hindu and Buddhist Traditions." In *Many Ramayanas: The Diversity of a Narrative Tradition in South Asia*, edited by Paula Richman. Berkeley and London: University of California Press, 1991: 50–59.

Rockhill, W.W. "Notes on the Relations and Trade of China with the Eastern Archipelago and the Coast of the Indian Ocean during the Fourteenth Century, Part II." *T'oung Pao*, vol. 16 no. 1 (March 1915): 61–159.

Rooney, Dawn. *Angkor: An Introduction to the Temples*. New York: W.W. Norton, 2004.
Rossabi, Morris, ed. *China Among Equals: The Middle Kingdom and its Neighbors, 10th–14th Centuries*. Berkeley: University of California Press, 1983.
Rossabi, Morris. *A History of China*. Chichester, UK: Wiley Blackwell, 2014.
———. *Khubilai Khan, His Life and Times*. Berkeley and London: University of California Press, 1988.
Sahai, Sachchidanand. *Les Institutions Politiques et l'Organisation Administrative du Cambodge Ancien (VIe–XIIIe Siècles)* [*The Political Institutions and Administrative Organization of Ancient Cambodia (6th–13th Centuries)*]. 1970: Paris, École française d'Extrême Orient.
Sarkar, H. B. "Chinese Texts on Chia-na-t'iao Kanthi." *Indologica Taurinensia*, Turin, vol. 21–22 (1996): 271–284.
Schafer, Edward. *The Golden Peaches of Samarkand: A Study of Tang Exotics*. Berkeley and Los Angeles: University of California Press, 1963.
———. *The Vermilion Bird: Tang Images of the South*. Berkeley and Los Angeles: University of California Press, 1967.
Schipper, Mineke. "Humanity's Beginnings in Creation and Origin Myths from Around the World". In *China's Creation and Origin Myths: Cross-Cultural Explorations in Oral and Written Traditions*, edited by Mineke Schipper, Ye Shuxian and Yin Hubin, 3–24. Leiden: Brill, 2011.
Schlegel, Gustave. "Geographical Notes III: Ho-ling 訶陵 Kaling." *T'oung Pao*, vol. 9 no. 4 (1898), 273–287.
Schottenhammer, Angela, ed. *The Emporium of the World: Maritime Quanzhou, 1000–1400*. Leiden: Brill, 2000.
Schottenhammer, Angela, "The Song 宋 Dynasty (960–1279)—A Revolutionary Era Turn?" In *China Across the Centuries: Papers from a lecture series in Budapest*, edited by Gábor Kósa, 133–173. Budapest: Eötvös Loránd University, 2017.
———. "China's Rise and Retreat as a Maritime Power." In *Beyond the Silk Roads. New Discourses on China's Role in East Asian Maritime History*, edited by Robert Antony and Angela Schottenhammer, 189–211. Wiesbaden: Otto Harrassowitz, 2017.
Schweyer, Anne-Valérie, "The Birth of Champa: Crossing borders in southeast Asian archaeology". *HAL open science*: halshs-00828812, Sept. 2010, 1–17.
———. "The confrontation of the Khmers and Chams in the Bayon period." In *Bayon: New Perspectives*, edited by Joyce Clark, 50–71. Bangkok: River Books, 2007.
Scott, Rosemary and John Guy, ed. *Southeast Asia and China: Art, Interaction and Commerce*. London: School of Oriental and African Studies, 1995.
Sen, Tansen. "Buddhism and the Maritime Crossings." In *China and Beyond in the Medieval Period: Cultural Crossings and Inter-Regional Connections*, edited by Dorothy Wong and Gustav Heldt, 39–62. New Delhi: Manohar, 2014.
———. "Chinese Sources on South Asia." In *Beyond National Frames: South Asian Pasts and the World*, edited by Rila Mukherjee, 52–73. Delhi: Primus, 2015.
———. "Early China and the Indian Ocean Networks." In *The Sea in History: The Ancient World*, edited by Philip de Souza and Pascal Arnaud, 536–547. Suffolk: Boydell and Brewer, 2017.
———. "Maritime Interactions between China and India: Coastal India and the Ascendancy of Chinese Maritime Power in the Indian Ocean." *Journal of Central Eurasian Studies*, vol. 2 (May 2011): 41–82.
———. "Maritime Southeast Asia Between South Asia and China to the Sixteenth Century". *TRaNS: Trans-Regional and -National Studies of Southeast Asia*, vol. 2, no. 1 (January 2014), 31–59.
———. "The Spread of Buddhism to China: A Re-examination of the Buddhist Interactions between Ancient India and China." *China Report*, 48, 1 & 2 (2012): 11–27.
———. "Yijing and the Buddhist Cosmopolis of the Seventh Century." In *Texts and Transformations: Essays in Honor of the 75th Birthday of Victor H. Mair*, edited by Haun Saussy, 345–368. Amherst: Cambria Press, 2018.
———. "Zheng He's Military Interventions in South Asia, 1405–1433." *China and Asia: A Journal in Historical Studies* vol. 1, no. 2 (December 2019): 158–191.
———. *Buddhism, Diplomacy, and Trade: The Realignment of Sino-Indian Relations, 600–1400*. Honolulu: University of Hawai'i Press, 2003.

Shaffer, Lynda Norene. *Maritime Southeast Asia to 1500*. Armonk and London: M.E. Sharpe, 1996.

Sharrock, Peter. "Cham-Khmer Interactions in 1113–1220 CE." In *Vibrancy in Stone: Masterpieces of the Đà Nẵng Museum of Cham Sculpture*, edited by Trần Kỳ Phương, Võ Văn Thắng and Peter D. Sharrock, 111–119. Bangkok: River Books, 2018.

————. *Banteay Chhmar: Garrison-Temple of the Khmer Empire*. Bangkok: River Books, 2015.

Shaughnessy, Edward. "Of Trees, a Son, and Kingship: Recovering an Ancient Chinese Dream." *The Journal of Asian Studies*, vol. 77 no. 3 (August 1918): 594–595.

Shiba, Yoshinobu. *Commerce and Society in Sung China*. Translated by Mark Elvin. Ann Arbor: University of Michigan Center for Chinese Studies, 1992 [1970].

Shin, Leo. *The Making of the Chinese State: Ethnicity and Expansion on the Ming Borderlands*. Cambridge: Cambridge University Press, 2012.

Shiro, Momoki. "'Mandala Champa' Seen from Chinese Sources." In *The Cham of Vietnam: History, Society and Art*, edited by Trần Kỳ Phương and Bruce Lockhart, 120–137. Singapore: NUS, 2011.

Shorto, H.L. "The 32 'Myos' in the Medieval Mon Kingdom." *Bulletin of the School of Oriental and African* Studies, University of London, vol. 26 no. 3 (1963): 572–591.

Shuen-fu Lin, "Professionalism and the craft of song" in *The Cambridge History of Chinese Literature*, vol. 1, edited by Kang–I Sun Chang and Stephen Owen, 520–532. Cambridge and New York: Cambridge University Press, 2010.

Sickman, Laurence and Alexander Soper. *The Art and Architecture of China*. Harmondsworth: Penguin Books, 1956.

Sihanouk, Norodom. *Shadow over Angkor: Memoirs of His Majesty King Norodom Sihanouk*, vol. 1. Translated and edited by Julio Jeldres. Phnom Penh: Monument Books, 2005.

[Sima Qian 司馬遷,] *Records of the Historian: Chapters from the Shih chi of Ssu-ma Ch'ien*. Translated and edited by Burton Watson. New York and London: Columbia University Press, 1969.

Sinn, Y.C. [Xian Yuqing 冼玉清]. "楊孚與楊子宅 [Yang Fu and Yang Zizhai]." *Lingnan Journal* 嶺南學報 (1952): 146–162.

Skaff, Jonathan. *Sui-Tang China and Its Turko-Mongol Neighbors: Culture, Power, and Connections, 580–800*. Oxford: Oxford University Press, 2012.

Smith, Anthony. *Nations and Nationalism in a Global Era*. Cambridge: Polity Press, 1995.

Smith, Monica. "'Indianization' from the Indian Point of View: Trade and Cultural Contacts with Southeast Asia in the Early First Millennium CE." *Journal of the Economic and Social History of the Orient*, vol. 42, no. 1 (1999): 1–26.

Smith, R.B. "Mainland South East Asia in the Seventh and Eighth Centuries". In *Early South East Asia: Essays in Archaeology, History and Historical Geography*, edited by R.B. Smith and William Watson, 443–456. New York: Oxford University Press, 1979.

Smith, R.B. and William Watson, eds. *Early South East Asia: Essays in Archaeology, History, and Historical Geography*. New York: Oxford University Press, 1979.

Smyth, D.A., ed. *Cambodian Linguistics, Literature and History*. London: School of Oriental and African Studies, 1993.

Soothill, W.E. and Lewis Hodous. *A Dictionary of Chinese Buddhist Terms: with Sanskrit and English Equivalents and a Sanskrit-Pali Index*. Delhi: Motilal Banarsidass, 1977 [1937].

Southworth, William. "The origins of Campā in central Vietnam: A preliminary review" (unpublished PhD thesis). London: School of Oriental and African Studies, 2001.

————. "River Settlement and Coastal Trade: Towards a Specific Model of Early State Development in Champa." In *The Cham of Vietnam: History, Society and Art*, edited by Trần Kỳ Phương and Bruce Lockhart, 102–119. Singapore: NUS Press, 2011.

Stadtner, David. "The Mon of Lower Burma." *Journal of the Siam Society*, vol. 96: 193–215.

Stark, Miriam. "Early Mainland Southeast Asian Landscapes in the First Millennium AD." *Annual Review of Anthrology* (2006): 21:1–21:26.

————. "Pre-Angkorian and Angkorian Cambodia." In *Southeast Asia—From prehistory to history*, edited by Ian Glover and Peter Bellwood, 89–119. Oxford and New York: Routledge Curzon, 2004.

————. "Southeast Asian urbanism: from early city to Classical state." In *The Cambridge World History, Vol. III: Early Cities in Comparative Perspective, 4000 BCE–1200 CE*, edited by Norman Yoffee, 74–93. Cambridge: Cambridge University Press, 2015.

Stark, Miriam. "The Transition to History in the Mekong Delta: A View from Cambodia." *International Journal of Historical Archaeology*, vol. 2, no. 3 (September 1998): 175–203.

————. "Universal Rule and Precarious Empire: Power and Fragility in the Angkorian State." In *The Evolution of Fragility: Setting the Terms*, edited by Norman Yoffee, 161–182. Cambridge: McDonald Institute for Archaeological Research, 2019.

Stein, R.A. "Le Lin-yi 林邑: sa localisation, sa contribution à la formation du Champa et ses liens avec la Chine [Linyi: its location, its contribution to the formation of Champa, and its ties with China]. *Han-Hiue* 漢學, *Bulletin du Centre d'Études Sinologiques de Pékin*, vol. 2, fascicules 1–3, 1947: 1–335.

Steiner, George. *After Babel: Aspects of Language and Translation*. Oxford: Oxford University Press, 1975.

Strange, Mark and Jakub Hruby. "*Nan shi* 南史." In *Early Medieval Chinese Texts*, edited by Cynthia Chennault et al., 209–216. Berkeley: University of California, 2015.

Stuart-Fox, Martin. *A Short History of China and Southeast Asia: Tribute, Trade and Influence*. Crows Nest, New South Wales: Allen and Unwin, 2003.

Stuart, G.A. *Chinese Materia Medica: Vegetable Kingdom*. Taipei: Southern Materials Center, 1987.

Tan, Ha Van. "Oc Eo: Endogenous and Exogenous Elements." *Vietnam Social Sciences*, vol. 1–2 (7–8): 91–101.

Tarling, Nicolas, ed. *The Cambridge History of Southeast Asia, Volume One: From early times to c.1500*. Cambridge: Cambridge University Press, 1999.

Taylor, Keith. "The Early Kingdoms." In *The Cambridge History of Southeast Asia, Volume One: From early times to c.1500*, edited by Nicholas Tarling, 137–182. Cambridge: Cambridge University Press, 1992.

Taylor, Keith. *A History of the Vietnamese*. Cambridge: Cambridge University Press, 2013.

————. *The Birth of Vietnam*. Berkeley: University of California Press, 1983.

Thant, Myint-U. *The River of Lost Footsteps: Histories of Burma*. New York: Farrar, Straus and Giroux, 2006.

Tilly, Charles. *Coercion, Capital and European States, AD 990–1992*. Oxford: Blackwells, 1992.

Tingley, Nancy, ed. *Arts of Ancient Viet Nam: From River Plain to Open Sea*. New Haven and London: Yale University Press, 2010.

Trainor, Kevin, ed. *Buddhism: The Illustrated Guide*. New York: Oxford University Press, 2001.

Trần, Kỳ Phương and Bruce Lockhart, ed. *The Cham of Vietnam: History, Society and Art*. Singapore: National University of Singapore, 2011.

Twitchett, Denis and Michael Loewe, eds. *The Cambridge History of China Vol. 1: The Chin and Han Empires, 221 BC–AD 220*. Cambridge: Cambridge University Press, 1986.

Twitchett, Denis and Paul Smith, eds. *The Cambridge History of China Vol. 5: The Sung Dynasty and its Predecessors, 907–1279, Part 1*. Cambridge: Cambridge University Press, 2009.

Twitchett, Denis, ed. *The Cambridge History of China Vol. 3, Sui and T'ang China, 589–906 AD, Part One*. Cambridge: Cambridge University Press, 1979.

Vickery, Michael. "A Misstep Toward a New History of Cambodia" (book review). *Zeitschrift der Deutschen Morgenländischen Gesellschaft*, vol. 155, no. 1 (2005): 239–251.

————. "A Short History of Champa." In *Champa and the Archaeology of Mỹ Sơn (Vietnam)*, edited by Andrew Hardy, Mauro Cucarzi and Patrizia Zolese, 45–60. Singapore: NUS Press, 2009.

————. "Coedès' Histories of Cambodia." *Silpakorn University International Journal* (Bangkok), vol. 1, no. 1 (Jan–June 2000): 61–108.

————. "Funan Reviewed: Deconstructing the Ancients." *Bulletin de l'École française d'Extrême Orient*, vol. 90–91, 2003: 101–143.

————. "Maritime Trade and State Development in Early Southeast Asia, by Kenneth R. Hall" (book review). *Journal of Asian Studies*: 211–213.

————. "Some Remarks on Early State Formation in Cambodia." In *Southeast Asia in the 9th to 14th Centuries*, edited by David Marr and Anthony Milner, 95–116. Canberra: Australian National University and Singapore: ISEAS, 1986.

————. "What and Where was Chenla?" In *Recherches nouvelles sur le Cambodge* [*New Research on Cambodia*], edited by François Bizot, 197–212. Paris: École française d'Extrême Orient, 1994.

————. "What to do about the Khmers" (book review). *Journal of Southeast Asian Studies*, vol. 27 no. 2 (Sept 1996): 1–20

Vickery, Michael. *Cambodia and Its Neighbors in the 15th Century*. Singapore: NUS Asia Research Institute Working Paper no. 27, 2004.

————. *Champa Revised*. Singapore: NUS Asia Research Institute Working Paper no. 37, 2005.

————. *Society, Economics, and Politics in Pre-Angkor Cambodia: The 7th–8th Centuries*. Tokyo: Toyo Bunko, 1998.

Vu Hong Lien, *The Mongol Navy: Kublai Khan's Invasions in Đại Việt and Champa*. Singapore: Nalanda-Sriwijaya Centre Working Paper No. 25, Jun 2017.

Wade, Geoff, ed. *China and Southeast Asia: Routledge Library on Southeast Asia* (6 volumes). London and New York: Routledge, 2009.

————. *Southeast Asia-China Interactions*. Singapore: NUS Press, 2007.

Wade, Geoff. "Beyond the Southern Borders: Southeast Asia in Chinese Texts to the Ninth Century." In *Lost Kingdoms: Hindu-Buddhist Sculpture of Early Southeast Asia*, edited by John Guy, 25–31. New York: Metropolitan Museum of Art, 2014.

————. "The 'Account of Champa' in the *Song Huiyao Jigao*." In *The Cham of Vietnam: History, Society and Art*, edited by Trần Kỳ Phương and Bruce Lockhart, 138–167. Singapore: NUS Press, 2011.

————. "The '*Ming shi-lu*' as a Source for Thai History: Fourteenth to Seventeenth Centuries." *Journal of Southeast Asian Studies*, vol. 31 no. 2 (Sep., 2000): 249–294.

————. "The Zheng He Voyages: A Reassessment." *Journal of the Malaysian Branch of the Royal Asiatic Society*, vol. 78., no. 1 (2005): 37–58.

————. *Champa in the* Song hui-yao*: A draft translation*. Singapore: NUS Asia Research Institute Working Paper no. 53, June 2003.

————. *Southeast Asia in the* Ming Shi-lu*: an open access resource*. Singapore: epress.nus.edu.sg/msl, 2005.

————. *The* Ming shi *Account of Champa*. Singapore: NUS Asia Research Institute Working Paper no. 3, June 2003.

————. *The Pre-Modern East Asian Maritime Realm: An Overview of European-Language Studies*. Singapore: NUS Asia Research Institute Working Paper no. 16, December 2003.

Walravens, Hartmut. *Paul Pelliot (1878–1945): His Life and Works—a Bibliography*. Bloomington: Indiana University Research Institute for Inner Asian Studies, 2001.

Wang Bangwei. "The Buddhist Connection between China and Ancient Cambodia: Śramaṇa Mandra's Visit to Jiankang." In *The Benefit of Broad Horizons: Intellectual and Institutional Preconditions for a Global Social Science*, edited by H. Joas and B. Klein, 282–291. Leiden: Brill, 2014.

Wang Gungwu, "Ming foreign relations: South East Asia." In *The Cambridge History of China, vol. 8: The Ming Dyasty, 1368–1644, Part 2*, edited by Denis Twitchett and Frederick Mote, 301–332. Cambridge: Cambridge University Press, 1998.

————. "Early Ming Relations with Southeast Asia: A Background Essay." In *The Chinese World Order: Traditional China's Foreign Relations*, edited by John K. Fairbank, 34–62. Cambridge: Harvard University Press, 1968.

————. "Introduction: Imperial China Looking South." In *Imperial China and its Southern Neighbours*, edited by Victor Mair and Liam Kelley, 1–15. Singapore: ISEAS Yusof Ishak Institute, 2015.

————. "Keynote address—Southeast Asia: Imperial themes." *International Journal of Asia Pacific Studies* 13 (2) (2017), 179–192.

————. "Some Comments on the Later Standard Histories." In *Essays on the Sources for Chinese History*, edited by Donald Leslie et al., 53–63. Canberra: Australian National University Press, 1973.

————. "The Nanhai Trade: A Study of the Early History of Chinese Trade in the South China Sea." In *Southeast Asia-China Interactions*, edited by Geoff Wade, 51–166. Singapore: NUS Press, 2007 [1958].

————. *The Chinese Overseas: From Earthbound China to the Quest for Autonomy*. Cambridge and London: Harvard University Press, 2000.

Wang Zhenping. *Tang China in Multi-Polar Asia*. Honolulu: University of Hawai'i Press, 2017.

Watters, Thomas. *On Yuan Chwang [Xuanzang]'s Travels in India*. Delhi: Munshiram Manoharlal, 1973 [1904–5])

Wechsler, Howard. "T'ai-tsung (reign 626–49) the consolidator." In *The Cambridge History of China, Volume 3: Sui and T'ang China, 589–906, part I*, edited by Denis Twitchett, 188–241. Cambridge: Cambridge University Press, 1979.

Wheatley, Paul. "Ch'ih T'u 赤土." In *Southeast Asia-China Interactions*, edited by Geoff Wade, 8–18. Singapore: NUS Press, 2007.

————. "Geographical Notes on Some Commodities in Sung Maritime Trade." In *Southeast Asia-China Interactions*, edited by Geoff Wade, 183–295. Singapore: NUS Press, 2007.

————. "The Malay Peninsula as Known to Third Century A.D. Chinese." In *Southeast Asia-China Interactions*, edited by Geoff Wade, 19–37. Singapore: NUS Press, 2007.

————. "The Mount of the Immortals: A note on Tamil cultural Influence in fifth-century Indochina." *Oriens Extremus*, vol. 21, no. 1 (1974): 97–109.

————. *Nāgara and Commandery*. Chicago: University of Chicago, 1983.

————. *The Golden Khersonese*. Kuala Lumpur: Penerbit Universiti Malaya, 1980.

Whitmore John. "Nagara Champa and the Vijaya Turn." In *Vibrancy in Stone: Masterpieces of the Đà Nẵng Museum of Cham Sculpture*, edited by Trần Kỳ Phương, Võ Văn Thắng and Peter D. Sharrock, 31–36. Bangkok: River Books, 2018.

————. "The Rise of the Coast: Trade, State and Culture in Early Đại Việt." *Journal of Southeast Asian Studies*, vol. 37, no. 1 (Feb. 2006): 103–122

Wicks, Robert. *Money, Markets, and Trade in Early Southeast Asia: The Development of Indigenous Monetary Systems to Ad 1400*. Ithaca: Cornell Southeast Asia Program, 1992.

Wilkinson, Endymion. *Chinese History: A Manual*, Fifth Edition. Cambridge: Endymion Wilkinson c/o Harvard University Asia Center, 2018.

Wolters, O. W. *Early Indonesian Commerce: A Study of the Origins of Srivijaya*. Ithaca, New York: Cornell University Press, 1967.

Wolters, O.W. *Early Southeast Asia—Selected Essays*. Edited by Craig Reynolds. Ithaca: Cornell University, 2008.

Wong, Dorothy and Gustav Heldt, eds. *China and Beyond in the Medieval Period: Cultural Crossings and Inter-Regional Connections*. New Delhi: Manohar, 2014.

Woodward, Hiram. "Bronze Sculptures of Ancient Cambodia." In *Gods of Angkor: Bronzes from the National Museum of Cambodia*, edited by Louise Allison Cort and Paul Jett, 30–77. Washington DC and Seattle: Smithsonian Institution and University of Washington Press, 2010.

————. "Dvaravati, Si Thep, and Wendan." *Bulletin of the Indo-Pacific Prehistory Association*, 30 (2010): 87–97.

Wright, Arthur. "The Sui Dynasty." In *The Cambridge History of China, Volume 3: Sui and T'ang China, 589–906, part I*, edited by Denis Twitchett: 48–149. Cambridge: Cambridge University Press, 1979.

————. *Buddhism in Chinese History*. Stanford: Stanford University Press, 1959.

Wu Guanghua 吴光華. *Han ying da cidian* 漢英大詞典 [*A Large Chinese-English Dictionary*]. Shanghai: Shanghai Yiwen chubanshe, 2009.

Xiao Tong 蕭統, ed. *Wen Xuan or Selections of Refined Literature* (3 volumes). Translated by David Knechtges. Princeton: Princeton University Press, 2014.

Xiong, Victor Cunrui. *Sui-Tang Chang'an: A Study in the Urban History of Medieval China*. Ann Arbor: University of Michigan, 2000.

Xu Xiqi 徐錫祺, ed. *Xin bian Zhongguo sanqiannian liri jiansuo biao* 新編中國三千年歷日檢索表 [Newly Compiled Search Table for Chinese Calendar Days for 3000 Years]. Beijing: Renmin jiaoyu chubanshe, 1992.

Xuanzang 玄奘 and Bianji 辯機. *The Great Tang Record of the Western Regions*. Translated by Li Rong. Berkeley: Numata Center for Buddhist Translation and Research, 1996.

[Xuanzang 玄奘 and Bianji 辯機.] *Si-yu-ki—Buddhist Records of the Western World*. Translated by Samuel Beal. London: Trubner & Co., 1884.

Yamagata, Mariko, Nguyễn Kim Dung and Bùi Chí Hoàng. "Development of Regional Centres in Champa, Viewed from Recent Archaeological Advances in Central Vietnam." In *Champa: Territories and Networks of a Southeast Asian Kingdom*, edited by Arlo Griffiths, Andrew Hardy and Geoff Wade: 47–62. Paris: École française d'Extrême Orient, 2019.

Yang, Bin. "The Bengal Connections in Yunnan." *China Report*, vol. 48, no. 1–2 (February 2012): 125–145.

————. *Between Winds and Clouds: The Making of Yunnan (Second Century* BCE *to Twentieth Century* CE). New York: Columbia University Press, 2009.

Yang Lihui and An Deming. "The World of Chinese Mythology: An Introduction". In *China's Creation and Origin Myths: Cross-Cultural Explorations in Oral and Written Traditions*, edited by Mineke Schipper, Ye Shuxian and Yin Hubin, 25–54. Leiden: Brill, 2011.

Yang, Lien-sheng. "Historical Notes on the Chinese World Order." In *The Chinese World Order: Traditional China's Foreign Relations*, edited by John K. Fairbank, 20–33. Cambridge: Harvard University Press, 1968.

Yang Xuanzhi 楊衒之. *A Record of Buddhist Monasteries of Luoyang*. Translated by Wang Yitong 王伊同. Princeton: Princeton University Press, 1984.

Yü, Ying-shih. *Trade and Expansion in Han China: A Study in the Structure of Sino-Barbarian Economic Relations*. Berkeley and Los Angeles, University of California Press, 1967.

Yule, Henry and A.C. Burnell. *Hobson-Jobson: A Glossary of Colloquial Anglo-Indian Words and Phrases, and of Kindred Terms, Etymological, Historical, Geographical and Discursive*. New Delhi: Munshiram Manoharlal, 1984 [1903].

Yung Wai-chuen, Peter. *Angkor: The Khmers in Ancient Chinese Annals*. Hong Kong: Oxford University Press, 2000.

Zakharov, Anton. "State Formation in First Millennium Southeast Asia: a Reappraisal." *Social Evolution and History*, vol. 18, no. 1 (March 2019): 217–240.

————. "Was the Early History of Campā Really Revised? A Reassessment of the Classical Narratives of Linyi and the 6th–8th-Century Campā Kingdom." In *Champa: Territories and Networks of a Southeast Asian Kingdom*, edited by Arlo Griffiths, Andrew Hardy and Geoff Wade, 147–158. Paris: École française d'Extrême Orient, 2019.

Zhang Xinglang [Hsing-lang Chang, 張星烺]. *Zhongxi jiaotong shiliao huibian* 中西交通史料匯編 [*Collection of Historical Materials on Sino-Western Relations*]. Edited by Zhu Jieqin 朱傑勤. Beijing: Zhonghua shuju, 2003 [1928].

Zhang, Cong Ellen. *Transformative Journeys: Travel and Culture in Song China*. Honolulu: University of Hawai'i Press, 2011.

"Zhong Jian zhongxin jiang yu jinnian wangong" 中柬中心將于今年完工 [Work to be Completed this Year on a China-Cambodia Center]. *Shitong haiwai* 世通海外, 29 January 2019.

Zhou Daguan 周達觀, *A Record of Cambodia:the Land and its People*. Translated and edited by Peter Harris. Chiang Mai: Silkworm Books, 2007.

[Zhou Daguan 周達觀.] *Customs of Cambodia—Zhou Daguan*. Translated by Beling Uk and Solang Uk and edited by Kent Davis. Florida: DatAsia, 2016.

[Zhou Daguan 周達觀.] *The Customs of Cambodia by Zhou Daguan* (*Chou Ta-kuan*). Translated by Michael Smithies. Bangkok: The Siam Society, 2001.

[Zhou Qufei 周去非.] *Das Ling-wai tai-ta von Chou Ch'ü-fei: Ein Landeskunde Südchinas aus dem 12. Jahrhundert* [*The Lingwai daida of Zhou Qufei: A South Chinese Geography from the 12th Century*]. Translated by Almut Netolitzky. Wiesbaden: Franz Steiner, 1977.

[Zhao Rugua 趙汝适.] *Chao Ru-kua: His Work on the Chinese and Arab Trade in the twelfth and thirteenth Centuries, entitled Chu-fan-chi*. Translated by Friedrich Hirth and William Rockhill. St. Petersburg: Imperial Academy of Sciences, 1911.

Zürcher, Erik. *The Buddhist Conquest of China*, 3rd edition. Leiden: Brill, 2007.

Endnotes

Introduction

1. The translations in this book are mine. For other works and authors mentioned in this introduction, see the bibliography.
2. Funan: 扶南; Zhenla: 真臘 (or 真蠟).
3. As noted in Chandler, *A History of Cambodia*, 18–21; Coe and Evans, *Angkor and the Khmer Civilization*, 74–80; and Briggs, The *Ancient Khmer Empire*, 42.
4. Vickery, "Funan Reviewed," 101; Gaudes, "Kauṇḍinya, Prey Thaong, and the 'Nāgī Somā,'" 341–343; Finot, "Sur quelques traditions Indochinoises," 32–33. See also chapter one.
5. Chandler, *A History of Cambodia*, 83–89; Coe and Evans, *Angkor and the Khmer Civilization*, 74–80.
6. Huo Liqiang and Li Yingqing, "Yunnan Firm Eyes Cambodian Park," *China Daily*, 11 March 2017; "Zhong Jian zhongxin jiang yu jinnian wangong 中柬中心將于今年完工 [Work to be Completed This Year on China-Cambodia Centre]," *Shitong haiwai* 世通海外 / *Shitong Overseas*, 29 January 2019.
7. On the centrality of Angkor to Cambodia's sense of modern nationhood, the Cambodian ruler Norodom Sihanouk (1922–2012) had this to say: "All Khmers are in love with Angkor . . . Angkor Wat, the purest gem of Angkor, remains for ever engraved on their hearts." Sihanouk, *Shadow over Angkor*, 182.

For an account of China's uneven relations with Cambodia since the 1950s, see Sophie Richardson's *Cambodia, China, and the Five Principles of Peaceful Coexistence* (New York: Columbia University Press, 2009).

8. Chandler, *A History of Cambodia*, 18–19.
9. Briggs, *Ancient Khmer Empire*, 12–36; Chandler, History of Cambodia, 18–27; Chen, *Suiqian Nanhai jiaotong shiliao yanjiu*, 73–90; O'Reilly, *Early Civilizations*, 92–111.
10. For example in Shaffer, *Maritime Southeast Asia*, 18–36.
11. For a discussion of why this break occurred see the beginning of chapter eight.
12. The name Zhenla still crops up in modern settings. For example it was used, incongruously, to describe the military offensives launched in 1970 by Lon Nol, then leader of Cambodia, against North Vietnamese forces inside Cambodia. These offensives were called Chenla I and Chenla II, Chenla being an old way of romanizing Zhenla. Becker, *You Don't Belong Here*, 178–180.
13. Briggs and O'Reilly take Zhenla to refer to the era between the demise of Funan and the rise of Angkor. Briggs, *Ancient Khmer Empire*, 37–87; O'Reilly, *Early Civilizations*, 11–126. Coedès treats Zhenla as the Chinese annalists do. Coedès, *Indianized States*, 65–70, 85–86, 93–94, 161, 166.
14. For a list of Chinese dynasties and Cambodian kings, see appendix two.
15. In an obituary of Michael Vickery, David Chandler notes the contrast between "slippery, stir-fry historical research" and Vickery's "densely argued, persuasive" work. Chandler, "Michael Vickery", 373.
16. *Zhengshi*: 正史; *tongshi*: 通史.
17. Gardiner, "Standard Histories," 49.
18. Wilkinson, *Chinese History*, 690. This far-ranging and meticulously compiled manual is a valuable guide to the vast corpus of Chinese imperial writings, as well as to numerous other matters.
19. Goodman, "*Jin shu*," 137–138.
20. *Shilu*: 實錄. Wang, "Some Comments on the Later Standard Histories," 54; Wilkinson, *Chinese History*, 690.
21. Wilkinson, *Chinese History*, 690.
22. For *Nan Qi shu*, see chapter two.
23. *Jizhuan*: 記傳.
24. Wilkinson, *Chinese History*, 691.
25. *Hui yao*: 會要.
26. The French version was published in 1883 by Marie-Jean-Léon Lecoq, the Marquis d'Hervey de Saint-Denys.

27. Tao Yuanming: 陶淵明. Wilkinson, *Chinese History*, 1081–1082. The original meaning of *juan* 卷 is "fascicle," and the term can be translated as "chapter," "volume" or "book," depending on context.

28. For the Chinese Text Project, see ctext.org/introduction.

29. Chen et al., *Zhongguo gujizhong*; Lu and Zhou, *Zhongguo gujizhong*.

30. The source is the seventeenth-century Chinese bibliophile Qian Zeng 錢曾. See chapter nine.

31. For works by these writers, scholars, and Buddhist monks, see chapters two and three.

32. *Yiwuzhi*: 異物志; *chuanqi*: 傳奇. Idema and Haft, *Guide to Chinese Literature*, 58.

33. The phrase "economic revolution" is Mark Elvin's, from *The Pattern of the Chinese Past*, 111.

34. The trend is discussed in Zhang, *Transformative Journeys*, 19–42.

35. Fan Chengda, *Treatises of the Supervisor*, xxxii–xli. Translator James Hargett uses the term "treatises" rather than "treatise" because while Fan's gazetteer as a whole constitutes a treatise, it includes a number of treatises on specific subjects.

36. For the gazetteers, see chapter eight.

37. See chapter nine.

38. Pelliot, "Le Fou-nan," 248–249 et seq.

39. Pelliot, "Quelques textes chinois," 251.

40. Coedès, *Indianized States*, 23, 35. The content of the 1968 English edition may be older than the publication date suggests. Michael Vickery notes that Coedès failed to update this edition to take it into account much of the scholarship of the period from 1948 to 1968. Vickery, "Coedès' Histories", 61–108.

41. Briggs, *Ancient Khmer Empire*, 24–25, 27.

42. J. C. van Leur, "On Early Asian Trade," 95. Cited in Mabbett, "The 'Indianization' of Southeast Asia," 144.

43. Mabbett, "'Indianization,'" 157–158, 160, 148.

44. Claude Jacques, "'Funan', 'Zhenla,'" 371–379.

45. Pollock, *Language of the Gods*, 122–134, esp. 123.

46. Vickery, *Society, Economics, and Politics*, 2. Also Vickery, "Funan Reviewed," 104, 111.

47. Vickery, *Society, Economics, and Politics*, 2.

48. Vickery, *Society, Economics, and Politics*, 200, 202. Also Coe and Evans, *Angkor and the Khmer Civilization*, 80–82.

49. Murphy and Lefferts, "Globalizing Indian Religions," 771. This is not to gainsay the importance of Indian influences in mainland and island Southeast Asia from the middle of the first millennium BCE on. See for example Bellina, "Southeast Asia and the Early Maritime Silk Road," 22–24; Glover, "Contacts between India and Southeast Asia," 130; Hung, "Cultural Interactions," 647–653.

50. Bourdonneau, "Culturalisme et historiographie," 1–2.

51. These specialists include Kenneth Hall, Li Tana, Geoff Wade, Wang Gungwu, Paul Wheatley, O. W. Wolters, and Xu Yunqiao (Hsu Yun-ts'iao), to mention only some. For details, see the bibliography.

52. The scholars include Rafe de Crespigny, Kenneth Gardiner, Wang Gungwu, and Endymion Wilkinson, as well as Damien Chassende, William Crowell, Stephen Durrant, Howard Goodman, and Johannes Kurtz. For details, see the bibliography.

53. It is complemented by Wang's more recent reflections on the Sinocentric perspective on China's relations with its Southern neighbors being just one historical perspective among a number. Wang, "Introduction," 1–15.

54. For details, see the bibliography.

55. *Fan*: 番, 蕃.

56. *Taiping yulan*, for example, makes scattered references to Kang Tai as the author of two works: *Funan tu su* 扶南土俗 [*Funan: the Land and its Customs*] and *Wu shi waiguo zhuan* 武時外國轉 [*A Record of Foreign States during the Wu Period*]. In addition, it cites a third work, *Funan zhuan* 扶南傳 [*A Record of Funan*], that is credited elsewhere to Kang Tai. See chapter one.

57. For a useful account of the evolution of spoken and written Chinese, see Wilkinson, *Chinese History*, 17–32. For a study of the elite and local vernaculars used in the Six Dynasties capital Jiankang, where some of the Chinese texts on Funan were written, see Chittick, "Vernacular Languages."

58. Karlgren, *Grammata Serica Recensa*, 4. Karlgren's reconstructions involve the use of colons (:) and hyphens (-) to indicate tones. For an explanation, Karlgren, *Grammata Serica Recensa*, 5.

59. Pulleyblank, *Lexicon of Reconstructed Pronunciation*; Baxter and Sagart, *Old Chinese*.

60. Da Qin: 大秦.

61. Coedès, *Indianized States*, 36.

62. "Zhi ba'nan guo jiu yun Funan" 至跋南國舊云扶南. Yijing, *Nanhai jigui neifa zhuan*, 17.

63. A visit recounted in *Nan Qi shu* (chapter two).

64. Zhenla: 真臘, variant 真蠟.

65. Antelme, "Quelques nouvelles pistes," 11–43. Beeswax as a commodity in Zhenla is not mentioned until the thirteenth century, when it is referred to by both Zhao Rugua and Zhou Daguan. For Zhao on wax, see chapter eight. For Zhou on wax, *Zhenla fengtu ji*, 141.

66. Ferlus, "Origine des noms anciens," 47–64.

67. Pelliot, *Mémoires*, 71–82. Elsewhere, Pelliot discusses what he calls "the intricacies involved in the name 'Čīn'" for China, as derived from the name of the Qin dynasty (221–206 BCE), and its use from the beginning of the first millennium CE onwards. Vickery, *Society, Economics, and Politics*, 420–421; Pelliot, *Mémoires*, 71; Pelliot, *Notes on Marco Polo*, 264–278.

68. The conflict in 713 is recorded in both the standard histories of the Tang dynasty, *Jiu Tang shu* and *Xin Tang shu*. According to these histories, a self-styled Black Emperor led four hundred thousand men from Zhenla, Linyi and others before being put down by the Tang general Yang Sixu (see chapter seven). Zhenla's name was already on record by that time in *Sui shu*, the standard history of the Sui dynasty, completed in 636.

69. Zhanla: 占臘; *la*: 臘. For *Ming shi* on Zhanla, see chapter eight.

70. Wade, "Beyond the Southern Borders," 26. The Khmer name Tonlé Sap means "large freshwater river."

71. *Guo*: 國; *cheng*: 城.

72. See, for example, the entries under *guo* in Luo et al., *Hanyu da cidian*.

73. For analyses of the composition and evolution of the Warring States, see Li, Early China, 183–206; Hui, *War and State Formation*, 54–108; Lewis, "Warring States," 587–644.

74. Tilly, Coercion, *Capital and European States*, 1–2.

75. *Wang*: 王.

76. In *Shuo wen jie zi*, *guo* 國 is defined as *bang* 邦, and *bang* 邦 is defined as *guo* 國. According to *Hanyu da cidian*, which is partly based on historical principles, *bang* meant "state" and "territory" in its earliest uses. [Xu,] *Shuo wen jie zi*, 280, 285. Luo et al.: *Hanyu da cidian*, entry under *bang* 邦.

77. Liu et al., *Jiu Tang shu*, 5272.

78. Xitu: 西屠. Li et al., *Taiping yulan*, 3502. In the earlier ms version of this book, the population of the Xitu states was mistakenly given as twenty rather than two thousand.

79. For an overview of the development of pre-state and state formations in Southeast Asia, including Cambodia, see Stark, "Early Mainland Southeast Asian Landscapes", 407–432, and the same author's "Southeast Asian Urbanism," 77–85.

80. *Zhu*: 主; *wang*: 王; *nü wang*: 女王.

81. For an account of these cities, see Michael Loewe, "The Heritage Left to the Empires" in *Cambridge History of Ancient China*, ed. Loewe and Shaughnessy, 1024–1028.

82. For *Sui shu* on Zhenla's thirty cities, see chapter six.

83. For *Liang shu* on the walls of Langyaxiu and Panpan, see chapter three. For *Nan Qi shu* on Funan's city walls, see chapter two.

84. For *Sui shu* on Īśānapura, see chapter six.

Chapter One

1. And not just in China. For example, the 2009 movie *Red Cliffs*, directed by John Woo, portrays the history of one of the greatest battles of this period.

2. Chen Shou: 陳壽. Born in present-day Sichuan, Chen served at the court of the recently established Jin dynasty in its capital Luoyang, where he worked on *San guo zhi* and two other histories, now lost. Cutter, "*San guo zhi*," 251.

3. *Hou Han shu* [*The History of the Later Han Dynasty*] records an eleventh-century BCE mission from Yueshang 越裳 to the Zhou court, but it does not mention Funan, which only appears in later commentaries. *Hou Han shu* describes Yueshang as being south of Jiaozhi—that is, the Red River Delta region. Fan Ye et al., *Hou Han shu*, 2835. For both the Yueshang legend about Funan and the account of tribute from Jiubuzhi 究不事, see Legge, *The Chinese Classics III: The Shoo King*, 535–536; and Pelliot, "Fou-nan," 249–251.

4. For the tribute from Jiubushi, see Fan et al., *Hou Han shu*, 2837. The name Kambuja (born of Kambu), from which the name Cambodia derives, is a term for the Khmers that first appeared in Cham and Khmer epigraphy in the ninth century CE. Vickery, *Society, Economic, and Politics*, 41.

5. Pelliot, "Fou-nan," 251, 303.

6. Chen et al., *Zhongguo gujizhong*, 1–2; Lu and Zhou, *Zhongguo gujizhong*, 1–2.

7. Various scholars, including Ian Johnson and Edward Shaughnessy, have described the extraordinary extent of these discoveries to date. Johnson, "Revolutionary Discovery," 53–56. Newly discovered texts are being published by the Center for Research on and Protection of Excavated Texts (Chutu wenxian yanjiu yu baohu zhongxin 出土文獻研究與保護中心) at Tsinghua University, Beijing. Shaughnessy, "Of Trees," 594–595.

8. Manguin, "Archaeology of Fu Nan," 107–108. For the two sites Angkor Borei and Óc Eo, see the introduction.

9. The two compilations are Wu Shu (947–1002)'s *Shi lei fu* and Li Fang (925–996)'s *Taiping yulan*. Both cite a work entitled *Yi wu zhi* 異物志 [*Annals of Strange Things*] as their source. Wu, *Shi lei fu*, 301; Li et al., *Taiping yulan*, 3133. In *Shi lei fu*, the last line of the passage on fans is missing.

10. Yang Fu, *Yi wu zhi*, 16–18, 25; Sinn, "Yang Fu and Yang Zizhai," 145–162. Sinn acknowledges that the evidence about Yang is not clear cut.

11. *Sui shu* describes him as having been a Court Gentleman for Consultation (Yi lang 議郎) during the Later Han, and having been the author of two works, *Yi wu zhuan* 異物傳 [*A Record of Strange Things*] and *Jiaozhou yiwuzhi* 交州異物志 [*Annals of Strange Things in Jiaozhou*]. Wei et al., *Sui shu*, 983. *Jiu Tang shu* lists him as the author of *Jiaozhou yi wu zhi*. Liu et al., *Jiu Tang shu*, *2015*. Court Gentleman for Consultation: Hucker, *Dictionary of Official Titles*, 267.

12. *Shi lei fu* and *Taiping yulan* both describe the passage as coming from a work called *Yi wu zhi* 異物志 [*Annals of Strange Things*]. In another citation from *Yi wu zhi*, not a passage about Funan, *Taiping yulan* mentions Yang Fu as *Yi wu zhi*'s author. But Chinese encyclopedias and compendiums contain hundreds of fragments from works with *yi wu zhi* in their title, many of them unattributed or attributed to authors with different names. *Taiping yulan*, for example, contains over two hundred quotations from works whose titles consist of or include the words *yi wu zhi*, some of them attributed to named authors, others unattributed, including the passage about Funan fans. Likewise in *Shi lei fu*, there are various references to books with *yi wu zhi* in the title, none of them naming Yang as the author.

13. "Zi Wudi yilai jie xianjian" 自吳帝以來皆獻見; Huangzhi: 黄支. Ban, *Han shu*, 1671. The passage is translated and discussed in Wang, "Nanhai Trade", 68–69. Wang argues that it is unlikely that all these states sent tribute during the Han, since except for a tribute mission from Huangzhi in 2 CE, such missions are not listed elsewhere in *Han shu*, as might have been expected.

Emperor Wu 吳 (Martial) is an abbreviated form of the Han emperor's posthumous title. Posthumous titles are used in this study for Chinese emperors from the Han to the Sui dynasties. From the Tang dynasty on, Chinese emperors are referred to by their posthumous temple titles (Xuanzong, Huizong, etc.). On imperial titles, see Wilkinson, *Chinese History*, xxi, 287–290.

14. Ban, *Han shu*, 1671.

15. These boat-building skills are summarized in Needham, *Science and Civilization, Vol. IV, Part III*, 441–442.

16. Nanyue: 南越; Panyu: 番禺.

17. Hong, "Archaeological Discoveries", 37–41.

18. The nine commanderies (*jun* 郡): Daner 儋耳, Zhuya 珠崖, Nanhai 南海, Cangwu 蒼梧, Yulin 鬱林, Hepu 合浦, Jiaozhi 交阯, Jiuzhen 九真, and Rinan 日南. Ban, *Han shu*, 188; Fan et al., *Hou Han shu*, 2835; Xiao, *Nan Qi shu*, 266; also Loewe, "Guangzhou," 59–64; Wang, "Nanhai Trade," 78.

19. Jiaozhou: 交州; *zhou*: 州. Loewe, "Guangzhou," 59.

20. Guangzhou: 廣州. Loewe, "Guangzhou," 59.

21. Loewe, "Guangzhou," 65–66.

22. "Jiaozhou huangdi shui yu tianjiwai jie nanyi baohuo suo chu shanhai zhenguai mo yu wei bi min shi xianyuan shu hao fanpan" 交州荒遰水與天際外接南夷寶貨所出山海珍怪莫與為比民恃險遠數好反叛. Xiao, *Nan Qi shu*, 266.

23. Sun Quan: 孫權; Lü Dai 吕岱. Wang, "Nanhai Trade," 79. For Lü Dai's biography in *San guo zhi*, which Wang cites, see Chen, *San guo zhi*, 1091–1093.

24. Wang, "Nanhai Trade," 79.

25. The Chinese title of the officer was Congshi nan xuan guohua 從事南宣國華. The date is from Wang, "Nanhai Trade," 79.

26. Chen, *San guo zhi*, 1092; Wang, "Nanhai Trade," 79. As far as the two other states that sent tribute are concerned, Tangming 堂明 has not been identified, while Linyi 林邑 was a newly emergent state in what is now central Vietnam (for a full discussion of Linyi, see appendix five).

27. Chen, *San guo zhi*, 920.

28. Yao, *Liang shu*, 783. *Liang shu* is the source for the description that follows of Kang's and Zhu's trip down South. Completed in 636, *Liang shu* is primarily a history of the sixth-century Liang dynasty and its foreign relations; but as in other standard histories it sometimes gives brief histories of foreign states, and this is the case here.

29. Yao, *Liang shu*, 783. Kang Tai 康泰's title in Chinese was Zhong lang 中郎 and Zhu Ying 朱應's was Xuanhua congshi 宣華從事. The term *xuanhua* 宣華 has the sense of "spreading or propagating [Chinese] civilization." The English titles are from Crespigny, *Men who Governed Han China*, 131–132, and the same author's *A Biographical Dictionary*, 1237, 1241. Nothing else is known about Kang Tai and Zhu Ying, although Kang's surname shows that he was Sogdian or of Sogdian origin. For ethnicons in Chinese

surnames—including Kang 康 for Sogdians and Zhu 竺 (as distinct from Zhu Ying's surname Zhu 朱) for Indians—see Zürcher, *Buddhist Conquest*, 281.

30. One hundred and twenty or 130 states, literally "a hundred and several tens of states" [*bai shu shi guo* 百數十國]. Yao, *Liang shu*, 783.

31. Kang Tai and Zhu Ying's journey must have started before 252, the year Sun Quan died, and could not have ended before Fan Xun became the king of Funan, since Fan Xun was ruling Funan during Kang Tai's visit there. According to *Nan Qi shu*, Fan Xun's predecessor Fan Zhan, who sent tribute to China in 243, reigned for a decade or so, and in that case Fan Xun would have become king no later than 252–253. (*Liang shu*, a later source, records that Fan Zhan ruled for twenty years, not ten, in which case Fan Xun might not have become king until the early 260s.) One complication is that according to *Liang shu*, Fan Xun did not send tribute to China until the 280s, suggesting that he might have become king somewhat later. *Jin shu* lists a tribute mission from Funan in 268 as well as missions in 285, 286, and 287, but without mentioning who sent them. Perhaps despite this Fan Xun sent his first tribute mission to China in 268 rather than in the 280s, and reigned for several decades from the 250s or 260s to the late 280s.

Another complicating factor is whether Fan Xun succeeded Fan Zhan immediately or after a period of time. Fan Zhan was killed by the assassin Chang, who was killed in turn by Fan Xun. The *Liang shu* account of the killing seems to suggest that Fan Xun acted swiftly, but if Chang did rule for a time, Fan Xun's accession might have been even later. Xiao, *Nan Qi shu*, 1014; Yao, *Liang shu*, 789; also Wang, "Nanhai Trade," 78–79. In Pelliot's view, the trip may have taken place between 245 and 250. Pelliot, "Fou-nan," 303. On the duration of the trip, the historian James Chin describes it as lasting twenty years, reflecting, he says, various views on the matter held by Chinese scholars. Chin, "Ports, Merchants, Chieftans, and Eunuchs," 222; also personal communication.

32. The traveling merchant's name was Jia Xiangli 家翔梨. For Kang Tai's comment on Jia Xiangli, see later in this chapter.

33. Yao, *Liang shu*, 783, 789, 798.

34. General for Pacifying the Waves: Fubo jiangjun 伏波將軍. The Hundred Yue (Bai yue 百越) was a general term for the peoples of the far south. The term Yue 越, which originally meant "very distant," came to be used during the Warring States period (656–221 BCE) as the name of a state in far southeast China, and from Han times onwards was applied to various peoples and cultures in the southernmost parts of China. Brindley, *Ancient China and the Yue*, 21–44.

Rinan 日南 was the southernmost commandery of China, established in Han times.

35. The Chinese name for the Roman Empire as given here and in later texts is Da Qin 大秦, generally thought to refer to the eastern Roman Empire. Likewise, the Chinese name Tianzhu 天竺, given here and in later texts, is generally agreed to refer to India or at least part of India. Wang, "Nanhai Trade," 73–74; Pelliot, *Notes on Marco Polo*, 439; Hudson, *Europe and China*, 83–85.

36. *Ganman* 干漫, also written *ganman* 干縵 and *duman* 都縵, seems to be a kind of breast-cloth. Pelliot notes that in Hokkien, *ganman* resembles the Malay term *kemban*, or woman's breast-cloth, a word still used today in Bahasa Melayu and Bahasa Indonesia. Misleadingly, the term *ganman* is usually translated into Chinese as *sarong*, despite the differences between *kemban* and *sarong*, and between both of these and the Cambodian *sampot*, which the *sarong* is sometimes confused with and which may be what is referred to here.

37. The Chinese word for envoy, *shi* 使, does not specify number, so here and in subsequent references to *shi* it is not clear how many people were involved. The name Andun, reprising a similar mention in *Hou Han shu*, has been taken to refer to the Roman emperor Marcus Aurelius Antoninus (r. 161–180 CE). It has been much cited in Western historical works as demonstrating that China and the Roman empire were directly in touch with one another. But according to *Hou Han shu*, the tribute bearers brought ivory, rhinoceros horn, and tortoiseshell—regional products that suggested they came from somewhere less distant than the Roman Empire. If so, they may have used Marcus Aurelius' name to bolster their status, rather than actually being sent by him. Fan et al., *Hou Han shu*, 2920; and Wang, "Nanhai Trade," 74, where Wang makes the point that the tribute goods were common ones, so that Marcus Aurelius' involvement must be in doubt.

38. Nothing is known about governor Wu Miao 吳邈, the merchant Qin Lun 秦論, or the officer Liu Xian 劉咸. Zhuge Ke 諸葛恪 hailed from an illustrious family; he was a nephew of Zhuge Liang 诸葛亮, renowned strategist of the Three Kingdoms state of Shu. Danyang 丹陽 was a city on the Yangzi River east of Jianye, present-day Nanjing; You 黝 and She 歙 were locations in eastern China; and Kuaiji 會稽 was a commandery in southeastern China.

After they are first mentioned in this passage, Sun Quan and Qin Lun are referred to by their given names only, as is customary in classical Chinese writings. I have added their surnames to make for easier reading.

39. The geographer Paul Wheatley argues that Juli 拘利 (Ki̯u lji- [K]) was another name for a polity on the Malay Peninsula variously called Juzhi 句稚, Jiuzhi 九稚, and Gouzhi 勾稚. Wheatley, "Malay Peninsula," 25–26. The great Indian river was clearly the Ganges. Coedès notes that the Indian king's name in Chinese was Maolun 茂論 (Mou-luan in Coedès, whose unacknowledged source was *Liang shu*), and plausibly suggests that it was the equivalent of Muruṇḍa, the name of a royal line ruling in northern India during this era. The Muruṇḍa were related to the Tokharians, called Yuezhi 月支 in Chinese. One of the Tokharians' chiefs founded the Kushan empire, which played a major role in the spread of Buddhism into Central Asia and China. Jacques suggests that the great river was the Indus rather than the Ganges, and that King Muruṇḍa was located in Gandhara, northwest of India rather than by the Ganges. But Jacques overlooks the fact that Su Wu traveled "directly northwest," a direction that would have taken him to the Ganges rather than the Indus. Coedès, *Indianized States*, 46; Yao, *Liang shu*, 798; Jacques, "China and Ancient Khmer History," 36. On the Yuezhi: Beckwith, *Empires of the Silk Road*, 84–85. On the Muruṇḍa: Kalia, *Bhubaneswar*, 17.

40. The name Chen Song 陳宋 may conceivably have referred to two envoys, Chen and Song, these being two common Chinese surnames. But the Indian king is unlikely to have sent Chinese, and the *Liang shu* text seems to indicate an individual called Chen Song and another person. The text reads, "two people, Chen Song and another" (Chen Song deng er ren 陳宋等二人). Yao, *Liang shu*, 798. The horses of Yuezhi or Tokharia were highly prized in China; this is the only mention in Chinese sources of horses in Funan.

41. Dudbridge, *Lost Books*.

42. On the history and nature of *lei shu* 類書, see Wilkinson, *Chinese History*, 1079–1089. Little remains of Zhu Ying's work, but it is listed in *Sui shu* and subsequent histories as *Funan yi wu zhi* 扶南異物志 [*Annals of Strange Things in Funan*]. Wei et al., *Sui shu*, 984.

43. As noted earlier, Kang Tai's work seems to have consisted of one book with several titles or else several books with one or more titles. The three titles most commonly associated with him are *Funan tu su*, *Wu shi waiguo zhuan*, and *Funan zhuan*. *Taiping yulan* describes him twelve times as the author of *Funan tu su*, three times with reference to Funan; it also mentions him, but only once, as the author of *Wu shi waiguo zhuan*. It mentions *Funan zhuan* a number of times, but never in association with Kang Tai's name. Another source, the early sixth-century *Shui jing zhu* [*A Commentary on the Classic of Waterways*], names Kang eight times as the author of *Funan zhuan*, and once as the author of *Funan ji* [*Record of Funan*], a work it attributes elsewhere to the fifth-century traveler Zhu Zhi.

44. Sources by passage are as follows.

- For passage nos. 1 and 13: Li, *Shui jing zhu*, 835, 7.
- For nos. 2–4, 6–12, and 16–20: Li et al., *Taiping yulan*, 4348, 4347, 4103, 3485, 3485, 3180, 3411, 1599, 3485, 3955, 2881, 3184, 3392, 3105, 1589. There are similar but shorter versions of passage no. 10 in *Bei tang shu chao* and *Shi lei fu*. For passage no. 12, the Song facsimile edition of *Taiping yulan* cites *Wu zhi yueguo zhuan* 吳志曰外國傳, clearly a copyist's error for *Wu shi waiguo zhuan* 吴时外國傳, one of the works attributed to Kang Tai. There is a shorter version of passage no. 16 in *Sou shen ji*.
- For no. 5, Yu, *Bei Tang shu chao*, *juan* 151, 6 verso; for 扶風 read 扶南.
- For no. 14, Ouyang, *Yi wen lei ju*, 1585.
- For no. 15, [Gan Bao et al.,] *Sou shen ji* and *Shi shuo xin yu*, 28. This *Sou shen ji* passage does not cite an earlier source; it is given here because the passage as a whole closely resembles passage nos. 16 and 17 as well as a shorter passage in *Taiping yulan*. Li et al., *Taiping yulan*, 4168.
- Passage nos. 1, 9, 10, and 12 to 20 are given (although not in the same order) in Chen and Tan, ed. "Funan ji 扶南記", 3–18.

45. It is not clear why Kang mentions Linyi as his point of reference, since while Linyi was earlier the southernmost district of Rinan commandery, by his time it was an independent state south of Rinan. As for the Rinan port of Lurong 盧容, according to *Shui jing zhu* Lurong was a river in Rinan that merged with the river Shouling 壽泠 shortly before flowing out to sea. The ?sixth-century Daoist work *Tai qing jin ye shen dan jing* 太清金液神丹經 [*Scripture of the Divine Elixir of the Gold Liquor of Great Clarity*] refers to the port of Shouling (see chapter two); perhaps Lurong and Shouling were two names for the same place. Li, *Shui jing zhu*, 833–834; [attr. Ge,] *Tai qing jin ye shen dan jing*, 14.

The port of Lurong seems to have been much used. Quoting *Linyi ji*, *Shui jing zhu* is apparently referring to Lurong when it describes a place that the ships of "many states ford and pass through" [*zhong guo jin jing* 眾國津逕]. Like other travellers, Kang and Zhu could have made Jiaozhi in the Red River Delta their starting-off point, but perhaps sea journeys in and out of Jiaozhi were made hazardous by coastal rocks, making Lurong a more convenient option. According to the historian Li Tana, "until the Tang dynasty the [Tonkin] Gulf was largely avoided in travel between Jiaozhi and China because of the huge rocks hidden along the coast . . . This obstacle was only overcome in the ninth century, when the rocks were removed." Even after the Tang rocks impeded shipping. According to *Song hui yao jigao* [*A Draft Edition of the Essential Documents and Regulations of the Song Dynasty*], rocky outcrops southeast of Jiaozhi still posed a hazard to shipping in Song times. Li, *Shui jing zhu*, 835; Li, "A View from the Sea," 84; Liu et al., *Song hui yao jigao*, 9831–9832.

46. According to Wheatley, Dukun 都昆 was a state located on the Malay Peninsula and can perhaps be identified with Qudukun 屈都昆, mentioned later in *Liang shu*. Wheatley, "Malay Peninsula," 24–25, 31. (For *Liang shu* on Qudukun, see chapter three.) The statement here that "Dukun is in Funan"—contradicted by the following passage on Dukun, which locates it at some distance from Funan—suggests something is missing from the first statement, which should perhaps read "Dukun is a dependency of Funan," or something of the kind.

The term "mint" is a loose rendition of *huo xiang* 霍香 (also written 藿香), *lophanthus rugosus* or Chinese patchouli, whose minty aroma made it attractive for use as a perfume and a medicine. Stuart, *Chinese Materia Medica*, 485; Yule and Burnell, *Hobson-Jobson*, 683–684; Li et al., *Taiping yulan*, 4347.

47. The Great Sea, Zhanghai 漲海 (also called Dahai 大海), seems to refer to Nanhai 南海, the Southern Sea, or perhaps the southern part of Nanhai and the waters beyond it. The Sea Drum was very large; its width of a hundred *zhang* 仗 (poles) was the equivalent of roughly 800 (US) feet. A *zhang* was ten *chi* 尺, or Chinese feet; at this time, one Chinese foot was equal to nine to ten (US) inches. (According to Wilkinson, one Chinese foot is estimated to have been equal to about nine (US) inches in Han and Three Kingdoms times, closer to ten (US) inches during the Six Kingdoms, twelve or so (US) inches during the Tang and Song dynasties, and nearly fourteen inches during the Yuan. Wilkinson, *Chinese History*, 612–613.)

48. Zhuzhuanbo 諸轉薄 was probably Java. Zhuzhuanbo may be an alternative for Zhubo 諸薄 (Tśi̯wo b'âk [K]), a place Kang Tai refers to several times. Pelliot tentatively identifies Zhubo with Java, noting that in other later sources the name also appears in another form, Dubo 杜薄 (D'uo: b'âk [K]). The late eighth-century *Tong dian* [*A Comprehensive History of Institutions*] describes Dubo as an island several weeks' sea journey east of Funan, with ten or so city-states (*guo cheng* 國城), each ruled by a king. Another name for Zhubo seems to have been Shepo 闍婆. In Wang Gungwu's view, Shepo referred to Java and, from about 820, to the state of Heling 訶陵 on Java. Shepo occurs in the twelfth-century writings of Zhou Qufei (discussed in chapter eight). It also occurs in the writings of Ma Huan (c. 1380–1460), aide to the Ming admiral Zheng He, who records that Shepo was an old name for Java. Ma Huan himself used the term Zhaowa 爪哇, the Chinese name for Java still used today. Pelliot, "Deux itinéraires," 269–273; Du, *Tong dian*, 5103; Wang, "Nanhai Trade," 127, 132–133; Ma, *Ying ya sheng lan*, 16.

The identity of Juji 巨迹, also apparently called Juli 拘利 and Juyan 巨延 (as in *Taiping yulan*), is not known. Li et al., *Taiping yulan*, 3502.

49. The location of Linyang 林陽 is not known for sure; perhaps it was in present-day Myanmar. The third-century writer Wan Zhen more or less repeats Kang Tai's report, describing Linyang as being seven thousand li to the west of Funan. Two centuries later, the traveler Zhu Zhi remarks that Linyang was two thousand li from Jinchen 金陳, and that it was only possible to travel from Linyang to Jinchen overland "by cart or by horse, there being no way by water." Li, *Shui jing zhu*, quoting Zhu Zhi's *Funan ji* 扶南記, 5. For Wan Zhen and Zhu Zhi, see later in this chapter.

Jinchen 金陳, also known as Jinlin 金林 or 金鄰, seems to have been on the mainland west or northwest of Funan. According to *Taiping yulan*, "Jinlin, also called Jinchen, is perhaps two thousand li or so from Funan. Silver comes out of the ground, and the people greatly enjoy hunting large elephants. They get to ride on the backs of the living ones, and take the tusks of those that are dead." Li et al., *Taiping yulan*, 3502. *Tong dian* mentions a great bay of Jinlin that travelers from Funan crossed in order to go south to Dukun and Juli, both probably places on the Malay Peninsula. If Jinlin was west or northwest of Funan, Linyang could have been farther west, in the center or south of present-day Myanmar. If so, seven thousand li—or three thousand five hundred kilometers—overestimated the distance by a factor of two. Du, *Tong dian*, 5103.

50. The term used here for monks is *shamen* 沙門, the Chinese transliteration of the Sanskrit word *śramaṇa*. *Śramaṇa* originally meant "seeker" or "ascetic," and came to be used in China as a term for Buddhist monk. The six days of Buddhist fasting were (and are) the eighth, fourteenth, fifteenth, twenty-third, twenty-ninth, and thirtieth of each month. The term used for perfumes and flowers, *xiang hua* 香華, has Buddhist connotations, and suggests that they were for placing before statues of the Buddha.

51. It is not clear where and what Piqian 毗騫 was. Wolters suggests it was "a remote place in the hinterland of Funan," but *Liang shu* calls it an island in the sea. The Chinese term for the gifts bequeathed (*yi* 遺) by the king of Funan—presumably the deceased king Fan Shiman—to the king of Piqian is the unusual word *duoluo* 多羅. *Liang shu* defines *duoluo* as a kind of cup, and *Sui shu* describes it as a gold leaf. Perhaps it was a gold-leaf cup. The state of Piqian was famous for its plentiful gold and its gifts of gold cups and plates to Funan. The seventh-century scholar Ouyang Xun quotes *Funan zhuan* to the

effect that "in the state of Piqian eating utensils are all made of gold," and *Liang shu* records Piqian's gifts of gold plates to Funan. So it is odd for the king of Funan to have bequeathed (or presented, an alterative meaning of 遺 when pronounced *wei*) gold cups to the king of Piqian. Perhaps the passage is garbled, with the names of the two kings inverted. Wolters, *Early Indonesian Commerce*, 260; Yao, *Liang shu*, 788; Ouyang, *Yi wen lei ju*, citing *Funan zhuan*, 1424. For the *Liang shu* account of Piqian, see chapter three.

52. The boats were twelve *xun* 尋 long, and a *xun* was seven to eight *chi* 尺 (Chinese feet). A *chi* being about nine (US) inches at the time, the boats were sizeable—some sixty to seventy (US) feet long and perhaps five (US) feet wide. They carried one hundred, fifty, or forty-two *ren* 人, "people." *Ren* is not gender-specific; later bas reliefs on Angkor temples seem to show boats carrying men. Wilkinson, *Chinese History*, 611–613.

53. Liuye: 柳葉 (Li̯əu: i̯äp [K]), meaning "willow leaf." Her name is given as such in *Nan Qi shu*, *Liang shu*, and other major sources. In *Jin shu* it is inverted to Yeliu 葉柳, meaning "leafy willow." Willows grow in cool and temperate climates, and are not known to have grown in Cambodia; this suggests that Liuye was a transliteration of a local name. Vickery notes that if this is so, it would be a name similar to other names such as Zhenla (Tśi̯ĕn lâp [K]) and Linyi (Li̯əm* ·i̯əp [K]) as transcribed into Chinese, "where the ancient Chinese shows that the local names ended in syllable final /p/, a common phonological trait in Khmer and other Southeast Asian languages." Vickery, "Funan Reviewed," 110.

Unlike Liuye, the Chinese characters for the name Hun Shen 混慎 (Yuən: Ź̯i̯ĕn- [K]) and its variants, like those for the names of other early Funan kings, have no obvious meaning. In the passages by Kang Tai, Hun Shen and Hun Dian 混滇 (Yuən: ? [K]) are clearly the same person, since in their written forms the two names differ only slightly. In later sources, the name takes two other forms, Hun Tian 混填 (Yuən: D'ien [K]) and Hun Kui 混潰 (Yuən: Yuâi- [K]). The name Hun Tian occurs in *Nan Qi shu*, *Liang shu*, and *Nan shi*; the name Hun Kui occurs in *Jin shu*, *Tong dian*, and the twelfth-century *Tong zhi*.

In all four variants of the name, the first character is the same, while the forms of the second character are similar and perhaps differ only because of copyists' errors. As to which form of the name is authentic, Kang Tai's version of the Liuye story is the earliest chronologically, but probably went through various redactions before appearing as a fragment in *Taiping yulan*, with the possibility of copying errors. This being the case, the most dependable early form of the name may be Hun Tian, the form found in *Nan Qi shu*. I have therefore referred to the person throughout to Hun Tian.

"Serving the gods" is a translation of the phrase *shi shen* 事神, in which the word *shen* 神 can mean either god or gods. I have followed Yao Silian, the editor of *Liang shu*, who clearly treats *shen* as plural, since he replaces the phrase *shi shen* with the more explicit phrase *shi gui shen* 事鬼神, "serving spirits and gods." Pelliot, "Quelques textes chinois," 245–246; Coedès, *The Indianized States*, 37; Yao, *Liang shu*, 788.

54. The state of Mofu 模趺 is not mentioned elsewhere and has not been identified; nor has the state of Wuwen 烏文. The use of the word *chu* 初, meaning "originally" or "previously", in the sentence about Wuwen suggests that Wuwen was the place Hun Shen first set out from. In their later accounts of the Hun Tian story, *Nan Qi shu* and *Liang shu* mention a third state, Jiao 激 (now also pronounced Ji) or 徼, rather than Wuwen, as Hun Tian's place of origin. The two histories give slightly different versions of the character for Jiao but are clearly referring to the same place. *Nan Qi shu* does not say where Jiao is; *Liang shu* describes it as being south of Funan. Otherwise, Jiao has not been identified. Pelliot considers possible identities and locations for Jiao as well as for Mofu and Wuwen, but does not reach any conclusions, other than tentatively identifying Mofu with Hengdie 横跌 on the east coast of the Malay Peninsula, on the basis of the Chinese characters for Hengdie and Mofu being similar. Xiao, *Nan Qi shu*, 1014; Yao, *Liang shu*, 788. Pelliot, "Quelques textes chinois," 247–249.

Here and in subsequent versions of Hun Tian's story, the ship he traveled to Funan in was *bo* 舶, a term that in Needham's view was used specifically for a junk or oceangoing ship. Needham, *Science and Civilization, Vol. IV, Part III*, 449–450.

55. For kings Pankuang 盤況, Fan Zhan 范旃, and Fan Xun 范尋 (Fan Xun being the king during Kang and Zhu's visit), see the accounts in *Nan Qi shu* and *Liang shu* in chapters two and three. The state of Tanxiang 嘾楊 where Jia Xiangli came from is unknown. His name was either Jia Xiangli 家翔梨 or just Xiang Li 翔梨, since *jia* 家 could either be a surname or read with the preceding character *ren* 人 to mean *renjia* 人家, "person."

As used here and later, the term Hindu is anachronistic, but is employed as a convenience to refer to the Indian pantheon of deities and associated beliefs. India's *dao fa* 道法, the law of the Way or dharma, could refer here to either Hindu or Buddhist beliefs, or both.

56. The spurs Fan Xun used on his fighting cocks were fake in the sense that they were artificially made and thus distinct from the natural, bony spurs on the birds' feet.

57. The mountain may have been called Great Creature (Da chong 大蟲) or Great Spirit (Da ling 大靈) because it was thought to be home to a god or to have magic qualities. *Chong* 蟲 usually means "insect" but can also be used more broadly to mean "creature."

58. Fan Xun's crocodiles and tigers, described here in a passage from the fourth-century *Sou shen ji*, also feature in shorter passages in the tenth-century encyclopedias *Taiping yulan* and *Taiping huanyu ji*. The *Taiping yulan* entry reads, "Large crocodiles are twenty to thirty feet long. They have four feet and look like [giant] geckos. They often swallow up people and eat them. Fan Xun, king of Funan, has lured some into being captured and put them in a water-filled ditch. If he is angry with someone, he ties them up to feed to the crocodiles. If they should die for their offense, the crocodiles eat them. If they are not eaten, they are released and are regarded as having committed no offense." Li et al., *Taiping yulan*, citing *Wushi waiguo zhuan*, 4168. The fact that *Taiping yulan* cites *Wu shi waiguo zhuan* suggests that *Wu shi waiguo zhuan* may also have been the source for the entry in *Sou shen ji*.

59. "Chopper" is a rough rendition of the rare term *zhi* 鑕, the instrument that in China was used to cut someone in two as a severe judicial punishment.

60. The repetitious and overlapping nature of the accounts of trial by ordeal may be the result of the two principal sources for these accounts, *Sou shen ji* (for the passage on tigers and crocodiles) and *Taiping yulan* (for the three following passages), drawing on different original sources. *Taiping yulan* cites *Funan zhuan* for two of its three passages and *Wu shi waiguo zhuan* for the third, while *Sou shen ji* seems to draw on *Wu shi waiguo zhuan*. This in turn suggests that *Funan zhuan* and *Wu shi waiguo zhuan* were two works by Kang Tai, rather than one work with two titles.

61. The term used for "decorated girdles of hide" (*gouluo dai* 鉤絡帶) is unusual. It is mentioned in *Taiping yulan*, which cites the fourth–fifth century scholar Zhang Bo 張勃 as saying that *gouluo dai* was a girdle made from hide used to decorate a horse's saddle. Variants for both the characters making up the word *gouluo* 鉤絡 are found in other sources; the term may be a transliteration of an unidentified foreign word. The remark about Funan people wearing girdles could suggest that they wore other clothes as well, in contrast with Kang Tai and Zhu Ying's remark in *Liang shu* about the people of Funan going around naked. Perhaps their comment should not be taken too literally. *Liang shu* also mentions that people in the nearby state of Langyaxiu wore belts (*luodai* 絡帶) made of gold cords.

Centuries later, girdles were an important article of clothing in the Kingdom of Angkor, though by no means the only one, as shown by statuary in Bayon, Angkor Wat, and other Angkor locations. Li et al., *Taiping yulan*, 3105; Yao, *Liang shu*, 789, 796; Boisselier, *La statuaire khmère*, 132–136.

62. *Chan* 蟬 (źi̯än [K]) means "cicada." In early Chinese Daoist theory, "cicada change" (*chan hua* 蟬化) refers to a form of magical transformation. But here źi̯än seems to be a transliteration of an unidentifiable local Funan term for a local practice. Another possible explanation, suggested by Warren Sun (personal communication), is that a giant cicada endemic to the region is said to secrete a sweat-like substance.

63. Li et al., *Taiping yulan*, citing *Waiguo zhuan*, 3502, 3482, 3482, 3482. The title *Waiguo zhuan* 外國傳 resembles the title of one of the works associated with Kang Tai, *Wu shi waiguo zhuan* 吳時外國傳. But it is also the title of works by two fifth-century Buddhist monks, Zhimeng 智猛 (?–453) and Tanjing 曇景 (479–502), so some or all of the fragments attributed to *Waiguo zhuan* in *Taiping yulan* may be their work rather than Kang Tai's. On Zhimeng, see Gernet, *History of Chinese Civilization*, 223. On Tanjing, see Wei et al., *Sui shu*, 985.

64. As noted earlier, Jinchen—also called Jinlin—may have been located west or northwest of Funan. Thanks to Kang Tai, perhaps, its name had some currency in third-century China, being one of the exotic places mentioned alongside Funan in a famous prose poem by the poet Zuo Si, discussed later in this chapter.

65. The carvings and engravings found on people's residences were almost certainly on wood, at least in part, since as *Nan Qi shu* confirms the people used wood to build their houses. But engravings may also have been on metal. In the phrase "carved patterns and engravings" (diaowen kelou 雕文刻鏤) the character *lou* 鏤 has a "metal" radical, and was defined in the Han dictionary *Er ya* to mean "carving metal."

66. For more on the kings' hunting habits, see the description by the third century scholar Wan Zhen later in this chapter.

67. "Handkerchiefs:" *shoujin* 手巾. On parrots and their popularity in China, see Schafer, *The Vermilion Bird*, 239; also appendix five, on the pleasure the great Tang emperor Taizong apparently took in receiving parrots from Linyi. Kang Tai does not make clear how the exchange of products, presumably between Funan and the locations mentioned, took place. Barter and cash transactions were both likely to have been used. Coins from Iran, India, and elsewhere have been unearthed at Óc Eo, and the Vietnamese archaeologist Lương Ninh reports that coins found at Óc Eo include coins from Funan itself. According to Ninh, the French archaeologist Louis Malleret neglected to analyze these when he first excavated sites at Óc Eo in the 1940s. Ninh, "Óc Eo," 44; Malleret, *L'archéologie du delta du Mékong*.

68. Yao, *Liang shu*, 798.

69. Yao, *Liang shu*, 788.

70. "Nüren wei zhu" 女人為主.

71. Vickery, *Society, Economics, and Politics*, 41, 267, 347, 349, 388; Gaudes, "Kauṇḍinya, Prey Thaong, and the 'Nāgī Somā'", 341–343. Īśānavarman is referred in *Sui shu*'s seventh-century account of Zhenla; see chapter six.

72. Quoted in Vickery, "Funan Reviewed," 101.

73. "Ainsi la légende de Kauṇḍinya et de Somā est originaire du Founan." Finot takes the story of Liuye and Hun Tian from the version told in *Nan Qi shu*. Finot, "Sur quelques traditions Indochinoises", 32–33. The stele was at Mỹ Sơn. (The earlier ms version of this book mistakenly gave another location.)

74. The identification is made, for example, in Coomaraswamy, *History of Indian and Indonesian Art*, 180; Coedès, *Indianized States*, 38–39; and Needham, *Science and Civilization in China, Vol. IV, Part III*, 449. Not everyone has subscribed to it, however. In her 2008 study of female power in Cambodia, Trudy Jacobsen perceptively distinguishes between the Liuye-Hun Tian and Soma-Kauṇḍinya legends, relating only the first to Funan. Jacobsen, *Lost Goddesses*, 19–20.

75. For (1) *Liang shu* on Panpan 槃槃, also written 盤盤 (in a passage missing from the Zhonghua shuju edition of *Liang shu*); and (2) the fifth-to-sixth-century traveler Zhu Zhi on Dunxun 頓遜, see Li et al., *Taiping yulan*, 3487, 3489. For Zhu Zhi, see later in this chapter. The locations of Dunxun and Panpan are discussed in chapter three.

76. Coedès goes further, arguing without any justification that Hun Tian was connected to an influential brahmin clan called Kauṇḍinya based in Mysore around the second century CE. Pelliot, "Fou-nan," 290–291, and "Quelques textes chinois," 245; Coedès, *Indianized States*, 30.

77. Vickery, "Funan Reviewed," 108–109, 114.

78. *Fan*: 范. Vickery, *Society, Economics, and Politics*, 50, 190–205.

79. *Fu*: 賦; *San du fu*: 三都賦; Zuo Si: 左思. Knechtges, "From the Eastern Han," 190. See also the translation of Zuo Si's *fu* in Xiao, *Wen Xuan*, vol. 1, 377–379. On the date of composition of the poem: Nienhauser, *Indiana Companion*, 806.

80. Xiao, *Wen xuan*, 106. Xiao Tong, crown prince of the ruling house of the Liang dynasty, compiled *Wen xuan*—including Zuo Si's "*Fu* on the Capital of Wu" [*Wu du fu* 吳都賦]—between 526 and 531, the year he died.

81. "Riyueqichu" 日月其除 from *Shijing* 詩經 [*The Classic of Poetry*]. Legge, *The Chinese Classics IV*, 174.

82. "Stately banners" (sigu 祀姑) were a form of royal banner associated with the state of Wu. See the entry under *sigu* in Luo et al., *Hanyu da cidian*; also the commentary by Li Shan 李善 (630–689), the early, respected Chinese commentator in *Wen xuan*, in Xiao, *Wen xuan*, 106.

83. Juqu 具區 was a marshland to the west of Wu, identified with Lake Tai in present-day Jiangsu. Xiao, *Wen xuan*, 106, 378.

According to *Taiping yulan*, Wuhu 烏滸 was a place of cannibals in the frontier region between Guangzhou and Jiaozhou. Catherine Churchman suggests that its inhabitants may have been precursors to the people known in Chinese sources as Li and Lao, who in her view developed their own enduring bronze drum culture in the same region. Li et al., *Taiping yulan*, 3479–3480; Churchman, *The People between the Rivers*, 86–87.

Nothing is known about Langhuang 狼荒. Huang should be written with the 月 radical, but this character is not available to print.

84. Commenting on Funan in this prose-poem, Li Shan makes the notable remark that the people of Funan "are especially talented and ingenious, unlike the other southern foreigners" (*te you cai qiao, bu yu zhong yi tong* 特有才巧不與眾夷同). Xiao, *Wen xuan*, 106.

85. Xitu 西屠 and Heichi 黑齒 are said by *Taiping yulan* to be two names for the same state, located beyond the bronze or copper pillars at "the southernmost extremity of China." The pillars were placed there to mark the extent of Han rule by the Han general Ma Yuan 馬援. According to *Taiping yulan*, Xitu/Heichi was a small state with ten or so dependencies, while the name Heichi, meaning "black teeth," derived from the fact that the people blackened their teeth by cleaning them with a certain type of grass. Li et al., *Taiping yulan*, 3502. For more on Xitu, evidently the home of soldiers in Ma Yuan's army who stayed behind, see appendix five.

As we have seen, Jinlin was located to the west or northwest of Funan.

86. Daner 儋耳 was one of the Han dynasty's southernmost commanderies, and if Xiang 象 refers to Xianglin 象林, which is likely, it was the Han dynasty's southernmost district, in the process of becoming the independent state of Linyi.

87. Funan: written as 夫南 rather than 扶南, the pronunciation for both being the same. On prose poems or *fu* 賦 (a different character from the *fu* of Funan): Idema and Haft, *Guide to Chinese Literature*, 109.

88. On Zuo Si's research: Knechtges, "From the Eastern Han," 190. Regarding Zuo Si's lack of knowledge of Funan: the only proviso is the fact that Zuo Si portrays the ruler of Funan riding on horseback. We know from Wan Zhen that the king of Funan went hunting and rode on elephants to do

so. And we know from *Liang shu* that in the third century, King Fan Zhan received a gift of fine horses from central Asia. Conceivably Zuo Si was aware of these reports.

89. Wan Zhen 萬震's name, the title of his book—*Nanzhou yi wu zhi* 南州異物志 [*Annals of Strange Things in the Southern Regions*]—and his official appointment are listed in Wei et al., *Sui shu*, 983. Governor: *Taishou* 太守. Hucker, *Dictionary of Official Titles*, 482.

90. There is an official record of Kang Tai and Zhu Ying having traveled abroad, and Zhu Zhi (see the end of this chapter) wrote about seeing something abroad firsthand. But there is no record of Wan Zhen making a foreign journey.

91. Rhinoceroses, elephants, skulls, swimmers, ships with cargo, and boats sailing with the wind are mentioned in Li et al., *Taiping yulan*, 3954, 3956, 1727, 1827/3568, 3412, and 3419, respectively. *Taiping yulan* sources all these fragments from *Wan Zhen nanzhou yi wu zhi* 萬震南州異物志 [*Wan Zhen's Annals of Strange Things in the Southern Regions*], except for the passages on ships and boats, which it sources from a book bearing the same title, *Nanzhou yi wu zhi* 南州異物志, but without Wan Zhen's name.

92. *Taiping yulan* describes it variously as *Wan Zhen nanzhou yi wu zhi* 萬震南州異物志, *Wan Zhen nanfang yi wu zhi* 萬震南方異物志 [both titles meaning *Wan Zhen's Annals of Strange Things in the South*], *Wan Zhen yi wu zhi* 萬震異物志 [*Wan Zhen's Annals of Strange Things*], and *Wan Zhen Nanzhou Rinan zhuan* 萬震南州日南傳 [*Wan Zhen's Record of the Southern Region and Rinan*]. As with Kang Tai's work, it is not clear whether there was one book with several titles or several books. The name most often cited in *Taiping yulan* and the name listed in *Sui shu* and subsequent standard histories is *Nanzhou yi wu zhi*, so it is the name used here.

93. Apart from *Taiping yulan*, several other sixth- to ninth-century collections and encyclopedias include references to *Nanzhou yi wu zhi*, but *Taiping yulan* is much the fullest source. For a first attempt to gather together the fragments of Wan Zhen's writings, including short passages on fifteen states, see Wan, *Nanzhou yi wu zhi*, edited by Chen Zhifu 陳直夫. Unfortunately, Chen's edition contains only one entry on Funan.

94. For passage nos. 1–3 and 5–6: Li et al., *Taiping yulan*, citing *Nanzhou yi wu zhi*, 3482, 3485, 3489, 4348, 3501.

For passage no. 4: Ouyang, *Yi wen lei ju*, 1674.

95. "Officers in charge" (*guanzhang* 官長) is an old term for the top-ranking official, used here for the various dependencies (*zhu shu* 諸屬). When *Sui shu* describes comparable officials in Zhenla, it uses the term *bu shuai* 部帥 (regional leaders).

96. For a discussion of the meaning of Kunlun 崑崙, 昆侖 (kuən li̯uĕn [K]), see later in this chapter.

97. As we have seen, Linyang may have been in the center or south of present-day Myanmar. In this case, seven thousand li consderably overestimates of the distance.

98. Dianxun 典遜 is a significant location that Wan Zhen is the first to mention. Dianxun is clearly an alternative form of the more commonly occurring name Dunxun 頓遜, and was probably in the north of the Malay Peninsula. *Liang shu* uses both names.

Liang shu describes King Fan Shiman with the same words that Wan Zhen uses, but records that he brought to submission ten or so neighboring states, not just Dunxun/Dianxun. Yao, *Liang shu*, 788.

99. "King of Funan" can also be read "kings of Funan," since *wang* 王 (king, monarch) can be singular or plural. Since Wan Zhen was a contemporary or near-contemporary of Kang Tai, the assumption must be that he is referring here to Fan Xun, the ruler of Funan during Kang Tai's visit there.

100. In the original Chinese, several parts of this passage about people who resemble animals are written in smaller script, indicating later comments; they have been omitted here. Two points from the comments are worth noting, however: (1) the people are said to live to the east of Funan; (2) their white teeth are contrasted with the teeth of people in other parts of Funan and beyond, which are said to be blackened with lacquer. (The phrase used for other parts of Funan and beyond is literally "beyond Funan" [Funan yiwai 扶南以外], but must have the sense here of "in the rest of Funan and beyond".) This is the only report of the inhabitants of Funan blackening their teeth.

101. This is according to Wilkinson, who suggests that half a kilometer may have been approximately the length of a *li* throughout imperial times, except during the Yuan dynasty, when it may have been shorter. But he cautions that while this equivalence has been customary in British and American writings on China, "the *li* was never a very exact measure." Wilkinson, *Chinese History*, 612.

102. For the accounts of Funan in *Tai qing jin ye shen dan jing*, see chapter two. "Rulers and high officials:" *junzhang* 君長.

103. Pelliot, "Deux itinéraires", 218–222; Pelliot, *Notes on Marco Polo*, 599–600; Chen, "*Funan shi chu tan*", 557–558; also Luo et al., *Hanyu da cidian*, entry under *kunlun* 昆侖.

104. Li et al., *Taiping yulan*, 3489, citing *Zhu Zhi Funan ji* [*Zhu Zhi's Record of Funan*].

105. Li et al., *Taiping yulan*, citing *Liang shu*, 3488. "*Qi yan kunlun gulong sheng xiangjin gu huo you wei wei gulong zhe*" 其言崑崙古龍聲相近故或有謂為古龍者. This passage is not in the Zhonghua shuju edition of *Liang shu*.

106. Li et al., *Taiping yulan*, citing *Sui shu*, 3482. The Chinese original reads, "*Qi wang xing Gulong zhuguo duo xing Gulong xun qilao yan Kunlun wu xing shi Kunlun zhi e*" 其王姓古龍諸國多姓古龍訊耆老言崑崙无姓氏崑崙之訛. The passage is not in the Zhonghua shuju edition of *Sui shu*.

107. "*Sui shi qi (guo) wang xing Gulong*" 隋時其（國）王姓古龍. For the *Tong dian* and *Tong zhi* comments, see chapter four.

108. Vickery, *Society, Economics, and Politics*, 188–189. Vickery notes that despite this translation of the term, its precise usage is uncertain. See also Pelliot, "Deux itinéraires," 229–230.

109. Vickery, "Funan Reviewed," 103.

110. Vickery, *Society, Economics, and Politics*, 185–187, 196–197, 217–219, citing views put forward by George Coedès and Claude Jacques.

111. *Funan ji*: 扶南記. Zhu Zhi's name is given as 竺枝 in *Shui jing zhu*, and 竺芝 in *Taiping yulan*. Another version of his name may be Zhu Jian'an 竺建安. *Liang shu* cites a comment on the state of Piqian by someone called Zhu Jian'an in a work entitled *Funan yinan ji* 扶南以南記 [*Record of Funan and Places to the South of It*]. Yao, *Liang shu*, 715. As Wheatley notes, the date of *Funan ji*'s composition can be roughly deduced from the fact that extracts from it are cited in *Shui jing zhu*, whose author Li Daoyuan died in 527. The extracts include mention of the 446 attack by the Chinese general Tan Hezhi 檀和之 on Linyi. So *Funan ji* was composed some time between these two dates.Wheatley, "Malay Peninsula," 34.

112. *Shui jing zhu* is one of two main sources for *Funan ji*, the other being *Taiping yulan*. The entries on Zhu Zhi are in Li, *Shui jing zhu*, 5, 35, 835, 840; and Li et al., *Taiping yulan*, 3489, 3501.

113. Zhu: 竺; Tianzhu: 天竺. Zürcher, *Buddhist Conquest of China*, 281.

114. Cited in Li, *Shui jing zhu*, 5. As noted earlier, Linyang may have been in the center or south of present-day Myanmar, while Jinchen, also called Jinlin, was west of Funan.

115. Li, *Shui jing zhu*, 840.

116. Cited in Li et al., *Taiping yulan*, 3489. *Taiping yulan* here gives Zhu's work yet another name, *Funan shi ji* 扶南史紀 [*Record of the History of Funan*].

Chapter Two

1. Taghbač is Christopher Beckwith's transliteration of the name, Tuoba 拓拔 in Chinese. In 386 the Tuoba in northern China established a dynasty known as Later Wei 後魏 (386–534). Rossabi, *A History of China*, 102; Beckwith, *Empires of the Silk Road*, 103.

2. The Eastern Jin was established in Jiankang 建康 following the Western Jin (265–316), which briefly reunited China before being driven out of north China by invaders. Eastern and Western Jin together comprised the Jin dynasty. With the Three Kingdoms state of Wu, the Eastern Jin, Liu Song, Nan qi, Liang, and Chen dynasties are collectively known as the Six Dynasties, all of them having Jiankang as their capital.

3. *Ethnie* is the sociologist Anthony Smith's term. Smith uses it to describe people with common ancestry myths and historical memories, elements of shared culture, some link with an historic territory, and some measure of solidarity, at least among their elites. Smith, *Nations and Nationalism*, 57.

4. Gernet, *A History of Chinese Civilization*, 202–237, esp. 262.

5. For what we know about the absorption of Funan by Zhenla, see chapter six.

6. The proper name of the Liu Song dynasty was the Song dynasty, but it is often called Liu Song after the family name of its founder Liu Yu 劉裕 to distinguish it from the later and much more illustrious Song dynasty (960–1279). Strictly speaking, *Jin shu* is not just a history of a southern court, since it covers both the short-lived Western Jin, with its capital at Luoyang, and its successor the Eastern Jin in Jiankang.

7. Gardiner, "Standard Histories," 48–49. Also Durrant, "Histories," 197–198.

8. For more on *Nan Qi shu*'s author Xiao Zixian 蕭子顯 and the *Nan Qi shu* account of Funan, see later in this chapter.

9. For the pre-eminent role played by Mahayana Buddhism in Funan by the early sixth century, see Wang, "The Buddhist Connection," 283. Also Chen, "*Pañcavārṣika* Assemblies," 45–46.

10. *Bao pu zi*: 抱朴子; *Tai qing jin ye shen dan jing*: 太清金液神丹經.

11. Zürcher, *Buddhist Conquest of China*, 18–80; Wang, "Nanhai Trade," 90–103; Sen, "Buddhism and the Maritime Crossings," 39–51. Also Wright, *Buddhism in Chinese History*, 42–64.

12. Sen, "Buddhism and the Maritime Crossings," 44.

13. Yijing 義凈, *Da Tang xiyu qiu fa gao seng zhuan* 大唐西域求法高僧傳 [*Great Tang Dynasty Biographies of Eminent Monks who went to the Western Regions in Search of the Dharma*], 247–252. Also Sen, "Yijing and the Buddhist Cosmopolis," 345–368.

14. [Faxian, 法顯] *Fo guo ji* 佛國記 [*A Record of Buddhist States*], 234–243. Also Sen, "Buddhism and the Maritime Crossings," 45; [Faxian,] *A Record of Buddhistic Kingdoms*, 111–115.

15. Yepoti: 耶婆提. [Faxian,] *Fo guo ji*, 238–239; Sen, "Buddhism and the Maritime Crossings," 45; Wang, "Nanhai Trade," 84–85.

16. One such individual, to be considered in the context of *Nan Qi shu* later in this chapter, was Nāgasena (Nagaxian 那伽仙), the Indian Buddhist monk who traveled to south China, then to Funan, then back to China in 484 as an envoy of King Kauṇḍinya Jayavarman to the Southern Qi court in Jiankang. Nāgasena is exceptional in that he gave the Southern Qi emperor a description of Funan, or at least of its devotion to its god Maheśvara. See the final part of this chapter.

17. Huijiao: 慧皎; *Gao seng zhuan*: 高僧傳; Daoxuan: 道宣; *Xu gao seng zhuan*: 續高僧傳. Wilkinson, *Chinese History*, 422.

18. Qiyu: 耆域. Huijiao, *Gao seng zhuan, juan*, 10, in Lu and Zhou, *Zhongguo gujizhong*, 50. For the occupation of Luoyang in 311 and Chang'an in 316 by descendants of the Xiongnu 匈奴, see Rossabi, *History of China*, 102.

19. Huijiao, *Gao seng zhuan, juan* 10, in Lu and Zhou, *Zhongguo gujizhong*, 50.

20. Senggapoluo: 僧伽婆羅; Mantuoluo: 曼陀羅. Tansen Sen, Wang Bangwei, and other specialists in the field accept the Sanskrit versions of the names given here, and of the name Boloumotuo/Paramārtha mentioned below, and I follow them. See in particular Wang, "The Buddhist Connection," 283–288. Also Daoxuan, *Xu Gao seng zhuan, juan* 1, in Lu and Zhou, *Zhongguo gujizhong*, 51–52.

21. Wang, "The Buddhist Connection," 281–283.

22. See chapter three.

23. Funan Office: Funan guan 扶南館. Daoxuan, *Xu Gao seng zhuan, juan* 1, in Lu and Zhou, *Zhongguo gujizhong*, 51; Wang, "The Buddhist Connection," 283.

24. Wang, "The Buddhist Connection," 283.

25. Boluomotuo: 波羅末陀. Daoxuan, *Xu Gao seng zhuan, juan* 1, in Lu and Zhou, *Zhongguo gujizhong*, 52–53. Wang, "The Buddhist Connection," 287–288.

26. Barrett, "Diana Y. Paul: Philosophy of Mind," 175. For more on Xuanzang, see chapters five and six.

27. With the exception, that is, of the envoy Nāgasena (see footnote 16 of this chapter, above). Nor, it seems, did the monks who traveled between China and Zhenla leave any record of Zhenla. See, for instance, the biography of the Chinese monk Punyodaya (Nati 那提), a scholar–monk from central India whose activities in spreading Tantric Buddhism during the Zhenla era took him first to Tokharistan, then to Ceylon, then to Zhenla and China. His biography in *Xu gao seng zhuan* has little to say about Zhenla. Daoxuan, *Xu Gao seng zhuan, juan* 4, cited in Chen et al., *Zhongguo guji*, 58–59. On Nati see also Sen, "Buddhism and Maritime Crossings," 51; Dudbridge, "Reworking the World System," 307–308.

28. In rendering the Chinese name Putibatuo 菩提拔陀 as Buddhabadra, I follow Jenner, *Memories of Loyang*, 249–250.

29. Yang, *Luoyang galan ji*, 250–251. Galan in the title of Yang's book is short for *senggalanmo* 僧伽藍摩, or sangharama, Sanskrit for "Buddhist grove" or "monastic community." Wilkinson, *Chinese History*, 820.

30. Yang, *Luoyang galan ji*, 250–251.

31. According to *Taiping yulan*, Geying 歌營 was a state south of Juzhi 句稚. Li et al., *Taiping yulan*, citing *Nanzhou yiwu zhi*, 3501.

The two Han dynasties were the Former and Later Han dynasties. Wei was the northernmost of the three states of the Three Kingdoms period, with its capital at Luoyang.

32. Gouzhi and Dianxun were both mentioned in chapter one. Gouzhi was probably located on the Malay Peninsula; Diansun 典孫 is an alternative form of the name Dianxun/Dunxun, the third-century dependency of Funan, and was also probably on the Malay Peninsula.

In "five thousand square li" the word *fang* 方 is written before the number, and may indicate area.

According to Wilkinson, "*fang* 方 (square) was used since earliest times to indicate both area and volume." But he adds that the use of *fang* to denote area only really came into use with the Jesuits in the late Ming. Before then standard measures were used to indicate distance, area, or volume without distinction. If *fang* does indicate area here, five thousand square li is roughly the equivalent of say 50 x 50 = 2,500 square kilometers. If this were a realistic indication of area, it could refer to the size of Funan's capital city. Wilkinson, *Chinese History*, 610.

33. Going north to Luoyang from Linyi, which by this time was independent of China, Buddhabadra would have traveled through southern China, then under the rule of the Liang dynasty, into an area controled by the Northern Wei (386–534), a Buddhist dynasty with its capital at Luoyang.

34. Panyu: 番禺. Daoshi, *Fayuan zhulin*, 474. According to *Fayuan zhulin*'s modern editors, the story was taken from an earlier compilation by the monk Daoxuan.

35. Monumentalism or gigantism in devotional statuary began to be evident in China at about this time, as exemplified by the huge fifth-century Buddha—"dull but extremely ruthless," as William Empson describes it—that dominates the Yungang caves near Datong in north China (shown in Fig. 8). Later, monumentalism was also a feature of Angkor, as attested by the stone faces on the entrances to Angkor Thom and the surfaces of the Bayon. As Chandler has remarked, the reasons for this passion for the gigantic have yet to be fully explained. Chandler, personal communication; Empson, *The Face of the Buddha*, 118. Also Sickman and Soper, *The Art and Architecture of China*, 97–101, 144.

36. For the text of *Bao pu zi*, see Ge, *Bai pu zi nei wai pian*. Also Nienhauser, *Indiana Companion*, 481–482.

37. On the development of Daoism during the Eastern Jin: Lewis, *China Between Empires*, 202. On Ge Hong's life and career: Campany, *To Live as Long as Heaven and Earth*, 13–17.

38. On southern traditions: Pregadio, *Great Clarity*, 123–139; also Gernet, *History of Chinese Civilization*, 210. On Jiaozhi and the final years of Ge Hong's life: Campany, *To Live as Long as Heaven and Earth*, 15–16.

39. From *Taiping yulan*. *Taiping yulan* has two similar quotations on Funan diamonds, both attributed to *Bao pu zi*. The passage here is the first of the two. I have not been able to locate these passages in the received text of *Bao pu zi* itself. Li et al., *Taiping yulan*, 3482, 3614–3615.

40. The terms translated here as "diamond" and "amethyst" are *jingang* 金剛 (or 金綱, as in the Song edition of *Taiping yulan*) and *zishiying* 紫石英 respectively. According to Needham, references to diamonds and amethysts—by which he evidently means *jingang* and *zishiying*, though he does not mention these two terms by name—occur in texts dating back to Han times or earlier. Needham also refers to an old Chinese belief that rams' horns could break up diamonds. Needham, *Science and Civilization in China*, Vol. III, 643, 669–671. The term *zishiying* has also been taken to refer to fluorite or fluoritum, a softer mineral. See for example Wu, *Han ying da cidian*, 2181.

A hundred poles (*zhang* 丈) were roughly 800 feet (US) deep, one pole being ten *chi* 尺or Chinese feet. The term used here for "stalactite," *zhong ru* 鍾乳, originally referred to the decorative protuberances on ancient drinking cups. Needham documents the use of the term for "stalactites" from pre-Han times on. Luo et al., *Hanyu da cidian*, entry under 鍾乳; Needham, *Science and Civilization in China, Vol. III*, 605.

41. Sometimes attributed to Ge Hong; for example by Lu and Zhou, *Zhongguo gujizhong*, 43. I learned about the Funan references in *Tai qing jin ye shen dan jing* from the Lu and Zhou anthology, where Ge Hong is given as the author. The fact that Ge Hong is quoted by name in the work indicates however that he may not, in fact, have been the author.

42. Pregadio, *Great Clarity*, passim.

43. Pregadio, *Great Clarity*, 57.

44. [attr. Ge,] *Tai qing jin ye shen dan jing*, 12, 14, 16. On what commends this version of *Tai qing jin ye shen dan jing*, given the many Chinese editions of the canon: Boltz, "*Daozang*," 28–33. Ellipses in the translations here indicate where other passages have been omitted.

45. The phrase "Jiaozhou and Lingnan" is a translation of the Chinese term Jiaoling 交嶺. Jiao 交refers to Jiaozhou; Ling 嶺 could refer to Wuling 五嶺 (the five mountains of south China) or Lingnan 嶺南 (South of the Mountains, a name for the region of southern China then called Guangzhou 廣州). Given Guangzhou's importance as a regional center, it seems likely that here the ling in Jiaoling refers to Lingnan—that is, Guangzhou. Guangzhou here refers to a region rather than the southern city of Guangzhou, whose name only came into use later.

46. Wulun: 無倫.

47. "Slowly, slowly you make your way along" is a line from *Shi jing* [*The Classic of Poetry*]. Legge, *The Chinese Classics IV*, 110.

Chuan 川, a Chinese word for "river" that is used here, can be either singular or plural. The river or rivers in question were no doubt the Pearl River of Guangzhou or the Red River of Jiaozhou or both.

48. Xianglin was the southernmost district of China in Han times that later became the state of Linyi.

The Southern Sieve (Nan ji 南箕, also known as the Sieve, Ji 箕) and the Great Fire (Da huo 大火, also known as Chen 辰 or Da chen 大辰) are two of the so-called twenty-eight mansions, or Chinese lunar constellations. Chen or Da chen is the mansion more commonly called Heart (Xin 心). Nan ji and Da chen are mentioned in Zhou dynasty texts: Nan ji in *Shi jing* and Da chen in the early historical annals *Chun qiu* [*Spring and Autumn Annals*]. Legge, *The Chinese Classics IV*, 347; Legge, *The Chinese Classics V*, 666–668. See also Luo et al., *Hanyu da cidian*, entry under *chen* 辰.

49. The kings and rulers of Funan may be one or many, as the number is not specified. Given what Wan Zhen writes about Funan, and what *Liang shu* adds later about Funan having had a number of kings, the plural seems more suitable.

"Ten thousand li of frontiers" is hyperbolic; ten thousand (*wan*) is a term often used to convey an immensely large number.

50. According to *Shui jing zhu*, Shouling 壽靈 was a river in Rinan that joined another river, Lurong 盧容, before flowing out to sea through a port at mouth of the estuary. Here the port is called Shouling; Kang Tai refers to a port called Lurong (see chapter one). Perhaps they were two names for the same place. Li, *Shui jing zhu*, 833–834.

51. Paodao 炮到 and Potan 鄱歎 are hard to decipher. They appear to be titles, but neither of them seems to correspond to any of the seventh- to eighth-century Khmer titles in Vickery's comprehensive analysis of such titles. Vickery does identify *po*, *tāṅ*, and *tāñ* as titles of rank, *po* as a Cham honorific and *tāṅ* and *tāñ* as etymological variants of a foreign loan word assimilated into Khmer, used over time in different ways for different ranks of women and men. Perhaps Potan is an amalgam of the two titles *po* and *tāṅ/tāñ*. On the other hand there is no correspondence between either of the two syllables of Paodao and any of the titles in Vickery's list. Vickery, *Society, Economics, and Politics*, 113, 214–216.

52. In the alchemy practiced by the Daoists of imperial China, cinnabar and sulphur were treated as ingredients of the elixir of immortality. Needham, *Science and Civilization in China*, Vol. V, Part IV, 40, 185, 303, and passim. The uses of cinnabar and sulphur in Chinese alchemy are also discussed in volume five, part five of Needham's *Science and Civilization in China*.

53. *Liang shu* refers to Fan Shiman attacking Dianxun, Qudukun, and Jiuzhi; here the writer refers to the same three places—Dianxun (also known as Dunxun), Dukun (a variant of Qudukun), and Juzhi (a variant of Jiuzhi)—and adds a fourth location, Bisong 比嵩, that has not been identified. The account given here of Fan Shiman's conquest of Dianxun is similar to the account given by Wan Zhen (see chapter one). Like Dianxun/Dunxun, Juzhi and Dukun seem to have been on the Malay Peninsula. Wheatley, "Malay Peninsula", 21–31.

54. As mentioned earlier, Wulun has not been identified. Linyang was possibly located in present-day Myanmar (see chapter one).

55. The merchant is initially just referred to as a "person" (*ren* 人); I have called him a merchant from the outset to make his identity clearer.

The state of Gunu 古奴 is mentioned earlier in this text as Gunusitiao 古奴斯調, perhaps a distorted reference to Jia'natiao 伽那調, a place mentioned in both *Shui jing zhu* and *Taiping yulan*. Pelliot tentatively identifies Jia'natiao with the old name Kanadvīpa (*dvīpa* being Sanskrit for "island"), as do O. W. Wolters and H. B. Sarkar. Wolters and Pelliot both suggest that Kanadvīpa may have been a place in northwest India; Sarkar argues for a location near the mouth of the Ganges. Pelliot, "Quelques textes chinois," 251–252; Wolters, *Early Indonesian Commerce*, 59; Sarkar, "Chinese Texts," 271–284.

56. "Mysterious and Yellow" (*xuan huang* 玄黄) was a lead-and-mercury mud or clay for lining crucibles used in making the elixir of immortality. Pregadio, *Great Clarity*, 9–10.

57. For Fang Xuanling 房玄齡's role as editor under Taizong's oversight, see Goodman, "*Jin shu*", 137–138. Goodman writes that '[w]e cannot determine precisely how the older proto-*Jin shu* materials were changed and refashioned'—or to put it another way, how much of *Jin shu* is based on earlier materials not subject to further editing. Goodman, *Jin shu*, 137.

58. Fang et al., *Jin shu*, 2547.

59. In the phrase "three thousand li in extent," the term translated as "extent" (*guangmao* 廣袤) is open to different interpretations. Its literal meaning is "length [*guang* 廣] and breadth [*mao* 袤]". It is clearly used in this sense, for example, in the second-century BCE compilation *Huainan zi*. But elsewhere its early usages vary. The dictionary *Hanyu da cidian* seems to cover the scope of its meanings by defining it as either "area," "breadth" or "extent." Which of these meanings applies here? We learn little by comparing this passage with passages about the size of Funan in other official histories and encyclopedias. *Liang shu*, *Tong dian*, and *Tong zhi* use the terms *guangmao*, *lunguang* 輪廣, and *guanglun* 廣輪 respectively, but as with *guangmao* the meanings of lunguang and *guanglun* are ambiguous.

If *guangmao* means "breadth," Funan would have stretched from, say, Óc Eo to Dunxun. If it means "length and breadth," as in *Huainan zi*, it would have measured, say, 2000 *li* from east to west and 1000 *li* from north to south. If it means "length plus breadth," as in circumference, it would have measured perhaps 1000 x 500 *li*. If it means "area," its size would have been perhaps fifty by sixty li—that is, twenty-five by thirty kilometers or 750 square kilometers, the size of a city and its environs. The latter may be the most likely interpretation. It would be consistent with the thirteenth-century gazetteer *Zhu fan zhi*'s description of Zhenla (Angkor)—a very large polity at the time—as 7000 *fang li* (square li). This roughly equates to say 70 x 100 li, that is, about 35 x 50 kilometers or 1750 square kilometers, a size suitable for the capital alone. All the same, it is hard to be sure which meaning applies here. Pelliot translates *guangmao* as "breadth" (largeur), and two leading specialists—Wilkinson and Chen Jiarong—take *guangmao* to convey a sense of extensiveness without being more precise. Luo et al., *Hanyu da cidian*, entries for *guangmao*, *lunguang* and *guanglun*; personal communications with Wilkinson and Chen.

60. "Cities and districts" is a translation of the Chinese term *cheng yi* 城邑, *cheng* 城 being "city" or "walled city" and *yi* 城邑 being "city", "district", or "village". In texts on Funan, and also in the case of

Linyi, *yi* seems to indicate either a city or a district, depending on context, though this interpretation is tentative.

61. Hu script probably refers to a writing system originating in India. There is another reference to Funan writings using Hu script in *Sui shu* (chapter four). One of several names used by the Chinese in imperial times to describe non-Chinese peoples, the term Hu tended to be applied to the peoples to the north and west of China. According to the dictionary *Hanyu da cidian*, until the Tang dynasty Hu also included the peoples of India.

Hu has often been translated into English as "barbarian," but the use of "barbarian" for any of the various imperial Chinese terms for "foreigner" has been questioned, notably by the historian and linguist Christopher Beckwith, who doubts whether it is suitable. He argues that while the ancient Greeks used one term—*βάρβαρος* or "barbarian"—the imperial Chinese used various names for different kinds of non-Chinese, and never employed one general term. In fact at least one Chinese word, *yi* 夷, originally meaning "eastern foreigner",came to be used in just such a general sense. An example of its use in this sense appears in the section of *Taiping yulan* that deals with foreigners, where they are called eastern and western *yi*. This does not, however, detract from the important point that imperial China used various terms to refer to foreigners, the ancient Greeks only one. This being the case in a Chinese context the term "barbarian" is indeed inadequate—though "foreigner", the term used in this study, is hardly sufficient either, since it does not distinguish among the various Chinese terms, and fails to capture the patronizing tone of some of them (for example, *man* 蠻, with its insect radical). Beckwith, *Empires of the Silk Road*, 355–362; Wilkinson, *Chinese History*, 384–385; Luo et al., *Hanyu da cidian*; Li et al., *Taiping yulan*, 3455–3557.

62. In its account of the foundation story of Liuye and Hun Tian, *Jin shu* inverts the name Liuye to Yeliu 葉柳 (leafy willow) and gives Hun Kui 混潰 as the name for Hun Tian. The written forms of Hun Kui and Hun Tian are similar; for further discussion, see chapter one.

63. "Her forces:" *zhong* 衆, literally, "mass of people." But in accounts of Linyi here and later the term zhong also carries the sense of "force", as in military force, as it does in early Chinese military texts. "Descendants:" *zisun* 子孫, literally, "sons and grandsons," a phrase sometimes used to refer to descendants or offspring more generally.

64. In a later passage, *Jin shu* records a tribute mission "at the beginning" of the Taishi reign period (265–274). Strictly speaking that would have been in 265 rather than 268, as recorded earlier. Fang et al., *Jin shu*, 58, 68, 77, 78, 202, 237.

65. In both accounts the sender's name is Zhu Zhantan 竺旃檀. The statement in the second account that he is "called king" (*cheng wang* 稱王) is an unusual turn of phrase that could indicate that his stature as king was somehow in doubt, and had not been endorsed by the Chinese court. Zhu Zhantan's family name, Zhu 竺, indicates that he was of Indian origin. As Pelliot and also Lu and Zhou note, one version of this *Jin shu* passage makes this more explicit by giving his name as Tianzhu Zhantan 天竺旃檀 (Zhantan of India). It is noteworthy that despite his Indian origins, Zhu did not assume a Sanskritized name, indicating that he was not subject to Indianizing influences as his fifth-century successor Kauṇḍinya (Jiaochenru) evidently was. Fang et al., *Jin shu*, 202; Lu and Zhou, *Zhongguo gujizhong*, 3; Pelliot, "Fou-nan," 252, 255. The *Liang shu* account of this event identifies Zhu Zhantan as king without qualification. For the *Liang shu* accounts of both Zhu Zhantan and Kauṇḍinya, see chapter three.

In Chinese the term for "elephant" (*xiang* 象) is not number-specific, so Zhu Zhantan may have presented one elephant or more than one.

66. On Emperor Dezong, see chapter seven. As Elvin notes, during the first millennium CE elephants were still a common feature of the southern Chinese landscape, especially its forests, though during the second millennium they were virtual exterminated on the Chinese mainland. Elvin, *Retreat of the Elephants*, 9–18, esp. the map on page 10.

67. See appendix four for a tabulation of the customs and people of Funan as recounted by Kang Tai and in *Jin shu*, *Nan Qi shu*, and *Liang shu*.

68. Chandler, personal communication.

69. "Levies and taxes:" *gong fu* 貢賦. The Chinese term suggests levies of produce from the land and other forms of tax paid to a king or lord. Like Angkor, Funan is generally believed to have been a cashless society, although as noted earlier, one Vietnamese scholar, Lương Ninh, claims to have found evidence of local coinage.

70. See chapter four.

71. The words are nearly the same as those used by the thirteenth-century envoy Zhou Daguan, by which time they had clearly become a trope or cliché. For the comment in *Liang shu*, see chapter three; for Zhou Daguan's comment, see chapter nine.

72. For *Wai guo zhuan*, see chapter one.

73. Shen Yue: 沈約. Nienhauser, *Indiana Companion*, 680–681; Chittick, "*Song shu*," 320–321; Knechtges, "From the Eastern Han," 234.

74. Chittick, "*Song shu*," 320.

75. Shen, *Song shu*, 2377 (on soldiers); 83, 85, 2379 (on tribute missions). Linyi's request to Funan to join an attack on the Chinese in Jiaozhou, though rejected, suggests that serious conflict between Cambodian rulers and the southernmost reaches of the Chinese empire was not entirely out of the question, and might have occurred at some early stage—for example, when the southern official Tao Huang was battling Funan and Linyi clans in the third century CE (see appendix five). If documented, such a conflict would strengthen Pelliot's suggestion that the name Zhenla could translate to "China defeated," as discussed in the introduction.

76. Chilibamo: 持梨跋摩.

77. Chilituobamo: 持梨陁跋摩; *bamo*: 跋摩.

78. Wang, "The Buddhist Connection," 286. Coedès offers two other Sanskrit equivalents without explanation: Śrī Indravarman or Śreshṭhavarman. He evidently takes Chili to be the equivalent of Śrī or Śre, thus leaving the single syllable *tuo* to be a transliteration of Indra or Shṭha, which is unsatisfactory. Coedès, *Indianized States*, 56.

79. William Crowell, "*Nan Qi shu*," 202.

80. Xiao Zixian: 蕭子顯. Crowell, "*Nan Qi shu*," 202; Berkowitz, *Patterns of Disengagement*, 188.

81. Emperor Wu's Buddhism: as Jinhua Chen explains, Wu was particularly devoted to the Prajñāpāramitā sūtra [Discourse on the Perfection of Wisdom]. Chen, "*Pañcavārṣika* Assemblies," 45–46. Grand rituals: Chen, "*Pañcavārṣika* Assemblies," 53, 55.

82. The contemporary Chinese scholar is Zhao Jihui 趙吉惠. Crowell, "*Nan Qi shu*," 206, citing Zhao.

83. Xiao, *Nan Qi shu*, 1014–1017.

84. "Flows from the west:" *xi liu* 西流. This is to give an awkward rendition of *xi liu*, which might otherwise be taken to read "flows west." The meaning is suggested by the similar passage in *Liang shu*: "*xibei liu dong ru yu hai*" 西北流東入於海 (flows from the north-west and enters the sea in the east) and the more explicit description of the river flowing west in *Nan shi*. For the *Liang shu* and *Nan shi* entries, see chapter three. Yao, *Liang shu*, 787; Li et al., *Nan shi*, 1951; Pelliot, "Fou-nan," 256.

85. In the Chinese text, *Nan Qi shu* makes an initial reference to Fan Shiman 范師蔓, after which it refers to him simply as Man 蔓. To make for easier reading, Fan Shiman's name is given in full throughout. The same is done in the extract from *Liang shu* in the next chapter. A fuller account of the genealogy of the early kings of Funan is given in chapter five.

86. Pelliot identifies the names Qiaochenru 僑陳如 (G'i̯äu đi̯ĕn ńźi̯wo [K]), Sheyebamo 闍耶跋摩 (Dź'i̯a i̯a ? muâ [K]) and Nagaxian 那伽仙 (Nâ ? si̯än [K]) with the Sanskrit names Kauṇḍinya, Jayavarman, and Nāgasena. These are very reasonable identifications; there is a good correspondence between the names' Ancient Chinese pronunciations and Pelliot's Sanskrit equivalents.

Kauṇḍinya was originally the name of a disciple of the Buddha. As noted earlier, Coedès associates the name with a brahmin clan in Mysuru (Mysore), India, which he claims without explanation was connected to Funan. Nāgasena was a popular name for Buddhist monks, having been the name of a second-century BCE Buddhist devotee from Kashmir. In *Nan Qi shu* Nāgasena is described as a Tianzhu *daoren* 天竺道人 (Indian man of the Way). The term *daoren* 道人 is sometimes used in early Chinese texts for a Buddhist disciple or monk; in later Chinese texts, it refers to some other kind of holy man or woman, perhaps Hindu. For more on *daoren*, see chapter six.

Nāgasena's name in Chinese is prefixed by Shi 釋 (Śākya), from the Buddha's Sanskrit name Śākyamuni (Sage of the Śākyas). Shi is the surname that the third-century Chinese Buddhist leader Daoan 道安 required all Buddhist monks in China to assume in place of their former surnames. When translating the names of Chinese monks into English it is customary to exclude the surname Shi, and I have followed this practice. Pelliot, "Fou-nan," 257; Coedès, *Indianized States*, 30; Zürcher, *Buddhist Conquest of China*, 189.

87. As mentioned earlier, Linyi was a state in the central part of present-day Vietnam. For details, see appendix five.

The mandate Nāgasena refers to was the Mandate of Heaven by which Chinese emperors claimed the authority to rule. The term used for China here is Zhongguo 中國 (Central State or, more likely at this time Central States, given that *guo* is not number specific, and during this era China was divided).

88. "Being transformed through drawing near the heavenly devas" is a tentative rendition of the Chinese phrase *hua lin zhu tian* 化鄰諸天. *Zhu tian* 諸天 refers to the various gods, or devas in Buddhist belief, and the literal meaning of *hua lin* 化鄰 is "transform and be near". Pelliot notes that the expression may have been a stock phrase, since it occurs in almost the same form just over a century later in an encomium in *Liang shu*. Pelliot, "Fou-nan," 258; Yao, *Liang shu*, 794.

89. Nothing is known about the person Jiuchouluo 鳩酧羅 (Ji̯əu ? lâ [K]) or his name. It is not a Chinese name, and its derivation is uncertain. As Pelliot observes, he (and we must assume it was 'he',

since the Chinese chroniclers do not say otherwise) seems to be the same person as Danggenchun, the Funan prince who usurped the throne of Linyi, probably in the 480s. According to *Nan Qi shu*, which calls him Fan Danggenchun 范當根純, Danggenchun was a foreigner (*yi* 夷) who seized Linyi, became king of Linyi himself, and sent tribute to the Chinese court in 491, only to be killed by offspring of the usurped king. *Nan shi* adds that Danggenchun was a son of the king of Funan. Pelliot, "Fou-nan," 25; Xiao, *Nan Qi shu*, 1013; Li et al., *Nan shi*, 1949. For more on Danggenchun, see chapter three.

90. Tan Hezhi 檀和之 was the Chinese general and governor of Jiaozhou who carried out a punitive attack on Linyi in 446 CE. His name was mentioned in chapter one, in the discussion on dating the work of the traveler Zhu Zhi (chapter one). Shen, *Song shu*, 2378. See also appendix five on Linyi.

91. The description of Funan and Linyi being adjacent contrasts with the statements in *Jin shu* and *Liang shu* that Funan was some three thousand li to the west or southwest of Linyi. Three thousand li may have been the distance between the principal cities of the two states, in which case their (ill-defined) frontiers could well have been adjacent.

92. A *bhara* was an ancient Indian measurement equal to just over 750 kilograms. I follow Pelliot, who suggests it here for the Chinese *poluo* 婆羅, a term used in early texts with various meanings. Five *bhara* would be well over four (US) tons—a huge amount perhaps not to be taken literally. Pelliot, "Fou-nan," 259, 270; Olivelle, King, *Governance and Law*, 457–458.

93. *Tan* 檀 is translated here as "rosewood," *dalbergia hupeana*, as distinct from "sandalwood" (*zhantan* 旃檀 and other names), though the two were sometimes confounded. Stuart, *Chinese Materia Medica*, 143, 360, 394. For sandalwood, see chapter four.

"Cotton" is a rendering of the term *gubei* 古貝 (kuo: pwâi- [K]), also written *guju* 古具 and *jibei* 吉貝. There is a description of this material in *Liang shu*, which says that it is "the name of a tree. When its flowers ripen they are like goosedown. You pull the end of the thread and weave it into cloth, which is pure white and not unlike ramie." Pelliot argues convincingly that *gubei* derives from *karpāsa*, the Sanskrit word for cotton. It is to be distinguished from another type of cotton (*baidie* 白疊) referred to in *Liang shu*, and from the later general word for cotton, *mianhua* 棉花, still in use today. Yao, *Liang shu*, 784–785; Li et al., *Taiping yulan*, 3134; Pelliot "Fou-nan," 60; Pelliot, *Notes on Marco Polo*, 426–531. Also Zhao, *Zhu fan zhi*, 192.

"Glass" is a translation of the Chinese word *liuli* 琉璃, which seems to refer to an opaque glass-like substance. In his discussion of the domestic and foreign origins of glass in China, Needham distinguishes between *liuli* and *boli* 玻璃, the latter being the Chinese term now used for glass. Needham writes that "broadly speaking one may consider *liu-li* as meaning opaque glass, and *po-li* [*boli*] as meaning more or less transparent glass. But the questions raised [by the two terms] are very complex, and the last word has probably not yet been said on them." Needham and Wang, *Science and Civilization in China, Vol. IV, Part I*, 104. There is also a long passage on *liuli* in Loewe, "Guangzhou", 75–77.

The word *suli* 蘇鉝, tentatively rendered here as "vessel", is rare, occurring only once in *Taiping yulan*, when it is mentioned as tribute sent to China by Linyi. Li et al., *Taiping yulan*, 3373.

94. The Chinese name Moxishouluo 摩醯首羅 (Muâ χiei *śi̯ôg lâ [K]) is commonly used in Chinese as a form of the title Maheśvara (Great Lord). The historian Wendy Doniger confirms that the name Maheśvara was probably used here to refer to the god Śiva. In his paean of praise, Nāgasena treats Maheśvara/Śiva as part of the Buddhist pantheon, at least in some sense. He describes the Great Lord as a compassionate Bodhisattva, although without actually calling him Lokeśvara, the Bodhisattva of compassion who was later to feature in iconography associated with Funan. Tingley, *Arts of Ancient Vietnam*, 174; Doniger, personal communication.

Modan 摩躭 (Muâ tậm [K]—tậm being Karlgren's reconstructed pronunciation for the character 耽, since he does not provide a pronunciation for 躭,) may conceivably be the Chinese name of the then capital or principal city of Funan, but if it is there does not seem to be an equivalent local name. Wheatley suggests that the name derives from the Tamil Mayentiram, meaning Śiva's abode. A relatively late source, *Xin Tang shu*, written some five centuries after the time of Nāgasena, gives the capital of Funan a quite different name, the City of Temu 特牧 (D'ək mi̯uk [K]) (see chapter four).

The location or locations of the capital of Funan has been the subject of some debate. Basing himself on the *Liang shu* description of the city of Funan being five hundred li from the sea, Pelliot places the capital in present-day Angkor Borei in southern Cambodia, a location accepted by Chandler and others. Taking into account the same *Liang shu* comment, Coedès prefers to place it at Ba Phnom, a hill southeast of Phnom Penh. Wheatley, "Mount of the Immortals," 106; Pelliot, "Fou-nan," 290, 295; Coedès, "La Tradition généalogique," 130; Coedès, *Indianized States*, 36–37; Chandler, personal communication. For *Liang shu* on the city of Funan being five hundred li from the sea, see chapter three.

95. In pentasyllabic rhyming verse. Pelliot's translation of this poem sometimes renders the meaning only imperfectly, and he offers little explanation of the various Buddhist terms, writing, "Je vois mal la suite des idees" (I find it hard to follow the train of thought). Pelliot, "Fou-nan," 260.

96. In the expression "Bodhi heart," Bodhi (Puti 菩提 in Chinese) means enlightened in a Buddhist sense. The term Two Vehicles (Er cheng 二乘) refers here to Theravada Buddhism and Mahayana Buddhism. The six pāramitās (*liu du* 六度) are the six qualities needed to become a Bodhisattva. With the exception of Shitihuan (for which see note 98 below), definitions of Buddhist names and terms given here are taken from Luo et al., *Hanyu da cidian*.

97. In Hindu and Buddhist theology, a *kalpa* (*jie* 劫) is an aeon, a great period of time.

98. "The six levels of existence:" literally, "the six roads or ways" (*liu dao* 六道, *ṣaḍgatīḥ* in Sanskrit), the six levels of existence in Hindu and Buddhist theology. The "ten stages," literally the "ten grounds" (*shi di* 十地, *daśabhūmi* in Sanskrit) are the final ten stages to be passed through before achieving enlightenment or Bodhisattva-hood. Here and later in this passage "karma" is a loose translation of *yuan* 緣, "causation" (*pratyaya* in Sanskrit), karma being the principle of ethical causation. The underlying meaning of "let the living world cross over" seems to be "let sentient beings cross over to an enlightened state of mind."

99. The Three Treasures (San bao 三寶) are the Buddha, the dharma (the law or teachings), and the sangha (the monastic order). Śakra, Lord of the Devas, refers to Indra, the lord protector of Devas, Devas being Hindu or Buddhist deities. Śakra is Shiti 釋提 in Chinese, a short form of Shittihuanyin 釋提桓因, Shi being Śakra, Tihuan being Deva, and Yin being Indra. Ren, *Fojiao da cidian*, 950; Soothill and Hodous, *Dictionary of Chinese Buddhist Terms*, 482.

100. Maritime interpreters were interpreters needed for the Chinese to communicate with the states of the south. There is mention in *Liang shu* and elsewhere of *chong yi* 重譯 (repeated interpretation), evidently meaning the need to for interpreters to go through more than one language before those they were interpreting for could be understood. For *Liang shu* on *chong yi*, see chapter three.

101. "Heaven's civilizing influence being renewed" is an allusion to the fact that Emperor Wu represented a new dynasty, the Nan Qi or Southern Qi in power in southern China. The meeting between Nāgasena and Wu, the second Nan Qi emperor, took place in the fifth year of the new dynasty.

102. Jiaozhou is referred to in the text as Jiaobu 交部 (the Jiao region). A reference elsewhere in *Nan Qi shu* shows that Jiaobu refers to Jiaozhou, the administrative region in the far south of China. By referring the matter to Jiaozhou, the emperor deflected the issue before him with the time-honored stratagem of passing it on to subordinates; there seems to be no record of a response from the Jiaozhou authorities. Pelliot misses the meaning of Jiaobu here. The term Central Land or Central Lands, Zhongtu 中土 (which is not number-specific), refers to China. At this time and for centuries afterwards Zhongtu was one of various ways of referring to the Chinese realm.

103. In the record of city walls here, the number of cities is not specified, so it is not clear whether what is referred to is one city or more than one.

The size of the bamboo leaves used for thatching houses is in Chinese feet (*chi* 尺). One *chi* being equal then to some ten (US) inches, the leaves were huge, somewhere between six-and-a-half and seven-and-a-half (US) feet or so long.

The term for storeyed buildings (*ge* 閣, a term sometimes misleadingly translated as pavilion), suggests houses on more than one level, perhaps houses raised on stilts of the kind still common in Cambodian villages today.

The description of the boats here seems to be taken from Kang Tai. One *zhang* (pole) being ten *chi* (Chinese feet), the boats were somewhere between sixty-five and seventy-five (US) feet long, roughly the same length as those described by Kang Tai. They were slightly broader, being perhaps six (US) feet wide, but given the approximate values of the measures concerned the difference is nugatory. The sentence about the heads and tails of the boats being shaped like a fish is the same as in Kang Tai's record.

104. Pomegranates are called here by a name sometimes used for them, *An shiliu* 安石榴 (literally, pomegranates from Anxi or Parthia). China here is Zhongguo 中國, the Central States or State (Zhongguo, like Zhongtu 中土, not being number-specific). "Mandarin oranges" is a translation of *jie* 桔, which is the most likely meaning here, though *jie* can also refer to balloon flowers. For *An shiliu* and *jie*, Luo et al., *Hanyu da cidian*; for *jie*, Stuart, *Chinese Materia Medica*, 18. For Anxi as Parthia, see chapter three.

105. Furen: 婦人.

106. Xiao, *Nan Qi shu*, 1014. For more on the status of women in Linyi, see appendix five.

107. "Pre-Angkorian society:" Vickery refers mainly to the seventh century, but by citing the example of Zhan, he implies that such matriliny may have been a feature of earlier centuries as well. Indeed, at one point he suggests that there may have been "a general matrilineal tendency throughout early Cambodian society." Vickery, *Society, Economics, and Politics*, 260–261, 326, 372–373. For *poñ/fan*, see chapter one.

108. On Indianization and the controversies surrounding it, see chapters one and eleven.

109. See chapter three.

110. Briggs writes that after eulogising Maheśvara, the monk "turns brusquely to the praise of Buddhism," thus obscuring this point. Briggs, *Ancient Khmer Empire*, 28.

111. For example by Manguin. Manguin, "The Archaeology of Fu Nan," 112–113.

112. *Sui shu* remarks that the people of Zhenla "respect the Buddhist dharma and place even greater faith in their holy men:" see chapter six. For Zhou's observations, Zhou, *Zhenla fengtu ji*, 94–95.

There has been some debate about the extent to which Hindu-Buddhist relations in premodern Southeast Asia were syncretistic or developed in parallel. Discussing Java, John Miksic argues in favor of parallel relations but notes the syncretic unity of Śiva and Buddha during the Majapahit era in Java (thirteenth to sixteenth century). Frank Reynolds analyses how Rama in the epic *Ramayana* sometimes had a clear Buddhist identity, a point also made by Penny Edwards. Miksic, *The Buddhist-Hindu Divide*, 2; Reynolds, "Three Ramayana," 50–59, esp. 50–55; Edwards, personal communication.

113. The tribute missions between 434 and 442: see the *Song shu* section of this chapter, the *Chen shu* and *Nan shi* sections of chapter three, and appendix three.

114. As noted in chapter one, Li Shan made this remark in a commentary on the third-century poet Zuo Si's prose-poem on the eastern capital of Wu state, which mentions Funan.

Chapter Three

1. Taizong and his father Gaozu 高祖 co-founded the Tang dynasty, the former encouraging the latter to rise up in rebellion against the declining Sui dynasty. Wechsler, "T'ai-tsung," 189–191.

2. Chassende, "*Liang shu*," 167–170, esp. 167; Chassende, "*Chen shu*," 44–47, esp. 44.

3. Graff, "*Bei shi*," 19–21; Strange and Hruby, "*Nan shi*," 210–211.

4. Yao Silian: 姚思廉. Yao Silan's father, Yao Cha 姚察 (533–606), began the work during the Sui dynasty. Chassende, "*Liang shu*," 167.

5. Chassende, "*Liang shu*," 167–168.

6. Yao Silian's biography in Liu et al., *Jiu Tang shu*, 2592–2593, and Ouyang et al., *Xin Tang shu*, 3978–3979. For the College of Literary Studies (Wen xue guan 文學館), see Liu et al., *Jiu Tang shu*, 2582 and Ouyang et al., *Xin Tang shu*, 3976. Yan Liben 閻立本's painting of the eighteen scholars is listed in Ouyang et al., *Xin Tang shu*, 1580. See also Wright, "The Sui Dynasty," 183; Sickman and Soper, *The Art and Architecture of China*, 160.

7. On Taizong and his times: Wechsler, "T'ai-tsung," 235; Lewis, *China's Cosmopolitan Empire*, 170–171. On the capital Chang'an: Xiong, *Sui-Tang Chang'an*, 236–251. During the Tang dynasty, Chang'an became the center for Chinese trade with central Asia, while Chinese trade with the southern states was conducted from Yangzhou on the lower Yangzi River. Wang, "Nanhai Trade," 112.

8. For the History Office (Shi guan 史館), set up in 629, Strange and Hruby, "*Nan shi*," 210; Gardiner, "Standard Histories," 48–49; Durrant, "Histories," 198.

9. During the Tang dynasty, a complete set of the *Histories of the Thirteen Dynasties* [*Shisan dai shi/shu*) 十三代史/書] took shape, covering all the history from *Shi ji* to *Sui shu*. Wilkinson, *Chinese History*, 694–695.

10. Li et al., *Bei shi*, 3159–3161 (Chitu), 3162–3164 (Zhenla); the texts taken from *Sui shu* are in Wei et al., *Sui shu*, 1833–1837.

11. For *Bei shi*, Graff, "*Bei shi*," 48–49. For *Nan shi*, see the sections on *Chen shu* and *Nan shi* later in this chapter.

12. It is part of *juan* 54 of *Liang shu*'s fifty-six *juan* of annals (*ji*) and biographies (*zhuan*). For *ji* and *zhuan*, see chapter one.

13. General Pacifying the South: Annan jiang 安南將. For Mandra, see chapter two.

14. Yao, *Liang shu*, 40, 52, 54, 57, 59, 63, 74, 79, 83, 40.

15. Islands: *zhou* 洲 (island or islands). The third-century BCE dictionary *Er ya* 爾雅 defines *zhou* as "an island in the water you can live on." The general description of southern states as large islands, while true to some extent, glosses over the fact that a number of states communicating with the Chinese through the Southern Sea, including Funan, were mainland polities. Evidently Yao Silian had only a vague knowledge of regional geography.

16. *Hainan zhuan*: 海南傳. Yao, *Liang shu*, 783.

17. Yao, *Liang shu*, 783, where *Liang shu*'s Zhonghua shuju editors put *Hainan zhuan* in the equivalent of italics as the title of a separate work. If it was a separate work, it has since been lost.

18. For Yueshang, see chapter one. Yao, *Liang shu*, 785.

19. *Ganlan* 干闌 was a traditional house raised high on a wooden frame. The received text erroneously has *yulan* 于闌 for ganlan.

20. For *ganman* or *duman*, see note 37, chapter one.

21. "*Qi da xing hao poluomen*" 其大姓號婆羅門, Yao, *Liang shu*, 786. The Chinese for brahmin (*poluomen* 婆羅門) is a frequently used transliteration. Educated Chinese at the time would have understood what a brahmin was. No doubt some would have read the seventh-century Chinese monk Xuanzang's account of his journey to India, in which he clearly explains the meaning of brahmin. [Xuan and Bianji,] *Da Tang xi yu ji*, 119.

22. Yao, *Liang shu*, 787–790.

23. As noted earlier, Pelliot argues that this would have placed the main city of Funan in Angkor Borei in southern Cambodia. Pelliot, "Fou-nan," 290.

24. "Lign-aloes" is one of several English names for *chenmuxiang* 沉木香, the substance referred to here, others being "aloeswood," "agarwood," and "gharu-wood." These English names all refer to the wood of the plant *aquilaria agallocha*, rather than the fragrances extracted from it, but here the term "lign-aloes" is used for both. The wood of the plant emits various fragrances, one of them akin to sandalwood, and has long been prized in China as a stimulant and a means to counter excess yin in the body. Lign-aloes is called by various other names in Chinese, including *chenshuixiang* 沉水香, *chenxiang* 沉香, and *zhanxiang* 蓌香 (also written 䅟香). These names were used by the Song gazetteer writers Fan Chengda and Zhao Rugua, both of whom treated lign-aloes as an important commodity. Stuart, *Chinese Materia Medica*, 44–45, where the entry is under *chenxiangmu* 沉香木. There is a helpful note on lign-aloes, or gharu-wood, as editor-translator James Hargett calls it in [Fan,] *Treatises of the Supervisor*, 35. For Fan Chengda's and Zhao Rugua's gazetteers, see chapter eight.

According to *Liang shu*, lign-aloes was also a product of Linyi and another early state, Langyaxiu.

The expression translated here as "kingfisher feathers" (*kong cui* 孔翠), could refer to peacocks, to peacocks and kingfishers together, or to the feathers of either. Kingfisher feathers were prized in imperial China from Zhou times on and were worn as capes and cloaks in the Tang court. Luo et al., *Hanyu da cidian*; Schafer, *The Vermilion Bird*, 238.

25. For Dunxun, see the writings of Wan Zhen in chapter one.

26. An alternative reading of the phrase "a thousand li in extent" is "a thousand square li", a far smaller amount, but this second reading seems inconsistent with the subsequent remark about Dunxun stretching a thousand li. The phrase in Chinese is "*difang qian li*" 地方千里 (territory of a thousand li, taking *difang* 地方 to mean "territory"), which can also be read "*di fang qian li*" (territory of a thousand square li, taking *di* 地 to mean "territory" and *fang* 方 to mean "square", indicating area).

27. The term "loosely dependent" is a translation of the term *ji zhu* 羈屬. This is redolent of the term *ji mi* 羈縻, "loosely reined or haltered," used to describe the imperial Chinese policy of exercising relatively loose control over frontier peoples, particularly during the Tang. On this Tang practice, see Lewis, *China's Cosmopolitan Empire*, 28–29.

28. The identification of Anxi 安息 with Parthia, the Iranian polity of the third century BCE to the third century CE, was made by the German historian Friedrich Hirth in 1885 and has since been generally accepted. Anxi is to be distinguished from Bosi 波斯, a Chinese name for Persia. According to Wolters, Bosi became current as the name for Persia in the fifth century CE, at which point Anxi fell into disuse. Pelliot notes that while Bosi seems to have referred to Persia in pre-Song texts, by the eleventh and twelfth centuries the name was sometimes applied to a state on the Malay Peninsula. Hirth, *China and the Roman Orient*, 139–143; Wolters, *Early Indonesian Commerce*, 45–46, 82, 141; Pelliot, *Notes on Marco Polo*, 87.

As Pelliot notes, the phrasing about Dunxun here suggests that it straddled the Malay Peninsula, enabling merchants to communicate in two directions—eastwards towards Jiaozhou in the far south of China and westwards towards "the various states beyond the frontiers" (*jiaowai zhuguo* 徼外諸國) of India and Parthia. The remark about ships not being able to go right across the Great Sea—here, it seems, Nan hai or the Southern Sea—seems to imply that in the sixth and seventh centuries, at any rate, goods were transported by land across the Malay Peninsula at Dunxun rather than carried by boats all the way round the peninsula. Pelliot, "Fou-nan," 263; Wolters, *Early Indonesian Commerce*, 46–47.

29. The term for "market" (*shi* 市) may be singular or plural. It is read as plural here, given the number of people and the scale of the activities involved.

30. The unknown identity of the curious state of Piqian, first mentioned by Kang Tai, is discussed in note 51, chapter one. The king as described here was ageless and preternaturally tall, so this *Liang shu* account of Piqian may be as much fantasy as reality, perhaps because no one dared visit it to see it firsthand.

"Pint" is *sheng* 升, an old measure of capacity. In the sentence on plates or cups, *ou* 塸 should read *ou* 甌. As mentioned earlier, *duoluo* 多羅 is a term that is not clearly understood. It may refer to a gold leaf, though in this instance casting a gold leaf in gold sounds superfluous.

Buddhist sutras are Buddhist scriptures or holy books. In Buddhist and Hindu doctrine, "pre-destined fate" (*su ming* 宿命) refers to the destinies of individuals determined by their actions in earlier lives.

31. Mawuzhou 馬五洲, or the Five Islands of Ma, may refer to Maluku. Pelliot takes the view that Mawuzhou may refer to Bali, in which case, he suggests, *wu* 五 would be a copyist's error for a character pronounced *li*. But there is a stronger case for the Five Islands of Ma referring to Maluku, the archipelago east of Java, which has several sizeable islands and a name beginning Ma. *Taiping yulan* quotes Kang Tai as writing that "to the east of Zhubo lie five islands that produce cloves [*jishexiang* 雞舌香], the trees of

which flower a lot but bear few fruit." Cloves are native to Maluku. Pelliot, "Deux itinéraires," 270–271; Li et al., *Taiping yulan*, 3485.

32. "Burned hemp:" a literal translation of *jiaoma* 焦麻, following Pelliot; nowadays identified with abaca or Manila hemp. The Great Island of Natural Fire (Ziran dazhou 自然大洲) is also mentioned in *Waiguo zhuan*, though not by name. It is clearly one of the volcanoes of Indonesia or the Pacific, but it is not clear which one it could have been. See *Wai guo zhuan* in chapter one. Pelliot, "Fou-nan," 265.

33. *Liang shu* remarks on their loose-hanging hair because it was not bound up in a knot in the proper Chinese fashion.

34. "The king who came after him" (*qi hou wang* 其後王) could also be read less specifically as "a king who came after him" or "a successor." The meaning of *qi hou wang* is ambiguous. The difference of interpretation matters because it affects how we reconstruct Funan's royal lineage.

If Hun Pankuang 混盤況 was Hun Tian's direct successor he could, of course, have been one of his sons, but there is no record in early Chinese sources to that effect. The various districts where he stirred up trouble presumably included the seven districts that Liuye and Hun Tian enfeoffed their sons with.

35. "Second-ranking king" is a translation of *xiao wang* 小王 (small king or queen) a title used elsewhere for a second-ranking or subordinate ruler. In *Bei shi*, for example, there is a description of Nü guo 女國 (Women's State), a matriarchal state in central Asia where the ruling queen was replaced on her death by two women from her clan, one the queen, the other a second-ranking queen called *xiao wang*. Li et al., *Bei shi*, 3189–3190, 3235–3236.

36. As in *Nan Qi shu*, Fan Man 范蔓 (that is, Fan Shiman 范師蔓) is referred to throughout simply by his second name, Man 蔓. Again, to make for clearer reading I have given his full name, Fan Shiman, instead.

37. As we saw earlier, the places Fan Shiman attacked—Qudukun (also known as Dukun), Jiuzhi (or Gouzhi), and Dianxun (or Dunxun)—were all probably located on the Malay Peninsula, while Jinlin (also called Jinchen) was evidently to the west of Funan.

The phrase "five to six thousand li," describing the territory opened up by Fan Shiman, raises in a different form the issue discussed earlier, namely what such an ambiguously phrased measurement might mean.

38. In Chinese, the name of Fan Shiman's son, Jinsheng 金生, means "Golden Born," and the name of Fan Zhan's assassin, Chang 長, means something like "Excelling". If Jinsheng and Chang were transliterations of local names, these names cannot be identified, although it is notable that "Golden Born" is similar to the meaning of mai ("Pure Gold") in Fan Yangmai, the name of two kings of Linyi (see appendix five).

Liang shu's account of the assassin Chang is sparer than *Nan Qi shu*'s. Like *Nan Qi shu*, *Liang shu* seems to suggest that after murdering Fan Zhan, Chang did not succeed to the throne before being killed himself, but it is not entirely clear on this point. Otherwise, *Liang shu* differs from *Nan Qi shu* in recording that Chang killed Fan Zhan some twenty years after Fan Shiman's death, rather than a decade or so after. *Nan Qi shu* was written closer in time to the events described than *Liang shu*, so *Nan Qi shu*'s decade or so may be more reliable.

39. The buildings constructed by Fan Xun 范尋 are called here *guange* 觀閣, a kind of high building often found in palaces.

40. The ordinary people are *minren* 民人 in Chinese, the only time the commonly used term *min* 民 (people) occurs in Chinese accounts of Funan.

Bananas and sugarcane were no doubt offered to the king not only as a sign of ritual respect but also because they were tasty. Perhaps the birds and tortoises or turtles (*gui* 龜, meaning either tortoise or turtle) were also for the king's consumption. In China tortoises and turtles were prized from early times on, their spirits admired or feared and their flesh consumed with relish. Tortoiseshell was also used for divination, jewelry, and ornaments. In Cambodia, a tortoise was portrayed many centuries later as a reincarnation of Viṣṇu in the east gallery bas relief in Angkor Wat. But we can only speculate as to whether tortoises or turtles had spiritual significance in the life of Funan. Schafer, *The Vermilion Bird*, 214–216; Rooney, *Angkor*, 144.

For bananas, read *jiao* 焦 as 蕉, as in the *Nan shi* version of this passage. Li et al., *Nan shi*, 1953.

41. Two poles (*zhang* 丈) were twenty Chinese feet (*chi*), and at this time one Chinese foot was the equivalent of nearly ten (US) inches. So the crocodiles were sixteen or seventeen (US) feet in length and their snouts some five to six (US) feet long. These huge creatures may have been the estuarine or saltwater crocodile, *crocodylus porosus*. The translation of the Chinese word *tuo* 鼉 as "alligator" is tentative. The Han dynasty dictionary *Shuo wen jie zi* 說文解字 defines *tuo* as a "water creature like a lizard, roughly one pole long, with skin you can make a drum from." Today *tuo* is the word used for the alligators in the Yangzi River. [Xu,] *Shuo wen jie zi*, 686.

42. Cangwu was a region in the far south of China, one of the southern commanderies during the Han dynasty. The foreign countries referred to here are the southern states beyond Cangwu and other parts of southern China. The subsequent paragraph in *Liang shu*, omitted here, is the second of the three passages in *Liang shu* devoted to Kang Tai and Zhu Ying, provided in chapter one.

43. Zhu Zhantan's unsuccessful attempt to give the emperor an elephant—or perhaps more than one (the Chinese is not specific)—is also described in *Jin shu* (see chapter two).

44. The expression *qi hou wang*, meaning either "the king who came after him" or "a king who came after him," occurs twice more in this section. The Chinese given in *Liang shu* for Kauṇḍinya, Jiaochenru 憍陳如 (Ki̯äu đi̯ěn ńźi̯wo [K]), is a little different from the Chinese given in *Nan Qi shu*, Qiaochenru 僑陳如 (K'i̯äu đi̯ěn ńźi̯wo [K]), there being a variation in the form of the first characters, 憍 and 僑.

45. As with the story of Hun Tian, the Chinese does not make clear whether there was one god or several.

"Went from the south"—literally "arrived from the south"—is the interpretation made here of the awkward phrase *nan zhi* 南至, following the example in *Nan Qi shu* of *xi liu* 西流, meaning "flows from the west." If Kauṇḍinya arrived from the south, he could have come from a community of brahmins on the Malay Peninsula which is attested to in Chinese records. For these brahmins, see chapter one.

46. Panpan 盤盤 (or 槃槃) seems to have been on the northern part of the Malay Peninsula. *Taiping yulan* cites *Liang shu* to the effect that Panpan was "on a large island in the Southern Sea, cut off from Linyi to the north by the Small Sea," which is mentioned elsewhere and was evidently today's Gulf of Thailand. According to this *Liang shu* account, Panpan was forty days away from Jiaozhou by boat and had cities encircled by wooden fences rather than walls. Wade suggests that Panpan may have been the present-day Thai province of Surat Thani, and notes that it was described many centuries later as a center for Buddhist studies with many Indian brahmins. Hsu Yun-ts'iao identifies it with present-day Pranburi in southern Thailand. Wade, "Beyond the Southern Borders," 28; Hsu, "Notes on Tan-tan," 40; Li et al., *Taiping yulan*, 3487.

The *Liang shu* comments quoted in *Taiping yulan* are not in the Zhonghua shuju edition of *Liang shu*. See also Wang, "Nanhai Trade," 102.

47. The law introduced by Kauṇḍinya, *fa* 法 in Chinese, probably refers to Buddhist or Hindu dharma rather than any form of secular law.

48. In rendering Chilituobamo 持梨陁跋摩 as Dhṛtavarman, I follow Wang Bangwei (see chapter two). The king is also mentioned in *Song shu*, where he is called Chilibamo 持梨跋摩.

49. The Chinese name for Jayavarman, Shexiebamo 闍邪跋摩 (Dź'i̯a i̯a ? muâ [K]), is written slightly differently here from the Chinese name for Jayavarman, Sheyebamo 闍耶跋摩 (Dź'i̯a i̯a ? muâ [K]), found in *Nan Qi shu*, there being a variation in the form of the second characters, 邪 and 耶.

The missions sent to China by Dhṛtavarman from 424 to 453 are evidently the three tribute missions sent in 434, 435, and 438 mentioned in *Song shu*. The mission sent to China by Jayavarman between 483 and 493 must have been the 484 mission by the Buddhist monk Nāgasena described in *Nan Qi shu*.

50. "Speaking through more than one interpreter" is a rendition of the term *chong yi* 重譯, which as noted earlier means literally "repeated interpretation."

51. The images of the gods were made from either bronze or copper, since the Chinese term *tong* 銅 can mean either; the more precise Chinese term for bronze, *qing tong* 青銅, came into use in Tang times (though the Yuan envoy Zhou Daguan continues to use just *tong* to describe parts of Angkor that were likely to have been bronze). Since bronze rather than copper was widely used for early Cambodian statuary, bronze is clearly the correct translation here.

There are numerous early bronze statues of four-armed gods associated with Funan. These include an image of Viṣṇu found in An Giang province of Vietnam, the province where Óc Eo is located (see Fig. 12). The statue, dating from the seventh century CE, has four arms bearing the customary conch, mace, and ball of earth; the fourth object customarily held, a cakra or wheel, is missing. A stone statue of Viṣṇu in Phnom Da dating from the late sixth to early seventh century has eight arms, three of them holding a flame, a deerskin, and a flask—objects not customarily carried by Viṣṇu. Another of Durgā from the Mekong Delta during the same period has four arms.

Could such images be what is referred to here? There are no extant statues carrying a boy, a sun, the moon, a bird, or an animal (though a deerskin comes close), and it is hard to know which Indian deities these descriptions might apply to. The reference to statues carrying small boys has an intriguing Christian overtone, though there is no other suggestion that Christianity could have spread from southern India (the most obvious possible point of contact) to Funan. Coedès suggests that being two faced, the statues were of Harihara, the Cambodian deity combining Viṣṇu and Śiva in a single divided face and body; but the statues could also have had faces pointing in different directions, like the four-faced Brahmā from Battambang dating from the late tenth to early eleventh century that is now housed in the National Museum in Phnom Penh. Tingley, *Arts of Ancient Vietnam*, 156–157; Jessup, *Masterpieces of the National Museum*, 26–27, 64–65; Coedès, *Indianized States*, 61.

For early Khmer bronzes, see Woodward, "Bronze Sculptures of Ancient Cambodia," 30–77; Bunker and Latchford, *Khmer Bronzes*, 43–125. Bunker and Latchford include an appendix with illustrations of seven Khmer bronze images of Śiva, each with five heads, but these are later works. Bunker and Latchford, *Khmer Bronzes*, 503–508.

52. "Women of the palace" is a translation of *pin* 嬪, a term that in China referred mainly to concubines.

53. The cotton cloth spread out in front of the king is called *baidie* 白疊 (white folds) and probably refers to another type of cotton (as distinct from *gubei* cotton, discussed in chapter two). In a later passage on baidie, *Liang shu* records "a grass seed like a silkworm cocoon, within which there is thread like fine hempen thread called *baidie* for making into a cloth that is very soft and white." Yao, *Liang shu*, 811; Pelliot, *Notes on Marco Polo*, 453–455.

54. The Great River (Jiang 江) was probably the Mekong.

55. I follow Pelliot in rendering the name Liutuobamo 留拖跋摩 as Rudravarman, meaning Protected by Rudra, Rudra being an aspect of the god Śiva.

The name of the envoy Dangbaolao 當抱老 (Tâng b'âu: lâu: [K]) being preceded by the character Zhu 竺 is unusual. The surname Zhu is associated with India, indicating that Dangbaolao was Indian, at least by origin. Ian Harris suggests Dangbaolao was a transliteration of Dharmapala, the name of a Buddhist monk, but the imperfect correspondence between *dang* (tâng [K]) and dharma, and the fact that the name of an earlier prince (Danggenchun 當根純) also begins with Dang makes this explanation unlikely. As Pelliot notes, names beginning Dang are unusual in Chinese records of Funan; Danggenchun is the only other person with a name beginning Dang mentioned in these records. According to *Nan Qi shu*, Danggenchun was a foreigner (*yi*) and contemporary of Kauṇḍinya Jayavarman, while *Nan shi* describes him as a son of an unnamed Funanese king. It is notable that if the two Dangs—one Indian (Dangbaolao), the other a foreign prince of Funan (Danggenchun)—were related, as their common surname Dang suggests, Kauṇḍinya Jayavarman or one of his immediate predecessors would have been of Indian origin. Xiao, *Nan Qi shu*, 1013; Li et al., *Nan shi*, 1949; Pelliot, "Fou-nan," 258, 270; Harris, *Cambodian Buddhism*, 242.

56. The statue of the Buddha sent as tribute is described as *rui xiang* 瑞像, literally an "auspicious statue," a phrase customarily used for a statue of the Buddha (a meaning Pelliot misses). Sandalwood is here called *zhantan* 旃檀.

Poluo 婆羅 is the name of an unidentified tree. *Taiping yulan* has a section on *poluo* or *mupoluo* 牧婆羅 trees, including an extract from a lost source, *Nan yi zhi* 南夷志 [*Annals of Southern Foreigners*], which says the trees were cultivated for the silken thread in their seeds. According to Pelliot, *poluo* was sometimes written in error for *suoluo* 娑羅, the sal tree, under whose branches the Buddha died. Li et al., *Taiping yulan*, 4267; Pelliot, "Fou-nan," 270.

Of the other gifts Kauṇḍinya Jayavarman sent to China in 519, the glass pearls and liquidamber are worth commenting on. "Glass pearls" is a rendition of *huoqi zhu* 火齊珠. *Zhu* 珠 means "pearl," and *huoqi* 火齊 seems to have been a colored vitreous material. *Taiping yulan* describes the use of *huoqi* in making screens and rings for fingers, and cites a third-century source (*Nan zhou yi wu zhi* 南州異物志 [*Annals of Strange Things in the South*]) as saying that *huoqi* is purple or gold in color and comes from India.

Liquidamber, a term generally used for a type of gum or the tree bearing it, is here a loose rendition of *suhe* 蘇合, described in *Hou Han shu* as a substance from Da Qin (the eastern Roman Empire) made from the ignited juices of a mixture of aromatic substances. *Liang shu* also mentions *suhe*, describing it as a mixed perfume from both central India and Da Qin. Fan et al., *Hou Han shu*, 2919; Yao, *Liang shu*, 797–798; Stuart, *Chinese Materia Medica*, 138–140, 243–244.

57. The number of rhinos is not specified; there could have been one or more.

At a length of twelve Chinese feet, the putative strand of the Buddha's hair would have spanned some ten (US) feet, more than long enough to pique the emperor's interest.

Nothing more is known about the monk Yunbao 雲寶, whether he successfully took the hair back to China, and if so what happened to it.

58. Gantuoli: 干陁利. Wang, "Nanhai Trade", 102, citing studies by Gabriel Ferrand and Jean Przyluski. Yao, *Liang shu*, 794–795. Here and in the passage on Langyaxiu, "cotton" is *gubei*. For *gubei*, see chapter two.

59. Yao, *Liang shu*, 795.

"Astride the neck of the Malay Peninsula:" Wang, "Nanhai Trade," 102. "In the northeast of the Malay Peninsula:" Hsu, "Notes on Tan-tan," 45–47; Wheatley, *The Golden Khersonese*, 252–265. Wheatley identifies Langyaxiu 狼牙脩 as the place called Langkasuka and similar names in Ming-era Arab and Javanese sources, as well as in undated Indian and Malay texts, and locates it in the vicinity of present-day Pattani.

60. Yao, *Liang shu*, 795–796.

A double entrance (*chongmen* 重門) consists of gateways lined up one inside another.

61. Funan's successive rulers are described further in chapter five and listed chronologically in appendix two.

62. For more on the ambiguity of the terms sheng zi 生子 and *qi hou wang* 其後王, see earlier in this chapter.

63. According to Vickery, the inscription is written in mid-sixth century script. Vickery, "Funan Reviewed," 121–122.

On K numbering for inscriptions: an inventory of ancient Sanskrit and Khmer inscriptions relating to Cambodia is maintained by L'École française d'Extrême-Orient, where the inscriptions are identified by the letter K, followed by a number. Most of these inscriptions were published by Coedès between 1937 and 1966 under École française auspices. Coedès, *Inscriptions du Cambodge*; see also Guy, *Lost Kingdoms*, xviii.

64. Manguin suggests the canals may have been used for drainage or transport. Manguin, "Archaeology of Fu Nan," 110–111.

65. See, for instance, the otherwise informative accounts of early Funan by the American historians Kenneth Hall and Lynda Shaffer, both of whom mention the story of Hun Tian drinking the water of Funan. Hall, Maritime Trade, 55; Shaffer, *Maritime Southeast Asia*, 25–26.

66. Manguin, "Archaeology of Fu Nan," 110.

67. For more on deities in Funan and Zhenla, see the note on bronze images of gods earlier in this chapter and the section on Hindu and local gods in *Jiu Tang shu*'s portrait of Zhenla in chapter seven.

68. Chassende, "*Chen shu*," 44–45; also Chassende, "*Liang shu*," 167.

69. Yao, *Chen shu*, 39, 81, 115.

70. Graff, "*Bei shi*," 18–21; Strange and Hruby, "*Nan shi*," 209–211. Li Dashi 李大師 (570–628) and Li Yanshou 李延壽 (d. 680) thus continued the father-son tradition begun in the Han dynasty by Sima Tan and Sima Qian, the authors of *Shi ji*, and continued by Yao Cha and Yao Silian.

71. Li et al., *Nan shi*, 1951–1957.

72. These amendments include (1) a change to the account of the great river of Funan, so that it is clearly described as flowing from west to east through the addition of the preposition *cong* 從 (from); (2) an account of General Fan Zhan's murder by Fan Shiman's son Chang that adds the word "attack" (*gong* 攻), suggesting a battle or violent event; and (3) a change in the name of the brahmin king Kauṇḍinya's successor from Chilituobamo 持梨陁跋摩 (Dhṛtavarman) to Chizaituobamo 持災陁跋摩, evidently a copying error, since the character for *zai* 災 (disaster) would be most unsuitable for transcribing the name of a friendly ruler.

73. The missions are listed in Li et al., *Nan shi*, 43, 44, 45, 48, 120, 187, 193, 194, 196, 197, 201, 207, 211, 214, 274, 294, 306. The mission sent in 442 is in Li et al., *Nan shi*, 48.

74. This seems to be the assumption, for example, in Charles Higham's otherwise illuminating account of early Cambodia. Higham, *Origins of the Civilization of Angkor*, 101–102, 104. Similarly, Briggs alleges that while Kang's and Zhu's works were later lost, "they were quoted by nearly all the Chinese dynastic histories after their dates." This seems to have been true of the Liuye story, but not very much more. Briggs, *Ancient Khmer Empire*, 21.

Chapter Four

1. Wei Zheng: 魏徵; Linghu Defen: 令狐德芬; Zhangsun Wuji: 長孫無忌. Xiong, "*Sui shu*," 330–331.

2. Wei Zheng's house was in the Yongxing ward 永興坊 of Chang'an. Xiong, *Sui-Tang Chang'an*, 1, 63, 218, map 2.1.

3. Xiong, "*Sui shu*," 330–331.

4. Funan music: Wei et al., *Sui shu*, 377.

5. Wei et al., *Sui shu*, 1833. The report is listed in Liu et al., *Jiu Tang shu*, 2016. Different type: *bie zhong* 別種. The term *zhong* 種 suggests ethnic or family ties. See 別種 in Luo et al., *Hanyu da cidian*.

6. Chitu's location: Wang describes locating Chitu as "one of the most difficult problems in the historical geography of Southeast Asia". In his view it "extended south-eastwards past Singora [present-day Songkhla] . . . and may have controlled some part of the west coast" of the Malay Peninsula. After a full review, Wheatley locates it in the northeast of the Malay Peninsula. Following a similarly exhaustive discussion, Hsu Yun-ts'iao locates it in Songkhla and Pattani.

In an interesting argument, Hoshino places it in a quite different location, at the ruined complex of Banteay Prei Nokor near present-day Kompong Cham, pointing out that, unusually, this complex has north-facing entrances, like the king's palace in Chitu. Hoshino argues that Chang Jun and the others crossed on foot from southernmost China into present-day Laos, then traveled by riverboat downstream on the Mekong. His argument is attractive—if Chitu was geographically close to Linyi, and so to southern China, it would help explain why Emperor Yang seemed to regard it as ripe for exploitation—but depends on awkward interpretations of parts of the Chinese text. Wang, "Nanhai Trade," 107–108, 110; Wheatley,

The Golden Khersonese, 26–36, esp. 36; Hsu, "A Study on Ch'ih-t'u," 10–11; Hsu, "Notes on Tan-tan," 45; Hoshino, "The Kingdom of Red Earth," 60–65.

7. On Emperor Yang and Sui ambitions: Wright, "The Sui Dynasty," 73–149. As given in the following *Sui shu* passage, the offices and titles of Chang Jun 常駿 and his fellow envoy Wang Junzheng 王君政 were Officer in Charge of State Farms (Duntian zhushi 屯田主事) and Officer in Charge of Forestry and Crafts (Yubu zhushi 虞部主事). Hucker, *Dictionary of Official Titles*, 179, 550.

8. Or perhaps even completed. For more on the timing of Funan's absorption by Zhenla, see later in this chapter and chapter six.

9. Linyi as Funan's neighbor: see, for instance, King Kauṇḍinya Jayavarman's description of Linyi to Emperor Wu of the Southern Qi in 484, as discussed in chapter two.

10. Glahn, *Economic History*, 183–184.

11. Hoshino, "The Kingdom of Red Earth," 58–60; Wright, "The Sui Dynasty," 109; Wei et al., *Sui shu*, 1832–1833.

12. Accounts of imperial Chinese missions to foreign states by both parties, the Chinese court and the recipient state, are rare but not unknown. For a study of an early Chinese mission to another Asian state, Ceylon, about which we are fortunate to have accounts by both sides—by Chinese chroniclers portraying an uplifting display of imperial Chinese power and patronage, and by Ceylonese recipients describing an ill-informed Chinese intervention in their affairs—see Timothy Brook's superb portrait of the Ming admiral Zheng He's escapades in Ceylon from 1410 to 1411. Brook, *Great State*, 91–100.

13. Wei et al., *Sui shu*, 1833–1835. The same passage is found in shorter form in *Bei shi*, *Tong dian*, *Taiping yulan*, and *Wenxian tongkao*. The *Sui shu* account of Chitu is the first account of Chitu in the standard histories; none of the earlier standard histories mention it. The account in *Tong dian* has minor variations, including mention of the fact that the capital "is also called Shizi [Lion] City", and that in Chitu "for playing there is double-six [an unidentified game] and chicken-bone divination; in midwinter your shadow is directly beneath you, and in midsummer your shadow is to the south, while the entrances all face north"—the comment about midsummer shadows suggesting that Chitu was south of the equator, beyond both present-day Cambodia and the Malay Peninsula. Du, *Tong dian*, 5094.

14. The locations and identities of Boluola 波羅剌, Poluosuo 婆羅娑, and Heluodan 訶羅旦 (also 訶羅單, 呵羅單) cannot be clearly identified. Citing *Nan shi*, *Taiping yulan* describes the capital of Heluodan as being the island of Shepo (Java), but this is clearly the result of a copying error. (The *Nan shi* entry lists the names of several states sending tribute missions, one of them Shepo, another Heluodan, and this is evidently what the entry in *Taiping yulan* should have read.) Da hai 大海 (Great Sea) is another name for the Southern Sea, or possibly in this instance (if we follow Hoshino) for Tonlé Sap Lake. Li et al., *Taiping yulan*, 3487, citing *Nan shi*. Li et al., *Nan shi*, 43.

15. The king's name, or perhaps title and name, are not possible to identify with any certainty. Hsu proposes plausibly that Qutan 瞿曇 (Guǎ dəm/dam [P]) is the ancient Indian honorific Gautama (Enlightened One) but is unable to explain Lifuduosai 利富多塞. Hoshino suggests less persuasively that Qutan is the royal title Steṅ/steñ. (Steṅ/steñ is Vickery's transcription; Hoshino writes Stan.) Qutan's reconstructed pronunciation, Guǎ dəm, is a poor match for Steṅ/steñ, besides which Vickery notes that the title Steṅ/steñ was not in use in pre-Angkorian times. Hsu, "A Study on Ch'ih-t'u," 13; Hoshino, "The Kingdom of Red Earth," 64; Vickery, *Society, Economics, and Politics*, 29.

16. The name of the capital, Sengzhi 僧祇 (Səŋ tɕiă/tɕi [P]) *cheng* 城, may mean Lion City, *sengzhi* being construed as a transliteration of the Sanskrit *siṃhá* (lion), *singa* in Malay, and *cheng* being the Chinese for "city". Du You, author of the late eighth-century *Tong dian*, certainly assumes as much, as he gives Lion City (Shizi *cheng* 獅子城) as the city's alternative name. Lion could have Buddhist overtones, since the Buddha was sometimes compared to a lion for his fearlessness. Hsu Yun-ts'iao confidently identifies Sengzhi *cheng* with the present-day city of Songkhla or Singgora, Lion City, in the south of present-day Thailand. An alternative explanation is that the city was called Eternal City, since *sengzhi* can be short for *asengzhi* 阿僧祇, Chinese for the Sanskrit *aśaṅkya*, meaning "innumerable" or "endless", often with respect to Buddhist and Hindu kalpas or aeons. Du, *Tong dian*, 5094; Hsu, "A Study on Ch'ih-t'u," 11–12; Soothill and Hodous, *Dictionary of Chinese Buddhist Terms*, 285, 324.

17. "Guardian spirits:" *jingang lishi* 金剛力士, literally "Vajra strongmen." The term is used to describe guardian spirits or idols at the entrance to Buddhist monasteries, and (as here) Buddhist pagodas. For Vajra, meaning "diamond" and by extension (because of its indestructible cutting power) "thunderbolt," see Zhou Daguan's description of the king of Zhenla as the bearer of the Vajra diamond, in chapter nine. Soothill and Hodous, *Dictionary of Chinese Buddhist Terms*, 282.

18. "Various aromatic woods:" *wu xiang mu* 五香木, literally "five aromatic woods," the five aromatic substances being variously defined, as noted earlier. *Wuxiangmu* is also a name for lign-aloes. Luo et al., *Hanyu da cidian*, entry under 五香木; Stuart, *Chinese Materia Medica*, 44.

19. The gold ox could well be Nandi, sacred bull of the god Śiva, which is often portrayed in a reclining position. Coedès convincingly proposes that the titles of Chitu's most senior officials are derived from Sanskrit, as follows: Sādhukāra (Doer of Good) or Sārdhakāra (Fellow Worker) for Satogaluo 薩陀迦羅; Dhanada (Dispenser of Good Things) for Tuonadayi 陀拏達義; Kamika (Agent) for Galimiga 迦利蜜迦; Kulapati (Head of the Family) for Juluomodi 俱羅末帝; Nayaka (Guide) for Nayega 那邪迦; and Pati (Chief) for Bodi 鉢帝. Coedès, *Indianized States*, 294.

20. "Light grey:" a guess at the meaning of *chaoyun* 朝雲, literally "morning cloud." The origin of this term is unclear.

21. Nanhai refers to the far south of China, being one of the southernmost commanderies established by the Han dynasty. Linyi was the state to the south of the southernmost part of China; at the time referred to here it was probably still occupied by Sui forces. Langyaxu 狼牙须 is a variant of Langyaxiu 狼牙脩, the state mentioned in chapter three that was probably located in the north of the Malay Peninsula.

Otherwise the locations of the places Chang Jun passed by—Jiaoshishan 焦石山 (Burnt Rock Mountain), Shizishi 師子石 (Lion Rock) and Jilong 雞籠 (Chicken Coop—are not possible to identify with any certainty.

The whereabouts of Linggabobaduo 陵伽鉢拔多 (Liṅgaparvata or Linga Mountain) is also unclear. In its account of Zhenla, *Sui shu* mentions a place called Linggabopo 陵伽鉢婆 (Liṅgaparvata), which Coedès identifies with the temple site at Wat Phu in present-day Laos but Vickery argues could well have been located elsewhere. The Tang dynasty geographer Jia Dan 賈耽 mentions a Ling Mountain (Lingshan 陵山, written with the same character *ling* 陵), located some eleven days' sail south of Guangzhou. This location is broadly consistent with that of the Linga Mountain that Chang Jun sailed by. There are also entries on a Ling Mountain (Lingshan 靈山, written with a different *ling* 靈), evidently located in today's Vietnam, in two much later sources: the Yuan merchant Wang Dayuan's *Dao yi zhi lüe* [*A Brief Record of the Foreigners of the Islands*] and the Ming mariner Fei Xin's *Xing cha sheng lan* [*The Overall Survey of the Star Raft*]. For Coedès and Vickery on Liṅgaparvata in *Sui shu*, see chapter six. For Jia Dan on Lingshan, see Ouyang et al., *Xin Tang shu*, 1153; also chapter seven. For *Dao yi zhi lüe* and *Xingcha shenglan* on Lingshan, Wang, *Dao yi zhi lüe*, 223–227; Fei, *Xingcha shenglan*, *qianji*, 7–8.

After the first reference to him, Chang Jun is referred to throughout as Jun. I have given his name throughout as Chang Jun.

22. The description of the last stage of the envoys' journey to Chitu reads literally, "After a month or so, he reached their capital." Here, the month or so evidently means from the time Chang Jun set out from the Nanhai commandery, rather than from the time he met the brahmin Jiumoluo 鳩摩羅 (Kuw ma la [P]).

Hoshino persuasively identifies Jiumoluo with the Sanskrit *kumāra*, meaning "prince" or "high-born son." So here it is a title rather than a name. Nayega, the name of the prince who welcomes Chang Jun at the final stage of his journey to Chitu, is written with the same Chinese characters as the official title Nayega/Nayaka (Guide) mentioned earlier, so again it is a title, not a name. Hoshino, "The Kingdom of Red Earth," 64.

23. As mentioned earlier, elsewhere *duoluo* 多羅 seems to refer to a gold leaf, or perhaps a gold leaf cup.

24. Jiaozhi was the Red River Delta region. Hongnong 弘農 was a prefecture near the city of Luoyang, which Emperor Yang of the Sui dynasty had made his capital on acceding to the throne a couple of years earlier.

For *wei* 尉 (guard) in the term Loyal Guards or Bingyiwei 秉義尉, see Hucker, *Dictionary of Official Titles*, 564 (*bingyi* 秉義, "loyal" or "righteous", is not in Hucker).

25. Luosha: 羅剎. Wei et al., *Sui shu*, 71, 687. Luosha's location east of Poli 婆利: *Sui shu* cited in Li et al., *Taiping yulan*, 3490, a passage not found in the received text of *Sui shu*. Poli on the island of Sumatra: Hsu, "Notes on Tan-tan," 43–44.

26. Li et al., *Taiping yulan*, 3490.

27. Zhandabo: 旃達鉢. The name is evidently a transliteration, but its original language and meaning has not been identified. Shizi: 師子 in *Liang shu*, 獅子 in *Cefu yuangui*. In one instance each, both sources call this place Shiziguo, the State of Shizi. Wei et al., *Sui shu*, 71, 72, 75; Ouyang et al., *Xin Tang shu*, 6299; Yao, *Liang shu*, 71, 800; Wang et al., *Cefu yuangui*, 11402, 11404.

28. Wei et al., *Sui shu*, 945.

29. As noted earlier, this passage of *Sui shu* seems to have survived only in a quotation in *Taiping yulan*. Li et al., *Taiping yulan*, 3482.

30. The report is in *Sui shu*'s separate entry on Zhenla. Wei et al., *Sui shu*, 1835–1836. The identification of Zhiduosina 質多斯那 (Tśi̯ět tâ si̯ẹ nâ [K]) with Citrasena is Pelliot's. Pelliot, "Fou-nan", 272. For Shali, see the following footnote. For more on Citrasena, see *Sui shu*'s account of Zhenla in chapter six. "Taken over": *jian* 兼. The other term used to describe Zhenla's takeover of Funan, for example in *Tang hui yao* 唐會要, is "annex" (*bing* 並). For a discussion of these terms, see chapter six.

31. Vickery, *Society, Economics, and Politics*, 22, 78. According to Vickery, before the death of his brother Citrasena had presided over a smaller realm, arguably giving him the status of a king, albeit a minor one. Citrasena's family name, Shali 刹利 (a short form of Shadili 刹帝利) or Kṣatriyaḥ, derives from the Sanskrit word for "rule" or "authority", and denotes the ruling or military varna or class in traditional Hindu society. In his seventh-century account of his visit to India, the Buddhist monk Xuanzang explains to his Tang readers what varna are. [Xuan and Bianji], *Da Tang xi yu ji*, 119. See also Mehta, *Foundations of Indian Political Thought*, 32.

32. Lu and Zhou, *Zhongguo gujizhong*, 61; Chen et al., *Zhongguo gujizhong*, 35.

33. For *shitong* 十通, see Wilkinson, *Chinese History*, 718–720.

34. For *Tong dian*, see Wilkinson, *Chinese History*, 719–720; Graff "*Tong dian*," 355–358; de Crespigny, "Universal Histories," 64–65. For *Tong zhi* and *Wenxian tongkao* on Funan, see later in this chapter.

35. Du You: 杜佑; Du Mu: 杜牧. Wilkinson, *Chinese History*, 718; de Crespigny, "Universal Histories," 65.

36. Border defense: *bian fang* 邊防.

37. Du, *Tong dian*, 5093–5094.

38. *Dai* 玳, the word used here for "turtle" or "tortoise" can also refer to their shells.

"Ornamental bridles" is a tentative translation of the term *ke* 珂, which can refer to various kinds of ornament used for horses' bridles.

39. The comment about the kings of Funan having the family name Gulong reproduces verbatim the comment about *gulong* in *Sui shu* as cited by *Taiping yulan*.

40. Envoy—or envoys: again, *shi* 使, "envoy", is not number specific.

41. Baitou 白頭 means "white head" or "white hair"; nothing is known about the Baitou state and its people (were they albinos?) beyond what is written in this entry in *Tong dian*, an entry repeated with minor modifications in *Xin Tang shu*.

42. Canban 參半 (Ts'ậm puân- [K]) has been variously located. *Jiu Tang shu* and *Xin Tang shu* place it to Zhenla's southwest and northwest, respectively. *Xin Tang shu* calls it a dependency of Wendan 文單 or Land Zhenla, the northern part of Zhenla. The modern Chinese scholar Yang Wuquan identifies it with the Sanbo 三泊 mentioned by Zhou Qufei, arguing that Sanbo is Sambor in Kratié province in present-day Cambodia. Hoshino locates it in the central plain of present-day Thailand. Li et al., *Taiping yulan*, citing [*Jiu*] Tang shu, 3483. Ouyang et al., *Xin Tang shu*, 6302. Hoshino, "Wen Dan and its Neighbours," 41; Yang Wuquan in Zhou, *Lingwai daida*, 82–83.

According to the eleventh-century compilation *Cefu yuangui*, Canban submitted tribute to the Chinese court just twice, in 625 and again in 628. Perhaps these two tribute missions from Canban, like the missions to and from Chitu in 607–610, were a reflection of unsettled conditions in Cambodia caused by the takeover of Funan by Zhenla. Wang et al., *Cefu yuangui*, 11397, reading 半 for 朱.

43. Wang et al., *Cefu yuangui*, juan 46.

44. Wilkinson, *Chinese History*, 717. Also Ng and Wang, *Mirroring the Past*, 131–133.

45. Work on *Tang hui yao* was begun by the brothers Su Mian 蘇冕 (d. 805) and Su Bian 蘇弁 (fl. 760–805), and continued by Cui Xuan 崔鉉 (fl. 840s–860s), who completed a first version in 853. For Su Mian and Su Bian, see Ng and Wang, *Mirroring the Past*, 132. For Cui Xuan, see Wilkinson, *Chinese History*, 717.

Wang Pu 王溥's biography is in Tuotuo et al., *Song shi*, 8799–8802.

On *Tang hui yao* being presented in 961, Wang, *Tang hui yao*, i.

46. Annex: bing 並. Wang, *Tang hui yao*, 1752.

The Chinese reads: "*Zhenla zai Linyi zhi xinan ben Funan zhi shuguo ye . . . Liang Datong zhong shi bing Funan er you qi guo*" 真臘在林邑之西南本扶南之屬國也 . . . 梁大同中始並扶南而有其國. Vickery notes correctly that this entry in *Tang hui yao* was "apparently missed by Pelliot". Vickery, "Funan Reviewed," 134.

47. *Shi*: 始.

48. Wang, *Tang hui yao*, 1798.

49. Li Fang: 李昉. On *Taiping yulan*, see Kurtz, "*Taiping yulan*," 343.

50. *Taiping yulan*'s sources for these references: (1) the use of gold: *Yi yuan* 異苑 [*An Anthology of the Unusual*], a lost work by a fifth-century writer, Liu Jingshu 劉敬叔; (2) the shipping of iron: the partially lost Six Dynasties work *Nanfang caowu zhuang* 南方草物狀 [*The Form of Plants, Animals and Other Creatures in the South*]; (3) the priceless mirror: the lost Tang dynasty work *Liang si gongzi ji* 梁四公子記 [*A Record of the Four Lord-Masters of the Liang Dynasty*]. Li et al., *Taiping yulan*, 3412, 3614, 3592.

51. The location of Danlan 耽蘭 cannot be identified.

52. *Taiping yulan*'s sources for these three passages: (1) Li et al., *Taiping yulan*, citing the lost early work *Shui jing* 水經 [*Classic of Waterways*], 4157; (2) Li et al., *Taiping yulan*, citing the third-century scholar Cui Bao 崔豹's lost work *Gu jin zhu* 古今注 [*Commentary on Old and New*], 4348; (3) Li et al., *Taiping yulan*, citing the Liang dynasty work Jin lou zi 金樓子 [*Master of the Golden Building*], 4349.

53. "Sandalwood" is here called *zizhanmu* 紫旃木, with the *Taiping yulan* passage noting that *zizhanmu* "is also called *zitan* 紫檀." Another name for sandalwood is *zhantan* 旃檀, the name used in the next *Taiping yulan* passage. "Frankincense" is *xunlu* 薰陸. Stuart describes it as olibanum. "Mint" is again *huo xiang* 霍香, Chinese patchouli, mentioned earlier by Kang Tai, who remarked that it came from Dukun. Stuart, *Chinese Materia Medica*, 71–72, 291, 360, 394.

54. There is one other passage on Funan in *Taiping yulan*, but it is clearly the result of a copyist's error, since there is an identical passage in *Liang shu*, reproduced in *Nan shi*, on the state of Fusang 扶桑, a quite different entity with a similar name to that of Funan. The *Taiping yulan* passage reads, "In Funan [Fusang] there are deer carts. The people of the state raise deer in the same way as in China people raise cows, making whey from the milk." Li et al., *Taiping yulan* citing *Nan shi*, 4017; Yao, *Liang shu*, 808; Li et al., *Nan shi*, 1976–1977.

55. Yue *Taiping huanyu ji*, 3359–3361.

56. Wang, "Some Comments on the Later Standard Histories", 54–57; Wilkinson, *Chinese History*, 824–825. On Ouyang Xiu, see also Nienhauser, *Indiana Companion*, 639–641.

57. Wang, "Some Comments on the Later Standard Histories", 54–56.

58. Central India: Zhong Tianzhu 中天竺. Liu et al., *Jiu Tang shu*, 5307; also Ouyang et al., *Xin Tang shu*, 6237.

59. Liu et al., *Jiu Tang shu*, 1070; Ouyang et al., *Xin Tang shu*, 479.

60. Liu et al., *Jiu Tang shu*, 5269–5288; Ouyang et al., *Xin Tang shu*, 6301.

61. Huanwang: 環王. Ouyang et al., *Xin Tang shu*, 6297–6299. *Xin Tang shu* records that Huanwang was "originally" (*ben* 本) Linyi, and was another name for the state of Zhanbulao 占不勞 or Zhanpo 占婆, the state or states usually known in English as Champa. *Xin Tang shu* adds that its king had several places of residence, the principal among them being Zhancheng 占城 or Cham City (again, a name usually translated into English as Champa). According to *Xin Tang shu*, Huanwang was the name for Champa from 756–757 onwards. The last tribute from Huanwang, recorded in *Taiping yulan*, seems to have been sent in 793. *Cefu yuangui* mentions it one final time with reference to an event in 838. See appendix five.

62. The comment about taxes (*shui* 稅) echoes the only other comment about taxes in Funan in official Chinese sources, the remark in *Jin shu* about levies and taxes (*gong fu* 貢賦) being paid with gold, silver, pearls, and perfumes.

63. "In a very short time" is a translation of the word *e* 俄, which can also mean "suddenly". Although e here refers only to the annexation of Temu 特牧 prior to Funan's move to Nafuna 那弗那, its description of a speedy process is in contrast to the entry in *Tang hui yao*, with its suggestion of a gradual takeover.

64. Vickery also questions whether *d'ək mi̯uk* is a rendition of the Khmer term *dmāk* or *dalmak/dalmāk*, and whether *dalmak/dalmāk* is the equivalent of the Sanskrit *vyādha* (hunter). He has no alternative explanation for the meaning of Temu, other than to suggest that *d'ək* might represent *dteuk*, the Khmer word for "water". Coedès, *Indianized States*, 36–37. Vickery, Society Economics, and Politics, 36; Vickery, "Funan Reviewed," 130.

65. See, for example, the entry on Funan in the 2019 online edition of *Encyclopedia Brittanica*.

66. Pelliot, "Fou-nan", 295; also Chen et al., "Gudai Nanhai diming huishi".

67. Zheng, *Tong zhi*, 3173–3174. Wilkinson, *Chinese History*, 718, 720.

68. For the question of whether he had one or seven sons, see the comments on the *Liang shu* account of Funan in chapter three.

69. At that time the Sui capital was Chang'an. Although the official purpose of *Chen shu* was to record events relating to the preceding Chen dynasty, the Sui dynasty established itself in Chang'an in 581, some eight years before the Chen dynasty's final collapse in south China, and *Chen shu* evidently went on recording foreign missions to Chang'an during the 580s even though the Chen court was no longer there.

70. Wlikinson, *Chinese History*, 719–720; de Crespigny, "Universal Histories", 67–68; Ma, *Wenxian tongkao*, 2601.

71. The sometimes slipshod translation into French was published in 1883 by Marie-Jean-Léon Lecoq, Marquis d'Hervey de Saint-Denys. Ma, *Ethnographie des peuples étrangers à la Chine*. Lecoq's translation of the section on Zhenla is in Part 2, 477–488.

Chapter Five

1. Coedès, *Indianized States*, 36–38, 40–42, 46–50, 55–62, 65–70; Briggs, *Ancient Khmer Empire*, 13–36. Both scholars depended on the work of Pelliot for their understanding of Funan. Being an overall review of the history of Funan, many of the footnotes in this chapter repeat sources and information given in chapters one to four.

2. According to Pierre Manguin, there are a few fifth-to seventh-century Sanskrit inscriptions that may relate to Funan, but their content is insubstantial. Manguin, "Archaeology of Fu Nan," 104.

3. Wan Zhen and *Jin shu* place it west of Linyi; *Liang shu* and Ge Hong (?) place it southwest of Linyi; Kang Tai, *Nan Qi shu*, and *Liang shu* place it south of Rinan. Li et al., *Taiping yulan*, 3482; Fang et al., *Jin shu*, 2547; Yao, *Liang shu*, 787; [attr. Ge,] *Tai qing jin ye shen dan jing*, 14; Xiao, *Nan Qi shu*, 1014; Li, *Shui jing zhu*, 835.

4. Linyi: Yao, *Liang shu*, 784. Rinan was a Han dynasty commandery: Ban, *Han shu*, 188; Fan et al., Hou Han shu, 2835; Xiao, *Nan Qi shu*, 266.

5. A date in brackets refer to the date of completion of a Chinese source, when known. See also appendix one.

6. Yao, *Liang shu*, 787.

7. Li, *Shui jing zhu*, 840.

8. Manguin, "Archaeology of Fu Nan," 107; Coe and Evans, *Angkor and the Khmer Civilization*, 75, 93.

9. Ba nam in the reconstructed pronunciation of Yijing's time. Yijing, *Nanhai jigui neifa zhuan*, 17.

10. Coedès, *Indianized States*, 37.

11. Yao, *Liang shu*, 783.

12. Li et al., *Taiping yulan*, 1599. Kang Tai's account of Liuye is repeated with minor variations in *Jin shu*, *Nan Qi shu*, and *Liang shu*.

13. Li et al., *Taiping yulan*, 1599. Different records give different versions of Hun Tian's name. Kang refers to him as Hun Shen and Hun Dian; *Jin shu* calls him Hun Kui. Hun Tian is the name given in *Nan Qi shu*, an early and so perhaps more dependable source.

14. The case, also, with the names of the early kings who succeeded Hun Tian.

15. Another suggestion, put forward by Pelliot, is that Hun Tian was a transliteration of the Sanskrit Kauṇḍinya. The suggestion is plausible but less convincing, for various reasons including the fact that Hun Tian's successor Pankuang may also have born the name or title Hun. Vickery, "Funan Reviewed", 108–109, 114; Pelliot, "Fou-nan", 290–291, and "Quelques textes Chinois", 245.

16. Wuwen: Li et al., *Taiping yulan*, 3485. Jiao or Ji: Xiao, *Nan Qi shu*, 1014; Yao, *Liang shu*, 788.

17. Kang Tai refers to *shen* 神 (deity, god) which can be either singular or plural. In its account of the story, *Liang shu* refers to *gui shen* 鬼神, "gods" in the plural. Li et al., *Taiping yulan*, 1599; Yao, *Liang shu*, 788.

18. Li et al., *Taiping yulan*, 1599. There are similar accounts in *Jin shu*, *Nan Qi shu*, and *Liang shu*.

19. Li et al., *Taiping yulan*, 1599; Yao, *Liang shu*, 788. By an altgernative reading of the phrase *sheng zi* 生子 they had only one son, who then became king of all seven districts.

20. Vickery, *Society, Economics, and Politics*, 41. Kambuja is the basis for the modern name Cambodia.

21. *Liang shu* calls him Hun Pankuang. Xiao, *Nan Qi shu*, 1014; Yao, *Liang shu*, 788. Also Li et al., *Taiping yulan*, 3955.

22. If he was Hun Tian's direct successor he could, of course, have been one of his sons, but there is no record of this being the case.

23. Yao, *Liang shu*, 788.

24. Li et al., *Taiping yulan*, 3955.

25. Yao, *Liang shu*, 788.

26. Yao, *Liang shu*, 788.

27. Vickery, *Society, Economics, and Politics*, 50, 190–205.

28. Li et al., *Taiping yulan*, 3489,

29. Li et al., *Taiping yulan*, 3489; Yao, *Liang shu*, 788.

30. Yao, *Liang shu*, 787.

31. Yao, *Liang shu*, 788.

32. Li et al., *Taiping yulan*, 4348, 4347.

33. Yao, *Liang shu*, 788–789, Xiao, *Nan Qi shu*, 1014. Jinsheng means "Golden Born". If it is the eqivalent of a local name, the name is unidentifiable. On matriliny and Fan Zhan: Vickery, *Society, Economics, and Politics*, 260–261, 326, 372–373.

34. Xiao, *Nan Qi shu*, 1014. *Liang shu* records that his reign lasted twenty years, but as a later source it may be less reliable. Yao, *Liang shu*, 789.

35. Chen, *San guo zhi*, 920.

36. The most colorful reference to musicians is in the two histories of the Tang dynasty (618–907). They mention Funanese dancers and musicians in the Tang court, the dancers in rose-colored costumes and red leather boots, the musicians playing on a variety of Indian-style instruments. Liu et al., *Jiu Tang shu*, 1070; Ouyang et al., *Xin Tang shu*, 479.

37. Xiao, *Nan Qi shu*, 1014. Chang is Chinese for something like "Excelling". If it is the equivalent of a local name, the name is unidentifiable.

38. Li et al., *Taiping yulan*, 1589.

39. Yao, *Liang shu*, 787, where Yao calls Diansun Dunxun.

40. Li, *Shui jing zhu*, 7.

41. Yao, *Liang shu*, 798. *Liang shu* does not explicitly state that Su Wu went to India after Fan Zhan's meeting with Jia Xiangli, but that must have been the sequence of events.

42. Yao, *Liang shu*, 798. Yuezhi as the Chinese name for the Tokharians: Beckwith, *Empires of the Silk Road*, 84–85. Maolun as Muruṇḍa: Coedès, *Indianized States*, 46. The Muruṇḍas and their connection with the Tokharians: Kalia, *Bhubaneswar*, 17.

43. Xiao, *Nan Qi shu*, 1014; Yao, *Liang shu*, 789. In the *Liang shu* account, Chang waited twenty years, from infancy to manhood, before killing Fan Shiman. I have followed *Nan Qi shu* here, as the source closer to the time of the event described. I have also assumed that Fan Zhan's assassin Chang did not live long enough to rule as king.

44. What remains of Kang's writings does not actually mention a meeting with the king, but since Kang and Zhu were imperial Chinese envoys a meeting must have taken place. Perhaps Kang's account of it is lost.

45. Yao, *Liang shu*, 798.

46. Yao, *Liang shu*, 783.

47. Huijiao, *Gao seng zhuan*, *juan* 10, in Lu and Zhou, *Zhongguo gujizhong*, 50.

48. Fang et al., *Jin shu*, 68, 77, 78. In different entries *Jin shu* gives two different dates for the first mission.

49. The source for these three missions is the much later, unofficial Song dynasty work *Yu hai*, so there must be some doubt about whether they took place. Wang Yinglin 王應麟, *Yu hai* 玉海, *juan* 152, cited in Chen et al., *Zhongguo gujizhong*, 119.

50. Fang et al., *Jin shu*, 68, 77, 78.

51. Yao, *Liang shu*, 789.

52. Ouyang, *Yi wen lei ju*, 1585. *Nan Qi shu* mentions that the Funanese enjoyed cockfights and pig fights. Xiao, *Nan Qi shu*, 1017.

53. Yao, *Liang shu*, 789.

54. Li et al., *Taiping yulan*, 3105.

55. Yao, *Liang shu*, 789.

56. Li et al., *Taiping yulan*, citing *Waiguo zhuan*, 3482. The dating of *Waiguo zhuan* is uncertain. The name *Waiguo zhuan* may have been a short form of Kang Tai's work *Wushi waiguo zhuan*; but *Waiguo zhuan* was also the title of two other books written by fifth-century Buddhist monks. So this and other *Waiguo zhuan* descriptions of Funan may date from two centuries later than Kang Tai.

57. [Gan et al.,] *Sou shenji*, 28.

58. Li et al. *Taiping yulan*, 3184, 3392.

59. Zhou, *Zhenla fengtu ji*, 128–129.

60. Li et al., *Taiping yulan*, citing *Waiguo zhuan*, 3482.

61. Xiao, *Nan Qi shu*, 1015.

62. Li et al., *Taiping yulan*, 3411.

63. Li et al., *Taiping yulan*, 4348.

64. Li et al., *Taiping yulan*, 3482.

65. Li et al., *Taiping yulan*, 3482.

66. For example in the pre-Tang Daoist text *Tai qing jin ye shen dan jing*. [attr. Ge,] *Tai qing jin ye shen dan jing*, 14.

67. Li et al., *Taiping yulan*, citing *Sui shu*, 3482. The passage is not in the Zhonghua shuju edition of *Sui shu*.

68. Vickery, "Funan Reviewed", 103, 188–189.

69. Yao, *Liang shu*, 789. In his record of his visit, Kang also remarks on the apparently contradictory fact that the people wear girdles. Li et al., *Taiping yulan*, 3105.

70. Xiao, *Nan Qi shu*, 1015.

71. Li et al., *Taiping yulan*, 3501.

72. Like the teeth of the Heichi (Black Teeth) people: Li et al., *Taiping yulan*, 3502.

73. Ouyang, *Yi wen lei ju*, 1674.

74. Fans: Wu, *Shi lei fu*, 301; Li et al., *Taiping yulan*, 3133. Diamonds: Li et al., *Taiping yulan*, citing Ge, *Bao pu zi*, 3482. Dangerous fish: Li et al., *Taiping yulan*, citing *Shui jing*, 4157. Sandalwood: Li et al., *Taiping yulan*, citing Cui Bao, *Gu jin zhu*, 4348.

75. Li et al., *Taiping yulan*, 4348, 4347, 4103, 3485, 3180.

76. Fang et al., *Jin shu*, 2547.

77. Effort: Yao, *Liang shu*, 789; harm: Fang et al., *Jin shu*, 2547. China's elephants: Elvin, *Retreat of the Elephants*, 9–18.

78. Fang et al., *Jin shu*, 2547.

79. Not to be confused with King Pankuang's son Panpan.

80. That is, the dharma of either Buddhist or Hindu belief. Yao, *Liang shu*, 789.

81. Fang et al., *Jin shu*, 2547. Hu as Indian: Luo et al., *Hanyu da cidian*, entry under Hu 胡. "Ugly and black:" Yao, *Liang shu*, 790.

82. Yao, *Liang shu*, 789; Wang, "The Buddhist Connection", 286.

83. Shen, *Song shu*, 83, 85, 2379; Yao, *Liang shu*, 789.

84. Xiao, *Nan Qi shu*, 1016–1017.

85. Xiao, *Nan Qi shu*, 1016–1017.

86. Xiao, *Nan Qi shu*, 1016.

87. Xiao, *Nan Qi shu*, 1017.

88. See chapter three.

89. Yao, *Liang shu*, 40, 52, 54, 57.

90. Yao, *Liang shu*, 790.

91. We must assume that the strand of hair was delivered. We know the emperor sent a monk called Yunbao to Funan to collect it, but there is no record of Yunbao taking it back to Jiankang. Yao, *Liang shu*, 790.

92. Chen, "*Pañcavārṣika* Assemblies," 45–46, 53, 55.

93. Daoxuan, *Xu Gao seng zhuan*, *juan* 1, in Lu and Zhou, *Zhongguo gujizhong*, 51–52; Wang, "The Buddhist Connection," 283–288.

94. The Funan Office: Funan guan 扶南館. Daoxuan, *Xu Gao seng zhuan*, *juan* 1, in Lu and Zhou, *Zhongguo gujizhong*, 51; Wang, "The Buddhist Connection," 283.

95. Daoxuan, *Xu Gao seng zhuan*, *juan* 1, in Lu and Zhou, *Zhongguo gujizhong*, 52–53. Wang, "The Buddhist Connection," 287–288. "Leading translator": Barrett, "Diana Y. Paul: Philosophy of Mind," 175.

96. Yang, *Luoyang galan ji*, 250–251.

97. Daoshi, *Fayuan zhulin*, 474.

98. Yao, *Chen shu*, 39, 81, 115. The fact that *Chen shu* reported the 588 mission implies that the mission was to the Chen dynasty, but *Tong zhi* describes the mission as going to Chang'an, which by that time was under Sui control. Zheng, *Tong zhi*, 720.

99. Du, *Tong dian*, 5094.

100. Ouyang et al., *Xin Tang shu*, 6301.

101. Ouyang et al., *Xin Tang shu*, 6301. Nafuna *cheng* as Navanagara (*cheng* meaning "city"): Pelliot, "Fou-nan", 295.

102. Wang, *Tang hui yao*, 1798.

103. Yao, *Liang shu*, 798.

104. Li et al., *Taiping yulan*, citing *Liang si gongzi ji*, 3592.

105. Li et al., *Taiping yulan*, citing *Yi yuan*, *Nanfang caowu zhuang*, and *Liang si gongzi ji*, 3412, 3614, 3592.

106. Xiao, *Nan Qi shu*, 1017; Yao, *Liang shu*, 787.

107. Tingley, *Arts of Ancient Vietnam*, 156–157; Jessup, *Masterpieces of the National Museum*, 26–27, 64–65; Woodward, "Bronze Sculptures," 30–77; Bunker and Latchford, *Khmer Bronzes*, 43–125.

108. Yao, *Liang shu*, 790; Xiao, *Nan Qi shu*, 1017.

109. Yao, *Liang shu*, 790. "Avalokiteśvara (Guanyin) at ease": my suggestion. See for example the tenth-century statue of Avalokiteśvara in the Denver Art Museum, denverartmuseum.org/object/1946.4.

110. Yao, *Liang shu*, 790.

111. Yao, *Liang shu*, 790.

112. Wei et al., *Sui shu*, 1833.

113. The location preferred by both Wheatley and Wang Gungwu. Wheatley, "Ch'ih T'u," 16; Wang, "Nanhai Trade," 107, 110.

114. Wang, "Nanhai Trade," 107–108; Hoshino, "The Kingdom of Red Earth," 58–60.

115. Wei et al., *Sui shu*, 1833–1835. The same passage in shorter form is found in *Bei shi*, *Taiping yulan*, and *Wenxian tongkao*. Chang's record: Liu et al., *Jiu Tang shu*, 2016.

116. Sengzhi *cheng* 僧祇城 (*cheng* meaning "city"): Lion City from the Sanskrit *siṃhá* (lion). *Tong dian* gives its alternative name as Shizi *cheng* 獅子城 (Lion City). Eternal City: from the Sanskrit *aśaṅkya*, meaning "innumerable" or "endless". Du, *Tong dian*, 5094; Soothill and Hodous, *Dictionary of Chinese Buddhist Terms*, 285.

117. Nayega: Coedès, *Indianized States*, 294. Nandi: my supposition.

118. Wei et al., *Sui shu*, 1833–1835.

119. Wei et al., *Sui shu*, 1835–1836. Vickery, *Society, Economics, and Politics*, 22, 78.

120. Ouyang et al., *Xin Tang shu*, 6301; Wang et al., *Cefu yuangui*, *juan* 999.

Chapter Six

1. For the customary dates of the Kingdom of Angkor, see Chandler, *History of Cambodia*, 35.

2. Notable among these historians are Coedès and Vickery, who hold quite different views on the nature of the Funan-Zhenla transition, basing their opinions on local inscriptions as well as translations of Chinese texts available to them. In *Indianized States*, Coedès states that Zhenla conquered Funan as the result of a dynastic quarrel that embodied a tension between two different geographical regions. Vickery argues more persuasively that the transition from Funan to Zhenla could have been a gradual one characterized by dynastic continuity. Coedès, *Indianized States*, 65–72; Vickery, "Funan Reviewed," 131–136.

3. Wang et al., *Cefu yuangui, juan* 46.

4. See chapter seven.

5. "An evil king": *e wang* 惡王.

6. Yijing, *Nanhai jigui neifa zhuan*, 17. Also, Wang, "The Buddhist Connection," 289–290.

7. Huanzhou 驩州 on the central coast of present-day Vietnam was the terminus of an overland route from the coast to Land Zhenla or Wendan, as described in *Jiu Tang shu*. See chapter seven. Wang Gungwu locates Bijing 匕景 to the south of Huanzhou, near present-day Danang. In doing so he cites Gu Jiegang 顧頡剛 and Shi Nianhai 史念海's 1938 work *Zhongguo jiangyu yange shi* 中國疆域沿革史 [*The Evolving History of China's Frontier Regions*]. Wang, "Nanhai Trade," 105, 109. "Fifteen days": the original says "half a month", referring to the lunar calendar. I have changed this to "fifteen days", a more natural expression in English.

8. The Sanskrit names of the two Buddhist schools are Saṁmitīya (Zhengliang 正量 in Chinese, short for Zhengliangbu 正量部) and Sarvāstivāda (Youbu 有部 in Chinese, short for Yiqiyoubu 一切有部). The first was a Mahayana sect, the second an early Hinayana sect. Wang, "The Buddhist Connection," 289; Soothill and Hodous, *Dictionary of Chinese Buddhist Terms*, 193, 215.

9. In Buddhist belief, Jambudvipa (Zhanbu 瞻部 in Chinese here, short for Zhanbuzhou 瞻部洲) was the southern of the four continents situated north, south, east and west of Mount Meru, the center of the universe. Soothill and Hodous, *Dictionary of Chinese Buddhist Terms*, 178.

10. On this thirteenth-century iconoclasm, Coe and Evans, *Angkor and the Khmer Civilization*, 158; Chandler, *History of Cambodia*, 72.

11. For *Nan Qi shu* and Zhou Daguan, see chapters two and nine, respectively.

12. Vickery, *Society, Economics, and Politics*, 25–26; Jacques and Dumont, *Angkor*, 42. Briggs also notes the existence of two Buddhist inscriptions dating perhaps to the early years of Jayavarman I's rule. Briggs, *Ancient Khmer Empire*, 55.

13. *Bing*: 並; *jian*: 兼; *gong, xi*, and *ji*: 攻, 襲, and 擊. Karlgren, *Grammata Serica Recensa*, 167–168; Luo et al., *Hanyu da cidian*, entries under 並 and 兼.

14. On Bhavavarman II and his dates, Vickery, *Society, Economics, and Politics*, 22.

15. Du, *Tong dian*, 5099; Wei et al., *Sui shu*, 90.

16. Wei et al., *Sui shu*, 1831.

17. On Water Zhenla and its location, see chapter seven.

18. Given that according to Vickery, Īśānavarman died some time after 637. Vickery, *Society, Economics, and Politics*, 79. Many dates of Cambodian kings are disputed, and unless otherwise specified, as in this case, the dates given in this work are taken from Coe and Evans, *Angkor and the Khmer Civilization*, 225.

19. Wei et al., *Sui shu*, 90.

20. "Southern foreigners:" *Nan man* 南蠻. As noted earlier, the character *man* 蠻 with its "insect" radical has disparaging overtones. Wei et al., *Sui shu*, 1835–1837.

21. "Southern foreigners of various different kinds, living intermingled with Chinese:" *nan min za lei yu huaren cuoju* 南蠻雜類與華人錯居. Wei et al., *Sui shu*, 1831.

22. "Far-off southern": *nan huang*: 南荒.

23. For the location of Poli 婆利, Hsu, "Notes on Tan-tan," 43–44.

24. Wei et al., *Sui shu*, 1835–1837. With a few minor omissions this passage is reproduced in Li et al., *Taiping yulan*, 3483. It is also reproduced with minor variations in *Tong zhi* and *Wenxian tongkao*. Zheng, *Tong zhi*, 3176; Ma, *Wenxian tongkao*, 2605.

25. Following the *Tong zhi* text, and so adding the phrase "get there" (*zhi* 至).

26. The identities and locations of Chequ 車渠 (Ki̯wo gi̯wo [K]) and Zhujiang 朱江 or 硃江 (Vermilion River) are unclear. Lu and Zhou write that Chequ is "generally regarded as having been in Tenasserim and the northern Malay Peninsula", but *Xin Tang shu* locates it to the east of Zhenla. The name Chequ 車渠 has no obvious meaning, but it is a homophone for *chequ* 車渠 or 蛼蟝, the name of a giant clam sought after in China. Could the place name have been based on this product? Luo et al., *Hanyu da cidian*, entry under 車渠; Lu and Zhou, *Zhongguo gujizhong*, 63; Wheatley, "Geographical Notes," 254–255. For *Xin Tang shu* on Chequ, see chapter seven.

27. Kṣatriyaḥ here is Shali *shi* 刹利氏, *shi* 氏 indicating family or clan rather than being a proper noun. The names Kṣatriyaḥ and Citrasena/Zhiduosina 質多斯那 were discussed in chapter four.

28. Yishe'naxian 伊奢那先 (·I śi̯a nâ sien [K]) is clearly a transliteration of the Sanskrit name Īśānasena. Jacques and Vickery both identify this name with the king Īśānavarman I, who is mentioned in contemporaneous inscriptions, some of them bearing dates. In Chinese, Īśānapura (the City of Īśāna) is Yishe'na *cheng* 伊奢那城, Yishe'na 伊奢那 being Īśāna and *cheng* 城 being "city", *pura* in Sanskrit. Jacques, Vickery, and Coedès all agree that Īśānapura was located near Sambor Prei Kuk, not far from present-day Kompong Thom. According to Paul Lavy, monuments at Sambor Prei Kuk that probably date from the seventh century bear Sanskrit inscriptions praising Īśānavarman by name.

Later in this passage the capital city is referred to as *du* 都 ("capital"), the first use of this term in Chinese texts on Cambodia. The term is used again later for the capital of Zhenla in *Jiu Tang shu*.

There is a rare Chinese reference to Īśānapura in the Buddhist monk Xuanzang's account of his early seventh-century journey to India. Xuanzang describes Īśānapura, which he calls Yishangnabuluo 伊賞那補羅 (·I śi̯ang: nâ puo: lâ [K]), as one of six states in the southeast corner of the Great Sea that he heard about but did not visit, "the ways to them being obstructed by mountains and rivers." Coedès, *Indianized States*, 69–70; Jacques, "Le pays Khmer avant Angkor", 70; Vickery, *Society, Economics, and Politics*, 79; Briggs, *Ancient Khmer Empire*, 46–47, 49; Lavy, "As in Heaven," 30; [Xuan and Bianji,] *Da Tang xi yu ji*, 595–596.

29. The Chinese term for regional leader, *bu shuai* 部帥, is unusual, and may reflect Wei Zheng and his colleagues' limited understanding of Zhenla's governance. The comment that official titles in Zhenla were the same as those of Linyi raises questions about how much the administrations of Linyi and Zhenla resembled each other. In Vickery's view, Linyi, like early Champa, was politically quite distinct from early Cambodia. Vickery, *Society, Economics, and Politics*, 51, 69. On the other hand, there were affinities, as suggested in appendix five.

30. In the Chinese text, "made of aromatic woods and precious stones" reads literally "five aromatics and seven jewels" (*wu xiang qi bao* 五香七寶), a phrase suggesting a luxurious assortment of aromatic substances including woods and herbs as well as precious stones. *Wu xiang* 五香 ("five aromatic substances") has been variously defined to include different kinds of precious perfumes, herbs, and medicines. *Qi bao* 七寶 ("seven precious things") can have Buddhist overtones and has been taken in Buddhist writings to refer variously to gold, silver, crystal, glass (*liuli* 琉璃), coral, amber, agate, and other kinds of pearl and precious stone. Luo et al., *Hanyu da cidian*, entries under 五香 and 七寶; Stuart, *Chinese Materia Medica*, 49.

31. The kind of cotton worn by the king differs in different contexts: it is *gubei* 古貝 when worn on formal occasions, and *baidie* 白疊 in more ordinary settings. For more on *gubei* and *baidie* cottons, see chapters two and three. "Jeweled tassels" follows the reading *yingluo* 纓絡 (sometimes written 瓔珞) for the puzzling *manluo* 瞞絡, following the *Taiping yulan* version of this text at ctext.org/taiping-yulan.

32. It is unclear from the Chinese text whether the official titles listed here—Guluozhi 孤落支 (Kuo lâk tśie̯ [K]); Gaoxiangping 高相憑 (Kâu si̯ang- b'i̯əng- [K]); Poheduoling 婆何多陵 (B'uâ yâ: tâ li̯əng [K]); Shemoling 舍摩陵 (Śi̯a- muâ li̯əng [K]); Randuolou 髯多婁 (Ńźi̯äm tâ li̯u [K]) (or Ranluolou 髯羅婁 (Ńźi̯äm lâ li̯u [K]), the title as given in *Tong zhi*)—each apply to just one person or more than one. They are clearly transliterations, but from which language is unclear. Only one of them seems to have an equivalent among the high-ranking titles in use at this time, as identified by Vickery in his analysis of local Sanskrit and Khmer inscriptions. According to Vickery the main high-ranking titles were *poñ*, *mratāñ*, *kuruṅ*, *kurāk*, *tāṅ*, *ge kloñ*, and *ācārya*. Of these only *kurāk* comes close to matching one of the Chinese terms, *guluozhi* (kuo lâk tśie̯ [K]). The first two syllables of *guluozhi* as pronounced in Ancient Chinese (kuo lâk) correspond with *kurāk*, although the final syllable, *zhi* (tśie [K]) is otiose. In Vickery's assessment *kurāk*, a non-Khmer word, was one of a group of titles indicating that "secular rulers were considered to belong to a single hierarchy uniting them with deities." Zheng, *Tong zhi*, 3176; Vickery, *Society, Economic, and Politics*, 175–255, esp. 205–206, 250. See also Aspell, *Southeast Asia*, 19.

33. "Close and friendly relations" (*heqin* 和親) was a term customarily used for relations cemented through arranged marriages. As noted earlier, Canban was somewhere to the west of Zhenla, while Zhujiang, which translates to Vermilion River, has not been identified.

34. Tuohuan 陀桓 or 陀洹 (Da ywan [P]) seems to have been some distance to the west or southwest of Zhenla. *Tang hui yao*, which refers to it as Noutuohuan 耨陀洹, describes it as being "five months by sea" from Guangzhou. *Xin Tang shu* locates it "in the sea southwest of Huanwang . . . ninety days from Jiaozhou." Lu and Zhou identify it with Dawei (Tuwa 土瓦 in modern Chinese), the city in the far south of present-day Myanmar. Given the similarity between the names Tuwa and Tuohuan/Da ywan, and Tuohuan's likely location, this is a plausible identification. Wang, *Tang hui yao*, 1779; Ouyang et al., *Xin Tang shu*, 6303; Lu and Zhou, *Zhongguo gujizhong*, 63. Also Wang, "Nanhai Trade," 139.

35. Over six centuries later, Zhou Daguan makes the same observation, explaining that some of the women of Angkor were as white as jade because they never saw the sun. But this implies that other Khmers were dark-skinned only because they were sunburnt. Some other explanation is clearly called for. Were the white women wearing makeup or covering their skin with a white paste? If so, did it serve to highlight blackened teeth? For Zhou Daguan, see chapter ten. For the prevalence of blackened teeth, see the *Taiping yulan* comment on Wan Zhen's writings, mentioned in chapter one.

36. "Pendant ears" is a translation of the term *chui er* 垂耳. The term *dan er* 儋耳, which has the same meaning, occurs in Zuo Si's prose poem on the Three Capitals. References to pendant ears occur elsewhere in early Chinese accounts of southern peoples, as Pelliot remarks. Pelliot, *Notes on Marco Polo*, 445. For Zuo Si's poem, see chapter one.

37. As Aspell notes, the practice of cleaning teeth with twigs from the willow was perhaps derived from an old Indian practice. The practice persists to this day, at least among rural communities in eastern India. Aspell, *Southeast Asia*, 19. Soothill and Hodous, *Dictionary of Chinese Buddhist Terms*, 402. Cleaning teeth with twigs today: personal observation.

38. "Milk products" is a translation of *sulao* 蘇酪 (reading 蘇 as 酥), which can refer to a variety of products, liquid and non-liquid, derived from the milk of cows, goats or sheep—though not sheep in this instance, since as Judith Jacob has shown in her study of Cambodians' lives during this era, there were no sheep in early Cambodia. Vickery may be right when he argues that this account of the food and drink of Zhenla is mistaken and perhaps the result of the authors of *Sui shu* "mixing sources" (an unusual but not unknown practice of Chinese official historians), since pre-Angkor and Angkor inscriptions in Khmer mention ghee, milk, and millet only rarely, and then only in accounts of temple offerings. In contrast, Vickery also notes that according to seventh-century inscriptions rice was the main crop for consumption, and that at least is consistent with the *Sui shu* account here.

"Rice, millet" is a translation of *geng su* 秔粟, a term that can refer to either rice or rice and millet. *Geng* 秔 is a type of non-glutinous rice; *su* 粟 can be either foxtail millet, unhusked rice, or grain in general. In the term translated here as "rice cakes", *mi bing* 米餅, *mi* 米 refers to husked rice, and is also used for husked fruit or grain of other kinds; *bing* 餅 means "biscuit" or "cake". Assuming *geng su* refers to both rice and millet, it is the first reference in Chinese records to Cambodian millet, mentioned again more clearly later in this passage. According to the archaeologist Charles Higham, the farmers who first cultivated the land on the plains of Cambodia planted millet as well as rice, so for early Cambodians millet was as old a crop as rice. Luo et al., *Hanyu da cidian*, entries for *sulao*, *geng*, *su*, and *mi*; Jacob, "The Ecology of Angkor," 293; Vickery, "What to do about the Khmers," 15; Stuart, *Chinese Materia Medica*, 294; Higham, *Origins of the Civilization of Angkor*, 35.

39. The practice of the man leaving home after marriage is the same as in Chitu. See the *Sui shu* account of Chitu in chapter four.

40. According to the *Tong zhi* version of this passage, the fasting lasted not seven but ten days. Zheng, *Tong zhi*, 3176.

41. The Chinese phrase used here for "monks, nuns, holy men" is *sengni daoshi* 僧尼道士, meaning Buddhist monks and nuns (*sengni* 僧尼) and masters of the way or dharma (*daoshi* 道士). *Daoshi* is a term whose early usage includes the meaning Buddhist monks, but here and later it seems to be used in distinction to them. In these instances its meaning is not entirely clear. (This applies both to *daoshi* and to terms similar to *daoshi*, namely *daoren* 道人 and *daozhe* 道者. Zhou Daguan also calls *daozhe/daoshi* by the name *basiwei* 八思惟.)

Pelliot is inclined to see *daoshi* and *basiwei* as referring to a Hindu cult, but without knowing which one; Coedès identifies Zhou's *basiwei* with the Sanskrit term *tapasvī*, ascetics, and more specifically worshippers of Śiva. Apart from the superfluous syllable *ta*, Coedès' identification is plausible, especially given the prevalence of Śiva worship in Funan and early Zhenla, as attested by *Nan Qi shu* and *Sui shu*. Zhou, *Zhenla fengtu ji*, 94; Pelliot, "Mémoire sur les Coutumes du Cambodge", 149–150; Coedès, "Nouvelles Notes", 224–225. In my earlier translation of Zhou's *Record*, I translated the terms *daozhe/daoshi* as "Daoist." My intention was to reflect the meaning of the text as understood by Chinese readers, but on reflection the translation was misleading, and here I translate *daoshi/daozhe* and *daoren* as "holy men". (This is not a very satisfactory term, since as Zhou Daguan notes, some *daoshi* were women. "Holy people" might be better, but somehow sounds clumsy.)

42. The various perfumes are *wu xiang* 五香, literally "five aromatic substances," the term used earlier to describe the king's luxurious surroundings. The "great waters" (*da shui* 大水) could refer to a great river, sea, or lake, here probably the Tonlé Sap Lake or River or the Mekong River. Sambor Prei Kuk is closer to the Tonlé Sap Lake than it is to the Mekong, so Tonlé Sap Lake may be what is referred to.

43. Large-grained millet, broomcorn millet, and foxtail millet are translations of the terms *liang* 粱, *shu* 黍, and *su* 粟 respectively. According to the agricultural historian Francesca Bray, *liang* is actually a sub-species of foxtail millet known for its large grains and fine flavor. Bray, *Science and Civilization in China, Volume VI, Biology and Biological Technology, Part II: Agriculture*, 437–441.

44. As noted earlier, Jiuzhen and Rinan were among the southernmost commanderies of China under the Han dynasty. Under the Sui, they were reinstated as Chinese prefectures, as was Jiaozhi in the Red River Delta. The three have long been regarded by the Vietnamese as part of their country, and are known in Vietnamese as Cửu Chân, Nhật Nam, and Giao chỉ. Taylor, *The Birth of Vietnam*, 166–167.

45. Some of the kinds of fruit listed here can be identified, others cannot. Jackfruit (*ponasuo* 婆那娑) clearly derives from the Sanskrit *panasa*. In the record of his travels to India, the monk Xuanzang gives a description of this fruit, which he calls *bannuosuo* 般橠娑. Wax gourds are known in Chinese as "winter gourds" (*donggua* 冬瓜), the term used in the original here. The word for "mango" used here, *anluo* 庵羅, is evidently derived from *āmra*, a Sanskrit word for mango. [Xuan and Bianji,] *Da Tang xi yu ji*, 128; Yule and Burnell, *Hobson-Jobson*, 440; Stuart, *Chinese Materia Medica*, 67, 259.

46. Aspell tentatively identifies *piye* 毗野 (b'ji i̯a: [K]) with the bael fruit, *bila* or *bilwa* in Sanskrit, and *potianluo* 婆田羅 (b'uâ d'ien lâ [K]) with the Indian date, *badarā* in Sanskrit. Quince is a rendition of *mugua* 木瓜, a term that in more recent times has also been a name for papaya. "Wood apple" is a translation of *gebita* 歌畢他 (kâ pi̯ĕt t'â [K]), which clearly derives from *kapitya*, the Sanskrit word for "wood apple." Wood apples are very large, as described here. *Linqin* 林檎 is a long-standing Chinese term for "crabapple." Pint is the measure of capacity *sheng* 升. Aspell, *Southeast Asia*, 21; Stuart, *Chinese Materia Medica*, 362–364; Luo et al., *Hanyu da cidian*, entry under *linqin*; Wilkinson, *Chinese History*, 612.

47. The fish called *jiantong* 建同 (ki̯an- d'ung [K]) and *fu hu* 浮胡 (b'i̯əu γuo [K]) are hard to identify. Perhaps *jiantong* were freshwater dolphins, a few of which are said to live still in the Mekong. The sea (*hai* 海) they lived in was probably the Tonlé Sap Lake.

48. *Sui shu* does not make it clear whether the sacrifices described here and in the following paragraph involved single animals and human beings or numbers of them. The Chinese terms for various grains and domestic animals consist of two stock phrases: *wu gu* 五穀, the five grains (variously defined); and *liu xu* 六畜, the six domestic animals (horses, oxen, goats, chickens, dogs and pigs). "The various grains do not grow" (*wu gu bu deng* 五穀不登) is a quotation from the Confucian philosopher Mencius. Īśānapura is here called *du*都 (capital), the first use of this term in Chinese texts on Cambodia. Luo et al., *Hanyu da cidian*, entries under *wu gu* and *liu xu*; Legge, *The Chinese Classics, II: The Works of Mencius*, 250.

49. Liṅgaparvata is Coedès' rendition of the Chinese name Linggabopo 陵伽鉢婆 (Liŋ gia pat ba [P]). Elsewhere, in its account of Chitu, *Sui shu* mentions a place with a similar name, Linggabobaduo 陵伽鉢拔多 (Liŋ gia pat bəit ta [P]). This second version corresponds particularly well with Coedès' Liṅgaparvata. Liṅgaparvata or Lingam Mountain derives from the Sanskrit *liṅga*, meaning "lingam" or "phallus", especially as a symbol for Śiva, and *parvata* meaning "mountain."

Bhadreśvara ("Prosperous Lord") is a name for Śiva, and is Coedès' proposed Sanskrit equivalent for the Chinese name Poduoli 婆多利 (B'uâ tâ lji- [K]) (Poliduo 婆利多 in *Tong zhi*). Coedès plausibly suggests that Poduoli is a transliteration of the first two syllables of Bhadreśvara.

Where was Linga Mountain with its shrine to Bhadreśvara? Coedès argues it was located at Wat Phu in Champassak in today's Laos, where an ancient mountain temple has long been associated with a Śiva cult worshipping Bhadreśvara. In his opinion this was where Zhenla's ruling family originated before moving south to establish the Zhenla capital at Īśānapura near present-day Sambor Prei Kuk. Vickery rejects this line of argument, suggesting that in pre-Angkor Cambodia the names Liṅgaparvata and Bhadreśvara may have been in quite common use, so that there could well have been a shrine to Bhadreśvara at Īśānapura (that is, Sambor Prei Kuk).

Jacques regards the record of human sacrifice to Bhadreśvara as implausible, particularly since Śiva is vegetarian. However, Chandler points out that human sacrifice in Cambodia was well documented as late as the nineteenth century.

Tong zhi puts the number of guards at the sacred temple on Mount Liṅgaparvata at two, not five thousand.

Wei et al., *Sui shu*, 1834; Zheng, *Tong zhi*, 3176; Coedès, *Indianized States*, 65–66, 69–70; Coe and Evans, *Angkor and the Khmer Civilization*, 101–103; Vickery, *Society, Economics, and Politics*, 38, 80–81; Jacques and Lafond, *The Khmer Empire*, 73; Chandler, "Royally Sponsored Human Sacrifices," 208–222.

50. "Every year" (*mei nian* 每年) follows the extract from *Sui shu* in the Song facsimile edition of *Taiping yulan*. An alternative reading, found in the received text of *Sui shu* and in *Taiping huanyu ji*, is "at year-end" (*nian bie* 年別).

51. "The Buddhist dharma" is here *fo fa* 佛法, literally, "the Buddhist law." "Holy men" is a rendering of *daoren* 道人.

52. For Zhou Daguan, see chapter nine.

53. As mentioned in *Liang shu*. Yao, *Liang shu*, 790. Rudravarman was the last king of Funan mentioned by name in Chinese sources, though clearly not the last ruler, given that tribute from Funan continued to be sent to China until the early seventh century.

54. For a full analysis of this inscription, K. 53, and a discussion of the name Citrasena-Mahendravarman, see Vickery, *Society, Economics, and Politics*, 41, 74–79, 370–372.

55. Vickery also refers to two other inscriptions, K. 44 and K. 1036, that in his view show a likely connection between the sixth-century Rudravarman of Funan and later Zhenla-era kings, Jayavarman I in one case and the twelfth-century Suryavarman II in the other. Vickery, *Society, Economics, and Politics*, 372; Vickery, "Funan Reviewed," 134–135.

56. Vickery, *Society, Economics, and Politics*, 74–78; Jacques, "Le pays Khmer avant Angkor," 68–69.

57. Vickery, *Society, Economics, and Politics*, 22, 335–339.

58. See chapter three.

59. Coedès, *Indianized States*, 74–76; Vickery, *Society, Economics, and Politics*, 80–81. Ma, *Wenxian tongkao*, 2605.

60. Vickery, *Society, Economics, and Politics*, 81.

61. This would be consistent with Vickery's view that "the economic conditions and increasing political integration of 7th-century and later Cambodia favored the dissolution of matrilineages and their replacement by patriliny." Vickery, *Society, Economics, and Politics*, 326.

62. Pollock believes that the Sanskrit used by the Khmers was entirely an elite language. In Pollock's words, "in Khmer country . . . Sanskrit was exclusively the cosmopolitan language of elite self-presentation." At first glance this view seems inconsistent with the Sanskrit-derived names of ordinary products recorded in *Sui shu*, but this is not necessarily so, since these names were probably those in use among the elite rather than ordinary people. Pollock, *Language of the Gods*, 125–130, esp. 129.

63. Slaves in Funan: there are references to slaves in *Waiguo zhuan* and in *Nan Qi shu*. See Chapters one and two. For Zhou Daguan on slaves: Zhou, *Zhenla fengtu ji*, 109–110.

64. For buildings and carvings in Funan mentioned in *Waiguo zhuan*, see chapter one. For buildings in Funan mentioned in *Jin shu*, *Nan Qi shu*, and *Liang shu*, see chapters two and three. For statuary in Funan mentioned in *Fayuan zhulin* [*Forest of Gems in the Dharma Garden*] and *Liang shu*, see chapters two and three.

65. The one partial exception being a single comparison between the living arrangements of the people of Zhenla and the people of Funan's offshoot Chitu.

66. See chapter nine.

Chapter Seven

1. These are *Tong dian* [*A Comprehensive History of Institutions*] (801), *Taiping guangji* [*Extensive Records Compiled during the Era of Great Peace*] (978), *Taiping yulan* [*{An Encyclopaedia} Compiled during the Era of Great Peace and Read by the Emperor*] (984), *Taiping huanyu ji* [*A Record of the World during the Era of Great Peace*] (late tenth century), and *Cefu yuangui* [*Outstanding Models from the Storehouse of Literature*] (1013). "The era of great peace" may be a general term descriptive of the Song, or a reference to the Taiping xingguo 太平興國 (Great Peace, Prosperous State) reign period (976–984) of the second Song emperor Taizong.

2. For a list of the missions and sources for them, see appendix three.

3. During the Six Dynasties, each of the five southern dynasties between the fourth and sixth century CE lasted an average of fifty-four years.

4. Liu Xu 刘昫 (887–946) lived through the end of the Tang dynasty in 907 and three of the five very brief "dynasties" or regimes in south China that succeeded it.

5. *Xin Tang shu* records that in 713 Mei Shuluan 梅叔鸞 (Mai Thúc Loan in Vietnamese), styled the Black Emperor (Hei di 黑帝), joined with Zhenla, Linyi, Jinlin, and other states and with a force of four hundred thousand occupied Hainan—Hainan meaning here "south of the sea," rather than the island known by that name—before being defeated by Chinese forces led by Yang Sixu 楊思勖. Taylor writes that the Black Emperor "seized all of An-nam." Liu et al., *Jiu Tang shu*, 4756; Ouyang et al., *Xin Tang shu*, 5857; Taylor, *The Birth of Vietnam*, 190–194.

6. Li Mona: 李摩那. Liu et al., *Jiu Tang shu*, 450. The two other tribute missions in 623 and 628 are also recorded in the longer *Jiu Tang shu* entry on Zhenla.

7. *Zhenla guo shi*: 真臘國事. Liu et al., *Jiu Tang shu*, 2016.

8. Liu et al., *Jiu Tang shu*, 5269–5287, on Zhenla 5271–5272. Part of this entry on Zhenla (from "In the second year of the Zhenguan reign period" to the end) is cited in Li et al., *Taiping yulan*, 3483.

9. As noted earlier, the term *kunlun* 崑崙 (the word as written here) had several different meanings. Among other things, it served as a generic term employed from the seventh century on for places and people in the Southern Sea, notably people formulaically described as having back skin and curly hair. This is clearly the meaning here. Elsewhere in chapter 197, *Jiu Tang shu* records that "from Linyi southwards, they all have curly hair and black bodies, and they are all called *kunlun*." Liu et al., *Jiu Tang shu*, 5270. See also the discussion of Wan Zhen's writings in chapter one.

The capital referred to here is presumably the Tang capital Chang'an. Aizhou was the name given in 622 by the Tang court to Jiuzhen, the southern Han commandery reisnstated by the Sui. It is located in the center-north of present-day Vietnam. As in *Sui shu*, the "sea" here may in fact be Tonlé Sap Lake. The numbers of animals sacrificed is unclear. Īśānapura is described here as *du* 都 ("capital"), the second time this word is used in Chinese records of early Cambodia, the first time being in *Sui shu*'s account of Īśānapura.

10. The people riding on howdahs on the backs of elephants are described as *ren* 人, which is not gender-specific. Later bas-reliefs at Bayon and Angkor Wat show that the people fighting battles on elephants were male, though as we have seen in Funan women could ride elephants too. Elephants are herbivores, so the authors of *Jiu Tang shu* were misinformed when recording that meat was fed to good-quality elephants (a comment repeated in *Xin Tang shu*).

11. Judging from inscriptions from this period, the heavenly deities that were revered were mainly from Indian Śaivaite and Viṣṇuite cults, though they also included other Indian gods as well as local deities. Extant stone statuary from the period portrays a range of gods from the Indian pantheon, notably Durgā, Gaṇeśa, Harihara, Indra, Kṛṣṇa, Rāma, Skanda, Varuṇa, and Viṣṇu. On the range of statuary: Jessup, *Art and Architecture*, 16, 43–60. On evidence pointing to both Indian and local deities being worshipped: Vickery, *Society, Economics, and Politics*, 140 et seq. See also the comments about the bronze images of gods in chapter three.

12. "Long and exhausting journey": taking the *Taiping yulan* reading *li yuan pilao* 歷遠疲勞 rather than the received text *luhai pilao* 陸海疲勞, "the exhaustion of land and sea." Li et al., *Taiping yulan*, 3483.

13. Jimie 吉蔑 is clearly a transliteration of the word "Khmer." Lu and Zhou, *Zhongguo gujizhong*, 68; Chen, "Funan shi chu tan", 558–560.

14. In this account of the division of Zhenla into Water Zhenla (Shui Zhenla 水真臘) and Land Zhenla (Lu Zhenla 陸真臘), also called Wendan (文單, alternatively pronounced Wenchan), the tenses of the verbs are not specified. I have used the past tense throughout, on the ground that by the time this account was written the division of Zhenla into two parts was no longer seen to be current. The absence of tense here is one of many instances in which an unspecific timeframe in Chinese sources poses problems.

15. "They both sent envoys": "both sent" is a translation of *bing qian* 並遣, an expression sometimes used when two or more tribute-bearers are recorded as sending tribute together. Here the meaning is evidently that from 650–683 to 713–755 both Water Zhenla and Land Zhenla sent envoys with gifts an unspecified number of times. The starting date of 650–683 for these joint efforts is confusing, since by *Jiu Tang shu*'s own account, the division of Zhenla into two did not take place until 705–706. As Hoshino notes, *Cefu yuangui* further complicates matters by recording that in 717, a decade or so after Zhenla had divided into two, "Zhenla and Wendan [Land Zhenla]" both sent envoys. Perhaps in this case *Cefu yuangui* uses the name Zhenla to mean Water Zhenla. Wang et al., *Cefu yuangui*, 11445; Hoshino, "Wen Dan and its Neighbours," 47.

16. The translation here follows *Taiping yulan* (and *Taiping huanyu ji*), which has *yue jie* 約皆 (each about), citing [*Jiu*] *Tang shu*, rather than *yue yuan* 約員 (all round about) as in the Zhonghua shuju edition of *Jiu Tang shu*. If *yue jie* is taken as the reading, Water Zhenla would have been a rectangle with each side measuring about eight hundred li, or four hundred kilometers, a land area of roughly 160,000 square kilometers. Li, *Taiping yulan*, 3483.

17. Bentuolang is written here Bentuolang *zhou* 奔陀浪州, *zhou* 州 being an administrative unit or region. Wang Gungwu identifies Bentuolang with Panduranga or Phan Rang on the southeastern coast of present-day Vietnam. At this time it was probably at or beyond the southernmost part of Champa. *Xin Tang shu* (which calls it Benlangtuo 奔浪陀) describes it as being to the south of Huanwang (Champa). There are various Chinese renditions of the name; *Song hui yao jigao* [*A Draft Edition of the Essential Documents and Regulations of the Song Dynasty*] refers to it as Bindalang 賓達榔. Wang, "Nanhai Trade," 136; Vickery, *Champa Revised*, 26–28, 80–81; Liu et al., *Song hui yao jigao*, 9831–9832. For *Xin Tang shu* on Benlangtuo, see appendix five. Also Chen et al., "Song yu Zhenlifu, Dengliumei, Pugan deng guo zhi guanxi."

Duoluobodi 墮羅鉢底 is usually identified with Dvaravati (*dvāravatī* being Sanskrit for "that which has gates"), the Buddhist Mon polity or polities located in the Chao Praya basin of today's Thailand and beyond, active during the second half of the first millennium CE. Various transliterated versions of Dvaravati's name are found in Chinese sources from the seventh century onwards, including later in *Jiu Tang shu*, where it is called Duoheluo 墮和羅, and in the early Tang writings of the Buddhist monks Xuanzang and Yijing, who refer to it as Duoluobodi 墮羅鉢底 and Duhebodi 杜和鉢底 respectively. [Xuan and Bianji,] *Da Tang xi yu ji*, 595–596; Yijing, *Nanhai jigui neifa zhuan*, 12–13. See also Wang, "Nanhai Trade," 123, 131; Indrawooth, "Archaeology of the Early Buddhist Kingdoms," 129–136.

The Small Sea—mentioned in *Liang shu*, *Tang hui yao*, and *Xin Tang shu*—is evidently the present-day Gulf of Thailand.

18. There is no other mention in the Tang standard histories or in *Taiping yulan* of the envoy Li Mona or Limona 李摩那. Li is a Chinese surname—indeed, the surname of the ruling house of the Tang—but the characters used for the full name suggest a transliteration, perhaps of an unidentified Khmer name.

19. The correspondence between Purandara and Poluotiba 婆羅提拔 is plausible except for the final syllable ba/bəɨt, which is problematic. *Taiping yulan* reproduces this *Jiu Tang shu* passage giving the alternative Poluoshiba 婆羅是拔, but the replacement of 提 with 是 is evidently a copying error. Vickery, *Society, Economics, and Politics*, 238, 352–356; Coedès, *Indianized States*, 86; Dupont, "La dislocation de Tchen-la," 27; Jacques and Dumont, *Angkor*, 41–42; Li et al., *Taiping yulan*, 3483.

20. Liu et al., *Jiu Tang shu*, 5273, 5285.

21. On Piao, perhaps Pyū: Wheatley, *Nāgara and Commandery*, 165–167, 188–190; Wade, "Beyond the Southern Borders," 28; Aung-Thwyn and Aung-Thwyn, *History of Myanmar*, 63–65. Aung-Thwyn and Aung-Thwyn have well-argued reservations about identifying Piao 驃 (also written 剽) with Pyū, but the two terms are so similar that it is difficult not to identify one with the other.

22. See the section on the Tang geographer Jia Dan in chapter seven.

23. *Sui shu* and *Tong dian* both describe Zhenla as being to Linyi's southwest. So do *Tang hui yao* (961) and *Taiping huanyu ji* (late tenth century).

24. For the founding of Angkor and the accession of Jayavarman II, Chandler, *A History of Cambodia*, 35–47; Coe and Evans, *Angkor and the Khmer Civilization*, 97–124; Briggs, *Ancient Khmer Empire*, 88–115. For Mahendraparvata as a royal capital, Higham, *The Civilization of Angkor*, 58–59; Chevance et al., "Mahendraparvata," 1303–1321.

25. Liu et al., *Jiu Tang shu*, 5271–5272.

26. *Yiqie jing yinyi*: 一切經音義; Huiying (fl. mid-seventh century): 慧英; Huilin (737–820): 慧琳. Cited in Lu and Zhou, *Zhongguo gujizhong*, 88–89.

27. *Gulun*: 骨論. Gemie: 閣蔑. Gemie is clearly the same term as Jimie meaning Khmer, as mentioned in *Jiu Tang shu*. As for the other terms, Sengzhi 僧祇 probably refers to the people of Chitu or Red Earth, described in *Sui shu*, since their capital was Sengzhi 僧祇. Lu and Zhou tentatively identify Tumi 突彌 with Tamils. Gutang 骨堂 has not been identified.

28. Yixin 邑心 may derive from Yishe'na or Īśānapura. The Three Treasures (San bao 三寶, Triratna in Sanskrit) are the Buddha, the dharma (the law or teachings), and the sangha (the monastic community). Lu and Zhou, *Zhongguo gujizhong*, 89; Soothill and Hodous, *Dictionary of Chinese Buddhist Terms*, 63.

29. Identification of the name Land Zhenla with Wendan 文單 is repeated in *Xin Tang shu*. Liu et al., *Jiu Tang shu*, 298–299, 320, 400; Ouyang et al., *Xin Tang shu*, 6301. An alternative pronunciation of *dan* 單 is *chan*, giving (jn today's pronunciation) the alternative name of Wenchan for Wendan.

30. Huanzhou 驩州 was the coastal terminus of the land route to Wendan mentioned by the Tang geographer Jia Dan (see later in this chapter). The circumstances surrounding the attempted seizure of Huanzhou by the Chinese are unclear. *Cefu yuangui*, *juan* 995, quoted in Chen et al., *Zhongguo gujizhong*, 104.

31. The scholars included Pelliot, Coedès, and Henri Maspero. Their views were summarized in the 1940s by Briggs in his history of the Khmer empire. Briggs published his work in 1951 but completed it in draft form eight years earlier, and although he included in it a brief discussion of Dupont's 1943 paper (see the following paragraph), he did not really take Dupont's argument into account. Briggs, *Ancient Khmer Empire*, 58–59; Chen, *Jianpuzhai erqiannian shi*, 195–204. On the date of Briggs' draft, Coedès, "The *Ancient Khmer Empire* by Lawrence Palmer Briggs (review article)," 115.

32. Dupont, "La dislocation de Tchen-la", 38–39.

33. Jacques, "'Funan', 'Zhenla'," 376; Vickery, *Society, Economics, and Politics*, 392; Vickery, "What and Where was Chenla?," 205.

34. Fan, *Man shu*, 245–247. Also [Fan,] *The Man shu*, 93.

35. *Man shu* lists seven cities in the Yunnan region, one called Zhenxi 鎮西 (guarding the west), the other called Kainan 開南 (opening to the south). In Lu and Zhou's view, Zhennan 鎮南 (guarding the south) mentioned in this passage refers to Kainan. Lu and Zhou, *Zhongguo gujizhong*, 86.

36. Pelliot, "Deux itinéraires," 213–215; Briggs, *Ancient Khmer Empire*, 59; Maspero, "La Frontière de l'Annam," 32; Stein, "Le Lin-yi," 41. For a skeptical assessment of Pelliot's view, Vickery, *Society, Economics, and Politics*, 103, 142.

37. Chandler, *History of Cambodia*, 33. Chandler here uses the name Land Zhenla, rather than Wendan.

38. For example Lu and Zhou, *Zhongguo gujizhong*, 68. In the considered view of the historian Chen Xiansi, there is not yet enough evidence to substantiate the identification with Vientiane/Wanxiang 萬象. Chen, *Jianpuzhai erqiannian shi*, 197–198.

39. Hoshino argues that Wendan's king and people spoke Tai, being recent Tai migrants, although according to Chandler the then inhabitants of the area probably spoke Khmer. Hoshino, "Wen Dan and its Neighbours," 39, 41, 44–46, 53–54; Chandler, personal communication.

40. The Tang geographer Jia Dan, cited in *Xin Tang shu*, describes a journey from Huanzhou to Wendan of 3 + 2 + 3 + 4 + 3 = 15 days to Wendan's outer city, and one more day to its inner city. According to Jia, overland travelers to Wendan from Huanzhou had to go via Tangzhou prefecture, which seems to have had its headquarters near Thakhek. After passing through a river gorge, they then had to travel a further seven or eight days before reaching the two main cities of Wendan. Jia makes no mention of these final days being passed on or by a river. Imprecise though it is, his account strengthens the case for Wendan being beyond the Mekong River in present-day Thailand. For *Xin Tang shu* on Jia Dan, see later in this chapter. For the *Taiping huanyu ji* reference, Yue, *Taiping huanyu ji*, 3273, cited in Pelliot, "Deux itinéraires," 213.

41. Pomi 婆彌 is evidently a transliterated name, but not one that has been identified. In Hoshino's view, Pomi's wife could have been the real ruler because of a matriarchal family system in the Wendan region before the arrival of Tai migrants. Hoshino, "Wen Dan and its Neighbours," 57.

42. This is Hoshino's explanation for Pomi's elaborate reception. According to *Cefu yuangui*, in 753 Wendan gave its support to a Chinese general called He Lüguang 何履光, who was one of the leaders of a Tang military assault on the state of Nanzhao 南詔 in present-day Yunnan. The recalcitrant state of Nanzhao resisted the assault and continued to wield power until it gave way to the kingdom of Dali 大理 in the tenth century. Wang et al., *Cefu yuangui*, 11405, 11458. Backus, *The Nan-chao Kingdom*, 75–78; Yang, *Between Winds and Clouds*, 87. For Wendan's role in the Nanzhao campaign, see also Hoshino, "Wen Dan and its Neighbours," 55–57.

43. Liu et al., *Jiu Tang shu*, 298; Wang et al., *Cefu yuangui*, 11719

44. Liu et al., *Jiu Tang shu*, 320. By one count: Wang et al., *Cefu yuangui*, 481.

45. Liu et al., *Jiu Tang shu*, 298–299. Commander Unequalled in Honor: Kaifu yitong sansi 開府儀同三司; Provisional Director of Palace Administration: Shi dianzhong jian 試殿中監. The English names for the titles are from Hucker, *Dictionary of Official Titles*, 275, 502. Hucker translates *shi* 試 as Probationary, its more literal meaning. The Palace Administration was a central agency in charge of administering the Tang emperor's palace; *shi* indicated a temporary appointment, which in Pomi's case was no doubt honorary rather than probationary—no one would have expected him to serve in a probationary role.

46. Hoshino, "Wen Dan and its Neighbours", 57.

47. The Jing Mountains or Jingshan 荊山 lay in the west of present-day Hubei province in central China. The maritime historian Lo Jung-pang writes that in Song times "tribute of elephants was time and again refused, because elephants were regarded as of no use to China." Despite this, the elephants kept coming. Hans Bielenstein calculates that from the Sui to the Song dynasties over a hundred and twenty elephants from Southeast Asia were gifted to the Tang and Song courts. Lo, *China as a Sea Power*, 201. Bielenstein, *Diplomacy and Trade*, 94–95. For unwanted elephants presented to China, see also chapter two.

48. Four of these five works—*Tang hui yao*, *Taiping yulan*, *Taiping huanyu ji*, and *Cefu yuangui*—were introduced earlier in the chapters on Funan. For the remaining work, *Taiping guangji*, see Li et al., ed., *Taiping guangji*; also Wilkinson, *Chinese History*, 724–725.

49. Wang, *Tang hui yao*, 1752. Nearly all these missions are also recorded in other official Chinese sources. See appendix three.

50. Wang, *Tang hui yao*, 1798.

51. The bird was called *lang* 浪, an unidentifiable name; the unidentified mountain was called Gelang 葛浪山. Li et al., *Taiping guangji*, 3371, 3813, 3973.

52. The miscellany is Duan Chenshi 段成式 (803–863)'s *Yuyang zazu* 酉陽雜俎 [*Youyang Miscellany*]. The collection of anecdotes is Zhang Zhuo 張鷟 (c. 658–730)'s *Chao ye qian zai* 朝野簽載 [*Brief Records of Court and Country*]. For both Duan and Zhang, see Owen, "The Cultural Tang," 357.

53. It is not possible to identify the *zifei* 紫鉗 or *lequ* 勒佉 (or *leiqu*) tree. *Zi* 紫 in *zifei* 紫鉗 means "purple;" *fei* 鉗 is a rare character, defined in the authoritative Kangxi Dictionary (1710) as a small nail. For Bosi 波斯 meaning Persia, see chapter three.

54. Nothing more is known about the monk Tuosha'nibatuo 陁沙尼拔陁, whose name is clearly transcribed from Sanskrit (拔陁 in names is a standard transcription of the Sanskrit -badra). His title, Garrison (more literally, Assault-Resisting Garrison) Militia Commandant (Zhechong duwei 折衝都尉), refers to his no doubt honorary position as one of the commanders of the garrison militias that complemented the military units defending Chang'an. Hucker, *Dictionary of Official Titles*, 119–20, 427, 545.

55. Huanzhou was the eastern terminus on the coast of present-day Vietnam for the overland route to Land Zhenla, as described in *Xin Tang shu* (see later in this chapter). Mention of it here in what may have been an early eighth-century source is significant; it suggests that its importance as a point of overland access to Zhenla dates back to this period.

56. "Camphor fruit" is a loose rendition of *longnao* 龍腦 (literally, dragon's brain), one of several Chinese terms for Borneo camphor (*dryobalanops aromatica*), whose small, hard fruits were served as a relish. Stuart, *Chinese Materia Medica*, 157–158. "Clams" here are *xiang ha* 香蛤, literally "fragrant clams," a variant of the more common *ha* 蛤 or *hali* 蛤蜊.

57. There is an additional final paragraph, which is apparently included in error. It reads, "The people of the country do not wear clothes, and when they see someone clothed they all laugh. They are without salt and iron, and shoot insects and birds using crossbows made of bamboo." Its inclusion here seems to be he result of a clerical mistake, with its comments being mistakenly applied to Zhenla rather than to Daoming 道明, a dependency of Land Zhenla that *Xin Tang shu* describes in almost exactly the same words (see later in this chapter).

58. Yue, *Taiping huanyu ji*, 3375–3377.

59. *Yuyan*: 語言. For Hoshino's view, see footnote 39 of this chapter.

60. Yue, *Taiping huanyu ji*, 3375–3377.

61. Wang et al., *Cefu yuangui*, 11259, 11289–11290, 11316.

62. Wang et al., *Cefu yuangui*, 11289. For the *Jin shu* reference to Hu script, see chapter three.

63. Missions listed in *Cefu yuangui* are in Wang et al., *Cefu yuangui*: 11351, 11395, 11397–11398, 11401, 11403–11404, 11413–11414, 11417, 11432–11433, 11461, 11719.

64. Li Touji: 李頭及; Commandant: Zhonglang jiang 中郎將. Wang et al., *Cefu yuangui*, 11462–11463; Hucker, *Dictionary of Chinese Titles*, 191. See also Hoshino, "Wendan and its Neighbours," 59.

65. Wang et al., *Cefu yuangui*, 11405, 11445.

66. Xinluo 新羅 is generally agreed to refer to Silla, the kingdom that ruled Korea from 668 to 935. Mohe 靺鞨 is thought to have been an early name for the Tungusic-speaking Jurchen people in the far east of present-day Russia. During the Song dynasty, these forest dwellers established their own Jin dynasty and in due course drove the Song out of northern China. The Jurchens' ancestors ruled the whole of China as the Manchus from 1644 to 1911. For Mohe see the entry in Luo et al., *Hanyu da cidian*.

67. *Bingzi* 丙子 was the name of a day in the sexagenary cycle of the traditional Chinese calendar, called in Chinese the *ganzhi* 干支 or root and branch cycle. On *ganzhi*, Xu, *Xin bian Zhongguo sanqian nian liri jiansuo biao*, 4–5.

68. Pledging loyalty to each new emperor is the underlying meaning of the term used here, *feng zheng shuo* 奉正朔, meaning literally "pledging loyalty on the first day of the first year." I am grateful to Warren Sun for pointing this out.

69. *Xin Tang shu* contains no information about either mission. Wang et al., *Cefu yuangui*, 11417.

70. The next mission—that is, apart from an apparently aborted mission in 1078. Liu et al., *Song hui yao jigao*, 9764–9765; see chapter eight.

71. Jia Dan 賈耽 (730–805)'s work is also referred to in *Taiping huanyu ji*, which calls it an account of ten routes (*Zhenyuan shidao lu* 貞元十道錄 [*A Record of Ten Routes of the Zhenyuan Reign Period*]) rather than seven. There is no record of an additional three routes, but perhaps the work referred to in *Taiping huanyu ji* treated three subsidiaries of the seven main routes as separate routes rather than subsidiaries. Ouyang et al., *Xin Tang shu*, 1146. Also Lo, *China as a Sea Power*, 104–105.

72. "Places:" literally, "prefectures and counties" *zhou xian* 州縣. *Xia*: 下. Ouyang et al., *Xin Tang shu*, 1146

73. Datong, Yunzhong: 大同, 云中. Uyghurs are referred to as Huigu 回鶻 rather than Weiwuer 維吾爾, the present-day name for Uyghurs in Chinese.

Annan 安南, often referred to in the context of Vietnamese history as An Nam or Annam, became a Tang protectorate in 679.

"Foreigners of the sea:" *Hai yi* 海夷. Ouyang et al., *Xin Tang shu*, 1111–1112.

74. Jia Dan's route south from Guangzhou is translated in [Zhao,] *Chau Ju-kua: His Work*, tr. Hirth and Rockhill, 10–14. Jia Dan's routes are also described and translated in Pelliot, "Deux itinéraires," 183–185, 210–213, 372, and discussed in Hoshino, "Wen Dan and its Neighbours," 50–53.

75. Pelliot locates Huanzhou 驩州 at Hà Tĩnh and Hoshino at Vinh. Pelliot, "Deux itinéraires," 184; Hoshino, "Wendan and its Neighbours," 51. See also Stein, "Lin-yi," 40.

76. Ouyang et al., *Xin Tang shu*, 1152–1153. See also Li, "A View from the Sea," 84–85.

77. The unusual reference to two cities, an outer city and an inner city, suggests that Jia Dan understood Wendan to have two main cities rather than one.

78. Some but not all of the geographical names mentioned in these itineraries can be identified. Tanglin 唐林 occurs elsewhere in *Xin Tang shu*, where it is described as a southern prefecture of China with a district called Anyuan 安遠, created in the early Tang and later abolished. Zhuya 珠崖 was one of the Han commanderies in the far south of China. *Xin Tang shu* refers elsewhere to the Wuwen 霧溫 Mountains as being "the Zhenla mountain range to the west of Huanwang [Champa]." Tangzhou 棠州 may also have been a short-lived southern Chinese prefecture, also called Changzhou 長/裳州, with its headquarters on the Mekong river near present-day Thakhek. The state of Luoyue 羅越 was probably

located in the southern part of the Malay peninsula. In his seventh, southern maritime route Jia Dan mentions Luoyue as being on the north side of a strait known to foreigners as Zhi 質,on the south side of which lay the state of Foshi 佛逝, that is, Srivijaya; this being so, the Zhi strait was the Malacca Strait, though Haw proposes instead that it was the Sunda Strait.

Other names on the route (Guluo 古羅, Tandong 檀洞, Danbu 單補, Riluo 日落, Luolun 羅倫, Shimi 石蜜, Gulang 古朗, Wenyang 文陽, Chichi 㮇㮇 (or by one version Maomao 犛犛), Suantai 算臺) have yet to be reliably deciphered, although various scholars (Chen Xiansi et al., Hoshino, Lu and Zhou, Pelliot and Stein) have all suggested possible local equivalents. If the names are transliterations of local place names, as seems likely, the transliterations are creatively done; the literal meanings of Tandong 檀洞 and Riluo 日落, for example, are Sandalwood Cave and Sunset.

On Tanglin and Wuwen: Ouyang et al., *Xin Tang shu*, 1114, 6297. On Tangzhou: Hoshino, 'Wen Dan and its Neighbours," 48–50; Lu and Zhou, *Zhongguo guji*, 70. On Luoyue: Wheatley, *Golden Khersonese*, 56–58; Haw, "Maritime Routes," 71.

79. Yue, *Taiping huanyu ji*, 3273; also earlier in this chapter.

80. Maspero, "Études d'Histoire d'Annam," 30, citing Lý Tế Xuyên 李濟川's fourteenth-century Vietnamese history *Việt Điện U Linh Tập* 粵甸幽靈集 [*A Collection of Dark and Spiritual Stories from the Viet Realm*]. Maspero's citation is referred to in Briggs, *Ancient Khmer Empire*, 58. As we have seen, *Jiu Tang shu* reports that at one point earlier on, Zhenla sided with the Black Emperor against the Chinese, rather than opposing him.

81. Hoshino, "Wen Dan and its Neighbours", 52.

82. Li, "A View from the Sea," 84–85.

83. Li, "A View from the Sea," 85. On the establishment of Đại Việt (Great Viet; in Chinese, Da Yue 大越) see Taylor, *History of the Vietnamese*, 72–73.

84. The missions are listed chapters two and three of *Việt Sử Lược* 越史略, whose editorship is traditionally attributed to Sử Hy Nhan 史希顏; these chapters are cited in Lu and Zhou, *Zhongguo gujizhong*, 118–122. According to the Song gazetteer Zhao Rugua, Zhenla also sent an annual tribute of gold to Champa from an unspecified date until 1177, when Zhenla and Champa went to war. See the account of Zhao Rugua's *Zhu fan zhi* in chapter eight.

85. [attr. Nhan,] *Việt Sử Lược*, chapter two, in Lu and Zhou, *Zhongguo gujizhong*, 119.

86. Đinh Tiên Hoàng was the Vietnamese leader's posthumous name. Vietnamese kings are referred to here by their posthumous names, to be consistent with the posthumous names used for Chinese emperors. Hoàng called his new state Đại Cồ Việt, a name that was modified to Đại Việt decades later, in 1054. Taylor, *History of the Vietnamese*, 72–73; Taylor, *The Birth of Vietnam*, 280–281. In subsequent references to Đại Việt, I often just use the term Vietnamese, a term that Churchman persuasively argues only really becomes credible from about this time on. Churchman, "Before the Chinese and Vietnamese," 37.

87. For *Xin Tang shu* on Zhenla's disputes, see later in this chapter. For *Lingwai daida* and the story of Zhenla's defeat in 1173 (or 1171, according to *Song shi*), and for the *Zhu fan zhi* account of Champa's naval attack on Angkor in 1177, see chapter eight.

88. With the exception of Touhe 投和 and Xiuluofen 修羅分, these entries repeat the places and locations given in *Jiu Tang shu* (see earlier in this chapter). Later, as we shall see, *Xin Tang shu* locates Zhenla somewhat differently, with reference to Pyū and three other locations, Chequ, Daoming, and Huanzhou. Ouyang et al., *Xin Tang shu*, 6302–6304.

89. The states' names in Chinese are 僧高 (Senggao), 武令 (Wuling), 迦乍 (Jiazha), 鳩摩 (Jiumo), and 富那 (Funa). The only comment that *Xin Tang shu* makes about any of them is that Senggao lay directly northwest of Water Zhenla, adding that its customs were the same as those of Huanwang (Champa). Ouyang et al., *Xin Tang shu*, 6299; also Ma, *Wenxian tongkao*, 2602.

90. "A strong centralizer:" Vickery's careful judgment. Vickery, *Society, Economics, and Politics*, 25–26. See also the remarks about Jayavarman I in chapter six.

91. Zhenla is recorded as sending a mission to China in 651, then not again until 682. See appendix three.

92. Ouyang et al., *Xin Tang shu*, 6301–6302.

93. As in *Jiu Tang shu*, Jimie clearly means Khmer. As with the same distance recorded in *Jiu Tang shu*, twenty thousand seven hundred li from Zhenla to Chang'an is unrealistic, and must be the result of a copying error or misunderstanding.

94. As noted in chapter six, the identity of Chequ is not known. *Sui shu* places it south of Zhenla, which might locate it on the Malay Peninsula, but if it was to the east of Zhenla, as recorded here, it could have been related to Champa. The location of Daoming is also unknown. Hoshino believes its name derives from a term for "vassal chief" in Tai and locates it on the Mekong north of present-day Vientiane. Hoshino, "Wen Dan and its Neighbours," 40.

95. Yijinna 伊金那 seems to refer somewhat inaccurately to Īśānasena (Yishe'na[xian] 伊奢那先). It is comparable to Yixin 伊心, the name found in the Buddhist work *Yiqie jing yinyi*, which also seems to refer to Yishe'na,

96. As noted in chapter four, Canban 參半 was evidently to the west of Zhenla; otherwise it has not been identified. As discussed in chapter six, Gantuohuan 乾陀洹 (or by an alternative pronunciation, Qiantuohuan) seems to have been another name for Tuohuan 陀桓, also to the west of Zhenla, perhaps in the Dawei area of present-day Myanmar. In a separate comment *Xin Tang shu* locates Tuohuan, "also called Noutuohuan 耨陀洹, in the sea southwest of Huanwang, adjacent to Duoheluo [Dvaravati] and ninety days from Jiaozhou." Ouyang et al., *Xin Tang shu*, 6303.

97. The measurements of Land Zhenla and Water Zhenla given here—seven hundred li and eight hundred li, respectively—pose the same problem as measurements given in earlier sources, since they are given without any indication as to whether they refer to length from east to west, area, or perimeter.

For Poluotiba/Purandarapura, see the discussion earlier in this chapter, expecially footnote 19.

98. The etymology of Land Zhenla's other name, Polou 婆鏤 (B'uâ lə̣u- [K]), is unclear. Vickery tentatively suggests a possible connection with *bruu*, a Katuic word for "mountain." Hoshino argues that it is a transliteration of the Sanskrit *pura* ("city"). The name or title of the king of Wendan, Daqu 笡屈 (? k'i̯uət [K])—or Danqu, according to an alternative pronunciation—is a transliteration, but of what is unclear. Hoshino believes it "sounds entirely Tai," but does not explain why he thinks this. Vickery's analysis of Khmer titles in the pre-Angkor and Angkor periods includes only one group of titles of possible relevance: *tāñ*, *tāṅ*, and *teṅ*, all deriving from a single foreign loan word and having a variety of functions; but in Vickery's analysis none of them occurs in combination with a second syllable resembling qu/k'i̯uət. Hoshino, "Wen Dan and its Neighbours," 41, 53; Vickery, *Society, Economics, and Politics*, 214–217, 224.

99. Courageous Commandant: Guoyi duwei 果毅都尉. According to Hucker, the rank of this position in Tang times was Vice-Commandant. One of Pomi's two titles, Bin han 賓漢, tentatively translated here as Distinguished Guest (reading han 漢 as person) is oddly formulated and differs from the titles for him mentioned in *Jiu Tang shu*. Hucker does not list the title. Hucker, *Dictionary of Official Titles*, 298 (for Guoyi duwei).

100. Coe and Evans, *Angkor and the Khmer Civilization*, 225.

Chapter Eight

1. That is, the then Bianliang. For the Jurchen, see esp. Beckwith, *Empires of the Silk Road*, 174–176, 224–226.

2. Lin'an: 臨安.

3. Polo, *The Travels of Marco Polo*, 209–225.

4. Chen Xiansi, *Jianpuzhai erqiannian shi*, 364–367.

5. Chen, *Jianpuzhai erqiannian shi*, 364. See also Franke and Twitchett, "Introduction," 4–6; Mote, *Imperial China, 900–1800*, 112 et seq. With respect to the period 755–960, Chen's argument is substantiated by Wang Gungwu's account of how China's Nanhai trade declined during much of this period as a result of unrest in China. Wang, "Nanhai Trade," 120–121.

6. See the list of tribute missions in Wang, "Nanhai Trade," 156. For Zhenla missions, see also appendix three.

7. Chen, *Jianpuzhai erqiannian shi*, 365–366.

8. Chen, *Jianpuzhai erqiannian shi*, 367. See also Zhou, *Lingwai daida*, 86.

9. See for example Shaffer, *Maritime Southeast Asia to 1500*, 29.

10. I rely here on the pathbreaking work of Derek Heng. Heng, *Sino-Malay Trade*, 76–77, 100–106.

11. Heng, *Sino-Malay Trade*, 85.

12. Vickery, *Society, Economics, and Politics*, 257, 406.

13. Wicks, *Money, Markets, and Trade*, 193–205. By contrast cash and later also paper money played a key role in commerce in Song China, while cash was also used in most other parts of Southeast Asia. Kuhn, *The Age of Confucian Rule*, 232–250; Wicks, *Money, Markets, and Trade*, passim.

14. Lieberman, *Strange Parallels* vol. 1, 223.

15. Hall, *A History of Early Southeast Asia*, 183. Vickery is critical of Hall's arguments regarding Suryavarman's commercial activities. He writes that Hall's "attempts to show the reign of Suryavarman I . . . as a period of royally sponsored commercial expansion . . . are wrong" in nearly every important detail. Michael Vickery, "Maritime Trade and State Development," 212.

16. My thanks to Penny Edwards for this suggestion.

17. "At least until the twelfth century:" References to Zhenla's trade by the gazetteers Zhou Qufei and Zhao Rugua, and to Zhenla's trade with China and elsewhere by the late thirteenth-century envoy Zhou Daguan, suggest that by their time trade, including foreign trade, had become a significant part of the Zhenla economy. See later in this chapter and chapter nine.

18. Shiba Yoshinobu discusses these "major changes" (Shiba's phrase) in his landmark work on the Song economy, first published in Tokyo in 1968 under the title *Sōdai shōgyō shi kenkyū* 宋代商業史研究, and published in an English translation in 1970. Shiba, *Commerce and Society*, 1. On the transformation of the Song economy, Elvin, *Pattern of the Chinese Past*, 113–199. On Southern Song merchants, Kuhn, *The Age of Confucian Rule*, 208–212.

19. Heng, *Sino-Malay Trade and Diplomacy*, 48–63, 150, 175–177. On Chinese junks and compasses, Shiba, *Commerce and Society*, 6–19; Needham, *Science and Civilization in China, Vol. IV, Part III*, 379.

20. *Zhi*: 志. There is no equivalent term for "travel diary" in Chinese; the term is Shuen-fu Lin's. Lin uses the term in inverted commas to describe various works written during the Southern Song that record journeys to places in and near China. Lin, "Professionalism," 531–532. Also [Fan,] *Treatises of the Supervisor*, xxxii–xli.

21. Fan Chengda 范成大 (1126–1193), *Guihai yuheng zhi* 桂海虞衡志; Zhou Qufei 周去非 (1135–1189), *Lingwai daida*: 嶺外代答 (*ling* 嶺 referring to Wuling 五嶺 [The Five Mountains], the mountain range formed by the five main mountain peaks of south China); Zhao Rugua 趙汝适 (1170–1231), *Zhu fan zhi* 諸蕃志.

22. [Fan,] *Treatises of the Supervisor*, xxx; Nienhauser, *Indiana Companion*, 372–373; Lin, "Professionalism," 531–532. Xiao, *Wen xuan*, 707; also Schafer, *The Vermilion Bird*, 195.

23. Nienhauser, *Indiana Companion*, 373.

24. [Fan,] *Treatises of the Supervisor*, xxviii–xxix, xxxv–xxxvi, xl–xli. Zhou Qufei and Zhao Rugua used parts of *Guihai yuheng zhi* in their own gazetteers.

25. Angela Schottenhammer, citing Lin Tianwei 林天尉. Schottenhammer, "Song Dynasty," 144–145.

26. Fan, *Guihai yuheng zhi*, 28. [Fan,] *Treatises of the Supervisor*, 38–39.

27. China is a translation here of Zhongzhou 中州 (The Central Region or Regions), another term for China. The phrase "ships from Guangzhou" leaves unclear whether the ships from Guangzhou were Chinese- or foreign-owned.

28. Dingliumei 丁流眉, which Fan later calls Dengloumei 登樓眉, and which is referred to variously in other sources as Dengliumei 登流眉, Danliumei 丹流眉, and Danmeiliu 丹眉流, was probably in the north of the Malay Peninsula. Zhao Rugua's *Zhu fan zhi* describes it as a dependency of Zhenla lying to the west of it. *Wenxian tongkao* locates it to the southwest of Zhenlifu 真里富, another Zhenla dependency located in the southwest corner of Zhenla. Pelliot places Dingliumei on the east of the Kra Isthmus, at Nakhon Si Thammarat in present-day Thailand. Hainan here means "south of the sea" and refers to other southern states. Zhao, *Zhu fan zhi*, 19, 28; Ma, *Wenxian tongkao*, 2605; Pelliot, "Deux itinéraires," 233–234.

29. It is given as a supplement in Fan, *Guihai yuheng zhi*, 165; Ma, *Wenxian tongkao*, 2593–2595, esp. 2594; [Fan,] *Treatises of the Supervisor*, 203.

30. The state of Foshi: Foshi *guo* 佛逝國. Zhao, *Zhu fan zhi*, 8, 11. Tuotuo et al., *Song shi*, 14,080. Coedès, *Indianized States*, 82, 125. Vickery writes that Coedès' identification of Foshi with Vijaya is confusingly sourced and should be rejected. But if we accept Coedès' argument that Foshi was a Chinese name for the Sumatran polity (Sri)vijaya, it is reasonable to suppose that Foshi was also a Chinese rendition of the name Vijaya used elsewhere, more specifically in Champa. Vickery, *Champa Revised*, 385–389. For Coedès' identifcation of Foshi with Srivijaya, Coedès, "*Le Royaume de Çrīvijaya*," 1–36; also Wolters, *Early Indonesian Commerce*, 175, 185.

31. Keith Taylor, *History of the Vietnamese*, 57; Coedès, *Indianized States*, 125. Taylor writes of Champa kings ruling in Vijaya from 999 on; Coedès mentions a new king of Champa establishing himself in Vijaya in the year 1000.

32. Fan, *Guihai yuhengzhi*, 142; [Fan,] *Treatises of the Supervisor*, 229–232. The thirteenth-century scholar was a man called Huang Zhen 黄震, and the work referred to is *Huang shi richao* 黄氏日鈔 [*Mr Huang's Daily Notes*], specifically *juan* 97, in *Siku quanshu zhenben erji*, 62–63; Wilkinson, *Chinese History*, 165.

33. The bronze or copper pillars on the southern extremity of the Han realm were the pillars set up by the Han dynasty general Ma Yuan. Dali refers to the state of Dali (937–1253) in present-day Yunnan. Dali succeeded Nanzhao, the state in Yunnan that the Tang court tried to suppress with the help of Land Zhenla in the ninth century. Turfan (Tufan 吐番 in Chinese) is a town on the northern rim of the Taklamakan desert in the present-day Chinese province of Xinjiang; according to *Hanyu da cidian* the name was also used in Song times to refer to the Himalayan plateau. As Hargett suggests, Xilan 細蘭 must be a transliteration of Ceylon.

34. Sanfoqi 三佛齊 is usually identified with Srivijaya.

35. The Chinese text reads, "*Nan da yanghaizhong zhuguo yi Sanfoqi wei da, zhu fan bao huo zhi duhui*" 南大洋海中諸國以三佛齊為大, 諸蕃寶貨之都會: Fan, *Guihai yuheng zhi*, 142; Zhou, *Lingwai daida*, 86.

36. Zhou, *Lingwai daida*, 5. Also Pelliot, "Mémoire sur les Coutumes," 132.

37. Zhou, *Zhenla fengtu ji*, 2.

38. Zhou, *Lingwai daida*, 4–5, 7.

39. Zhou, *Lingwai daida*, 4–5, 7, 13–14

40. Zhou, *Lingwai daida*, 81.

41. The description of Zhenla as being far from Champa yet abutting on to it suggests that Zhou Qufei regards the two states' capital cities as being far apart.

42. Wali 窊裏 in present-day Myanmar (or Laos, another possibility discussed): [Zhao,] *Chau Ju-kua: His Work*, tr. Hirth and Rockhill, 25, 56. Wali on the Kra isthmus: Lu and Zhou, *Zhongguo gujizhong*, 98.

43. Xipeng: 西棚; Sanbo/Sanpo, Sanluo: 三泊, 三濼; Malan, Maluowen, Moliang: 麻蘭, 麻羅問, 莫良; Dilata: 第辣撻.

44. Zhou Daguan on Moliang 莫良: Zhou, *Zhenla fengtu ji*, 172. Malyan on inscriptions: Pelliot, "Mémoire sur les Coutumes," 173. Malyan in Battambang: Vickery: *Society, Economics, and Politics*, 442.

45. For his various possible identifications Yang cites the work of the Chinese scholars Lin Jiajing 林家勁, Cen Zhongmian 岑仲勉, Xu Zhaolin 許肇琳, and others; Yang in Zhou, *Lingwai daida*, 82–83. Sanbo and Malian by slightly different names: Zhao Rugua's *Zhu fan zhi* mentions two places called Sanluo and Maluowen which are probably Sanbo and Malian. See later in this chapter.

46. *Zhou fa*: 咒法.

47. *Daoshi* 道士, *daoren* 道人: see the discussion in chapter six. *Ling shen*: 靈甚.

48. Zhou, *Zhenla fengtu ji*, 94.

49. Nüwa: 女媧. For Nüwa in early myths, Schipper, "Humanity's Beginnings in Creation and Origin Myths," 19–20. For Nüwa becoming an historical figure, Yang and An, "The World of Chinese Mythology," 35.

50. Sanfoqi: 三佛齊; Shepo: 闍婆.

51. For Zhao Rugua on Zhenla's dependencies, see later in this chapter. For Zhou Daguan, see chapter nine. See also Jacques and Dumont, *Angkor*, 96–97, 108.

52. Zhou, *Lingwai daida*, 241, 428–429. Jianyu: 肩輿.

53. China here is again the term Zhongzhou, The Central Region(s), used earlier by Fan Chengda.

The description of how the palanquin is carried suggests that two people carried the palanquin along after two others had lifted it off the ground. A frieze on the Bayon temple in Angkor Thom shows palanquins carried by two people, and Zhou Daguan describes them as being carried by either two or four people. Zhou, *Zhenla fengtu ji*, 167.

54. Zhou, *Lingwai daida*, 77, 80.

55. Min refers to the region of southeast China centered on the present-day province of Fujian.

"To be a senior military official" is a paraphrase of the original, which reads literally, "to be among the West Class." The West Class (Xi ban 西班) and The East Class (Dong ban 東班) were categories of Chinese officials in the Song court, West Class officials being military and East Class officials being civil. The Jiyang 吉陽 Army was based on the island of Hainan and responsible for China's southern maritime frontier; its Military Director-in-Chief (Du jian 都監) was a high-ranking officer. Zhou, *Lingwai daida*, 80; Hucker, *Dictionary of Official Titles*, 362, 537.

56. Qiongguan 瓊管, also called Qiongzhou 瓊州, was another place on Hainan, on the north side of the island. There is a similar account of these events in *Song shi*, which dates the Chinese officer's arrival in Champa to 1171 rather than 1173. 1173 must be the preferred date, given that *Lingwai daida*'s account is contemporaneous. The French sociologist Paul Mus cites part of this passage in his study of military equipment as portrayed on the Bayon temple in Angkor Thom. Mus, "Les Balistes du Bàyon," 338.

57. Zhanlipo: 占里婆: Zhou, *Lingwai daida*, 434.

58. Zhou, *Lingwai daida*, 434.

59. Zhenlifu: 真里富. Ma, *Wenxian tongkao*, 2605; Tuotuo, *Song shi*, 14,086–14,087. [Zhao,] *Chau Ju-kua: His Work*, tr. Hirth and Rockhill, 56. Lu and Zhou take the same view: Lu and Zhou, *Zhongguo gujizhong*, 93, 101.

60. This is the view of Almut Netolitzky, the translator into German of *Lingwai daida*. [Zhou,] *Das Ling-wai tai-ta von Chou Ch'ü-fei*, 291.

61. Edwards' suggestion, personal communication.

62. Zhao, *Zhu fan zhi*, 1.

63. Zhao, *Zhu fan zhi*, 2. For an illuminating portrait of Song and Yuan dynasty Quanzhou, see Schottenhammer, *The Emporium of the World*.

64. [Zhao,] *Chau Ju-kua: His Work*, tr. Hirth and Rockhill, 38.

65. [Zhao,] *Chau Ju-kua: His Work*, tr. Hirth and Rockhill, 37. See also Wheatley, "Geographical Notes", 184–187.

66. Zhao, *Zhi fan zhi*, 18–19.

67. Pugan 蒲甘 refers to Bagan or Pagan in the center-west of today's Myanmar on the Ayeyarwady (Irrawaddy) River, an important polity in the eleventh century that went into decline in the late thirteenth

century, partly because of attacks by the Mongols. Aung-Thwyn and Aung-Thwyn, *History of Myanmar*, 77–106, esp. 105–106; Thant, *The River of Lost Footsteps*, 56–59; Taylor, "The Early Kingdoms," 164–168.

Jialuoxi 加羅希 (加囉希 in *Shuyu zhaozi lu*), which Zhao writes later in this passage was a dependency of Srivijaya, has not been firmly identified; Yang Bowen suggests it may have been present-day Chaiya on the east side of the Kra Isthmus, but without explaining the basis for his suggestion. Zhao, *Zhu fan zhi*, 22.

In the phrase translated seven thousand or so li in area, the word *fang* 方 before the number may indicate area. Seven thousand li in area or say 70 x 100 li would refer only to the size of the capital city. By contrast, Zhou Daguan cites *Zhu fan zhi* as saying the size of Zhenla was seven thousand li in breadth (*guang* 廣), but no doubt we should rely on the original source rather than Zhou's citation of it. Zhou, *Zhenla fengtu ji*, 16; Wilkinson, *Chinese History*, 610.

68. Hirth and Rockhill take the phrase "districts and towns" (*xianzhen* 縣鎮) to refer to the state's administrative divisions. So far as is known, these consisted of provinces, which Zhou Daguan calls "prefectures" (*jun* 郡), and villages. [Zhao,] *Chau Ju-kua: His Work*, tr. Hirth and Rockhill, 52. Zhou, *Zhenla fengtu ji*, 172. For a summary of what is known about the administration of the Angkor kingdom, see Coe and Evans, *Angkor and the Khmer Civilization*, 176–180.

69. The length of the golden bridge—thirty poles or so long, the equivalent of about 300 (US) feet or 91 meters—does not quite match the larger of the two ponds in the royal palace at Angkor Thom, which is 125 meters long. Glaize, *Les Monuments*, 144.

70. Zhao's definition of *a'nan* 阿南, a term of unknown derivation, suggests they were the equivalent of *devadāsī*. *Devadāsī*, literally female servants of the deity, were Hindu temple dancers associated with palace rituals. In the twentieth century they were still active in some Hindu temples in India, for example the Jagannath temple in Puri, Odisha. [Zhao,] *Chau Ju-kua: His Work*, tr. Hirth and Rockhill, 55. *Devadāsī* in Puri: personal observation. For an anthropologist's account of the Puri *devadāsī*, see Marglin, *Wives of the God-King*.

71. In this account of punishment by amputation or branding, the "or . . . or" translation could equally well be "and . . . and," since the Chinese text does not make it clear whether the punishments were imposed severally or all at once.

72. In the phrase "an ounce of lead"—evidently a substitute for cash—"ounce" is *liang* 兩, a term also sometimes translated "tael," and "peck" is *dou* 斗. One *liang* was the equivalent of forty grams or 1.4 (US) ounces, and one *dou* was roughly the equivalent of seven liters or fifteen (US) pounds. Wilkinson, *Chinese History*, 612–613.

73. The three kinds of lign-aloes mentioned here are described later in *Zhu fan zhi* in a long section on this aromatic substance. This later section starts by describing different kinds of first-class lign-aloes or *chenxiang* 沉香, then goes on to discuss other lower-quality varieties, including those called *zhan* or *jian* 箋 (small bamboo), *su* 速 (rapid) in its fresh and ripe forms, *zan* 暫 (short-term), and *huangshu* 黃熟 (yellow ripe). According to Zhao the best lign-aloes—both *chenxiang* itself and its rapid and yellow ripe varieties—all came from Zhenla. Zhao, *Zhu fan zhi*, 173–177.

Kingfisher feathers (*cui mao* 翠毛), prized in China at this,time, were referred to centuries earlier in the *Liang shu* account of Funan.

Dammar is a translation of *dunou nao* 篤耨腦 and follows Rockhill and Hirth, who argue that *dunou* is a transliteration of *damar*, the Malay word for the dammar tree. (The third syllable, *nao* or "brain," seems superfluous.) Dammar is a source of resin used for cosmetic purposes as well as for pitch and turpentine. Others identify *dunao* variously with terebinth or the sal tree. As for gourd dammar, Zhao Rugua explains this later as referring to the gourds that local people stored dammar resin in. These were then shipped abroad in porcelain jars. [Zhao,] *Chau Ju-kua: His Work*, tr. Hirth and Rockhill, 199–200; Zhao, *Zhu fan zhi*, 168–169; Wu, *Han ying da cidian*, 390. Sal tree: Stuart, *Chinese Materia Medica*, 406–407; Yule and Burnell, *Hobson-Jobson*, 294–295.

Benzoin is a translation of *jinyanxiang* 金顏香, *jinyan* 金顏 meaning gold in color and *xiang* 香 meaning aromatic substance. Rockhill and Hirth and Yang Bowen agree that *jinyanxiang* refers to styrax benzoin, a tree native to Sumatra and the benzoin resin it produces, used for perfume, incense, and medicine. In Bahasa Melayu the resin is known as *kemenyan*, probably cognate with *jinyan*. [Zhao,] *Chau Ju-kua: His Work*, tr. Hirth and Rockhill, 198–199; Zhao, *Zhu fan zhi*, 167.

Sappan wood is *sumu* 蘇木, also called *sufangmu* 蘇枋木 or *sufang* 蘇枋 wood, *sufang* being from the Malay sepang. Sappan wood (*caesalpinia sappan*) was used for medicinal purposes and as a sedative. [Zhao,] *Chau Ju-kua: His Work*, tr, Hirth and Rockhill, 198–199; Zhao, *Zhu fan zhi*, 167; Stuart, *Chinese Materia Medica*, 78.

Cotton cloth here is *mianbu* 綿布, which Zhao describes later as being the third strongest of four types of *jibei* 吉貝 (cotton, also called *gubei* 古貝). Earlier the word *mian* was used for floss silk, but by this time it was being used for cotton as well. Zhao, *Zhu fan zhi*, 192–193; [Zhao,] *Chau Ju-kua: His Work*, tr. Hirth and Rockhill, 217–220; Pelliot, *Notes on Marco Polo*, 459.

74. China here is Zhongguo 中國 (Central State or, more loosely, Central Kingdom), the first clear use in these texts of this term with the meaning of a single central state, as it is still used today. It is notable that the first use of Zhongguo meaning Central State occurs in an early thirteenth century text, following many centuries in which various other terms were used to describe what later became conceived of as China.

75. Pelliot's reasoning is that the ṅ in **lukṅut* (Pelliot's rendition of the contemporary pronunciation of Luwu 祿兀) was a weak nasalization with a guttural element, while in Tang northern dialects a final *t* came close to a final *r*, so that **lukṅut* became **lukgut* or **lukgur* which was *nagara*. Pelliot, "Friedrich Hirth et W.W. Rockhill, 'Chau Ju-kua,'" 466–467; also Chandler, *A History of Cambodia*, 45; [Zhao,] *Chau Ju-kua: His Work*, tr. Hirth and Rockhill, 54.

76. Pugan: 蒲甘. This point is made in [Zhao,] *Chao Ju-kua: His Work*, tr. Hirth and Rockhill, 56. See also Aung-Thwyn and Aung-Thwyn., *History of Myanmar*, 77–106, esp. 105–106; Thant, *The River of Lost Footsteps*, 56–59; Taylor, "The Early Kingdoms," 164–168.

77. Bosilan: 波斯蘭; Luohu: 羅斛; Zhenlifu: 真里富 (or Zhenfuli 真富里); Lüyang: 綠洋; Tunlifu: 吞里富; Duhuai: 杜懷; Xunfan: 潯番.

78. Ma, *Wenxian tongkao*, 2605.

79. This account of Luohu 羅斛, Xian 暹, and Xianluo 暹羅 is taken from Pelliot. Pelliot, *Notes on Marco Polo*, 768. See also Geoff Wade, "The 'Ming shi-lu' as a Source for Thai History," 249–294, esp. 257–258

80. Zhao, *Zhu fan zhi*, 27.

81. This is Yang's view, apparently based on the limited similarity between the name Xunfan and Jianpen 尖噴, one of the Chinese names of Chumphon (the name of a present-day Thai province). Zhao, *Zhu fan zhi*, 27. For Tuohuan, see chapter six.

82. Surprisingly, however, neither Zhao Rugua nor subsequently Zhou Daguan, who also remarks on the fine buildings, makes any mention of the great size of the settlement around Angkor Thom, whose extensive dimensions have been clarified by recent LIDAR (Light Detection and Ranging) lasar mapping. See, for example, Evans et al., "Uncovering archaeological landscapes," 12,595–12,600.

83. For Phnom Bakheng see Glaize, *Les Monuments*, 95–99. Groslier, *The Art of Indochina*, 102–104; Jacques and Dumont, *Angkor*, 58–62. Another candidate for Zhao's description could be the Baphuon, built around 1060 by Udayādityavarman II (r. 1050–1066), but this great structure, praised by Zhou Daguan, lies northwest of the center of Angkor Thom, not to its southwest.

84. Mouhot, *Travels in Siam*, 237–240.

85. According to Coedès, the 1177 attack resulted in the death of Tribhuvanādityavarman, king of Zhenla. Coedès cites Lecoq's translation of this passage in *Wenxian tongkao*, which takes the passage verbatim from Zhao. But Zhao does not report that the king was killed, writing only that the Champa forces '*sha zhi* 殺之', "killed him or them", without recording the identity of the person or people killed. To complicate matters, Lecoq's translation is loosely written at this juncture, and does not actually mention a king of Zhenla at all. It refers only to the king of Champa having attacked the Zhenla capital and "enlevé les richesses que cette ville renfermait" (taken away the riches this city contained). So the source of Coedès' assertion is unclear. Coedès, *Indianized States*, 164–166; Ma, *Ethnographie des peuples étrangers à la Chine*, tr. Lecoq, 487.

86. Yet other accounts of the events involving Khmers and Chams at this time can be found in Whitmore, "Nagara Champa," 32–33; and Sharrock, "Cham-Khmer Interactions," 117–118.

87. Maspero, *The Champa Kingdom*, 78–80. Maspero describes the attack in 1177 in terms that are colorful but not always reliable. In a story that has often been repeated—an example of "stir-fry research"—he writes that a shipwrecked Chinese guided the Cham forces to the capital of Angkor, citing *Lingwai daida* as his source. But the story—inherently unlikely, since the Cham would surely have known where the capital was—does not feature in *Lingwai daida*, at least in the received text. Maspero, "Le Royaume de Champa: Chapitre VII", 307–308.

88. Maspero, *The Champa Kingdom*, 80.

89. Vickery, *Champa Revised*, 74–75.

90. Vickery, *Champa Revised*, 75. Also Vickery, *Cambodia and Its Neighbors*, 5-6, and Vickery, "A Short History of Champa," 55.

91. Vickery, *Champa Revised*, 74.

92. Schweyer, "The confrontation of the Khmers and Chams," 67–70.

93. The products listed here are not in the order Zhao lists in the second part of his book, but in the order he lists them in his earlier passage on Zhenla. Zhao, *Zhu fan zhi*, 207, 173–178, 215, 210–211, 167, 168–169, 191–192. Cardamom: *doukou* 豆蔻; called here white cardamom or *bai doukou* 白豆蔻, presumably because the seeds of one type of cardamom, green cardamom, turn white. Zhao, *Zhu fan zhi*, 195; [Zhao,] *Chau Ju-kua: His Work*, tr. Hirth and Rockhill, 221–222; Stuart, *Chinese Materia Medica*,

30–31. Musk wood: a literal translation of *shexiangmu* 麝香木. Zhao, *Zhu fan zhi*, 184–185; [Zhao,] *Chau Ju-kua: His Work*, tr. Hirth and Rockhill, 212.

94. Ye Tinggui: 葉廷珪; *Xiang lu*: 香錄, also called *Nanfan xiang lu* 南蕃香錄 [*A Record of Southern Foreigners' Aromatic Substances*]. Lu and Zhou, *Zhongguo gujizhong*, 116–118, citing entries from Ye's work in *Xin zuan xiang pu* 新纂香譜 [*A Newly Compiled Register of Aromatic Substances*], a twelfth-century work by Chen Jing 陳敬 and Yan Xiaoqing 嚴小青. Gourd fragrance: *piao xiang* 瓢香; Borneo camphor and musk: 腦麝, short for *longnao shexiang* 龍腦麝香. Luo et al., *Hanyu da cidian*, entry under 腦麝; Stuart, *Chinese Materia Medica*, 231.

95. Lou Yue 樓鑰, *Gongkui ji* 攻媿集 [*The Collected Works of Lou Yue*], *juan* 88, quoted in Lu and Zhou, *Zhongguo gujizhongi*, 114–115.

96. Wang Yinglin 王應麟, *Yu hai* 玉海, *juan* 152, quoted in Chen et al., *Zhongguo gujizhong*, 119. For *Yu hai* see also Wilkinson, *Chinese History*, 1082.

97. Ma, *Wenxian tongkao*, 2605. The mission began in the twelfth month of the sixth year of the Zhenghe reign period (1111–1118)—that is, sometime between the first week of January and the first week of February 1117. Xu, *Xin bian Zhongguo sanqian nian liri jiansuo biao*, 199–200.

98. Ma, *Wenxian tongkao*, 2605; Tuotuo et al., *Song shi*, 14,087. For the *Song hui yao jigao* entry see later in this chapter.

99. The Qingyuan prefecture—in fact a county from 1197—was in the southeastern Chinese port city of Mingzhou.

100. *Rui xiang* 瑞象 (auspicious elephant); *rui xiang* 瑞像 (statue of the Buddha): see *Liang shu* in chapter three.

101. Heng, *Sino-Malay Trade*, 101–102.

102. Wilkinson, *Chinese History*, 845–846; Wang, "Some Comments on the Later Standard Histories," 60–62.

103. Xu Song (1781–1848): 徐松. Wilkinson, *Chinese History*, 846–847; Wade, "The 'Account of Champa,'" 139.

104. Liu et al., *Song hui yao jigao*, 9787. This event is also recorded in Li Dao 李燾 (1115–1184)'s annals of the Northern Song. Li Dao, *Xu zizhi tongjian changbian* 續資治通鍵長編 [*Long draft of a Continuation of The Comprehensive Mirror to Aid Governance*], *juan* 69, cited in Lu and Zhou, *Zhongguo gujizhong*, 117. For this work, see Wilkinson, *Chinese History*, 847.

105. Tuotuo et al., *Song shi*, 14084. *Song hui yao jigao* also records these remarks, though its account describes the commissioner as saying that neither Zhanla nor Champa customarily engage in warfare. Liu et al., *Song hui yao jigao*, 9812. For the use of the name Zhanla 占臘 for Zhenla 真臘, see later in this chapter.

106. Taylor, *History of the Vietnamese*, 74.

107. Tuotuo et al., *Song shi*, 289–290. On the war, Taylor, *History of the Vietnamese*, 83–84.

108. Liu et al., *Song hui yao jigao*, 9813. This incident is also recorded in Li, *Xu zizhi tongjian*, cited in Chen et al., *Zhongguo gujizhong*, 117–118. See also Wade, *Champa in the* Song hui-yao, 20.

109. Liu et al., *Song hui yao jigao*, 9813.

110. Bandit Suppression Commission: Zhao tao si 招討司. Chief Attendant: (Si) hou (司) 候. Hucker, *Dictionary of Official Titles*, 117, 446. Warship: *zhanzhuo* 戰棹.

111. Port: *gang* 港—perhaps a settlement near the mouth of the Mekong. The Yuan envoy Zhou Daguan relates that with the wind behind him the sea journey from Champa to the frontier of Zhenla took about half a lunar month. Zhou, *Zhenla fengtu ji*, 15.

112. Liu et al., *Song hui yao jigao*, 9764–9765.

113. Secretariat: Zhong shu 中書, in Song times short for Secretariat-Chancellery, Zhong shu menxia 中書門下. Visitors' Bureau: Ke sheng 客省. Hucker, *Dictionary of Official Titles*, 193, 280.

114. For example, by Coe and Evans, *Angkor and the Khmer Civilization*, 142.

115. The two names given in different parts of the same passage—Xinzhumosengke (新祝摩僧可) and Jiumosengge (鳩摩僧哥)—may be variants of the same name.

Civilization-Promoting Commandant: Fenghua langjiang 奉化郎將. Mojunmingjisi: 摩君明稽 田思. Civilization-Pacifying Commandant: Anhua langjiang 安化郎將. Tuotuo et al., *Song shi*, 14086, 14087; Liu et al., *Song hui yao jigao*, 9765. Hucker, *Dictionary of Official Titles*, 213, 301 (where Tucker translates *hua* 化 as Culture). Hucker's *Dictionary* does not list the term Anhua, literally "Pacifying Civilization."

116. Liu et al., *Song hui yao jigao*, 9765.

117. Molamotu: 摩臘摩禿. The name may be garbled; it is followed by the character *fang* 防, which in the *Song hui yao jigao* account of the same mission becomes the unidentified title *fangshouguan* 防授官, held by a third participant in the mission. In that account the mission leader's name is given as Molafu 摩臘富, and Motu 摩禿 is listed as another person. Tuotuo et al., *Song shi*, 14087, 14100; Liu et al., *Song hui yao jigao*, 9765.

118. *Song shi* gives the name of the king as Jinshuaibinshen 金衰賓深. The account in *Song hui yao jigao* also includes this four-character term. Jinshuaibinshen is hard to decipher, and bears no resemblance to the name of the then king of Angkor, Sūryavarman II. Given that *jin* 金 means "gold" and *bin* 賓 is a polite word for "guest", it could perhaps be a corrupted rendition of an honorific or title, though nothing like it is listed in Hucker's *Dictionary of Official Titles*. Tuotuo et al., *Song shi*, 14087; Liu et al., *Song hui yao jigao*, 9765. See also Coedès, *Indianized States*, 334.

119. Both sources record that in 1155 Luohu as well as Zhenla submitted tribute. For the Zhenla dependency of Luohu in present-day Thailand, see the discussion of Zhao Rugua's *Zhu fan zhi* earlier in this chapter. Tuotuo et al., *Song shi*, 397, 407, 583; Liu et al., *Song hui yao jigao*, 9765, 9964, 9966. Accounts of the tribute missions sent in 1117 and 1120 were first given in Ma, *Wenxian tongkao*, 2605.

120. "One of the greatest Khmer rulers:" Coe and Evans, *Angkor and the Khmer Civilization*, 141–142.

For all its grandeur, Angkor Wat is not mentioned in Chinese sources until it is remarked on by Zhou Daguan. Zhou, *Zhenla fengtu ji*, 44.

121. Taylor, *History of the Vietnamese*, 93. Also Maspero, *The Champa Kingdom*, 75–76. Maspero's account and the dates he gives differ from those of Taylor.

122. The passage is not in the received text of *Guihai yuheng zhi* but is cited in *Wenxian tongkao*, which gives it in full. It is included as a supplement in Fan, *Guihai yuhengzhi*, 166. Ma, *Wenxian tongkao*, 2595; also [Fan,] *Treatises of the Supervisor*, 205–207.

123. Fan, *Guihai yuhengzhi*; 3, 166; [Fan,] *Treatises of the Supervisor*, xxviii, 205–206.

124. Fan, *Guihai yuhengzhi*, 166.

125. *Luowo* 羅我 is an unusual term, and seems to refer to an ornate form of saddle, rather than a full howdah. In the Chinese text, *luowo* is not number specific, but the use of the color vermilion, exclusive to the emperor, indicates there was only one.

126. Tuotuo et al., *Song shi*, 14087. The account is repeated in *Song hui yao jigao*, which adds that before being nearly exterminated Champa surrendered to Zhenla. (In the *Song hui yao jigao* account I follow Lu and Zhou read *yuansha* 元殺 as *jiaosha* 剿殺, the term used in *Zhu fan zhi*.) Liu et al., *Song hui yao jigao*, 9820–9821.

127. Tuotuo et al., *Song shi*, 14085.

128. Tuotuo et al., *Song shi*, 14086.

129. Zhanla: 占臘; *zhan*: 占.

130. Zhang et al., *Ming shi*, 8394.

131. Pelliot, *Mémoires*, 71–81. As noted earlier, Pelliot carries his logic further and suggests intriguingly that Zhenla might translate to "China defeated." See the introduction.

132. Ganbozhi: 甘孛智; Ganpuzhi: 澉浦只. This is the first reference in Chinese sources to the name Ganbozhi and its variant Ganpuzhi, clearly derived from the old name Kambuja (born of Kambu) found in Cham and Khmer epigraphy from the ninth century CE on. Vickery, *Society, Economics, and Politics*, 41.

133. Ganbozhi: 甘孛智; Ganpozhe 甘破蔗; Jianpuzhai: 柬埔寨. Zhang et al., *Ming shi*, 8395.

134. Liu et al., *Song hui yao jigao*, 9831–9832.

135. Lakawood or *jiangzhen* 降真 is an aromatic wood, sometimes conflated with lign-aloes. Black ebony is *wuwen* 烏紋 (also 烏文). Coarse incense is a near-literal translation of *cu xiang* 麤香. "coarse aromatic". Stuart, *Chinese Materia Medica*, 428, 253.

136. The Kunlun Sea is clearly the South China Sea, or at least the area off the southeastern coast of present-day Vietnam. As noted earlier, Bindalang seems to refer to Phan Rang in today's southern Vietnam. The location of the rocky outcrops called Wanli 萬里 has not been identified. It could be any of the island groups in the South China Sea.

137. Liu et al., *Song hui yao jigao*, 9831–9832. The tribute given in 1200, 1202, and 1205 consisted in all of five elephants, two elephant drapes, twenty-two elephant tusks, sixty rhino horns, forty pieces of local cloth, and ten lengths of Indian cotton (here *douluomian* 兜羅棉). The name of the king whose anniversary was celebrated in 1200 is given as Moluobaganwuding Ensilifangmozhi 摩羅巴甘勿丁 恩斯里房麾蟄, an indecipherable name, or title and name. Liu et al., *Song hui yao jigao*, 9831. Reading *Douluomian* to mean Indian cotton follows (1) *Hanyu da cidian*, which defines *duoluo* as a transliteration of the Sanskrit *tūla* (cotton) and *mian* (cotton, floss); (2) Pelliot, who argues that in late Song times, *douluomian* was used in Chinese lay texts to refer to certain special types of cotton goods. Luo et al., *Hanyu da cidian*, entry under *douluomian*; Pelliot, *Notes on Marco Polo*, 430–432.

138. Wang, "Early Ming Relations," 47–48.

139. Wheatley, *Golden Khersonese*, 62.

140. For a fine portrait of the sophisticated but inward-looking intellectual culture of the Song elite, see Bols, "*This Culture of Ours*,", esp. 148–344.

141. Heng, *Sino-Malay Trade*, 62.

142. Leys, "The Chinese Attitude towards the Past", 287, 289. Leys attributes his views partly to those of the French writer Victor Segalen (1878–1919).

Chapter Nine

1. Zhou Daguan: 周達觀; *Zhenla fengtu ji*: 真臘風土記.

2. Zhou, *A Record of Cambodia*. This was the first translation of Zhou's work from Chinese into English. A second translation from Chinese into English, by the Cambodian scholars Beling Uk and Solang Uk, was published in 2016, and includes helpful comments about the Khmer language and local conditions. Zhou, *Customs of Cambodia*, tr. Uk and Uk. The Uks' translation of Zhou was the second by a Cambodian scholarly team or scholar; the first, into Khmer, was done by Ly Thiam Teng and published in Phnom Penh by Moha Leap in 1973.

3. Pelliot, "Mémoire sur les Coutumes," 132, citing the beginning of *Zhenla fengtu ji* in *GuJin shuo hai*.

4. Zhou, *Zhenla fengtu ji*, 16. The standard history of the Yuan dynasty, *Yuan shi*, makes no mention of this or any other mission involving Zhenla. Notably, however, it records that at the outset of the Yuan dynasty (1271–1368) it was decided that Zhenla, along with Champa and Jiaozhi (the Vietnamese), would submit an annual tribute of elephants to be kept and led out by foreign riders during imperial ceremonies. No further mention is made of this plan, so it may not have materialized. Song et al., *Yuan shi*, 1974; Mote, *Imperial China*, 469. Also Zhou, *Zhenla fengtu ji*, 16; Maspero, *The Champa Kingdom*, 82–86; Taylor, *History of the Vietnamese*, 125–139.

5. The third-to-last Angkor ruler known by name, followed by Indravarman IV (1308–1327) and Jayavarmādiparameśvara (1327–?), unless we also include Huerna, the king who sent a tribute mission to the Ming court in 1373, when he may still have been living at Angkor, since a Ming envoy visited either him or his successor at Angkor in 1403. Coe and Evans, *Angkor and the Khmer Civilization*, 281; also appendix two. For Huerna, see chapter ten.

6. Wu Qiuyan: 吾邱衍. Wu refers to Zhou as Zhou Dake: 周達可. The anthology was called *Zhu su shan fang ji* 竹素山房集 [*An Anthology of Writings from the Mountain Dwelling of Bamboo Purity*]. Xia Nai suggests that Dake may have been Zhou's alternative name. Zhou, *Zhenla fengtu ji*, 2. Pelliot, *Mémoires*, 37–38.

7. Xia Nai lists fifteen works, five of them Yuan and Ming dynasty editions. Zhou, *Zhenla fengtu ji*, 191–192.

8. The miscellany was compiled by a scholar called Lin Kun 林坤, who came from the same place as Zhou Daguan and Zhou Qufei. This was Kuaiji 會稽, present-day Shaoxing, between Wenzhou to the south and Hangzhou to the north. *Cheng Zhai zaji*: 誠齋雜記. Zhou, *Zhenla fengtu ji*, 2.

9. Pelliot, *Mémoires*, 39–40; Zhou, *Zhenla fengtu ji*, 3.

10. Zhou, *Zhenla fengtu ji*, 191–194.

11. Tao Zongyi: 陶宗儀. *Shuo fu*: 說郛. Pelliot, *Mémoires*, 39–40; Zhou, *Zhenla fengtu ji*, 191. Also Wilkinson, *Chinese History*, 878.

12. Lu Ji 陸楫; *GuJin shuo hai*: 古今說海. A facsimile edition of a 1909 version of the book was published by Shanghai wenyi chubanshe in 1989.

13. Pelliot, *Mémoires*, 39–40; Zhou, *Zhenla fengtu ji*, 191–192, 196–198.

14. Wu Guan: 吳琯; *Gujin yi shi*: 古今逸史. Pelliot, *Mémoires*, 43–45; Zhou, *Zhenla fengtu ji*, 192.

15. Chen Menglei: 陳夢雷; *Qin ding gujin tushu jicheng*: 欽定古今圖書記成. Wilkinson, *Chinese History*, 1084; Pelliot, *Mémoires*, 46; Zhou, *Zhenla fengtu ji*, 193.

16. Qian Zeng: 錢曾; Zhou Jianguan: 周建觀. The text of Qian Zeng's entry is in Zhou, *Zhenla fengtu ji*, 189.

17. Abel-Rémusat, *Description du royaume de Cambodge*; Pelliot, *Mémoires*, 46.

18. Pelliot, "Mémoire sur les Coutumes", 123–177; Pelliot, *Mémoires*, passim. The *Mémoires* are preceded by an informative foreword by Coedès and Paul Demiéville: Pelliot, *Mémoires*, 5–6.

19. Zhou, *Zhenla fengtu ji*, 203.

20. It is notable that when the Ming scholar Yan Congjian reproduced a large part of *Zhenla fengtu ji* in his *Shuyu zhouzi lu* [*A Record of Various Views on Distant Regions*,] he treated it as a single long text, with no sub-headings. Yan, *Shuyu zhouzi lu*, 270–278.

21. The sacred dynasty is the Mongol Yuan dynasty. "The scriptures of the western foreigners" (*xi fan jing* 西番經) probably refers to Buddhist texts. As noted earlier, Ganpuzhi 澉浦只 and Ganbozhi 甘孛智 are Chinese transliterations of the name Kambuja, meaning "born of Kambu," Kambu being a founding ancestor.

After "almost the same as Ganbozhi," a textual variant includes another sentence, which reads, "To the south of it there is a large river with *an* 洝—*an* means 'warm water.'" This is probably a reference to the Mekong. Pelliot, *Mémoires*, 83; Rossabi, *Khubilai Khan*, 192–198; Vickery, *Society, Economics, and Politics*, 41. Zhou, *Zhenla fengtu ji*, 22.

22. Compass points are given here in north-south-east-west terms, but Zhou actually names two of the points on a twenty-four-division compass, *dingwei* 丁未 and *kunshen* 坤申. By the thirteenth century magnetic compasses with twenty-four divisions were in regular use. On twenty-four-division compasses, Needham and Wang, *Science and Civilization in China*, *Vol. IV*, *Part I*, 279–293.

Min and Guang were regions in southeastern and south China. "The various overseas ports," more literally "the various *zhou* ports for overseas," refers to the various international ports whose names end in *zhou* 州 along the southeastern and southern coasts of China, from Wenzhou to Guangzhou. The Seven Islands Sea (Qi zhou yang 七洲洋) was a name commonly used for the part of the South China Sea nearest China. The exact location of Zhenpu 真蒲 is not known; perhaps it was in the area of present-day Vũng Tàu.

"About fifteen days": literally, "half a month". Zhou uses the Chinese lunar calendar, which has twelve months in the year, alternately twenty-nine or thirty days long.

23. This paragraph has been moved forward from section 18 of the original text, where it was out of place.

24. The long river, *chang jiang* 長江 in Chinese, is clearly the Mekong. This is also the Chinese name for the Yangzi River and so conjures up in the Chinese reader's mind an image of the Yangzi's own massive outlet to the sea. At this time the li may have been the equivalent of slightly less than half a kilometer. Wilkinson, *Chinese History*, 612.

25. The Chinese word *niu* 牛 can mean both "ox" or "cow" and "buffalo" (the latter called more precisely *shui niu* 水牛), whereas the Khmer have different words for them (*goa* for "cow" and *grabay* for "buffalo".) Reliefs at Angkor show both, and presumably the herds Zhou saw could have been of either.

26. Zha'nan 查南 is hard to identify; perhaps it is Kampong Chhnang, the present-day town beyond the southern end of Tonlé Sap Lake, given a resemblance between the names Zha'nan and Chhnang. Here and later Zhou calls Zha'nan a *jun* 郡, in Yuan times an archaic word for "prefecture." Zhou later uses the same term, *jun*, when writing of Zhenla's "ninety or so prefectures." Coedès, "Notes sur Tcheou Ta-Kuan," 4–5; Pelliot, *Mémoires*, 96.

The names Halfway Village (Banlu cun 半路村) and Buddha Village (Fo cun 佛村) may be unidentified proper names or just descriptive. Freshwater Sea (Danyang 淡洋, called Danshui yang 淡水洋 later on) must be Tonlé Sap Lake. Tonlé Sap is the only name of Zhou's that comes close to its Khmer equivalent, Tonlé Sap being Khmer for Freshwater River. Ganpang 干傍 is hard to identify. It could be the Khmer word that is usually written *kompong or kampong*, which originally may have meant a pier or landing, and which is found today in many Cambodian place-names. If so it is not clear which *kompong* is referred to. On *kompong/kampong*: Vickery, *Society, Economics, and Politics*, 440–441.

In alluding to the capital, Zhou uses the term *cheng* 城 ("city") rather than *du* 都 ("capital").

27. *Zhu fan zhi* is the gazetteer by Zhao Rugua discussed in chapter eight. It records that Zhenla "may be some seven thousand li or so in area," referring perhaps to the area of the capital city. In Zhou's discussion of the distances of Zhenla from its neighbors, he is probably referring to distances from main city to main city.

28. As noted earlier, Xianluo 暹羅 is a composite word for the polities named Xian 暹 and Lavo (Luohu 羅斛 in Chinese). It did not come into use until more than half a century after Zhou visited Cambodia, when Lavo was taken over by Xian. The use of the word here suggests either that Zhou was still editing his book half a century after his trip or that someone amended it after his death. Later, Zhou also refers to the people of Luo (*luoren* 羅人). Pelliot, *Mémoires*, 98; Coedès, *Indianized States*, 235; Wade, "The *Ming shi-lu* as a Source,“ 257–258.

It is not possible to identify Panyu 番禺 (alternatively pronounced Poyu or Fanyu), the place ten days' journey south, perhaps on the Malay Peninsula.

29. Suodu 唆都 was the Chinese name of the Mongol commander Sögätü. He played a leading role in defeating the Song dynasty, then led a successful punitive attack on Champa. He was killed by the Vietnamese in 1285. His biography is in Song et al., *Yuan shi*, 3150–3153.

"A general and a senior commander" is a paraphrase of the Chinese text, which describes the Chinese military commanders sent to Champa by rank, given in terms of their insignia and the men (called households) under their charge. The insignia took the form of tallies—a miniature tiger or a piece of gold or silver—that were cut in two, one half being given to the commander and the other being kept in court. According to Zhou, the first commander had a tiger tally and ten thousand households, making him roughly the equivalent today of a general in charge of a division. The second had a gold tally and a thousand households, roughly the equivalent of a colonel in charge of a regiment. *Ci hai*, 5237; Zhou, *Zhengla fengtu ji*, 38–39, 119–123; Song et al., *Yuan shi*, 4660; Pelliot, *Notes on Marco Polo*, 836–837.

The sacred Son of Heaven was Temür, the Chengzong Emperor.

30. Zhou writes of leaving the port city of Mingzhou 明州, present-day Ningbo, but of returning to Siming 四明. Siming was another name for Mingzhou. Converting the dates Zhou gives to those of the Western calendar, he left Wenzhou on March 24, 1296, arrived in Champa on April 18, 1296, and reached Zhenla at the beginning of August that year. He set sail for home again sometime between June 21 and July 20, 1297, arriving back in Mingzhou on August 30, 1297. So he was in Zhenla for just less than a year.

31. Zhou refers to the capital city here as *zhoucheng* 州城, which has the sense of a regional city or capital. He does not name it. The capital at the time of Zhou's visit was evidently called Yaśodharapura, after king Yaśovarman I (r. 889–c. 900), the name Yaśodharapura having been found on an early fourteenth-century inscription. If as seems plausible the name Luwu referred to by Zhou's predecessor Zhou Qufei was a transliteration of Angkor, by Zhou's time the capital may also have been called Angkor. Higham, *The Civilization of Angkor*, 138. On Luwu as Angkor, see *Lingwai daida* in chapter eight.

32. The snakes or nagas that are still in place today seem to have only seven heads, but Uk and Uk point out that there are the faint remains of two more heads on the nagas guarding the south gate (something I missed during my visits there). They note that the French explorer Francois Garnier, who visited Angkor in 1866, wrote of dragons with nine heads on each side of the entrance to Angkor Thom. Zhou, *Customs of Cambodia*, tr. Uk and Uk, 17; Francois Garnier, *Voyage d'Exploration en Indo-chine*, 47.

33. Zhou's description of the four walls facing the cardinal points (following Pelliot and reading *xifang* 西方 as *sifang* 四方) and five gates with elephants carved on to them conforms to what exists at Angkor Thom today. So does his description of the fifty-four stone figures pulling a snake on either side of the city bridges. On the other hand, the five gateways in the city walls are all clearly surmounted by four heads rather than five. So did Zhou recall wrongly the number of heads? We know that the stonework of the city was reworked by successive kings, so perhaps Zhou did see five faces, which were later modified. Images with five heads or faces were certainly not unknown at the time; there are several in the National Museum in Phnom Penh. Zhou's text is ambiguous as to whether all five heads above the gateways were decorated with gold or only the middle one. The absence of the adverb *jie* 皆 (all) suggests only the middle one was gilded. Pelliot, *Mémoires*, 128.

34. The sentence about criminals is out of place in the original and has been moved up to go with the sentence about dogs.

The towers on the four sides of the city wall probably refer to the temples with small towers dedicated to Lokesvara still found at each corner of the walls of Angkor Thom. Here, as later, Zhou uses the term *ta* 塔 for "tower". For him *ta* would have meant both tower and Buddhist stupa, which in China often took the form of a pagoda. *Ta* in Zhou's text is translated as "tower" or "pagoda" depending on context.

35. The gold tower Zhou refers to is evidently the Bayon. There is now a stone terrace rather than a bridge on the east side of it. The gold Buddhas have gone, but the terrace is still guarded by two lions, now just of plain stone. The number of towers on the Bayon has been variously calculated; according to a recent estimate by Olivier Cunin, it consists of sixty structures, forty-nine of which are face towers. Zhou's figure of twenty or so may correspond to the main towers in the inner part of the building. His description of the Bayon being at the center of the state evidently means that it was at the center of the capital city, which it was. Cunin, "The Bayon," 146.

36. The bronze tower is clearly Baphuon, though Baphuon lies northwest of Bayon rather than north of it. In my earlier translation of Zhou's *Record* I tentatively identified the structure described in *Zhu fan zhi* as Baphuon, but as discussed in chapter eight, on further consideration that structure seems more likely to have been Bakheng.

37. The king's residence (*lu* 廬) evidently refers to the royal palace or perhaps more specifically to the king's dwelling place within the palace precinct. Here and elsewhere, Zhou uses the terms *guozhu* 國主 (ruler of the state) and *zhu* 主 (ruler) when referring to the king, perhaps out of consideration for Chinese protocol. (The title *wang* 王, king, was only used in Chinese records when conferred by the Chinese court, which may not have been the case with Indravarman III, the king during Zhou's visit, probably because he had only recently come to power.) In this translation, I render *guozhu* and *zhu* as king. Zhou does use the term *wang* twice, but only in chapter three when he mentions Cambodia's "foreign king" (*fan wang* 番王).

The gold tower in the king's sleeping quarters was evidently the structure now known as Phimeanakas in the precincts of the palace.

38. Stone Tower Mountain is probably Phnom Bakheng.

By Lu Ban 魯班's tomb Zhou clearly means Angkor Wat. This is his only reference to this structure, completed more than a century before his visit. It is astonishing that he says so little about so dramatic a site, while being so impressed by other less extraordinary places such as Bapuon. Perhaps he wrote more extensively about it but what he wrote was later lost.

Zhou's references to Lu Ban, a semi-mythical carpenter from the ancient Chinese state of Lu, are puzzling. As the Ming writer Yan Congjian remarks nearly three centuries later, "Lu Ban was originally a man of Lu, so how could he have a tomb in Zhenla? Nowadays it seems the immortal Lu Ban is always with us. There is nowhere he hasn't gone. Wherever there is a fabulously built palace, temple, pagoda, or bridge, it is sure to be Lu Ban's work, not only in China but also among the foreigners. How absurd!" Perhaps Zhou was a victim of this thoughtless adulation of Lu Ban. Another possible explanation, put forward by the French archaeologist Louis Finot, is that Zhou confused the ubiquitous Lu Ban with another god, Visvakarman, the Hindu god of carpenters. According to this explanation, Zhou then mistook Visvakarman for Suryavarman II, the king who had Angkor Wat built, perhaps as his own mausoleum. Visvakarman was popularly known in Cambodia as Brah Bisnukar, and the name Brah Bisnukar was almost the same as Brah Bisnulok, the popular form of Suryavarman II's posthumous title Parama-Visnuloka. Yan, *Shuyu zhouzi lu*, 271; Finot, "The Temple of Angkor Wat", 125–128.

Its builder apart, the fact that Zhou describes Angkor Wat as a tomb lends weight to the view that it was constructed as a mausoleum.

39. The East Lake is the East Baray, at the center of which is East Mebon temple. There is nothing to suggest that the temple housed a reclining Buddha. On the other hand, part of a reclining bronze Vishnu was recovered on the other side of Angkor Thom, near the West Mebon temple in the West Baray. Conceivably this is what Zhou was referring to. There is another short passage in the text at this point that is found only in the Yuan miscellany *Cheng zhai za ji* [*Cheng Zhai's Miscellany*]. The passage reads: "There is a stone tower in Zhenla, and in the tower is a bronze reclining Buddha. Water continually flows from its navel. It tastes like Chinese wine, and easily makes people drunk." Lin Kun 林坤, attr., *Cheng zhai zaji* 誠寨記 (ctext.org/wiki.pl?if=gb&res=278847); Pelliot, *Mémoires*, 55–61; Freeman and Jacques, *Ancient Angkor*, 188; Glaize, *Les Monuments du Groupe d'Angkor*, 270.

40. The square, in fact cruciform gold tower, is evidently Neak Pean, built in the last part of the twelfth century during the reign of Jayavarman VII. Neak Pean is in the middle of the man-made lake Jayatataka Baray, northeast of Angkor Thom. As the site is now, it consists of a tower in the middle of a pond, which is linked to smaller ponds by four small chapels. All four chapels contain stone images with mouths that serve as water-spouts. They include images of an elephant, a lion, and a horse, as Zhou says. The site apparently represents the sacred Himalayan lake of Anavatapta, famous as the source of four great rivers issuing north, south, east, and west from the mouths of a lion, an elephant, an ox, and a horse respectively. For some reason the elephant and the lion in Neak Pean have exchanged places, and instead of an ox in the east chapel there is the head of a man.

41. "Ninety or so prefectures": different versions of the text read "ninety or so" (*jiushi yu* 九十餘) and "altogether ten or so" (*fan shi yu* 凡十餘), the characters for "nine" (九) and "altogether" (凡) being very similar. Ten or so are surely too few, given that Zhou lists ten and adds that he cannot recall the names of the others. Ninety or so seems more likely, although it is a very large number. No doubt much depends on the size of the unit of administration that Zhou calls prefecture (*jun* 郡).

Some, though not all, of the places Zhou names can be tentatively identified today. As we saw in Zhou's General Preface, Zhenpu may have been located at the present-day Vũng Tàu, and Zha'nan at the present-day Kampong Chhnang. Zhou later mentions that like Zhenpu, Bajian 巴澗 was on the coast, though he does not say where. As discussed in chapter eight, Moliang may have been the place known in inscriptions as Malyan, located in present-day Battambang or Pailin. Baxue 八薛 could perhaps be the present-day Pakse, a city in southern Laos near Wat Phu, the temple discussed in chapter seven as a possible location for Wendan.

Pumai 蒲買 seems to be Phimai, the temple complex in eastern Thailand that was a center of Angkorian royal patronage from the late eleventh century on. Zhigun 雉棍 may be Saigon, now Ho Chi Minh City in southern Vietnam; according to the Chinese scholar Xu Zhaolin 許肇琳 the Vietnamese once called Saigon Chaigun 柴棍, while overseas Chinese called it Zhaigun 宅棍. Laigankeng 賴敢坑 has not been clearly identified. Basili 八廝里 is probably the Basilan mentioned in *Zhu fan zhi*, the polity adjacent to Zhenlifu in the southwest corner of Zhenla. Zhou, *The Customs of Cambodia*, tr. Smithies, 87; Freeman, *A Guide to Khmer Temples*, 70–89; Xu Zhaolin cited in Zhou, *Zhenla fengtu ji*, 173.

The phrase in Chinese for their officials, *guan shu* 官屬, can also refer to officials and their subordinates.

42. Buddhist temples and pagodas in the villages: as noted earlier, the precise meaning of the term *ta* 塔, translated here as "pagoda", is uncertain. It could conceivably refer to non-Buddhist structures of some kind, though "pagoda" seems more likely. *Maijie* 買節 (mai tsiet [K]) may correspond to the Khmer *mai s'rok* (headman of a village or district) or *mé jee* (respected elder). *Senmu* 森木 (ṣi̯əm muk [K]) may be *samnak*, the Khmer word for "temporary stay". (Karlgren's sound reconstructions are given here but are only of limited value, since they refer to the Chinese spoken in Chang'an during the Sui, six centuries earlier.) *Mé jee* and *samnak*: Zhou, *Customs of Cambodia*, tr. Uk and Uk, 119 (the Uks' transliterations).

Stele inscriptions tell of the importance to Angkor at this time of rest houses, built by Jayavarman VII along the main roads between the capital and other locations, including Champa and Phimai, one of the "prefectures" of Zhenla mentioned here. On the road to Champa there were at one time fifty-seven rest houses at regular intervals. The stone remains of some rest houses are still standing. The Chinese postal stations to which Zhou compares these resting-houses were an equally important element of the Chinese state, and were rapidly developed during Mongol times. Chandler, *History of Cambodia*, 61–62; Rossabi, *Khubilai Khan*, 124.

43. This brief reference to the devastating effects of repeated military conflicts with the Luo people, later to become the people of Xianluo or Siam, suggests that at the time of Zhou's visit the Kingdom of Angkor beyond the capital was under pressure from the Siamese and in a precarious condition.

44. The old king was Jayavarman VIII (r. 1243–1295). His replacement Indravarman III (r.c. 1296–1308) was the king Zhou describes.

45. "Died" (*cu* 殂) is a textual variant. Other versions read "loved his daughter" (*ai nü* 愛女) so that the text would read, "His wife's father loved his daughter, and she secretly stole . . ." "Died" seems marginally more plausible, since if the old man had loved his daughter she might not have needed stealth. Zhou, *Zhenla fengtu ji*, 183.

46. It is not clear whether the dignitaries and royal relatives were in front of the whole procession or in front of the king and behind the soldiers. The procession of Suryavarman II (r. 1113–c. 1149) shown on a relief in Angkor Wat, the only known portrait of a royal procession at Angkor, shows the king surrounded by his army, with soldiers taking up the whole of the front part of the procession.

47. "He only used a gold cart . . .": this sentence has been moved forward from later in this section, where it was out of place.

48. *Sanba* 三罷 is the Khmer word *sompeeah*, the term for the respectful gesture described.

49. The precise sense of the phrase ". . . without anything fixed in writing", *wu ding wen* 無定文, is unclear. Perhaps it indicates that the king's pronouncements were made without prior agenda or documentation, or without being noted down as they were made, or both.

50. "Uncouth foreigners:" Zhou here uses the composite term *manmo* 蠻貊, *man* 蠻 meaning "southern foreigners" and *mo* 貊 being another word used for outsiders in general and more specifically for certain northern and southern tribes called Mo (Muk [K]). Both terms had disparaging overtones, as reflected in the "insect" radicals (虫, 豸) in the characters used to write them. On the Mo, Schafer, *Vermilion Bird*, 50–53, where using a southern Chinese pronunciation he calls them Mak.

51. The foreign king who enjoys a nightly tryst in the gold tower in the palace, evidently Phimeanakas, is of course the king of Angkor. *Shang* 上 (at the summit) is a variant reading. Other texts have *xia* 下 (at the base). The structure of Phimeanakas as it is today is such that the chamber at the top would have been suitable for the tryst.

52. For southern foreigners Zhou again uses the disparaging term *man* 蠻. The description of early Cambodians as ugly and black was, as we have seen, a trope dating as far back as *Jin shu* and *Liang shu*.

53. *Nanpeng* 南棚, literally "southern canopy," may be a transliteration of a Khmer word, but if so it is not clear which one. The gloss in the text explaining *nanpeng* is in Zhou's original. As noted earlier, the light skins of some of the women cannot just be explained by their seclusion away from the sun. Perhaps they were wearing makeup of some kind.

54. Given the adjective Zhou uses (*su* 酥, meaning smooth like milk or butter) when writing about the tops of bodies being uncovered, he has been taken to refer to the smooth breasts of women. However, his text refers to men and women with equal emphasis, and uses a term for "chest" (*xiong* 胸) that is gender-neutral.

55. The king's "one principal wife": Zhou actually writes "one for the main room" (*zheng shi* 正室). This is a common term for first wife, but in this context suggests that the king's sleeping quarters may actually have been constructed with a central room and rooms on each side of it pointing north, south, east, and west. "Several thousand" reads more literally "three to five thousand", "three to five" being a phrase in Chinese often used to indicate a small number.

56. *Chenjialan* 陳家蘭 (đi̯ĕn ka: lân [K]) has not been satisfactorily explained. It has been identified with several possible words in Khmer and Sanskrit, including the Sanskrit *śṛṅgāra*, meaning "beauty" or "erotic love". The northerners are evidently those living in north China. Zhou's "open canal" (*kai shui dao* 開水道) style of hair may refer to some form of back-shaving or parting, though precisely what is not clear. *Chenjialan*: Xia citing Pelliot and Coedès in Zhou, *Zhenla fengtu ji*, 10.

57. "Epicene individuals:" *er xing ren* 二形人, literally "individuals with two forms or appearances." In my earlier translation I took the term to refer to men, but it is gender-neutral, so I have modified the translation to take this into account.

58. Of the official titles given here, Pelliot suggests that *bading* 巴丁 (pa tieng [K]) is the equivalent of *mratāñ* (Vickery's transliteration), a title that according to Vickery was used for high dignitaries until the reign of Sūryavarman I (r. 1002–1049). Otherwise the equivalents of the titles *anding* 暗丁 and *siladi* 廝辣的 cannot be firmly identified. *Anding* occurs with a quite different meaning later in this section, suggesting a textual corruption in one usage or the other. Pelliot, *Mémoires*, 65; Vickery, *Society, Economics, and Politics*, 190; Zhou, *Customs of Cambodia*, tr. Uk and Uk, 33. See also Zhou, *Zhenla fengtu ji*, 93.

59. The words "except for" have been added here.

60. "Hair wound up in a knot": the Chinese phrase used here, *zhui ji* 椎髻, suggests hair bound up into a tall knot or bun resembling a club or cudgel, which is the basic meaning of *zhui*. Reliefs at Bayon

and Angkor Wat show a variety of hair styles, including a small, neat bun or topknot. The term used for "cloth" (*bu* 布) does not specify what the cloth was made from.

61. As mentioned earlier, a Chinese ounce or *liang* was the equivalent of forty grams or 1.4 (US) ounces. There were sixteen ounces in a *jin* or catty, and the weight of a catty was about 630 grams or 1 1/3 lbs (pounds avoirdupois).

The Western Seas, a vague term in Chinese as in English, may refer here to India.

62. "Holder of the Diamond:" More literally, the text reads, "Like what is worn on the head of the *vajra* [*jingang* 金剛]." *Jingang* or *vajra* means "diamond" and also "thunderbolt." Here Zhou's *jingang* seems to be referring to Jingang chi 金剛持, the Holder of the Diamond, Vajradhāra in Sanskrit. The Holder of the Diamond is the form of the Buddha, sometimes called the Primordial Buddha, that is often associated with Vajrayāna or Diamond Vehicle beliefs—tantric beliefs that were widespread in east Asia in the thirteenth century and that later became a central influence in China during the Manchu dynasty. By comparing Indravarman III to the Holder of the Diamond, Zhou may simply be using a trope for indestructible power, but he may conceivably be indicating that tantric Buddhism was an element of the king's worldview. Ren, *Fojiao da cidian*, 788, 796; Trainor, *Buddhism*, 162–165.

63. The term *anding basha* 暗丁八殺 seems to mean literally "not knowing the language," since *anding* may be a corruption of the Khmer for "not knowing", while *basha* is clearly *peeasaa*, the Khmer word for "language," from the Sanskrit *bhasa*. Pelliot, *Mémoires*, 64–65; Chandler, personal communication.

In this passage, Zhou makes his first reference to local Chinese. The term he uses here and later, Tang ren 唐人 (people of the Tang) is still used today in the Chinese expression for Chinatowns in England and America, Tang ren jie 唐人街 (Streets of the People of the Tang). The term Tang ren was widely used from the Song dynasty onwards. As *Ming shi* puts it, "Foreigners all call Chinese people (*huaren* 華人) people of the Tang. It is like that in all the overseas states." Zhang et al., *Ming shi*, 8395.

64. Zhou uses the same term for "missile-throwing engine" or "trebuchet," *pao* 砲, as he does in his description of the fireworks on New Year's Day in the following section. Here it is contained in the term *pao shi* 砲石, meaning literally "trebuchet-thrown rocks".

65. Jiade 佳得 (Kai tək [K]) is clearly a transliteration of Karttika, the Hindu lunar month which starts in late October by the Gregorian calendar. The second day of Karttika marks the end of the festival of Divali, so called from the Sanskrit for "row of lights". Perhaps there is a connection between the lights of Divali and the lanterns and fireworks Zhou describes. Xia citing Pelliot and Coedès in Zhou, *Zhenla fengtu ji*, 122–123.

66. "A large stage": the term *peng* 棚, translated here as "stage", also occurs in part seven, where it is used in its usual sense of canopy or canopy framework. Here the meaning seems closer to the sense of a covered framework or stage. In the Chinese for the phrase "scaffolding used to make a pagoda", *zao ta pu gan* 造塔撲竿, the second character is read 塔 rather than the alternative 搭, and *pu* 撲 is taken to mean "stick" or "pole." Zhou, *Zhenla fengtu ji*, 120–121.

67. The firework display must have been put on either inside the palace walls or in front of the Elephant and Leper King terraces just to the east of the palace. The distance of the bank from the palace of 20–30 poles or *zhang*—some seventy to 100 meters or 230 to 350 (US) feet—would put the bank within the palace walls, somewhere near the large pond on the northeast side of the palace compound. The pond with its finely decorated stone walls, still extant, is thought to have been built by Jayavarman VIII, the king whose reign ended shortly before Zhou's visit. Otherwise the bank would have been immediately outside the eastern entrance to the royal palace, near the Elephant and Leper King Terraces.

68. Coedès identifies *ya lie* 壓獵 ('ap li̯äp [K]) with the Khmer words *roa-up* (count) and *ree-up* (arrange), and suggests that *ya lie* was a kind of annual population review or census, comparable to a similar activity in Siam during the Ayutthaya kingdom founded in the following century. Coedès, "Nouvelles Notes," 229.

69. *Lan* 藍 *in ailan* 挨藍 ('ậi lâm [K]) is clearly *râm*, the Khmer word for "dance." Opinions differ as to the likely meaning of *ai* 挨; perhaps it represents *ngai*, the Khmer word for "day." Coedès, "Notes sur Tcheou Ta-Kuan," 8–9; Pelliot, *Mémoires*, 22; Zhou, *Customs of Cambodia*, tr. Uk and Uk, 65.

70. "Their long and short months": in Chinese the text refers to the large and the small (*da xiao* 大小). I follow Pelliot, who takes large and small here to refer to the long 30-day and short 29-day months of the Chinese lunar calendar. Pelliot, *Mémoires*, 22.

Intercalary months are extra months added to lunar calendars to make up the eleven-day difference between the lunar and solar years. By Zhou's time the Chinese had developed a system of intercalation that did not depend on the insertion of a month at a particular, fixed point in the year, hence Zhou's surprise at the Cambodian practice of intercalating the ninth month and no other. With regard to the divisions or watches of the night, the customary practice in China at the time was to have five, hence Zhou's remark about four.

The "open, shut . . . set up, take away" cycle is an *Old Chinese* twelve-day cycle. It relates to the twelve branches and ten stems that make up the sixty-year cycle that is a core element of Chinese astronomy and counting systems. (The Chinese associate each of the twelve branches with an animal, a practice replicated in Angkor—and taken from the Chinese?—as Zhou notes later in this section.) In the Chinese calendar, each of the twelve branches or days has a label that describes it with a quality such as "open" or "shut". These labels date back at least as far as the second-century compilation *Huainan zi* [*Master Huainan*]. In *Huainan zi* the labels begin with *jian* 建 (set up) and *chu* 除 (take away), and end with *kai* 開 (open) and *bi* 閉 (shut). Zhou has the labels the other way round—his text reads *kai bi jian chu* 開閉建除—but the intention is clear enough. I have added the words "cycle of twelve days" to make the text more explicit. Liu et al., *Huainan zi*, 148; Dubs, *History*, vol. 3, 255–257.

For many centuries the Chinese used the twelve-day cycle alongside two other day cycles, a seven-day cycle and a ten-day cycle. The seven-day cycle (or week) came into use in the Song dynasty, well before Zhou's time, though he does not seem to have been familiar with it. As for the ten-day cycle, it derives from the thirty-day Chinese month and has a long history. It persists today in the common Chinese word for ten days, *xun* 旬. Needham, *Science and Civilization in China, Vol. III*, 396 et seq.

71. The Khmer words for "horse", "chicken", "pig", and "cow" are *seb*, *moaun*, *j'rook*, and *goa*. Apart from an extra *bu* in *busai*, Zhou's transliterations are close to their originals. The translaterations are *busai* 卜賽 (horse); *man* 蠻 (chicken); *zhilu* 直盧 (pig); and *ge* 箇 (cow). Zhou gives the animal names in accordance with the orthodox Chinese astronomical expressions (*sheng xiao* 生肖). Amending my earlier transcription, I have read *man* 蠻 for *luan* 欒. Xu citing Pelliot in Zhou, *Zhenla fengtu ji*, 127.

72. In writing of slaves, Zhou uses a signifier that is more usually used for small objects than for human beings, and pronouns that are used for animals.

Uk and Uk identify the Zhuang 撞 of Zhenla with the Choang, one of the Stieng group of minority peoples in Cambodia today. The present-day pronunciation of the Zhuangs' name in Chinese is similar to those of the Zhuang 壯 people of southwest China, but there is no connection between the two, the Zhuang of China being Tai speakers and Stieng being a type of Mon-Khmer. Uk and Uk in Zhou, *Customs of Cambodia*, tr. Uk and Uk, 50.

73. "Cloth" here is *bu* 布. The Taiwan scholar Jin Ronghua argues that *bu* here refers to cash, but this is doubtful. While *bu* can have an alternative meaning of "cash," it had this meaning in China a millennium earlier, in the first millenium BCE. Moreover, elsewhere Zhou uses the term *bu* to mean "cloth," and in his later description of Zhenla, the Yuan dynasty merchant Wang Dayuan describes trade transactions being done with gold, silver, beads, or various kinds of cloth (see chapter ten). Jin Ronghua in Zhou Daguan, *Zhenla fengtu ji*, 56.

74. Uk and Uk suggest that *batuo* 巴駝 is a transliteration of the word *bétôr* or *bédôr* (their transliterations), a Pali word for "father" now only used on ceremonial occasions. *Mi* 米 is close to *mai*, "mother" in Khmer. Zhou, *Customs of Cambodia*, tr. Uk and Uk, 51.

75. If the term *zhentan* 陣毯 derives from Khmer, its derivation has not been clearly identified. The Yuan merchant Wang Dayuan reports the same ritual, and writes that it was called *lishi* 利市, a Chinese term meaning "good fortune." Wang's modern editor Su Jiqing argues that in the Wenzhou dialect spoken by Zhou Daguan the pronunciation of *zhentan* was similar to the Khmer term *suosdey*, also meaning "good fortune." Wang, *Dao yi zhi lüe*, 69, 77.

76. One picul or *dan* 擔, the term Zhou uses when assessing the size of family donations, is usually regarded as consisting of a hundred catties or *jin*—that is, about 64 kilos or 144 pounds. One hundred piculs would thus have been a scarcely feasible amount, well over six tonnes. So something seems to be wrong here. Perhaps Zhou was using the term *dan* in its older sense of "what a man can shoulder" (which also happens to be the earlier meaning of the word "picul", from the Malay word *pikul*, "what a man can carry on his shoulder".) All we can reliably take from this passage is that the largest donations were very large indeed. For the kilogram and (US) pound equivalents of *dan* in Yuan times, Wilkinson, *Chinese History*, 613.

77. That is, the night of April 29–30, 1297.

78. Zhu Maichen 朱買臣 was a second-century BCE Chinese official who was abandoned by his wife. Zhu's full story, related in *Han shu*, is that when he was poor his wife left him, thinking he would never become wealthy; he then became a high official and filled with remorse, she committed suicide. Zhu's biography is in Ban, *Han shu*, 2791–2793; see also Zhou, *Zhenla fengtu ji*, 105–106.

79. "Lepers" is a translation of the Chinese *binglaizhe* 病癩者 (those with leprosy, *binglai* 病癩; *binglai* also occurs in the inverted form *laibing* 癩病, the term for leprosy used in China today.) *Laibing* 癩病 dates back at least as far as the seventh century when it featured in a study by the Chinese physician Chao Yuanfang 巢元方 (fl. 614), who describes it as a disease with a variety of symptoms including numbness. They are consistent with leprosy, though they could have been of other skin diseases too. Some think that the king who contracted leprosy was Jayavarman VII, but Chandler argues that if there was a leper

king it is more likely to have been Jayavarman VIII, the king who reigned from 1243 until 1295. Chao, *Zhubing yuan hou lun*; Chandler, "Legend of the Leper King", 3–14; Pelliot, *Mémoires*, 23–24; Zhou, *Zhenla fengtu ji*, 132. See also Zhou, *Customs of Cambodia*, tr. Uk and Uk, 70–71, where the Uks argue that Zhou's *binglai* was a skin ailment such as flavus.

80. The three words used here probably refer to pundits, Buddhist monks, and Saivite holy men—and women too, according to Zhou. The first, *banjie* 班詰 (pwan k'i̯ĕt [K]), seems to derive from the Sanskrit *paṇḍita* (though the aspirated 'k' is incongruous), meaning "pundit" or "learned man". The second, *zhugu* 苧姑, seems to be the same as *chaoku*, the respectful term used for Theravada Buddhist monks in Siam, and also the old Khmer term *chaukov* for "abbot". As for *basiwei* 八思惟 (pwăt si i̯wi [K]), Coedès argues that it is a transcription of the last two syllables of the Sanskrit word *tapasvi*, meaning "ascetic". He notes that there are inscriptions at Angkor referring to *tapasvi*, one of them identifying these people as Śaivites—that is, worshippers of Śiva. Śaivites are lingam-worshippers, and Zhou's description of *basiwei* as stone-worshippers also suggests they were Śaivites. Zhou, *Zhenla fengtu ji*, 96; Pelliot, *Mémoires*, 65; Coedès, "Nouvelles Notes," 224–225; Zhou, *Customs of Cambodia*, tr. Uk and Uk, 37 (for *chaukov*, their transliteration).

81. Sakyamuni, one of the Buddha's commonest epithets, means Sage of the Sakyas and refers to the fact that he was from the Sakya clan. Bolai 孛賴 (B'uət lâi- [K]) may be the word Prah, a word used in one form or another for the Buddha in Cambodia, Thailand, and Myanmar.

82. The leaves of the fan-palm or palmyra, palmyra being a Portuguese word meaning palm tree, have been used to write on since the fifth century CE. Buddhist sutras brought to China from India were written on them, making them greatly treasured, so much so that during the Tang dynasty a palmyra was planted in the Chinese capital Chang'an. To make the material for a manuscript, the leaves are cut into rectangular strips and threaded together in a form still found today.

83. The word Zhou uses for "tall headdress" is *gugu* 罟姑, the Chinese word (written with various characters) for a particular form of Mongolian headdress, a tall, hollow structure sometimes reinforced with wire.

Zhou refers to Tartars rather than Mongols, but seems to be using be the term Tartar to indicate Mongols, rather than referring specifically to the Tatar tribe of the steppes.

84. Zhou's transliterations of Khmer numbers from one to ten are quite easily recognizable, the numbers in Khmer being *mooay*, *bpee*, *bay*, *booun*, *bprum*, *bprum mooay*, *bprum bpee*, *bprum bay*, *bprum booun*, and *dop*. The same applies to his transliterations of Khmer terms for father, mother, elder brother, and younger brother. The term *chilai* 吃賴 (ki̯ət lâi- [K]) for uncle is slightly less clear; perhaps it derives from *k'lai*, an old pronunciation of *t'lai*, Khmer for brother-in-law. Pelliot, *Mémoires*, 20, 69; Zhou, *Customs of Cambodia*, tr. Uk and Uk, 53.

85. Zhang San 張三 means Zhang the Third and Li Si 李四 means Li the Fourth, informal names indicating that their owners are the third- and fourth-born in their families.

86. The etymology of Beishi 備世 is unclear. There seems to be no record elsewhere of a word resembling Beishi being used as a name for China. Its pronunciation B'ji- śi̯äi- as reconstructed by Karlgren has some affinity with the word Vijaya, a name associated with Vijaya in Champa and Srivijaya in Sumatra, but neither of these associations makes any sense here. One possibility, suggested by Coedès, is that Beishi is the Sanskrit word *viṣaya*, realm or kingdom, used here as a respectful metonym for China. Pelliot, *Mémoires*, 66; Coedès, "Nouvelles Notes," 225–226.

87. Muntjaks or barking deer are a small Southeast Asian deer, the male with tusks and small antlers. *Suo* 梭 is similar to a word for "chalk" in Thai.

88. The Uyghurs, now the principal ethnic group in Chinese Xinjiang, were important advisers to the Mongols in China in the thirteenth century. There is no known connection between Uyghur and Khmer scripts, or indeed between the two languages. The script used by the Uyghurs in Zhou's time was based on the old Turkic alphabet. The script used by the Khmers was ultimately derived from the ancient Indian Brahmi script. (The Brahmi script was written horizontally from left to right, hence the Cambodian practice of doing the same. Zhou called it writing from back to front, since the Chinese wrote from right to left and top to bottom.) As for the two languages, they are quite distinct, Uyghur being a Turkic language and Khmer being one of the Austroasiatic languages. On Uyghur support for the Mongols: Allsen, "Rise of the Mongolian Empire," 349–350.

89. Who was Esen Khaya (Yexian Haiya 也先海牙 in Chinese)? Could he have been head of the delegation to Cambodia that Zhou took part in? Zhou's passing reference to him here suggests some familiarity, and the fact that Esen Khaya could compare Khmer and Mongolian suggests that he had firsthand experience of both. Esen Khaya is not among the biographies of officials in *Yuan shi*; but two people with the name Esen Khaya are listed in the repertory of Yuan names compiled by Igor de Rachewiltz, an authority on Mongol names. The first was a *darughachi* or "resident commissioner" or local chief administrator for the Mongols; the other was a middle-ranking Uyghur official. It is not

known whether either of these men was ever an envoy to Southeast Asia. Conceivably Esen Khaya was related to one of the two military officers Khubilai Khan sent south into Annam in 1286–1287 following the death of General Suodu. The names of these officers were Esen Temür and Arigh Khaya. Rachewiltz and Wang, *Repertory of Proper Names*, vol. III, 2289, 2700; vol. IV, 778; Rossabi, *Khubilai Khan*, 218; personal communications from the late Igor de Rachewiltz.

90. A textual variant has it that there were indeed such shops. Zhou, *Zhenla fengtu ji*, 119.

91. The towers where the two disputants were lodged are clearly Prasat Suor Prat, the twelve towers, still extant, in front of the Leper King and Elephant Terraces near the eastern entrance to the royal palace.

92. In Yuan times, seven to eight poles or *zhang*, the height of Tonlé Sap Lake at high water, was the equivalent of some 80–90 (US) feet or about 25–29 meters. The depth of Tonlé Sap Lake at its driest, three to five Chinese feet, was about one to two metres or three-and-a-half to six (US) feet.

93. The use of night soil or human excrement was a basic element of Chinese farming for many centuries. Its use as fertilizer was promoted in the early years of Communist rule but was reduced after agricultural reforms in the 1980s.

94. Lakawood, cardamom, gamboge, lac, and chaulmoogra oil all yield resins as well as seeds or oils for medicinal use. Lakawood, also called rosewood, is one of the English names for *jiangzhenxiang* 降真香. It is sometimes conflated with lign-aloes. Gamboge is Pelliot's suggestion for *hua huang* 畫黃, which is otherwise hard to identify. Gamboge is an orange-colored medicinal resin which, as its name suggests, is closely associated with Cambodia. (Stuart identifies gamboge with *tenghuang* 籐黃.) Lac is the resin secreted on certain trees by the lac insect and used as a varnish. It is not related to lakawood. The crude form of lac is stick lac. When the stick lac is melted, the red dye in it forms thin flakes called shellac, from which the colored varnish called lacquer is made. The chaulmoogra is a tree whose seed oil was once used to treat leprosy. Yule and Burnell, *Hobson-Jobson*, 177, 499; Stuart, *Chinese Materia Medica*, 182, 201, 428. Pelliot, *Mémoires*, 26.

95. If his figures for beeswax are accurate, Zhou is describing a serious trading business. Given that one catty or *jin* was the equivalent of about 630 grams or twenty-two ounces, a trading junk carrying three thousand combs of beeswax, each weighing forty *jin*, would be carrying a cargo weighing seventy-five tons or 165,000 pounds—a massive load. Perhaps Zhou wrote "every year" (*mei yi nian* 每一年) rather than "every junk" (*mei yi chuan* 每一船), though there is no textual variant to support this.

96. The thickness of lakawood trees is given here in Chinese inches or *cun* 寸. There are ten *cun* to a *chi* 尺 or Chinese foot, which in Zhou's time was the equivalent of about fourteen (US) inches.

97. Mulberry mistletoe is called *sang jisheng* 桑寄生, "mulberry parasite" in Chinese, and that is what it is. The peppers Zhou writes about are not capsicums but black peppers, which grow green on the vine and turn black when picked and dried. Wild hops is one of the English names for *lü cao zi* 綠草子, also known as Japanese hops. Stuart, *Chinese Materia Medica*, 209.

98. Ramie is *zhuma* 苧麻 in Chinese, the English name coming from the Malay *rami*. It is a tall plant that, like hemp, produces a strong fiber. It is not clear why Zhou mentions the fact that the Luo people making silk have to do without ramie and hemp—perhaps the satiny silk *ling* 綾 that he refers to was blended with them, given that it is often blended. The text here may be flawed: Zhou inverts *zhuma* and writes *mazhu* 麻苧. Moreover *zhu* 苧 has uncertain connotations, being used by Zhao later in the indecipherable term *hezhu* 合苧 to describe the size of alligators.

99. The five main colors were dark green, vermilion, yellow, white, and black.

100. The cities Zhou mentions were and are all cities in southeast China. Most of them were involved in trade with Southeast Asia and farther afield. Zhenzhou, now part of the city of Yicheng, was up the Yangzi River from Shanghai, not far from Nanjing. The port of Wenzhou was in the area Zhou came from. Quanzhou was the great metropolitan port southwest of Wenzhou. Chuzhou, inland from Wenzhou, was the site of the Longquan or Dragon Spring kilns where celadon was made, and also a center for porcelain and lacquer production. Mingzhou, now called Ningbo, was the port north of Wenzhou that Zhou set out from.

The term celadon, *qingci* 青甆 (green pottery) in Chinese, comes from the name of the green-clad hero of a work by the now-forgotten seventeenth-century French writer Honoré d'Urfé, which happened to be vogue in Europe at the same time as *qingci* was. Archaeologists excavating the royal palace in Angkor Thom have found remains of Chinese porcelain dating from Song, Yuan, and Ming times. Zhou, *Zhenla fengtu ji*, 149.

Saltpeter or potassium nitrate was used for medicine and gunpowder. Lovage, more specifically Sichuan lovage, is one of the English names for *chuanqiong* 川芎, a herb used to cure aches and pains and improve blood circulation. The Zhou text has *caoqiong* 草芎 rather than *chuanqiong*, but the two may be the same. According to Jin Ronghua, yellow grass cloth or *huang caobu* 黃草布 was a fabric made in Gui'an, a former county of Zhejiang. The word translated here as "copper" (*tong* 銅) could also mean bronze. The tung or *tong* 桐 tree is a tree of the genus *aleurites*, whose seed oil is good for varnishing.

"Wheat" is a translation of *mai* 麥, which can refer to either barley (*da mai* 大麥) or wheat (*xiao mai* 小麥). Here Zhou clearly means wheat, given the absence of wheat as an ingredient for soy sauce that he mentions later on. Zhou, *Zhenla fengtu ji*, 150; Stuart, *Chinese Materia Medica*, 123; Jin Ronghua in Zhou, *Zhenla fengtu ji* (Taipei), 91.

101. Evidently because of trade restrictions imposed by the Chengzong Emperor.

102. *Yangtao* 羊桃 here can refer either to starfruit (carabola) or to Chinese gooseberry, often known nowadays as kiwifruit. As Uk and Uk point out, *yangtao* here must refer to starfruit rather than Chinese gooseberry, starfruit being a tropical fruit. Xia citing Pelliot in Zhou, *Zhenla fengtu ji*, 151; Zhou, *Customs of Cambodia*, tr. Uk and Uk, 91.

103. *Mei* 梅 (prunus mume) and *li* 李 (prunus salicina) are usually both translated as "plum," but to distinguish between them here I have translated *mei* by one of its other names, "flowering apricot."

104. A siskin is an olive-green songbird like a goldfinch.

105. "Leopards" is a translation of *bao* 豹, which can mean either leopard or panther (*heibao* 黑豹, black leopard.) Similarly "goat" here is a translation of *yang* 羊, which can mean either sheep or goat (*shanyang* 山羊, mountain sheep.) In her analysis of Angkor inscriptions, Jacob lists goats but not sheep, so I have opted for goats. However she does not mention either leopards or panthers, so the choice of translation in that case is more arbitrary. Jacob, "The Ecology of Angkor," 293.

106. Another explanation for the special treatment of cows is the Hindu reverence for cows, still reflected today in the sacred cows of the royal palace in Phnom Penh.

107. Winter gourds, also known as wax gourds, are large, fast-growing gourds that can be stored for months, hence their name. Snake gourds (*wanggua* 王瓜 in Chinese) are a member of the cucumber family, with fruit that can grow to up to two meters long, and can be eaten like green beans. *Xiancai* 莧菜 can be identified with a type of amaranth. *Kumai* 苦蕒 can be identified with chicory or endive. Stuart, *Chinese Materia Medica*, 33, 229–230.

108. Gudgeons or gobies (*tubu* 吐哺) are a freshwater fish, usually quite small. They often swim close to the bottom of the river or lake, and this may account for a variant form of the fish's name, *tufu* 土附 (literally, earth hugger.) The weight of large gudgeons, two catties or more, was nearly three pounds or nearly one and a half kilos.

109. "As big as large pillars" is a guess at the meaning of *da ru hezhu* 大如合苧, taking *hezhu* to refer to a homophone *hezhu* 合柱 meaning a hollow jointed pillar. Perhaps the text here is corrupt, or *hezhu* is a word whose meaning is now forgotten. The expression *liucang zhi gui* 六藏之龜, a turtle or tortoise with six internal organs (reading *cang* 藏, meaning "conceal," as *cang* 臟, meaning "internal organ",) is also odd. By the Chinese reckoning of the time there were five internal organs—heart, liver, spleen, lungs, and kidney—rather than six, though the expression six internal organs was sometimes used because the two kidneys made up two organs not one. But why describe a turtle this way? Perhaps it was a way of referring to the whole turtle, offal and all. To this day tortoise meat and offal are regarded as a delicacy in Cambodian villages. An alternative suggestion, made by Jin Ronghua, is that *liucang zhi gui* is just another way of saying "tortoise," with *liucang* 六藏 taken literally to mean the six concealed parts of the tortoise—head, tail, and feet—hidden under its shell. Jin in Zhou, *Zhenla fengtu ji* (Taipei), 96–97.

110. Zhou calls goose-necked barnacles by the name they are apparently given in Wenzhou: *gui jiao* 龜腳 or *gui zu* 龜足 (turtle feet). Goose-necked barnacles or goose barnacles are crustacean delicacies in the form of barnacles anchored by a thick, flexible stalk that looks a little like a goose's head and neck. The inches here are Chinese inches. Zhou, *Zhenla fengtu ji*, 158.

Zha'nan, Zhenpu, and Freshwater Lake (as well as Bijian later in this section) are all places Zhou mentioned earlier. In his preface Zhou refers to Zha'nan as being south of the Freshwater Lake (that is, Tonlé Sap Lake) and indicates that Zhenpu was on the southeast coast near the Mekong Delta. He lists Bajian as one of Zhenla's "prefectures" and mentions that, like Zhenpu, it was the coast.

111. "Razor clams" (*cheng* 蟶) follows the text in Xia's edition of Zhou. A variant reading is *du* 肚 (stomach,) which would refer to the stomach of the crocodiles. Zhou, *Zhenla fengtu ji*, 157.

112. The leaf *pengyasi* 朋牙四 has not been identified with any certainty. *Baolengjiao* 包稜角 (paw ləŋʻ kjaw [P]) may be a composite term for the Khmer words for cooked rice (*bai*) and husked rice (*onggor*), or more likely the word for husked rice with an unidentified first syllable. "A type of palm" is a translation of the Chinese term *jiao* 茭. *Jiao* is usually the name of a type of wild rice, but here it is generally taken to refer to a palm tree, perhaps the stemless nipa palm. Zhou, *Zhenla fengtu ji*, 160; Yule and Burnell, *Hobson-Jobson*, 139–140.

113. No prohibition on salt works: unlike in China, where salt manufacture was under strict government control, with salt manufacture authorized under licence.

114. When referring to tamarind, Zhou transliterates a Khmer word rather than using the Chinese word for tamarind. The transliterated word is *xianping* 咸平 (yăm b'i̯wɐng [K]); the Khmer word for tamarind is *om-bpeul*.

115. The wine yeast that Zhou refers to here is a Chinese yeast for making wine, usually a byproduct of wine already made.

116. *Qia* 恰 (or variants *ha* 恰 or *ge* 蛤), the pewter vessel, has not been identified with a Khmer term with any certainty. The word Zhou uses for the pot for pouring wine, *zhuzi* 注子, describes an old-fashioned vessel, usually made of gold, bronze, or earthenware, shaped like a kettle.

117. The Cambodian scholar Ly Thiam Teng identifies *xinna* 新拿 with *sândâr*, a Khmer word for a medium-sized boat. Uk and Uk suggest plausibly that *pilan* 皮闌 is *prânaing*, a Khmer term for canoe. In Xia's view, *pilan* may be related to *perahu*, the Malay word for boat, or else to a south Indian word for rowing boat from which the archaic English term balloon (rowing vessel) is derived. Zhou, *Customs of Cambodia*, tr. Uk and Uk, 115, citing Ly Thiam Teng; Zhou, *Zhenla fengtu ji*, 171.

118. Judging from reliefs at Bayon, the bend in the palanquin pole was typically upward in the middle, rather than downward, so that the pole as a whole was shaped like the letter W.

119. It seems that Champa kings—like Chinese and Europeans—regarded gall as a source of bravery and courage. *Ming shi* tells how the Chams themselves collected gall from unwitting travelers for the king of Champa, who drank it and even bathed in it so that "his body was permeated by it." According to *Ming shi*, the Chams prized Chinese gall above all others. In an account of his travels in Indochina in the mid-nineteenth century, the French priest Charles Emile Bouillevaux (1823–1913) wrote that the custom of stealing gall still existed. In 2015 a former detainee of the Khmer Rouge accused Khmer Rouge guards of consuming human gall bladders steeped in wine to bolster their strength. Zhang et al., *Ming shi*, 8392–8393. Wade, *The Ming shi Account of Champa*, 19. For Bouillevaux, Zhou, *Zhenla fengtu ji*, 177–178. For Khmer Rouge guards, Charlie Campbell, "Cambodian Guards Drank Wine With Human Gallbladders, Says Genocide Survivor" in *Time*, 22, January 2015.

120. Zhou's term for the person who had sexual relations with his sister is *manren* 蠻人 (southern foreigner). Presumably he was a Khmer. Zhou's fellow countryman Mr Xue 薛 was a *xiangren* 鄉人, a person from Zhou's own locality, meaning that he came from Wenzhou or thereabouts.

121. See appendix four for a comparison of Zhou's *Record* with other, earlier sources.

122. Zhou, *Zhenla fengtu ji*, 109–110, 43–44, 64–65, 136–137, 146–147, 174.

123. For the *Sui shu* account see chapter six.

124. Zhou, *Zhenla fengtu ji*, 107, 119, 137.

125. Zhou, *Zhenla fengtu ji*, 43–44.

126. Lu Ban: 魯班. Zhou, *Zhenla fengtu ji*, 44.

Chapter Ten

1. Su in Wang, *Dao yi zhi lüe*, 9–11.

2. Su in Wang, *Dao yi zhi lüe*, 9–11; Rockhill, "Notes," 61–63. Rockhill mentions that Wang describes ninety-nine places, but Su Jiqing's 1981 Zhonghua shuju edition of *Dao yi zhi lüe* has a hundred entries. Wang, *Dao yi zhi lüe*, passim.

3. Wang, *Dao yi zhi lüe*, 69–70.

4. In the opening sentence, literally "the gate to the south of the *zhou*," the term *zhou* 洲, (read here as *zhou* 州 or administrative region) clearly means city, like the *zhou* in Mingzhou, Hangzhou, etc. It is used again later in this passage, in the reference to a city with a hundred towers.

"A stone river:" evidently a river whose bed and banks were made of stone—in other words, a stone-lined moat, no doubt the moat around Angkor Wat.

5. Four hundred thousand elephants is an improbably large number, twice the number recorded over a century earlier by Zhao Rugua. The annual gathering seems to be the ninth-month royal review that Zhou Daguan calls *ya lie*. The peacocks and oxen as Wang describes them were no doubt live animals decorated with jade and gold. The array of twelve silver towers guarded by bronze elephants contrasts with the array of twenty-four bronze towers guarded by eight bronze elephants recorded by Zhao Rugua.

6. "Buddhist pagodas" is a translation here of *futu* 浮屠, a Buddhist term derived from the word Buddha and used to refer to the Buddha, Buddhist pagodas, etc. Masi 馬司 Green Lake and the Sangxiang Buddha Hall (Sangxiang Foshe 桑香佛舍) cannot be clearly identified, although Sangxiang Foshe has come over time to be taken to refer to Angkor Wat. The modern Chinese scholar Su Jiqing notes that Sangxiang Foshe is a name associated with Angkor Wat, as do Lu and Zhou, but without explaining why. These sources also identify Masi Green Lake with Zhou Daguan's North Lake [Jayatataka], but again without explanation. Plausibly enough, Rockhill reads the *she* 舍 in Foshe 佛舍 not as "hall" but as "Buddhist relic," apparently taking *she* to be short for *sheli* 舍利 or *śarīra*, a Biddhist term derived from Sanskrit meaning "relic," "ashes" or "body". In his interpretation it is the relic, not the bridge, that is wrapped in gold. Su in Wang, *Dao yi zhi lüe*, 76–77; Lu and Zhou, *Zhongguo gujizhong*, 151; Rockhill, "Notes," 100; Soothill and Hodous, *Dictionary of Chinese Buddhist Terms*, 279.

7. "Buddhist doctrine" is a translation of *fan fa* 梵法, a term referring to the doctrines of Hindu or Buddist sutras or classical texts. The implication here is that Buddhist doctrine included precepts relating to this coming-of-age ritual.

"Good fortune" here is a translation of the Chinese term *lishi* 利市, as compared with the term *zhentan* 陣毯 that Zhou Daguan uses for the same ceremony. As noted earlier, Su Jiqing surmises that *zhentan* is a transliteration of a Khmer term meaning "good fortune." Su in Wang, *Dao yi zhi lüe*, 77; see chapter nine.

8. For "chief," Wang writes *qiu* 酋, a term meaning chief or tribal chief, which in his usage would have been a more demeaning term than *zhu* 主 (ruler) or *wang* 王 (king.) For "pearls on [the] eyebrows and forehead," one textual variant reads *zhu* 朱 meaning vermilion instead of *zhu* 珠 meaning pearls.

For amputations of the foot, arm or leg, the Chinese text does not specify in each case whether the punishment is applied to one or both limbs. Chinese here are again Tang ren, People of the Tang. Jianning is the name of a place in present-day Fujian province of China. "Cloth" (*bu* 布) may refer to cotton cloth, but is not specific.

9. Rockhill, "Notes", 106.

10. To these might be added *Da Ming yitong zhi* 大明一統志 [*The Gazetteer of the Unified Great Ming*], the 1461 official gazetteer for the territories under the aegis of the Ming, which includes an entry on Zhenla. The gazetteer's entry on Zhenla does not, however, add to what is known about Zhenla from earlier sources, including Zhou Daguan, from whom the gazetteer's editors take much of their information. Li Xian et al., *Da Ming yitong zhi* in Lu and Zhou, *Zhongguo gujizhong*, 174–175.

11. On foreign trade and tribute during the Yuan and Ming, see for example Brooke, *The Troubled Empire*, 219–221; Mote, *Imperial China*, 719–721; Wang, "Ming foreign relations", 301–332, esp. 302; Chaffee, "Song China," 34–54, esp. 48.

12. The years of the voyages were 1405, 1409, 1413, 1417, 1421, and 1431. The final voyage in 1431 was commissioned by Yongle's grandson the Xuande Emperor (r. 1425–1435). A seventh voyage, second chronologically (it took place in 1407–1409), was under Zheng He's charge, but not one he actually participated in. Mills in Ma, *Ying-yai Sheng-lan*, 10–22.

13. Wang Gungwu makes a strong case for the Yongle Emperor being an aggressive man, more so than his father, the first Ming emperor. This personality trait would help explain his decision to commission the Zheng He expeditions, as well as his ill-fated decision to attack the Vietnamese, whose country his forces clumsily and ultimately unsuccessfully occupied between 1407 and 1427. Wang, "Ming foreign relations," 315–322.

14. In its biography of Zheng He, *Ming shi* lists "thirty or so" states that Zheng He passed through, among them Zhenla. Zhang et al., *Ming shi*, 7768.

15. In *Ming shi* the Yongle Emperor is explicitly described as wanting Zheng He to "display China's wealth and power (*fu qiang* 富強)." Zhang et al., *Ming shi*, 7766. For the motives and conduct of Zheng He's expeditions, including their coercive aspects, see Dreyer, *Zheng He: China and the Oceans*, 33–34; Mills in Ma, *Ying-yai Sheng-lan*, 1; Sen, "Zheng He's Military Interventions," 158–191; Wade, "The Zheng He Voyages," 37–58; Wang, "Ming foreign relations," 319, 320.

16. Ma Huan: 馬歡. Mills in Ma, *Ying-yai Sheng-lan*, 34–36, 76.

17. Fei Xin 費信 also took part in a fourth overseas expedition, one that was not led by Zheng He.

18. Fei, *Xingcha shenglan, hou ji*, 1–2. The comment about the length of the sea journey from Champa is found in a variant version of the text: Fei, *Xingcha shenglan, hou ji*, 2. The sea mentioned in the poem could be a reference to Tonlé Sap Lake.

19. "Short upper garment": shan 衫; "elegant cloth": *qiao bu* 俏布, reading *qiao* 俏 for *shao* 梢.

20. Huang, *Xiyang chaogong dianlu*, 7. Also Wilkinson, *Chinese History*, 901. In his introduction to Huang's work, Xie Fang remarks that "a relatively salient shortcoming" of Huang's book "is that the writer is not familiar with overseas geography." Xie in Huang, *Xiyang chaogong dianlu*, 5.

21. Huang, *Xiyang chaogong dianlu*, 14–18.

22. As the gazetteer *Zhu fan zhi* records (see chapter eight), there were several sought-after types of the aromatic substance lign-aloes, among them the *su* 速 (rapid) and *zan* 暫 (short-term) varieties, with the best lign-aloes coming from Zhenla. Huang's names for the three types of lign-aloes relate to the places they come from: the Zhenla dependency Lüyang (for *lüyang* 綠洋) for the best, Sanfoqi or Srivijaya (? for *sanle* 三濼) for the second-best, and the unidentified place Boluo (for *boluo* 勃羅) for the worst. His record conforms largely with the earlier record of the gazetteer *Lingwai daida*, which notes that the best, second-best, and worst lign-aloes come from Dengliumei (rather than Lüyang), Srivijaya, and Boluo, respectively. There are several textual variants here for the sentence about *su* 速 and *zan* 暫 lign-aloes; I have dropped the first *xiang* 香. Xie in Huang, *Xiyang chaogong dianlu*, 16.

23. Dammar, dammar in gourds, and sappan wood are all described in the gazetteer *Zhu fan zhi* (chapter eight). Wood apple, piye (possibly bael fruit), mangoes, and the two types of fish called *jiantong* and *fuhu* are all mentioned in *Sui shu* (chapter six.) "Ebony" here is *wumu* 烏木 (*maba ebenos.*)

"Yellowflower wood" is a literal translation of *huanghuamu* 黄花木, which today is sometimes described as a type of piptanthus but whose meaning here is not known. "Local lakawood" is a tentative translation of *tu jiangxiang* 土降香, *tu* 土 meaning "indigenous" or "local" and *jiangxiang* 降香 being similar to *jiangzhenxiang* 降真香, the term Zhou Daguan uses for lakawood. Huang, *Xiyang chaogang dianlu*, 17; Stuart, *Chinese Materia Medica*, 253; *Hanying da cidian*, 1718.

24. Huerna 忽兒那 and Naiyiji 奈亦吉 (whose name is followed by *lang* 郎, a term of respect) may be transliterations of Khmer names, but if so they are hard to decipher. Coedès tentatively identifies Huerna with Sūryavaṃśa Rājādhirāja, who according to Coedès regained Angkor from temporary Siamese occupation in 1357; but *Ming shilu* refers to Huerna as "the king of Zhenla at Bashan [Ba Phnom]," suggesting he may have ruled from Ba Phnom in the Phnom Penh area rather than Angkor. The name Huerna is notable for the fact that it does not end in *varna* (protected by) and thus breaks with a long-standing practice of Khmer kings. Coedès, *Indianized States*, 236. For *Ming shilu* on Huerna see later in this chapter.

Shali or Kṣatriyaḥ refers to the first ruler of Zhenla mentioned in *Sui shu*, namely king Citrasena (Zhiduosina) whose family name was Kṣatriyaḥ (Shali).

25. "Its territory is . . .": Huang's final remarks are not time-specific; the tenses he uses could be either present or past. I have opted for the present tense on the assumption that in Huang's view Zhenla still existed as a large, strong state. "Working through more than one interpreter", more literally "with repeated interpretation", is a phrase encountered earlier that evidently means using interpreters who interpreted from Khmer to an intermediate language, and then from that language to Chinese.

26. Passing the imperial examination means here that he achieved the status of *jinshi* 進士 (presented scholar), the highest level in the imperial examination system. Yu in Yan, *Shuyu zhouzi lu*, 1.

27. Yan, *Shuyu zhouzi lu*, 270–278.

28. Funan as Xiangpu 象浦: Yan, *Shuyu zhouzi lu*, 270. "Treats as Zhenla's precursor": as do later Ming writers, for example Luo Yuejiong, author of *Xian bin lu* (see below.)

29. *Tongyi li*: 統一曆.

30. Tang Jing: 唐敬.

31. Yin Shou: 尹綬; Imperial Historian: Yu shi 御史. The holder of this official title was a government inspector rather than a historian.

32. Putisa: 菩提薩; Puti means Buddha; the derivation of the name as a whole is unclear. Tonlé Sap Lake: Danshui 淡水 or Freshwater Lake, this being the name used for the Tonlé Sap Lake by Zhou Daguan.

33. Yan, *Shuyu zhouzi lu*, 271. According to Coedès, the name Chao Ponhea Yat corresponds with local sources and refers to a king otherwise known as Suryavarman who moved the Cambodian capital to Phnom Penh. Coedès, "La Fondation de Phnoṃ Pen," 6–11; Coedès, *Indianized States*, 237.

34. Yan's asides: *Shuyu zhouzi lu*, 271 (on the origin of the magnetic compass), 272 (on Lu Ban), 277–278 (on Pagan.)

35. Yan, *Shuyu zhouzi lu*, 277–278. For the status of Pagan, see also the section on Zhao Rugua in chapter eight.

36. Chandler suggests this as a reason for the large number of Cambodian tribute missions to China at this time. Chandler, *History of Cambodia*, 92.

37. Yu in Luo, *Xian bin lu*, 6.

38. Luo, *Xian bin lu*, 138–143.

39. The work is cited in Li et al., *Taiping yulan*, 3592. See chapter four.

40. For *fengmu* 風母 and animals with similar names: *Taiping yulan* cites four sources, including Ge Hong's Daoist work *Bao pu zi*, but none of them mentions Funan. Li et al., *Taiping yulan*, 4026. The animal *quechenshou* 卻塵獸 is not mentioned in *Taiping yulan* or similar sources.

41. Wilkinson describes it as the most comprehensive description of its kind. Wilkinson, *Chinese History*, 901.

42. Xie in Zhang, *Dongxi yangkao*, 5–7; Wilkinson, *Chinese History*, 901.

43. Zhang, *Dongxi yangkao*, 48–54.

44. This comment about Ganpozhe 甘破蔗 and Jianpuzhai 柬埔寨 recalls Zhou Daguan's remark that the local name for Zhenla was Ganbozhi 甘孛智, and that Ganpuzhi 甘破蔗 was an error for Ganbozhi.

45. Zhang, *Dongxi yangkao*, 49, 51, 52, 55.

46. *Qiuzhang*: 酋長. The term *qiuzhang*, meaning chieftain or tribal chief, is similar to the term *qiu* 酋 used earlier by Wang Dayuan to refer to the Cambodian king. So *qiuzhang* here could also refer to a local king.

47. For Yan Congjian, see earlier in this chapter.

48. "Crane crest" plum seems to be what is referred to by *heding* 鶴頂 (also pronounced *haoding*, meaning literally "crane's crest"), which can be a type of plum or a name for goosefoot plants. Black horn and white horn were presumably taken from cows or deer, either for medicinal or decorative purposes. Musk wood (*shexiangmu* 麝香木) is an unidentified substance mentioned earlier by the Song gazetteer writer Zhao Rugua. Stuart, *Chinese Materia Medica*, 475; Luo et al., *Hanyu da cidian*.

49. Mao, *Huangming xiangxu lu* in Lu and Zhou, *Zhongguo gujizhong*, 203–205. Xiangxu 象胥: Interpreter, as in Hucker, *Dictionary of Imperial Titles*, 231. There is an illuminating portrait of Mao Ruizheng, his family and his milieu in Papelitzky, "Gui-an as a Centre for Writing," 107–135.

50. The *Ming shi* account of Zhenla is in Zhang et al., *Ming shi*, 8394–8396. *Ming shi* records of missions to and from Zhenla are in Zhang et al., *Ming shi*, 26, 29, 33, 35, 45–48, 82, 84, 94, 97, 99. Fuller records are in *Ming shilu* as cited in Chen et al., *Zhongguo gujizhong*, 168–174. A invaluable English translation by Geoff Wade of the *Ming shilu* entries on Southeast Asia is available as an online resource in Wade, *Southeast Asia in the Ming shi-lu*.

The only other tribute mission from Zhenla thay may have been sent during the Ming is one mentioned by Zhang Xie in *Dongxi yangkao* as taking place in 1452. This mission is not listed in official sources.

51. According to *Ming shi*, Siam for example sent thirty-four.

52. These were in 1371, 1373, 1377–1378, 1380, 1383, 1387, 1388, 1389 (three times), 1390, 1404, 1405, 1406, 1408, 1414, 1417, 1419, and 1435–1436.

53. These were in 1370, 1383 (twice), 1386–1387, 1403 and 1405–1406.

54. For a wideranging discussion of these, see especially Brooks et al., "Interpolity relations", esp. 58–70.

55. *Ming shilu, juan* 55, 69 in Chen et al., *Zhongguo gujizhong*, 168; Zhang et al., *Ming shi*, 26. "Venerable hill:" Coedès considers Ba Phnom to have been a possible site for the capital of Funan. Coedès, *Indianized States*, 36–37. See also the discussion of *Nan Qi shu* in chapter two.

56. The gradual shift of the locus of Cambodian authority from Angkor to Phnom Penh during the fourteenth and fifteenth centuries, and the reasons for its occurrence, have been much discussed. For appraisals of what happened and why, Chandler, *History of Cambodia*, 93–94, 313; Lieberman, *Strange Parallels*, vol. 1, 236–239.

57. *Ming shilu, juan* 116, 134 in Chen et al., *Zhongguo gujizhong*, 169; Zhang et al., *Ming shi*, 33, 35. The Hongwu emperor renouncing war: Wang, "Ming foreign relations," 311–312. The Hongwu Emperor on reducing tribute: Zheng et al., *Ming shi*, 8397. Samdach Kambuja-dhirāja is the name Coedès suggests for the transliterated name Canda Ganwuzhe Chidazhi 參答甘武者持達志, Samdach being an honorific and Ganwuzhe/Kambuja meaning Cambodia.

58. *Ming shilu, juan* 153, 156 in Chen et al., *Zhongguo gujizhong*, 169.

59. *Ming shilu, juan* 179, 190, 193 in Chen et al., *Zhongguo gujizhong*, 170; Zhang et al., *Ming shi*, 8385.

60. Zhu Yuan: 祝原. *Ming shilu, juan* 149 in Chen et al., *Zhongguo gujizhong*, 173; Zhang et al., *Ming shi*, 94.

61. *Ming shilu, juan* 193 in Chen et al., *Zhongguo gujizhong*, 171; Zhang et al., *Ming shi*, 46.

62. *Ming shilu, juan* 190 in Chen et al, *Zhongguo gujizhong*, 170–171; Zhang et al., *Ming shi*, 82. This and the following story are also told by Yan Congjian. For Yan Congjian, see earlier in this chapter.

63. *Ming shilu, juan* 44 in Chen et al., *Zhongguo gujizhong*, 173.

64. As the record of its tribute missions in *Ming shi* shows.

65. Coedès, *Indianized States*, 236.

66. Zhang et al., *Ming shi*, 8400.

67. Chandler, *History of Cambodia*, 92.

68. For the Ming's surprisingly uncensorious views of Ayutthaya (Siam)'s aggressive tendencies, see also Wang, "Ming foreign relations", 329–330.

Chapter Eleven

1. As we have seen, the most informative texts included those found in *Taiping yulan* (for most of Kang Tai's writings), *Nan Qi shu*, *Liang shu*, *Sui shu*, and Zhou Daguan's *Zhenla fengtu ji*, and to a lesser extent *Jin shu*, *Jiu Tang shu*, *Xin Tang shu*, and Zhao Rugua's *Zhu fan zhi*. Appendix four provides a table with the content of principal sources for Funan and Zhenla, showing how they resemble or differ from each other.

2. For the comment in *Liang shu*, see chapter three.

3. Manguin, "Archaeology of Fu Nan," 103; Vickery, "Funan Reviewed," 112.

4. Vickery, "What and Where was Chenla?," 205. Vickery qualifies his comment by adding that two Austronesian terms assimilated to Khmer in Khmer inscriptions in southern Cambodia show that Khmer had been in touch with Austronesian languages "since Funan, or even pre-Funan times." Vickery, "What and Where was Chenla?," 215.

5. See chapter three.

6. See appendix four.

7. See appendix four; also the comparison of *Sui shu*'s portrait of Zhenla and Chinese accounts of Funan in chapter six.

8. Dependency: *shu* 屬.

9. See chapter eight.

10. For example, in Shaffer, *Maritime Southeast Asia*, 20–24; Hall, *History of Early Southeast Asia*, 49, 54–59; Sen, "*Maritime Southeast Asia*," 40.

11. For a list of tribute missions and what they consisted of, see appendix three.

12. For the attitude of Song scholars towards trade, see chapter eight.

13. Vickery, "Funan Reviewed", 102–103, referring to Coedès, *Indianized States*, 36–38.

14. See chapter three. This textual evidence of Indian influence in Funan from the fifth century on is consistent with Pollock's view that "public Sanskrit [was present] in Khmer country . . . from about the fifth century" onwards. It is also consistent with archaeological evidence that, according to Manguin, shows the spread through mainland Southeast Asia of Sanskrit inscriptions of Buddhist texts from the fifth to seventh centuries. Pollock, *Language of the Gods*, 125, 127; Manguin, "Pan-Regional Responses," 171–181, esp. 172.

15. See the section on the transition from Funan to Zhenla in chapter six.

16. See the introduction and chapter seven.

17. Though in another passage it refers to a king of Funan, his subordinate and the rulers of Funan's dependencies. See chapter two.

18. Loewe, "Knowledge of Other Cultures," 75.

19. Ge, *Zhai zi Zhongguo*, 45. See also Ge, *Here in 'China' I Dwell*, 32–33.

20. In *Jin shu* and *Xin Tang shu*. See chapters two and seven.

21. Issues relating to irrigation and water management in Angkor are summarized in Coe and Evans, *Angkor and the Khmer Civilization*, 182–184.

22. On matrilineal succession in Funan, see chapter two. For a pathbreaking study that helps redress the gender imbalances in histories of early Cambodia see Trudy Jacobsen, *Lost Goddesses*.

23. Zhou, *Zhenla fengtu ji*, 101–102, 121, 146, 179.

24. *Nan man*: 南蠻. As noted earlier, the radical element of the character *man* is 虫, *hui* or *chong*, meaning "insect."

25. *Xuanhua*: 宣華.

26. Mabbett, "The 'Indianization' of Southeast Asia," 148.

27. Or perhaps the middle of the fourth century, if Zhu Zhantan, the Funan king from India, is taken into account.

Appendix 5

1. Linyi [lim ?ip (P)]: 林邑. In Chinese *Lin* 林 means "forest" and *yi* 邑 means "city", "district" or "village" according to historical context. Stein argues that Linyi/Lim ?ip may be a transliteration of a local ethnic name. But it seems just as likely that the name simply derives from the Chinese name Xianglin 象林, Elephant Forest, a name for one of the five districts of Rinan, the southernmost commandery of the Han dynasty. Stein, *Lin-yi*, 209–241, esp. 225–226.

Champa: in Chinese, Zhancheng 占城 [Cham city]; also Zhanbulao 占不勞, Zhanpo 占婆. For the treatment of Linyi as part of the early history of Champa, see for instance Maspero, *The Champa Kingdom*, 39–52; Coedès, *Indianized States*, 42–45, 47–50, 56–58, 94–95.

2. In 2005 Vickery wrote: "[E]arlier . . . I proposed that Linyi was linguistically Mon-Khmer, but I would accept that part of its area may have been absorbed by Champa at a time when the Chinese were still using the name Linyi, and that this is reflected in the invasion of 605 . . . I would still prefer to argue that the main ethno-linguistic group of Linyi was Mon-Khmer." Vickery, *Champa revised*, 17.

3. This is not to mention archaeological findings, or later Vietnamese sources that refer back to this era. For an overview of recent archaeological achievements, see Griffiths, Hardy and Wade, *Champa: Territories and Networks*.

4. See chapter two.

5. For this tribute mission, see chapter one. Linyi is often described as an independent state, and this will do as a rough description of its status. But during and after the Han dynasty, entities that the Chinese called *guo* 國 presided over by rulers they called *wang* 王 or "king", as Linyi was, ranged from enfeoffed

territories within the imperial realm to truly foreign or independent states. Tribute submission was an important indication that the Chinese court regarded the state concerned as foreign, though often still under Chinese sway.

6. Fang, *Jin shu*, 2545–2547. As in subsequent standard histories, the account of Linyi comes first among the history's accounts of various southern foreigners.

7. Xianglin district: Xianglin *xian* 象林縣. Xianglin was a district of Rinan, Rinan being the southernmost commandery under the Han dynasty. Rinan was known earlier as Xiang 象: according to *Han shu*, the Qin dynasty established the Xiang commandery (Xiang *jun* 象郡) and the Han dynasty renamed it Rinan after conquering the southern state of Nanyue. *Han shu* also mentions Xianglin 象林, referring to a journey to "the Xianglin frontier of Rinan". Ban Gu, *Han shu*, *juan* 6–7, 28. For Ma Yuan, who erected bronze pillars marking the southern frontier of the Han, and Nanhai, one of the other nine southern Han commanderies, see also chapter one.

8. Labour Section: Gong cao 功曹, a local Chinese agency in charge of labour gangs. We can assume that the person referred to here was the administrator, the head of the agency at the district level, though *Jin shu* does not mention a title. Hucker, *Dictionary of Official Titles*, 296.

區: Ou [ʔəw (P)], the modern pronunciation of this character when used as a Chinese surname. An alternative modern pronunciation, adopted by Pelliot, Maspero, Taylor and others, is Qu [k'i̯u (K)]. Lian [li̯än: (K)]: 連. In *Shui jing zhu* and *Liang shu*, Lian 連 is written 逵 (Kui) and 達 (Da) respectively. In all three cases the Chinese characters are similar, and assuming *Jin shu* to be the earliest source I have taken Kui and Da to be copying errors. Using the transliteration Qu rather than Ou, Pelliot identifies Qu Lian 區連 with a Qu Lian 區憐 mentioned in *Hou Han shu* as a foreigner who launched an attack from beyond the frontier of Xianglin in Rinan in 136 CE. But this date is too early for Pelliot's Qu Lian to be the Ou/Qu Lian of Linyi, given that the latter was active at the end of the Han. Pelliot, "Deux itinéraires", 189–190, 382. For *Shui jing zhu* and *Liang shu*, see below.

Maspero seeks to identify Qu Lian (as he calls him) with Śrī Māra, whom he describes as the likely founder of Champa. Māra's name is mentioned on the renowned Sanskrit stele found at Võ Cạnh, which probably dates from the late third or fourth century CE. But as Vickery remarks, there is no reliable basis for such identifications of early Chinese names with names found on inscriptions. Maspero, *The Champa Kingdom*, 26; Vickery, *Champa revised*, 19–21.

Ou Lian is sometimes known as Khu Liên, the modern Vietnamese pronunciation of Qu Lian. Vietnamese pronunciations of Linyi names in Chinese records are not usually given here. The Vietnamese language, like the languages of the Chinese, has evolved over time, and only the reconstructed sounds of Ancient Chinese can give us some sense, albeit limited, of how Linyi names were pronounced at the time. The same applies to the names of local officials serving the southern Chinese courts, given here *faute de mieux* with modern Chinese pronunciations rather than their Vietnamese equivalents. A further caveat is that if the local language of Linyi was not Chinese, but was rather a form of Mon-Khmer or Cham, Ancient Chinese pronunciations may have been transliterations or translations of non-Chinese names, adding further uncertainty.

9. "Sons and grandsons": *zisun* 子孫, a term also just meaning "son". Assuming that here it means "sons and grandsons", it is not clear how many of these succeeded Ou Lian, or whether the daughter was his or a subsequent king's. Fan Xiong [b'i̯wɒm: ji̯ung (K)]: 范熊. Yi [i̯et (K)]: 逸, referred to later in *Jin shu*, just once, as Fan Yi [b'i̯wɒm: i̯et (K)] 范逸.

10. In the original this significant sentence reads *gui nü jian nan* 貴女賤男.

11. The Chinese text here seems incomplete; judging from the fuller version in *Nan Qi shu*, its meaning is as is given in English here. Xiao, *Nan Qi shu*, 1014.

12. "Precious flowers": often a term used to describe flowers with Buddhist connotations. Cotton: *jiapan* 迦盤. *Jiapan* may be derived from *karpāsa*, the Sanskrit word for cotton, perhaps via Cham or Khmer. *Jia* 迦 is often used for the Sanskrit *ga*, and cotton is *kabbas* in modern Khmer, while Pelliot notes that the Chams of central Vietnam call cotton *kapaḥ*. Pelliot, *Notes on Marco Polo*, 442. Similar descriptions of cotton in *Nan Qi shu* and *Liang shu* use the terms *jialan* 迦藍 and *jibei* 吉貝 respectively. Xiao, *Nan Qi shu*, 1014, Yao, *Liang shu*, 786.

13. Sun Quan 孫權 (182–252) was the founder of the Three Kingdoms state of Wu. Perhaps we should take the *Jin shu* comment literally. The envoys mentioned in *San guo zhi* clearly did not travel all the way to Sun's court in Jianye, present-day Nanjing; instead, they delivered their tribute to Lü Dai, Sun Quan's official in Jiaozhou. Likewise, Linyi's tribute to Emperor Wu could have been delivered to an intermediary, rather than carried all the way to Wu's court in distant Luoyang.

14. According to earlier passages in *Jin shu*, Linyi first sent envoys with tribute in 268 (with Funan) and again in 284. Fang, *Jin shu*, 58, 75.

15. Wen: 文 [mi̯uən (K)]. The original Chinese meaning of *wen*, which came to mean "culture" and "literature", is "ornate", "embellished". In *Jin shu*, Wen, his son Fo, and Fo's son Huda (mentioned later) are

all given the family name or title Fan 范. Fan Chui [b'i̯wɒm: ď'wi (K)]: 范椎. Xijuan: 西卷. According to an early source cited by *Shui jing zhu*, Xijuan became the location of the capital of Linyi. Li, *Shui jing zhu*, 833, citing the lost work *Jiaozhou waiyu ji* 交州外域記 [*A Record of the Outer Regions of Jiaozhou*].

"Foreign" here is *yi* 夷. In the account of Wen given in his history of Champa, Maspero describes him as Chinese, but there is nothing to suggest this here. As a slave born in Yangzhou (see note 35 below), Wen could have come from a variety of backgrounds. If he was *yi* like his master Fan Chui, he was a non-Chinese foreigner who from the Linyi perspective could have been a local. Then again, perhaps he had Indian connections. It is notable that the name of his grandson Huda 胡達 includes the word Hu 胡, a term for foreigners that often referred to Indians. Maspero, *The Champa Kingdom*, 27.

The year Fan Yi died, 336, Linyi again sent tribute (from Wen?) in the form of a tame elephant. Fang, *Jin shu*, 182. In this passage Yi is referred to as Fan Yi; when his name occurs later as Yi, I have added Fan.

16. Again, the Chinese capital, here a synecdoche for China itself.

17. By piecing together inscriptions and Chinese sources, Maspero seeks to divide his history of Champa into fourteen dynasties. For the Linyi period, he conceives of five dynasties. In his estimation Qu Lian (Śrī Māra in his view) founded the first, Wen the second, Fan Yangmai the third, and Rudravarman the fourth, with Huanwang constituting the fifth. Maspero, *The Champa Kingdom*, 23–51. But there is nothing in Chinese records to suggest the existence of these five dynasties, or indeed anything other than a single line of Linyi kings called Fan 范 stretching from early times until the death of Fan Zhenlong in 645 or soon thereafter, followed by Huanwang a century or so later.

18. "Wife": or "wives", the noun not being number-specific.

19. Greater Qijie 大岐界, Lesser Qijie 小岐界, Shipu 式僕, Xulang 徐狼, Qudu 屈都, Qianlu 乾魯 and Fudan 扶單: none of these states can be identified; perhaps like the dependencies of Xitu (see below), they were villages or clan settlements rather than fully-fledged states.

20. Hu 胡: "foreign", probably referring here to India.

21. Xia Houlan: 夏侯覽. Jiuzhen was one of the nine commanderies established during the Han dynasty, situated immediately north of Rinan commandery.

22. Zhu Fan: 朱蕃. Regional Inspector: Cishi 刺史, a senior local disciplinary official. Hucker, *Dictionary of Official Titles*, 558. The Heng Mountains: Heng shan 橫山, Hoành Sơn in Vietnamese, a mountain range running from the Annamite Range to the South China Sea. The range divides the northern and central regions—that is, Hà Tĩnh and Quảng Bình provinces—of present-day Vietnam.

23. Jiang Zhuang: 姜壯; Han Ji: 韩戢.Governor: Taishou 太守, the head of a local commandery. Hucker, *Dictionary of Official Titles*, 482.

24. Xie Zhuo: 謝擢.

25. Protector-General: Duhu 督護, a senior military official having regional responsibility for overseeing non-Chinese under imperial control. Hucker, *Dictionary of Imperial Titles*, 539–540. Liu Xiong: 劉雄.

26. Lurong: 盧容. This was the port that Kang Tai and Zhu Ying set out from to visit Funan in the third century CE. See chapter one.

27. Teng Jun: 滕畯. The Protector-General of the West would normally have been stationed in the western regions, in what is today Xinjiang. The assignment in the western regions was a demanding one, and Teng was no doubt a capable administrator. His transfer to the south probably reflected the difficulty the Chinese authorities were facing in their efforts to subdue the local peoples there.

28. An account of Wen's last battle in *Shui jing zhu* says that he died of injuries. Li, *Shui jing zhu*, 834.

29. Fo [[but (P)]: 佛. The original Chinese meaning of Fo is "Buddha". Teng Han: 滕含. This official has the same surname as Teng Jun, so was probably related to him. I have added Teng to his name the second time it is mentioned. *Shui jing zhu* recounts that three years earlier, in 358, Fo unsuccessfully defended the city of Linyi against forces led by another southern Chinese official, Wen Fangzhi 温放之. Elsewhere in *Jin shu* there is also a passing reference to this campaign, where it is dated 359. Fang, *Jin shu*, 204.

30. Elsewhere *Jin shu* records a tribute mission from Linyi in 372. Fang, *Jin shu*, 221.

31. "He": the subject of this sentence is not given, but seems to be Fo, as in the previous sentence, suggesting that Fo lived well into the 400s. Jiude 九德 was a commandery created out of part of Jiuzhen during the Three Kingdoms period. Despite these attacks, *Jin shu* records Linyi as sending a tribute mission to China in 414. Fang, *Jin shu*, 264.

32. Huda [γuo d'ât (K)]: 胡達. As noted earlier, Hu 胡 means "foreign", often Indian. It is the term used earlier to describe the written script Wen used. The original Chinese meaning of *da* 達 is "reach, penetrate". *Liang shu* records the name of Fo's successor as Xuda 須達, which it describes as his grandson. The characters *hu* 胡 and *xu* 須 are not too dissimilar, so Huda and Xuda may be the same person. Yao, *Liang shu*, 765.

33. Homer, *Odyssey*, 404; Malory, *Morte Darthur*, 8–9.

34. As well as other tales of endurance, especially of babies surviving in the wilds. Beckwith, *Empires of the Silk Road*, 2–12.

35. Citing the lost work *Jiangdong jiu shi* 江東舊事 [*Old Affairs of the Eastern Yangzi*], *Shui jing zhu* relates that Wen was from the port city of Yangzhou on the lower Yangzi River and was sold into slavery in Jiaozhou, where he was ill-treated and escaped to sea with merchants before going to Linyi. There he served the king for ten years before the king died and he usurped the thone. Li, *Shui jing zhu*, 837.

36. Notable among them Vickery and Southworth. Vickery, *Society, Economics, and Politics*, 200, 202; Southworth, "Origins of Campā", 371–374.

37. Vickery, *Society, Economics, and Politics*, 200, 202. Also Coe and Evans, *Angkor and the Khmer Civilization*, 80–82. Fan 范 is also a Chinese surname; but Vickery's case, built largely around the prevalence of Fan in the names of early kings of Funan, deserves serious consideration. See also chapter one.

38. Yao, *Liang shu*, 786.

39. For possible matrilineal influences in Funan, see chapter two.

40. *Lou chuan*: 樓船.Tao Huang: 陶璜.

41. Fang, *Jin shu*, 1560. Pelliot, "Fou-nan", 255. Pelliot translates 且連接扶南 as "De plus, il (le roi de Linyi) touche au sud au Fou-nan" (Furthermore, he [the king of Linyi] touches on Funan in the south). *Lianjie* 連接 means more than just touch on, having a sense of link with or connect up with. Pelliot's "au sud" (in the south) is not in the received text.

42. For comparable tables that differ in some details, see Pelliot, "Deux itinéraires", 383–384; Maspero, *Champa Kingdom*, 119.

43. Shen, *Song shu*, 79,82, 83, 85, 86, 88, 95, 122, 169.

44. Li, *Shui jing zhu*, 839.

45. Fan Yangmai [b'i̯wɒm: i̯ang ngât (K)]: 范陽邁; Du Huidu: 杜慧度. Shen, *Song shu*, 2377–2379. This is the main *Song shu* entry on Linyi. Earlier on, *Song shu* provides some brief comments about Linyi during the last years of the preceding Eastern Jin dynasty (317–419). During this period, *Song shu* relates, Linyi was engaged in conflict with Jiaozhou for over a decade—evidently in the early 400s—at which point Fan Huda (as *Song shu* calls him) attacked Rinan, Jiude and Jiuzhen before being defeated by a local governor, Du Yuan 杜瑗. Subsequently, Du Yuan was appointed Regional Inspector of Jiaozhou, and soon after his death in 410 his son Du Huidu 杜慧度 assumed the same position. *Song shu* and *Shui jing zhu* relate that in 413 and 415 Du Huidu was involved in further conflicts with Linyi. In 413 he engaged in two battles. In the first, Fan Huda's two sons were taken and beheaded, and Fan Huda himself fled—and, as Taylor puts it, "was not heard of again". In the second, Du's forces fought below the walls of Linyi's capital city for several days before withdrawing. Shen, *Song shu*, 738, 2263–2264; *Shui jing zhu*, 835, citing *Linyi ji*;. Taylor, *Birth of Vietnam*, 113.

For a full and informative account of the Du family including Du Huidu, see Taylor, *Birth of Vietnam*, 109–115. Taylor reads the Dus' names in Vietnamese, so that Du Huidu, for example, is Đỗ Tuệ Độ. In Taylor's view the Du/Đỗ family "was unquestionably the most Vietnamese of all the imperial clans to govern Vietnam", in other words were the most locally-rooted Chinese administrators to rule over today's northern Vietnam.

46. 420, according to *Nan shi*. Li, *Nan shi*, 25.

47. For *Nan Qi shu*, see below. Maspero calculates that the elder Fan Yangmai died in 421 and was replaced ten years later by the younger Fan Yangmai. Coedès writes that the younger Fan Yangmai followed the elder one when the latter died in 421. As his Chinese sources Maspero cites *Nan Qi shu*, *Liang shu*, *Nan shi*, *Shui jing zhu* and *Wenxian tongkao*, but none of these contains relevant dates; Coedès provides no references. Both writers add that the younger Yangmai was nineteen when he succeeded his father—a fact which is recorded in *Shui jing zhu*, but which does not help date his succession. Maspero, "Le Royaume de Champa: Chapitre III", 491; Maspero, *The Champa Kingdom*, 119, 150; Coedès, *Indianized States*, 57; Li, *Shui jing zhu*, 839.

48. The account that follows is from Shen, *Song shu*, 2377–2378, with Li, *Shui jing zhu*, 836.

49. Yuan Mizhi: 阮彌之. Ousu [k'i̯u si̯wok (K)]: 區粟. For the likely location of Ousu, often transliterated Qusu (using *qu*, the alternative pronunciation of 區) see page 235. For a full description of the campaign, see Taylor, *Birth of Vietnam*, 116.

50. Shen, *Song shu*, 2377.

51. 435 is the date given, rather than 434 as earlier recorded.

52. Tan Hezhi: 檀和之.This is the same General Tan whose campaign against Linyi was praised by the Funan envoy Nāgasena in 484. See chapter two.

53. Zong Que: 宗慤; Xiao Jingxian: 蕭景憲.

54. Qiang Zhongji: 羌仲基. Fortress of Zhuwu: 朱梧戍, *shu* 戍 being a frontier garrison or fortress, here presumably a structure on the frontier between Linyi and the Jiaozhou commandery of Rinan. This is the only time Zhuwu is mentioned in official Chinese sources.

55. Fan Fulongda: 范扶龍大; Fan Fulong 范扶龍 in *Liang shu*. In another reference to him elsewhere in *Song shu* he is called Fan Pishada 范毗沙達. Shen, *Song shu*, 1971.

56. Shen, *Song shu*, 1971–1972.

57. Harris, *Sun Tzu, The Art of War*, passim.

58. Aide: Zhangshi 長史. Fan Longba: 范龍跋; Fan Shencheng: 范神成. Shen, *Song shu*, 2379; Hucker, *Dictionary of Official Titles*, 112.

59. See *Shui jing zhu*, below.

60. Ousu: 區粟; Ouli: 區栗; Wuli: 烏里. Li, *Changing Landscape*, 7 et seq.

61. Stein, *Lin-yi*, 1–52, esp. 52; Taylor, *Birth of Vietnam*, 115; Southworth, "Origins of Campā", 272. Stein calls the city K'iu-sou, while Taylor and others call it Khu-tuc, its name in Vietnamese.

62. Dianchong 典冲 means Dian Torrent, the *chong* 冲 in Dianchong meaning "rushing water". In *Shui jing zhu* the name is used to refer to the river as well as the area around it. The account in *Shui jing zhu* is worth quoting in full: "The Regional Inspector of Jiaozhou, Tan Hezhi, destroyed Ousu, then with flying pennants covering the sea [that is, with a naval fleet] he went on to Dianchong, where at the pagoda above Penglong bay he engaged in a big battle with Linyi. He then went back across Dianchong. Linyi ['s soldiers] entered the estuary and its army made a large advance before suffering the same afflictions it had endured before. The capital [*du*] of Linyi is to the west of the estuary and controls Dianchong. It is forty li from the sea cliffs . . . To the east [Linyi] borders on the sea, to the south it is adjacent to Funan, to the west it is next to Xulang [an unidentified state], and to the north it connects with Jiude." Li, *Shui jing zhu*, 836–837.

63. Li, *Shui jing zhu*, 839.

64. Southworth, "Origins of Campā", 274–275. See also Yamagata, "Development of Regional Centres", 48. This is not the place to address the complicated problem of trying to matching possible locations of early Linyi cities and fortresses with archaeological sites. For a helpful tabulation of sites and historical records, including those relating to Linyi, see Dung, "Champa Settlements of the First Millennium", 44–46.

65. *Shui jing*: 水經. For the authorship, content and different editions of *Shui jing zhu*, see Huesemann, "*Shui jing zhu*", 311–314; also the entry on *Shui jing zhu* in Nienhauser, *Indiana Companion*, 710–712.

66. Li, *Shui jing zhu*, 830–841.

67. Tan Hezhi's campaign in Linyi: Li, *Shui jing zhu*, 834, 839.

68. Li, *Shui jing zhu*, 833–834.

69. This suggests that if it was roughly rectangular in shape, the city was twice as wide as it was long. At this time one li was the equivalent of 300 paces or 1,800 feet (*chi*). Wilkinson, *Chinese History*, 612.

70. *Wuyu*: 屋宇.

71. Li, *Shui jing zhu*, 834.

72. Li, *Shui jing zhu*, 838.

73. Huai: 淮. The two Huai rivers are called Da yuan Huai shui 大源淮水, Great Source Huai River, and Xiao yuan Huai shui 小源淮水, Little Source Huai River. A river called Huai is today a tributary of the Thu Bồn river at Hội An. Li, *Shui jing zhu*, 838.

74. At the time, two poles (*zhang*) were the equivalent of 16 to 17 feet (US). Owls' tails were *chiwei* 鴟尾, a homonym for *chiwei* 蚩尾, meaning tails of a sea creature called *chi* 蚩. These *chiwei* were decorations dating back to Tang times and earlier that consisted of the tails of sea creatures added to rooftops to ward off disaster. Luo, *Hanyu da cidian*, entry under *qiwei* 蚩尾; Wheatley, *Nāgara and Commandery*, 390–391, citing Stein and Marcel Granet.

75. "Local": *yi* 夷, literally, "foreign". "Foreign" in the next paragraph is also *yi*.

76. The two Huai: presumably, the large and small Huai rivers that merged somewhere near the city.

77. Wen Fangzhi: 温放之. *Jin shu* dates this campaign to 359. *Jin shu* has no further record of Wen Fangzhi. As noted earlier, according to *Jin shu*, Fo was again attacked in 361, this time by the southern Chinese official Teng Han.

78. It is not clear whether this refers to the whole city, or to the small city, evidently some kind of palace complex, within the larger city. In context it seems to refer to the small city.

79. "Wife" or "wives", the noun not being number-specific. "No distinctions among the palace women": *pinying wu bie* 嬪媵無別, *pinying* 嬪媵 meaning "concubines and serving maids", and *wu bie* 無別 meaning "being without distinction or difference".

80. A distancing similar to the one described in *Jin shu*.

81. "District": here, *yi* 邑 as in Linyi 林邑. In this instance, *yi* could refer to the city itself.

82. See *Jin shu* on Linyi, above.

83. This is not the view held by either Wheatley or Southworth. Wheatley argues that the two accounts describe two cities, the first being Qusu [Ousu], the second the capital city. He explains away their similarities by calling them a mixture of "fact and folklore". Going further, Southworth argues that *Shui jing zhu* engages in a "hypothetical montage" of several different fortresses and cities at different times, among them Qusu [Ousu] and the capital city as they were both known in 446, the year of Tan Zhihe's campaign. Wheatley, *Nāgara and Commandery*, 384–392, esp. 392; Southworth, "Origins of Campā," 274–275. I see no particular reason to accept their arguments, as explained in the main text.

There is one anomaly in *Shui jing zhu*'s two accounts of Linyi's city, and that is the mention of an "eastern city." Is this a reference to another city, or is it a name for the city being described? Either way, it implies that Linyi's main capital was complemented by a second city—Ousu, perhaps. Chinese reports of an early state having more than one main city or capital are not unknown. In its account of Wendan (Land Zhenla), for instance, *Xin Tang shu* records that the state had two cities. And *Xin Tang shu*'s account of Linyi's successor Huanwang notes that the king had residences, implying perhaps cities, in three locations. For Wendan see chapter seven; for Huanwang see below.

84. Li, *Shui jing zhu*, 840–841. The source quoted is the lost work *Yu Yi qijian* 俞益期牋 [*Yu yi's Diary*]. Similar accounts of Xitu are given in *Liang shu*, *Xin Tang shu* and (as we saw earlier) *Taiping yulan*. As noted earlier, the *Taiping yulan* description of Xitu refers to Xitu's ten or so small dependent states, numbering some two thousand foreign families in all. These dependent "states" or statelets were probably formed by each of the original ten or so 'Ma stay-behind' families.

85. Xiao, *Nan Qi shu*, 1012–1014.

86. Pure gold: literally, purple-ground gold, *zimo jin* 紫磨金. According to *Shui jing zhu*, *zimo jin* was a commonly used term for high-quality gold, *shang jin* 上金. Li, *Shui jing zhu*, 829.

87. Duo: 咄. *Duo* means "a crying sound", making Duo a name suitable for a child. The phrasing here is confusing, and words may be missing, as indicated in square brackets.

88. "Gold mountains": *jin shan* 金山. *Jin shan* gives no indication of number, and there could have been one gold mountain or more than one. Given Linyi's wealth in gold, I have assumed the latter.

Nirgrantha, Nigan 尼乾 in Chinese (also written Nijian 尼健,尼揵 in other contexts) is short for Nirgrantha-Jñātīputra, meaning "free from all ties" in Sanskrit. It is the Buddhist name for followers of Mahāvīra, the founder of the Jain religion. Mahāvīra was regarded by early Buddhists as heterodox, and was included in early Buddhist texts as one of six non-Buddhist teachers. Soothill and Hodous, *Dictionary of Chinese Buddhist Terms*, 185; Buswell and Lopez, *Princeton Dictionary of Buddhism*, 586–587. *Liang shu* repeats this report about Linyi's religion, recording that the king of Linyi was a follower of Nirgrantha. Yao, *Liang shu*, 786. The term Nigan/Nirgrantha is not found in other early standard histories.

"Enormous": *shi wei* 十圍 or ten *wei*, *wei* being a general term for the girth or circumference of an object that could be encircled with both arms. Wilkinson, *Chinese History*, 612.

89. For the Cham word for gold, Edwards and Blagden, "Chinese Vocabulary of Cham", 84.

90. Quan (Dog) fortress: Quan shu 犬戍. Ouli 區栗: as Li Tana notes, here and later *Nan Qi shu* writes Ouli 區栗 rather than Ousu 區粟. Li, *Changing Landscape*, 7. "Inestimably large amounts": Xiao, *Nan Qi shu*, 1013.

91. "Foreign": Hu 胡, probably meaning Indian.

92. *Yi*: 夷. "Foreign", in this instance meaning someone who was neither from Linyi nor from China. Circumstantial evidence suggests that Danggenchun 當根純 was the same person as Jiuchouluo 鳩酧羅, the slave (or son, according to *Liang shu*) of Kauṇḍinya Jayavarman, king of Funan, who left Funan without the king's authorisation and took over Linyi in the early 480s. (If the two names refer to the same person, the reason for this is unclear.) Incensed by Jiuchouluo's impudence, Kauṇḍinya Jayavarman sent Nāgasena to the Southern Qi court in 484 to ask Emperor Wu to send an army to overthrow him, just as Tan Hezhi had earlier defeated Linyi. The story is told in *Nan Qi shu*, 1015–1016; see chapter two.

93. Fan Zhunong: 范諸農 [b'i̯wɒm: tśi̯wo nuong (K)]. Wenkuan: 文款 [mi̯uən k'uân: (K)].

94. "Lordly teachers": *shi jun* 師君, literally "teacher lords".

95. "Good fortune": *jili* 吉利. The term is similar to the term *lishi* 利市 mentioned by Wang Dayuan in his account of Zhenla's coming-of-age ritual. See chapter ten.

96. This description of a gnomon may derive from *Shui jing zhu*, which describes the same thing. Li, *Shui jing zhu*, 834. *Nan Qi shu* again gives the name Ouli 區栗 not Ousu 區粟.

97. For Xiao's Buddhism, see also Chapter two.

98. Yao, *Liang shu*, 38, 50, 52, 54, 70, 71, 78, 787.

99. Yao, *Chen shu*, 69, 81. The 572 mission was sent "jointly with Funan". Coedès, following Maspero, supposes the missions from Linyi were sent by Rudravarman. Maspero cites a Mỹ Sơn inscription to identify Rudravarman's son as Shambhuvarman, and identifies Shambhuvarman with the Linyi king Fanzhi, but the only basis for him doing so is a loosely defined chronology. Maspero, *Champa Kingdom*, 43, 156–157; Coedès, *Indianized States*, 70–71. For King Fanzhi, see the section on *Sui shu* below.

100. Yueshang: 越裳. *Shang* 裳 can also be pronounced *chang*. Yao, *Liang shu*, 784.

101. In reproducing this passage, *Nan shi* gives the name Xitu 西圖 for Xi 西. In *Shui jing zhu*, *Xin Tang shu* and *Taiping yulan* the state is referred to as Xitu 西屠. Li, *Nan shi*, 1948, 1965; Li, *Taiping yulan*, 3502. Ouyang et al., *Xin Tang shu*, 6297. For the *Xin Tang shu* account of Xitu, see page 251.

102. Ou Da: 區達. The character *da* 達 may be an error for *lian* 連, which it resembles.

103. Yao, *Liang shu*, 784.

104. The text reads: "At the beginning of the Shengping reign period of Emperor Ai". Ai appears to be in error for Mu, since at this time Emperor Mu was still on the throne.

105. Dizhen: 敵真 [d'iek tśi̯ĕn (K)], literally "Enemy Truth"; Dikai: 敵鎧 [d'iek k'ậi: (K)], literally "Enemy Armour". In both cases the literal meanings are incongruous; they could conceivably be intended to convey the idea of "truth against the enemy" and "armour against the enemy". In the name of the later king Gaoshi Shengkai, Pelliot suggests that *kai* 鎧 is a translation of the Sanskrit -*varman*. If that is so, the name Dikai could be a translation from a Sanskrit name.

106. According to Southworth, the inscription is Mỹ Sơn inscription C96. The identification with Gaṅgārāja was first proposed by Maspero. Accepting the identification, Southworth argues that "this is . . . the earliest, clear correspondence between a king of Linyi known from Chinese sources and a ruler listed in epigraphy from the Thu Bồn valley". Adding to this, Vickery notes that Gaṅgārāja is mentioned by similar names in two other inscriptions, C73A and C81, and remarks that in his view Gaṅgārāja was "a mythical ancestor of the first Thu Bồn lineage"—that is, the first lineage from the Thu Bồn River valley in central Vietnam, rather than a lineage from the area north of the Hải Vân pass between Danang and Hué, which is often associated with early Linyi. Zakharov queries the identification of Dizhen with Gaṅgārāja, arguing that Dizhen was not the founder of a dynasty, and not known to be a pilgrim. But if Dizhen represents the intrusion into the Chinese annals of a lineage based in the Thu Bồn valley, he could indeed have been its founder, real or mythical. Maspero, *Champa Kingdom*, 30; Southworth, "Origins of Campā", 304; Vickery, *Champa Revised*, 20; Zakharov, "Was the Early History of Campa Really Revised?", 150. For Gaṅgārāja, see also Louis Finot, "Notes d'Épigraphie, III", 206–21.

'C' listings for Sanskrit and Cham inscriptions relating to Champa and Linyi are taken from *The Corpus of the Inscriptions of Campā*, an online publication of L'École francaise d'Extrême-Orient in collaboration with the Institute for the Study of the Ancient World at New York University. isaw.nyu.edu/ publications/ inscriptions/campa

107. Wendi: 文敵 [mi̯uən d'iek (K)], literally " Culture Enemy". Again, this is an incongruous name. It is notable that Dizhen, Dikai and Wendi are all referred to without the name Fan.

108. This seems to have been the conclusion that Maspero drew. Maspero, *Champa Kingdom*, 119. Vickery, *Champa Revised*, 20.

109. Southworth, "Origins of Campā", 304–305.

110. The tribute would presumably have been sent in 492, when according to *Nan Qi shu* Fan Zhunong was recognised as king of Linyi after Danggenchun's ouster. Pelliot tentatively but plausibly identifies Fan Wenzan 范文贊 [b'i̯wɒm: mi̯uən tsân- (K)] with Fan Zhunong's son Wenkuan 文款 [mi̯uən k'uân: (K)] as mentioned in *Nan Qi shu*. If we accept the *Nan Qi shu* version of events, Wenkuan/Wenzan did not replace his father until the latter drowned in 498. Perhaps he sent the tribute on behalf of his father before his father's death, or there is some other, unknown reason for the discrepancy on this point between the accounts in *Nan Qi shu* and *Liang shu*. Pelliot, "Deux itinéraires", 384.

111. General Overawing the South: Weinan jiang 威南將軍; General Soothing the South: Suinan jiangjun 綏南將軍. Earlier on, *Liang shu* gives the date of the tribute sent in 511 as 512. Tiankai: 天凱 (t'ien k'ậi: [K]); Bicuibamo: 弼毳跋摩 (b'jĕt ts'jwäi- ? muâ [K]); Gaoshi Shengkai: 高式勝鎧 (kâu śjiək śjəng- k'ậi: [K]); Gaoshi Lütuoluobamo: 高式律陁羅跋摩 (kâu śjiək ljuĕt ḍię: lâ ? muâ [K]) . Drawing on Pelliot, these names can be explained as follows: (1) reading *kai* 鎧 for *kai* 凱, Tiankai 天凱 may be a translation of Devavarman, *tian* meaning "heaven", *deva* in Sanskrit, and *kai* meaning "armour", *varman* in Sanskrit; (2) Vijayavarman may be a transliteration of Bicuibamo, Vijaya being a possible reading of *bicui* 弼毳 (b'jĕt ts'jwäi-) and *varman* being the standard reading of *bamo* 跋摩; (3) Gaoshi Shengkai may be a part-transliteration, part-translation of Kū Śrī Jayavarman, Gaoshi 高式 being Kū Śri, an honorific derived from Sanskrit, and Shengkai 勝鎧 being Chinese for "victorious armour", Jayavarman in Sanskrit; (4) Gaoshi Lütuoluobamo is likely to be a transliteration of Kū Śri Rudravarman. Pelliot proposes that Bicuibamo (Vijayavarman) and Gaoshi Shengkai (Kū Śrī Jayavarman) were the same person; but judging from Funan and Zhenla lineages, or the case of the two Linyi rulers called Fan Yangmai, the names could equally well refer to two kings with similar names. Pelliot, "Deux itinéraires", 384.

112. Vickery, *Champa Revised*, 21. For the inscription, on a stele at Mỹ Sơn, see Finot, "Notes d'Épigraphie, III", 206–213; Maspero, *The Champa Kingdom*, 156. The dates for Rudravarman given on the inscription are in general conformity with the dates given in Chinese records.

113. See footnote 74.

114. See below for the *Jiu Tang shu* report on this, repeated in *Xin Tang shu*.

115. Li Bi/Lý Bi: 李賁. For the background to this event, see the account in Taylor, *Birth of Vietnam*, 135–144, esp. 138.

116. Yao, *Liang shu*, 785–786.

117. "Buddhist attire": *fafu* 法服. *Fafu* can mean Buddhist, Daoist or any officially regulated dress; here the sense is clearly that the dress is Buddhist.

118. "Cotton": *jibei* 吉貝.

119. "Good fortune": *jili* 吉利.

120. Wei et al., *Sui shu*, 1831–1832.

121. Wei et al., *Sui shu*, 1832–1833.

122. "Area": *yanmao* 延袤. "Area" is a tentative translation of this term, whose literal meaning is "length and breadth". See the discussion of *guangmao* 廣袤 and related terms in chapter two.

123. Sinapodi (siei nâ b'uâ tiei- [K]): 西那婆帝; Sapodige (? b'uâ d'i- kâ [K]): 薩婆地歌. These and other titles—if they are titles—of officials seem to be transliterations from Sanskrit. Aspell convincingly identifies Sinapodi with Senāpati, an old Sanskrit title meaning "general" or "commander", and suggests that Sapodige is the Sanskrit term Sarvādhikārin, meaning "general superintendent". Aspell, *Southeast Asia in the Sui shu*, 9.

124. Lunduoxing: 倫多姓 (li̯uĕn tâ si̯äng- [K]); Gelunzhidi: 歌倫致帝 (kâ li̯uĕn t̂i- tiei- [K]); Yitagalan: 乙他伽蘭 (li̯uĕn t'â ? lân [K]). The Sanskrit or other origins of these three titles or terms are unclear.

125. Local officials: *wai guan* 外官, literally "outside officials", that is, officials serving outside the capital. Sections: *bu* 部, a term that can mean divisions or parts, depending on context. Here it seems to encompass a sense of geographical location. Foluo: 佛羅 (b'i̯uət lâ [K]): Aspell identifies Foluo with the Sanskrit *putra*, son, and plausibly suggests that here *putra* could mean prince. Kelun: 可輪 (k'â: li̯uĕn [K]): *kelun* seems to be a transliteration of *kloñ/khloñ*. As noted earlier, Vickery identifies *kloñ/khloñ* as a title, perhaps Mon-Khmer in origin, that was used in pre-Angkor and Angkor epigraphy to refer to various people at different hierarchical levels. Another, less likely equivalent for *kelun* is the term *kuruṅ*, which is usually translated "king" or "to rule" but whose usage, Vickery notes, was not always consistent.

"Heads of regions and districts": *mu zai* 牧宰, a reference to senior (regional) and junior (district) administrators in China. "Difference in rank": reading差 here as *ci*, meaning rank or status. The comparison made with Chinese regional and district officials—regional heads were few in number, district heads much more numerous—suggests that there were only a few *foluo*/*putra* and many more *kelun*/*kloñ*, perhaps as many as two hundred or so. In this case perhaps the *kelun*/*kloñ* were village chiefs, and hence had a local (Khmer?) rather than Sanskrit title. Aspell, *Southeast Asia in the Sui shu*, 9; Vickery, *Society, Economics,, and Politics*, 188–189, 196–197. For *kloñ* and *kuruṅ* see also chapter one.

126. "A scholar's cap": *zhangfu* 章甫, a term dating back to the second-millennium BCE Shang dynasty. "Rose-colored": *chaoxia* 朝霞, literally "dawn-rose", a term also used in *Sui shu* for the clothing of the king of Chitu (see chapter four). The Buddhist monk Xuanzang mentions the same term *chaoxia* as an Indian name, perhaps Sanskrit in origin, for the colour of clothing. [Xuanzang and Bianji], *Da Tang xi yu ji*, 226–227.

127. "Lute": *qin* 琴. "Pipa": 琵琶, an instrument, usually four-stringed, that is sometimes translated zither; "five-stringed pipa": *wuxian* 五絃, literally "five strings", an old, smaller version of the pipa. The word for China here is Zhongguo 中國.

128. "Large noses": *gao bi* 高鼻, literally "high noses".

129. "Bound up in a knot": *zhuiji* 椎髻, an expression suggesting a tall topknot. Zhou Daguan uses the same expression to describe the hair of women in thirteenth-century Angkor: see chapter nine.

130. Wei et al., *Sui shu*, 40. Maspero attributes the mission to Fanzhi, but *Sui shu* does not record who sent the mission. Maspero, *Champa Kingdom*, 43.

131. As mentioned in chapter four.

132. Liu Fang: 劉方.

133. Wei et al., *Sui shu*, 1358. Fanzhi: 梵志, Zhi 志 meaning "will" or "purpose", and Fan 梵 meaning "brahmin", "sacred," "Sanskrit". Fan 梵 is to be distinguished from Fan 范, the title or name given to earlier kings. Drawing on Finot's analysis of a Mỹ Sơn inscription, Maspero identifies Fanzhi with Śaṃbhuvarman, son of Rudravarman, and dates Śaṃbhuvarman to some time between 578 and 678. *Liang shu* records tribute from Rudravarman in 530 and 534, and *Sui shu and Jiu Tang shu* record tribute from Fanzhi in 605, 623 and 625. So if Rudravarman lived a very long life Maspero's identification is conceivable. But Chinese records would be expected to note that Fanzhi was Rudravarman's son, and they do not. Finot, "Notes d'Épigraphie, XI", 897–977, esp. 900; Maspero, *The Champa Kingdom*, 43, 157; Coedès, *Indianized States*, *70–71;* Liu, *Jiu Tang shu*, *5270*.

134. In its biography of Liu Fang. Wei, *Sui shu*, 1358. The remaining sentences in this paragraph draw on both *Sui shu* sources.

135. Duli: 闍黎. This could conceivably be a longer version of a name of a river called Li 黎 (Lê in Vietnamese). Hardy and Đông tentatively locate a Li or Lê River south of the Thu Bồn River, but if the Linyi capital was in the Thu Bồn region, this would put Hardy and Đông's Li River too far south. Hardy and Đông, "Peoples of Champa", 140–141.

136. In Chinese this important sentence reads, "*Huo qi miaozhu shiba mu, jie zhu jin wei zhi, gai qi you guo shiba ye yi*" 獲其廟主十八牧, 皆鑄金爲之, 蓋其有國十八葉矣.Wei et al., *Sui shu*, 1833.

137. Wei et al., *Sui shu*, 1833. For Liu Fang's campaign, including his death from sickness on the way home, see also Maspero, *Champa Kingdom*, 43–44; Taylor, *Birth of Vietnam*, 164–165.

138. Ouyang et al., *Xin Tang shu*, 6298. "Governor": (here) Shouling 守令. Hucker, *Dictionary of Official Titles*, 433, 482. "City": here, *yi* 邑.

139. Not to mention the doors in the Funan offshoot Chitu (Red Earth).

140. Liu, *Jiu Tang shu*, 5269–5270.

141. *Yanmao*: 延袤.

142. Liu, *Jiu Tang shu*, 5269–5270.

143. Fan Touli: 范頭黎. Touli means "black-haired" or "black-headed". In each case there may have been more than one rhino, pearl and parrot, the number not being specified. Drawing on Finot's analysis of a Mỹ Sơn inscription, Maspero and Coedès identify Fan Touli with Kandarpadharma, son of Śaṃbhuvarman (in their view, Fan Fanzhi). Maspero also identifies Fan Touli's son Fan Zhenlong with Bhāsadharma, who he describes as the son of Kandarpadharma. According to Finot, the Mỹ Sơn inscription concerned mentions Kandarpadharma as having a son, but does not give him a name. *Finot*, "Notes d'Épigraphie, XI", 900; Maspero, *Champa Kingdom*, 44– 45; Coedès, *Indianized States*, 71.

144. Liu, *Jiu Tang shu*, 5270.

145. Fan Zhenlong: 范鎮龍. Zhenlong means "suppressing the dragon". In another section of *Jiu Tang shu*, Linyi is recorded as sending tribute missions in 639 and 653. The first of these could have been from Fan Zhenlong. Liu, *Jiu Tang shu*, *juan* 3, *juan* 4.

146. Liu, *Jiu Tang shu*, 5270; Ouyang, *Xin Tang shu*, 6298. Mohemanduogadu: 摩訶漫多伽獨. Maspero suggests plausibly that this is a transliteration of the title Mahamantrakri, or Great Councillor, similar to the modern Khmer title Moha Montrei.

147. Finot, Maspero and Coedès pay little attention to these significant remarks. Southworth notes that Fan Zhenlong's death resulted in "a major domestic crisis", but without mentioning the end of the Fan clan or title. Southworth, "Origins of Campā", 315. Schweyer notes that according to inscription C 96, a minister ordered the death of "all male descendants" of the lineage of Bhadreśvaravarman, rather than Fan Zhenlong. Schweyer, "The Birth of Champa", 12.

148. "*Jin zhi Huanwang guozhu ji Fanzhi zhi hou* 今之環王國主即范志之後," reading *ling* 令 in the original as *jin* 今 and *tu* 土 as *wang* 王. Li, *Taiping yulan*, 3481, citing [*Jiu*] *Tang shu*. This comment is not in the Zhonghua shuju edition of *Jiu Tang shu*.

149. Liu, *Jiu Tang shu*, 5270.

150. Maspero, following Finot, identifies this brahmin with Bhadreśvaravarman, who according to Finot is described on the same inscription as the nephew of Kandarpadharma's son. Maspero, *The Champa Kingdom*, 45; Finot, "Notes d'Épigraphie, XI", 900.

151. Ouyang et al., *Xin Tang shu*, 6298.

152. Zhugedi (tśi̯wo kât d'i- [K]): 诸葛地. Finot, Maspero and Southworth all identify Zhugedi with Jagaddharma, a person named on the Mỹ Sơn inscription that also lists Rudravarman, Śaṃbhuvarman and others. The identification is plausible, since Zhugedi corresponds well with Jagad-, the first part of Jagaddharma. After Lutuoluobamo/Rudravarman I, this would therefore be only the second instance of a name in a Chinese record of Linyi that corresponds with a name on a local inscription.

According to Finot, who Maspero and Coedès follow, the place Jagaddarma/Zhugedi fled to was Cambodia (Zhenla). There he married king Īśānavarman I's daughter, and their son later became king of Champa. "Married the queen" in the *Xin Tang shu* account suggests, of course, that the woman Jagaddharma/Zhugedi married was Fan Touli's daughter. Perhaps he married both women, or one of these accounts is wrong. Finot, "Notes d'Épigraphie, XI", 900; Maspero, *The Champa Kingdom*, 45; Coedès, *Indianized States*, 71; also Southworth, "Origins of Campā", 315.

"Father's sister": *gu* 姑. *Gu* can refer to more than one kind of relative, including the sister of a father or husband; "father's sister" seems the most likely meaning here.

153. See chapter seven. Ouyang, *Xin Tang shu*, 5857. Also Taylor, *Birth of Vietnam*, 192. Annan (Pacifiying the South) was the name of the protectorate in the far south of China established by the Tang.

154. Tribute sent from Huanwang in 793 is recorded in *Taiping yulan*. It included a rhino that died three years later. Li, *Taiping yulan*, 547.

155. Zhang Zhou: 張舟. According to Maspero, Huanzhou and Aizhou were taken over by Harivarman I, then king of Huanwang. Maspero, *The Champa Kingdom*, 50–51.

156. Wang et al., *Cefu yuangui*, *juan* 970.

157. Ouyang et al., *Xin Tang shu*, 6297–6298. In translating this passage I have used the present tense, since although Huanwang was defunct by the time *Xin Tang shu* was written (it is last mentioned in *Cefu yuangui* with respect to an event that took place in 838), Champa was not. *Cefu yuangui* in Chen et al., *Zhongguo gujizhong*, 104.

158. The Wuwen Mountains were mentioned by the Tang geographer Jia Dan; see chapter four. Benlangtuo *zhou* 奔浪陀州 is evidently one of various names for Phan Rang on the coast of central-south Vietnam, (*zhou* here meaning region). Great river estuary: *da pu* 大浦. The editors of the Zhonghua shuju edition of *Xin Tang shu* take this to be a proper name, but it could just be a descriptive term.

159. This account of Xitu was first given in *Shui jing zhu* and repeated with minor variations in *Liang shu* and *Taiping yulan*.

160. Huanwang: 環王. Zhanbulao: 占不勞; Zhanpo: 占婆. *Ming*: 明; *hu*: 胡."Mingda [Huda?], king of Linyi, made a tribute gift of gold finger rings": *Linyi wang Ming* [*Hu*] *da xian jingang zhihuan* 林邑王明 [胡?] 達獻金鋼指環. The word *huan*, ring, does not indicate singular or plural, but doubtless he gave the Chinese court more than just one.

161. Champa Mountains: Bulao Shan 不勞山, Bulao derives from Zhanbulao, Champa.

162. *Yangpubu* [*i̯ang p'uo: puo* (K)]: 陽浦逋; *tuoyang'axiong* ((? *i̯ang ·â ji̯ung* [K]): 陀陽阿熊; *achangpu* (*·â d'i̯ang puo* ([K]): 阿長逋; *pomandi* (*b'uâ muân- d'i-* [K]): 婆漫地. For *pubu/pu poṅ*, see Edwards and Blagden, "Chinese vocabulary of Cham", 89. The king's residences: Zhancheng 占城 is Cham city, the Chinese term usually rendered in English as Champa. Qiguo (Dz'iei kwək [K]) 齊國, literally "the state of Qi", is a curious name, Qi having been an ancient Chinese state with no known connection with this region. Perhaps it is the transliteration of an unidentified local name. Pengpishi (b'ung b'jiç śi̯äi- [K]) 蓬皮勢 is an unidentified name, perhaps also a transliteration of a local name.

163. The envoys and tribute are listed in Wang, *Tang hui yao*, 2076–2077; Wang et al., *Cefu yuangui*, 11401–11405, 11409–11410, 11413. According to *Cefu yuangui*, between 650 and 750 Linyi sent tribute to China 25 or 26 times, in 653, 654, 657, 669, 670, 686, 691, 695 (twice), 699, ?702 (the year given is 703, but seems to be in error for 702), 703 (twice), 706, 707, 709, 711, 712, 713, 714, 731, 734, 735 (twice within a short time, perhaps the same mission), 748 and 749. During this period Linyi sent tribute to China far more often than any other southern state: compare for example the tribute from other states listed in Smith, "Mainland South East Asia", 44.

164. Wang et al., *Cefu yuangui*, *juan* 46.

165. In Wang Gungwu's view, this flow of tribute reflected Linyi's involvement in a lively system of regional trade. He remarks that "[t]he prosperity of Linyi must be recognised as a major factor in making the . . . century after 623 the most successful period of the Nanhai trade". Wang, "Nanhai Trade", 128.

166. Bogashebomo: 钵迦舍波摩 (Bogashebamo 钵迦舍跋摩 in *Cefu yuangui*); Jianduodamo: 建多達摩; Lutuo(luo): 盧陀 (羅). Coedès and Maspero, who Coedès follows, both blur any residual distinction between Linyi and Champa by describing these figures as kings of Champa, rather than Linyi, and focusing on the Sanskrit versions of their names rather than their names as given in Chinese. Maspero, *Champa Kingdom*, 45, 161; Coedès, *Indianized States*, 71–72.

167. Maspero, *Champa Kingdom*, 45.

168. Vickery, *Champa Revised*, 23.

169. The comment comes at the end of *Nan Qi shu*'s account of Funan. Xiao, *Nan Qi shu*, 1017.

170. Wei et al., *Sui shu*, 1836.

171. This generalization is mainly based on comments in *Jin shu* and *Liang shu*. *Liang shu* states unequivocally that Linyi's entrances face north, *Jin shu* records that its entrances face north, but notes that some entrances also face in other directions. A third source, *Shui jing zhu*, is less clear. It implies that north is the primary direction when it notes that in the palace precinct (?) the southern walls have no windows, and notes that the doors of the Ousu fortress face north. But it also records that the doors of Linyi's palace face south, and describes the capital's main gate as facing east (the north gate being blocked, evidently to prevent river access).

172. Fang, *Jin shu*, 2545.

173. Li, *Shui jing zhu*, 840; Yao, *Liang shu*, 784; Ouyang et al., *Xin Tang shu*, 6297; Li et al., *Taiping yulan*, 3502

174. Fang, *Jin shu*, 2545–2546; Li, *Shui jing shu*, 837; Yao, *Liang shu*, 784.

175. Fang, *Jin shu*, 2546; Li, *Shui jing zhu*, 834.

176. Fang, *Jin shu*, 2546–2547; Li, *Shui jing zhu*, 834, 838.

177. Yao, *Liang shu*, 785.

178. Fang, *Jin shu*, 1560.

179. Fang, *Jin shu*, 2545; Xiao, *Nan Qi shu*, 1013–1014; Yao, *Liang shu*, 785–786;

180. Shen, *Song shu*, 2377; Xiao, *Nan Qi shu*, 1013.

181. Shen, *Song shu*, 2378.
182. Xiao, *Nan Qi shu*, 1013; Yao, *Liang shu*, 784.
183. Xiao, *Nan Qi shu*, 1013.
184. Yao, *Liang shu*, 784.
185. LI. *Shui jing zhu*, 834, 836–837, 839.
186. Li, *Shui jing zhu*, 833, 838.
187. Li, *Shui jing zhu*, 838.
188. Shen, *Song shu*, 2379.
189. Xiao, *Nan Qi shu*, 1013, 1015–1016.
190. Xiao, *Nan Qi shu*, 1013.
191. Xiao, *Nan Qi shu*, 1014; Yao, *Liang shu*, 786.
192. Yao, *Liang shu*, 786–787.
193. Wei, *Sui shu*, 1832–1833. Glahn, *Economic History*, 183–184.
194. Wei, *Sui shu*, 1832; Ouyang et al., *Xin Tang shu*, 6298.
195. Wei, *Sui shu*, 1358, 1833.
196. Ouyang et al., *Xin Tang shu*, 6298.
197. Liu, *Jiu Tang shu*, 5270.
198. Liu, *Jiu Tang shu*, 5270; Ouyang et al., *Xin Tang shu*, 6298.
199. [*Jiu*] *Tang shu* cited in Li, *Taiping yulan*, 3481.
200. Liu, *Jiu Tang shu*, 5270; Ouyang et al., *Xin Tang shu*, 6298
201. Wang et al., *Cefu yuangui*, 11401–11405, 11409–11410, 11413.
202. Ouyang et al., *Xin Tang shu*, 6297.

Index

This index relates to the main text, with selective references to the endnotes. The index does not include references to Appendix 5 on Linyi and other appendices. For unlisted book titles refer to the name of the author or editor.

A

Abel-Rémusat, Jean-Pierre 168
Africa, African ivory 23, 198
Aizhou 121, 123, 132
An Lushan rebellion 140
Ancient Chinese 14
Angkor xi, xii, 1, 2, 5, 7, 10, 11, 140–141, 147, 149–151, 153, 204
  capital called Luwu 150–152, 352 n. 75
  increasing size 147
  The Kingdom of Angkor 17, 124, 194, 215
Angkor Borei, location of main city of Funan 4, 10, 22, 91, 93
Angkor Wat 161, 171, 194, 202
  associated with carpenter Lu Ban 171, 194, 202, 357–358 n. 38
Annan or Annam 132–133, 144, 147
Annamite Mountains 134
Arabs or Dashi, Arab world 140, 198
Atelme, Michel 15
Austronesian languages 17, 211, 219
Avalokiteśvara or Guanyin 73, 104, 148
Aymonnier, Étienne 9

B

Ba Phnom, Ba Shan, Ba Mountain 122, 206
Baitou (White Hair) people 87, 90, 92, 102, 207
Bajian, Angkor prefecture 172
bang or territory 16
Banteay Prey Nokor 122
Bao pu zi see Ge Hong
Bakheng, Phnom 153, 171, 194
Baphuon 171
Basili, Angkor prefecture 172
Baxter, William 14
Baxue, Angkor prefecture 172
Bayon 171, 194, 357 n. 35
Bei shi (*The History of the Northern Dynasties*) 43, 64, 67, 77
Beijing 206
Bentuolang, perhaps Phan Rang 122, 136, 343 n. 17
Bhadreśvara or Poduoli, name for Śiva 115, 117, 130, 150, 152, 341 n. 49
Bhavavarman I, king of Zhenla 116–117
Bhavavarman II, king of Zhenla 109, 135
Bijing 108, 338 n. 7
Bisong 49
Bohai Sea 132
Boluola 80
Bosilan 151–152
Bourdonneau, Éric 11
Briggs, Lawrence Palmer 10
  The Ancient Khmer Kingdom 10
Buddhabadra or Putibatuo 7, 45, 102–103, 219
  account of Funan 45–46, 102
Buddhist and Buddhism 3, 5, 7, 18, 42, 43–46, 62, 67, 80–81, 100, 108, 115, 216, 360 n. 62
  Avalokiteśvara or Guanyin 73, 104
  Buddhist monks 7, 43–46
  colossal statues 46, 102
  first mentioned in the context of Funan 25, 96
  long strand of hair of the Buddha 74, 101
  Mahayana Buddhism 43, 44, 54
  Vajrayana Buddhism 360 n. 62
Bureau of Military Affairs, central Chinese authority 160

C

Cambodia xi, 1, 2, 7, 11, 13, 23, 107, 116, 195, 204–207
  collections of early Chinese texts on 7
  other Chinese names for 107, 163, 169, 204
  see Funan, Zhenla
Canban, dependency of Wendan 87, 113, 135, 136–137, 333 n. 42
Canda Ganwuzhe Chidazhi, perhaps Samdach Kambuja-dhirāja 207
Cangwu, Han dynasty commandery 24
Canlie Popiya, king of Zhenla, perhaps Samdach Chao Ponhea 202, 367 n. 33
Canlie Zhaopingya, king of Zhenla, perhaps Samdach Chao Ponhea Yat 202, 207, 367 n. 33
Cefu yuangui (*Outstanding Models from the Storehouse of Literature*) 6, 84, 87, 89, 105, 108, 128, 131
Ceylon or Xilan 144, 198, 331 n. 12
Cham, Champa 15, 108, 126, 133, 134, 143–144, 147, 149–151, 153–154, 159, 170, 192, 198, 201–202, 204. 207, 209
  cavalry 148
  conflict with Zhenla see Zhenla
  tribute from Zhenla 153
  see also Huanwang

Chandler, David xi, xii, 3, 11, 127
A History of Cambodia 11
Chang, Fan Shiman's son 55, 71
Chang'an, present-day Xi'an 14, 92, 121, 123, 134, 136
Chang Jun, envoy to Chitu 79, 81–84, 104–105, 110, 210
Chen dynasty 42
Chen Jiarong (Chan Kai Wing) 11, 320 n. 59
Chen Menglei 167
Qin ding gujin tushu jicheng (A Collection of Illustrations and Books Old and New, Imperially Authorised) 167
Chen Shou, Indian envoy 21
Chen shu (The History of the Chen Dynasty) 18, 43, 64, 76–77, 102
Chen Song, king of India's envoy to Funan 25, 27, 96
possibly two people, Chen and Song 311 n. 40
Chen Xiansi 11, 125, 140
Chen Xujing 11
Cheng, Han dynasty emperor 203
cheng or city, meanings of the term 17
Cheng Zhai za ji (Cheng Zhai's Miscellany) 167
Chequ 112, 135–137
Chichi or Maomao gorge 133
China xi, 2, 3, 7, 16, 21, 44 and *passim*
called Beishi by Cambodians 184
China Text Project 6–7
Chitu or Red Earth 67, 79–84, 104–105, 112, 210, 216, 330 n. 6, 331 n. 13
Buddhism 80–81
brahmins 81–83
funeral practices 81
marriages 81
names or titles of state officials 81
products 81
Sui shu portrait of 79–84
see also Sengzhi City
Chola in southern India 140
chuan qi, strange stories 8
Cinnamon Sea 142
Citrasena (Zhiduosina), family name Kṣatriyaḥ (Shali), also called Mahendravarman, king of Zhenla 84, 87–88, 105, 109, 113, 116–117, 205, 212, 333 n. 31
Coedès, George 9, 10, 15, 117, 122, 143, 144. 202, 214, 341 n. 49
The Indianized States of Southeast Asia 10
Coe, Michael 11
Angkor and the Khmer Civilization 11
College of Literary Studies, Tang dynasty 65
compasses, magnetic 142

D
Da Qin or (eastern) Roman empire 14, 25, 45, 48, 49, 89, 94, 103, 213
Đại Cồ Việt, later Đại Việt 134, 144, 158
see also *Vietnam, Vietnamese*
Daizong, Tang dynasty emperor 128, 136
Dali, successor to Nanzhao 144, 349 n. 33
Danbu garrison 133
Daner, Han dynasty commandery 24, 37
Danlanzhou, source of iron 88
Daoist and Daoism 3, 7, 18, 42, 46–50, 217
Daoist writings on Funan 46–50
Daoming, dependency of Wendan 135, 136–137
Daoshi, monk 46
Fayuan zhulin (Forest of Gems in the Dharma Garden) 46
Daoxuan, monk 44
Xu gao seng zuan (More Biographies of Eminent Monks) 44
Daqu, name or title of Wendan king 136–137
Datong 132
Dezong, Tang dynasty emperor 52, 128, 132, 136
Dhṛtavarman or Chilibamo/ Chilituobamo, king of Funan 53, 72, 100
Dilata 145–146
Dingliumei or Dengloumei, Dengliumei, etc. 143, 145–146, 151–152, 349 n. 28
Đinh Tiên Hoàng, emperor of Đại Cồ Việt 134
Du Mu, late Tang poet 85
Du You, author of *Tong dian* 85
Dubo see Java
Dudbridge, Glen 28
Dukun or Qudukun 28, 49, 71, 95, 312 n. 46
Dunxun or Diansun or Dianxun, Funan dependency 20 (map), 35, 38, 41, 45, 48, 49, 69, 71, 76, 95–96, 212–214, 216, 326 n. 26
Duoluobodi or Duoheluo, Dvaravati 122, 123, 126, 135, 137, 343 n. 17
Dupont, Pierre 122, 125
Dutch, the 204

E
East Baray 217
East Mebon 171
Edwards, Penny xii
Encyclopedias and compendiums 6, 13
Esen Khaya or Yexian Haiya 184, 194, 362 n. 89

F
Fairbank, John K. 12
fan as title see *pōn*
fan meaning foreign 13
Fan Chengda, author of *Guihai yuheng zhi* 8, 18, 142, 145, 161
Fan Chuo 126
Man shu (Book of the Southern Foreigners) 126
Fan Shiman or Fan Man, king of Funan 33, 36, 38, 49, 55, 71, 95, 211, 216, 219
Fang Xuanling, author of *Jin shu* see *Jin shu*
Fan Xun, king of Funan 26, 30, 36, 38, 51, 71, 96–98
Fan Zhan or Zhan, king of Funan 25, 27, 29, 33, 35–36, 95, 213–214
Faxian, monk 44
Fei Xin 198
Xingcha shenglan (An Overall Survey of the Star Raft) 198
Ferlus, Michel 15
Finot, Louis 9, 10, 34
Five Dynasties and Ten Kingdoms 140, 219
Funan xi, 2, 4–11, 14, 15, 19, 20 (map), 21–25, 28–39, 41, 43–50, 52–53, 54–63, 67–77, 79, 84–92, 93–106, 107–109, 203
appearance of the people 51, 53, 72, 100, 316 n. 100
boats 29, 33, 60, 88, 98, 103
teeth, blackened 98

Funan (*continued*)
Buddhism 7, 42–46, 55–56, 58–62, 101–102, 108–109, 214, 219, 325 n. 112
carved wood and perhaps metal 32, 51, 314 n. 65
character of the people 39, 51, 59, 74, 76, 90, 100–101
cinnabar 49
city walls and moat 60, 71, 76, 101
clothing 26, 59, 310 n. 36
connections with Zhenla 87, 116–117, 211–213
derivation of name 15, 93
diamonds 47, 90, 98, 319 n. 40
elephants 29, 61, 90, 98
fans 22–23, 98
funeral practices 74, 105
gold 88, 103
Hindu and other gods and their images 62, 72, 104, 328 n. 51
housing 60, 101
hunting 32, 38, 98
kings called Paodao and Potan 48–49, 320 n. 51
kings' names in Sanskrit 6, 99
Liuye–Hun Tian foundation story 29, 34–35, 51, 54, 70, 94
location and size 17, 53, 54, 88, 93, 99–100, 211, 219, 320 n. 59,
matrilineal customs 61, 95
mentioned by the poet Zuo Si 36–37
musicians and dancers 90
overland route 41
ploughing and planting practices 51, 52, 90, 100
products 61, 69, 323 n. 93
queen as first ruler 34, 70
sandalwood 89, 98–99, 103
slaves 56, 59, 97
taxes and levies 51, 52, 90, 100
trade, including foreign trade 61, 76, 89, 99, 101, 103, 219
trials by ordeal 30, 32, 59–60, 71, 97
turtles' shells 85
wells and water usage 72, 76, 104
women 59, 61, 94
written records and script 51. 52, 84, 100, 130, 321 n. 61

G

Ganges, the 96
Ganpang 170
gazetteers of the Song dynasty 8, 11, 142–156
Gaozong, Tang dynasty emperor 77, 122
Gaozong, Song dynasty emperor 161
Gardiner, Kenneth 4
Ge Hong 13, 46–47, 217
Bao puzi (*The Master who Embraces Simplicity*) 43, 47, 85, 90
Ge Zhaoguang 216
Gender issues, the role of women 217–218, 220
Geying 45
Gernet, Jacques 42
Guangxi region 143–144, 145
Guangzhou city 142, 143, 155, 201, 213, see also Panyu
Guangzhou region 24, 44, 132
Guian county, Zhejiang province 205
Guihai yuheng zhi (*The Treatise of the Supervisor and Guardian of the Cinnamon Sea*) 8, 142–144, 149, 161
lign–aloes 143
gulong 39–40, 84, 86, 92, 98, 212
Guluo river 133
guo or state, meaning of the term 16–17, 215
Gutang people 124

H

Hainan, or South of the Sea; also island 143
Jiyang army 147–148
Hainan zhuan (*A Record of South of the Sea*) 68
Hall, Kenneth 141
Han dynasty 3, 12, 19, 21, 22, 45, 144
Han shu (*The History of the Former Han Dynasty*) 22, 23
Hangzhou, earlier called Lin'an 139, 142, 166, 198, 201
Hargett, James 8
Harṣavarman III, king of Zhenla/Angkor 158, 160
He, Later Han dynasty emperor 26
Heluodan 80
Heng, Derek 12
Hepu, Han dynasty commandery 24
Hokkien 16
Hongwu, emperor of the Ming dynasty 206–207, 209
Hou Han shu (*The History of the Later Han Dynasty*) 22
Huangzhi 23
Hongnong, near Luoyang 83, 105
Hoshino, Tatsuo 11, 79, 127, 134, 330 n. 6
Huan, Later Han dynasty emperor 26, 27
Huang Xingzeng 199–200
Xiyang chaogong dianlu (*Records of Tribute from the Western Ocean*) 199–200
Huanwang, early Chinese name for Champa 90, 334 n. 61
see also Appendix 5
Huanzhou, near present-day Vinh 108, 127, 133, 135, 345 n. 55
uses of the Huanzhou–Wendan route 134
Huerna, king of Zhenla 200, 205
Huijiao, monk 44
Gao seng zhuan (*Biographies of Eminent Monks*) 44
Huiying and Huilin, monk authors of *Yiqie jing yinyi* (*The Pronunciations and Meanings of All the Sutras*) 124, 212
Huizong, Song dynasty emperor 145, 160–161
Hun Tian, also called Hun Shen, Hun Dian, Hun Kui, first king of Funan 29, 34–35, 51, 53, 54, 94, 213–214, 219, 313 n. 53
Kauṇḍinya suggested as meaning of name 35, 214
later lineage, according to *Liang shu* 75

I

India or Tianzhu 2, 9, 15, 25, 27, 40, 43, 48, 88, 89, 94–96, 103, 132, 144, 198, 203, 213–214
caste or class system of 9, 86
Gunu or Kanadvīpa 49, 320 n. 55
Indianization debate 9–11, 214–215, 307 n. 49
Indian law introduced into Funan 72
Su Wu sent as Fan Zhan's envoy 27
Indra 122
Indravarman I, king of Zhenla/Angkor 137

Indravarman II. king of Zhenla/ Angkor 154
Indravarman III, king of Zhenla/Angkor 166
Iśānapura or Yishe'na *cheng* 17, 86, 113, 115, 121, 123–124, 339 n. 28
see also Sambor Prei Kuk
Iśānasena (Yishe'naxian) or Kṣatriyaḥ Iśānasena, Iśānavarman I, king of Zhenla 105, 108–109, 113, 116–117, 122, 126, 135, 200–201, 339 n. 28

J
Jacques, Claude 10, 109, 122, 125, 215, 339 n. 28
Jambudvipa 109
Japan 2, 204
Java or Dubo, Zhuzhuanbo, Zhubo, Shepo 2, 29, 33, 140, 146, 198, 312 n. 48
perhaps Yepoti 44
Heling, Javanese state of 123, 134
Jayatataka or North Lake/North Baray, with Neak Pean 172, 194, 217
Jayavarman I, king of Zhenla 109, 116, 126, 135, 141
Jayavarman II, king of Zhenla, founder of Kingdom of Angkor 124–126, 137
Jayavarman VII, king of Zhenla/ Angkor 154–155, 163, 217
Jia Dan, Tang court geographer 132–134, 345 n. 40
Jia Xiangli or Xiangli, travelling merchant 29, 33, 35, 96, 213–214
Jialuoxi, dependency of Srivijaya 149, 151, 202, 351 n. 67
Jianye or Jiankang, later called Nanjing 21, 24, 36–37, 42, 44, 47. 57, 101–102, 202, 206
Funan Office (Funan guan) 44, 101
Jiaoshishan (Burnt Rock Mountain) 82
Jiaozhi, originally a Han dynasty commandery 24, 47, 90, 144, 146, 158–159, 169, 204
Jiaozhou region 20 (map), 24, 47, 100, 158, 324 n. 102
population in fifth century 24
Jiaxing, on the Grand Canal 201
Jilong (Chicken Coop) island 82
Jin dynasty 27
Western Jin dynasty 44
Eastern Jin dynasty 42
Jin shu (*The History of the Jin Dynasty*) 4, 18, 19, 42, 90, 99, 103, 210–211
description of Funan 51–53
Jinchen or Jinlin 71, 312 n. 49
Jinsheng, Fan Shiman's son 71, 95
Jiubuzhi 22, 308 n. 3
Jiuchouluo, Funanese king of Linyi 56, 322–323 n. 89
Jiumoluo, Chitu brahmin 82
Jiuzhen, Han dynasty commandery 24, 110
Jiu Tang shu (*The Old History of the Tang Dynasty*) 16, 18, 25, 52, 78, 119–128, 156, 216
description of Zhenla 120–125
account of Water Zhenla and Land Zhenla 125–128
Khmers or Jimie/Gemie 124
mention of book on Zhenla, *Zhenla guo ji* 121, 123
Zhenla's plan to join in an attack on Chinese Annam 120–121
Juji or Gouzhi, Juzhi, Jiuzhi, an island 29, 71, 95
Jurchens 139, 140, 143

K
Kaifeng 139, 160
Kambuja, Kambu 22, 94
Kang Tai, Chinese envoy 2, 6, 7, 9, 13, 18, 19, 21, 22, 24–36, 40, 77, 78, 94–99, 101, 103, 116, 210–211, 213–214, 217–218, 309–310 n. 29, 311 n. 43
likely dates of trip south 25, 310 n. 31
account of Funan 28–30, 32–36
see also Zhu Ying
Karlgren, Bernard 14, 40
Kauṇḍinya or Jiaochenru, brahmin king of Funan 62, 72, 99, 106, 214, 322 n. 86
similarities with Hun Tian 75, 99, 214–215
Indianizing influence 72, 99
Kauṇḍinya (Qiaochenru) Jayavarman (Sheyebamo), king of Funan 55, 57, 59, 67, 72, 74, 100, 116, 213
inscription linking to son Rudravarman 75, 117
General Pacifying the South 72
Kingdom of Angkor, The see Angkor
Khmer, Khmers xi, 4, 10, 195, 212, 217
called Jimie, Gemie 124–125, 135
Khmer inscriptions 122
Mon–Khmer languages 10, 17, 152, 212, 219
king see *wang*
Korea 44, 132
Kra Isthmus 147, 149
Kṣatriyaḥ 121
Kṣatriyaḥ Citrasena see Citrasena
Kṣatriyaḥ Iśānasena see Iśānasena
Kublai Khan, Yuan dynasty emperor 139, 209
kunlun 38–40, 49, 98, 124–125, 342 n. 9
equivalent of *kuruṅ* or other local terms 40
mistaken for *gulong* 39–40, 86, 98
Kunlun Sea 169
Kumārajīva, monk 45

L
Laigankeng, Angkor prefecture 172
Land Zhenla or Lu Zhenla 119, 125, 126–127, 135–137, 201, 216–217, see also Wendan
Langyaxiu or Langyaxu 74, 82
Later Han dynasty 23
Lecoq, Marie-Jean-Léon, Marquis d'Hervey 117
lei shu, categorized works 28
Leur, Jacob van 10
Leys, Simon, on buildings and the imperial Chinese world view 165
Li Dashi and Li Yanshou, authors of *Nan shi and Bei shi* see *Nan shi*, *Bei shi*
Li Fang, author of *Taiping guangji* and *Taiping yulan* see *Taiping guangji and Taiping yulan*
Li Shan, *Wenxuan* commentator 142

Lý Thánh Tông, Vietnamese king 158
Liang dynasty 42
Liang shu (*The History of the Liang Dynasty*) 5, 18, 19, 25–26, 35, 43, 44, 53, 61, 64, 84–85, 93, 95, 97, 99, 101, 103–104, 210–215, 217
  on Kang Tai in Funan 26
  on kings of Funan 36, 70–74
  description of Funan 69–74
Li Mona, envoy 121–122, 131
Li Tana 134
Lieberman, Victor 141
Limu or Bamboo Fence Wood city 204
Liṅgaparvata or Linggabobaduo/Linggabopo 82, 115, 332 n. 21, 341 n. 49
Lingnan 47
Lingwai daida (*Representative Responses to Questions about Regions beyond Wuling*) 8, 134, 145–149, 152
Linyang 29, 33, 312 n. 49
Linyi, state of 24, 38–39, 45, 48, 49–50, 56, 69, 82, 85, 90, 108, 110, 112, 113, 144
  compared to Funan 51, 68
  compared to Zhenla 110, 113
  described in *Liang shu* 68
  Indian influence in 69
  women 61
  requests Funan's help in attacking Jiaozhou 53
  invaded by the Sui dynasty 79–80
  plan to join Zhenla in attack on Chinese Annam 120–121
  see also Appendix 5 for the account of Linyi in Chinese records
Liu Fu, recruitment officer in Guangzhou 159–160
Liu Song dynasty 42, 53
Liu Xian 26
Liu Xu, author of *Jiu Tang shu* see *Jiu Tang shu*
Liuye, also called Yeliu, queen and first recorded monarch of Funan 17, 29, 51, 53, 54, 94, 201, 313 n. 53
  identified with Somā the naga queen 34
Loewe, Michael 216
Lou Yue 156
Lovek 151
Lü Dai 24
Lu Ji. editor of *Gujin shuo hai* (*A Sea of Stories Old and New*) 167
Wu, Kingdom of 24, 27
Lu Zhenla see Land Zhenla, Wendan
Luo Yuejiong 203
  Xian bin lu (*A Record of All Foreign Guests*) 203
Luohu 151–152
Luolun river 133
Luosha 83
Luoyang 44, 45, 87, 92, 97, 102
Luoyue 133
Lurong port 28, 311 n. 45
Lüyang 151–152

M

Ma Duanlin, author of *Wenxian tongkao* see *Wenxian tongkao*
Ma Huan 198, 199
  Yingyai shenglan (An Overall Survey of the Ocean's Shores) 198
Ma Yuan, Han dynasty general 144
  set up bronze pillars 144
Mabbett, Ian 10, 219
Ma Duanlin, author of *Wenxian tongkao* 157
  see *Wenxian tongkao*
Malan or Maluowen, Moliang, Angkor prefecture 145–146, 151–152, 172
Maluku or Mawuzhou 70, 326–327 n. 31
Mahendraparvata, first capital of the Kingdom of Angkor 124
Maheśvara or Moxishouluo, name for Śiva 54, 58–59, 62, 100, 215, 323 n. 94
Manchus 139
Mandra or Mantuoluo, monk 44, 101
Marcus Aurelius Antoninus or Andun, Roman emperor 26, 310 n. 37
Manguin, Pierre-Yves 10, 22
Mao Ruizheng 205
  Huangming xiangxu lu (*The Record of an Interpreter of the August Ming Dynasty*) 205
Maolun or Muruṇḍa, king of India who met Su Wu 33, 96, 311 n. 39
Marco Polo 139
Maspero, Henri 127, 134, 153
Mekong River 1, 4, 17, 93, 127, 133, 169
Ming dynasty 3, 8, 12, 18, 107, 195–197, 204–205, 210
Ming shi (*The History of the Ming Dynasty*) 15, 157, 163, 195, 196, 198, 206
  Zhanla meaning "Champa defeated" 163
Ming shi lu (*Ming Veritable Records*) 195, 196, 206
Mingzhou, also called Siming, present-day Ningbo 142, 170
Modan mountain in Funan, mentioned in *Nan qi shu* 58, 90, 100, 323 n. 94
Mofu 29, 35
Molamoto, Zhenla envoy 161
Mon see Khmer
Mu, Jin dynasty emperor 52, 72
Mujinbo, Angkor prefecture 172

N

Nafuna City, perhaps Navanagara or New City 90–91, 103, 108
Nāgasena or Nagaxian, monk envoy of Funan 15, 55–62, 100, 217, 322 n. 86
Naiyiji, officer of King Huema 200
Nan qi or Southern Qi dynasty 42
Nan Qi shu (*The History of the Southern Qi Dynasty*) 4–5, 13, 18, 19, 24, 35, 43, 54–63, 85, 94, 103, 109, 210–211, 213–214, 217
  description of Funan 54–63
Nan shi (*The History of the Southern Dynasties*) 18, 43, 64, 67, 77
Nanhai, Han dynasty commandery 24, 82
Nanhai or Southern Sea, also called the Great Sea, Jiaozhi Sea, Kunlun Sea 21, 22, 39, 41, 68–69, 74, 80, 99, 108, 123, 124, 132, 133, 144, 199
Nanjing see Jianye
Nanyue, state of 23
Nanzhao, state of 128
Nayega, Nayaka in Sanskrit, prince of Chitu 82–83, 104
Ningzong, Southern Song dynasty emperor 157
Northern Wei dynasty 46, 102
Nüguo, Women's State 17

Nüwa, mythical Chinese figure 145
nü wang, queen 17

O
Óc Eo 4, 10, 22, 93
Ouyang Xiu, author of *Xin Tang shu* see *Xin Tang shu*
overseas Chinese 110, 145, 193

P
Pagan or Pugan 147, 149, 151–152, 202
Pankuang or Hun Pankuang, king of Funan 29, 35–36, 54, 70–71, 94, 216
Panpan, son of Pankuang 26, 71, 95
Panpan 35, 72, 99, 328 n. 46
Panyu, present-day Guangzhou city 23, 46, 102
Panyu, place south of Zhenla 170
Paramārtha or Boluomotuo 45, 102
Parthia or Anxi 69, 326 n. 28
Pelliot, Paul 1, 9, 10, 15, 22, 34, 127, 167–168, 214
parrots 28, 33
Persia or Bosi 23, 129, 326 n. 28
Phimeanakas 171, 174, 194
  site of Angkor king's trysts with female naga 174, 359 n. 51
Piao, perhaps Pyū 123, 135, 137
Piqian, state of 29, 33, 41, 69–70, 312 n. 51
  Indian script in 70
Poli 112
Pollock, Sheldon 10
  The Language of the Gods in the World of Man 10
Poluosuo 80, 331 n. 14
Poluotiba or Purandara(pura), royal city of Water Zhenla 122–123, 136, 344 n. 19
Polou, another name for Land Zhenla 136, 348 n. 98
Pomi, king of Wendan, and his unnamed queen 126–127
pōn, Khmer title, perhaps Chinese *fan* 10, 35–36, 95, 98, 212
Pregadio, Fabrizio 47
Pulleyblank, Edwin 14
Pumai, Angkor prefecture 172
Punyodaya or Nati, Buddhist monk 318 n. 27

Q
Qian Zeng see *Zhenla fengtu ji*
Qin dynasty 15
  original of the name China 15, 308 n. 67
Qin Lun 26
Qiyu, monk 44, 96–97
Quanzhou 42, 149, 204
Qutan Lifuduosai, king of Chitu 80, 104

R
Record of Cambodia: the Land and its People, A see *Zhenla fengtu ji*, Zhou Daguan
Rinan, Han dynasty commandery 24, 26, 69, 93, 110, 112, 211
Rockhill, William and Friedrich Hirth 149
Roman empire see Da Qin
Rossabi, Morris 12
Rudravarman or Liutuobamo, last named king of Funan 74–75, 101–102, 116, 212
  inscription linking to father Kauṇḍinya Jayavarman 75
Rudravarman III, king of Champa 158

S
Sakyamuni Buddha, called Bolai 183
San guo zhi (*The Annals of the Three Kingdoms*) 21, 22, 24, 25
Sambor Prei Kuk, location of the early Zhenla city Iśānapura 124, 339 n. 28
Saṃgapāla or Senggapoluo 44, 101
Sanbo or Sanluo 145–146, 151–152
Sanskrit 4, 10, 11, 43, 99, 103, 104, 118, 214, 219
  inscriptions 116–117, 122
  names of Funan kings 215
Schweyer, Anne-Valérie 154
Sea Drum 28
Secretariat, imperial government 160
Sen, Tansen 12
Sengzhi City, capital of Chitu 80, 104, 331 n. 16
  Sengzhi people 124
Shen Yue, author of *Song shu* see *Song shu*
Shenzong, Song dynasty emperor 158–159, 217
  urges Zhenla to join attack on Vietnamese 158
Shiba Yoshinobu 12
Shi ji (*The Record of the Historian*) 22
Shi lei fu (*A Prose-Poem on Categories of Things*) 22
Shimi mountains with Gulang caves 133
Shizi 84
Shizishi (Lion Rock) 82
Shouling port 48, 320 n. 50
Shu, Kingdom of 21
Shui Zhenla see Water Zhenla
Shuo wen jie zi, early dictionary 16
Siam see Xian
Siem Reap 2, 15
Sima Qian, author of *Shi ji* see *Shi ji*
Śiva 60, 104, 115, 122, 215
  see Maheśvara, Bhadreśvara
Six Dynasties 7–8, 213, 317 n. 2
Sogdians 25
Skaff, Jonathan 12
Small Sea, present-day Gulf of Thailand 133
Song dynasty, including the Southern Song 8, 11, 15, 19, 139, 155, 213, 217, 219
Song Qi, co-author of *Xin Tang shu* see *Xin Tang shu*
Song hui yao jigao (*A Draft Edition of the Essential Documents and Regulations of the Song Dynasty*) 131, 141, 156, 158–160
Song shi (*The History of the Song Dynasty*) 18, 139, 141–142, 152, 156–158, 161–162
  limited coverage of Angkor at its height 165
  lack of comment on Angkor's buildings 163
Song shu (*The History of the Liu Song Dynasty*) 5, 18, 25, 42, 53–54, 99
  references to Funan 53–54
Southern Sea see Nanhai
Srivijaya or Foshi, Sanfoji 2, 140, 144, 146, 151
Stein, R. A. 127
standard histories or *zhengshi* 3, 4–5
  ji (annals) and zhuan (biographies and records) 5
  partiality of 4
  veritable records or shilu 4
  written by committee 43
Stark, Miriam 10

Su Wu, King Fan Zhan's envoy to India 25, 27, 95–96
Sui dynasty 42, 64, 79–80
Sui shu (*The History of the Sui Dynasty*) 5, 17, 18, 25, 40, 79–85, 104–105, 107–108, 110–116, 119–120, 131, 152, 156–157, 194, 210, 212, 215–217
  description of early Zhenla 112–116
Sumatra 44, 74, 82
Sun Quan 24–25, 26
Suodu, Yuan dynasty general 170
Suryavarman I, king of Zhenla/Angkor 141
Suryavarman II, king of Zhenla/Angkor 161
Suzhou 143, 198

T
Taizhou 149
Taiping guangji (*Extensive Records Compiled during the Era of Great Peace*) 128, 133
Taiping huanyu ji (*A Record of the World during the Era of Great Peace*) 78, 89, 127–130
  strange tales about Zhenla 128–130
Taiping yulan (*An Encyclopedia Compiled during the Era of Great Peace and Read by the Emperor*) 6, 7, 8, 16, 22, 25, 28, 38, 78, 88–89, 130, 213
  accounts of Funan by Kang Tai and others 26–32, 88–89
Tai qing jin ye shen dan jing (*The Scripture of the Divine Elixir of Great Clarity*) 43, 47–50
  descriptions of travels to Funan 47–50, 211
Taizong, Song dynasty emperor 6, 149
Taizong, Tang dynasty emperor 50, 64–67, 87, 108, 110
  Taizong's commissioning of history books 65
Taizu, Song dynasty emperor 87, 88
Takeo province xi
Tan Hezhi, general 56
Tandong river 133
Tang Jing, Ming envoy to Zhenla 201, 207
Tangming 24
Tang dynasty 4, 8, 14, 15, 16, 18, 28, 42, 43, 64, 219
Tang hui yao (*Essential Documents and Regulations of the Tang Dynasty*) 6, 78, 87–88, 103, 105, 108–109, 128, 211, 215
  Zhenla's takeover of Funan 87–88, 105
Tanglin prefecture 133
Tangzhou, with Riluo and Wenyang districts 133
Tanyang 29
Tao Yuanming, poet 6
Tao Zongyi, author of *Shuo fu* [*Environs of Stories*] 167
Taylor, Keith 144, 158, 161
Temu, capital of Funan mentioned in *Xin Tang shu* 62, 90–91, 102, 108
  questionably identified with Vyādhapura 91
Temür Khan, Chengzong, Mongol Yuan dynasty emperor 166
Thakhek 127
Three Kingdoms, the 21, 24
tianxia or all-under-heaven 12
Tianzhu see India
Tilly, Charles 16, 215
  definition of state 16, 215
Tong Dian (*A Comprehensive History of Institutions*) 6, 25, 40, 78, 85–87, 92, 102, 120
Tong zhi (*A Comprehensive Treatise on Institutions*) 6, 40, 78, 85, 91–92, 139, 141, 156
Tonlé Sap 16, 170, 185, 201
  Putisa city 201
Touhe 135
translation issues 12–15
tribute 12
  from Funan to China 51, 53, 56–57, 67–68, 72–74, 76–77, 86–87, 96–97, 99, 101, 156, 199
  from Wendan to China 127–128, 135–136
  from Zhenla to China 110, 115, 121–122, 129–131, 135, 156, 159–161, 200–201, 202, 206–209
  from Zhenla to the Vietnamese 134
  from five small states to China during early Zhenla 135
  of elephants, including description of them 51–52, 72, 161–162
Tribhuvanādityavarman, king of Zhenla/Angkor 161–162
  unreliable account of his death 352 n. 85
Tumi, perhaps Tamil people 124, 344 n. 27
Tunlifu 151–152
Tuoba or Taghbač people 42
Tuohuan or Gantuohuan, perhaps Duhuai, Dawei 113, 134, 135, 151–152, 339 n. 34
Tuosha'nibatuo, monk envoy 130
Tuotuo or Toqto'a, author of *Song shi* 157 see *Song shi*
Turfan or Tufan 144

U
Uk, Beling and Solang Uk 168
universal histories or *tongshi* 3
Uyghurs 132, 184, 362 n. 88

V
Varadagrāma 122
Vickery, Michael 10, 11, 34, 35, 40, 61, 84, 88, 95, 109, 116–117, 122, 125, 141, 153, 214–215, 333 n. 31, 339 n. 28
  on *hun* and *fan* as local titles 35–36, 95
  arguing Zhenla gradual consolidated its authority 125–126
Vietnam, Vietnamese 157–159, 161–162
Vientiane or Wanxiang 127
Việt Sử Lược (*A Brief History of Vietnam*) 134
Vijaya or Foshi, Xinzhou 143–144, 153–154, 158, 349 n. 30
volcanic islands 32, 70
Vyādhapura see Temu

W
Wade, Geoff 15
Wai guo zhuan (*A Record of Foreign States*) 31–32, 53, 97
Wali 145–146, 151–152
Wan Zhen 7, 13, 21, 22, 37–39, 40, 88, 95, 98, 116, 211, 217
  Nanzhou yiwu zhi (*Annals of Strange Things in the Southern Regions*) 38–39
wang, king 16
Wang Bangwei 53

Wang Dayuan 196–198
Dao yi zhi lüe (A Brief Record of the Foreigners of the Islands) 196–198
Wang Qinruo, author of *Cefu yuangui* see *Cefu yuangui*
Wang Gungwu xii, 11, 12, 165
"The Nanhai Trade" 11
Wang Junzheng, envoy to Chitu 79, 81
Wang Pu, author of *Tang hui yao* see *Tang hui yao*
Wang Yinglin 156
Yu hai [Sea of Jade] 156
Warring States, The 16
Wat Phu 115, 127, 341 n. 49
Water Zhenla 16, 110, 119, 122, 125–126, 131, 136, 201, 216
small city states in its east 126
size 131, 136
Wei, Kingdom of 21, 27, 45
Wei Zheng, Linghu Defen, Zhangsun Wuji, authors of *Sui shu* see *Sui shu*
Wen of the Liu Song dynasty, emperor 72
Wen of the Sui dynasty, emperor 79
Wendan, another name for Land Zhenla 119, 125, 127–128, 136–137
location, probably in today's north-east Thailand 127
size 131, 136–137
Suantai district and two unnamed cities 133
Wenxian tongkao (A Comprehensive Study of Institutions on the Basis of Authoritative Documents) 6, 78–79, 85, 92, 117, 134, 139, 141, 143, 148, 152, 156
Wenxuan (Selections of Literature) 37, 142
Wenzhou 142, 145, 166, 169–170
Yongjia county
Wicks, Robert 12, 141
Wilkinson, Endymion 14, 320 n. 59
Wu, Former Han dynasty emperor 23, 26
Wu Guan 167
Gujin yishi (Other Histories Old and New) 167–168
Wu, Jin dynasty emperor 72
Wu, Kingdom of 24, 27
Wu, Liang dynasty emperor 5, 45, 54, 64–65, 67, 101–102
Buddhist monks at the Liang court 44, 65
Wu, Nan Qi dynasty emperor 55, 64–65, 218
Wu Qiuyan 166
Wulun 48
Wuwen Mountains 133
Wuwen 29
Wu Zetian, empress 122, 128

X

Xia Nai 167–168
Xian, Luo or Xianluo, later Siam 152, 154, 170, 176, 187, 194, 208–209, 356 n. 28
Xianglin, early name for Linyi see Linyi
Xiangpu, Ming name for Champa 201
Xiao Zexian, author of *Nan Qi shu* see *Nan Qi shu*
Xiaozong, Southern Song dynasty emperor 161
Xin Tang shu (The New History of the Tang Dynasty) 8, 25, 52, 62, 78, 84, 102, 105, 109, 120, 127, 132–136, 156, 201, 215–216
description of Zhenla 135–136
Xinzhou or New City see *Vijaya*
Xinzhumosengge or Jiumosengge, Zhenla envoy 160
Mojunmingjisi, his deputy 161
Xiongnu 44
Xipeng 145–146, 151–152
Xitu, state of 16, 37, 315 n. 85
see also Appendix 5
Xiuluofen 135
Xu Song 157
Xuanzang, monk 45, 86
Xuanzong, Tang dynasty emperor 122
Xunfan 151–152

Y

Yan Congjian 201–203, 207
Shuyu zhouzi lu (A Record of Various Views on Distant Regions) 199–203
Yan Liben, Tang court painter 65
Yang Bowen 143
Yang Fu 7, 23, 309 n. 12
Yang, Sui dynasty emperor 79–83, 104–105, 110
Yang Wuquan 146
Yang Xuanzhi 45
Luoyang galan ji (A Record of the Monasteries of Luoyang) 45
Yangzi River 21
Yao Silian, author of *Liang shu and Chen shu* see *Liang shu, Chen shu*
Yao Cha, father of Yao Silian 65
Yaśodharapura 151
Yaśovarman I, king of Zhenla/Angkor 137, 151, 217
Ye Tinggui 155
Xiang lu (A Record of Aromatic Substances) 155
Yijing, monk 7, 15, 43, 93, 108–109, 215
Nanhai jigui neifa zhuan (A Record of Buddhist Precepts Sent Home from the Southern Sea) 108–109, 215
yi wu zhi, annals of strange things 8
Yin Shou, Ming envoy to Zhenla 201–202
Yongle dadian (Great Comendium of the Yongle Era), Ming encyclopedia 145, 149
Yongle, Ming dynasty emperor 198, 201, 209, 366 n. 13
Yuan dynasty 3, 8, 12, 14, 15, 18, 107, 139, 145, 163, 165, 195, 205
Yueshang, state of 22, 308 n. 3
Yuan shi (The History of the Yuan Dynasty) 5, 163
Yue Shi, author of *Taiping huanyu ji* see *Taiping huanyu ji*
Yuezhi (Tokharian) people and their horses 27, 96
Yulin, Han dynasty commandery 24
Yunbao, monk 74
Yunzhong 132

Z

Zha'nan, Angkor prefecture 170, 172
Zhang, Later Han dynasty emperor 23
Zhang Tingyu 15
Zhang Xie 204
Dongxi yang kao (On the Eastern and Western Oceans) 204–205
Zhangzhou 204
Zhao Rugua, also romanised Zhao Rukuo 8, 18, 116, 142, 146, 149–156, 165, 196, 217
Zhu fan zhi 116, 134, 146, 149–156, 163, 170, 194, 217–218

Zheng He, Ming admiral 197–199, 209, 366 n. 12
Zhenla xi, 2, 4–9, 11, 14, 15, 17–19, 67 and *passim*
  appearance of the people 114
  bathing 192
  beeswax 150, 154
  boats 191
  Buddhism, Buddhist monks, called *zhugu* 121, 123, 145, 150, 152, 179–180, 182–183, 193, 203
  buildings including king's palace 150, 152–153, 171–174, 194, 196, 203
  calendars 178
  capital city 163, 170–171, 196, 217
  carts 192
  character of the people 113
  childbirth 181, 194
  Chinese in Angkor 193, 196, 360 n. 63
  compared with Funan 117–118
  compared with Champa 150
  conflicts with Champa 142, 151, 153–154, 162, 201, 352 n. 85, 352 n 87
  conflicts with Xian, later Siam, laying waste to the land 172, 194
  connections with Funan 87, 116–117, 211–213
  disputes and criminals 184–185, 196
  derivation of name 15
  doors or houses facing east 123, 135
  dress 175–176
  education of boys 183
  elephants for fighting 121, 123, 147, 150, 196, 200
  farming 150, 185–186
  festivals and celebrations, including New Year 177
  flora and fauna 188–190
  food 150, 152
  funerals 114
  gall, consumed by Champa kings 192, 365 n. 119
  guests' treatment 130, 135
  Hindu and other gods 121, 123, 343 n. 11 see also Bhadreśvara
  holy men and women, called *basiwei* 115, 146, 152, 179–180, 362 n. 80
  kings see buildings including king's palace
Zhenla (*continued*)
  language and writing 130, 183, 194
  lapse for three centuries of relations with China 137, 140–141
  latrines 186
  learned men, called *banjie* 182–183
  leprosy, illness and death 181–182, 361–362 n. 79
  lign-aloes (and in Funan) 147, 150, 326 n. 24, 366 n. 22
  location 121, 125–127
  marriages 11
  names 178
  officials, including titles 113, 175–176
  overland route to and from southern China 123–124, 132–134
  palanquins 147, 175–176, 191–192
  patrilineage 113, 117
  purple pin fungus 129–230
  products 114–115, 150, 152, 154–155, 186–187, 190, 196, 199, 202–203
  royal audiences 113, 150
  royal lineage, archaeological link with Funan 116–117
  sexual relations 130, 181, 193, 196
  slaves and savages 178, 194, 207, 218
  takeover of Funan 84–85, 105, 107–110, 215, 219
  trade, including foreign trade 146, 151–152, 156, 158, 188, 196, 204–205, 213–214
  trials by ordeal 150, 185
  utensils and furnishings 190–191
  village officials, called *maijie* 172
  women, including palace women and traders 172–175, 187–188, 194
    dancing girls 150
    girls' coming-of-age ritual 179, 194, 196, 217
  Zhanla as another name 15, 158, 163
  see also Water Zhenla, Land Zhenla
Zheng Qiao, author of *Tong zhi* see *Tong zhi*
Zhenla fengtu ji (*A Record of Cambodia: the Land and its People*) xii, 1, 2, 166–167, 168–193, 195, 205, 213
  complete text, rearranged 168, 169–193
  date of composition 166–167
  lacunae in extant text, according to Qian Zeng 167
  sources for extant text 167
  see also Zhou Daguan
Zhenlifu *or* Zhanlipo 148, 151–152, 156–157
  female Buddha 148
Zhennan city 126
Zhenpu, Angkor prefecture 169, 172
Zhenzong, Song dynasty emperor 157
Zhigun, perhaps Saigon, Angkor prefecture 172, 358 n.41
Zhonghua shuju or Zhonghua Book Company 6, 7
Zhou Daguan, author of *Zhenla fengtu ji* xi, 1–3, 5, 7, 8, 11–13, 18, 62, 97, 107, 109, 116, 118–119, 145–146, 149, 156, 157, 163, 165, 194–196, 202, 203, 205, 210, 213, 217–218
  place of origin 166
  mission to Zhenla 166, 170
  see also *Record of Cambodia: the Land and its People, A*
Zhou dynasty 16
Zhou Qufei, author of *Lingwai daida* 8, 18, 142, 144, 145–146, 166
Zhu Dangbaolao, Funan envoy 74
Zhu Maichen 181, 361 n. 78
zhu, ruler 17
Zhu Ying, Kang Tai's fellow envoy 7, 1`3, 25, 26, 94, 97, 103, 210, 213, 218
Zhu Yuan, Ming envoy 207
Zhu Zhi 7, 13, 21, 40–41, 211
Zhu Zhantan, king of Funan 52, 72, 99, 321 n. 65
Zhuang people 178
Zhujiang 113
Zhuya, Han dynasty commandery 24, 133
Zuo zhuan (*The Commentary of Zuo*) 16
Zuo Si, poet 21, 36
  San da fu (*Prose-Poem on the Three Capitals*) 36–37